Off the
Beaten
Path

As seen from Leonard Harrison State Park, Pine Creek wends its way through Pennsylvania's Grand Canyon.

READER'S DIGEST

Off the Beaten Path

A guide to more than 1,000 scenic and interesting places still uncrowded and inviting

The Reader's Digest Association, Inc.

Pleasantville, New York / Montreal

Off the Beaten Path

Project Editor: Carroll C. Calkins
Project Art Editor: Gilbert L. Nielsen
**Associate Editor and
Project Coordinator:** Noreen B. Church
Associate Editor: W. Clotilde Lanig
Research Editor: David P. Palmer
Picture Editor: Robert J. Woodward
Picture Researcher: Margaret O. Mathews
Art Associate: Henrietta Stern
Editorial Assistant: Ann Rafferty

Contributing Editor: Margaret Perry
Contributing Copy Editor: Harriet Bachman
Contributing Researcher: Nathalie Laguerre
Contributing Writers: Charles C. Bricker, Jr.,
Kent Dannen, Tom Dickey, Don Earnest,
James Forsht, Mark Gasper, Brenda Hirsch,
B. Cory Kilvert, Jr., Linda Lee, Alan Linn,
George Marsden, Richard Marshall,
Barbara Rogan, Marie Walborn, Daniel Weiss
Indexer: Sydney Wolfe Cohen

READER'S DIGEST GENERAL BOOKS

Editorial Director: John A. Pope, Jr.
Managing Editor: Jane Polley
Art Director: Richard J. Berenson
Group Editors: Norman B. Mack, John Speicher,
David Trooper (Art), Susan J. Wernert

The acknowledgments and credits that appear on page 374 are hereby
made a part of this copyright page.

Library of Congress Cataloging in Publication Data

Off the beaten path.

At head of title: Reader's digest.
✓ Includes index.
1. United States—Description and travel—1981–
Guide-books.   I. Reader's Digest Association.
E158.033   1987   917.3'04927   86-11372
ISBN   0-89577-253-1

The Concept

Many of the destinations included on these pages, as you will see on the state maps, are literally off the beaten path. Others are in towns or on main routes but have an unusual or specific appeal. Among the latter are museums featuring tureens, teapots, rare dolls, old telephones, clocks, fire engines, steam tractors, antique cars, and many other offbeat attractions. In treating well-known places, such as national parks, we have selected the areas that are less frequented but interesting in their own right.

Planning a book on this subject is not without its problems. There's the obvious factor of self-destruction, which is to say that publicizing a place can remove it from the category that qualified it for inclusion. Then, too, what may be off the beaten path for some travelers may be a well-known destination to those who live in the area.

We are, however, undaunted, and we believe that our inclusion of more than 1,000 interesting places that are widely distributed and widely different serves to diffuse the impact on any one place.

How the book was developed

The editors studied the map and history of every state and made a list of intriguing places that are geographically out of the way or that have subject matter beyond the mainstream. We also chose places in all parts of each state so that no matter where the reader might be, a place of interest could be found within a reasonable distance.

Our final list was then sent to the travel department in each state with a request for confirmation of the places we had chosen or for any needed additions or deletions. We evaluated the responses and established a master list of potential entries.

We knew from the beginning that the only way to give the reader the most accurate and up-to-date information would be to have a driver file a firsthand report. We assigned drivers to visit each and every place and send us road information, all available brochures and leaflets, and a personal evaluation. They were also asked to recommend appropriate deletions and additions.

The master list was sent to more than 200 photographers all across the country, and we were rewarded with well over 31,000 color photographs, from which we selected about 380 for the book. Before we could write about all these places, our researchers had to confirm countless names, dates, and other bits of information. To accomplish this, they spent more than 16,500 minutes on the telephone.

We are proud of the book. But careful as we have been, it is not unlikely that you will encounter the unexpected somewhere along the way. Things change: roads deteriorate or close, opening hours and admission charges are adjusted, new managements take over, services may be curtailed, places may close down. But if you use this volume in the spirit of adventure that it is intended to engender, your appreciation of this fascinating country will be greatly enhanced.

—*The Editors*

Information at end of entries

Symbols (right) are shown when relevant. Opening times, such as Mon.–Fri., Apr.–Oct., are inclusive—meaning Monday through Friday, April through October. Road directions are not given in the text when the location is obvious on the map. If admission fees are not mentioned, they are not required. Information about reservations is given only where needed.

 Picnicking

 Camping

 Trailers

 Hiking

 Backpacking

 Binoculars desirable

 Horseback riding

 Bicycling

 Swimming

 Rowboating

 Canoeing

 Fishing

Cross-country skiing

Winter sports

Washington (322)

Montana (276)

North Dakota (234)

Minnesota (184)

Oregon (330)

Idaho (282)

Wyoming (290)

South Dakota (240)

Iowa (200)

California (344)

Nevada (338)

Utah (296)

Colorado (302)

Nebraska (246)

Arizona (316)

New Mexico (308)

Kansas (254)

Oklahoma (260)

Texas (266)

Hawaii (364)

Alaska (354)

Contents

This topographic map reveals the network of waterways and the striking variety of landforms in the United States. Page numbers for the chapter openings are in parentheses.

Maine (8)
Vermont (22)
New Hampshire (16)
Massachusetts (28)
Wisconsin (192)
New York (46)
Rhode Island (36)
Connecticut (40)
Michigan (128)
Pennsylvania (66)
New Jersey (56)
Illinois (206)
Indiana (144)
Ohio (136)
Maryland (80)
Delaware (76)
West Virginia (86)
Virginia (92)
Missouri (214)
Kentucky (152)
North Carolina (98)
Arkansas (222)
Tennessee (162)
South Carolina (106)
Mississippi (178)
Alabama (170)
Georgia (112)
Louisiana (228)
Florida (120)

Maine

The Pine Tree State is best known for its scenic rockbound coast, but the forests, lakes, and many other attractions should not be overlooked.

Maine was not an easy land to settle, and some of the hard work is memorialized in the farm museums, blacksmith shop, and the logging museum that vividly recalls the labor involved in cutting the original stands of timber here. The parks and recreation areas, by the sea and in the remaining wilderness, reveal a little of what so much of this northeastern area was like in times gone by. Here too are a couple of islands whose inhabitants exemplify the kind of rugged individualism on which state-of-Mainers still rightly pride themselves.

1. Fort Kent Blockhouse Historic Site.
Blockhouse Rd. This area was first settled in the early 1800's by French colonists who were forced from their Canadian homes in Acadia (now the Maritime Provinces) when they refused to pledge allegiance to the conquering British.

The great stands of timber attracted lumbermen from Canada and the United States, and border disputes soon developed. Concerned about its interests, the state of Maine dispatched troops to the area and built a fort at a strategic juncture of the Fish and St. John rivers. Completed in 1840, the fort was named for Gov. Edward Kent. It was armed and manned, but the boundary disputes were settled in 1842 and no shots were ever fired.

The blockhouse was restored by Boy Scouts and is maintained by a local troop. The wide stone steps lead to a six- by six-foot plank door hung on heavy hand-wrought hinges. A collection of antique hand tools is displayed inside.

Parking spaces, water taps, picnic tables, and fireplaces are available in a grove of oaks and white pines on the bank of the Fish River. True to its name, the river yields salmon and trout. *Open Memorial Day–Labor Day.*

2. Nylander Museum.
393 Main St., Caribou. In the words of the director, this museum serves as "a window on the world" for the citizens of northern Maine and as a point of interest for tourists passing through.

It is also a tribute to one man's lifelong curiosity about the world around him. At the age of 10, Olof Nylander, the son of a shoemaker in a small Swedish town, sold his collection of local Stone Age and Bronze Age implements to the museum in the nearby city of Ystad.

He came to America in his teens and developed a consuming interest in geology. Before his death in 1943 at age 79, he had established a reputation as a tireless and innovative field worker and had published many articles in scientific journals. His wide-ranging personal collection of geological and marine life specimens, as well as Indian and other artifacts, is housed in the museum.

The tidy white clapboard structure was built in 1938 by the Works Progress Administration, a federally funded organization established to provide much-needed employment during the Great Depression. In addition to the extensive Nylander collections, the museum houses permanent displays of butterflies, Indian artifacts made by the local Micmac and Malecite tribes, tools and utensils from the early days of settlement here, and weapons and other objects used by the citizens of Aroostook County in the Civil War. Special exhibits are mounted during the summer season. *Open Wed.–Sun., Memorial Day–Labor Day.*

---

3. Baxter State Park. *South Branch Pond.*
Few governors have been more generous to their constituents than Percival P. Baxter. Between 1930 and 1962 he bought and gave to the state of Maine some 200,000 acres of wilderness and set up trust funds to defray the costs of development and maintenance. The state has kept faith with the intent of the gift, and it strictly enforces the rules that sustain the spirit of wilderness here.

No pets or other domestic animals and no motorcycles, trail bikes, or other all-terrain vehicles are allowed in the park. Snowmobiles are strictly limited to specific areas. Hunting, trapping, and the use of

3. *Here's the essence of peace and quiet as seen from the west shore of South Branch Pond. The misty heights of Black Cat Mountain rise in the background.*

weapons—including slingshots—are prohibited except in certain areas during hunting season. In only one campground (Kidney Pond) can visitors play radios, record or cassette players, or TV's. For anyone seeking peace and quiet, these are welcome regulations.

Vehicles more than 9 feet high and 22 feet long are not allowed. Maximum length for a car and trailer is 44 feet.

At South Branch Pond, in a tranquil woodland setting, you can rent a canoe, enjoy one of the inviting picnic spots, with fieldstone fireplaces, or spend the night in a lean-to shelter (available by reservation) in a grove of white birches. The five hiking trails in this area range in length from less than half a mile (to South Branch Falls) to almost 10 miles (to Russell Pond). *Park open for day use, Apr.–Dec.; campgrounds open mid-May–mid-Oct. Admission charged. Reservations suggested. For information call (207) 723-5140.*

4. Lumberman's Museum. *Patten.* Before the Revolution, when Britannia ruled the waves, the great stands of pine along the coastline were reserved by the Crown, to be used as masts for the mighty ships of the line.

The product has changed in size, from 75-foot masts to the toothpicks now made here by the billions, but the material is the same: pine, from the Pine Tree State. It is fitting that the history of lumbering is commemorated here in Patten, where the industry still survives and logging trucks now roar by.

Of the 3,000 artifacts on display, a goodly percentage are from the collection of the late Dr. Lore Rogers. They include tools and equipment for every imaginable lumber-camp chore.

One of the nine buildings on the site is a reconstructed 1820 logging camp, where crew members once slept on rows of evergreen boughs. The limited space reveals how short of stature these men must have been and belies the public image of the giant lumberjack.

Photographs, dioramas, and working models illustrate how standing timber was felled and converted to lumber in the early days. A featured display is the old and rare Lombard Steam Log Hauler. As the predecessor of the continuous-tread bulldozer and the military tank, it has been declared a national historic mechanical engineering landmark. *Open Tues.–Sun. and all holidays, Memorial Day–Labor Day; weekends only, Labor Day–Columbus Day. Admission charged.*

5. Lily Bay State Park. This is a pleasant place to sample the appealing character of the rugged Maine woods, and with almost 1,000 acres in the park, crowding is not a problem. The moose in the area frequently favor a bog beside the Mud Bank picnic area. Although any moose in the wild is a memorable sight, they are at their most impressive here when autumn nights foreshadow the coming of winter and the animals begin to group together.

Also unforgettable is the haunting cry of the loon, a beautiful diving bird with a distinctive white necklace in sharp contrast to its black plumage.

Fishermen here try for lake trout, known locally as togue, brown and brook trout, salmon, perch, and suckers.

The views of Moosehead Lake and Big Squaw Mountain to the southwest are magnificent. The park offers a pebbled swimming beach and a small field for Frisbee, volleyball, and other games. *Open Ice-Out in spring to Oct. 15.*

6. Moosehead Marine Museum. *Greenville.* The museum houses a small onshore collection of marine memorabilia, but the centerpiece here is a 110-foot lake steamer. The steel-hulled *Katahdin* was built in 1914 to take tourists to the luxurious Mount Kineo Resort and other destinations on Moosehead Lake. The lavishly appointed ship, with fixtures and furnishings of brass, mahogany, leather, and velvet, was queen of the Maine lake-steamers for more than 20 years. When the resort failed after World War I, the *Katahdin* was reduced to the hard service of towing log rafts on the lake. Then environmental considerations put a stop to the rafting of logs, and it seemed that this historic ship (the oldest surviving steel hull built by the Bath, Maine, Iron Works) was headed for the scrap heap.

She was saved, however, by a group of local enthusiasts who incorporated to preserve the ship as a floating museum and put her back in service on the lake. This has been done, and the refurbished *Katahdin* is now available for short cruises

7. *How aptly named are the cathedral pines rising majestically over the camping area. Missing in the picture are the fragrance and the sound of the wind.*

and group charters. In addition, a number of interesting marine artifacts are displayed on board.

From the deck of the original passenger carrier here, one can see the sleek seaplanes that now serve the lakeshore and the wilderness beyond. *Open Ice-Out in spring–Labor Day. Admission charged.*

---

7. Cathedral Pines. This camping area is named for the towering red pines that create the illusion of soaring cathedral vaults as you look up at the arching canopy of foliage some 70 feet overhead.

Near the entrance to the grounds are picnic tables, fireplaces, and an office where firewood and ice are available.

Beach Road leads to the swimming area and campsites on Flagstaff Lake. Bigelow Road leads to additional tent sites on and adjacent to another waterfront area on this large lake. *Open mid-May–Sept.*

8. Wyman Lake. Few hydroelectric projects relate so well to their surroundings as does this one. For 16 miles along its high eastern shore, superb panoramic views of Wyman Lake and its somber background of timbered mountains await the visitor. History is remembered here, and at a scenic outlook about four miles south of Caratunk a tablet marks the place where Benedict Arnold and more than 1,000 men left the Kennebec River on an expedition to Canada in 1775. Their mission was to participate in an assault on Quebec.

From the scenic outlook a steep, short path leads to the lakeshore. South of here on Route 201 are other, easier points of access and an inviting spot for picnicking in a grove of white pines and hardwoods.

The views are less spectacular along the road that follows the west shore, but other attractions are found, including bathing beaches and, seven miles north of the dam, another picnic area. Of interest to birders are the shrikes seen here. These predators store their small prey on thorns and twig ends after killing it.

---

9. The Blacksmith Shop Museum. *Chandler Rd., Dover-Foxcroft.* Before the days of mass production, mail-order parts,

9. Most of the objects shown here have parts made of iron. The blacksmith had to know how to make them and how to fix them when they broke.

paved highways, and automobiles, every small community had to be largely self-sufficient, and the skills of the ironworker were much in demand. The village smithy in earlier times was as essential to the community as the general store.

Here in a small shingled barn, where the fires of the forge went out in 1905, the tools of this demanding and disappearing craft are displayed along with some of the handmade iron objects that were used for farming, transportation, recreation, and everyday living. A harness-repair bench, a cheese press, and other old-time implements remind the visitor of a less complex time—when horsepower was provided by horses instead of machines. *The building is never locked; admission is free, but donations are accepted.*

---

10. Moosehorn National Wildlife Refuge. *Baring Unit.* Anyone interested in seeing northeastern wildlife in its natural habitat would be well advised to spend some time here. The refuge, one of more than 400 across the nation, is on the Atlantic Flyway and provides feeding and resting grounds for great flights of migratory birds. It also supports a sizable resident population: more than 200 species have been observed here, and most of these,

including the osprey and bald eagle, are commonly seen. The refuge puts a major emphasis on determining and providing for the ecological needs of the American woodcock. This interesting bird has been declining in numbers as its woodland habitat is encroached upon.

The various tracts in the refuge total about 2,500 acres and support some 40 kinds of mammals the year-round. At the Edmunds Unit, 20 miles to the south, harbor seals and Atlantic porpoises are seen offshore. The bear, moose, fox, bobcat, deer, and beaver are to be expected in this environment; but that supposed westerner, the coyote, is something of a surprise. Vose Pond and Bearse Lake are recommended for fishing. Snowmobiling is also popular here. *Open year-round.*

---

11. Quoddy Head State Park. A bit of the Maine wilderness can be sampled in this 485-acre park, which includes the easternmost point of land in the United States. Here in the spruce woodlands, deer and an occasional moose may be seen, but predatory bobcats and coyotes are said to be reducing their number. Porcupines and rabbits range through the park, and

11. *The rocks of Quoddy Head, for all their rugged appearance, are being weathered away by the wind and sea and covered by trees gaining footholds in the cracks and crevices.*

12. *A lush stand of meadowsweet has established itself here by Englishman's Bay. Notice the thin layer of soil supporting the tall, slender trees.*

the usual birds of the northeastern woods and meadows are abundant.

One of the inland trails includes a section of boardwalk beside a peat bog, with signs to identify the wildflowers that grow here in profusion. The main trail that runs for about 1½ miles around the head offers good views of nearby West Quoddy Head Light, where a beacon has served mariners since 1805. The sunrise can be spectacular here and often has an interesting greenish cast. In summer this is a favorite place for whale watching. *Open mid-Apr.– Dec., weather permitting.*

12. Roque Bluffs State Park. The 800 acres that make up this relatively new coastal park were acquired in 1968 and converted for recreational use a decade later. Roque Bluffs is still quiet and infrequently visited, partly because it is often enshrouded by fog. July is the best month to enjoy its half-mile crescent beach, but even then the waters of Englishman's Bay are chilly. The shore affords pleasing views of several wooded islands, one of which is Roque Island.

The park includes the six-acre Simpson's Pond, where swimming and fishing are permitted. The most frequent catch is brown trout. The pond is also home to otters and beavers, and beaver lodges are

visible from the beach. Among the park's many species of winged residents is the endangered bald eagle.

At several spots there are well-equipped picnic sites, one of which has a playground. The park has boardwalks but no hiking trails or camping facilities. *Open May 15–Sept. 30; accessible year-round.*

13. Schoodic Peninsula. The only part of Acadia National Park on the mainland, Schoodic Peninsula has fewer tourists than the larger, more diverse, and better-known Mount Desert Island. But something of the special character of Acadia is perhaps more beguiling here, where headlands of weathered rock reach down to the water; and farther out, at Schoodic Point, the ocean is tumultuous and spectacular. The heavy seas thunder headlong into great shelves of pink granite and spray high into the air.

John G. Moore acquired the peninsula to use as a wild park adjacent to a resort he was planning to build. But he died in 1899, and the property went to his heirs. They offered it as an addition to the existing Lafayette National Park on Mount Desert Island, with the stipulation that the name of the park be changed. By an act of Congress in 1929, the peninsula was added, and the name of the park was changed to Acadia.

From Route 186 the entire rugged shoreline is paralleled by a six-mile-long stretch of well-maintained, one-way road that drivers share with cyclists. At frequent turnouts splendid seascapes break through the forest wall and offer views of reed bogs, stony coves where shorebirds feed, bays dotted with lobster boats, and wooded islands in the distance. A mile-long gravel road climbs to the summit at Schoodic Head, where on clear days the coastal view is magnificent.

The Blueberry Hill parking area is the departure point for hiking trails ascending inland through stands of spruce and across open hillsides dotted with low-bush blueberries. One steep trail ascends 180 feet to a promontory called The Anvil. One can also walk down toward the water to view marine flora and fauna. Shorebirds are abundant here, and bald eagles are occasionally sighted. *Open year-round, dawn to dusk.*

14. Stanwood Homestead Museum and Birdsacre Wildlife Sanctuary. *Ellsworth.* This property was owned and cared for by one family for more than 100 years, and one member of that family devoted her lifetime to the careful study of nature. It is not surprising, therefore, to find here a delightful aura of tranquillity. Capt. Roswell Stanwood built his simple white frame cottage in 1850. Fifteen years later a daughter, Cordelia, the first of five children, was born in that house.

The surrounding woods, the spring, the stream, and the ponds attracted Cordelia Stanwood, and she developed a deep appreciation of the ways of nature—and especially of birds. Her inquiring mind and compelling interest in the subject led her to become an accomplished amateur ornithologist.

She lived and worked here for more than 50 years. It is fortunate indeed that others can now visit the rooms, walk the paths, and share a legacy of peace and quiet in a place where nature was studied, respected, and preserved.

The complex includes the unpretentious house with its comfortable, lived-in quality, the nature trails and bird sanctuary, and the Wildlife Recovery Center. The center is licensed to care for and release orphaned, sick, or injured wildlife, and there are usually a number of patients in residence. The gift shop has many bird-related items for sale. *Buildings are open daily June 15–Oct. 15. Admission is free, but donations are encouraged.*

15. Lake St. George State Park. This attractive lakeside park is a pleasant place for picnicking, swimming, and fishing. Its handsome administration buildings are reminiscent of the 19th-century architecture prevalent in the area.

Of the three main picnic areas, one is adjacent to the lake. It is shaded by young oaks and maples, has bathhouses for swimmers, and a camper parking area that accommodates small- to average-size vans and trailers.

About 100 yards of the pebbly shoreline serve as a swimming beach. Granite slabs provide easy access to the water, and a string of buoys outlines the safe area.

13. *Schoodic Peninsula, in its communion with the sea, offers many opportunities to enjoy the spectacular vignettes of tide pools, rocks, grasses, reeds, shrubs, and trees.*

Fishermen here catch mostly bass and landlocked salmon. Boat launching is permitted, and canoes and rowboats are available for rent. In addition, the park offers a softball field, swings, seesaws, and trails for snowmobiles. *Open for fishing Apr.–Sept.; for camping May–Sept.*

16. Norlands Living History Center. *Off Rte. 108, Livermore.* This impressive complex was built for the Washburns, a remarkable family of 19th-century political, military, and business leaders.

The Washburn house is a fine example of the Italianate style. Pure New England, however, are the farmer's cottage and the large barn attached to the house in deference to the hard winters here.

The library, built in 1883 to serve the family and the community, is a handsome granite building in the High Victorian Gothic style. Architecture of an earlier day is also exemplified by the old-time schoolhouse and the white clapboard church with tall, narrow arched windows, ornate latticed bell tower, and a steeple crowned with a gilded dolphin weathervane.

The term "Living History" refers to a variety of programs in which the past is creatively reenacted here. "History on the March" presentations take about an hour,

"Time-Machine Journeys" last up to four hours, and the "Adult Live-Ins" continue for a few days. In the last-named, paying guests assume the roles of people who lived and worked in the area in the 19th century. Children's programs include a day in a one-room schoolhouse of 1842.

An old-time working farm is maintained on the grounds, and hayrides and tours of the buildings are offered. Picnic tables are pleasantly situated in a grove of tall pines. *Open Wed.–Sun., July–Aug. Fees charged. For dates and fees for Live-Ins and special events, call (207) 897-2236.*

17. Crocker Pond Campground. *Off Rte. 5, south of Bethel.* This campground, near the boundary of the 3,000-acre Patte Brook Multiple Use Management Area, has seven developed sites—each of them with tent pads, picnic tables, fireplaces, water, and toilet facilities. There is also a small field where you can pitch a tent or park a trailer.

Crocker Pond and the nearby Broken Bridge Pond have been stocked with brook trout. Round Pond, also good for fishing, is reached by a pleasant half-mile walk along Albany Brook. The many kinds of conifers, hardwoods, and undergrowth in the area provide browse and

shelter for deer, hares, moose, black bears, and wildfowl. About a half-mile west of Crocker Pond Road is the old Pingree Mine, where rock-hounds can go to look for specimens of mica, beryllium, and other minerals. *Accessible year-round. Campground open mid-May–mid-Oct.*

18. The Jones Gallery of Glass and Ceramics. *Douglas Hill Road.* People have been making useful objects of glass for more than 3,000 years. From the very beginning, its plasticity in the molten state and its receptivity to color have inspired artisans to create an astounding variety of decorative and functional objects.

In this museum, which also includes ceramics, the pieces shown—ranging from early Egyptian to modern-day examples—reveal the beauty and utility of both materials. In keeping with the gallery's educational aims, the exhibits, selected from some 4,000 pieces on hand, are usually related to a specific theme.

The 2,000-volume library, 300 microfiche, and some 6,000 color slides are available to researchers and members of the museum. The shop here features glass and ceramic antiques—not reproductions. You may bring glass or ceramic objects to the museum for identification; this

16. *Reliving a moment in the history of threshing: this machine is a vast improvement on the hand-held flail but a far cry from the efficiency of the giant combines of today.*

18. *Typical of the fine work displayed here is this 1920's free-blown vase.*

service is free to members, but a donation is requested from others.

The Jones Gallery collection is of remarkable quality and scope, reflecting the knowledge and experience of the founder, Dorothy-Lee Jones. *Open May 1–Nov. 15. Admission charged.*

---

19. Eagle Island. *Accessible in summer by ferry from Mackerel Cove on Bailey Island.* Eagle Island, about three miles offshore, was the lifelong retreat of Adm. Robert E. Peary, who discovered the North Pole on April 6, 1909. The celebration Peary expected on his return did not take place because another explorer claimed to have been there first.

Scientific evidence and a congressional inquiry later confirmed, however, that Peary's expedition was the first to raise a flag at the Top of the World. Peary, when he was a young man, built the house on Eagle Island and spent most of his summers here. He left the place to his daughter, who donated it to the state of Maine for use as a park.

The large house, with a three-sided fireplace in the living room and a big restaurant-style stove in the kitchen, has an aura of hospitality that belies the admiral's reputation as a stern authoritarian.

Peary was an amateur taxidermist, and he prepared many of the arctic and Maine birds displayed in the house.

A small ocean beach is open to swimmers willing to brave the chill waters, and the woods offer a pleasant choice of short nature trails.

If you plan to stop over, bring food and refreshments. Nothing is sold on the island. *The Kristy K, running mid-June–Labor Day, weather permitting, leaves Bailey Island at noon and reaches Eagle Island at 12:30 (en route to Portland). On the return trip it stops at Eagle Island at 3:30 and arrives at Bailey Island at 4. Adults about $10, children under 12 about $5.*

---

20. Monhegan Island. Situated 10 miles out in the Atlantic, this 650-acre isle epitomizes the beauty of windswept Maine, with its rocky coasts, rugged headlands, moors, and forests of spruce and balsam. The surrounding ocean surf is calm enough for fishing or an invigorating dip on some beaches, but turbulent and un-

20. *Aerial view highlights the informal scattering of houses on the inhabited side of Monhegan Island, and the lobster boats in the harbor indicate the major business here.*

predictable on the seaward sides. Here also, the traditional Maine industry of lobster fishing has been refined to a science with an enforced shortened season to sustain the size and quality of the catch.

In its remoteness, Monhegan has resisted two pervasive features of modern life: electricity (there is no electric power except for privately owned generators) and automobiles, which cannot be brought to the island. The attractions are to be enjoyed on foot. Of the 15 miles of trails, some are quite rough, marked only by stacked rocks. In the village, as dusk descends, most residents light up their gas or kerosene lamps to accompany the stars and moonlight. For generations artists have summered on the island and contributed to a prodigious output of coastal landscapes and seascapes. Beginning in July, many of these works are on display

in the Monhegan Museum, the Plantation Gallery, and artists' studios.

Among the most interesting of the various birds and animals seen here are harbor seals, best observed at half tide at the northern end of the island.

Inns, guesthouses, and cottages offer accommodations, and there are a few restaurants. There are no bars, and liquor is not sold. Camping and backpacking are not permitted. *From mid-June through Sept. boats make daily round trips, for which advance reservations are strongly advised. From Port Clyde call (207) 372-8848, and from Boothbay Harbor call (207) 633-2284. You can also phone these numbers to ask for "An Introduction to Monhegan Island," which includes information on places to stay.*

New Hampshire

With its stretch of seashore, vast national forest, and hundreds of lakes and ponds, this is truly a state for all seasons.

Where there's such a wealth of waterways, a great forest, and a seashore, scenic beauty is expected. But there are also some man-made attractions. These include an archeological mystery—still unsolved—and a castle built by a man who dreamed of beauty on every side and made the dream come true. Beauty and grace were the concerns of a renowned sculptor whose studio and home are now on public view. President Franklin Pierce's homestead is here, as is the birthplace of Daniel Webster, the great orator and champion of national unity.

1. Lake Francis State Park. The park is situated on an inlet of Lake Francis where the Connecticut River enters from the First and Second Connecticut lakes. From the park you can view the rapids in the river. Here it is a juvenile stream unimaginably different from the wide expanse it becomes on its seaward course. And yet the young river gathers itself in Lake Francis into a tranquil, expansive body of water, stretching beyond the horizon as if to preview what it will become a few hundred miles downstream. So to stand at the inlet is to see in one glance both the youth of a great river and a prefiguration of its maturity. Wildlife is a major attraction here: 123 different species of birds have been sighted, including bald eagles, loons, and endangered woodpeckers. Deer and moose are frequent visitors, and bears are occasionally seen at a dump only a few miles away.

For hikers there are several possibilities. An easy trail runs through the woods along the Connecticut River, leading from the campground to a covered bridge 1½ miles away. Another trail provides a three-mile hike up the slopes of Mount Galloway, the highest mountain in the area. Although the last mile is quite steep, the spectacular view from the top makes the effort worthwhile. The old logging roads that wind in and around the park are enjoyed by both hikers and bicyclists.

Fishing is good in Lake Francis, and you can rent a boat or canoe nearby; the park has a public boat launch. Within a mile or so of the park are a swimming beach, a stable that rents horses, and riding trails. *Open early May–Columbus Day; accessible year-round.*

2. Coleman State Park. This small, remote park is in a beautiful, almost alpine setting on the shore of Little Diamond Pond, high in the White Mountains (1,700 feet). From it there is a beautiful view across the wooded slopes of Dixville Notch. The park, some 2,500 acres in extent, is sufficiently isolated that bear and moose may be seen; sometimes moose come down to the pond in the evening to feed. Loons settle on the pond, and eagles occasionally circle overhead.

The camping area is a large, grassy field with a scattering of fragrant balsam trees and hardwoods. There are no hookups for trailers, but each campsite has a fireplace with a grill, and during the camping season water is piped in from a spring. If you are lured by the prospect of catching rainbow trout or squaretail brook trout to grill over your campfire, you may want to bring a boat, which you can launch at the small beach. Boats can also be obtained from a privately owned rental outfit a short way down the road.

From Little Diamond Pond the road continues on to Big Diamond Pond a mile away, providing an enjoyable walk and a good chance of seeing deer. For a more rigorous outing you can hike the fairly steep trail, roughly half a mile long, from the campground up Sugar Hill. In winter the park is an ideal place for cross-country skiing, snowshoeing, and snowmobiling.

The park, which is reached by a good paved road, is accessible year-round. *Open for camping late May–mid-Oct.*

3. Norton Pike. *Littleton. Go north from the center of Littleton on Rte. 116 (Union St.), and turn right on Reddington St.; cross the river and the railroad tracks, and then make an immediate right turn on Brook Rd.;*

Norton Pike is on your right. This division of the Norton Company is probably the largest manufacturer of sharpening stones in the world. The roots of this subsidiary go back to 1823, when a farmer in the village of Pike discovered a kind of sandstone on his land that was good for sharpening blades. He began to sell the stone locally, and after his death his widow expanded the business. The company grew, and in 1917 it was bought by the Norton Company, thus becoming Norton Pike. The present factory was built in 1947.

During your tour, you will see both "natural" and "artificial" sharpening stones being made in innumerable shapes and sizes. The natural stones are made from hard and soft Arkansas rock, shipped to the factory in roughly quarried lumps. The rock is first cut into thin slabs of approximately the desired size by an array of gang saws. Final cutting to size is done by hand; the stones are then ready to be cleaned, dried, and oiled.

A more elaborate procedure is required for the artificial stones, which are made from two kinds of coke derivatives, silicon carbide and aluminum oxide. These are ground into powder and mixed with a bonding material. This mixture is next put into molds in presses that exert from 25 to 75 tons of pressure. The formed stones are then dried at 1200° C and ground to their final size and shape.

The tour of the factory, which lasts about an hour, is not only fascinating but oddly appealing—perhaps because one finds in these old processes an understandable technology and a level of craftsmanship that is easy to admire. *Open weekdays except holidays.*

4. Shelburne Birches Memorial Forest. Flanking the highway for nearly one-fifth of a mile at Shelburne is a dense stand of paper birches, dazzlingly graceful throughout the year in their white bark, and especially ravishing in spring or autumn, when their leaves are in the first delicate flush of green or the last glory of gold and yellow.

This is the kind of tree from which the

4. *A few conifers and other hardwoods have established a foothold, but the woods here near Shelburne are dominated by the dramatic paper birch.*

LEGEND

NUMBERED ATTRACTIONS DESCRIBED IN TEXT **1**

HIGHWAY MARKERS

INTERSTATE **70**   UNITED STATES **40**   STATE **53**

ROAD CLASSIFICATIONS

Interchanges

CONTROLLED ACCESS HIGHWAYS
(Entrance and Exit only at Interchanges)

OTHER DIVIDED HIGHWAYS

PRINCIPAL THROUGH HIGHWAYS

OTHER THROUGH HIGHWAYS

CONNECTING HIGHWAYS

MILEAGES

LONG DISTANCE MILEAGES SHOWN IN RED
35

MILEAGE BETWEEN DOTS

ONE MILE EQUALS 1.6 KILOMETERS   ONE KILOMETER EQUALS .6 MILES

SPECIAL FEATURES

STATE PARKS ▲ With Campsites △ Without Campsites   RECREATION AREAS ▲ With Campsites △ Without Campsites

POINTS OF INTEREST

© THE H.M. GOUSHA COMPANY · SAN JOSE, CALIFORNIA

SCALE IN MILES AND KILOMETERS
ONE INCH 20 MILES 0   5   10   15   20
ONE INCH 32 KM 0 5 10 15 20   32

North American Indians made their birchbark canoes, and some of the ones growing here are giants—among the largest to be found in the eastern United States. An especially rare thing to see along a well-traveled highway, the forest, a commemoration of Shelburne citizens who served in World War II, was established soon after the war's conclusion.

5. Greeley Ponds. The entrance to the pond trail is at a small parking lot about four miles west of Kancamagus Pass on the south side of the road. Note: the sign

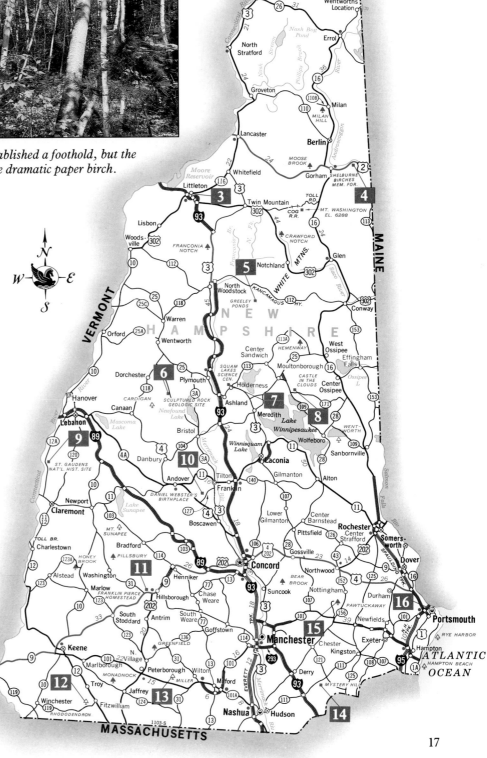

9. The garden was designed by the sculptor and members of his family. The brooding figure below is a bronze casting of the memorial commissioned by Henry Adams for his wife Marian. The original is in Rock Creek Cemetery, Washington, D.C.

is parallel to the road and quite easy to miss. There is also an access from Waterville Valley to the south.

The trail to the first of the two ponds from Kancamagus Highway is about 2½ miles long; the second pond is almost half a mile farther. It is fairly easy walking. There are no extreme gradients; log bridges span streams and swampy places; and the trail is clearly marked with yellow blazes on the trees. The only obstacles for hikers are the knotted tree roots that crisscross the path almost every step of the way. But in winter the trail is excellent for cross-country skiing. The forest here is a mixture of conifers and deciduous trees, with a notably dense stretch of waist-high young hemlocks.

The Restricted Use Scenic Area (where fires and camping are not allowed) is more open than the rest of the forest, and as you enter it you begin to glimpse the cliffs towering above you and realize that you have been walking up a wide valley. Near the first pond a steep trail leads to a peak on

one of these ridges, Mount Osceola. The ponds themselves are dark green and still, protected from passing winds by the trees around them. As you approach the first, look for the mature hemlock growing atop a seven-foot-high boulder. The roots reach down the rock to the earth like muscular boa constrictors. *Accessible year-round, weather permitting.*

6. Sculptured Rock Geologic Site. At this intriguing stretch of the Cockermouth River, the stream has worn a chasm some 100 feet long and 30 feet deep. Its granite walls, striated in pale colors, have been carved and polished by the water into a fantasy of bowls, beaks, curves, and swirls. Here too are ferns that have somehow established a precarious foothold in the rock.

The best vantage point is from a bridge spanning the river. If you face down-

stream and look directly below, you can see the shape of a lion's head in the rock, with its nose at the stream and a round hole marking the gape of the mouth. Elsewhere, as you look down, you can see what appear to be toad and lizard heads, primeval shell creatures with bulging eyes—and whatever else your imagination and the water level at the time may permit. The gorge is estimated to be about a million years old. *Open year-round.*

7. Science Center of New Hampshire at Squam Lakes. A lovingly tended place, the center's purpose is to introduce the visitor to a variety of natural environments and the creatures that live in them.

An exhibit trail, which is open from May 1 to November 1, leads from the visitor center across rocky meadowland through which a small stream flows. The stream drains another ecological zone, an area of marsh, and finally flows into a trout pond. The attractive expanse of water, with white granite boulders at its edge, mirrors venerable white pines and paper birches on its dark surface. Nearby are enclosures for bears, deer, owls, raccoons, and a bobcat. Farther along the trail are a forestry exhibit and a hundred-year-old steam-powered sawmill.

In July and August live animals are displayed during talks given by naturalists about the local wildlife. For the rest of the year the center has special programs for school groups. *Open year-round. Admission charged May 1–Nov. 1.*

8. Castle in the Clouds. *Moultonborough.* This lovely place in the Ossipee Mountains edging Lake Winnipesaukee is the dramatic expression of a desire that is easy to understand and all but impossible to fulfill. The project that achieved this purpose was the creation of Thomas Gustave Plant, a multimillionaire whose dream was to have an environment in which he could behold nothing but beauty. Purchasing 6,000 acres of woodland and sparing no expense, Plant built his mansion on a promontory with views of the island-studded lake below and the White Mountains looming in the distance. To achieve the perfection he required, Plant utilized the skills of vast numbers of European artists and craftsmen. The estate, completed in 1910 at a cost of $7 million, was named Lucknow after a castle in Scotland.

Exploring the grounds, one can only agree that Plant realized his dream. Miles of carriage roads and riding trails wind through quiet woods fragrant with pine to waterfalls, ponds, streams, and hilltops with breathtaking views of the surrounding countryside. There are garden walks and tours of the mansion, whose stained glass windows depict some of the scenery here. The best time to visit is from the third week of September to mid-October, when the autumn foliage is brilliant and the crowds have dwindled. *Open weekends early May–mid-June; daily mid-June–mid-Oct. Admission charged.*

9. Saint-Gaudens National Historic Site. *Just off Rte. 12A, 2½ miles north of Windsor, Vt. (location of the longest covered bridge in the United States).* This fine house—a large, elaborate structure set on high ground and circled by lawns and distant views of the Vermont hills—was once the home of one of America's most distinguished sculptors, Augustus Saint-Gaudens. Originally a coach inn on the old stage road between Windsor and Meriden, it was bought by Saint-Gaudens in 1885 for a summer place, but from 1900 until his death in 1907 the estate served as his permanent home.

Here he combined his interests in gardening and the styles of the classical Greek and Roman periods to create a fairyland of porticoes and wide vistas, of colonnades and formal gardens. On the property are two studios, the Gallery, the Temple (where the artist is buried), and some of Saint Gaudens's most famous works.

Saint-Gaudens's father, an immigrant shoemaker, had encouraged his son's artistic interests; remembering this, the sculptor named the estate Aspet, after his father's birthplace in France. Saint-Gaudens was an inspirational teacher, and many young artists studied with him at Aspet. He encouraged students and apprentices to follow his personal inclination "to develop technique and then to hide it." *Open daily Memorial Day–mid-Oct. Admission charged.*

10. Birthplace of Daniel Webster. *Go south on Rte. 127 about 2½ miles from its junction with Rte. 3 and take the third hard-top road on the west (the first with a road sign for a junction); go 3/4 mile on this road to find the house, which is signed.* Daniel Webster was born here on January 18, 1782. The son of a poor farmer, he became one of America's preeminent statesmen. Throughout his long career as lawyer, legislator, Cabinet officer, and presidential aspirant, he was renowned for his oratorical eloquence, powerful presence, and championship of national unity. For 40 years he was New England's most respected and influential spokesman. Webster, who died in 1852, was elected to the Senate Hall of Fame in 1957.

His birthplace, a small, single-story building of dark gray clapboard with cedar shingles, is an essay in simplicity. The two-room interior is simple in the extreme, with wide board floors, a brick

10. This humble cabin in the woods retains the sense of remoteness that was all too real in the late 1700's, when Daniel Webster was a youngster here.

19

fireplace, a bench, and a table. The house, in its modesty, is in telling contrast to the eminence that Daniel Webster later achieved. *Open Wed.–Sun., late June–Labor Day. Admission charged for persons over 17; senior citizens free.*

11. Franklin Pierce Homestead. *Hillsborough.* This gracious white clapboard Georgian-style mansion was completed in 1804 by Benjamin Pierce, a prosperous politician. That same year saw the birth of a son, Franklin, who later became the 14th president of the United States. The Pierces were a sociable family, and many great men of the time, including Daniel Webster, visited them during Franklin's youth. Handsome, intelligent, and well liked, Franklin rose quickly in politics and left home in 1833 to serve as a Democratic congressman in Washington, D.C.; 20 years later he was inaugurated president. Unable to deal effectively with the issue of slavery, he lost the support of his party, gave up politics in 1857, and retired to Concord, New Hampshire.

The interior of the homestead at Hillsborough, now a national historic landmark, has been largely restored to its original appearance. Of special interest is the elegant ballroom on the second floor, with hand-stenciled walls. Here Benjamin

Pierce, a Revolutionary War veteran, used to drill the local militia. Among the antique items in the barn is Franklin Pierce's fine old horse-drawn sleigh, decorated with painted flowers. The homestead is managed by volunteers from the Hillsborough Historical Society. *Open Fri.–Sun. and holidays, Memorial Day–Labor Day. Admission charged.*

12. Rhododendron State Park. In these 294 rolling acres of the Monadnock Hills is a 16-acre stand of *Rhododendron catawbiense* and *Rhododendron maximum*. The stand of *R. maximum* is the largest to be found at such a northerly latitude. The shrubs, blooming in July, create a flowering canopy 15 feet high.

The park had its origin in 1902, when Mary Lee Ware bought the land to preserve the rhododendrons from the damage that would ensue from a proposed lumbering operation. The following year she donated the land to the Appalachian Mountain Club, which gave it in turn to the state of New Hampshire in 1946.

The rhododendron trail is easily walked in about an hour, and even when the shrubs are not in flower it is a very pleasant excursion: the woodland is fairly open, and from the higher parts of the trail you can look down on the carpet of

rhododendrons that elsewhere arch above your head.

Just off the path leading to the picnic area is a wildflower trail established and maintained by the Fitzwilliam Garden Club, where an interesting selection of wild plants—ginger and Indian tobacco, for example—has been planted and labeled. *Open year-round.*

13. Miller State Park. The park lies on Pack Monadnock Mountain, and the road to it is very steep, with numerous hairpin bends. Though paved, it is unsuitable for buses or campers, or for any driver not confident of his vehicle's brakes. But the drive up the mountain is of particular interest because you rapidly ascend through clearly distinct zones of vegetation that reflect the dramatic influence of altitude on the climate and the plants that thrive. The view from the summit is superb, and from an observation tower you have an even loftier perspective of the surrounding mountains and valleys.

You can picnic at the peak, but be aware that it will be several degrees colder there than at the foot of the mountain, and that the wind can be fierce. *Open year-round but impassable during snow and ice. Admission charged daily in summer; on weekends late spring and early autumn.*

14. Mystery Hill. Scattered over about 20 acres on this lightly wooded hilltop are several curiously placed stone slabs and tumbled stone walls that form higgledy-piggledy avenues. For visitors, perhaps the greatest interest here is in the claims made for the place and the prolonged debate it has provoked.

According to some investigators, this is the most significant pre-Columbian site in North America, clear evidence of a great civilization that flourished here, perhaps, in the Bronze Age, long before Europeans "discovered" the New World. Those who support this view call the place America's Stonehenge, comparing it to England's famous Stonehenge, a megalithic monument from prehistoric times. According to the others—the majority of academic archeologists—the complex dates from the colonial period and no earlier, being the

11. *The generous proportions, and the inviting entry-garden, recall the hospitality of the homestead where President Franklin Pierce spent his early years.*

13. *Villages, farms, lakes, woodlands, and distant hills—the essence of New England—are all in evidence here.*

work, perhaps, of an eccentric and imaginative farmer. If his purpose was to mystify, he certainly succeeded.

At the visitor center, evidence for both schools of thought is displayed in museum cases containing finds from this and other "pre-Columbian" sites, including what some claim are inscriptions in runic, Punic, and other ancient Old World scripts. Tour guide maps, available at the visitor center, explain the various features found along the path looping the area. *Open daily May–Oct.; weekends Apr. and Nov., weather permitting. Admission charged.*

15. Pawtuckaway State Park. A rolling road through this varied park, with more than 5,000 acres of unspoiled nature, takes you to picnic grounds and campsites on a promontory above Lake Pawtuckaway. On the way you pass two large swamps, picturesque with sedge and cattails, and a beaver pond where the skeletons of drowned trees rise starkly from the water. At the boundary of the park, and visually a part of it, is Mount Pawtuckaway, with its granite cliffs.

The woodland here, primarily composed of oak, white pine, and birch, is especially interesting for the many large glacially deposited boulders that are scattered throughout the area. The shores of the lake are also strewn with boulders. Fishermen come for the bass and pickerel, while birders look for the blue herons, eagles, and Canada geese that frequent the area. In winter the park is opened only when there is snow; the parking area is plowed to give access to trails for cross-country skiing and snowmobiling. *Open for camping mid-May–Columbus Day.*

16. The Wentworth-Coolidge Mansion. *Portsmouth.* Back in colonial times this handsome, green-shuttered frame house, sprawling over a knoll facing Little Harbor, was a hub of social and political activity in New Hampshire. As the residence of Benning Wentworth, a native of Portsmouth who became New Hampshire's first royal governor, it was the colony's seat of government from 1741 to 1767. Here, in the room used as a council chamber, Wentworth granted large parcels of land, signed charters incorporating new towns, and arranged trade alliances, all of which had an immense impact on the colony's development.

Governor Wentworth also gave a great deal of attention to the development of his mansion. He employed the best artisans he could find to embellish the interior with elaborate woodwork, the beautifully carved pine mantelpiece that adorns the council chamber, and other architectural grace notes. The results attest to the skills of 18th-century craftsmen.

Since 1816 the Wentworth estate has been owned in turn by the Cushings of Massachusetts and the J. Templeman Coolidge family, who presented the property to the state of New Hampshire in 1954. The house has remained almost intact. Some of the rooms are now refurbished to appear as they did when the Wentworths lived here, while others reflect the times of the Cushings and the Coolidges, thus providing a fascinating view of changing lifestyles over a period of nearly 250 years.

You can take a self-guided tour of the mansion, enjoy a picnic on the 100-acre estate with its rolling lawns and profusion of lilacs (in early May), stroll through a recreated 18th-century garden, and amble down to the dock to see the old boathouse and a small schooner. *Open weekends Memorial Day–late June; then daily through Labor Day. Admission charged.*

Vermont

The fall color, white church steeples, maple syrup, cheese, and good skiing might well be enough—but there's more.

Among the surprises along the byways of the Green Mountain State are two attractions dedicated to the spirit: one is a shrine where healing is said to take place, the other a church built in the round to (perhaps) keep the devil from lurking in corners. More earthly concerns are recalled in a tavern-museum, a cheese factory, and a marble exhibit. Here are the homestead of a man who had a great idea for education and the boyhood home of our 30th president. Art is acknowledged in a petroglyph site and a display of works by a famous grandmother.

1. St. Anne Shrine. *Isle La Motte.* Vermont's oldest white settlement was founded here at the water's edge in 1666, when a French officer, Capt. Pierre La Motte, built Fort St. Anne as a bastion against the Mohawk Indians. The fort was needed for only a short time, but soon afterward Jesuit priests built the first Christian chapel on the site.

Within the small cruciform chapel is a simple wooden altar with the figures of St. Anne and the Virgin Mary. To the left another altar is dedicated to St. Anne; on the walls near it hang abandoned crutches and plaster casts, evidence of the healings that are said to take place here. A rustic grotto near the chapel shelters a figure of the Virgin Mary. Also close by is an A-frame shrine that houses a marble statue of St. Anne. On the hill behind the chapel are other shrines that are dedicated to Sts. Anthony and Francis.

In a grove of pine trees on the site of the old stockade is the Gethsemane Garden, where the stations of the cross are inscribed on copper tablets. Beyond the Gethsemane Garden stands a granite statue of Samuel de Champlain, in a canoe with an Indian companion, marking the site of his landfall at Isle La Motte in 1609. Because of the crowds attracted to the shrine on weekends and holidays, it is best to visit the place on weekdays. *Dock facilities are available for those who come by boat. Open May 15–Oct. 15.*

2. Missisquoi National Wildlife Refuge. *Swanton.* The Indian name Missisquoi, meaning an area of "much waterfowl" and "much grass," well describes this place. Vast numbers of migratory waterfowl traveling the Atlantic Flyway stop to feed and rest here on some 5,600 acres of marsh, open water, and woodland. The best months to see them—black ducks, mallards, wood ducks, Canada geese, and many other species—are May into June and mid-September to early October. Among the nearly 200 species of birds observed here are great egrets, bald eagles, and pileated woodpeckers.

The Black Creek and Maquam Creek nature trails, together about 1½ miles in length, are easily walked. They follow the course of two woodland creeks whose waters are darkened by decaying vegetation. Points of interest along the way, numbered and described in the trail brochure, include muskrat burrows, woodpecker feeding stations, and duck "loafing sites." Beavers are abundant here, and signs of their activities—felled birch trees, wood chips, scent mounds, runs, and lodges—are everywhere, most dramatically in the many bone-white birch limbs floating in the black water.

White-tailed deer, red fox, raccoon, otter, and mink are in residence; and among the fish are northern pike, walleye, bass, salmon, and carp. But whether you fish or simply walk and look about you, the Missisquoi Refuge provides a fine opportunity to view nature as a network of interdependent communities. *Open year-round, but the trails may be flooded in spring.*

3. Big Falls. *North Troy. On Rte. 101, just south of the junction with 105, turn right on Veilleux Rd. (dirt). Follow this across a covered bridge and take the first left. Go about 1½ miles, then look (and listen) for the falls on your left. The first pull-off on the left after you see the falls gives access to the best viewing spots, which are above the waterfall.* Just upstream from the falls, the Missisquoi River divides around a rocky island

topped by small conifers. The scene is elegant enough to have been designed by a Japanese gardener. Below this the river plunges, boils, fumes, and roars into a narrow chasm perhaps 60 feet deep, and then continues wide and placid between banks set with hemlock and juniper.

There are no facilities for tourists here, but the falls may be seen at any time of the year. In wet weather they should be approached with *extreme caution:* the granite underfoot can be very slippery. The height and plunge of the falls could make one dizzy, and the spectacle is so attractive as to tempt the unwary viewer beyond a safe foothold.

4. Brighton State Park. *Island Pond. Signed on Rte. 105 just west of the town; where the road forks, keep to the left.* The park is small but charmingly situated on the shore of Island Pond Lake. Adjacent to the white sandy beach are picnic tables and a bathhouse, fine views of the conifer-clad island from which the lake takes its name, and the surrounding hills.

The town of Island Pond, with its white church, which would seem at home in the Swiss Alps, is attractively situated at the far end of the lake and adds to the appeal of the setting. *Open May–mid-Oct.; accessible year-round.*

5. Grand Isle State Park. This agreeably spacious campground spreads down a gently sloping hillside overlooking Lake Champlain and the mountains beyond its eastern shore. The terrain is an open mix of light woodland and rough pasture, with an ancient split-rail zigzag fence running along the north and west boundaries.

Easily reached by ferry from Plattsburgh, New York, or by road and bridge from the south, the park provides an idyllic central location from which to explore the bays, inlets, beaches, islands, and small villages for which the Champlain area is famous. Facilities include 31 lean-tos, some with access for the handi-

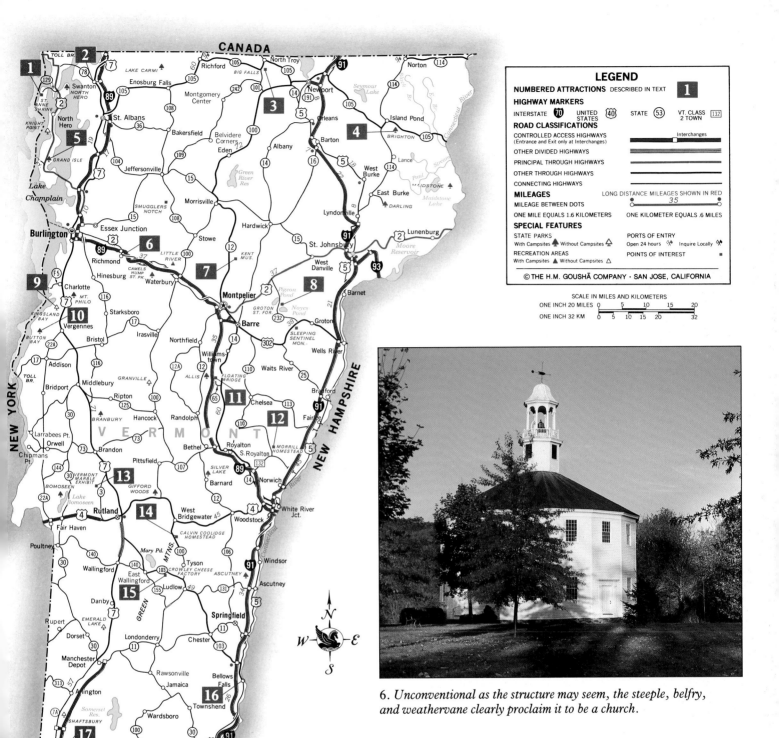

6. *Unconventional as the structure may seem, the steeple, belfry, and weathervane clearly proclaim it to be a church.*

capped. To reserve a shelter, call (802) 372-4300. *Swimming and rental boats for campers only. Open Memorial Day–Columbus Day; accessible year-round.*

6. Old Round Church. *Richmond. Heading south on Rte. 2, turn right onto Bridge St. at the center of Richmond. Pass the post office, cross the railroad tracks and the bridge spanning the Winooski River, and continue to the Old Round Church.* From the time it was built in 1813, this remarkable 16-sided, two-story frame building has attracted comment. The reason for its shape is not certain. Local lore says it was to keep the devil from lurking in corners or to prevent an enemy from hiding around a corner. Another suggestion is that 16 men each built a side and a 17th added the belfry. A page from the account book of William Rhodes, the head carpenter, lists 17 workers in addition to himself. But the most likely explanation is that it was modeled after a round church in Claremont, New Hampshire, where Rhodes's parents lived.

The Old Round Church was built to serve as both a house of worship and a town hall. Five denominations cooperated to raise money for its construction by selling pews. Regular church services ceased around 1880, but town meetings were held here until 1973, when the church was

8. *This white-tailed deer expresses concentrated interest in a strange intruder.*

declared structurally unsafe. Since then it has been completely restored. Of special interest are the box pews, the hand-wrought hinges, and the hand-painted wood graining on both the pulpit and the horseshoe-shaped balcony. *Open daily July 4–Labor Day; weekends only late spring and early autumn.*

7. Kent Museum. *Kent's Corner, Calais.* Lost today on an old gravel road between Maple Corner and East Calais, this handsome brick house has a vibrant past. Back in the 1830's the Montreal–Boston coach road passed this way on the lap between the Vermont towns of Hardwick and Montpelier. Since the stagecoach required a change of horses and Calais was about midway, Abdiel Kent, a local young entrepreneur, decided to build a tavern to meet this need.

Almost all the materials used in the building's construction—bricks, granite, and lumber—were produced and fashioned in the immediate vicinity. "A. Kent's Hotel"—complete with a tap-room, ballroom, and an attached store—opened in 1837 and remained in operation until 1846, when the proprietor married and converted it into a family home. Soon afterward the stage route was replaced by the railroad. Owned by the Vermont Historical Society since 1944, the tavern has

been restored as a museum with furnishings, toys, and implements in a homelike setting portraying the lifestyle of 19th-century Vermonters. *Open P.M. Tues.–Sun., July–Aug.; weekends only late Sept.–early Oct. Admission charged.*

8. Groton State Forest. The nine recreation areas in this beautiful forest offer opportunities for a variety of outdoor activities, summer and winter. The forest, a mix of hemlocks, birches, maples, and other hardwoods, is threaded with trails

for hiking, snowmobiling, and nature study. In several of the areas inviting campsites are to be found.

The Boulder Beach Day Use Area is on Lake Groton, the largest body of water in the forest. Here the dense woods, which elsewhere come right down to the edge of the lake, have given way to a pleasant small, sandy beach studded with large boulders deposited by a glacier thousands of years ago. On your way to the beach, look for a massive boulder with a large paper birch growing from the top. A briskly bubbling stream runs alongside.

Dedicated trout fishermen may want to seek out Noyes Pond in the Seyon Fly-Fishing Area, where fly casting is permitted only from boats and canoes. ("Seyon" is "Noyes" spelled backwards.) *On Rte. 302, about 1½ miles west of its junction with Rte. 232, watch for the sign to the Seyon Area. Take the dirt road here, turn right at the signed fork, then left at the next unsigned fork. Rental boats. Boulder Beach Area open early June–Labor Day; accessible year-round. Seyon Area open early May–Oct.*

9. Kingsland Bay State Park. This exceptionally pretty park is set on an inlet on the east shore of Lake Champlain, a place of quiet green water and gray pebble beaches strewn with small boulders and bleached driftwood. Ledges of granite, clothed in juniper and arborvitae, project into the lake from miniature headlands; far beyond are the peaks of the Adirondacks.

The road into the park, running along

10. *Sailboat confirms the connection of the bay to the waters of Lake Champlain.*

11. *It seems like an illusion, but the Brookfield bridge is actually afloat. Hinged ends allow for changing water level.*

and above the shore, is fringed on the lakeside by wild grape, white pine, bittersweet, and arborvitae; on the other side lie open meadows. The road leads to a picnic area where there are tables and charcoal grills. There is also a small beach where boats can be launched.

If you continue a few hundred yards beyond the park entrance and take the first turn to the right, you will come immediately to an informal parking area at the head of the inlet. From here, there are fine views and access to the water. *Rental boats and canoes. Open Memorial Day–Labor Day; accessible year-round.*

---

10. Button Bay State Park. Button Bay, a wide inlet on the east shore of southern Lake Champlain, is approached across an alluvial plain that becomes a patchwork of vivid green meadows and cultivated fields in the spring. On the western side of the lake are the undulating foothills of the Adirondacks. At a distance to the east rise the Green Mountains—which from here take on a lovely shade of blue.

The 236-acre park wraps around the shore of Button Bay, which is relatively open, with conifer woods to the north and south. There are well-arranged tent and trailer sites and several lean-tos, as well as

a picnic area and boat-launching sites. Nature trails, including one for the blind, and a small nature museum add to the park's appeal. *Rental boats. Open late May–mid-Oct.*

---

11. Floating Bridge. *Brookfield.* Brookfield is a charming village of white clapboard houses and well-trimmed lawns nestling beside the dark waters of Sunset Lake. In 1820 Luther Adams built a floating bridge across the lake here, and since then people, animals, carts, and cars have crossed the water—a journey of about 100 yards—by this curiously intimate means.

The present bridge, built in 1978 by the Vermont Agency of Transportation, is the seventh at the site. Made of pressure-treated timber, the roadway is supported by 380 floating polyethylene drums filled with polyurethane foam. Driving across the bridge, which barely skims the lake, you see the water so close to eye level that the sensation is rather like being in a boat. At each end is a hinged ramp, and at these points the water can be as much as five inches deep. Check your brakes after crossing in these conditions. For pedestrians, there are walkways on each side, raised eight inches above the driving lane.

---

12. The Justin Smith Morrill Homestead. *Strafford.* On July 2, 1862, President Lincoln signed the Morrill Act, a measure that contributed mightily to the cause of higher education by granting public lands to the states to help finance colleges offering courses in "agriculture and the mechanic arts." Representative Justin Morrill worked on his far-reaching legislation here in the house he designed and built for himself in 1848–51. A wood cottage painted rosy pink to simulate stone and adorned about its windows, porches, and gables with Carpenter Gothic trim, it seems as visionary in its setting as the schools that Morrill proposed.

The land rises to fields and woods behind the house, and not far up the hill are several farm buildings, also pink. From the hillside may be seen the Strafford Town House, erected in 1799 as a meetinghouse for local officials, and as a place of worship for all denominations. The view is charming, as is a little man-made waterfall tumbling through the hole of a lichened millstone. This small detail evokes the kind of loving care that Morrill gave to his home.

The furnishings include pieces from Morrill's Washington home as well as family memorabilia. Among the intriguing features of the house are the screens on the parlor and dining room windows. They have romantic landscapes hand-painted on the outside to keep people from looking in while allowing those inside to see out. The property is now a national historic landmark. *Open Wed.– Sun., mid-May–mid-Oct.*

---

13. Vermont Marble Exhibit. *Proctor.* There are extensive deposits of marble in Vermont's Green Mountains, and most of the stone quarried there is processed in the village of Proctor, the largest center for such work in North America. The Vermont Marble Exhibit, also the largest of its kind, documents every aspect of this remarkable stone and many of the ways in which it is used.

Among the displays are walls of marble of different kinds from all over the world: Peru, Golden Vein, Carolina Rose, Minnesota Flambeau, Andes Black, and many others are as varied, intriguing, and beautiful as their names. Exhibits include tabletops, baths, flooring, and a complete series of relief busts of the presidents of the United States. Other exhibits, as well as films, explore the geology of marble and quarrying and production methods.

13. Sculptor Alan Dwight uses an air-powered pneumatic hammer to create a lifelike iguana in Vermont marble.

14. The furnishings are those of a person content with simple surroundings. They were used, surprisingly, by the 29th president of the United States.

A gallery overlooks a shop where the marble is finished.

In a sculptor's studio you can also watch granite being chiseled and carved and see an exhibition of modern granite sculpture and statuary. *Open daily late May–Oct. Admission charged.*

---

14. Calvin Coolidge Homestead. *Plymouth.* Shortly after midnight on August 2, 1923, Vice President Coolidge, who was vacationing at his boyhood home in Plymouth, was awakened when a courier brought word that President Warren G. Harding had suddenly died. By the light of a kerosene lamp in the sitting room, Coolidge was sworn into office as the new president by his father, a notary public. During his five years as Chief Executive Coolidge returned here for vacations, content with the simplicity of the house and its air of peacefulness. Not until 1932 did he install electricity and other modern amenities. He was buried, as he requested, in the cemetery nearby in 1933.

The small white farmhouse stands in a spacious meadow at the edge of Plymouth village. There are no elaborate gardens or stands of ancient trees to soften its spartan quality, or to detract from the plain and simple ambiance that makes it so appealing—particularly when one considers the eminence of its owner.

Nearby is a handsome large barn that

houses a Farmers Museum. The homestead, barn, and the white frame church that Coolidge attended now constitute a national historic landmark. *Open daily mid-May–mid-Oct. Admission charged.*

---

15. Crowley Cheese Factory. *Healdville.* At Vermont's oldest cheese factory, Colby (a kind of cheddar, but with a creamier, more open texture) is still made every day by hand, just as it was a hundred years ago. Visitors can see the curds being cut and raked in the big vats, then hand-worked and formed in hand-cranked presses. The tools, techniques, and product haven't changed.

The factory was built by Winfield Crowley in 1808, when his business outgrew the farm kitchen where he had by then been making cheese for almost 60 years. The establishment today is still redolent of the less hurried, more peaceful time when it got its start. A collection of old cheesemaking tools—curd knives, a cheese press, and a centrifuge—is on display. You can sample the product or buy it at the gift shop, along with candy, maple syrup, jams, and baked goods. *Factory open Mon.–Sat.; shop open daily.*

---

16. Indian Petroglyphs. *Bellows Falls.* The best vantage point is about 50 feet downstream from the Vilas Bridge on the west side of the Connecticut River. Looking over the riverbank, just beyond a white fence, you can see a boulder with yellow paint marks and several petroglyphs deeply incised in the rock, covering a surface about 15 feet in breadth and 6 feet in height, probably carved by the Pennacook Indians.

The petroglyphs represent heads—probably human, but perhaps not. Several of them have a pair of horns, or feathers, projecting from the crown, and two are connected by a kind of cord. The most prominent figure in the group is a head adorned by six horns and supported by a neck and shoulders. If they represent humans, the carvings are a little larger then life-size. Possibly the petroglyphs commemorate periods when local tribes would suspend hostilities and gather here to fish for salmon on their spawning run up the Connecticut River. But what the staring-eyed faces represent, or when or why they were carved, we may never know. They may simply be an example of early American graffiti. *Accessible year-round.*

---

17. Grandma Moses Gallery and Schoolhouse. *Bennington.* A hardworking farm woman most of her life, Grandma Moses began to paint in oils at the age of 78. Although she had no technical training, her farm scenes and rural landscapes had a cheerful, naive quality that soon won her acclaim as a "primitive." She completed more than 1,000 works before her death in 1961 at the age of 101. Some 30 paintings by Grandma Moses are displayed in the gallery, along with plates and tiles ornamented with scenes from her paintings and the tilt-top pine table she used as an easel (with side panels decorated in her inimitable style).

Adjoining the gallery is the schoolhouse Grandma Moses attended as a girl in Eagle Bridge, New York. It was also the school for four of her nine grandchildren and nine great-grandchildren. Built in 1834, the schoolhouse was moved to Bennington in 1971 and now serves as a museum of Grandma Moses memorabilia. In it is a stained glass window from the W.D. Thomas Pharmacy in Hoosick Falls, New York, where her work was first shown. The main part of the room re-creates the appearance of the old schoolhouse, with church pews (instead of benches) and antique desks.

The Grandma Moses Gallery and Schoolhouse are associated with the well-known Bennington Museum, which has fine collections of pottery and glass, furniture, paintings, costumes, and musical and medical instruments on display. *Open daily Mar.–Nov. excluding Thanksgiving Day. Admission charged.*

---

18. Molly Stark State Park. Situated in a beautiful valley on the west side of Mount Olga, this small park has several appealing features. The local roads are favored by cyclists, and in winter the countryside is inviting for skiers and snowshoers. In addition, the forest of hardwoods and pines harbors deer, raccoons, Cooper's hawks, and other wildlife of interest to nature lovers. The park's campsites are set in the woods around a pleasant clearing dotted with apple trees.

Perhaps the main attraction, however, is the trail leading from the campground to the summit of Mount Olga. About three-quarters of a mile long, it is easy to follow, although it is somewhat steep near the summit. From the mountaintop the view is of wooded hills and valleys with an occasional barn roof glinting in the sun. On a clear day you can see the states of New York, Vermont, New Hampshire, Massachusetts, and Connecticut. For even better views you can climb the ladder of the fire tower located at the summit. *Open for camping late May–early Oct.*

ADVENTURE—Off the Beaten Path

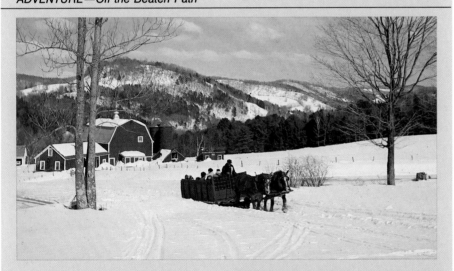

In a Horse-Drawn Sleigh

When it took two men a good 20 minutes to hitch up the sturdy team of Belgians that would pull the 14 of us over hill and dale here in eastern Vermont, we knew we were slipping into the unhurried pace of a bygone era.

As soon as we were comfortably seated on bales of hay and tucked under lap robes, the driver—with a hearty "giddiyap"—started our heavy two-horsepower conveyance on its way. As we glide across the fields, the only sounds we hear are the jingle of sleigh bells on the harness, the heavy breathing of the horses, and the crunch of snow under the runners. The trees, stark against the whiteness, move by at a leisurely rate, and the clouds seem stationary in the sky. Heading into the woods, we're assailed by the heavenly fragrance of the pines. We do not just glance at the snowy world around us; we have time to take it in, soak it up, and make it a part of us.

At the top of the hill we take a leg-stretching walk and enjoy the magnificent view of Woodstock in the valley below. Headed back toward the farm, the horses settle into their 19th-century pace, and we savor the gentle movement, warmth of the sun, and chill of the wind. Later, driving home on a busy road in my speeding steel box insulated from the elements, I feel a haunting sense of loss.   —D.G. Barker

For reservations call (802) 457-2221.

Massachusetts

Concern for its citizenry—expressed by land for public use and in memorials to its heroes—is a hallmark of the Bay State.

Despite a growing population, Massachusetts maintains many superb parks, preserves, and wildlife sanctuaries. Nor does it neglect its prominent leaders. Here you will find the home base of the remarkable Adams family and a historic house directly linked to John Alden, a signer of the Mayflower Compact. The John Greenleaf Whittier home features memorabilia of this influential poet and abolitionist. Early industry is represented by the Saugus Iron Works and the Lowell Historical Park, each of which contributed to the Industrial Revolution.

1. Mount Greylock State Reservation.
Accessible from Rte. 2 near North Adams or from Rte. 7 near Lanesboro. If you take the road from Route 7, stop at the visitor center, which offers a good introduction to the native flora and fauna. A map available here shows campgrounds, picnic areas, and hiking trails in the reservation.

As you drive the steep, winding road up the mountain from either direction, notice how the change in altitude affects vegetation. As the lush hardwood forests at the lower levels give way to the low-growing, wind-sculpted evergreens at the summit, you can see how a relatively small rise in altitude creates conditions of climate and growth similar to the environmental changes that gradually occur hundreds of miles to the north.

Greylock, at 3,491 feet, is the highest peak in Massachusetts. On the summit is a 90-foot stone tower commemorating the citizens of the Commonwealth who died in war. Weather permitting, the top of the tower offers an incomparable panorama of the lovely green-clad mountains and valleys of Massachusetts, New Hampshire, Vermont, Connecticut, and New York.

Among the hiking paths in the reservation is a section of the Appalachian Trail, on which you might meet some of the hardy backpackers going the full distance between Mount Katahdin in Maine and Georgia's Springer Mountain.

The weather at the summit may be quite different from that at the lower levels. Even in summer it is a good idea to take a sweater or windbreaker. The road is closed to cars from first snowfall until about mid-May. Snowmobiles use it in winter. Check road conditions at the visitor center, which is usually open except on major holidays. *Reservation open year-round; campground open mid-May–Oct.*

2. Pleasant Valley Wildlife Sanctuary.
Take West Dugway Rd. about three miles south of Pittsfield. Most animals are secretive in their ways. But the lifestyle of that busy builder and hydraulic engineer, the beaver, is out in the open for all to see. Here at Pleasant Valley you will get a close-up look at the gnawed stumps of their building material and the complex dams they make to control the water level in their mounded lodges.

Beavers were introduced here along Yokun Brook in 1932, and their dams have made ponds that now provide excellent

1. *From Mount Greylock the lush foliage of New England is on magnificent display.*

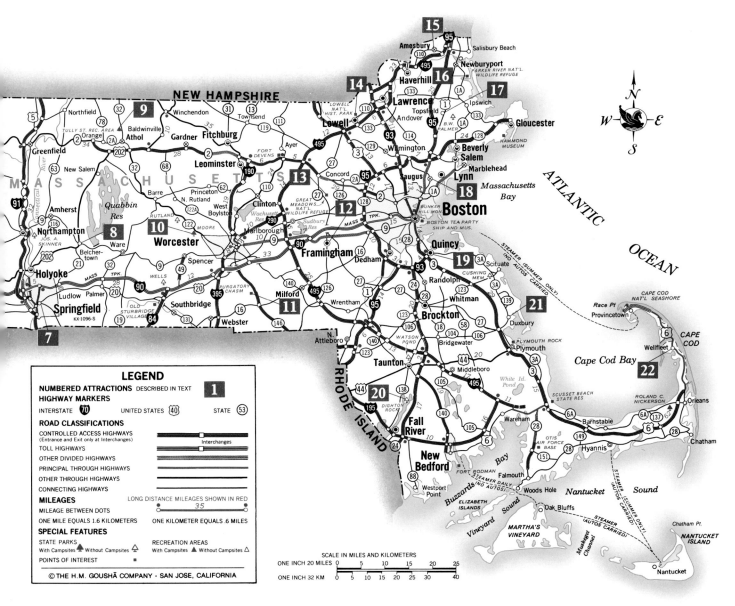

habitats for migrant waterfowl and other birds. Because the sanctuary is at a relatively high elevation, such birds as the hermit thrush, winter wren, and slate-colored junco, normally rare to this area, stay here in spring and summer instead of pushing on farther north to their usual nesting grounds.

The 730-acre area is laced with some seven miles of trails winding past ponds and waterways and through meadows and woods. The Trail of Ledges, which leads to a fire tower and a fine view, is steep in places and should probably not be tried by those unaccustomed to uphill hiking.

A hummingbird garden attracts numbers of these jewellike flyers from June through August. A trail-side museum has natural history exhibits and provides pamphlets describing the water cycle, the numerous plants that grow here, and the

beavers' feats of construction. *Sanctuary open year-round. Museum open Memorial Day–Labor Day.*

---

3. Gingerbread House. *Tyringham.* It is not surprising that this unique structure, with its undulating eaves and oddly shaped windows, set artfully behind interesting constructions of rock, was designed by a sculptor. It was the studio of Henry Hudson Kitson, whose best-known works include the "Minuteman" in Lexington, and the "Pilgrim Maid" in Plymouth.

While the house is reminiscent of the witch's seductive cottage in the fairy tale "Hansel and Gretel," the attraction here is not gingerbread but modern art. After Kitson's death in 1947, the house was

bought by an artist and is now a gallery dealing in sculpture, prints, and paintings by modern artists. Behind the house are two round silolike structures with conical roofs reinforcing the otherworldly aspect. One, attached to the house, is part of the gallery; the other, standing free in the garden, is used as a studio by the owner for his own work. Although known as the Gingerbread House, the official name is the Tyringham Art Gallery. *Open daily June–Aug.; weekends only Sept.–Oct. Admission charged.*

---

4. Bartholomew's Cobble and Colonel Ashley House. *Take Rte. 7-A to Ashley Falls and watch for signs to the Cobble.* This site is best known for the remarkable diversity of its ferns, wildflowers, trees, shrubs, and vines and the many species of

4. The severely symmetrical Ashley house, circa 1735, adjoins Bartholomew's Cobble (right). This rocky outcrop is but one of the interesting topographic features here.

birds they attract. One need not be a naturalist to appreciate the topography of the land here, with its steep cliffs and spines of marble and quartzite interspersed with open glades studded with rocks.

"Cobble" is the New Englander's word for rocky outcrops that rise steeply, like islands of stone, from adjacent bottomlands. This one, named for George Bartholomew, who farmed the surrounding fields in the 1800's, is a natural rock garden of grand proportions.

At the small museum of natural history, you can learn more about almost everything you will see here. Walking the self-guiding, interpretive Ledges Trail takes approximately an hour and provides a concise, delightful experience of small-scale craggy grandeur and botanical variation. A somewhat longer trail leads down to the meandering Housatonic River and a classic oxbow lake. A mile-long uphill path goes to the high pasture that spreads over the top of Hulburt's Hill.

The nearby Colonel Ashley House, built in 1735, is the oldest still standing in Berkshire County. Col. John Ashley was a member of the local committee that, in 1773, drafted resolutions against British tyranny, foreshadowing the Declaration of Independence written in Philadelphia three years later. He acquired holdings of more than 3,000 acres and was among the first slave owners in Massachusetts to accept the idea of abolition.

In the house you will see handsomely finished period rooms, a pottery collection including fine examples of redware, and 18th- and 19th-century tools of many kinds. *Cobble open year-round. Natural history museum open Wed.–Sun., Apr. 15–Oct. 15. Ashley House open P.M. Wed.–Sun. and all holidays, Memorial Day–Columbus Day. Admission charged.*

5. Mohawk Trail State Forest. Here you will walk on paths where from time immemorial the Indians walked, following the course of the river through the steep wooded valley. The pioneers heading west through this opening named it Pioneer Valley, and they aptly called the water course the Cold River.

Flowing past the picnic area and campsites, the Cold River here is swift and boulder-strewn except for a pool for swimming. To the north rises the pine-covered bulk of Mount Todd. Three paths are available to the hiker. You can take a trail to the summit, follow the Indian Trail, which branches off to the left to a high viewpoint, or choose the one-mile trail to the south (the longest of the three), leading to Totem Lookout.

6. Chesterfield Gorge Reservation. *A mile or so west of Chesterfield, go left for two miles to the gorge.* The dramatic power of nature is demonstrated here where the action of ancient glaciers and the erosive force of the Westfield River have cut a gorge about 100 feet deep through solid granite. The river today cascades between vertical cliffs into a deep green pool. Stunted evergreens cling precariously to crevices and ledges on the sheer sides of the gorge.

The charm of the place is its unexpected appearance. The gorge lies hardly 50 yards from a road running through farmland that offers no clue to the powerful natural forces that created it. The ample parking and picnic facilities are a further invitation to stop off here. *Accessible year-round. Warden on duty weekends May 1–Oct. 15. Admission charged.*

7. Indian Motocycle Museum, *33 Hendee St., Springfield.* In 1901 two bicycle enthusiasts, George M. Hendee and Oscar G. Hedstrom, opened the Indian Motocycle Manufacturing Company. (The *r* was dropped to set their product apart.)

The first motorcycles built in America were Indians, and for more than 50 years they were perhaps the world's best-known engine-driven bikes.

The permanent collection in the museum, located on a street named for one of the partners, includes one of every model of Indian Motocycle, from the 1901 Indian to the Chief, produced in 1953. Exhibits are rotated, along with other American makes of the same period.

Here too are other examples of early motor vehicles: the first motorcycle ever built—a Daimler manufactured in Germany in 1885—and the first of all snowmobiles, made at the request of the Canadian government for patrolling the wilderness. Adding to the early 1900's atmosphere are a nickelodeon and a hurdy-gurdy. Hundreds of pamphlets and photographs and a collection of toy motorcycles are also on display.

An Indian X-4 Dog Roadster, an automobile made in 1928, has been restored and is on view. Few of these were produced, and a year later this enterprise was nipped in the bud by the Depression.

A motorcycle festival is held annually on the third Sunday in July. Enthusiasts come on bikes of many different makes to compete for prizes as the oldest, the largest, the best restored by a woman, the farthest driven, the best preserved, and so on. *Open year-round except Thanksgiving Day, Christmas, and New Year's Day. Admission charged.*

8. Charles L. McLaughlin Trout Hatchery.
Belchertown. Trout fishing, one of the world's favorite sports, depends on well-stocked waterways. This hatchery, named for a former director of the state's Division of Fisheries and Wildlife, raises more than a million trout annually just for this purpose. The fry are hatched indoors in fiberglass troughs, transferred to nursery tanks, and then, when they reach the size of fingerlings, released to develop in outdoor concrete raceways.

The most impressive of these three breeding facilities are the 200 50-foot raceways set along a shallow slope, each swarming with rainbow, brook, and brown trout. Although rainbow trout normally breed in the spring, a fall-breeding strain has now been produced.

After a year in the hatchery for some and two years for others, special conveyors lift them to aerated tank-trucks that take them to selected lakes and streams.

For a dime you can buy a handful of food pellets and watch the water swirl and surge as the trout rush to feed.

The water, maintained year-round at a temperature of 48° F, comes from two gravel wells and is sometimes supplemented by a pumping station on the nearby Swift River. *Open year-round.*

9. Tully State Recreation Area. *On Rte. 32, three miles north of Athol.* In the 19th century waterpower was used directly to turn the wheels and run the machinery. For power in the 20th century, water is mostly used to turn the turbines that generate the electricity that runs the machines. Here, in this watery domain, both of these eras are represented.

At the dam on Tully Lake, which was originally built for flood control, a hydroelectric plant is planned. At nearby Doane's Falls a water-driven mill was built in the mid-1700's.

Tully Lake is used mostly for canoeing and fishing. The 21 campsites here are not accessible by car, although none is more than 100 yards from the parking area.

Tully Lake Brook, which flows between Tully Lake and Long Pond about 2½ miles upstream, appeals to paddlers who like a gentle stream with no white water. Tully Brook is stocked with rainbow and brook trout. The lake is equally favored for bass fishing, and pickerel and perch are also taken.

From the lake it's an easy walk to Doane's Falls, where the mill once stood and where millstones and the remains of foundations can still be seen. From beneath a small bridge, Lawrence Brook cascades dramatically for 150 feet or so through a narrow granite gorge. The surrounding woods consist of pines and mixed hardwoods such as oak, maple, beech, and birch; and the predominant wildlife includes red fox, white-tailed deer, otter, beaver, ruffed grouse, woodcock, and pileated woodpecker. Ice fishing and snowmobiling are popular sports in winter. *Recreation area open Memorial Day–Labor Day. Fee for camping.*

10. Moore State Park.
Long forgotten in this peaceful setting are the strident sounds of the sawmill, corn mill, and triphammer shop for which the waterways here were originally built.

Turkey Hill Brook, the source of power for the mills, flows into the 25-acre Eames Pond, then down a succession of three cascades, and on through the park.

An inviting walking trail follows the edge of the pond, where fishermen try for pickerel, perch, and bass.

The exterior of the sawmill that was first operated in 1747 by Jaazaniah Newton has been restored with siding of weathered wood, and the remains of the old water-driven turbines can still be seen. An old schoolhouse is also being restored in the park.

In the well-tended naturalized gardens are great drifts of azalea and mountain laurel, but the star performers here are the rhododendrons. The many species and hybrids produce a profusion of flowers from mid-May through mid-June.

Among the birds to be seen here are chickadees, goldfinches, nuthatches, bluebirds, cardinals, mourning doves, and scarlet tanagers. The park superintendent proudly calls this "a botanical garden in a mill-village setting." It is certainly a serene and pleasant place to break a journey. The park is named for Maj. Willard Moore, a Paxton patriot who led the local farmers to fight the British at Bunker Hill. *Open year-round.*

11. Purgatory Chasm. *The turnoff for the chasm is clearly marked on Rte. 146 about 10 miles south of Worcester.* On venturing into Purgatory Chasm, one is likely to agree that it is well named. Although it is only about 50 feet wide, it reaches a depth of 100 feet or so between precipitous walls accentuated by tall cedars growing from seemingly solid rock.

From the parking lot the chasm is reached by a half-mile-long descending trail that is quite steep: the posted warnings about slippery rocks and uncertain footing should be well heeded. On reaching the bottom, one has the awesome feeling of having plunged suddenly into the earth's rocky body. From the bottom, trails lead along the edge of the chasm and circle back to the parking lot, thus avoiding an otherwise difficult climb. The site also has a recreation area with picnic tables. *Open year-round.*

12. Macomber Farm. *Framingham. From Interstate I-90 take the Framingham exit and watch for signs.* This unique 46-acre

13. *Making good use of local materials, the muskrat builds a home of reeds and mud.*

complex offers not only a visit to a working farm but also an opportunity to see and experience various aspects of farm life from the animals' point of view. The ingenious devices created for this purpose are fun for adults as well as children.

You can, for example, look through binoculars that show the world as seen by a pig. On a ramp nearby you can try "pig walking," placing your hands and feet in bronzed hoofprints labeled to show the proper sequence. Then you are invited to practice sniffing at a stand of pipes emitting various scents, until you can identify those that are the same, as pigs are able to do. Playing a video game that shows large full-color slides of pigs, you learn how piglets struggle to establish their position in the group.

You can also play seeing and walking games related to horses, cows, and other farm animals. In the fowl barn, games demonstrate the body language of chickens and turkeys, and the meaning of the term "pecking order." At the horse barn you are invited to test your own "horsepower" and join in the game of "working like a horse."

Wide walkways lead to the clean and airy barns, fragrant with fresh hay, and to the cattle pens, milking parlor, veterinarian facilities, and other attractions. *Open daily Apr. 1–Oct. 30. Admission charged.*

13. Great Meadows National Wildlife Refuge. *To reach the visitor center here, follow Rte. 27 north from Wayland for 1.7 miles; turn right on Water Row Rd. and continue until it ends (1.2 miles). Turn right on Lincoln Rd., drive ½ mile, and then turn left on Weir Hill Rd.* These freshwater wetlands, flanking the Sudbury and Concord rivers, were created inadvertently more than a century ago when a mill dam was built, causing an overflow. Rendered useless for farming, the wetlands became popular for hunting and fishing. Since 1944 the U.S. Fish and Wildlife Service has acquired about 3,000 acres of the area, including a tract of floodplain called the Great River Meadows by early settlers.

In this world of marshes and ponds— the domain of deer, foxes, small mammals, and birds—there is scarcely a hint that metropolitan Boston is only 20 miles away. The beauty of the place and the abundance of the wildlife belie its location, just as its present purpose—to serve as a habitat for wildlife—belies its earlier use by hunters.

The refuge consists of two units. In the Weir Hill Area, you can explore woodlands and fields as well as the river and marshes. The Dike Trail Area (the original Great Meadows) is especially good for observing wildlife. The Dike Trail, one of several here, is a dry pathway bordered by reeds and the American lotus. It loops

around a pond rimmed by oaks and maples and dotted with reed islands and numerous muskrat lodges. Many kinds of migrant waterfowl stop here, including Canada geese and several species of ducks. *Open daily spring–fall; weekdays except holidays during winter.*

14. Lowell National Historical Park. For anyone concerned with America's heritage and with community revitalization, Lowell is a place of special interest. Sometimes referred to as "the birthplace of the American Industrial Revolution," the town has a proud past as a model industrial community of the early 1800's. A further source of pride was the Lowell mill girls— young farm women who came here by the thousands to operate the power looms in the textile mills and live in the strictly supervised company boardinghouses. In the 1920's, as New England's textile industry declined, the town began its downward trend. Efforts to reverse that trend now include the establishment of the Lowell Heritage State Park and the Lowell National Historical Park, a cooperative undertaking of the city, the state, and the National Park Service. The process of repair and renovation in the historic district is well under way, especially along the canals that were Lowell's source of power and that also served as a means

14. *Handsome proportions and fine brickwork are typical of Lowell's mills.*

16. *The old boat serves as a blind, not for hunters but for those who wish to observe the birds that flock to the refuge.*

of transportation in the city's heyday.

At the park visitor center, located at Market Mills, a restored mill complex, you can arrange to take a 2½-hour tour, by trolley, barge, and on foot, that reveals the city's past. The old mill buildings, immaculate with their spanking new paint and clean brickwork, stand out against the rest of the urban architecture and give the curious impression of two contrasting cities, the one resuscitated by a tranfusion of galleries, shops, offices, and fresh paint being the sanitized ghost of the time-worn city that surrounds it. *Open year-round; tours daily, May 26–Oct. 8.*

---

15. The Whittier Home. *Amesbury. From Rte. 110 turn onto Main St. and follow it to Market Square. Go around the rotary until you face back the way you came; then look for the fork with a sign to the Whittier Home.* For 56 years this was the home of John Greenleaf Whittier, an active abolitionist, a founder of the Republican Party, and one of America's best-known poets. The house was simply a four-room cottage when Whittier bought it in 1836. Over the years he added the portico, the upper stories, and the summer kitchen.

By the time of his death in 1892, Whittier was quite famous. Only four years later his niece (to whom he had bequeathed the property) opened his home as a muse-

um. This continuity ensured that the Whittier memorabilia remained largely intact. It is the completeness of the personal belongings and furnishings (hats, boots, shaving brush, books, manuscripts, portraits, letters, even the original wallpaper) that gives the place its particular intimate charm. The rooms are small but comfortable, and on the walls there is ample evidence of Whittier's work as a writer and abolitionist.

The house is now a registered national historic landmark. Just up the street is the Friends Meetinghouse, which Whittier, a Quaker, attended, and which served as a station of the Underground Railroad. *Open P.M. Tues.–Sat., May 1–Oct. 31; in winter by appointment only.*

---

16. Parker River National Wildlife Refuge. This 4,650-acre refuge, which lies on the Atlantic Flyway, is a magnificent place to visit, especially during the spring and fall migrations. Most of the preserve is on Plum Island, which is about six miles long and a mile wide. A road runs its entire length. On the left, going south, are sand dunes dotted with wild roses, scrub pines, dune grasses, bayberry, black cherry, and beach plum. On the right there are fresh- and saltwater marshes, and beyond are the waters of Broad Sound, a long, narrow inlet. The beach, one of the finest on the

eastern seaboard, is reached by access roads tightly controlled to preserve the delicate ecology of the dunes, which act as a barrier to the sea.

Self-guiding nature trails lead to various ecological niches within the refuge. The longest is a boardwalk trail that wanders for two miles through Hellcat Swamp, where a freshwater swamp and cranberry bogs are pocketed among the dunes. At the end of the trail is an observation blind for bird-watchers. More than 300 species regularly frequent the refuge to rest and feed, including large numbers of migrating warblers, Canada geese, black ducks, and green-winged teals. Among the mammals here are deer, foxes, muskrats, minks, and weasels, but they are rarely seen during the day. In winter, harbor seals come to sun themselves on the beaches.

The refuge is very popular in summer, but the best seasons to visit are in the early spring and in fall, after the September harvesting of cranberries and plums. Fishing permits may be obtained at the refuge gatehouse. *Open year-round, weather permitting.*

---

17. Ipswich River Wildlife Sanctuary. *Topsfield. From Rte. 1 turn east on Rte. 97 at the traffic light. Then turn left on Perkins*

Row, where there is a sign to the sanctuary entrance. Occupying about 2,000 acres, this is the largest of the 14 sanctuaries supervised by the Massachusetts Audubon Society. It is also the most varied, not only because of the number of wildlife habitats that are represented here but also because of the extensive landscaping that has been carried out.

In the early 1900's the land was bought by Thomas Proctor, a wealthy Bostonian who applied himself with zeal and openhandedness to the creation of a private arboretum with an enormous rock garden—called the Rockery—as its centerpiece. In effect, the Rockery, set by a small lake, is a small man-made mountain, complete with little gorges, caves, and paths and profusely planted with exotic trees and shrubs. Among the trees Proctor imported for his arboretum, cork, magnolia, Korean pine, and Sawara cypress are especially notable. A fine grove of pine trees stands on the hill above the Rockery.

The other notable rocky feature is a stony embankment, about 20 feet high and 30 feet wide, that runs for miles through the swamp. It appears to be man-made but is actually a natural formation caused by streams flowing beneath Ice Age glaciers.

There are 10 miles of trails in the area and a causeway crossing a large pond to an island covered with beech trees. The woodlands are carpeted with partridgeberries, starflowers, and wintergreen, while masses of blue irises grow in the marshy areas and a wildflower garden offers its special beauty. The sanctuary, which is a major courting and breeding ground for the American woodcock, has wildfowl impoundments, a special area for bird-watching, and an observation tower overlooking a meadow. Canoe and cabin rentals are available. *Open Tues.–Sun. year-round. Admission charged.*

18. *Charm was not a criterion when the ironworks was built—but it was attained.*

18. Saugus Iron Works. *Saugus.* This national historic site is a full-scale working replica of the original ironworks founded here in the early 1640's by John Winthrop, Jr., son of the governor of Massachusetts Bay Colony. Since the 1630's the small colony had been in an economic slump, suffering from a sharp decline in immigration. With fewer ships arriving from England, there was a serious scarcity of iron products—tools, nails, hinges, pots, and kettles—all of which had been imported. To meet that need, young Winthrop sailed to England to obtain capital and a team of skilled ironworkers. Securing both, he returned home, chose a site where waterpower, wood for charcoal, and iron ore were available, and built an up-to-date plant and company houses for the workers. The community was known as Hammersmith. In the 1650's the ironworks failed because of production costs and an insufficient market for its products. But its employees trained others in their skills and thus helped to establish an iron industry in America.

The whole complex has been re-created with wonderful precision and thoroughness. A small museum explains the early process of ironmaking with a 10-minute slide show and exhibits. From the museum a path leads to the smelting furnace, and from there to the "finery." Draft for the furnace was provided by huge bellows driven by waterpower from the Saugus River. Waterpower also drove a huge hammer, used to pound the brittleness out of the cast pig iron and turn it into wrought iron. The machinery in the rolling and slitting mill, where sheets and rods of iron were made, also depended upon waterpower. Worth visiting too are the blacksmith shop and the ironmaster's house, which was Hammersmith's social and business center. Three rooms have been restored in a "high 17th-century" style with elaborate furnishings.

In addition to the remarkable authenticity of the site, Saugus Iron Works is rewarding to visit because the processes displayed are easily understood, unlike modern high technology, and one has the feeling that with a little application one might have invented the whole business oneself. *Open year-round.*

19. Adams National Historic Site. *Quincy. From Rte. 3-A (Hancock St.) go west on Newport Ave. to the corner of Adams St.* For four generations, America's most distinguished family lived on the land here, building and rebuilding to suit the changing needs of their remarkably active lives.

The family saga begins, however, about a mile south on Franklin Street (ask at the historic site for directions), where two 17th-century houses stand side by side. John Adams, second president of the United States, was born in one house and his son, John Quincy Adams, the sixth president, in the other.

The Old House, on Adams Street, was built as a country villa in the 1730's and bought by John Adams in 1787, when he and his wife, Abigail, returned from diplomatic service abroad. It is interesting to consider the contrast between the grandeur of public life enjoyed by the great and powerful in 18th-century America and the modesty of their domestic arrangements, especially compared to the estates of their counterparts in Europe. This contrast, in fact, was duly noted by

Abigail Adams upon her return from the Court of St. James's in London.

Among the members of the family based here were a remarkable number of accomplished statesmen, educators, historians, lawyers, and authors dedicated to demanding intellectual pursuits and compassionate service to their fellow men.

The furnishings in the Old House reflect the various tastes and interests of a widely traveled family over a period of 150 years. No other house in America offers a personal historic record of such impressive scope. The trees planted by John Quincy Adams in the garden behind the house have established firm roots and grown strong, as has the country that he and his family served so well. *Open daily Apr. 19–Nov. 10.*

---

20. Dighton Rock State Park. In the picturesque woodlands of this small, inviting park is one of the most tantalizing mysteries of America's early exploration. Dighton Rock, a 40-ton boulder originally partly submerged in the nearby Taunton River, is engraved with ornate signs and symbols that scholars even today have been unable to decipher.

In 1963 the rock was raised from the river, and later on a small museum was built to shelter the engravings and the exhibits explaining the four contending theories of their origin. One theory attributes the inscriptions to Phoenician explorers. Another suggests that they were executed by the Norse, and then there were those who said the mysterious signs were American Indian symbols. Perhaps the most popular theory attributes the engravings to a lost 16th-century Portuguese explorer who, it is claimed, ended his days among the local Wampanoag tribe. The strongest evidence for this proposal is the supposed inscription of the date 1511 and a suggested similarity between certain Portuguese words and words in the Wampanoag language. Whatever theory is correct, the conjecture is fascinating, and the park's ample and quiet picnic grounds make this a refreshing stop. *Park and museum open daily mid-May–early Oct. Admission charged.*

---

21. John Alden House. *Duxbury. From Rte. 3 take Exit 34 east to Alden St. and watch for the signs.* This shingled saltbox house is a direct link with the first coloni-

zation of America. John Alden, one of the voyagers on the *Mayflower,* was a signer of the Mayflower Compact, a leader of the Plymouth Colony, and the suitor of Priscilla Mullins. The story of their romance, as recounted in Henry Wadsworth Longfellow's poem "The Courtship of Miles Standish," may or may not be true. But they did indeed marry, and they settled in Plymouth. Like many of the colonists, the Aldens had a farm plot in Duxbury. And it was here in the town that he and Capt. Miles Standish had founded that John Alden and his son Jonathan built their house in 1653.

The house has an off-center entry and chimney rather than the strictly symmetrical design of the classic saltbox. The name is derived from the long slope of the roof in back, which resembled the hinged lid of early-day salt containers. John Alden, the longest-lived of the founding fathers, lived in this house until he died in 1687 at the age of 89.

Now administered by the Alden Kindred of America, the house contains some handsome Early American fixtures and furnishings. *Open Tues.–Sun., late June – early Sept. Admission charged.*

---

22. Wellfleet Wildlife Sanctuary. Five miles of easy trails meander through the fields and pinewoods, along the ponds,

streams, moorlands, salt marshes, and beaches in this beautiful 700-acre preserve on Cape Cod.

The World of Water Trail, installed by the Massachusetts Audubon Society, shows what happens when salt water and fresh water meet. A detailed guide, available at the visitor center, explains, for example, how salinity and temperatures vary with the tides, how the two environments sometimes overlap, and how *Spartina,* the most abundant marsh plant, has the unique ability to draw fresh water from salt water, discarding the salt crystals through its foliage.

But you needn't have such specialized interests to enjoy a visit here. It is a serene place for quiet strolling, where you will see sandpipers, plovers, and whimbrels feeding at the water's edge, and rabbits and foxes scurrying through the woods. And if you step softly at low tide, you can perhaps catch a glimpse of the shy fiddler crabs as they emerge from their holes in the bank of a creek.

A picnic area in a fine grove of white pines overlooks the salt marsh and the beach at Wellfleet Bay. *Open year-round except Mon. in winter. Camping open only to members of the Massachusetts Audubon Society. Admission charged.*

19. *The Adams house clearly defines the unique shape of the classic saltbox.*

Rhode Island

*Although dominated by busy Narragansett Bay and the seashore,
our smallest state offers some rewarding inland discoveries.*

This is one of our most densely populated states, but consistent with its traditional independence, it takes a strong stand regarding the importance of nature and wildlife—as evidenced by the state forests, bird sanctuaries, and a fish hatchery. A related interest is expressed in a superb topiary garden where plants are artfully trimmed to geometric and animal forms. The changing seasons here are celebrated by a succession of harvest festivals sponsored by an Indian museum, and the pioneer heritage is represented by an inviting 17th-century farmstead.

1. George Washington Management Area. *Rte. 44, West Glocester.* Land for the camping area in the 3,300-acre park was donated to the state in 1933 to honor the bicentennial of our first president's birth, which was observed the previous year.

There are 55 camping sites near the tip of Bowdish Lake, where a sandy beach invites swimmers, and fishermen are likely to catch largemouth bass, yellow perch, and pickerel. A launching ramp may be used by boats with motors under 10 horsepower. The picnic ground on Peck Pond, at the other side of the management area, also has a sandy beach and a supervised swimming area. This pond is stocked with trout.

Access to the more remote regions of the forest is provided by the Walkabout Trail, an easy eight-mile loop with several cutoffs allowing shorter hikes. The trail, built in 1965 with the help of Australian sailors, takes its name from the traditional wanderings of Australian aborigines.

Winter is one of the best seasons here. Many snow-covered gravel roads, accessible from the campground, are open for snowmobiling; and in the area around Peck Pond four trails, ranging from three-quarters of a mile to more than four miles in length, are groomed for cross-country skiing. Ice fishing is also popular. A warming house is maintained for relief from the winter's cold. *Open year-round. Camping May–Sept. Use fee charged.*

1. A secluded cove with a choice of sun or shade attracts swimmers at Bowdish Lake.

2. Diamond Hill State Park. *Rte. 114, Cumberland.* Traditionally a favorite spot for collecting minerals, the large crag dominating this 373-acre park is highlighted by patches of roseate quartz crystals, part of a vein a mile long and some thousand feet wide. In the sunlight the crag glitters as if sprinkled with diamonds—which accounts for the name.

The park provides a pleasant setting for family day trips. Fifty-five picnic tables are spaced around a small man-made skating pond at the base of the hill.

Mineral collecting and ball games are popular summertime activities. On Sunday afternoons in July and August, concerts are given in an outdoor theater. For winter fun two sled runs have been built on the slopes. *Open year-round.*

3. Arcadia Management Area. *Rte. 165.* This 12,000-acre, multiple-use forest management area is administered to enrich its timber, water, wildlife, and recreational resources. The carefully balanced

program is intended to preserve the primitive beauty of the forest while providing varied opportunities for outdoor activity.

Swimming is allowed at two sandy beaches, one on Beach Pond and the other on the smaller and more secluded Browning Mill Pond. Both beaches have lifeguards. Fishermen will appreciate the many small streams and ponds, several stocked with trout, while canoeists enjoy the run on Wood River.

Most of the roads in the area are gravel, requiring low speed. Twenty sites for family camping are provided at the Tefft Hill Campground; for those who seek greater solitude the Stepstone Falls camping area offers four primitive campsites accessible only by backpacking. Well-marked hiking trails of varying length thread through forests and pine groves with rhododendron thickets, and lead to waterfalls and scenic overlooks. Many of the roads and trails provide fine cross-country skiing and snowmobiling in the winter. *Open year-round. Camping May–Sept.*

SCALE IN MILES AND KILOMETERS
ONE INCH 10 MILES
ONE INCH 16 KM

seen. The hatchery's capacity of about a million trout helps to stock Rhode Island's streams for the enjoyment of an estimated 40,000 fishermen. The place, charming in appearance, is fascinating to see.

Since the fish are accustomed to being fed by humans, they boil to the surface as one approaches the edge of the tree-shaded, dark green pond. To discourage depredation by herons, the pond and raceway are covered with green netting and wire. Each section of the raceway contains hundreds of trout of approximately the same size in order to minimize their cannibalistic behavior. *Open year-round.*

6. New England Wireless and Steam Museum. *East Greenwich. On Frenchtown Rd., west off Rte. 1.* The power of steam and the development of wireless communication have led to a series of inventions that have vastly changed the world. This museum celebrates the subjects and a few of the inventors, and exhibits some of their most significant creations.

Displays in two buildings deal with the history of communications from telegraph to television and include crystal sets, vacuum tubes, transoceanic cable equipment, and a variety of other antiques.

Radio Station PJ, one of the earliest stations, has been moved to the museum grounds from its original site at Point Judith and restored to its 1907 condition.

In the steam engine building three engines made by the George H. Corliss Steam Engine Company of Providence are on display along with others, all in running order. A library focusing on steam power and communications is housed in an 1822 New England meetinghouse.

An annual highlight is the Yankee

ciated with the harvesting of important crops: maple sugar in March, strawberries in June, string beans in July, and cranberries in October. In addition, the Nickomo festival is celebrated in early December with an exchange of gifts.

These gatherings offer feasting on the seasonal foods and Indian dances, led by local Narragansetts, in which visitors are encouraged to participate. *Open P.M. daily except in Feb. Donation requested.*

5. Lafayette State Trout Hatchery. *Off Rte. 4, south of Lafayette.* Also known as Goose Nest Spring Hatchery, this complex, founded in 1922, is one of the oldest hatcheries in the country. It consists of a large spring-fed pond, a raceway about half a mile long, and buildings in which tanks containing fingerling trout may be

4. Tomaquag Indian Memorial Museum. *Summit Rd., Arcadia Village.* Situated amid the Arcadia Management Area, this small, cedar-shingled building houses several cabinets containing Indian artifacts from various North American tribes, with a focus on those of the Northeast. In addition to stone tools and leather strapwork by Plains Indians, weavings by Navajos, and baskets by northwestern tribes, the collection features ash splint basketwork of the Mohegans, Scaticooks, and local Narragansetts. *Tomaquag* is the Narragansett word for beaver.

The museum serves as a focal point for four annual festivals of thanksgiving asso-

Steam-Up on the last Saturday in July. Many of the museum's steam engines are fired up on this occasion, and steam buffs are invited to bring their own equipment to operate at the fair. *Open P.M. Sun., June–Labor Day. Admission charged.*

---

7. Green Animals. *Cory's Lane, off Rte. 114, Portsmouth.* Thomas E. Brayton, a Massachusetts manufacturer, purchased this seven-acre estate in 1872 and summered here until his death in 1939.

Exquisite evidence of Brayton's interest in topiary (the ancient art of training and pruning plants into geometric designs or animal shapes) may be seen today as one wanders through the gardens. But it was his daughter, the late Alice Brayton, an amateur horticulturist, who helped bring these 100 forms to their present perfection, putting them in a class with the nation's best examples of topiary.

Among the animal shapes are a camel, a giraffe, a horse and rider, and a mountain goat. A fat bear is especially appealing. The animals are all fashioned from California privet; the geometric designs are made of sheared boxwood.

Elsewhere, perennial, biennial, and annual flower beds, as well as plantings of ferns, shrubs, and fruit trees, create a subtle blend of scent and sight, as if taken from the pages of a Victorian novel.

From the clapboard main house there is a lovely view of Narragansett Bay. Inside, a small toy collection is displayed, including an impressive exhibit of toy soldiers. *Open daily May–Sept.; weekends in Oct. Admission charged.*

---

8. Norman Bird Sanctuary. *Third Beach Rd., Middletown.* George Norman was a late 19th-century Newport merchant who made a fortune in waterworks and utilities. His daughter donated the land for this sanctuary in 1949. Eleven trails, from one-tenth of a mile to 1.3 miles in length, lead through the 450-acre site, where birders can look for many common and some unusual species. This is an interesting landscape because it includes virtually every type of terrain found in New England, from lofty crag to meadow, woodland, dense thicket, freshwater swamp, and pond.

Each trail has its own appeal, which may include sightings of woodcock, green-backed herons, great blue herons, snowy owls, and other less common birds. Red foxes are known to lurk within the sanctuary and often may be seen.

Legend maintains that veins of quartz in the rocks along Indian Rock Trail were a source of stone for Narragansett arrowheads. A popular hike leads to Hanging Rock, beside a large pond. It is believed by some that criminals were once hanged here. The curious conglomerate structure, with its overhang, rises 70 feet above sea level and provides fine views.

The sanctuary has a shop where bird-feeding supplies are sold. In the nearby outbuildings, birds brought in to recover from injuries are cared for and may often be observed. *Open year-round.*

7. Because of the skill and labor required to create and maintain hedges, edgings, and topiary, there are not many gardens as richly detailed as these.

9. Wilbor House and Barn Museum. *Little Compton.* Samuel Wilbor, the first white settler on this land (bought from the Sakonnet Indians in 1673), built a house here in the 1680's and farmed the surrounding 122 acres. The house, which originally had two rooms, one above the other, and an attic, has been enlarged many times through the years as it passed

8. *There are almost always birds to be seen in the sanctuary, but even when they are scarce the scenic views are a delight.*

from father to son for eight generations.

The property, presented to the Little Compton Historical Society in 1955, now serves as their headquarters. Except for the two rooms built in the 1680's, which have been restored to their original condition, the house and barn are now as they were in the 18th century.

The plain and simple house is typical of early New England. The oldest rooms have exposed corner posts, low, unplastered ceilings, and small windows. Outside is a well with a well sweep to raise the bucket. Some of the period furnishings were donated by Wilbor descendants.

The barn faithfully reflects Rhode Island's agricultural past, with numerous implements, carriages, sleighs, a formal coach, and an original one-horse shay.

Also in the barn is the Portuguese Room, commemorating the customs and traditions brought to Little Compton by the Azoreans who came here some hundred years ago. *Open daily July–mid-Sept. Admission charged.*

10. Kimball Wildlife Refuge. *Charlestown. Exit from Rte. 1 near Windswept Farm at the sign for Burlingame State Park Picnic Area. Take first left onto Montauk Rd. and then turn left again at the pond.* The land for this 29-acre woodland sanctuary was bequeathed by William Hammond Kimball, a summer resident of the area, to the Audubon Society of Rhode Island in 1924. Two years later Everett and Mary Southwick became the caretakers. Today's well-tended trails and the garden memorializing past benefactors reflect this naturalist couple's lifelong devotion to the development of the refuge.

Situated on a glacial moraine deposited some 12,000 years ago, the sanctuary invites contemplation of a glacier's irresistible force. One trail leads past several bowl-shaped kettle holes carved as the giant ice sheets receded. Indeed, Toupoyesett Pond here is really a large kettle hole deep enough to reveal the water table. In May and June, starflowers, Canada mayflowers, and pink lady's slippers are in bloom along the quiet trails, and the memorial garden is occasionally visited by ruby-throated hummingbirds. The refuge offers a number of nature programs throughout the year. In July and August there is a nature day-camp for children. *Open year-round.*

9. *Heating in the 17th century was minimal, thus the curtain-enclosed bed.*

Connecticut

Gracefully spanning the centuries, the Constitution State is a pleasure to explore, from charming small towns to centers of technology.

The Audubon Center here is one of the best of its kind, as is the collection of early-day tools at the Sloane-Stanley Museum. Connecticut's contribution to Yankee ingenuity is acknowledged in the Lock Museum and the American Clock & Watch Museum. A colonial copper mine, which also served as a prison, is now open for visitors. Further examples of the variety available here are an Indian museum, a museum for children, a dollhouse museum (for children and adults), a museum of contemporary art, an opulent mansion, and some appealing historic houses.

1. Northeast Audubon Center. *Sharon.* Here on some 700 acres of woodlands, ponds, open fields, and marshes is a microcosm of 19th-century Connecticut. Habitats for the great variety of plants and wildlife found here are fast disappearing.

The property, donated by Mrs. Clement R. Ford, includes the Ford home, which now houses the center's offices, library, classrooms, and display areas.

Among the exhibits are specimens of the local plants and flowers as well as live turtles, frogs, snakes, and salamanders, all found nearby. In the farm area barnyard animals can be seen.

In the Discovery Room, a section for children, sets of simulated animal tracks disappear behind a door. When you open the door the creature that makes them is identified. On a "please touch" table examples of fur, bark, and animal bones invite inspection, while silhouettes of birds suspended from the ceiling show their various sizes and shapes.

Workshops, nature classes, films, guided field trips, training programs and internships, and seasonal bird counts are all part of the center's program. And in early spring visitors can watch the making of maple syrup with sap collected from local trees. *Open year-round. Admission charged.*

2. Sloane-Stanley Museum. *Kent.* Eric Sloane, the late Connecticut artist and writer, started the museum as a tribute to

1. *Canada geese on Ford Pond. Closeup observation is common at Audubon Center.*

the ingenuity and craftsmanship of the early settlers in New England. It houses his extensive collection of tools made by these inventive Yankees. Household equipment and tools for the seemingly countless outdoor chores are on display here. The objects range from pots and baskets to axes and wheelbarrows.

Several of Mr. Sloane's still lifes are shown, along with the objects portrayed.

The wooded property and the barn that houses the museum were donated by the Stanley Works of New Britain to celebrate its 125 years as a maker of hand tools.

Next to the museum Mr. Sloane built a small cabin, using only old tools and local lumber and stones and referring to an 1805 farm boy's diary as a guide. The cabin has an unusual chink-log chimney, a dirt floor, bottle-glass windows, and a small herb garden in the dooryard.

During the 19th century this was the site of the Kent Iron Furnace. Down a slight slope from the museum are the ruins of the sturdy granite structure, with its

Gothic arch, now undergoing restoration.

The museum is set on a wooded hillside overlooking the Housatonic River. Although the foliage in summer is so dense that the river is lost to view, the shady rise is an ideal setting for the picnic tables scattered there. *Open Wed.–Sun., May–Oct. Admission charged.*

3. The Aldrich Museum of Contemporary Art. *258 Main St., Ridgefield.* The contrast between the traditional exterior of the pre-Revolutionary building and the 20th-century art it contains is an unexpected pleasure here. The museum, founded about 20 years ago by Larry Aldrich, a collector of contemporary art, is known for its exhibits focusing mainly on major trends in today's art world and the works of undiscovered artists.

Behind the museum, on a sloping lawn surrounded by flowering trees and

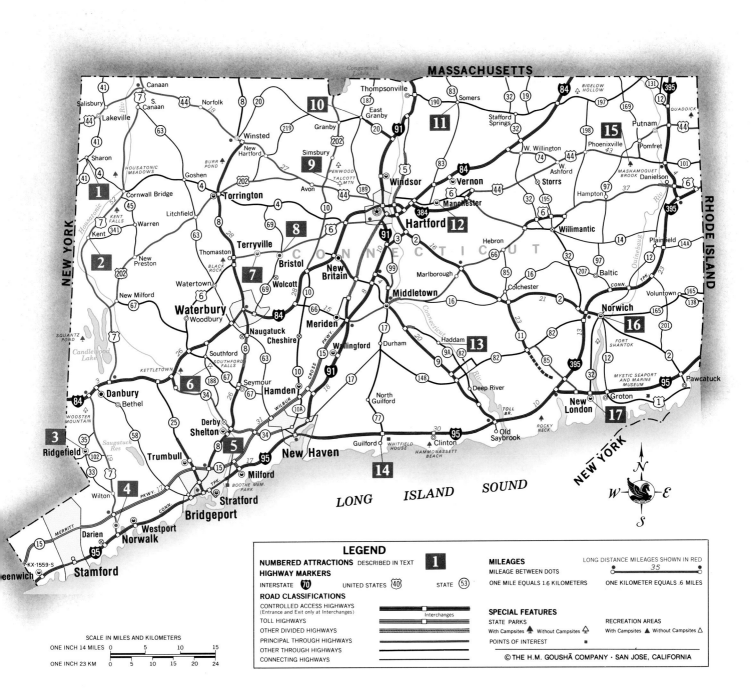

MASSACHUSETTS

NEW YORK

RHODE ISLAND

NEW YORK

LONG ISLAND SOUND

shrubs, are sculptures by some 15 contemporary artists. The terrace overlooking the garden is a pleasant place to sit and view the collection.

Among the museum's activities is the "Artreach" program, a series of lectures, films, and slide shows given by art teachers and historians. It is offered to local schools as part of a year-long schedule of cultural events, including group tours to museums and art galleries as well as private collections in New York City and throughout New England. *Open weekends year-round; weekdays by appointment. Admission charged.*

4. Lockwood-Mathews Mansion Museum. *295 West Ave., Norwalk.* LeGrand Lockwood, who had grown up in Norwalk and left home, returned as a millionaire in 1864 and built the grandest house in town, a magnificent 60-room mansion on a hill overlooking the Norwalk River.

With towers, turrets, arches, and iron grillwork on the rooftop, the granite building resembles a European castle overlaid with Victorian elegance. The four-story house, whose interior is decorated with exceptionally fine frescoes, marble carvings, etched glass panels, marquetry, and parquetry, has a skylighted rotunda 42 feet high. Many of the rooms

open onto a balcony that surrounds this great hall. Sweeping up from the rotunda to the balcony is the main stairway, whose carved walnut banister has an elegant inlay of boxwood in the Greek key design. A peacock of blue stones inlaid in a garland of marble decorates one of the mansion's 25 fireplaces.

Shortly after the house was completed, the Lockwoods lost their fortune, and the Charles D. Mathews family of New York bought the estate and occupied it for more than 60 years. Now completely restored, it is a museum. *Open Tues.–Fri. and Sun., Mar.–mid-Dec. Admission charged.*

5. Boothe Memorial Park. Situated on a hill overlooking the Housatonic River, the park is maintained as a memorial to two eccentric bachelor brothers, David and Stephen Boothe, who willed the property to the town of Stratford. Despite the sign on the gate (when this was written) indicating that only town residents may enter, the park is open to all.

On the 44 acres of their estate the brothers assembled an amazing collection of 19 buildings. Included is a Dutch windmill, a six-story bell tower that is slightly out of plumb, a miniature lighthouse, and a pagodalike redwood cathedral.

A 77-foot clock tower and belfry known as the Anniversary Tower houses family heirlooms gathered from cousins far and near, along with the family genealogy.

The brothers' collecting extended to whatever caught their fancy—from baskets to pioneer bonnets—and the assorted buildings contain quantities of the miscellany that they could not resist.

Walking trails wind through the park to the various exhibits and to a rose garden and a sundial set in a circle of stones. Picnic tables under the trees overlook the river. *Open year-round.*

---

6. Southford Falls State Park. The waterfall that gives the park its name is on Eight Mile Brook, which flows from Lake Quassapaug to the Housatonic River, a distance of eight miles. The plunging and cascading falls once drove a waterwheel that powered a sawmill, a gristmill, and a fulling mill for finishing wool cloth. Almost all that remains of these 19th-century industries is a grindstone, a part of the sluiceway, and a few foundation walls.

Several trails loop through the woods, along the stream, and above the falls to Papermill Pond, formed by a dam across the brook. Here a quiet, woodsy expanse has picnic tables and barbecue pits. The pond, stocked with trout, is popular with fishermen, who try their luck in both summer and, through the ice, in winter.

A loop trail about a mile long leads to a lookout tower, which can be climbed for an overview of the park.

A recent addition here is a picturesque covered bridge spanning the stream near the bottom of the falls. It is a replica of a laminated arch structure designed in 1804 by Theodore Burr, a well-known early

American bridge builder. The late Eric Sloane, a noted Connecticut artist, was the consultant in the building of Southford's bridge. *Open year-round.*

---

7. Lock Museum of America. *Terryville.* In the 19th century the Connecticut Yankees' mechanical skills were convincingly demonstrated by their work as locksmiths. With a nucleus of some 5,000 old locks donated by the Eagle Lock Company of Terryville, the Lock Museum of America opened in 1972 in a building that once had served as the town hall.

News of the museum spread quickly among collectors, and donations began to pour in. Ten years later, when more space was needed, a permanent home for the collection was built.

Every one of the locks in the original 5,000 was manufactured in Connecticut during the 19th century. Today's collection, numbering more than 23,000, represents manufacturers from all across the country, and although the emphasis is still on antique locks, many from the early 20th century are included.

Thousands of keys and other related objects are on display, and the museum library includes lock catalogs from many early American lock manufacturers.

At the time of this writing, Thomas

Hennessy of Bristol, a well-known collector of locks and author of books on the subject, was the curator of the museum, which houses his own extensive collection. *Open Tues.–Sun., May–Oct.*

---

8. American Clock & Watch Museum. *Bristol.* Before they were electrified, digitalized, mass-produced, and taken for granted, clocks and watches were objects of beauty and wonder. This museum pays tribute to that earlier era. Here you will see an exceptional collection of American timepieces, along with memorabilia of many of their creators.

The museum is housed in an 1801 building called the Miles Lewis House. The addition of the Ebenezer Barnes Wing, whose paneling comes from a 1728 house of that name, extends the museum into the garden area.

The collection includes examples from early American clockmakers, many of whom lived in Bristol and nearby towns, as well as timepieces of the 20th century.

Among the exhibits are hundreds of watches displayed in glass cases, several early shelf clocks lined up on a wall in the summer kitchen of the old mansion, and a

8. *These timepieces, simple and complex, set the stage for the collection here.*

9. *View from the mountain overlooks fields, fall foliage, and the town of Avon. Boardwalk is part of a nature trail.*

mirror clock, flanked by two banjo clocks, hanging above an antique chest.

The Edward Ingraham Library, named for the museum's first president, is located in the fireproof basement of the Barnes Wing. Open only to horological researchers, it has a valuable assortment of reference books, diaries, photographs, and other historical material. *Open Apr.–Oct. Admission charged.*

---

9. Talcott Mountain State Park. The park extends for more than three miles along a wooded ridge named for John Talcott, a Revolutionary War hero. There is something about high places that impels mankind to go the forces of nature one better and build something higher. The park has as its centerpiece the Heublein Tower, a famous landmark in the Farmington River valley. Perched on Mount Philip, the park's highest peak, the 165-foot tower was for 30 years the home of Gilbert Heublein, who built it in 1914.

To reach the tower, one must climb the trail winding up the craggy mountainside from the parking lot at the foot of the ridge. The hike has special rewards in spring, when the trilliums, wood anemones, trout lilies, and other native wildflowers are in bloom. Wildlife, too, can be seen along the way, and from the top, bird-watchers often catch glimpses of bald eagles and turkey vultures.

In one room of the tower is a museum that presents the history of the building, which includes its use during World War II as a radio transmitter station.

The trail leads to a shelter with picnic tables and then winds back down the mountain by another route to the parking lot. *Park open year-round; tower open daily Memorial Day–Labor Day; weekends late spring and early fall.*

---

10. Old New-Gate Prison and Copper Mine. *East Granby.* The mine, the first of its kind in the American Colonies, was opened in 1707 by a group of Simsbury citizens, and it continued in operation under various lessees, including Governor Belcher of Massachusetts, for more than 65 years. At the height of its productivity, more than 20 miners worked here.

Although there had been several attempts to smelt copper ore in America, most of them failed, and the ore from this mine was shipped to England for processing. After two valuable consignments of copper were lost at sea, it was decided that shipping was uneconomical, and the mine was closed in 1773.

In that year the Connecticut colony designated the copper mine as a prison for burglars, horse thieves, robbers, and counterfeiters and named it for the infamous Newgate Prison in London. In 1776 New-Gate became the first state prison in America. During the American Revolution a number of Tories and captured British soldiers were sent here. About 50 years later, when the prison at Wethersfield was built, New-Gate was closed.

There are guided tours through the tunnels where prisoners were confined. Temperatures range in the low 40's and sweaters are recommended. *Open Wed.–Sun., mid-May–Oct. Admission charged.*

---

11. Somers Mountain Indian Museum. *Turnpike Rd., Somers.* What you will see here is the result of one man's consuming interest in the subject of American Indians. James R. King, 90 years old at the time of this writing, has created a museum of unusual scope. He started collecting artifacts at the age of eight, and his interest grew. He studied and learned and lived on a number of Indian reservations from Alaska to Mexico. The collection includes objects from every major North American Indian culture and is so extensive that only about half of it can be shown here at any one time.

The displays are of such remarkably varied items as beadwork and the porcupine-quill work that preceded it; wampum, including stone wampum from 300 B.C.; arrowheads from Canada and from every state in the continental United States; war bonnets; weapons; peace pipes, some of them around 2,000 years old; papoose carriers; saddles made of buffalo bone and hide; and the newspaper, dated July 6, 1876, from Bismarck, Dakota Territory, that reported the dramatic news of Custer's last stand.

The gift shop sells contemporary Indian handicrafts. These include such traditional items as beadwork, barkwork, totem poles, and moccasins. *Open year-round.*

14. *The saltbox house and the flowering lilac are New England classics.*

12. Lutz Children's Museum. *247 South Main St., Manchester.* Named for Helen Lutz, who founded the museum in 1953, the collection covers the fields of art, history, and the natural sciences, and features rotating exhibits and projects in which children are encouraged to participate. But don't let the name mislead you; adults will find it interesting too.

Among the displays is a group of puppets and a puppet theater where children can put on a performance; a train composed of an engine, a passenger car, and a caboose; a collection of fluorescent minerals; and a menagerie of live turtles, woodchucks, snakes, and a horned owl.

The museum has available for rent a variety of educational kits containing objects from the collection and suggested craft projects for children. Also offered are group classes, craft workshops, field trips for both adults and children, and during school vacations, films for children.

Morning sessions are held for preschoolers, with a program of simple craft projects, storytelling, and an introduction to a live animal.

At the museum's outdoor center, located at 269 Oak Grove Street, nature trails wind through 53 acres of rolling fields, woodlands, and swampy areas. Printed guides to the trails are available at the museum headquarters. *Open Tues.–Sun. year-round. Admission charged.*

13. The Thankful Arnold House. *Haddam. On the corner of Hayden Hill and Walkley Hill Rds.* The house as it stands today has a remarkable unity, considering the history of its construction. Built in 1794–95, the place had only two rooms and a loft, all stacked against the chimney wall. It was bought four years later by Joseph Arnold, a descendant of one of the founders of this community on the Connecticut River, shortly before his marriage to Thankful Clark.

In their 15 years of marriage before Joseph died at age 49, the Arnolds had 11 children, and the house, as can be imagined, had to be expanded. The additions, made about 1798 and 1810, were skillfully handled and brought the structure to its present size and shape.

The widow Arnold lived here for 26 years after the death of her husband, and the house was known locally as hers. All

told, it was occupied by members of the family for more than 150 years.

The pumpkin-colored clapboard dwelling, which New Englanders call a bank or hillside house, has three stories in front and two on the slope at the back. Its restoration in the 1960's was sponsored by Isaac Arnold, a direct descendant, who turned it over to the Haddam Historical Society. The house, furnished with period pieces, is the society's headquarters and museum. The adjacent Wilhelmina Ann Arnold Barnhart Memorial Garden is named for the Isaac Arnolds' daughter.

It's worth a stroll up Walkley Hill Road, beyond the Arnold House, to see the many lovely old homes along the way. *Open P.M. Sat. and Sun., June–Sept. Admission charged.*

14. Thomas Griswold House. *Guilford.* The white clapboard saltbox, built about 1774 by Thomas Griswold III for his two sons, stands on a gentle rise called the Griswold Ledge above the Old Post Road. It started life as a double house of the classic saltbox design, and for almost 200 years was lived in by the Griswold family.

In 1958 Robert Griswold DeForest sold the property to the Guilford Keeping Society, an organization dedicated to the preservation of the town's historic beginnings, and the Griswold House became the society's headquarters.

Through the years many changes had been made, with an ell, dormer windows, a shed, and a porch added. The society undertook a complete restoration in 1974, returning the saltbox to its original design.

During the restoration the 10-foot-wide kitchen fireplace was opened and was found to have two beehive ovens as well as a warming oven. Other features include a double-batten door, a round-back Guilford cupboard, and a few pieces of the original Griswold furniture, among them a 1760 cherry lowboy and a ladderback "Pilgrim" chair.

One of the special features of the 1825 blacksmith shop, which was brought from Rhode Island and restored by the society as a working shop, is the ox sling used as an integral part of the framework. *Open Tues.–Sun., mid-June–mid-Sept.*

15. Mashamoquet Brook State Park. *Near Pomfret.* These rolling hills were once the territory of the Mohegan Indians, who were forced out by early settlers. An occasional arrowhead or well-trodden footpath remains as a poignant reminder of the time when this land was theirs.

Two color-coded trails wind through the park's 960 acres—a three-mile Red and a four-mile Blue—taking hikers over terrain that is sometimes steep and rocky.

A self-guiding nature trail crosses a swampy area formed by an old beaver dam. The beavers are gone, but the results of their diligent work are plainly visible. Numbers posted along the way correspond to those in a booklet identifying the plants, trees, and wildlife found in this area, including herons, wood ducks, bluebirds, and swallows.

Mashamoquet Brook, a trout stream that flows through the park and joins Wolf Den Brook, is stocked twice a year, drawing fishermen particularly in spring and fall. Picnic tables are set under evergreens beside the brook.

Some of the campsites are shady, and others are in open fields. For cross-country skiing the area north of Wolf Den Drive is best. At Bypass Pond, a man-made lake, swimmers enjoy a sandy beach. *Park open year-round; camping late Apr.–Columbus Day. Admission charged weekends and holidays in summer.*

16. *The tavern room looks much as it did from 1701 to 1830 when this was a stage stop.*

16. Leffingwell Inn. *348 Washington St., Norwich.* This historic hostelry began as a simple saltbox home, built in 1675 by Stephen Backus, son of a Norwich founder. Although extensive additions were made by later owners, the interior was never remodeled. The beams, wainscoting, and wide floorboards remain intact.

Thomas Leffingwell bought the house in 1700 and turned it into an inn with a tavern room. It soon began to flourish. In 1715, when more space was needed, a second saltbox was attached as an ell to the original, giving the inn two identical facades as viewed from the corner.

Some years later Thomas's grandson, Christopher Leffingwell, a prominent Norwich businessman, added the rear section, which includes the North Hall, the kitchen, and the George Washington Parlor—named for the general, who was entertained in that room during the Revolutionary War. The once simple saltbox, so much enlarged, became the town house of a leading Norwich family.

Today the inn, completely restored, contains many fine examples of 17th- and 18th-century furniture, some of it from the Norwich area. At least one piece, the grandfather clock that still stands in the George Washington Parlor, was made to Christopher Leffingwell's specifications. *Open June–Labor Day. Admission charged.*

17. Lyman Allyn Museum. *625 Williams St., New London.* The museum, founded in 1932, was built in memory of Lyman Allyn, a prosperous New London whaling captain, by his daughter, Harriet U. Allyn. The original building, a large granite structure with a pillared entrance, has been enlarged several times and now has ten galleries for the permanent collection and four for changing exhibits, as well as classrooms and an auditorium.

Although its primary focus is on paintings by Connecticut artists, particularly of the Old Lyme School, and antique Connecticut furniture, the museum also has 17th- and 18th-century silver, pre-Columbian art, Greek and Roman sculpture, and early Christian and Renaissance paintings.

The doll museum has a magnificent collection of miniature furniture arranged in period rooms in a dollhouse. The pieces include quilts, dishes, pots and pans, miniature paintings, tiny books with illustrated text, and a deck of playing cards laid out on a table of corresponding size. A second dollhouse is purely Victorian.

The Allyn home, an 1826 Federal stone building now called the Devon-Allyn House, is on the museum grounds and has been renovated and furnished with outstanding 19th-century furniture. *Museum open P.M. Tues.–Sun. year-round; house open by appointment.*

New York

The ocean, the lakes, and the rivers that border the state offer watery retreats to complement the attractions of the interior.

Populous though it is, the Empire State has a surprising number of getaway places that offer a wide variety of choices for relaxation and recreation. There are beaches on the Atlantic and on lakes Ontario and Erie, islands in the St. Lawrence River, and some inviting small towns on the banks of the Hudson. Scattered across New York are hundreds of sizable lakes. The vast wilderness areas in the Catskills and Adirondacks are laced with streams, waterfalls, and hiking trails. Thoughtful perusal of the map and some exploration of the smaller back roads can reveal discoveries to supplement the numbered highlights on the following pages.

1. Iroquois National Wildlife Refuge. These 10,818 acres of marsh, swamp, wet meadow, and pasture are set aside to offer food, rest, and protection for more than 200 species of birds, especially during the spring and fall migrations. In early to mid-April, the peak of the spring season, as many as 40,000 Canada geese may be seen feeding at a single time. And flights of great blue herons, which nest here, are a common sight. Although fewer numbers of migrating birds pass this way in autumn, it is the best time for observing ducks, especially wood ducks, mallards, and blue-winged teal. At any time of the year birders can expect to see a number of permanent residents, including great horned owls and downy woodpeckers.

The refuge is a place for a peaceful, leisurely visit. The trails, overlooks, and roadside vantage points give access not only to its population of birds and small mammals, but also to a splendid variety of landscapes; and the skyscapes are spacious over this flat land. Except for roads and designated trails, the refuge is closed to visitors from March 1 to July 15, the waterfowl nesting season. *Headquarters open Mon.–Fri. except holidays.*

2. Long Point on Lake Chautauqua State Park. This pleasant day-use park is water-oriented, with an extensive marina, a

2. Sailors and fishermen at the end of a pleasant day on Lake Chautauqua.

swimming beach with a bathhouse, and a large parking area for cars and boat trailers. Fishing is quite good for northern pike, perch, and muskellunge. "Muskies" from 48 to 60 inches long have been taken here. In winter ice fishing is popular.

The park has several trails: some follow the scenic lakeshore, and one, flanked by fine old willows, goes out to the end of a long, narrow point projecting about a quarter-mile into the lake. At the end of the point you can stand on a small boulder to enjoy the sensation of being entirely surrounded by water and to savor the sweeping view of the lake and encircling hills. *Open year-round. Admission charged daily in summer, and on weekends and holidays May–late June.*

3. Griffis Sculpture Park. *Ashford Hollow. Reached by Ahrens Rd. off Rte. 219. Towering sculptures at either side of the road mark the entrance.* Delightfully displayed in a sylvan setting is a collection of 150 objective and nonobjective sculptures fashioned of aluminum, bronze, steel, cast iron, and wood, the creations of several

different artists. Trails crisscross the park's 400 acres of meadows, ponds, and lightly wooded slopes. As you walk along, abstract forms and surreal figures come boldly into view or lurk to astonish you among the trees.

Particularly striking are the sculptures of a giant woman striding across a field and a bishop confronting a king and queen. Farther on you come upon a flight of giant geese, a life-size giraffe browsing twigs at the edge of a woods, and in the woods a huge, silvery crab with a gigantic, rust-colored mantis and a king cobra for companions. At a pond you see glistening aluminum bathers.

The creation of the Ashford Hollow Foundation for the Visual and Performing Arts, the park is altogether unique and

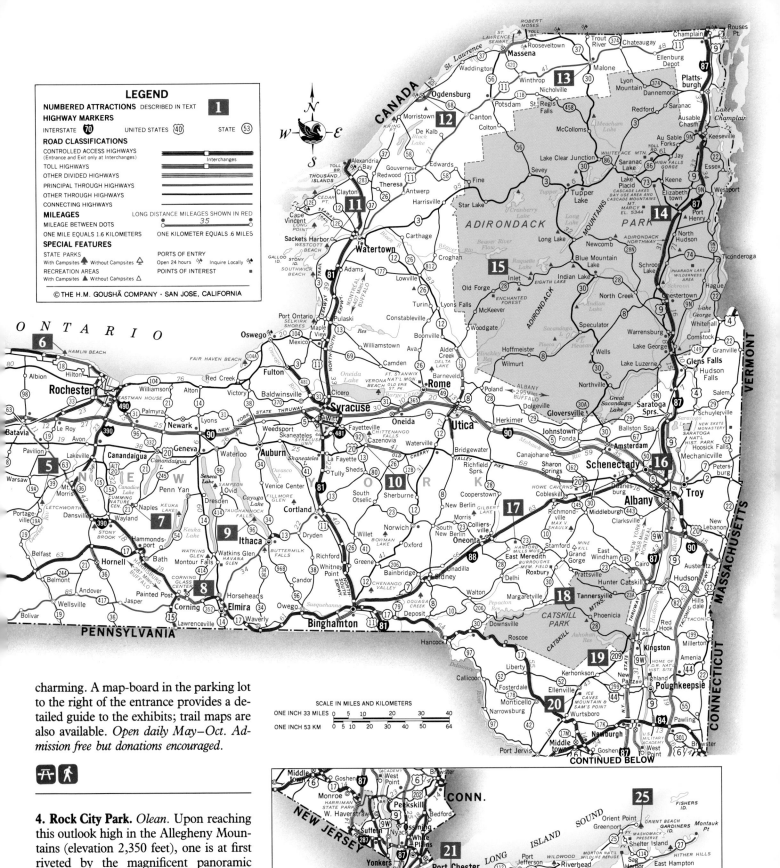

charming. A map-board in the parking lot to the right of the entrance provides a detailed guide to the exhibits; trail maps are also available. *Open daily May–Oct. Admission free but donations encouraged.*

4. Rock City Park. *Olean.* Upon reaching this outlook high in the Allegheny Mountains (elevation 2,350 feet), one is at first riveted by the magnificent panoramic views. But the gigantic boulders of dramatic shapes and formations found here are the featured attraction.

Estimated to be 500 million years old, the rocks, known as pudding stone, are a quartz conglomerate formed at the bottom

5. *Idyllic is the word, and the scale is grand—note the people in the distance.*

Letchworth's home, to rustic cabins and campsites. One of the many picnic areas in the park is on the site of a "ghost town" abandoned in the mid-1800's with the failure of the Genesee Valley Canal. Remains of the canal can be seen in the park.

White-water rafting trips are arranged during the spring and summer, and a winter recreation area is maintained for cross-country skiing, skating, snowmobiling, and tube-sledding. *Open year-round. Admission charged mid-May–Oct. Museum open mid-May–Oct.*

6. Hamlin Beach State Park. Stretching for three miles along the breeze-swept shore of Lake Ontario, this park is especially appealing in summertime. It has a mile of sandy beach, picnic tables, a ball field, walkways along the water's edge, campsites with electrical hookups, and a launching area for car-top boats. Fishermen here are likely to catch trout, bullheads, bass, and salmon.

The park's most unusual and interesting feature, however, is the Yanty Creek Nature Trail, designed for use by both sighted and blind visitors and, for part of its length, for wheelchairs. The trail, nearly a mile long, leads through various ecological environments: deciduous woods, marshland, a coniferous woodlot, an old field returning to scrub and wood, and a pond. At frequent intervals the path is posted with signs, in both braille and print, describing what you can—or are likely to—see, hear, touch, and even smell at a particular spot at different seasons. Shelves beneath some signs hold dried specimens of local flora and fauna. An information hut on the trail posts a list of the 74 species of birds sighted in the park, among them the bald eagle. In the springtime the pleasure of the walk is enhanced by the wild roses and dogwood blossoming beneath the oaks and white pines. *Accessible year-round; picnic area open mid-Apr.–mid-Oct.; campground open May–Columbus Day. Admission charged during camping season.*

7. Cumming Nature Center. *Gulick Rd., Naples.* This area of wooded hills and marshland is an appealing place for a fam-

of a prehistoric sea. During the uplifting of this mountain system, the rocks were exposed to the surface. When the shale beneath the pudding stone began to erode, the rocks toppled, creating the unusual forms seen today. The trail, winding through Rock City, starts and ends near Signal Rock, once used by Indians for their signal fires. Walking single file, you squeeze through narrow passageways, pass beneath great overhanging boulders, and descend into crevasses carved out by extinct waterfalls. On the last leg of the trail you climb a stone stairway said to have been built by the Indians for easier access to the top, which served as a fortress. (The trip takes about 45 minutes; walking shoes are advised.)

In June, pink and white mountain laurel blooms in profusion, and many other plants flower beneath the maples, hemlocks, pines, and oaks on the hillsides. *Open daily May–Oct. Admission charged.*

5. Letchworth State Park. Rich in history and scenic beauty, this 14,350-acre park stretches along 17 miles of one of the most spectacular gorges in the eastern United States. Three waterfalls accent the twisting Genesee River as it cascades through valleys and canyons where the cliffs at some places tower nearly 600 feet. This awesome natural setting, together with the area's Iroquois and pioneer heritage, has helped to make the 1906 gift of land from Buffalo businessman William P. Letchworth a diverse park with year-round recreational opportunities.

The roadway wandering through the center of the park provides easy access to scenic vistas, the highly developed recreation areas (including two swimming pools), the extensive system of 20 hiking trails, a fishing pond stocked with trout, and the Pioneer and Indian Museum, which highlights the culture of the region's original inhabitants, the Senecas, and the lifestyle of the early pioneers. On a bluff near the museum a statue marks the grave of Mary Jemison, known as "the White Woman of the Genesee." Captured as a young girl by the Senecas during the French and Indian War, Mary adopted tribal ways, married, and bore eight children to two Seneca husbands.

Accommodations in the park range from the Glen Iris Inn, originally Mr.

ily outing any day of the year. The preserve, a branch of the Rochester Museum and Science Center, is on some 800 acres of land donated in 1972 by Mr. and Mrs. Howard Cumming and has been designated a national environmental study area by the National Park Service.

Several trails meander through the nature center, each with a different environmental theme. The Pioneer Trail, about a mile long, leads to a reconstructed 1790 log homestead, with farm animals and implements, that realistically portrays some aspects of life on an 18th-century plantation. To see an example of what beavers can do with sticks, stones, and mud, take the 1½-mile trail to Beaver Pond.

The Iroquois Trail, a loop of about half a mile, features the history of the Six Indian Nations of New York State as depicted in Ernest Smith's paintings, which are posted along the path.

From spring through fall the visitor center offers film programs, nature displays, conducted nature walks, and oxcart rides. In winter cross-country skiing, snowshoeing, and old-fashioned sleigh rides are enjoyed. To round out the year, maple-sugaring demonstrations are given in March, along with a pancake buffet. *Open year-round.*

8. Montour Falls. *West Main St., Village of Montour Falls.*

Almost as high as Niagara, these beautiful falls descend in three tiers to form a dramatic all-seasons backdrop for the village, spectacular in summer and sparkling with sheets of ice in winter. A sketch of the falls, made in 1820 by Louis Philippe, later King of France, hangs in the Louvre Museum in Paris.

The falls were named She-qua-gah (Tumbling Waters) by the band of Seneca Indians brought here from Pennsylvania in the 1760's by their matriarch, Queen Catharine Montour. The queen, of French and Indian descent, had taken charge of the small group following the death of her husband, a Seneca chief. Intelligent and progressive, she traveled extensively as a representative of her people and was popular in society.

Forced to move westward during the American Revolution, Catharine returned to this beloved spot after the war to live out her life. She died in 1804 at the age of 94. A marker in her honor is found in Cook Cemetery in the village of Montour Falls. The whites, who settled here after the exodus of the Indians, called their community Mills Landing and Havana. Later it was renamed in honor of the Indian queen. (Several other places also perpetuate her name.)

The village's historic district is known for its handsome Greek Revival buildings. Several of these are in the national register of historic places. They include the public library, built in 1864 in the form of a Greek cross with a porch supported by Doric columns, and the 19th-century county clerk's office, a porticoed building of mellow red brick that is now used as a private law office.

At Havana Glen, a two-mile-long ravine on the edge of the village, a series of low waterfalls cascades through the woods, forming an occasional quiet pool. The tranquil beauty of this landscape has made it a favorite place with nature lovers from the time of the Senecas. An inviting picnic and camping area is located among the trees at the lower end of the ravine. *Open daily May–Oct.*

9. Taughannock Falls State Park. *Rte. 89, eight miles north of Ithaca.*

In 1779, when the Continental Army marched through the area of Taughannock Falls and Gorge, they drove away the Indian tribes, including Taughannocks and Iroquois, who had lived here for hundreds of years, farming the land and fishing the waters of Cayuga Lake.

During the 19th century the falls were used to power mills and a gun factory, and in the 1880's a resort was developed in the area. As tourism here declined, the resort failed, and in 1925, on a tract of 69 acres, the state park was established. Today it includes almost 800 acres.

The falls, 48 feet higher than Niagara, plunge 215 feet into a natural amphitheater created by thousands of years of erosion and the effects of seasonal melting and freezing. They are named, according to legend, in memory of a Taughannock Indian who was thrown over the cascade to his death after a disastrous battle with the Iroquois. Hiking trails lead along the north and south rims of the gorge and to the foot of the falls.

Taughannock Creek empties into Cayuga Lake, where a delta formed by the stream provides a site for picnic grounds, boat launches, and a swimming beach.

The park has campsites, cabins, bathhouses, and a marina, and in winter offers cross-country and downhill skiing and ice skating. *Park open year-round; campsites open Apr.–mid-Oct. Admission charged.*

10. Lorenzo. *Cazenovia.*

Sent to America in 1790 by Dutch investors to find land for development, John Lincklaen reached the rolling hills at the tip of Lake Cazenovia and stopped. "Situation superb, fine land," he wrote back. Authorized to proceed, he purchased 120,000 acres, laid out the village of Cazenovia (named for his company's manager), built roads and mills, and promoted the development of the region.

On a knoll overlooking the lake Lincklaen built for himself a magnificent Federal-style mansion in 1807 and named it Lorenzo, apparently after Lorenzo de' Medici. Formal and gracious, with a severe brick façade highlighted by delicately proportioned blind arches, the house pro-

9. *Amidst the drama of spray and sound, don't overlook the beauty of the stone.*

12. *In "Howl of the Weather," depicting Chippewa Indians braving the St. Lawrence River, Frederic Remington shows his mastery of detail and movement.*

vided an appropriate setting for entertaining the notables of his time.

The property, occupied by the Lincklaen family for 160 years, was purchased in 1968 by the state of New York as a historic site. Now a museum, it is furnished with family possessions. On the surrounding grounds are formal gardens, groves of trees, walks, and a carriage house containing a wonderful collection of 19th-century horse-drawn vehicles.

During your visit, allow time for a tour of Cazenovia. One of the most beautiful villages in the Northeast, it has a charming main street and hundreds of fine old houses, mostly Victorian and carefully maintained. *Open Wed.–Sat., P.M. Sun., and Mon. holidays, Memorial Day–Labor Day; grounds open year-round.*

11. Sackets Harbor. This small lakeside village with its calm, relaxed air was not always so. During the War of 1812 the settlement, situated beside a bluff commanding access to the St. Lawrence River and blessed with a fine harbor, became an important naval base for the United States, which hoped to take Canada and expel the British. Soldiers, sailors, marines, and shipbuilders arrived here by the thousands; timber was cut, barracks flung up, a shipyard established, and a fleet built. Twice the British attacked, each time unsuccessfully, but the second assault, in May 1813, left Sackets Harbor almost demolished.

With the approach of winter in 1814, nearly 3,000 workers were engaged in constructing two vessels that would each carry 1,000 men. News of peace arrived before the ships were completed, and the young nation's largest shipbuilding venture was halted. Sackets Harbor, however, remained an active naval yard until the late 1800's.

The battlefield, a state historic site, is now a waterfront park offering views of Lake Ontario and a few reminders of the past. Nearby are officers' quarters built in 1847 and the 1817 Union Hotel, now a visitor center with exhibits that give a view of life here during the War of 1812. Among the displays are the colorful tunics, breeches, smocks, pantaloons, and feathered hats worn then—a startling contrast to the drab practicality of uniforms today. *Grounds open year-round. Visitor center open Wed.–Sat., P.M. Sun., and major summer holidays, late May–mid-Oct. Admission charged.*

12. Frederic Remington Art Museum. *303 Washington St., Ogdensburg.* Housed in a white Victorian mansion, the home of George Hall, a boyhood friend of Remington's, the museum contains a most comprehensive collection of the artist's work.

Known as the foremost artist of the Old West, Frederic Remington was born in Canton, New York, in 1861 and spent most of his youth here in Ogdensburg, a town that claims him today as a native son. At 17 he left home to attend Yale University, where he studied art. His classes there were the only formal training he ever had—he was much more interested in boxing and football than in school. He soon headed west, where he began to work as an illustrator and artist.

The museum's collection of 70 Remington oils includes "The Charge of the Rough Riders at San Juan Hill," which stirringly depicts the famous battle in Cuba during the Spanish-American War, when Remington was a war correspondent for the Hearst newspapers. Fourteen bronzes (among them "The Bronco Buster"), 140 watercolors, and many pen and ink sketches are also on display.

Remington died in 1909 in Ridgefield, Connecticut. His last studio is reconstructed at the museum, and here you will see many of his personal belongings, including his rifles, Indian weapons, and over the rough stone fireplace a stuffed buffalo head.

In addition to the Remington works, a collection of period glass, china, silver, cameos, and a group of 19th-century American and European paintings and sculptures are shown. *Open year-round except major holidays.*

13. Ballard Mill. *Williams St., Malone.* Communities looking for ways to make good use of abandoned industrial buildings that are still sturdy, spacious, and attractive can take heart from the story of Ballard Mill.

Jay O. Ballard, who built the mill on the Salmon River in 1901, produced a high-quality woolen fabric known throughout America as Malone Cloth. But the competition from other places using more modern and sophisticated equipment gradually increased, and the mill that was once the mainstay of the town became unprofitable. In 1965 it closed.

The mill remained empty until 1975, when the Malone Extension Division of North Country Community College saw the old red brick building as the perfect site for a proposed working arts center. With funds from various foundations and local industries and the assistance of local volunteers, Ballard Mill and nearby buildings were converted for use as an arts and crafts center. In the main building the techniques of quilting, woodworking, jewelry making, weaving, and printing are taught, along with classes on how to market the products. Studio space in the other buildings is rented to professional artists and craftsmen who gather here.

On an island formed by the millrace, an old airplane hangar has been refurbished as a theater for plays and concerts. Classes in ballet are held here, as are the annual crafts festivals.

The old mill wheel has been restored and once again turns, this time to produce electricity for the center. *Open daily Apr.– Oct.; Mon.–Sat., Nov.–Mar.*

---

14. Cascade Lakes Day Use Area and Cascade Mountain. *Keene. Watch for the lakes and the unmarked turnoff from Rte. 73.* These two woodland lakes, together stretching for over two miles, and the trail up the nearby 4,100-foot peak provide a quiet, uncrowded setting for an invigorat-

ing day in the Adirondack wilderness.

The rustic day-use area is unstaffed by park personnel. Located on a slender spit of land between the lakes, it contains picnic tables, fireplaces, and a dock. The lakes are stocked with trout, and boating and fishing are encouraged, although motors are prohibited. Swimmers can dive from the dock or enter the water from the pebbly shore.

The trail up Cascade Mountain starts from a small parking lot on the south side of Route 73 about a mile west of the day use area. This 2½-mile trail is relatively steep in places but moderate compared to others in the vicinity, and it rewards the hiker who reaches the treeless summit with a spectacular view of the Lake Placid region in the valley below. *Accessible year-round, weather permitting.*

15. Eighth Lake Public Campsite. *Off Rte. 28.* Adirondack Park is such an enormous wilderness, with 2,800 lakes and ponds, 31,000 miles of rivers and streams, and 42 mountains above 4,000 feet, that singling out a place from which to enjoy it can be a challenge. One delightful place is the Eighth Lake Public Campsite, which extends from Seventh Lake to Eighth Lake, the easternmost of a series of lakes connected by the streams that form the Fulton Chain.

The campground has 121 sites, about 40 of which can accommodate trailers up to 35 feet in length. The sites, some close to the water, are inviting alcoves in the forest offering privacy, cooking facilities, and picnic tables, but no hookups. Campers and day users will also find picnic areas, swimming beaches, and boat launches here.

Surrounded by quiet forests, the Fulton Chain offers beautiful, unspoiled waters

---

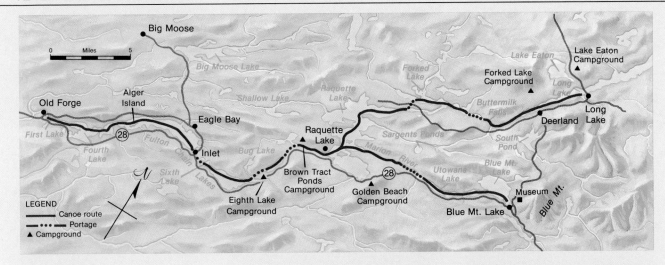

Canoeing in the Adirondacks

We rented a canoe at the livery in Old Forge and had a talk with the manager about the distances we should plan to make each day. We took his (excellent) advice, lightened our packs in anticipation of the places where we would have to carry the canoe, and pushed off into a small pond. Our course led us up a winding stream to First Lake and then through woodland lakes connected by narrow stretches of water, bringing us to the broad expanse of Fourth Lake.

We were warned that the water can be rough when the winds are high, but fortunately it was a calm day.

Our first portage was at the foot of Sixth Lake, and we found that seven-tenths of a mile can seem twice as far when you are carrying all your gear and a canoe. Pitching camp in a lean-to at the Eighth Lake Campground, we were tired and hungry but proud of having made our goal of 18 miles the first day.

After talking to some experienced canoeists at the campground we changed our plans. We decided to take the route to Forked Lake rather than go down the Marion River to Blue Mountain Lake,

which we had seen when we visited the excellent Blue Mountain Museum.

The next morning we followed the advice given us and crossed Raquette Lake early, before the wind came up. From the north end of the lake we had a half-mile portage to Forked Lake. It was easy paddling to Buttermilk Falls and then another short carry to good water, leading to the takeout point at Long Lake. Happily, as we had arranged at our starting point, a truck awaited to take us and our trusty canoe back to Old Forge and civilization.—*H.K. Stern*

For reservations call (315) 369-6286.

19. *The Huguenots were excellent craftsmen. The Hasbrouck house, above, dates from the late 17th century, and the restored church reveals the original character of the masonry.*

for canoeing and a sense of remoteness, which is often heightened by the accompaniment of ducks or an occasional deer at the shore. Fishing is quite good, especially in the Seventh and Eighth lakes, which are cold enough for lake trout. Also caught here are smallmouth bass and occasionally landlocked salmon. Among the many trails in the area is one to Black Bear Mountain, two or three miles away, a suitable place for mountain climbing. Campsites may be crowded on weekends. *Open daily early Apr.–mid-Nov.*

16. National Bottle Museum. *20 Church Ave., Ballston Spa.* The fascination with the infinite variety of shapes, sizes, colors, and uses of bottles, jars, insulators, and any number of other glass objects is evidenced by the growing number of people who seek them out.

Collectors, potential collectors—and even visitors with a more casual interest—will be intrigued by the examples on display here. The pieces, mostly organized by kind, range from milk bottles and fruit jars to bitters bottles, soda bottles, and candy containers. One exhibit is a reconstructed pharmacy with bottles large and small, quaint and colorful, created for a remarkable variety of nostrums both herbal and alcoholic. Glassblowing tools and equipment are also shown.

The museum is in the handsome, hundred-year-old Verbeck House, which is in the national register of historic places. The house was built in 1889 as a home for James W. Verbeck, a prominent Saratoga County lawyer. It remained in the immediate family until 1977; in 1979 the heirs, Abba and Katherine Newton, donated the building to the Federation of Historical Bottle Clubs.

All phases of the bottle-collecting hobby are covered in the books, articles, and other research materials in the library. Lectures and slide programs are offered at the monthly meetings of the National Bottle Museum Society. *Open daily June–Labor Day. Admission charged.*

17. Hanford Mills Museum. *East Meredith.* Eight historic buildings preserved and restored here offer a vivid insight into the development of rural American industry and technology in the last century. The original water-powered mill, built on the banks of Kortright Creek sometime between 1820 and 1840, was first used to saw lumber. Later a gristmill was added. Then in 1860 David Josiah Hanford purchased the property and created a multifaceted business, adding a supply store and a woodworking shop that produced everything from architectural trim to milk boxes and buggy parts. Around the turn of the century Hanford's sons were among the first to harness the flow of water to

generate power for rural electrification.

Today this rich heritage can be appreciated in a fine collection of over 200 antique milling machines, including the 12-foot-wide, 10-foot-diameter waterwheel, shingle mills, barrel-top shapers, handhole cutters, and the eight-kilowatt dynamo that was used to produce electricity. A collection of early photographs provides a unique view of the social history of a rural area typical of the Northeast.

Special events are organized on many summer weekends, including a fly-fishing clinic on the mill pond in June, an old-fashioned July 4 celebration, the August children's fair, and an antique-engine jamboree in September. *Open daily mid-May–mid-Oct. Admission charged.*

18. Burroughs Memorial Field. *Off Rte. 30, two miles west of Roxbury.* Boyhood Rock, the boulder where the young John Burroughs often sat to contemplate the natural world around him, reminds us that one need not seek inspiration in distant places. For it was here in the small area of woods and farmlands around Roxbury that the great American naturalist and philosopher first became aware of the mysteries he would pursue for a lifetime.

Burroughs was born on a farm in Roxbury in 1837, and all through his 84 years he returned again and again to his native countryside, finally to be buried, as he had requested, in a field not far from the rock he considered his own.

During the Civil War Burroughs worked at the Department of the Treasury in Washington. Afterwards he was sent by the government to the British Isles, a land he saw as much inferior to his beloved Catskills. Later the naturalist moved to West Park in the hills of New York State, where he farmed, kept a vineyard, and continued to explore and write about the wonders of nature.

Finally, in his 70's, he returned to Roxbury and renovated an old house that he named Woodchuck Lodge, just over the hill from his birthplace; here he lived and worked for the rest of his life.

Memorial Field lies in a slight fold of "Old Clump," a mountaintop in the Catskills. From the parking lot a path leads through woods to the rock and, in a clearing across the path, to the stone-encircled grave site. This place and the hills and fields beyond marked the center of Burroughs's world. *Open daily Apr.–Oct, weather permitting.*

19. Huguenot Street. *New Paltz.* Even before King Louis XIV banned their religion (in 1685), many French Protestants, known as Huguenots, had exiled themselves, finding refuge in neighboring countries. In 1677 several Huguenot families from *die Pfalz* (the Rhine-Palatinate) arrived in the Hudson Valley. They bought land from the Indians, built log huts, and named their settlement after their previous home. In the 1690's they replaced the huts with steep-roofed stone houses much like those of the Palatinate.

Several of these quaint, medieval-looking dwellings remain on Huguenot Street, designated a national historic landmark with the claim of being "the oldest street in America with its original houses."

These were originally one-room structures, and the large family kitchens with enormous fireplaces and cupboards displaying pottery and old pewter are especially appealing. Also on Huguenot Street are the old stone church (1717), which has been carefully restored, and the DuBois Fort (1705), used formerly as a meeting place and now as a restaurant.

The visitor center has a gallery of historic pictures and offers tours of the site. The place is heavily visited on Heritage Day, the first Saturday in August, and is often visited by school groups on weekdays in June and September. *Open daily late May–late Sept. Admission charged.*

20. Ice Caves Mountain National Landmark. The rising and falling of mountain ranges and the prehistoric existence of vast inland seas are almost incomprehensible to the human mind. Therefore any clues to the time span and geologic forces involved in the natural history of the earth are to be treasured. That is why this area is a registered national landmark. For here on this flat-topped mountain in the Shawangunk Range are massive rocks that were at the bottom of the sea 330 million years ago; a lost river, the source of which is still unknown; a dead lake; tunnels and deep, narrow chasms; ice caves; and layers of shale containing the million-year-old bones of mammoths.

But apart from its geological interest, the magnificent scenery and the dramatic rock formations at Ice Caves Mountain make it an exciting place to visit. From the visitor center a scenic loop road brings you to the major attractions—the ice caves and Sam's Point. You may not find ice in the caves (it melts in summer), but they are still intriguing to explore. The most breathtaking spot, however, is Sam's Point. This enormous monolith, 2,255 feet above sea level, gives a view of five states that is especially glorious during the fall, when the foliage changes color. The point is named for Sam Gonzalez, a fur trapper who is said to have leaped from the point into the treetops far below to escape a pursuing party of Indians and survived, suffering only a broken leg.

Nature trails through woodland lead to springs, chasms, and other scenic spots. Pink azaleas and mountain laurel bloom in the woods from late May into early June, and in late July masses of blueberries ripen on the mountaintop. During spring and fall great numbers of migrating hawks may be seen. *Open Apr. to snow. Admission charged; children under six free.*

21. Sagamore Hill National Historic Site. *End of Cove Neck Rd., Oyster Bay.* Sagamore Hill was built in 1884 for Theodore Roosevelt, who in 1901 was to become the 26th president of the United States. The large, rambling house and its surrounding 155 acres served as an idyllic setting for Roosevelt's large family and, for the years of his presidency, as the summer White House.

The future president's specifications for the 23-room house included a big piazza facing west to view the sunset, a drawing room across the entire west end, and a library with a bay window facing south.

The piazza, overlooking Oyster Bay

21. *Inviting indeed is the covered porch from which the president enjoyed the sunset.*

22. Bronze Buddha graces a quiet corner at the Center of Tibetan Art.

and Long Island Sound, was the scene of many historic events, including the day in 1904 when Roosevelt, having served as president for three years after McKinley's assassination, learned he had been nominated to serve again.

On the library mantel the "ting-tang clock," so named by the Roosevelt children because of its unique sound, still ticks off the hours. Most imposing is the North Room, a 30- by 40-foot hall added in 1905, which became the center of family activity. Paneled in black walnut, swamp cypress, hazel, and mahogany, it contains Roosevelt's many hunting trophies, paintings, books, and other treasures and faithfully reflects the life of the active family, with four boys and two girls, that lived here.

Old Orchard, the Georgian brick home that Mr. and Mrs. Theodore Roosevelt, Jr., built on the grounds in 1937, is now a museum, exhibiting mementos of the president's political and family life. The small library of books and pamphlets by and about Theodore Roosevelt is available to researchers by appointment. *Sagamore Hill open daily Apr.–Oct.; Tues.–Sun., Nov.–Mar. Old Orchard open daily Apr.–Dec.; weekdays Jan.–Mar. Admission charged; senior citizens and children free.*

22. Jacques Marchais Center of Tibetan Art.
338 Lighthouse Ave., Staten Island. Two stone buildings, designed to resemble a Tibetan Buddhist *gompa*, or monastery, are sited on a terraced hillside, with stone-paved garden walks, planted patios, a lotus pond, and a magnificent view of New York City's Lower Bay. These buildings house the only museum in the United States that concentrates on Tibetan and Buddhist art.

The center, opened in 1947, was the vision of Jacqueline Norman Klauber, who used the professional name Jacques Marchais. She designed the buildings and assembled the collection, including an extensive library on Oriental art, philosophy, and history. The serenity here has impressed even visitors from Tibet.

The main museum building, a replica of a Tibetan temple, features a large tiered platform with ritual figurines and objects arranged like a Tibetan altar. Colorful *tankas* (temple paintings on cloth) depicting Buddhas, bodhisattvas, and other deities decorate the walls. Among other highlights in the museum are a jewel-encrusted Nepalese shrine, Tibetan musical instruments, and a group of silver objects that once belonged to the Panchen Lama and are used in the Buddhist fire ritual ceremony. The center sponsors various public programs on weekends. *Parking may be a problem. Open P.M. Fri.–Sun., Apr.–May, Oct.–Nov.; Wed.–Sun., June–Sept. Admission charged.*

23. Jamaica Bay National Wildlife Refuge.
Perhaps the most singular feature of this watery wilderness is its contrast to the surrounding cityscape. In spring and fall thousands of birds swoop down to these wetlands for shelter and food, unfazed by the millions of people rumbling by in cars and trains and the jets roaring overhead. In close proximity, humans and birds follow their own rhythms, largely unaffected by one another.

For city people, the 9,155-acre refuge (which has seven miles of paths) offers easy access to the natural world. Most visitors come during the migratory seasons, when herons, egrets, hooded mergansers, warblers, hawks, and roughly 150 other feathered species are seen here.

But the summer and winter are also rewarding times to visit the refuge, not only for birding but for enjoying the scenery, the relative peace, and the pleasant illusion of being nowhere—but still within sight of Manhattan's magnificent skyline.

23. An American egret works the waters of Jamaica Bay, seeking an evening meal.

The refuge is particularly lovely in wintertime, when crystals of ice form on the trees and grasses and the sense of solitude is heightened. *Open daily except Christmas and New Year's Day.*

24. Bayard Cutting Arboretum. *Oakdale. Off Rte. 27A. Take the Southern State Parkway to Exit 45.* In the mid-1700's, English gardening was revolutionized by the informal, parklike landscape designed by Lancelot ("Capability") Brown. One of his admirers a hundred years later was Frederick Law Olmstead, the landscape architect best known as the creator of New York City's Central Park.

When William Bayard Cutting established his arboretum in 1887, he employed Frederick Law Olmstead's firm to design it. The garden, much in the style of Capability Brown, is a magnificent 690-acre park of evergreen and deciduous specimen trees, rhododendrons, azaleas, and many other shrubs, wildflower plantings, small ponds, and wide lawns that sweep down to the Connetquot River.

The names of the five trails through the grounds indicate the special characteristics of each: Pinetum, Wildflower, Rhododendron, Bird-Watchers', and Swamp Cypress. All are detailed on a map available at the arboretum center.

The estate, donated to the Long Island State Park and Recreation Commission by Mrs. William Bayard Cutting and her daughter, Mrs. Olivia James, includes the former Cutting home, which now serves as a center for the arboretum. The interior is noted for the ornate oak paneling, stained glass windows, and handsome antique fireplaces. On display are extensive collections of mounted birds, American Indian artifacts, and interesting plants. Near the entry is a spectacular specimen of a weeping European beech.

Rooms in both the mansion and the carriage house are reserved for concerts, classes, and horticultural exhibits. *Open Wed.–Sun. and legal holidays. Admission charged mid-Apr.–mid-Nov.*

25. Orient Beach State Park. That a state park exists here is due to the foresight of local farmers some 60 years ago. At that

25. *From the destructive forces of wind, water, and sun, beauty may also come.*

time the land was owned by the Male Taxpayers of Orient, a farmers' organization with an interest in preserving this marshy peninsula as a barrier protecting their farms from the sea. In the late 1920's the organization donated the land to the state, hoping that the government would take over the burden of maintenance. The farmers' plan worked, and in the early 1930's the park was established.

Today this 357-acre park is an inviting place for a family day trip. The five-mile-long peninsula in quiet Gardiner's Bay provides 10 miles of sand-and-pebble beach, a small portion of which is reserved for swimming. The lifeguards on duty and the gentle waters here make it suitable for children. The large picnic area is shaded by a grove of cedars. Fishing is allowed from the shore, but boats may not be launched. Flounder and snapper are the likely catch. Great blue herons are often seen stalking the shore. *Open Wed.– Mon., Apr.–Labor Day; Thurs.–Mon., Labor Day–Mar.*

26. Morton National Wildlife Refuge. *Noyack Rd., Sag Harbor.* Long before the 17th century, when the white man invaded eastern Long Island, this narrow strip of land between Little Peconic and Noyack bays was the home of the Montauk and Shinnecock Indians, who farmed and fished and traded with the Corchaugs,

their relatives on the North Shore. The property was deeded in 1679 to John Jessup, who had come here from Massachusetts some 40 years earlier. Known as Jessup's Neck, the peninsula has 187 acres of woodlands, salt marshes, sandy shores, and a freshwater pond.

After almost 200 years of private ownership and use as farmland, the property was given by Mrs. Elizabeth Morton to the United States Fish and Wildlife Service in 1954; the land is now slowly reverting to its natural state.

The refuge is an important resting and feeding stop for birds on their seasonal migrations. Since 1956, when the refuge was established, more than 200 species of waterfowl, songbirds, hawks, and waders have been observed. Black ducks, goldeneyes, and scaups are among those staying in the area all winter. An observation blind on the bank of the small pond is a great boon to bird-watchers.

The refuge also harbors white-tailed deer, foxes, raccoons, and opossums, and the tidal waters abound with bluefish, weakfish, clams, scallops, and oysters.

A one-mile self-guiding nature trail leads through woods of oak, sumac, and juniper, and past quiet ponds and marshes to the beach. Numbered posts along the trail are keyed to the descriptions given in a pamphlet available at the visitor center. *Open year-round.*

New Jersey

If you are one of those to whom "Jersey" means turnpike, it's time to seek out some of the delights to be found off that beaten path.

The Great Swamp, the Pine Barrens, and Sandy Hook are celebrated New Jersey landforms, but even so, sections of each are not unduly crowded. Also closely identified with the state is a celebrated general. It was here that George Washington experienced a dramatic escape from the British (see entry No. 5), had a frustrating near-victory at Monmouth battlefield, enjoyed a pleasant sojourn at the Wallace house, and saw his troops endure a bitter winter near Morristown.

New Jersey's natural resources and numerous waterways made it an early leader in industry, as evidenced by the ironworks at Allaire, Batsto, and Ringwood, and the Delaware and Raritan Canal. Spacious parks and preserves for wildlife and a treasure trove of Victoriana add further scope to the state's appeal.

1. High Point State Park.
In the late 1800's this magnificent tract of land on the crest of the Kittatinny Ridge was part of an elegant private resort. A carriage road wound up the forested slopes to High Point Inn. A short walk then led to New Jersey's highest peak (1,803 feet), where guests enjoyed cool breezes and panoramic views of the New Jersey, New York, and Pennsylvania countryside. Years later the inn was partially dismantled and converted to a smaller lodge; in the 1920's the property was given to the state of New Jersey and opened to the public.

The most prominent feature in the 14,000-acre park is the granite-faced obelisk that soars 220 feet from the top of High Point. Interior stairs lead to the top of the monument, from which you can see for some 40 miles. It is said that on very clear nights the lights of New York City are visible.

With its forests, lakes, creeks, glens, swamp, and old farm fields, the park is a haven for wildlife, especially for white-tailed deer, which often dart across the park roads. A few black bears roam in some areas, steering clear of people, and once in a great while a bobcat is sighted. Several species of hawks and other raptors wheel about, and bluebirds and wild turkeys are regularly seen.

The park has nine hiking trails of varying lengths and ease, each with its own rewards. Trail guides are available at the visitor center near the entrance. The Old Trail, for example, utilizes a former horse-and-buggy road through a pleasantly open forest for half a mile, and is easy to walk. The more arduous and scenic Monument Trail goes around Cedar Swamp, where you can find pitcher plants and sundews—carnivorous plants that are uncommon in this region. The Appalachian Trail also runs through the park.

The park's day-use area includes spring-fed Lake Marcia (with a beach for swimmers) and tree-shaded picnic tables. Sawmill Lake, two or three miles from the day-use area, provides a private retreat for campers only. The lake is stocked with trout, bass, and pickerel, and on winter weekends many come here for ice fishing. *Open year-round. Admission charged.*

2. Wawayanda State Park.
Well signed on Rtes. 23, 94, and 513. Spaciousness and excellent upkeep are an immediate impression of this fine park, partly because of the manicured entrance grounds and the two miles of excellent road rolling from the park headquarters to the parking lot on Wawayanda Lake. The lake, about 1½ miles long, has a lovely prospect, with several islands, a shoreline edged with forests, coves, and cliffs, and a swimming area with a sandy beach. Picnic tables are located in the wooded areas nearby.

A short walk from the beach is a marina where canoes, rowboats, and live bait are available. Several species of trout and bass are caught in the lake, as well as pike, pickerel, and muskellunge. Ice fishing is a popular sport in winter.

More than 20 miles of hiking trails lead to small ponds, a swamp, and scenic outlooks. The park is an excellent place for riding, and horses are available from stables nearby. Bird-watching is another favorite recreation; warblers are frequently seen, as well as hawks and other raptors, including an occasional eagle. To prevent crowding, the park gates are closed when visitors reach a certain number. *Open year-round. Admission charged.*

3. Ringwood State Park.
On a gentle slope in the Ramapo Mountains stands a rambling, white-stuccoed manor house whose history is intertwined with that of America's first large-scale iron industry.

In 1740 the Ringwood Company acquired several rich mines in this vicinity and established an ironworks here on the present manor grounds. During the American Revolution the company supplied the army with ordnance, hardware, and camp stoves. The ironmaster, a topographical engineer, prepared military maps for General Washington.

The original house, where Washington sometimes stayed, was replaced in 1810 by the ironmaster Martin Ryerson, who built a fine 10-room house in the Federal style. In 1853 Ringwood was purchased by Peter Cooper (the founder of Cooper Union Institute), who turned the property over to his son-in-law, Abram Hewitt, one of the great ironmasters of that time. Making Ringwood their residence, the Hewitts gradually added 41 rooms. The house today is a charming mix of styles. The exterior unabashedly combines gables, Ionic columns, and Victorian filigree, and the interior, furnished with choice antiques, is equally intriguing.

In front of the house spacious lawns sweep down to a small brook and lake picturesque with water lilies and resident geese and ducks. In contrast are the formal gardens behind the house. Everywhere are reminders of the past, including the blacksmith shop where Washington's horses were shod. The 579-acre park offers hiking trails, a children's playground, and dozens of picnic tables spaced along a woodland stream. *Open daily except Mon.; house open for tours May 1–Oct. 31. Admission charged.*

1. *Looking across Lake Marcia toward Kittatinny Ridge. Note the obelisk silhouetted against the skyline.*

4. Steuben House. *1209 Main St., River Edge. Leave Rte. 4 at the Riverside Square Mall and follow Hackensack Ave. North for ½ mile. Turn right onto Main St. in River Edge and continue to the house.* Located on the bank of the Hackensack River, the golden sandstone house and the adjacent undeveloped acreage form an oasis of quiet in the midst of a heavily populated area. Two centuries ago, however, this was the site of a small but busy inland port and a strategic point for both sides in the ebb and flow of the conflict in this region during the Revolution. A few yards from the house are the old wharf and an iron swing

bridge built in 1888 to replace a wooden span called New Bridge, which was built in 1744. In November 1776 Gen. George Washington led his Continental Army across New Bridge in a dramatic escape from the British at Fort Lee, and the structure became known as "the bridge that saved a nation."

In 1777 the owner of the house, Jan Zabriskie, was accused of passing military intelligence to the British. His property was subsequently confiscated and presented in 1783 to the Prussian officer Major General Baron von Steuben as a reward for his services to the Continental Army. Five years later Steuben sold the estate back to the Zabriskie family.

Acquired by the state of New Jersey in 1928 as a historic shrine, part of the two-story, 12-room house is now a museum for artifacts of local manufacture, charmingly displayed. Found here are fine examples of matchstick furniture, pottery, textiles, antique dolls, folk art, and a well-stocked medicine cabinet. Near the hearth in the keeping room stands an oak settee with an unusually high back that forms a cabinet in which hams were cured. The museum also houses a splendid dugout canoe that was unearthed nearby. *Open Wed.–Sat. and P.M. Sun. year-round. Admission free but donations encouraged.*

---

5. Delaware Water Gap National Recreation Area. Winding through a deep, narrow rent in the Kittatinny Mountains, the Delaware River creates a vista that draws thousands of tourists annually. But just north of the water gap lies a seldom-visited recreation area of unspoiled beauty. Flanking the Delaware River for some 35 miles as it flows between the Kittatinny Ridge in New Jersey and the Pocono Mountains in Pennsylvania, the largely wooded hills and vales include ponds, brooks, gorges, waterfalls, swimming beaches, and many kinds of wildlife.

On the New Jersey side a blacktop road traverses the length of the recreation area, overlooking the river part of the way. Going north from the water gap, the narrow lane threads through the fern-carpeted Worthington State Forest and passes bucolic farmland, a re-created 19th-century farm community (open in summer), and a crafts center. The absence of traffic and the rural peace and quiet everywhere are reminiscent of earlier times and places.

From the roadside, trails lead to cool glens, swift brooks, and scenic points along the Delaware River, where on summer weekends several hundred canoes may be seen gliding downstream.

An ideal and well-marked picnic spot is found at Watergate, where the trees open upon a large, rolling meadow bordered on one side by a pond and on the other side by a brook overhung with trees. The small dam here, with two miniature stone towers, gives the place its name. In summer the air is heady with the scent of mown grass drying in the sun; birds sing, and the brook ripples musically by. It's so blissful here that, for the time at least, all seems right with the world. Picnic tables with charcoal grills are widely spaced beneath shade trees.

Maps and trail guides are available at the Kittatinny Information Center in New Jersey, just off I-80 at the water gap. *Open year-round.*

---

6. Morristown National Historical Park. *From Rte. 287 take Exit 32 to reach Washington's headquarters. To visit Jockey Hollow, return to Rte. 287 and go south to Exit 26B. Watch for the signs.* With the approach of winter in 1779, General Washington needed an encampment for the Continental Army from which close watch could be kept on the British in New York City. Morristown was a strategic location, and Mrs. Jacob Ford, Jr., whose husband

had died during one of the early campaigns, offered the use of her home to General and Mrs. Washington.

The elegant, Georgian-style frame mansion is furnished approximately as it was when it served as the general's headquarters. Walking through the rooms, you can visualize the activity here, with the Washingtons, Mrs. Ford and her four children, the many officers, visitors such as the Marquis de Lafayette, and some 20 servants at work. In the dining room, which also served as the conference room, take note of the Chippendale mirror, which has a phoenix rising at the top. In 1780 the phoenix motif evolved into the national symbol, the American eagle.

Leaflets for a self-guiding tour of the house are available at the headquarters museum; here too a film is shown (every half-hour) that portrays life at the headquarters and at Jockey Hollow, where 10,000 ill-clad, starving soldiers endured one of the worst winters of the century.

Although it was an hour's ride by horse from headquarters, Jockey Hollow was chosen for the encampment because it had sufficient timber for the construction of nearly 1,200 huts and for firewood. Today it is a serene 1,800-acre park with woodlands, brooks, and meadows. From the entrance a pleasant road loops through the area, passing several reconstructed cabins and the parade ground. The 26 miles of trail in the park are used for hiking, horseback riding, and cross-country skiing. Behind the Jockey Hollow visitor center are

6. *Winter's light reveals the handsome details under the eaves and by the entry.*

7. *Between these dramatic seasonal effects are the constant subtle changes that make the Great Swamp so fascinating.*

open fields, an old apple orchard, a re-creation of an 18th-century farm garden, and the sturdy Wick farmhouse, where Gen. Arthur St. Clair headquartered.

The park may be heavily visited on spring and fall weekends and on Washington's birthday. *Headquarters open year-round except Thanksgiving Day, Christmas, and New Year's Day; admission charged. Jockey Hollow open year-round.*

7. Great Swamp National Wildlife Refuge.
From Rte. 287 take Exit 26 and follow Maple Ave. half a mile. Turn left onto Madisonville Rd., then right on Pleasant Plains Rd. Continue about two miles to the refuge. Established in 1960, the refuge has 6,793 acres of cattail marshes, grassland, and swamp woodlands, most of which has been designated a wilderness area for white-tailed deer, red and gray foxes, muskrats, minks, and other mammals. It is also frequented by 200 species of birds, both migratory and resident.

The refuge headquarters supplies trail maps and brochures that list the wildflowers, mammals, birds, and reptiles found here season by season. Don't miss the Wildlife Observation Center, where a boardwalk crosses a small swamp to a duck observation blind. The swamp, marvelously beautiful, is filmed over by bright neon-green algae sprinkled in May with tiny yellow flowers and clumps of delicate purple iris. Here and there are open spots where turtles can be seen napping in the murky water. From peepholes in the blind one overlooks a larger swamp filled with pond lilies. The croaks and peeps of frogs and calls of birds are the only sounds in this mysterious and fascinating place.

The best viewing times are early morning and late afternoon. Visitors should cover their arms and legs completely to protect them from mosquitoes and ticks; the latter can cause Lyme disease. *Open year-round, dawn to dusk.*

8. Clinton Historical Museum Village.
The buildings comprising this picturesque community are remindful of the life, work, and customs in the area from the mid-18th century to the early 1900's.

The centerpiece is the old Red Mill on Spruce Run. Local enterprises such as this were indispensable in the days when transportation was slow and uncertain. The mills would grind whatever might be profitable at the time. This one, built in the 1760's, first ground flaxseed to make linseed oil; in later years it ground grain and then limestone; and from 1903 until it closed in 1920 it was used for grinding talc and graphite. Today it serves as a museum. On the top floor is a working model of a typical mill. The other three floors are devoted to room settings of tools and equipment, fixtures and furnishings, toys, and decorative objects illustrating the early-day life in this area.

Other attractions along Spruce Run are an old schoolhouse, a blacksmith shop, a general store and post office, a log cabin, and the stone crusher and kilns used to process limestone quarried from the cliffs that parallel the river. Weekends, when special events are frequently held, are more crowded than weekdays. *Open P.M. daily Apr.–Oct. Admission charged.*

8. *The dam on Spruce Run diverts water to the mill's undershot wheel.*

9. Wallace House. *Somerville.* The months Gen. George Washington spent in this house, from December 1778 to June 1779, must have been among the most pleasant in his years of service to the Continental Army. He had endured the hardships and frustrations of the previous winter with his ill-equipped army at Valley Forge. Then in June 1778, at the Battle of Monmouth, he and his troops had successfully harried the British as they retreated from Philadelphia (see entry No. 12). Now, with the enemy engaged to the north and in the south, and his own troops well established in the nearby Watchung Mountains, Washington was able to savor the mild winter weather and enjoy the chance to entertain in the finest house in the vicinity.

The eight-room house was built in the Georgian style for John Wallace, a Philadelphia tea merchant, but before he could take possession arrangements were made for its use as Washington's headquarters. After the army moved north to White Plains, New York, the Wallaces moved in; the house stayed in their family until 1801. In 1897 the Revolutionary Memorial Society bought the place and in 1946 gave it to the state of New Jersey. It has been restored as faithfully as possible to its 18th-century appearance, although the original Wallace furnishings were perhaps more elegant. The guided tours of the house provide an insight into the life and style of that era. *Open Wed.–Sat. and P.M. Sun. year-round. Admission charged.*

---

10. Delaware and Raritan Canal State Park. As early as 1676 William Penn is said to have considered building an inland waterway across the narrow "waist" of New Jersey to expedite the trip from Philadelphia to New York. More than 150 years were to pass, however, before work began on a canal connecting the Delaware River north of Bordentown and the Raritan River at New Brunswick. This 44-mile waterway (7 feet deep and 75 feet wide) required 14 locks to complete its course. The water came from a feeder canal 22 miles farther up the Delaware. Largely dug by hand by Irish immigrants, these giant trenches extracted a high price. Construction costs soared above $2.8 million, and scores of workers housed in labor camps died of cholera.

By way of the canal, which opened in the spring of 1834, the trip from Borden-

10. *The lush growth of trees and shrubs is naturalizing the man-made canal.*

town to New Brunswick took the better part of two days. The waterway remained in operation for nearly 100 years.

Since 1974 large sections of the canal have been set aside as a unique state park, whose character varies with its changing surroundings as it wanders through central New Jersey. The canal's towpath is enjoyed by joggers, hikers, cyclists, and horsemen. Canoes can be rented near Bull's Island, where a campground is maintained, and at several towns along the canal, including Titusville, Kingston, and Griggstown. Sections of the canal are stocked with trout, and fishermen are also likely to catch bluegill, perch, pickerel, and largemouth bass.

---

11. Sandy Hook Unit, Gateway National Recreation Area. For more than 200 years this sandspit in lower New York Bay has been identified with military defense and the saving of lives at sea. In colonial times the shallows here were known as a graveyard for ships, and in 1764 a lighthouse was constructed that could cast a light visible for 15 miles. Following the outbreak of the Revolution, the light was of primary value to the British, and the colonists attempted to destroy it. They were unsuccessful, however, and the light was saved by the enemy. The installation, maintained by the Coast Guard, is now the oldest working lighthouse in the country, and is designated a national historic landmark. Because ocean currents have deposited sand at the end of the peninsula, the octagonal structure is today about 1½ miles back from the edge of the point.

Another witness to the perils of the high seas is the U.S. Lifesaving Service, now the visitor center. Established in 1849 to rescue victims of shipwrecks, it was one of the first such stations in the nation.

Of the many military defense systems that have been installed on the peninsula, the most colorful is Fort Hancock, which was built in the late 19th century and kept in use until the 1970's, when the last of the Nike missiles were removed. You can explore the barracks, mess halls, officers' houses, and other buildings of this old army town. Also worth seeing are the 20-inch Rodman gun (1869) and the massive concrete mortar battery (1894).

But Sandy Hook has much more to offer. Its miles of ocean beach, dunes, and salt marsh (home for egrets, ospreys, and many other protected birds) invite exploration by pleasure seekers and nature lovers. Trails lead through the dunes and to a unique holly forest on the bay side. The best times to visit are summer weekdays and the off-season months, when there are no crowds. *Open year-round. Admission charged for beach areas.*

12. Monmouth Battlefield State Park.
The battle here on June 28, 1778, enhanced the morale of the Continental Army: for the first time the colonials engaged the British in open field combat and stood them off. Historians, however, consider the Battle of Monmouth a missed opportunity for a stunning American victory. At a critical point in the conflict Maj. Gen. Charles Lee retreated instead of attacking as ordered, and the British, after a day of fighting, were able to move out under cover of darkness and safely make their way north. General Lee was court-martialed and found guilty of disobedience and misbehavior.

An illuminated diorama in the visitor center shows the sequence of the battle hour by hour. The center also provides information on historic Craig House and Owl Haven nature center, either of which can be reached by car or by trails in the park. If you walk, you'll see the land much as it was on that historic day in 1778. John Craig, a paymaster for the local militia, was involved in the battle; his shingle-and-clapboard house on the battlefield has been restored. Built in 1710, it has seven rooms, three fireplaces, a cold cellar, and a sleeping area for the slaves.

The nature center displays live owls, reptiles, and amphibians, as well as mounted birds and other nature-related specimens. Nature walks, seasonal exhibits, and interpretive talks are also offered. *Park open year-round. Craig House open Thurs.–Sun., June–Labor Day; weekends Labor Day–May. Owl Haven open Tues.–Sun. year-round.*

13. Turkey Swamp Park. *Georgia Rd., Freehold.* Long ago the town of Adelphia was called Turkey, and the surrounding thickly forested, swampy lands and bogs were known as Turkey Swamp. The name was adopted by the park, which now encompasses more than 500 acres.

Several self-guiding nature trails around the lake and bogs lead through the woodlands of oak and pitch pine, with their undergrowth of blueberry and pepperbush. The Fit-Trail, with 20 illustrated exercise stops along the 1¼-mile route, circles the entire park.

The park features a shelter, open in summer, enclosed and heated in winter, with a fireplace, picnic tables, and a kitchen. Available for general use during the day, it can be rented for private evening parties from mid-March to mid-December. Family campgrounds are located in the woodlands. Wilderness campgrounds in a remote section of the park may be reserved by groups.

Canoes, rowboats, and paddleboats are available for rent, and there are children's playgrounds, picnic groves with grills, and fields for soccer and other sports. *Open year-round; camping March–Nov. Fees for camping and special facilities.*

14. Allaire State Park. The park, with some 3,000 acres laced with roads and trails, watered by two rivers, and with campgrounds and a golf course, is a major attraction. And here too is the ongoing restoration of a small early-19th-century company town.

In 1814 the first furnace was built here to extract ore from local deposits of bog iron. The industry expanded, and by 1836–37 this was a busy community of about 60 buildings and 400 people employed by the Allaire Works. But great improvements in smelting were being made elsewhere, and the Allaire furnace could not compete after a while.

11. *Although it is more than 200 years old, the lighthouse at Sandy Hook still warns mariners of the offshore shallows.*

Were it not for the generosity of Mrs. Arthur Brisbane, widow of the famous journalist, who deeded the village and surrounding land to the state, and the active interest shown by the local Boy Scouts and service clubs, Allaire would simply have disappeared, as did so many similar communities in New Jersey.

The serenity of the tree-shaded grounds and well-tended 19th-century buildings belie the din, smoke, and hard, grimy labor involved in turning bog iron into the pots, kettles, pipe, hand irons, and other products made here. A sawmill, a gristmill, and a blacksmith shop contributed to the din. The smelter roared night and day for months on end, and the scores of charcoal pits making fuel for the furnace added a pall of pungent, acrid smoke.

If we have learned to appreciate the labors of our forebears, it is partly because of restorations such as this. Keep in mind, too, that if you purchase something in a specific store, it's because you choose to. In this and other company towns all across the nation years ago, workers had no choice; they were usually paid in scrip redeemable only at the company store.

As another reminder of earlier days, you'll hear the distinctive sound of a real steam whistle as the narrow-gauge Pine Creek Railroad runs past the village.

The park office provides lists of the species of wildflowers (206), birds (163), mammals, reptiles and turtles, and fish (about 20 each) that inhabit the park. The nature center displays fossils and mounted animals from the area and shows slides of the flora and fauna. For the half-mile nature trail there are cassettes, pamphlets, and braille markers. Canoes are available for rent nearby, and some of the trails are suitable for cross-country skiing. *Open year-round. Admission charged.*

15. Double Trouble State Park. This wilderness of woods and marsh in the Pine Barrens is a nature lover's delight at all times of the year, and on a grey day it has a misty, almost other-worldly aura that is especially appealing.

The park's history goes back to the late 18th century, when a sawmill was built and a dam constructed for waterpower. According to local lore, muskrats repeatedly gnawed through the dam, causing leaks that were announced with the cry "Here's trouble" and quickly repaired. One day the owner found two gaps in the dam and shouted to his men, "Here's double trouble!"—thus the name.

Faced with a dwindling supply of timber around the end of the 19th century, people began to grow cranberries to augment their incomes. The land was sold to the state in 1965, but the sawmill and the cranberry operation are still in business.

Within the park's 5,000 acres are a general store, cranberry packinghouse, one-room schoolhouse, migrants' cottage, and other early-day buildings, which are now being restored.

From the cranberry processing plant a self-guiding nature trail about 1¼ miles long crosses Cedar Creek, winds around the bogs, and ends at the sawmill. The red tint in the creek is caused by cedar bark and iron deposits. The air is aromatic with cedar, and in season rhododendrons, mountain laurel, sweet bay, and fragrant honeysuckle bloom beneath sassafras trees, pitch pines, and red maples. Also growing in this moist environment is the carnivorous sundew.

Great blue herons, egrets, pigeon hawks, and quails are seen here. Fishermen can expect pickerel and catfish. Cedar Creek is very popular with canoeists, and canoes can be rented nearby. The park is especially enjoyable in springtime and in autumn, when the cranberries are harvested. In summer bring insect repellent. *Open year-round.*

16. *Here is a dramatic illustration of contrasting edges created by the ocean and the bay. Barnegat Light (right) which is south of this road, marks a break in the barrier beach.*

16. Island Beach State Park. On leaving New Jersey's heavily developed coast, you will find Island Beach State Park a pleasant surprise, with its miles of undeveloped seashore. The southern end of a long barrier beach, this area became an island in 1750, when raging seas broke through the narrow bar of land at Seaside Heights. The inlet was open until 1812, when another storm closed it.

In the 1950's, to preserve the fragile environment of dunes and grasses found here, the state of New Jersey purchased 2,694 acres for a park with a botanical preserve, a recreation zone, and a wildlife sanctuary. The nature center at the north end of the park offers guided walks and has exhibits of the shells, butterflies, and primitive maritime vegetation found here.

A paved road lined with dunes and beach heather leads from the park entrance to the recreation zone (a marvelous stretch of white, sandy beach on the ocean) and continues to the wildlife sanctuary, which is also open to visitors. At the end of the road the Barnegat Lighthouse can be seen 1½ miles in the distance. A beach buggy is required to reach Barnegat Inlet.

The park is especially lovely in autumn, which can extend until Thanksgiving. The water stays warm, the beaches are empty of people but filled with shells, swarms of monarch butterflies cling to the branches of goldenrod, and the southbound birds are on the wing. *Open year-round. Admission charged.*

17. Wharton State Forest. *On Rte. 542 off the Garden State Parkway.* In this large forest (composed mostly of pines, with some cedar and mixed hardwoods) are the Batsto and Mullica rivers, Atsion Lake, several streams, nature trails, a long hiking trail, and a number of campgrounds. But the major feature is the restored iron-making village of Batsto.

The combination of iron ore from the local bogs and fuel from the dense forests led to the establishment of many small iron-producing centers in southern New Jersey in the 18th century. Local forges made water pipes, stoves, firebacks, kettles, and other homely necessities; and during the Revolution and the War of 1812, they supplied firearms and ammunition. When coal from the Pennsylvania

17. *Bog ore (foreground) was the source of life at Batsto. In background is a pile of wood to burn for charcoal, and the ironmaster's imposing residence.*

mines became available, the wood-burning forges could not compete. Glass factories were built here in the mid-1800's, but they too failed. Batsto would have disappeared, as did similar villages in the area, had it not been for Joseph Wharton of Philadelphia, who bought the property and started redevelopment in 1876. The 39 buildings include the ironmaster's handsome mansion, the general store, post office, sawmill, smithy, shops, barns, and ironworkers' houses. Various early American crafts are demonstrated in the village during the summer. An ore boat, the charcoal kiln, and the furnace site are silent reminders of the hot and noisy work that once prevailed here.

A nature area adjoins the village, and the 40-mile Batona Wilderness Trail swings by. The Atsion Lake area, about a 20-minute drive from Batsto, has a playground, picnic area, swimming beach, and canoes and boats for rent. The forest offers shelter for many birds and other wildlife. Fishing is good, mainly for pike, pickerel, perch, and bass.

The 500 miles of sandy roads in the forest are open for hiking, horseback riding, four-wheel-drive vehicles, and snowmobiles in season.

Atsion Lake is likely to be crowded on summer weekends. *Open daily except Thanksgiving Day, Christmas, and New Year's Day. A parking fee is charged on weekends at village, daily at lake, Memorial Day–Labor Day.*

18. Edwin B. Forsythe Wildlife Refuge. *Watch carefully for the sign on Rte. 9.* Among the most effective conservationists are those who serve in Congress—where environmental concerns can be translated into law. It is only fitting that those who have served well should be remembered. The late Congressman Edwin B. Forsythe worked diligently to protect the natural environment, and in 1984 the already established Brigantine and Barnegat Wildlife Refuges were renamed in his honor.

The area now includes more than 34,000 acres of bays, channels, salt marshes, barrier beaches, dunes, upland fields, and woodlands. The refuge is a major stop on the Atlantic Flyway. The peak of north-bound migration is mid-March to mid-April. During the summer warblers, shorebirds and wading birds are abundant. The south-bound migration is from mid-October to mid-December, with spectacular concentrations of ducks, geese, and brant in early November. Dur-

18. *Among the surprises in this wild setting is the colorful marshmallow.*

ing the winter as many as 150,000 birds stay in the area. At the visitor center you can get a list of the 289 species observed here. Leaflets are also available for an eight-mile, self-guiding auto tour; the suggested stops along the way include observation towers, a pool covered with water lilies, a nesting area where 600 Canada geese are hatched every year, and other areas where bald eagles, ospreys, and wood ducks may be seen.

For hikers, the self-guiding People's Trail leads through a typical coastal woodland, while the Leeds Eco-Trail penetrates an estuarine environment where incoming tides mix with freshwater streams flowing seaward. *Open year-round.*

---

19. Fort Mott State Park. The strategic importance of the Delaware River was recognized as early as 1838, when the federal government purchased land here at Finns Point. The first guns were installed in 1878. In 1895 strong American sympathy for the Cubans, revolting against their Spanish rulers, led to the likelihood of war with Spain. As a precaution, naval defense guns were placed here and Fort Mott was constructed. (It was named for Maj. Gen. Gersham Mott of New Jersey, who had distinguished himself in the Mexican War and the Civil War.) During the brief conflict with Spain that ensued in 1898, the enemy fleet was destroyed off the coast of Cuba, and this fort was never used. The garrison was gradually reduced and the

guns removed; in 1951 the abandoned fort became a state park.

The shot rooms, the ammunition and powder magazines, and the range-finder tower can still be seen. But the attraction today is the peaceful setting, where one can savor the expanse of sky and see the oceangoing ships sailing the waters of the Delaware. In midstream on Pea Patch Island is Fort Delaware, the site of a Civil War prison camp. In the national cemetery adjacent to the park is a memorial to Confederate soldiers and, in particular, to those prisoners who died at Fort Delaware. Another monument is dedicated to Union soldiers buried here.

A (literal) highlight in the area is Finns Point lighthouse. The 115-foot wrought-iron tower, built in 1876, is listed in the National Register of Historical Sites. The schedule may change, but at this writing you can climb to the top (on the third Sunday of the month, June–October) for a spectacular view. The park may be crowded on weekends. *Open year-round.*

---

20. Hancock House. *Hancock's Bridge.* In 1675 John Fenwick and a group of fellow Quakers established a colony in this part of the Delaware Valley. As the settlers prospered, they built a number of handsome brick homes. One of the first was the house built by Judge William Hancock in 1734 and attached to a simple structure erected a few years earlier. The community and the drawbridge here on

Alloway Creek were named for the judge.

The exterior of the two-story house is a fine example of the ornamental brickwork favored in this region. Colored (vitrified) brick was combined with standard red clay brick in various patterns. The corners of the Hancock house feature a striped zigzag pattern in blue and red, with a checkerboard effect in front. The building date is on one corner, along with the initials W—H—S, for William and his wife Sarah. The interior is furnished with pieces typical of their time.

During the Revolutionary War a tragic incident occurred in the house. About 30 Quakers, assigned to defend the drawbridge, were garrisoned here. The British, who were foraging in the area, had lost a battle at Quinton's Bridge on March 18, and were seeking revenge and a victory over the local militia. Just before dawn three days later, a force of 300 British troops and local loyalists surprised the two sentries on duty at Hancock's Bridge and, without firing a shot, used their bayonets to massacre the small garrison asleep in the house. *Open Wed.–Sun. year-round.*

---

21. Parvin State Park. In this quiet retreat it is hard to imagine that this was once the site of a busy gristmill and sawmill. The Parvin family operated the mills, and the original millpond, created by damming Muddy Run, was given their name.

Although Parvin Lake and the smaller Thundergust Lake are major attractions, the eight miles of trails winding through the swamps, groves, thickets, and forest in this 1,125-acre preserve are of special interest to nature lovers. The woods include some 40 kinds of trees, 60 different shrubs, more than 200 flowering plants, and many ferns and mosses. Birders have spotted 123 species in the park; and deer, raccoons, squirrels, and other small mammals may be seen. A naturalist conducts informal walks, depending on interest and the weather.

The inviting picnic grounds and play areas on Thundergust Lake are sensibly separated. In summer a lifeguard is on duty at the swimming beach on Parvin Lake. Boats and canoes are available for rent, and the fishing is considered to be good. Ice fishing and skating are popular in winter. *Open year-round.*

---

22. Wheaton Village. The first successful glassworks in America was started here in southern New Jersey in 1739 by Caspar Wistar. A rapidly growing population soon created a good market for bottles and window glass. Southern New Jersey, with its abundant silica sand, plentiful wood for the furnaces, and excellent waterways, became a major center for glassmaking. In the late 1800's some 70 glassworks were flourishing here, including the T.C. Wheaton Company.

Theodore C. Wheaton, a physician, pharmacist, and drugstore owner, recognized the growing importance of glass containers, and in 1888 he bought an existing glassworks in Millville. As the T.C. Wheaton Company, the business prospered from the start, and today Wheaton Industries is the largest family-held glass producer in the world.

The centerpiece of Wheaton Village, established in 1968, is a working replica of the original factory. Glassblowers (gaffers) are at work here using the old tools and equipment. For a fee, you can make your own paperweight under their guidance.

The Museum of American Glass, on the village grounds, has some 7,000 pieces displayed in cases and in period settings of a kitchen and a pharmacy that effectively show their function.

Although glassmaking is the focus of the village, the 19th-century architecture, the tinsmith's and potter's shops, a printshop, a schoolhouse, and a general store help to create the ambience of an earlier era. The opportunities to order from an authentic old-time soda fountain, ride a half-scale railroad, and watch a live medicine show are further diversions to enjoy here. *Open daily Apr.–Dec.; Wed.–Sun., Jan.–Mar. Closed Easter, Thanksgiving Day, Christmas, and New Year's Day. Admission charged.*

23. Dennis Creek Wildlife Management Area. *Dennisville. The entrance is at the end of Jake's Landing Rd., one-third mile east of the junction of Rte. 47 and Rte. 557.* Peaceful, secluded, quiet, this area of some 5,000 acres of forest, reed thickets, and salt marsh (one of the finest in New Jersey) is penetrated by Dennis Creek as it gently flows toward Delaware Bay. It is an ideal spot for those who long to get away from the noise and confusion of modern life and immerse themselves in nature, with all its tranquillity.

The one-mile drive along Jake's Landing Road takes you through a magnificent pine grove in a section of Belleplain State Forest to the creek, where you will find two boat ramps. Fishing is excellent in both creek and bay, with plenty of white perch, striped bass, weakfish, black drum, flounder, and shad. Crabbing, too, is popular in these tidal waters.

The Dennis Creek area is good hunting territory, especially in the nearby forest, where quails, rabbits, woodcocks, and the white-tailed deer (which sometimes wander into the salt marsh) are abundant.

Birders often come to observe the waterfowl, which include black ducks, pintails, shovelers, goldeneyes, Canada geese, and the hooded merganser.

Although no information center and no facilities or cleared and marked trails are provided at Dennis Creek, visitors can enjoy exploring the great expanse of marsh and woodlands and perhaps have a picnic on the shores of the bay.

24. Cape May Point State Park. *Two miles west of the city of Cape May.* Tranquillity is the keynote today at this 190-acre park of ever-changing shorelines, dunes, freshwater marshes, ponds, and woodlands. But during World War II, when the region served as a coastal defense base, it was a busy place. A concrete bunker was installed some 900 feet back from the beach for protection against possible enemy attack. During the Korean War the bunker served as a radio transmitter station, and when that conflict ended, the property was given to New Jersey as a recreational area.

Today, because of sea and sand erosion, the bunker stands at the water's edge, providing an unobstructed view of the bay and an ideal fishing "pier" from which to try your luck in the surf.

Guided bird walks are given weekly from August to October, the best time to observe migrating songbirds, waterfowl, and seabirds. An observation platform overlooks the freshwater marsh, a favorite place to see migrating hawks, and observation blinds are located along the more than three miles of trails.

The so-called Cape May diamonds—clear quartz crystals found along the beaches—are on display at the Nature Center. Here too is a saltwater tank with fish species that flourish offshore.

Although picnic tables and grills are provided near the park entrance, many visitors prefer to picnic on the wide, sandy beach. *Open year-round.*

24. *The inviting essence of the seashore—and the realm of Cape May diamonds.*

Pennsylvania

For 300 miles, from east to west, the state spans a fascinating range of history, culture, industry, agriculture, and landforms.

Pennsylvanians' interest in preserving the natural scene is confirmed by more than 100 state parks. Reclamation is also of primary concern, as you will see at a tree farm and a fish hatchery that support this purpose. In one state park are a restored glacial lake and a beautiful landscape once scarred by strip mining and oil drilling. Museums in the state fulfill a diversity of interests—such as trolley cars, toy trains, dolls, watches, antique tools and implements, and Little League baseball. A valued cultural contribution, by a family of renowned American artists, is the showplace created for their works, many of which were inspired by the beauty of the Pennsylvania countryside.

1. Presque Isle State Park.

Miles of white sand beach can be enjoyed in this 3,200-acre park on a peninsula jutting into Lake Erie. It's a great place for walking at almost any time of the year, regardless of the weather. In winter, when the park is almost deserted, Presque Isle is a wonderland, with trees and ground mantled by sparkling white snow. From the inland side of the peninsula, which hooks back toward the mainland to form Erie Harbor, the city of Erie serrates the horizon when the weather is clear.

In addition to the swimming beaches, reached by a loop road, the park has about 20 miles of hiking trails, some leading through woodlands sheltering an array of wildflowers. Several ponds and lagoons offer excellent fishing, especially for salmon, perch, walleyes, and muskies. During winter ice fishing is popular. Rental boats and boat launches are available, as well as a 498-boat marina.

Although the park is crowded on weekends in summer, when the beaches are open for swimming, it offers quiet and solitude at other times. *Open year-round.*

2. Baldwin-Reynolds House Museum.
639 Terrace St., Meadville. Henry Baldwin, a United States Supreme Court justice from 1830 to 1844, based the design

of his stately three-story home on a Southern mansion. It sits on a gentle rise in the midst of landscaped grounds with a commanding view of French Creek, once the major trading route in the area. The pre–Civil War Southern culture and lifestyle are represented in this impressively elegant frame structure.

After Baldwin's death in 1844, the house was bought by a relative, William Reynolds. Members of his family lived here until 1963.

The 19th-century kitchen and servants' lodgings are tucked away on the ground floor and in the basement. Massive, high-ceilinged rooms with arched doorways, parquet floors, Italian marble fireplaces, doors with satin glass floral designs, and incredibly delicate cherry, ash, and walnut woodwork combine to give each room its own delightful character.

The total effect is one of an opulence in which every conceivable personal whim is fulfilled. There are secret compartments in the library where important papers could be hidden, and specially designed false pillars that can be removed to reveal a small proscenium-style arch for family entertainment and performances.

The museum also contains a number of historical and antique displays. Among the items exhibited are a large collection of souvenir spoons and many examples of

early American paper currency. In a room devoted to the home textile industry demonstrations are periodically given of its looms and spinning wheels.

Next door to the Baldwin-Reynolds house is the newly restored Dr. Mosier office, circa 1938, containing the doctor's accoutrements, including a medical skeleton and a ledger indicating fees and treatments. *Open Wed., Sat., Sun., Memorial Day–Labor Day. Admission charged.*

SCALE IN MILES AND KILOMETERS

ONE INCH 33 MILES 0 5 10   20   30   40

ONE INCH 53 KM 0 5 10   20   30   40   50   64

LEGEND

NUMBERED ATTRACTIONS DESCRIBED IN TEXT **1**

HIGHWAY MARKERS

INTERSTATE **70**   UNITED STATES **40**   STATE **53**

ROAD CLASSIFICATIONS

CONTROLLED ACCESS HIGHWAYS
(Entrance and Exit only at Interchanges)   Interchanges

TOLL HIGHWAYS

OTHER DIVIDED HIGHWAYS

PRINCIPAL THROUGH HIGHWAYS

OTHER THROUGH HIGHWAYS

CONNECTING HIGHWAYS

MILEAGES   LONG DISTANCE MILEAGES SHOWN IN RED

MILEAGE BETWEEN DOTS   35

ONE MILE EQUALS 1.6 KILOMETERS   ONE KILOMETER EQUALS .6 MILES

SPECIAL FEATURES

STATE PARKS   RECREATION AREAS
With Campsites Without Campsites   With Campsites ▲ Without Campsites △

POINTS OF INTEREST ■

© THE H.M. GOUSHÃ COMPANY · SAN JOSE, CALIFORNIA

3. Moraine State Park. Through the marvels of environmental engineering, what was once an ugly, man-made hole in the ground has been transformed into a serene recreational park. Moraine State Park is located upon land used for coal mining, strip mining, and gas and oil drilling. The reclamation was accomplished by sealing off the abandoned mines, plugging the depleted wells, and dramatically altering the physical landscape.

A glacial lake that existed 10,000 years ago was re-created by damming existing streams. Lake Arthur covers more than 3,000 acres, has 40 miles of shoreline, and is well stocked with bass, walleye, muskellunge, and channel catfish. The lake's seven-mile length makes it ideal for canoes, kayaks, rowboats, and sailboats. Motor-powered boats up to 10 horsepower are also permitted here.

Although the lake is the centerpiece, creeks, swamps, marshes, thickets, hard-

3. *This charming cove is in the Pleasant Valley recreation area on Lake Arthur.*

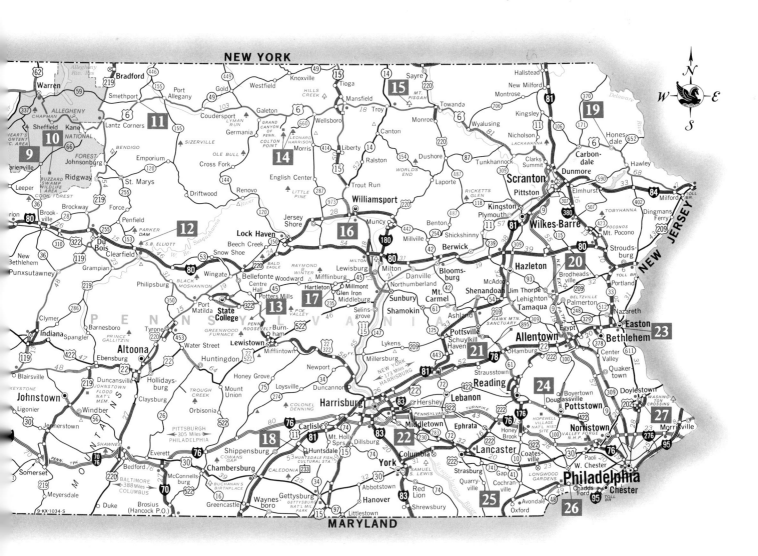

4. *Patience is rewarded in this moment of pleasure shared with a monarch butterfly.*

wood forests, and mud flats add variety to the natural environment here. More than 150 different species of birds, including hawks, loons, owls, blue jays, and herons, can be spotted at the park, many of them year-round.

Marked hiking trails extend throughout the park. The relatively short Hilltop Nature Trail takes hikers through land cleared for farming that is slowly reverting to its natural state.

More ambitious hikers can tackle the seven-mile-long Glacier Ridge Trail, a segment of the projected North Country Trail, a 3,200-mile hiking route from Crown Point, New York, to Lake Sakakawea, North Dakota. *Open year-round.*

4. Raccoon Creek State Park. Although most of the land surrounding man-made Raccoon Lake is landscaped, much of the remaining 6,500-acre area is in its heavily forested natural state. In the fall the foliage of 42 different kinds of trees turns color in a spectacularly vivid display of nature's diversity.

Hikers can follow the five miles of trail crisscrossing a 314-acre wildflower reserve where more than 500 species of flowering plants can be found. The peak blooming seasons are mid-April to mid-May and August through October. One of the other hiking trails includes a tour of the Frankfort Mineral Springs. During the 19th century the mineral water here was reputed to possess healing powers, and the springs were quite famous. The annual winter freeze forms tremendous ice sculptures that stand immobile until they melt in the spring thaw.

The lake yields bluegills, sunfish, bullheads, brook and rainbow trout, walleye, crappies, largemouth and smallmouth bass, and yellow perch.

For visitors not solely concerned with recreational activities, the park offers a wide variety of interpretive and educational programs, including scheduled walks for bird-watchers, night hikes, snowshoe hikes, four self-guiding nature trails, and a Christmas bird count. *Open year-round; camping Apr. 15–Oct. 15.*

5. Meadowcroft Village. *Avella.* To preserve some aspects of a bygone era, the village includes restorations of a one-room schoolhouse, a covered bridge, a general store, and a blacksmith shop, all of which are furnished with appropriate artifacts.

Here too are various living-history craft demonstrations of a blacksmith plying his trade or the operation of a spinning wheel. Such special events as a cornhusking bee, a fiddlers' competition, clog dancing, and Indian handicrafts are scheduled throughout the year.

Racing fans will be interested in the Miller Museum, which includes an unofficial harness-racing Hall of Fame. Delvin Miller's racing career is explored in great detail. Dan Patch, a world-famous racehorse at the turn of the century, is fea-

5. *The Pine Bank bridge boasts both hand-hewn timbers and hand-wrought ironwork.*

tured in a colorful exhibit of photos and memorabilia. An extensive collection of harness carriages includes examples from the earliest models to the present day. *Open Wed.–Sat., P.M. Sun., May–Oct. Admission charged.*

6. The Arden Trolley Museum. *Rte. 18, Washington.* For about the first half of the 20th century—after the horse-and-buggy era but before the automobile completely took over—the electric trolley was a popular form of public transportation.

The streetcars were used in cities, between cities, and on dead-end lines to amusement parks. The Arden Trolley Museum is devoted to the restoration, display, and appreciation of the equipment that served this bygone era.

The highlight here is a one-mile trip in a trolley car. Riding in a beautifully restored turn-of-the-century streetcar, with its polished woodwork and shiny chrome, is a pleasant step back in time.

You can also visit the large, hangarlike shed that houses the museum's collection of electric cars. There are nine fully operational streetcars, and some 16 others in stages of restoration. You can watch the volunteer workers as they repair engines and overhaul the car interiors. Although most of the cars saw service in Pennsylvania, trolleys from Boston and New York and a streetcar from the famous Desire line in New Orleans are also on display. *Open P.M. daily July 4–Labor Day; weekends and holidays May, June, and Sept.*

7. Nemacolin Castle. *Front St., Brownsville.* Named for the Indian leader Nemacolin, who established the first English trading route between Ohio and Maryland, Nemacolin Castle is an imposing brick edifice set on a hill with a commanding view of the Monongahela River. The early trading route connected with the river at present-day Brownsville. In 1806 it became part of Route 40, the country's first east-west national highway.

What is now the castle started as a simple trading post on the site of old Fort Burd, which guarded the trade route. As the post prospered, its owner, Jacob Bowman, gradually added onto the original stone structure, turning it into a red brick Tudor-style castle with a crenellated oc-

tagonal tower and 22 rooms. The guest bedroom in the tower is especially memorable; an immense canopied bed is swallowed up by the room's sheer size. The room gives a wonderful view of the property and has a ladder leading to a second level, which overlooks the entire town.

Most of the rooms contain original 19th-century furnishings. In the "bishop's bedroom" are a rare Napoleonic rosewood bed and a flawless 30-square-foot mirror made in 1850. Marble fireplaces and delicate mahogany woodwork add to the air of 19th-century opulence.

Visitors are invited to picnic on the grounds outside the castle and contemplate the steady flow of the Monongahela River. *Open P.M. Sat., Sun., Easter–May 29; P.M. Tues.–Sun., May 30–mid-Sept. Admission charged.*

8. Fort Necessity National Battlefield. *Rte. 40.* A replica of the hastily constructed Fort Necessity marks the site of the opening battle of what would become the French and Indian War. The original fort was built by Virginia militiamen under the command of George Washington, then a 22-year-old lieutenant colonel, to bolster a tenuous defensive position against an attack by a superior French force. Although Washington's first com-

mand ended in the only surrender of his career, this battle and Washington's previous skirmish at Jumonville Glen started the future Revolutionary War commander on his distinguished military career.

At the visitor center the National Park Service uses a 15-minute slide show, dioramas, and light-table displays to recount the chain of events leading up to the battle. Fort Necessity, a small, palisaded log structure, has been reconstructed on its original site. Although the landscape surrounding the fort has been altered since Washington's day, a half-mile walking tour effectively details the progress of the battle; a series of informative plaques marks the halting, gradual approach of the French troops as they slowly overwhelmed the English defenders.

Overlooking the battlefield is the Mount Washington Tavern, which was built in the 19th century as a stagecoach stop on the old National Road. The tavern served as a restaurant and hotel and provided a much-needed respite for weary travelers. It was named for George Washington, who bought land where his first major battle was fought. The Mount Washington Tavern Museum has a number of period rooms and an authentic Conestoga wagon in the front yard. *Battlefield and tavern open year-round.*

8. The replica of Washington's fort was not so hastily constructed as the original.

9. Heart's Content Recreation Area. *Allegheny National Forest.* Nestled inside the extensive Allegheny National Forest is this heavily forested primitive area. Although most of the old-growth timber was cut by the prosperous logging industry in the 19th century, Heart's Content has been maintained as a representation of the original western Pennsylvania wilderness.

A 1¼-mile interpretive trail winds through a remnant of the original stand of hemlock, white pine, sugar maple, beech, and black cherry trees, some of which are 3 feet in diameter and 100 feet high.

The trail plunges deep within the forest, and after a short walk the explorer feels a solitude that becomes all-encompassing. The deep shade reduces the underbrush, and the dense foliage overhead seems to shut out all traces of a world beyond the forest. At the end of the trail is an early-day logging exhibit.

Nearby mountain streams are stocked during the spring, which is the best time for fishing. *Open year-round; camping mid-Apr.–mid-Dec.*

10. Buzzard Swamp Wildlife Area. *Allegheny National Forest.* This is an excellent place to see wildlife in its natural environment. Motorized vehicles are not allowed to enter this huge, quiet, and undisturbed marsh, which is maintained as a migratory waterfowl propagation area.

Owing to the massive beaver dams, most of the water in the swamp lies still and unmoving. Among the birds to be seen in this environment are ducks, geese, white herons, whistling swans, and sandhill cranes. Here too are hawks and other raptors, including an occasional osprey. Although there is a resident population of Pennsylvania songbirds, most of the species are migratory. Early spring and early fall are the best times to visit.

Backpackers are welcome and permitted to camp at most places inside Buzzard Swamp. The park provides a well-marked 1½-mile interpretive hiking trail called the Songbird Sojourn. Along the trail visitors encounter a wood duck home, a woodpecker tree, a spring that does not freeze over, and a variety of coniferous and deciduous trees. *Open year-round.*

11. McKean County Historical Society Museum. *County courthouse, Smethport.* Housed in the confined, slightly musty basement of the county courthouse is a charming, informative, and superbly well-organized museum devoted to the history of this part of northwestern Pennsylvania. It clearly and concisely chronicles the social, cultural, economic, and geographical influences on the development of the area from frontier times to the present.

First in the exhibits is an extensive display of photographs grouped to show the evolution of the major centers. The pictures include portraits of home and farm life, views of factories, mines, logging camps, mills, and railroad stations, and panoramas of emerging communities. A light-table map serves to connect the towns historically.

Much of the museum is devoted to displays of old articles relating to the lumber industry; the oil business, which flourished in the 19th century; the Bradford, Bordell and Kinzua Railroad; and the extensive McKean County blown-glass and molded-glass industry.

Putting together furniture, household objects, tools, and clothing collected from the surrounding area, the historical society has captured the character of life in the 18th and 19th centuries in displays of a general store, an early farm, a Victorian living room, and other settings.

The museum also houses an extensive firearms collection ranging from 1640 flintlock pistols to an 1880 Smith and Wesson .32-caliber revolver, with a large assortment of American and European muskets and rifles as well. All in all, the museum gives a vivid impression of what life has been like in the county since colonial times. *Open P.M. Mon.–Fri. in summer; P.M. Tues. and Thurs. in winter.*

9. Moss and ferns on the fallen tree will create a seedbed for future hemlocks.

14. *Pine Creek continues to scour its time-worn course through the heavily forested slopes of Pennsylvania's Grand Canyon.*

12. S.B. Elliott State Park. Formerly a climax forest of huge pines and hemlocks, this area was devastated by the logging industry by the turn of the century. In 1911, when the timber was gone and most of the land was deserted by the lumber companies, the conservationist Simon B. Elliott prompted the Pennsylvania legislature to establish a tree nursery here. During the Great Depression in the 1930's the Civilian Conservation Corps (CCC) built six log cabins (which can be rented) and a picnic area adjacent to the nursery.

In today's thickly forested park there are eight well-marked and well-maintained hiking trails. They range from strolls over rolling terrain to tough hikes through heavy foliage and underbrush. They are not long, however, and all eight could be walked in one day.

Most of the large trees in the park are hardwoods, principally red oak, white oak, and sugar maple; there are also some fine stands of pine. Trailer sites are pleasantly situated among the trees.

The primitive, natural state maintained here is attractive to such wildlife as beavers, turkeys, foxes, squirrels, deer, and black bears. Many of the mountain

streams surrounding the park are stocked with trout. *Open year-round; campground open mid-Apr.–late Dec.*

13. Penn Roosevelt State Forest Picnic Area. *This may still be unmarked. Heading east on Rte. 322, turn right about 18 miles from State College, just before passing a huge reservoir on the left. Take the rutted road for a quarter-mile, turn right onto the blacktop, and follow the signs.* Featured here are picnic spots and primitive camping grounds centered around a small, spring-fed lake with a dam in a peaceful, isolated mountain setting. Although the place is only five miles from the highway, the constant, gentle splash of water over the dam into the mountain stream is the only sound that penetrates the stillness of the surrounding forest.

Penn Roosevelt Lake is used mostly for swimming. It is not stocked, so any trout caught here are native to the lake and stream. A hiking trail leads deep into the forest, where rhododendrons and laurel grow in profusion. Deer, turkeys, grouse,

and raccoons prosper, and black bears are sometimes seen. One caution: keep an eye out for the occasional copperhead snake or timber rattler. *Open year-round; camping mid-Apr.–mid-Dec.*

14. Leonard Harrison State Park and Colton Point State Park. Occupying mountains on opposite sides of Pine Creek Gorge, each park offers breathtaking views of the Grand Canyon of Pennsylvania and the course of Pine Creek as it snakes its way between heavily forested ridges. In the distance mountain ranges seemingly stretch to infinity.

Although family camping facilities are available, both parks are largely in their natural state. Rhododendrons, azaleas, and wild laurel, which usually bloom in mid-June, abound. Both parks offer a variety of hiking trails. Those at Colton Point are somewhat more challenging.

The great stands of pine for which the creek was named were logged off in the 19th century. Today's second-growth forest includes black cherry, aspen, sugar maple, red oak, black birch, beech, white ash, shagbark hickory, sassafras, and sycamore. In autumn this diversity creates a broad palette of colors that dominate the landscape as far as the eye can see.

Mountain streams and creeks are stocked with trout and other freshwater fish. The best angling begins after mid-June, when the creek begins to dry up. Rafting should be enjoyed earlier.

Both supervised and unsupervised white-water raft trips down Pine Creek are arranged by a local concessionaire. *Open year-round. Winter access is limited.*

15. Mount Pisgah State Park. *Watch for signs on Rte. 6.* The 75-acre Stephen Foster Lake, named for the Pennsylvanian who wrote "Old Folks at Home" and other popular songs about the Old South, is the central feature of the park. Stocked with bass, chain pickerel, crappie, sunfish and bullhead, the lake offers good fishing, particularly in spring. Boats and canoes are for rent, or visitors can launch their own—but motors are prohibited. In winter the frozen lake is popular for ice fishing and skating.

A mile-long self-guiding nature trail and other longer trails pass through wooded acres, open farmland, and marshes. Since much of this countryside was once under cultivation, the emphasis of the trail signs is to explain farming's effects on plants, animals, and terrain.

On the last two weekends in March and the first in April, the park sponsors a demonstration of maple-syrup making. Both the traditional bucket and spile technique of collecting sap and the modern method of using plastic hose are employed. Visitors can help collect the sap from the sugar maples and watch as it is boiled, reboiled, and boiled yet again, to yield the much reduced flavorful product. Sampling is part of the fun. *Open year-round.*

16. Peter J. McGovern Little League Baseball Museum. *Williamsport.* Opened in 1982, the museum chronicles the development of Little League baseball from the first eight-team league that started here in Williamsport in 1939 to the present-day organization with 7,000 teams in 24 countries. The man for whom the museum is named served from 1952 until his death in 1984 as the first full-time president of the Little Leagues.

Incorporating the latest in design, exhibit, and display techniques, the Little League Baseball Museum was created for fans of all ages. The hands-on displays include: light-box questionnaires on Little League rules; 10-foot-tall track-mounted sliding panels with special baseball tips; and pitching and batting cages where prospective hurlers and hitters can study their styles with the aid of 90-second videotapes of themselves in action.

Inside the "play-it-safe room" are life-sized murals demonstrating 10 important warm-up exercises for young athletes. Here too are exhibits showing the evolution of Little League safety equipment such as batting helmets, shin guards, and chest protectors. One exhibit includes mementos of current major league players who began as Little Leaguers. Any young player is likely to be inspired by the sight of his idol as a youngster, wearing a Little League uniform.

Highlights of championship games in the past are shown on videotape. Team pictures of the winners dating back to 1947 are on display in the Little League World Series Room.

Behind the museum is the stadium where the annual Little League World Series is played. For ballplayers young and old, the sight of the empty baseball diamond can conjure up stirring visions of what might have been—or what might yet come to pass. *Open daily except major holidays. Admission charged.*

---

17. Millmont Covered Bridge. *At Hazelton, take Rte. 45E toward Millmont. Turn right at the sign "Glen Iron-4."* In the days when lumber from local mills was the only available building material, bridges were often covered to protect and preserve their supporting timbers. The value of this practice is demonstrated here by the excellent condition of this 151-foot structure spanning the Penn River.

Bridge builders developed many truss systems. The one used here was patented in 1817 by Theodore Burr. The truss was so widely used in this state that Pennsylvania covered-bridge enthusiasts call their organization the Burr Society.

20. Clock tower and Asa Packer mansion express Jim Thorpe's distinctive character.

The graceful lines of the bridge stem from the slight arch that compresses the structure between stone buttresses, increasing load-bearing capacity. This is a fine example of the beauty derived when form follows function. The gentle, soothing sound of water flowing below the bridge counterpoints the echo of one's own footsteps on the heavy wooden planks. Sunlight cuts in through wall openings near the roof, and even at midday the interior is bathed in a spectral, warm light. Inside, one can see how the vertical and horizontal beams are secured—by iron spikes—and appreciate the general quality of the craftsmanship.

---

18. Huntsdale Fish Cultural Station. *Rte. 233, Carlisle.* If you have ever wondered where fish used to stock streams and lakes come from, a visit to this facility will answer your questions. The spawning, fertilization, incubation, and maturation of freshwater fish all take place in the 160-acre Huntsdale hatchery. This is one of the largest fish-culture facilities in the country, and more than a million fish are produced each year to stock lakes and streams in Pennsylvania state parks. Most of the fish here are trout, walleye, tiger muskies, and muskellunge fingerlings—although other warm-water species such as shad and crappie are sometimes raised.

A brochure available at the reception area explains the breeding and fingerling procedures step by step. Most impressive here are the 22 raceways, each of which may contain as many as 10,000 fish. The best seasons to visit are in early spring and early fall, when the fish are approaching full size and stocking has not yet begun.

The entrance to Kings Gap Environmental Education and Training Center, a half-mile drive on Pine Road, is a fastidiously maintained nature study area in a natural forest preserve. More than 15 miles of hiking trails circling up a mountain provide a clear picture of indigenous plant and animal life.

Wildlife abounds. Deer, wild turkeys, ruffed grouse, raccoons, and gray squirrels may often be seen on a day's hike. At the top of the mountain a stone mansion housing the Education Center offers a commanding view of the Cumberland Valley. *Both facilities open year-round.*

19. Wayne County Historical Society Museum. *810 Main St., Honesdale.* In a superb 150-year-old brick building that was once the office of the Delaware and Hudson Company, the Wayne County Historical Society Museum recalls the rich economic, geographical, and cultural history of the area.

When the eastern Pennsylvania anthracite mining industry started to prosper in the early 19th century, Honesdale became a focal point of commercial transport. Mined anthracite coal was taken to the town of Carbondale and then hauled to Honesdale by the Gravity Railroad, the first commercial American locomotive line. From Honesdale the coal was shipped by boat through the 108 locks on the Delaware and Hudson Canal to the markets in New York State.

The museum has an exhibit showing how the railroads linked the entire country. The old photographs of bridge construction, relay designs, train stations, lumber camps, factories, and burgeoning towns show how challenging engineering problems were solved back then, and how the railroads influenced the development of new communities.

The major industries of Wayne County are also explored. One room displays the work of craftsmen in the glass-cutting factories that once dotted the vicinity. Here too is a glassblower's typical work station, complete with all the tools required to blow and shape glass.

Next to the museum is the recently restored Torey House, the 19th-century land office that served Honesdale and most of the county. On the streets of Honesdale one can still find many splendid early 19th-century buildings. Inquire at the museum about walking tours of the town. *Museum open Mon.–Sat., Apr.–Dec.; Tues., Thurs., Sat., Jan.–Mar. Admission charged.*

---

20. Jim Thorpe. At about the time the legendary American Indian athlete, Jim Thorpe, died in 1953, the Pennsylvania towns of Mauch Chunk, East Mauch Chunk, and Upper Mauch Chunk were seeking a solution to their economic decline. It was suggested by Mr. Thorpe's widow that a consolidated town named for her husband would be a fitting tribute as well as an aid to tourism. The idea was accepted, a memorial was built, and in 1954 the towns combined under the name

Jim Thorpe. The community bearing his name became Jim Thorpe's final resting place. All this may have helped, but the major attractions are the old buildings and the beauty of the surrounding mountains, particularly in the fall.

The Mauch Chunk Historical District still exudes a quiet elegance. Millionaires Row is a series of lavishly appointed brick town houses built for the most prominent families. Just two blocks away is Stone Row, with modest, three-story stone row houses built by Asa Packer, president of the Lehigh Valley Railroad, for the line's foremen and engineers.

Many of the public and commercial buildings are handsome examples of 19th-century architecture. Inside the Carbon County Courthouse is an oak-paneled courtroom with an elaborate spindled backdrop and a stained-glass skylight. The Dimmick Memorial Library has attractive terra cotta panels and a plush two-story reading room.

The Asa Packer mansion, perched on a steep hill overlooking the town, was the home of a local self-made millionaire and entrepreneur. The rambling, three-story Italianate mansion, a frame structure, has been maintained in its original state since the death of its owner in 1879.

The 20-room interior contains intricately hand-carved Honduras mahogany wood paneling and beautifully crafted rosewood furniture. The building and the well-groomed surrounding grounds all have an air of 19th-century elegance. *Mansion open Tues.–Sun., Memorial Day–Oct. Admission charged.*

---

21. Hawk Mountain Sanctuary. One of the few sanctuaries in the world set aside for migrating birds of prey, Hawk Mountain is a favorite site for birders. From this 1,500-foot ridge one can watch for more than 200 species of birds that frequent the area, as well as 14 species of raptors—including eagles, ospreys, hawks, and falcons—on their flights to their winter or summer ranges.

The mountain is named for the birds that wing their way through here in great numbers in spring and fall. A ¾-mile trail on the heavily wooded slopes winds past two very good viewing points. The northern overlook is recommended for the fall migration. During this season, from late August to the end of November, the greatest number of birds pass overhead. The

21. *A short hike from the parking lot at Hawk Mountain rewards you with this view.*

sanctuary is less crowded during the smaller spring migration, however, and open vantage points are easier to find.

Hunting is not permitted, and deer, chipmunks, squirrels, and raccoons are plentiful here. After the mountain laurel blooms in early summer, nesting warblers and other songbirds take up residence on the tranquil mountain and fill the air with their gentle calls.

To enhance your appreciation of this unique environment, see the interpretive displays at the visitor center. *Open year-round. Admission charged.*

22. Watch and Clock Museum. *514 Poplar St., Columbia.* Appropriately, you are given a card and must punch in on an industrial time clock when entering the museum. The National Association of Watch and Clock Collectors manages the museum, which traces the history of time measurement—from a reproduction of the incredible nonmechanical Rhodes Antikytheron clock, circa 79 B.C., to the most sophisticated modern atomic clock.

Among the musical clocks played here are a 1770 Glune glass bell clock, an 1840 organ clock, a 1903 Regina music box, and a 1905 Symphonion/Leipzig German

clock with 10 interchangeable discs, each with a different melody. The massive inner works of large tower clocks are contrasted with the delicate mechanisms of small pocket watches. On display also are clocks with Japanese characters, mantel clocks of various styles, mirror clocks, master-and-slave clocks, banjo clocks, a lantern clock, a Swiss water clock, and all sorts of novelty timepieces.

Many items are exhibited in glass cases so that the inner movements of wood, iron, and brass may be studied from all sides. Most of the clocks are originals, although a few of the older models are replicas made by members of the association.

Nearly all of the clocks and watches are in working condition. The museum is so filled with the various pitches and rhythms created by the precise mechanical measure of time that one is acutely aware of the passing of each second. If you are in the museum at noon, you will hear the cacophony of chimes, rings, and gongs announcing the hour of 12. *Open daily except Sundays and major holidays.*

23. Troxell-Steckel House and Barn. *Egypt.* During the 18th and 19th centuries the Lehigh Valley was settled primarily by farmers from Germany. In 1756 the son of one of these immigrants, John Peter Trox-

ell, built a medieval-style German farmhouse near what is now the town of Egypt. Fifteen years later the house and surrounding property were sold to Peter Steckel—thus the name.

The fieldstone farmhouse has been restored and furnished to suggest the lifestyle of the German settlers in the area. The austerity of the home reflects the simple and rigorous lives of its inhabitants; a telling feature is a box built into a wall for the reverent storage of the family Bible.

The 18-acre property includes a small stream, an idyllic meadow, and a field that is still farmed. Beside the stream is a springhouse where dairy products were stored in the old days.

In the Swiss-style bank barn, built in 1875, each stall has its own exterior door; the animals were fed from a wooden platform above the stalls. An earthen ramp against the rear side of the barn provides wagon-access to the upper storage area. Farming equipment, hand tools, and a collection of horse-drawn carriages and sleighs are displayed inside the barn. *Open P.M. Sat.–Sun., June–Oct.*

24. Mary Merritt Doll Museum. *Douglasville.* The more than 2,500 examples here, dating mostly from 1725 to 1900, are good evidence of the widespread appeal of toys made in the human image. Along the walls are eight-foot-tall glass cases filled with dolls, dollhouses, and doll accessories and furnishings from all over the world—collected by Mrs. Mary Merritt, a lifelong doll enthusiast.

The dolls and settings shown, mostly made during the 19th century, represent a variety of cultures and lifestyles. The simple Mennonite bedroom in one dollhouse, for example, contrasts dramatically with the decor of the lavish Victorian parlor in another miniature setting.

The huge collection includes a replica of a real Georgian-style house, authentically furnished with miniature pieces, a number of superb wax baby dolls, an eighth-century Egyptian doll, Queen Anne dolls, French fashion dolls, china dolls, mechanical dolls, and dolls with two faces (one smiling and one crying).

Many 19th-century dolls were made at home by doting parents, using whatever material was handy–cornstalks, dried apples, beeswax, rags, to name a few.

The admission fee includes a visit to the Merritt Museum of Childhood next door. The museum, which evokes a nostalgic sense of an early 20th-century toy store, also displays a fascinating miscellany that includes old cavalry rifles, Indian artifacts, pottery, baskets, antique pewter, and china goods. *Open daily except major holidays. Admission charged.*

---

25. Toy Train Museum, Red Caboose Motel, and Strasburg Railroad. *Strasburg.* This attraction will appeal to anyone nostalgic for or curious about the era of the great steam locomotives—and the wonderful toys they inspired.

The historical section of the Toy Train Museum has examples of all types of trains from 1880 to the present. Each era of development, including the standard-gauge classic period, is represented. Three complex operating layouts have push-button controls with which visitors can activate the trains and accessories.

Adjacent to the Toy Train Museum is the Red Caboose Motel. Overnight guests can stay in a refurbished N-5 caboose. Meals are served in two original Victorian dining coaches decorated with velvet curtains and brass Pullman lanterns.

The Strasburg Railroad—a coal-burning turn-of-the-century steam locomotive pulling antique cars—runs past the Red Caboose siding. The century-old station for the train ride is reached by a ¾-mile walk alongside the tracks or a short drive west on Route 741.

The locomotive, hissing steam and belching black smoke, pulls an eight-car train along a nine-mile track through the Amish farmland. The wooden 19th-century coaches are period pieces complete with coal-oil lamps and potbelly stoves. For railway enthusiasts especially, this is a bit of the real thing. *Toy Train Museum open daily May–Oct.; weekends Apr.–Nov. Strasburg Railroad open daily May–Oct.; weekends late Mar.–Apr. and Nov.–Dec. Admission charged.*

---

26. Brandywine River Museum. *Chadds Ford.* A century-old gristmill overlooking the Brandywine River has been handsomely renovated with a circular wing to make a spacious and airy three-story museum with informal galleries for the display of paintings and sculptures.

Major works of art from three generations of the Wyeth family are featured, including paintings by N.C. Wyeth, his son Andrew, and his grandson Jamie. The renowned commercial illustrations of N.C. Wyeth and Howard Pyle, the father of modern American illustration, and works by Pyle's students are also shown.

Much of the museum is devoted to the art of the Brandywine region, and to the still life and landscape painters and sculptors associated with the "Brandywine Tradition." The collected works represent more than 100 years of activity, and the tradition continues.

Part of each floor serves as a lobby where visitors can rest and enjoy the enchanting views of the Brandywine countryside through floor-to-ceiling windows. Sunshine washes through a skylight, warmly bathing these areas with light. The effect helps provide an understanding of the source of inspiration for this celebrated school of painting, with its emphasis on natural light.

The Brandywine River Museum is named for the adjacent river. Visitors are encouraged to picnic on its banks, enjoy the wildflower gardens and nature trail, and discover for themselves the beguiling character of a place that has influenced so many artists. *Open daily except Christmas. Admission charged.*

---

27. The Mercer Museum. *Pine St., Doylestown.* A visit to this unique museum is a packrat's dream. Imagine having the foresight and resources, at the turn of the century—when America was in the throes of technological change and discarding an entire way of life—to collect and store unwanted relics of the past. This was the visionary enterprise of Henry Chapman Mercer, a pioneering archeologist and anthropologist born in 1856. He saw that the essence of our culture is to be found in its tools and equipment, and collected more than 40,000 artifacts from the 18th and 19th centuries.

Mercer then designed and supervised the construction of a museum to accommodate the vast accumulation. The medieval-looking edifice was built according to specifications he carried in his head, without benefit of blueprints. Finished in 1916, it was the most creative use of poured concrete so far attempted.

The exhibition hall is a gigantic, barn-like room. Each of the six levels has a balconylike corridor and small exhibit rooms. Each room contains tools and objects representing some 60 crafts and trades, or facets of early American life, with incredible completeness.

The place is packed with everything imaginable. Many items—stagecoaches, sleighs, Conestoga wagons, a whaleboat, iron stoves—are suspended from the walls and ceiling by iron rods set in the concrete, to be seen from all angles. The museum is a national historic landmark. *Open Mon.–Sat. and P.M. Sun., Mar.–Dec. Admission charged.*

26. *The regional mill is appropriate to the character of the art displayed inside.*

Delaware

What the places may lack in remoteness, they make up for in variety, in this small state with its excellent network of roads.

Although about half the perimeter of this long, narrow state is bounded by water—the Delaware River, Delaware Bay, and the Atlantic Ocean—there's an engaging diversity of attractions to be enjoyed here. In addition to the dunes and beaches, there are forested hills, meadows and marshes, and historic homes and gardens. And in one 16,000-acre wildlife preserve more than 300 species of birds may be observed. The Lewes Historic Area recalls the town's venerable past. Included here is a charming small church built more than 300 years ago.

1. Walter S. Carpenter, Jr., State Park. *Newark.* You can look into Pennsylvania and Maryland from this pleasant park nestled in the northwestern corner of Delaware where the three states come together. Their meeting point, known as The Wedge, was once popular with bandits, who could quickly escape the law of one state by crossing the boundary into another. The park has only 425 acres but seems more spacious, partly because it rises to about 300 feet—which is high for Delaware—and offers long views of the surrounding countryside.

Horseback riding is a popular activity here. A stable next to the park rents horses, offers riding instruction, and has a jumping course as well as a riding ring. Two miles of bridle trails meander through farmland and forest.

Those who prefer to go on foot can take the nature trail or try the more rugged route designed for fitness enthusiasts. In the spring fishermen like to cast for trout from the banks of a creek that runs alongside the park. A small pond also offers good fishing. And in winter the slopes provide fine tobogganing.

The park has a primitive campsite, available to youth groups, and a picnic area. *Open year-round. Admission charged.*

2. Brandywine Creek State Park. *Wilmington.* Named after the small river that almost bisects its 784 acres, this park has open meadows, hills, wooded trails, a floodplain, marshland, and a majestic stand of tulip poplars, some of them more than 160 years old, in an area known as Tulip Tree Woods.

The park also contains Delaware's first nature preserve, which includes the state's largest freshwater marsh. Here the patient observer may see the secretive Muhlenberg's turtle. For dedicated birders, one hilltop offers a superb vantage point for viewing migrating hawks in late autumn as they follow the course of the Delaware River southward.

Guided walks are led by members of the park's nature center, which also features films and displays. One can also hike independently along eight miles of nature trails, jog over a fitness course, have a picnic, fly kites, and toss Frisbees in some of the wide-open spaces.

The river is open to canoeists, and fishermen can angle for crappies, bluegills, rock bass, and—in spring—trout. Several bridle paths through groves of tulip, beech, and oak trees invite riders, and in winter the park attracts sledders and cross-country skiers. Primitive camping facilities are available for youth groups. *Open year-round. Admission charged.*

3. George Read II House and Garden. *New Castle.* This handsome red brick mansion, one of the finest examples of Federal architecture in the United States,

4. Mirror image of a great egret. It is for moments like this that birders seek out the quiet byways and backwaters of Bombay Hook National Wildlife Refuge.

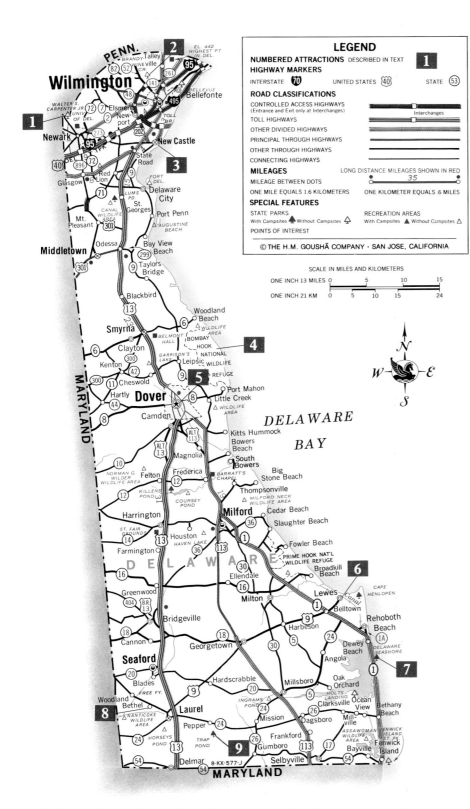

Mr. and Mrs. Philip D. Laird, who refurbished the house and furnished it in Colonial Revival style. They extended their taste for Colonial Revival to the garden as well, adding the formal brick paths. The Lairds were also instrumental in preserving the historic district of New Castle, settled by the Dutch in 1651.

When Mrs. Laird died in 1975, the estate was donated to the Historical Society of Delaware, and the house has since been restored to its original Federal-style elegance. In tribute to Mr. and Mrs. Laird, three rooms are maintained just as they furnished them.

Guided tours of the mansion are conducted by the historical society. Also available are guided walking tours of New Castle, including visits to three of the town's 18th-century buildings. *Open Tues.–Sun. except holidays, Mar.–Dec.*

4. Bombay Hook National Wildlife Refuge. *Smyrna.* Kahansink Indians were the first known occupants of this appealing sprawl of marshland, tidal stream, freshwater ponds, and timbered swamps. In 1679 the Indians sold part of the area to Dutch settlers from New York, who hunted birds, trapped muskrats, and cut salt hay from the marshes.

Bombay Hook now encompasses 16,280 acres and is one link in a chain of waterfowl refuges established in the 1930's along major migratory routes. Some 300 species have been observed since the refuge opened. Waterfowl abound, especially in March and November; shorebirds, wading birds, and songbirds are most evident during May, August, and September. Others for whom this is a haven include owls, hummingbirds, woodpeckers, and several varieties of vultures and hawks.

Short walking trails and a long, winding automobile trail lead through the area, which is a habitat for foxes, river otters, beavers, and varieties of turtles, snakes, salamanders, and frogs. An information center is open on weekdays.

The Allee House, also in the refuge but reached from Route 9, is a superbly preserved mid-18th-century plantation home with a brick exterior and fine original woodwork within. *Park open year-round; Allee House open P.M. weekends.*

was built in 1804 by George Read II, a prominent Delaware lawyer whose father was a signer of the Declaration of Independence. George Read married his cousin, Mary Thompson, and they brought up their seven children in this house.

Situated on the banks of the Delaware

River, the 14-room mansion is known for its elaborately carved woodwork, handsome relief plasterwork, and delicate fanlights. Its second owner, William Couper, who bought the property in the 1840's, added the garden of intricate parterres.

The property was bought in 1920 by

5. John Dickinson Mansion. *Dover.* One of America's founding fathers, John Dickinson, grew up in this spacious brick home that looks across cultivated fields to the St. Jones River. Dickinson was often called "the Penman of the Revolution" for the many pamphlets and articles he wrote about American independence. After the Revolution he served in the legislatures of both Delaware and Pennsylvania and was among the framers of the Constitution.

The house, built in 1740 by Dickinson's father, Samuel, is not as grand as Monticello or Mount Vernon, but it provides an insight into the comfortable lifestyle of a prosperous colonial landowner.

In 1804, when much of the interior of the building was destroyed by fire, a document listing the entire contents of the house was found. Several of the original pieces are on display today in the beautifully proportioned rooms. Volunteers from the local historical society offer detailed tours of the mansion. *Open daily except Mon. and holidays.*

5. Brick façade and boxwood plantings exude the charm of the colonial South.

6. Lewes Historic Area. Two Dutchmen purchased this spot in 1629, giving it the poetic name Zwaanendael—Valley of the Swans—even though the nearest valley is miles away. The Dutch had no lack of competitors in the area, and during the next 150 years they endured a series of confrontations, raids, and takeovers.

The first settlers, who arrived in 1631, were wiped out by Indians. After the Dutch sent replacements, a contingent of Swedish newcomers tried to capture the area. The British also constantly argued with Holland over ownership of the whole territory. And because the town was an important seaport, the most frequent visitors for a time were buccaneers, among them Capt. William Kidd, who reputedly buried his treasure here.

Shortly after Pennsylvania annexed Delaware in 1685, the town received its present name (pronounced Lewis) from William Penn.

Visitors to Lewes can retrace its colorful past in the historic area, to the left off Route 9 as you enter the town. The Zwaanendael Museum, built in 1931 and modeled after the town hall in Hoorn, Holland, has a number of exhibits illustrating Lewes's heritage.

Several notable old houses are open to visitors. The Cannonball House, shelled by the British during the Revolution, still has in its foundation the ball for which it was named. A blacksmith shop, plank house, creamery, a doctor's office, the ferry house, and the Burton-Ingram House, which contains a marine museum, have all been carefully restored.

St. Peter's Church, part of which dates to 1681, is a gem; and along Pilottown Road there are several fine old homes, most of which are privately owned. Guided tours of the historic area are offered Tuesday, Thursday, Friday, and Saturday mornings. *Museum open Tues.–Sun. year-round. Admission charged for tours.*

7. Delaware Seashore State Park. Six miles of beach stretch between ocean and bay in this extensive park just south of Rehoboth Beach. The bay side is usually quieter than the ocean shore, although the highway is never far off—U.S. Route 1 runs down the center of the entire sandy strip—and the whole area is crowded in

7. The hopes of fishermen spring eternal and are often rewarded in this park.

the summer season. But in spring and fall, when the park is often quite deserted, the beaches are excellent for strolling, shelling, and birding.

Permits are not needed to go surf fishing for sea trout, bluefish, flounder, striped bass, and other game fish. A campground on the bay side has 300 sites for tents and trailers, almost half of them equipped with water and electricity. Also on the bay is a picnic shelter.

At the well-equipped marina you will find fishing tackle, small boats for rent, and a launching ramp. *Open year-round; camping mid-Mar.–mid-Oct. Admission charged in summer.*

8. Historic Bethel on Broad Creek. The history of this picturesque little town and its role in early American shipping began in 1795, when Kendall M. Lewis built a small dock here on Broad Creek, a tributary of the Nanticoke River.

The dock became the busy center of the town, whose primary industry was transferring cargoes from large ships to shallow-draft scows that could reach the towns farther upstream on Broad Creek.

In 1869 a shipyard was constructed in Lewisville, as the town was called, and five years later the first vessel to be built here was launched.

In 1880 the town's name was changed to Bethel, "the sailor's retreat" (according to the Bible), and in 1889, when the flat-bottomed Chesapeake Bay sailing ram was designed here, Bethel's reputation as a shipbuilding town was assured.

Although the shipyard was dismantled in the 1940's, the historic town remains a colorful place to see. A small museum displays local maritime artifacts. *Museum open P.M. Sun. in summer.*

9. Trap Pond State Park. This thousand-acre wooded park, ideal for a family outing, surrounds a small, attractive lake where fishermen angle for perch, catfish, bass, pickerel, and sunfish. Rowboats, canoes, paddleboats, and small sailboats are available for rent, and boat owners can launch their own. Two self-guiding mile-long nature trails lead through the forest of evergreens and mixed hardwoods, a habitat enjoyed by several species of birds, including the pileated woodpecker and the bald eagle.

The Cypress Point Trail takes you to the watery world of the bald cypress, where you will find the northernmost stand of these southern trees, and through groves of dogwood, sweet gum, holly, myrtle, and magnolia.

On the side of the lake reserved for swimming are a sandy beach and a lakeside picnic grove shaded by tall loblolly pines; both spots are popular, especially on summer weekends. Campsites, beneath a canopy of pines, are offered on a first-come basis. *Park open year-round; facilities available Apr.–Oct.*

9. *Enchanting scenes like this one—at Trussum Pond—are duplicated in the watery environs of nearby Cypress Point Trail.*

Maryland

From the coastal plain to the Appalachian Mountains, this state has all the natural regions that typify the eastern United States.

Endowed with a diversity of landforms—including the Piedmont, the Blue Ridge province, and the Ridge and Valley province—within its irregular borders, Maryland offers spectacular mountain scenery, lakes, streams, beaches, and a seaside cliff rich with Ice Age fossils. The state also supports an important refuge for waterfowl. Here on the Atlantic Flyway it is not surprising that the art of decoy carving was highly developed. Two museums are dedicated to the subject. Another attraction is a town that claims to be the seafood capital of the world.

1. Swallow Falls State Park. This peaceful woodland park on the rocky banks of the swift-running Youghiogheny River contains some of Maryland's most spectacular scenery. It has been a longtime favorite with campers. A plaque marks the site where John Burroughs, Thomas Edison, Harvey Firestone, and Henry Ford camped in 1918.

Today the park contains two large camping areas. Hiking trails, which cut through a stand of 300-year-old virgin hemlocks towering above verdant expanses of ferns, mountain laurel, and rhododendrons, connect to an extensive system of paths and old logging roads in adjoining Garrett State Forest.

The Canyon Trail, considered to be one of the most beautiful in the state, leads from Swallow Falls to Muddy Creek Falls. Along the rocky ledges are many plant fossils. Another hiking trail crosses a swinging bridge above sparkling Muddy Creek Falls and loops around to the pool below. The highest vertical waterfall in Maryland, with a plunge of 64 feet, it is seen to best advantage from its base. In these deep, quiet woodlands the visitor is likely to observe deer, wild turkeys, beavers, and an occasional fox. Black bears also roam the forest.

The Youghiogheny River, a favorite with fishermen, is stocked with trout several times a year. *Park open year-round; camping May–Nov.*

2. New Germany State Park. *New Germany Rd., Grantsville.* Located on the site of several abandoned 19th-century mills in the midst of the Savage River State Forest, this 210-acre park is a favorite family recreation area.

The lake here was created in the mid-1800's, when John Swauger dammed Poplar Lick Run to provide waterpower for his sawmill and gristmill; now it is a pleasant setting for picnicking, swimming, boating, and fishing. Trout and bass are the favorite game fish, and rowboats are available for rent.

Hiking trails of varying levels of difficulty wind through the park and connect with other paths in the surrounding forest (Maryland's largest state forest), where deer, turkeys, and grouse abound. A 17-mile trail provides spectacular vistas along the crest of Big Savage Mountain. In winter many of these trails are used for cross-country skiing or snowmobiling.

Camping facilities range from rustic but comfortably equipped log cabins and a spacious family camping area in the park to primitive sites in the more remote regions of the forest.

Both sailboating and canoeing are permitted on the 350-acre Savage River Reservoir, and during certain times of the year white-water canoeing is possible below the dam. *Park open year-round; camping May–Oct. Admission charged.*

3. Washington Monument State Park and Appalachian Trail Crossing. In 1827, when memories of the Revolutionary War were still fresh, several hundred townspeople from Boonsboro, including three veterans of the war, built a stone tower on top of nearby South Mountain—possibly the country's first monument to the memory of George Washington.

The tower slowly deteriorated over the years and in 1882 had to be restored. After 10 years or so, a crack developed, and the tower again fell into disrepair and lay in ruins for many years. The present 35-foot

5. Figures in background help to confirm the size of these rocks in Deer Creek.

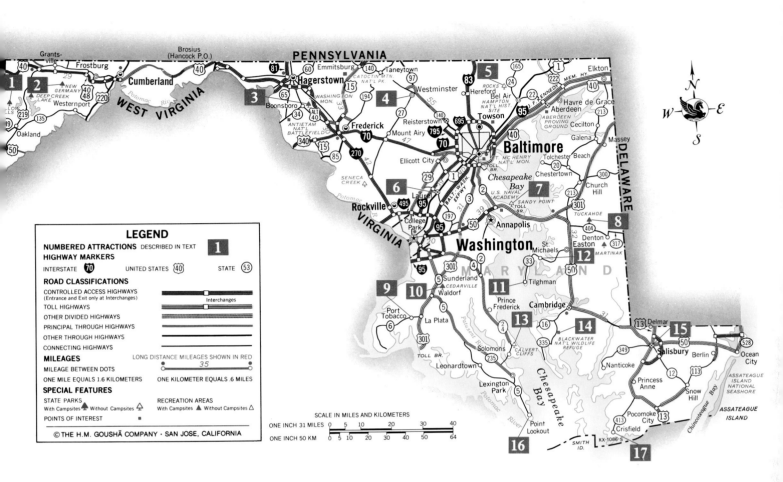

monument, built by the Civilian Conservation Corps, was dedicated on July 4, 1936, just 109 years after the patriotic citizens of Boonsboro first gathered in the town square and, to the sound of fife and drum, shouldered their pickaxes and marched up the mountainside.

The tower is reached by a fairly steep, well-surfaced trail lined with plaques highlighting George Washington's life. Inside, a winding staircase leads to the top, which affords a remarkable view of the countryside to the northwest.

The Appalachian Trail passes the tower and can be walked for a few miles within the park. The Cumberland Valley is on a major north-south flyway for migrating hawks and eagles, which can be seen from about the middle of September through November. The visitor center houses a small collection of firearms, Indian relics, and Civil War memorabilia. *Park open year-round; visitor center Apr.–Oct.*

4. Carroll County Historical Society (Shellman House) and Doll Museum. *206 E. Main St., Westminster.* In the days when Westminster was a trading center for grain-laden wagons bound from central Pennsylvania to the port of Baltimore, one of the finest buildings on Main Street was No. 206. The handsome Georgian town house was built in 1807 by Jacob Sherman, a German settler from Pennsylvania, as a wedding gift for his daughter.

Now called the Shellman House after a subsequent owner, the 2½-story brick mansion houses the historical society's collections, including a 19th-century sampler, local quilts and coverlets, early farm tools, and a notable Eli Bentley grandfather clock. One of the early owners of the house was the country's first switchboard operator, to whom Alexander Graham Bell presented a miniature gold telephone, which is on display.

Next door, in the Kimmey House (circa 1800), is Miss Carroll's Children's Shop, a permanent exhibit of about 200 dolls and dollhouse furniture from various parts of

the world. *Open Tues.–Fri. year-round; also Sat. and P.M. Sun., June–Sept. Closed holidays. Admission charged.*

5. Rocks State Park. Atop a 100-foot cliff, overlooking the rolling hills of Deer Creek valley, looms an enormous, thronelike rock formation known as the King and Queen Seat, so named, it is said, for the ceremonial meetings held here by the Susquehannock Indians.

The rock formation is only a short walk from the ridgetop parking lot; five other trails of varying length and steepness lead up the cliff from the road in the valley below. Delightful picnic spots are set along the banks of Deer Creek, a lovely little mountain stream that winds among steep-sided hills clad with mixed evergreens and hardwoods. *Open year-round except Thanksgiving Day and Christmas week. Admission charged.*

8. *The yellow dodder accents this scene of nature's wild abandon on Crouse Mill Lake.*

8. Tuckahoe State Park. *Rte. 404, Queen Anne.* The rolling, wooded hills and open meadows of this 3,408-acre valley, traversed by quiet, lovely Tuckahoe Creek, create a remarkably attractive and varied park. It has a well-labeled half-hour nature trail that includes one of the nation's largest overcup oak trees—118 feet high with a trunk 27 feet in circumference.

For more vigorous workouts, a two-mile, 20-station exercise course and two playgrounds are provided. If you have your own canoe, you can try the 5½-mile trail on Tuckahoe Creek. And for nature lovers, the 500-acre Adkins Arboretum (the first to be built in Maryland) will include, when completed, all the trees, shrubs, and plants indigenous to the state.

A dam across Tuckahoe Creek forms Crouse Mill Lake, at the end of which is a flooded forest. A pair of bald eagles may be seen here, perched on the spectral white trunks rising from the water.

One of Tuckahoe's open fields is reserved for hot-air ballooning; an annual meet is held here in the spring. *Park open year-round; camping Apr.–Nov.*

6. Montpelier Mansion. *Rte. 197, Laurel.* This beautifully proportioned Georgian house was built for Maj. Thomas Snowden just after the Revolution. It is an elegant structure situated on a high knoll. Its English boxwood gardens, planted in the 1700's, are considered to be among the loveliest in America.

Major Snowden's marriage in 1774 to Ann Ridgely, a rich heiress, supplemented his already considerable estate. It also gave the vast plantation a name—Montpelier—in honor of his bride's birthplace in Anne Arundel County.

George and Martha Washington occasionally visited Montpelier, as did Abigail Adams, who praised the "large, handsome, elegant House" and the Snowdens' "true English Hospitality."

Montpelier passed from the Snowden family to several other owners before it was acquired by the state in 1961. *House open P.M. Sun.; gardens open year-round. Admission charged for house tours.*

7. Sandy Point State Park. Located only a few miles from Annapolis, and just off the main route from Washington to Rehoboth Beach, Delaware, and Maryland's Ocean City, where Washingtonians summer, the 785-acre waterfront park is usually crowded on summer weekends.

The park has two swimming beaches—one with a spectacular view of the Chesapeake Bay Bridge-Tunnel and the other

quieter, less crowded, and a bit more remote. Both offer crabbing and fishing.

But when the crowds leave in the fall and the air is a bit nippy, Sandy Point can't be surpassed as a place for viewing the birds migrating south along the Chesapeake. The Atlantic Flyway is directly above. *Open daily Memorial Day–Labor Day; weekends and holidays Labor Day–Memorial Day. Admission charged.*

9. Port Tobacco. As early as 1608 an Indian settlement called Potopaco was noted here on a map drawn by Capt. John Smith. In the 1630's an English community was established, and about a hundred years later the town of Port Tobacco be-

came the seat of colonial government in Charles County. The burgeoning tobacco trade brought the planters modest prosperity, and a few handsome homes were built. Some have been restored and can be seen today around the village green and scattered through the town.

The reconstructed Old Courthouse, an unusual blend of late medieval and classic Georgian styles of architecture, now includes a 19th-century courtroom and a museum of Indian artifacts, Civil War relics, and local memorabilia.

Although the canal and river that provided access to the Potomac and the sea are now filled with silt, Port Tobacco still retains the quiet charm of an 18th-century seaport village and is a delight to see. *Old Courthouse and Museum open Wed.–Sun., June–Aug.; weekends Apr.–May, Sept.–Dec. Admission charged.*

9. *Among Port Tobacco's architectural delights is the Chimney House, circa 1765.*

---

10. Cedarville State Forest. A scant 25 miles southeast of the nation's capital, this extensive forested area, once the favored winter hunting grounds of the Piscataway Indians, provides a welcome contrast to the pace, hard edges, and noise of the city. Within the 3,510 acres are 20 miles of marked trails for hiking and horseback riding (but no rentals), self-guiding nature trails, picnic sites, a four-acre fishing pond stocked with bluegill, catfish, and bass, an old kiln where charcoal was once made, and an enclosed area where white-tailed deer roam in their natural habitat.

Cedarville is also the site of the headwaters of the mile-wide, 20-mile-long Zekiah Swamp. A few drainage ditches are the only remaining evidence of backbreaking efforts in colonial times to drain the swamp for cultivation. The labor was in vain, and the wooded bottomland remains a haven for abundant wildlife. *Park open year-round; camping May–Nov.*

11. Tilghman Island. Tilghman (pronounced *Till*-man) is an island in name only, separated as it is from Maryland proper by Knapp's Narrows, which is in reality a creek. But the designation typifies local flavor here on the Eastern Shore.

Along the bay is the tiny town of Tilgh-

man, where fishing boats are docked in view of the main street, and backyards are piled high with crab pots.

The area boasts two pleasant parks for picnicking. Tilghman Park has an observation deck providing a sweeping view of the marshlands that stretch out to the shores of Chesapeake Bay. Here birders come to watch the waterfowl as they feed. Kronsberg Park, a little smaller, is an enclosed woodland setting.

---

12. St. Michaels. This charming colonial town on the Miles River, an inlet from Eastern Bay, is centered at St. Mary's Square, the original "green" around which the town was built. Here you will

11. *Harvesters of the sea at rest. Powerboats tend the crab pots, and skipjacks under sail dredge for the oysters.*

12. *The long, elegant bowsprit and the rake of the mast mark the* Rosie Parks *as a Chesapeake Bay skipjack.*

find some of the best preserved and most picturesque 18th- and 19th-century houses on the Eastern Shore.

Along the harbor 18 waterfront buildings have been incorporated into the Chesapeake Bay Maritime Museum, where the fascinating lore of the tidelands is featured. These include the boat-builder's shop with its completed watercraft on display; the historic Colchester Beach bandstand; an 18th-century corn-crib, which houses small gunning boats; and the Hooper Strait Lighthouse, moved from its original site on Hooper Island.

The waterfowl building contains a splendid collection of decoys, hunting guns, and the sneakbox and sinkbox boats once used by commercial duck hunters. *Museum open Tues.–Sun. year-round.*

13. Calvert Cliffs State Park. These steep-sided, 60- to 75-foot-high cliffs, which dominate the western shoreline of Chesapeake Bay for 30 miles, are dramatic reminders that a warm, shallow sea covered this area some 15 million years ago.

During the subsequent ice ages the sediments were compressed. As the ice finally receded, the land was uplifted, the sea level lowered, and the ancient seafloor was exposed to the forces of wind and water, which created the cliffs.

More than 600 species of fossils have been identified here, but because of erosion, climbing on the cliffs and digging for these relics is prohibited. They can, however, be picked up on the beach. Sharks' teeth are the most abundant, but various kinds of fossil shells are also found. An easy two-mile trail leads to the beach.

The park also has a one-acre fishing pond, picnic tables and grills, a playground, and a self-guiding nature trail. Ranger-guided nature walks are given during the summer. *Open year-round.*

14. Blackwater National Wildlife Refuge. This 14,000-acre preserve consists mostly of salt marsh and saltwater ponds interspersed with stands of pine and mixed

woodland. It is on the Atlantic Flyway and attracts vast numbers of migratory waterfowl. Many species, including whistling swans, geese, and some 20 kinds of ducks, winter here. Found here too are great blue herons, bald eagles, peregrine falcons, and the fish-eating ospreys, for which nesting platforms are built. All told, more than 241 species have been identified on the refuge, which is an obvious destination for birders.

A five-mile auto drive traverses the best of the area. A short walking trail winds through a typical section of woodland, and a marsh-edge trail on a boardwalk puts you right into the marshy habitat.

Mammals here include the muskrat, otter, skunk, opossum, deer, and red fox. The Delmarva fox squirrel, a large light gray species, is on the endangered list, and its habitat here is being expanded.

An observation tower provides a wide view of the refuge and its various inhabitants. *Open year-round.*

14. *The waving fronds of reed grass contribute their warm seasonal color to the otherworldly environment of the refuge.*

15. The North American Wildfowl Art Museum. *Holloway Hall, Camden Ave., Salisbury State College.* The Ward Foundation, named for the late Steve and Lem Ward, is the sponsor of this unusual museum dedicated to the craft and art of decoy carving. The brothers, who began carving and painting decoys in 1918, were acknowledged masters, and their work now brings high prices. The museum features a replica of the Wards' workshop at Crisfield in southern Maryland.

The Wards fashioned both the classic working decoys and the remarkably lifelike decorative models. Fine examples of both styles—and the work of many others—are on display.

Using decoys to attract live ducks and geese is a practice of long standing. Shown here are specimens made of rushes by American Indians about 1,000 years ago. Here too are boats and blinds, firearms, carver's tools, and a video presentation of a typical waterfowl habitat.

The foundation sponsors competitions and workshops to further the arts of decoy carving and painting, and examples are available in the gift shop. *Open Tues.–Sat. and P.M. Sun. except major holidays. Admission charged.*

16. *The osprey sits grandly on its ragged nest, oblivious of the tiny intruder.*

15. *Decorative decoy of the blue-winged teal—remarkably like the real thing.*

16. Point Lookout State Park. Point Lookout, a peninsula with Chesapeake Bay on one side and the wide estuary of the Potomac River on the other, has had a long and checkered history. It was ex- plored by Capt. John Smith in 1612, granted by the crown to George Calvert, Lord Baltimore, in 1632, and claimed in 1634 by Calvert's son, the first governor of Maryland, as a site for the mansion he planned to build for himself.

During the Revolution the peninsula was used by the colonists as a watch post for English raiding ships, and it was occasionally fired upon and plundered by the British. During the War of 1812 the British again attacked the point and in the summer of 1813 occupied the area.

In 1830 the government built a lighthouse, which still stands but is no longer used. By the time the Civil War began in 1861, Point Lookout had become a popular resort with a hotel and cottages. In 1862 the Union government leased the resort and built an army hospital. Of innovative design, the structure had ward buildings radiating out from the center like the spokes of a wheel. Before long the Union began to use the place as a prison camp. From 1863 to the end of the war in April 1865 nearly 3,500 rebel soldiers died here as a result of exposure, disease, and starvation. Two monuments in the park commemorate them.

Today the point is a 495-acre park offering historical interest, recreational opportunities, and scenic beauty. Swimming, surf fishing, crabbing, and oystering are all popular. The park also has a large lake for freshwater fishing, rental boats, launch ramps, a camping area, playgrounds, and miles of hiking trails, including one to the remains of an old Civil War fort. *Open year-round. Admission charged in summer; weekends and holidays in May, Sept.*

17. Crisfield. The large marina, public boat landing, wholesale and retail fish markets, and numerous crab houses and restaurants support the town's claim to be the seafood capital of the world.

Three small museums add to the interest of this very picturesque town and the locale. One is the Ward Museum, a branch of the North American Wildfowl Art Museum, which displays decoys and related items. It was in Crisfield that the Ward brothers, famous decoy carvers, lived and worked.

For good tidewater swimming, crabbing, and fishing, the Jane's Island State Park beach is accessible by ferry from Memorial Day to December. The park campground, on the mainland side, is open from March to December.

Crisfield is also the point of departure for boat trips to nearby islands. To reach Smith Island, which has three quaint fishing villages and bus service, call Tyler's Cruises (301) 425-2771.

Tangier Island has a number of restaurants, craft shops, and guesthouses, and can be toured by six-passenger beach buggies. Call Tangier Island Cruises (301) 968-2338. *Boats run May–mid-Oct.*

West Virginia

Deep in the forested hills and valleys are rewarding encounters with nature—and with the vibrant history of a hard-won land.

Spectacular waterfalls, a great hemlock forest, and a high plateau accent the dramatic natural scene in this mountainous state. The abundant game that made this rugged land a favorite hunting ground for many Indian tribes is still appreciated—and has been protected in a game preserve and fish hatchery. The demanding life of the early pioneers is depicted in two excellent farm museums. The prehistoric Mound Builders, who were the first inhabitants, seem to have had an easier time. The very earliest intruders here were glaciers that left a charming botanical gift from the Ice Age.

1. Grave Creek Mound State Park. *Moundsville. Take 8th St. off Rte. 2 in Moundsville and continue to Jefferson St.* The largest conical mound in the Americas, Grave Creek Mound rises impressively to a height of 69 feet from a base 295 feet in diameter. It contains an estimated 60,000 tons of earth, all of it carried in baskets from the encircling moat and the nearby borrow pits. At an average load of 40 pounds per basket, the construction required 3 million basketfuls.

Built about 2,000 years ago by Indians of the Adena culture (which blossomed in the Ohio Valley), the structure was discovered in the early 1800's by white settlers. Its first excavation, in 1838, revealed two burial chambers containing human remains, ornaments, tools fashioned of bone, stone, and shell, and a small tablet of sandstone inscribed with signs that have been interpreted as a kind of pre-Columbian writing.

On climbing the spiral path to the top and looking down upon the Ohio River and the surrounding hills, one can't help wondering what inspired the Mound Builders to create their massive works. The mound provokes a perplexed melancholy over a mystery that may never be solved and a people lost forever.

Adjacent to the mound is the Delf Norona Museum and Cultural Centre, which contains artifacts and other displays dealing with the mound, the Adena, and associated cultures in the vicinity. Among the exhibits is a replica of the Grave Creek

2. One can imagine a fisherman here with an eye to the best place for the first cast.

tablet. *Open Mon.–Fri. and P.M. Sat., Sun. except on major holidays. Admission charged for Adena culture exhibits.*

---

2. Valley Falls State Park. This was once the site of the largest Cherokee village in the area. The Indians called the place Evil Spirit Falls; white explorers called it Hard Around Falls, and later, Falls of the Big Muddy, or Monongahela; still later, the falls took the name of David Tygart, a pioneer settler.

At the head of a long canyon a series of two falls flows over beds of rock, as smooth as if they had been cast from a mold, into a large pool below. From the broad, flat rocks on the riverbank you can get an eye-level view of the upper falls: thin tongues of polished rock, over which a filigree of water and air rushes in a billowing curve, to surge against the rocks at your feet in a churning swirl of pale, glass-green waves and sparkling bubbles. The roar and flow of the falls is hypnotic, and you soon wonder whether the water or the rock you stand on is moving.

You can also see the grooves where rock was cut for a millrace in 1837. In the past 150 years the rock has hardly worn at all. Its comparison with the slick, smooth surface at the lip of the falls is a reminder of the incomprehensible span of geologic time. A bridge crosses the millrace to the remnants of a gristmill built about the same time.

The 1,145-acre park offers a small picnic ground near the falls and five hiking trails in woodlands where wild turkeys, white-tailed deer, and red foxes may be seen. Walleyed pike, channel catfish, and smallmouth bass are likely catches in the stream. Spring is the best time to visit for good weather and the greatest volume of water. *Open year-round.*

---

3. Cathedral State Park. *Aurora.* The name of the park is fully justified by the great upward loom of the giant hemlocks, the subdued light, and the enduring silence here. The majestic trees, estimated

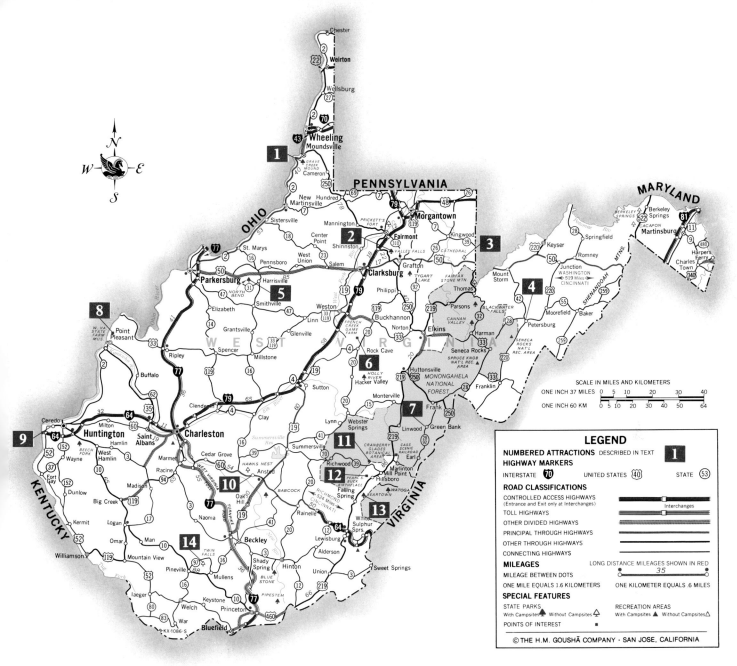

to be 350 years old, reach up to 90 feet in height with trunks 21 feet in girth. Among them is the largest hemlock in the state. One of the last living stands of the virgin hemlocks that once flourished in the highlands, the forest was proclaimed a natural history landmark in 1966.

Cathedral Trail makes a loop through the 133-acre park. For part of the way it follows the course of fern-bordered Rhine Creek. Pathways wander off to the side and then return to the main trail, allowing one to explore further. In the grove of huge trees the light is a soft, subaqueous green, and the understory is spacious. Each tree is in its own clearing, and many are encircled at a respectful distance by rhododendrons. A wide variety of wildflowers adds beauty to the scene. Nature is allowed to take its course in the park

with little human intervention. At least one giant has become entirely stripped of bark and stands like a skeleton among its living relatives. Here and there one finds a fallen tree clothed in soft green moss.

The park provides charcoal grills and a shelter in the picnic area and a playground. Spring and summer are especially lovely here, but the park is also inviting in the fall, when it is less frequented. *Open year-round.*

---

4. Petersburg State Trout Hatchery. Regardless of whether you prefer trout in a stream or on a dinner plate, it is fascinating to see how the demand for that prized fish is met. At this hatchery (one of nine in

the state) 1 million trout, rainbow and golden, are raised every year for introduction into West Virginia's streams. The golden trout were bred selectively in Petersburg from a gift of 10,000 rainbow fry given to the hatchery in 1949, and were introduced on a large scale into West Virginia's rivers in 1963, the state's centennial year. The golden is indeed a shining gold color with red-striped sides and red-veined fins and tail.

The grown fish and breeding stock are kept in four large, dark pools constantly aerated by fountains, side sprays, and a stream flowing through. The trout can be seen swimming in shoals, darting, or resting. Younger trout—which are 1½ to 2 inches long and dark brown in color—are kept in two raceways, each holding some 100,000 of the fish. The fry that grow into these fingerlings are raised indoors in shallow tanks about 20 feet long.

The trout to be released in streams are transported in stocking trucks through which water is constantly circulated by an electric pump. About 90 percent of the fish will be caught by anglers.

Perhaps the most interesting time to visit the hatchery is September, when spawning and hatching occur. *Open year-round. Admission charged.*

5. North Bend State Park. In this beautiful 1,405-acre park one has the sensation of wandering a high plateau. The central area lies on a bluff at a horseshoe bend in the North Fork of the Hughes River, flowing placidly several hundred feet below. A scenic trail, overhung by large sycamores and hemlocks, skirts the rim of the escarpment, sometimes descending into and climbing out of the miniature valleys that score the sides of the bluff and run down to the river's edge. Other trails through the woodlands lead to a variety of overlooks and dramatic rock formations. The woods are inhabited by white-tailed deer that are remarkably unafraid.

In addition to the accommodations provided by the North Bend Lodge, which is

6. *White-tailed deer browsing. The antlers are in their July and August velvet stage.*

5. *Among the stone formations at North Bend is this "devil's cup and saucer."*

situated on a ridge overlooking the river valley, the park offers vacation cabins and tree-shaded campsites. A nature trail for the handicapped with information stations in print and braille, outdoor games and equipment for the blind, a swimming pool, and playgrounds are among the many facilities found here. Bicycling can be enjoyed along the roads and three of the trails in the rolling terrain of the park. *Open year-round.*

6. French Creek Game Farm. *On Rtes. 4 and 20.* At this well-kept, parklike zoo you can see the wild animals and birds that once were—and mostly still are—native to West Virginia. The 329-acre farm was started in 1923 to protect diminishing wildlife and to pen-raise animals and game birds for release into the countryside. That program was eventually discontinued, and in recent years the place has been devoted to education and recreation. Native wildlife wander freely in the fenced natural habitats arranged along a mile-long loop walk.

The most spectacular of the creatures to be seen are the mountain lion of formidable size, a very large black bear, elks, and bison. Among the more engaging specimens are white-tailed deer, coyotes, raccoons, and showy ring-necked pheasants. Wild turkeys, foxes, timber wolves, opossums, and other species are also at home here. In addition, the game farm main-

tains a stocked trout pond, open to fishermen, and a spacious picnic area. *Open year-round; admission charged Apr.–Nov.*

7. The National Radio Astronomy Observatory. *Green Bank.* The enormous discs and antennas of this observatory loom from the valley floor to tune in to distant galaxies, quasars, and pulsars. The NRAO, which is operated by a private consortium of universities, also maintains research facilities in Arizona and New Mexico. It chose this secluded valley for one of its sites because the surrounding hills provide a shield from harmful radio interference from nearby towns.

The working equipment here includes a 140-foot equatorially mounted telescope (the largest of its type in the world), used to study the energetic cores of quasars and radio galaxies; a 300-foot transit telescope (with a surface of almost two acres), which collects radio signals from quasars and pulsars; and the interferometer, which makes use of four telescopes together. The center also has several historical telescopes and antennas, including an exact replica of the Jansky telescope. Karl Jansky's study of the Milky Way in 1930–32 led to the recognition that radio signals are produced by natural processes in the galaxy.

Learning of the mind-boggling work that goes on here and seeing the sci-fi landscape and equipment give one a thrilling and yet eerie awareness of remote worlds. An hour-long narrated bus tour of the site, following a 15-minute movie on radio astronomy, is offered free of charge. The tours begin on the hour and depart from the observatory. Cameras are permitted. *Open Wed.–Sun., mid-June–Labor Day; weekends only Sept.–Oct.*

8. West Virginia State Farm Museum.

Just off Rte. 62, four miles north of Point Pleasant. This memorial to America's early-day farmers and pioneers takes one back to the time when there were no shopping malls, and do-it-yourself was a way of life. The demonstrations of broom making, quilting, and other such activities (given at special times) bring the scene to life. In early autumn you can see the steam engine and belt-driven threshing machine in action and buy the cider, apple butter, and molasses made here.

Among the 31 buildings on the farm's 50 acres are an 1805 log cabin, a one-room schoolhouse, an operating blacksmith's shop, a country store that is stocked with nostalgic items and includes a post office, and a replica of a Lutheran church built in 1815. The church, a simple log cabin, has a safety balcony for women and children and a musket rack by the entrance—reminders of the conflicts between the Indians and the encroaching white settlers.

Also found here are fascinating collections of household and farm equipment of the 1800's, barnyard animals, and a museum with a taxidermic collection of birds and animals. With advance notice you can arrange to purchase a lunch of corn bread and pinto beans and a piece of cornmeal pie at the store. *Telephone (304) 675-5737. Open Sat. and P.M. Sun. Admission free but donations encouraged.*

9. The Pilgrim Glass Corporation. *Ceredo. Take the airport exit off I-64 west of Huntington; watch for the factory before the airport entrance.* From the windowed observation deck you can listen to a recorded history of glass and glassmaking while watching the craftsmen ply their ancient trade on the floor below.

As is the case with almost every difficult activity, when it is done by an expert it looks easy. Here it seems quite simple to take a glob of molten orange glass from the furnace and stretch, turn, shape, clip, and score it to produce glass elephants and unicorns, or whatever else may be the order of the day.

By contrast, the task of replacing the firebrick in one of the furnaces being used seems more difficult. But of course it takes years of training to become a professional gaffer, as master glassblowers are called.

West Virginia is a major center for the craft, and there are a number of factories in the northwestern quadrant of the state. The specialty at the Pilgrim factory is cranberry glass; its rosy hue is achieved by fusing pure gold with lead crystal. *Open Mon.–Sat. and P.M Sun. except Thanksgiving Day and Christmas.*

10. Contentment Museum Home. *On Rte. 60 in Ansted.* The antebellum house, restored one-room schoolhouse, and small museum that make up this complex provide an insight into the quiet rural life of 19th-century West Virginia.

The house, built about 1830 with a white-columned veranda across the front, was named Contentment by the wife of a Confederate officer who acquired the property in 1872. One can easily imagine the serenity the couple found in this setting. Among the modestly elegant antique furnishings one particularly charming piece is the fainting sofa, popular generations ago, when ladies were expected to be creatures of delicate sensitivity.

The schoolhouse, with its benches, desks with inkwells, Burnside stove, and bell tower, evokes the days of blue-back spellers and *McGuffey's Readers.* At the back of the building are the privies that were required before the advent of indoor plumbing. Among the museum displays are moonshiners' copper stills, confiscated by the revenuers, an 1880's wedding gown, a quaint Godey trunk, old pictures of the region's mining camps, Civil War memorabilia, and Indian artifacts. *Open Mon.–Sat. and P.M. Sun., June–Sept. Admission charged; those under 12 free.*

11. Cranberry Glades Botanical Area.

Reached by the park road from the visitor center at the junction of Rtes. 150 and 39. One walks in wonder here in an open, treeless basin completely out of character with the dense surrounding forest of evergreens and hardwoods.

In the four bogs that make up the glades are species of cranberries, bog rosemary, mosses, lichens, and deep layers of peat that are native to the Canadian muskeg some 800 miles to the north.

There are two major theories about this intriguing island of botanical nonconformity. The more prosaic conjecture is that the deep layers of sphagnum moss developed over the centuries in shallow basins

7. This transit telescope—100 yards across—seeks signals from outer space.

Running the New River

White water! The very word conjures up thoughts of roaring rapids, jagged rocks, foam, spray, and the excitement of pounding through the standing waves. I had long promised myself that I'd give it a try—sometime, maybe. And then one spring morning there I was—sitting on the edge of an inflatable raft with my life jacket on, paddle in hand, and butterflies in my stomach.

We put in near the old boomtown of Thurmond and head down the New River. There are six other landlubbers aboard and our leader, Phil. He has made this run countless times before, and fortunately his good cheer and confidence are contagious.

You hear the big ones before you see them. As the roar increases, apprehension builds. We enter the rapids on a V-shaped tongue of smooth water. Phil tells us when to paddle to avoid the standing rocks, the sleepers (shallow-underwater rocks), and the holes that form behind big submerged rocks. The safest and most exciting route is often right down through the large waves.

Between the rapids are smooth, quiet stretches where your pulse returns to normal and you can contemplate the cliffs, wooded hills, and abandoned mines along the river. About midday we pull up on a beach for lunch.

Most rapids have names and reputations. I had heard about the dread Keeney's: Upper (rough), Middle (steep and fast), and Lower (even worse). Next there's Double Z, a tricky troublemaker that calls for some hard paddling.

We are drenched, buffeted about, white-knuckled, and more than a little scared. But when we see the arch of the New River Gorge Bridge at the end of the run, it seems all too soon. The river has performed its special brand of magic. There are hugs and handshakes. Addresses are exchanged. But best of all is the little core of confidence we've all gained.   —Dolores Damm.

For reservations call (304) 252-2244.

---

created by the shifting sedimentation of the local streams; plants able to tolerate the extremely acid conditions eventually became established. The more romantic supposition is that more than 100 million years ago, as the glaciers slowly pushed their icy fingers into this area, the arctic microclimate that accompanied them supported the plants that created the bogs. When the climate changed and the glaciers retreated, this botanical gift was left here in the hills of West Virginia.

In any event, the Glades are here to be enjoyed. In the botanical area, which encompasses 750 acres, a half-mile-long boardwalk with interpretive signs gives you a close view of two of the bogs, with their cranberry vines, thickets of swamp rose and speckled alder, spongy mosses, grasses, sedges, and flowers. Among the latter are showy swamp candle, orchids, trilliums, lady's slippers, hepatica, jewelweed, and the carnivorous sundew.

The adjacent 35,600-acre Cranberry Wilderness Area (which is within a black bear sanctuary) offers more than 70 miles of trails varying in length from 3 to 13.5 miles and primitive campsites for backpackers. Adjoining the wilderness area is the Cranberry Back Country, whose 20,000 acres are laced with trails and abandoned roads suitable for hiking, riding, and cross-country skiing. The visitor center has information on all three areas. *Accessible year-round, weather permitting. Visitor center open daily Memorial Day–Labor Day; weekends Sept.–Oct.*

---

12. Pearl S. Buck Birthplace. *Hillsboro.* Pearl Comfort Sydenstricker, who is better known under her married name, was born here on a small farm in 1892. The writer, who won acclaim in the 1930's for her novel about China, *The Good Earth,* became the only American woman to receive both the Pulitzer Prize (in fiction) and the Nobel Prize (in literature).

The gracious white frame homestead, with its balconied portico, built in the 1840's by her mother's family, the Stultings, is furnished approximately as it was in 1892. Much of the furniture was built by Mrs. Buck's grandfather. The memorabilia displayed include photos of the author during her years in China and the Bible that her father, a missionary, had transcribed into Chinese.

On the property is the Stulting barn, which has been restored and contains an assortment of farm implements of the same period. The Sydenstricker house, in which Pearl Buck's father was born 40 miles away, has been relocated here as part of this interesting historical farm complex. *Open Apr.–mid-Nov.*

---

13. Beartown State Park. Except for the boardwalk, this area of unusual rock formations is entirely the creation of nature. The rock is droop sandstone, which tends to break up into huge blocks along nearly vertical planes. As the result of erosion, these blocks have shifted downward, causing deep fissures of varying width and sheer cliffs. Some of the cracks are two or three feet wide with flat floors, suggesting streets running between buildings. Colonies of black bears are said to have lived among these rocks, hence the name.

To see this fascinating place one goes by a sturdily railed boardwalk over torrents of fallen rock and deep, mossy, straight-walled crevasses. Tall, feathery hemlocks grow from towering wedges of rock as though from the prows of ships; the roots of the trees are sometimes high above you, sometimes below, and often crawling down the sides of the rock like writhing snakes. Rock-cap ferns, light green and heavy-textured, grow like small trees on many rocks, bewildering one's sense of scale. In accompaniment to this grandeur, windsong fills the air in the trees and crevasses and among the boulders.

The boardwalk crosses miniature canyons and valleys in the rock, their sides occasionally blushed with patches of pale red, yellow, and orange and streaked with mineral deposits. Then, at ground level, the boardwalk ends, and you stroll through a deep crevasse, its rock walls pocked with skull-like depressions and erosion holes and worn into soft pleats, folds, and bony skeletal formations. The way out connects with the boardwalk and thence back to the parking lot, where you can have a refreshing drink of water from a hand-pumped fountain. The half-mile walk has interpretive signs. The favored season for the avoidance of crowds is autumn. *Open year-round.*

14. Twin Falls State Park. Woodland streams, two waterfalls, a beautiful gorge, forests carpeted with ferns and mosses, rhododendron thickets, old fields, a rustic pioneer farmhouse, rural peacefulness, and a small museum are among the remarkably varied offerings in this splendid 3,775-acre park. A number of trails and park roads (mostly paved) bring you within easy reach of all the attractions.

To take the Falls Trail, which is lovely during any season, you can park a short distance from Cabin Creek Falls. About 20 feet high, the falls tumble down overhanging ledges to a green pool rimmed by rhododendrons. The path continues along Marsh Fork stream through a lightly wooded valley and then follows a climbing course above Black Fork stream to Black Fork Falls, a fine outfling of water rather more spectacular than the first falls. The trail, about 1½ miles long, is not a loop and requires backtracking.

The Twin Oaks Braille Trail offers a three-eighths-mile loop around a clearing in woodland of oak and beech. Blind people guide themselves by holding on to a cable guide rail, along which they encounter plaques in braille describing the environment. This is a pleasant stroll for the sighted as well.

The Pioneer Farm, a restored log-and-chink farmhouse with outbuildings and small fields enclosed with split-rail fences, is marvelously picturesque. The farmhouse is occupied and not open for inspection, but you can lean on the fence and contemplate the charms of rural life.

The park also has a lodge with a restaurant, tennis courts, a golf course, a pool, a playground, camping areas, and picnic spots. *Open year-round.*

14. *Black Fork Falls (above). The peaceful setting at Pioneer Farm (right) has changed little in the last 100 years.*

Virginia

*From the Tidewater to the Blue Ridge the landscape of the
Old Dominion is suffused with its historic past and gentle beauty.*

Many facets of Virginia's long and varied history are revealed in out-of-the-way museums. A house that confirms the comfort and elegance enjoyed by a fortunate few in the plantation era also displays artifacts created by Indians who roamed these hills and valleys more than 11,000 years ago. Another museum retains the character of a typical small farm and honors the black slave who labored there beside his master and went on to become an influential educator.

Aspects of the Civil War, which was heavily fought on Virginia soil, are memorialized. Among reminders of an earlier America are two gristmills, one of which belonged to a successful miller who was also a noted surveyor, soldier, and president of the United States.

1. Southwest Virginia Museum Historical State Park. *Wood Ave., Big Stone Gap.*

Much of the history of southwestern Virginia is told in this museum, from the time of the Cherokee and Shawnee Indians to the boom days of the 1890's—when hopeful developers flocked to the area.

One who came to seek his fortune was Rufus Ayers, attorney general of Virginia from 1886 to 1890. The ornate three-story house of native stone that he built in 1893 for his family now houses the museum. With an interior of handsomely carved red oak woodwork, marble fireplaces, and a wide, elaborate stairway, the building is uniquely suited to display the wide assortment of historical and cultural material in the museum's collection, which was begun by Mrs. Janie Slemp Newman and her brother, C. Bascom Slemp.

On the ground floor are mountain musical instruments—dulcimers, guitars, fiddles, autoharps—along with 19th-century medical and surgical equipment, mustache cups, firearms, picture hats, and a quilt with red squares made from Martha Washington's brocaded silk petticoat. Rooms donated by the Daughters of the American Revolution and the United Daughters of the Confederacy contain mementos of the Civil War.

Spinning wheels, a loom, carders, and early sewing machines are displayed on the third floor, and in the basement one can see a homemade whiskey still, antique kitchen equipment, and representing the coal industry of the area, a 1,100-pound lump of coal. *Open daily Memorial Day–Labor Day; Tues.–Sun., Mar.–Memorial Day, Labor Day–Dec.*

---

2. White's Mill. *White's Mill Rd., five miles north of Abingdon.*

Built in 1790 and seemingly unchanged for 200 years, the picturesque four-story working gristmill is set among gently folded hills. It leans slightly over a wooden raceway that brings water to the overshot wheel. Below the waterwheel the stream flows into a trout pond and hatchery.

The mill's floors and woodwork, worn smooth and polished by the two centuries of use, are dusted with a fine mist of flour, giving it an authentic character that no museum could duplicate.

On the floor beneath the entrance level, with a sound that is constant but unobtrusive, the wheel drives the shaft that rotates the gears that turn the millstones upstairs. Here on this floor is the miller's office, a

2. The overgrown raceway leaks a little, but the wheel turns and the mill grinds.

large, comfortable room heated in winter by an open fire.

Freshly ground cornmeal, both white and yellow, popcorn meal, and whole wheat and buckwheat flours are sold at the mill. Visitors may fish for trout and pay for their catch. *Open year-round.*

3. Shot Tower Historical Park. *Wytheville.* This fortresslike stone shot tower, one of only three remaining in the United States, was built in 1807 by Thomas Jackson, a skilled mine operator and part owner of the lead mines in nearby Austinville. The 20-foot-square, 70-foot-high structure stands on a bluff overlooking the New River.

The tower was operated until 1839, when, according to local lore, it was closed because shot was being made at the site of the mines. Although there is no proof, it is also believed that the tower was used to produce shot for the Confederate Army during the Civil War.

In the early 19th century, a drop of some 150 feet was required to turn droplets of molten metal into the round shape required for shot. To achieve this drop, a 75-foot shaft was sunk into the hillside from the floor of the tower and, to give access to the shaft, a horizontal tunnel was dug from the base to the riverbank.

Lead was carried from the mines, four miles away, to the tower, hoisted up to the balcony by a system of ropes and pulleys, and melted in a fireplace at the top. The molten lead was then poured through a sieve, the size of its holes depending on the kind of shot needed, dropped through the tower into the shaft, and caught in a container of water at the bottom.

On display inside the tower is a plaque marking it as a national historic mechanical engineering landmark. For panoramic views of the surrounding farmland, visitors are invited to climb the winding stairway to the melting platform, which opens onto the balcony. A short walking trail winds through the grounds to a picnic area with a pleasant overview of the river. *Open daily Memorial Day–Labor Day; weekends Apr.–Memorial Day, Labor Day–Oct. Admission charged.*

4. Smithfield Plantation House. *Blacksburg.* This white clapboard plantation house was built in 1772, on Virginia's

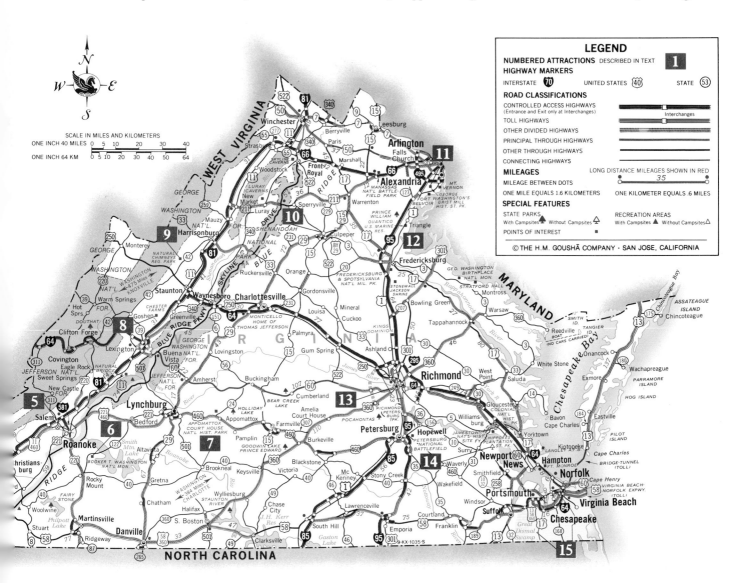

western frontier, by Col. William Preston, who was at one time a member of the Virginia House of Burgesses.

Named Smithfield in honor of Colonel Preston's wife, Susanna Smith, the plantation remained in the family for almost 200 years. In 1959 Mrs. Janie Preston Boulware Lamb, a great-great-granddaughter of the builder, presented the house and four acres of land to the Association for the Preservation of Virginia Antiquities, and the house was restored and opened to the public in 1964.

The interior of the 1½-story dormer-windowed house is notable for its Chinese Chippendale staircase, its handsome drawing room mantelpiece, and the dining room corner cupboard, which was made on the plantation.

Reflecting the simplicity of the late 18th and early 19th centuries, the kitchen garden contains turnips, beans, herbs, and various fruits along with primula and foxglove. The garden was restored in 1982 by the Garden Club of Virginia.

In the basement is the Michael-Schultz collection of Indian artifacts, some from 9500 B.C., found in southwest Virginia. *Open Wed., Sat., Sun., mid-Apr.–Oct. Admission charged.*

---

5. Roanoke Transportation Museum. Roanoke's identification with railroads dates from the 19th century, when the city was headquarters of the Norfolk and Western Railway Company. This aspect of Virginia's heritage is vividly evoked here. The railroad section of the museum ranges from antique passenger cars and engines to the computer-run miniature HO scale model *Alleghany Western.* Buffs can bring their own miniature train units to run on the 1,400 feet of track, complete with turnouts and assembly yards. On the fourth weekend of each month passengers can ride steamers on the park's narrow-gauge railway.

Among the antique cars are the slate-blue Wabash 1009 passenger car, the Chesapeake and Ohio's steam engine No. 1604, several freight and tank cars of the Norfolk and Western Railway Company, and a group of brightly colored railroad maintenance wagons.

There's more romance here, too, for those interested in the American genius for transportation. Machines such as a 1938 Cadillac fire truck and a 1957 Studebaker Commander, designed when gas was still cheap enough to carry the weight of surplus chrome, are displayed along with a Canadian dogsled, an 1870 surrey, stock racing cars, and on special occasions the Budweiser Clydesdale horses.

Also on display are planes and helicopters and, towering above the exhibition grounds like a giant exclamation point, a black and white Jupiter rocket. *Open daily May–Labor Day; Wed.–Sat., Labor Day–May. Admission charged.*

6. Split-rail fence and chinked log cabin are accurate reproductions of the original.

6. Booker T. Washington National Monument. *Rte. 122 between Bedford and Rocky Mount.* Burroughs Plantation, where Booker T. Washington was born in 1856 to Jane Ferguson, the plantation's cook, was a poor, small 19th-century farm with master and slave working side by side. At the end of the Civil War, when Booker was nine years old, liberation came, and Jane and her two sons and daughter moved to West Virginia.

The plantation has been reconstructed, and once again it has the character and appearance that it had when Booker was a child. None of the original buildings remain, but the same chinked log construction has been used in the restoration. Racks of drying leaves hang in the tobacco barn; chickens and turkeys wander around freely; and European wild boars, which resemble the almost extinct Arkansas razorbacks once raised here, now occupy the hogpen.

A walking trail winds through the grounds. At the visitor center you will find a printed guide to the trail, marked with red symbols that indicate where, at the push of a button, dramatized readings about life here in the 19th century can be heard. The guide also gives highlights of Mr. Washington's life and career.

5. Few machines can equal the impression of power inherent in a steam locomotive.

Jack-o-Lantern Branch Trail, named for the small stream that flows through the fields and forests surrounding the plantation, is an easy walk. A detailed guide to the path is available at the Environmental Education and Cultural Center. *Open daily except Thanksgiving Day, Christmas, and New Year's Day. Admission charged.*

7. Red Hill Shrine. *Brookneal.* After many years of public life as one of the founding fathers of our country and Virginia's five-term governor, Patrick Henry, revolutionary patriot and statesman, bought Red Hill Plantation in 1794 and retired there to continue his practice of law. He died five years later and was buried in a small cemetery on the grounds beside his second wife, Dorothy.

The plantation, now restored, is a complex of several buildings, including the main house, a two-story structure rebuilt on its old foundations from the original blueprints; the kitchen; the carriage house, where a carriage dated 1800 is on display; and the office where Patrick Henry practiced law.

Dominating the entire scene is an Osage orange tree. With a 90-foot spread and a height of 54 feet, it is said to be the largest and oldest Osage orange in the country. The American Forestry Hall of Fame lists it as both the Virginia champion and national champion of its kind.

At the visitor center a collection of Patrick Henry memorabilia is on display, including his flute, cuff links, salt dishes, an ivory letter opener, wine glasses, and his house keys. A printed guide to the walking trail through the grounds is available at the visitor center. *Open daily except Christmas. Admission charged.*

8. Chester Farms. *Raphine.* In the early 1960's, Francis Chester, a New York attorney, decided to leave the law profession and raise sheep. This 350-acre farm, set in rolling hills in one of the major sheep-breeding areas of the East, is now unique in the way it produces wool and yarn.

The flock of 450 sheep is made up of white columbias, a breed developed by the U.S. Department of Agriculture, and black Afghan karakul sheep (also called broadtails), which have a tightly curled fleece. Crossbreeds of these two species are used at the farm to produce brown and gray wools. By mixing the different colors, the yarn workers can create a wide variety of natural shades.

Chester Farms spins its wool on a mule, a rare turn-of-the-century machine that twists the fibers much as hand spinning does. This process stretches and then relaxes the yarn before it is wound on spools, giving it a soft, fluffy texture with more elasticity than wool spun on modern, high-speed equipment. The soft yarn is particularly well suited for hand weaving and knitting.

The most interesting times for visiting the farm and penning areas are during the lambing season, December to May, and for the shearing, the last weekend in April. *Open Mon.–Fri. year-round.*

9. Natural Chimneys Regional Park. *Mt. Solon.* Soaring above the surrounding plain like a great medieval castle, the chimneys are a strange remnant of the time, countless centuries ago, when an ocean covered the Shenandoah Valley, leaving behind these rocks etched by the forces of nature.

It takes little imagination to see in these weathered, highly textured formations such shapes as turrets, gargoyles, distant cities, or perhaps menacing fortifications. Small junipers growing among the rocks help to create a curiously deceptive scale.

Since 1821, on the third Saturday of August a jousting tournament has been held on the plains below the chimneys. Modern-day knights, with lances poised and chargers galloping, try to spear three steel rings hanging from crossbars suspended over the 75-yard course in the meadow that is known as the National Jousting Hall of Fame.

Self-guiding nature and biking trails wander through the fields and woodlands. The park also has 120 tree-shaded campsites, a swimming pool, picnic areas, and a children's playground. *Open year-round. Admission charged.*

10. Culpeper Cavalry Museum. *Chamber of Commerce Building, Davis St., Culpeper.* Although the museum is small, it contains a collection that belongs to an event and an era of great importance in modern history. At various times during the Civil War both Union and Confederate forces occupied Culpeper, the site of some of the war's fiercest fighting. In 1861 the Battle of Brandy Station, with 19,000 mounted men, took place five miles from town. It remains the biggest cavalry encounter ever fought in the Western Hemisphere. The museum, founded in 1977, commemorates that battle and documents the town's involvement in the war.

9. Ancient seas left the layers of rock that record the imponderable age of the earth.

11. *This sturdy stone reconstruction portrays the elegance of the original. The raceway goes under a bridge into the arched opening.*

Much of the museum's collection of bayonets, sabers, knapsacks, stirrups, firearms, and other items of warfare was found on the battlefields in the countryside surrounding Culpeper. Paintings, hundred-year-old maps, and many photographs decorate the museum's walls.

A slide show of the Battle of Brandy Station and Culpeper's role in the Civil War is also shown. *Open year-round.*

---

11. George Washington's Grist Mill Historical State Park. This impressive reconstruction gives us a unique view of the private life and interests of our first president. Based on archeological investigations and plans and papers found among his personal effects, the gristmill is a detailed replica of one Washington built and operated for almost 30 years.

Originally, Mount Vernon was the estate of Washington's half-brother, Lawrence. Washington inherited the property in 1761 and with it a deteriorating and inefficient water mill. Always a clever entrepreneur, the future president was sensitive to northern Virginia's agricultural transition from tobacco to wheat, and in 1770 he decided to abandon the old mill

and build a new one in order to be better able to capitalize on the region's changing economy. Washington operated the mill successfully for the rest of his life, including the eight years of his presidency, and at his death willed it to a nephew.

A tour through the mill's five floors, from the 16-foot breast-shot waterwheel on the ground floor to the grinding, sifting, and packing areas above, provides a vivid picture of late 18th-century American industry—a picture made all the more intriguing by the thought that this busy enterprise was a product of the same insight, determination, and stamina with which our first president helped to forge a new nation. *Open daily late May–Labor Day. Admission charged.*

---

12. The Copper Shop. *701 Sophia St., Fredericksburg.* Owned and run by coppersmiths Allen H. Green II and Allen III, the shop offers a fascinating look at how, in early America, simple tools and materials were used to create objects both beautiful and useful. It is one of the few places in the country where one can still see swell-bodied weathervanes and other copper objects being made.

The work is done entirely by hand, from making the pattern to cutting the copper sheets and hammering them to shape on hard sandbags. Traditional designs are used for many of the objects, and most are made to order.

One of the specialties of the shop is the Fredericksburg Lamp, an elegantly designed candleholder with a slim hurricane chimney created by the elder Mr. Green in 1976. It comes with or without a reflector in six different versions, including a patio lamp, a chandelier, and a table lamp. The Island Sconce, fashioned by Allen III, has recently been added to the collection of copperware.

The shop is housed in an old square building with a pillared porch overlooking the tree-bordered Rappahannock River. Visitors are welcome. *Open year-round.*

---

13. The Edgar Allan Poe Museum. *East Main St., Richmond.* A building known as the Old Stone House, dating from the 1730's, is one of five houses devoted to the memorabilia, the life, and the times of Edgar Allan Poe. Behind the stone house is the small, wall-enclosed Enchanted Garden inspired by two of Poe's poems, "To

One in Paradise" and "To Helen." The garden is planted with evergreens, rhododendrons, and ivy-bordered lawns, with wrought-iron benches. Altogether, the atmosphere of the Poe Museum seems imbued with the spirit of its subject.

The museum's most elaborate display is a large painted clay model of Richmond as it was in the first half of the 19th century. Museum guides point out the places where Poe lived and worked.

Also on display are Poe's walking stick, a pair of boot hooks, and his wife's trinket box and mirror—suitable mementos, perhaps, of a man whose life was that of a wanderer and whose temperament was insuperably romantic.

The collection contains a number of photographs and drawings of Poe and his circle of friends and includes a strange, ethereal sketch of his wife Virginia. Facsimiles of the first editions of his works and of his manuscripts include a handwritten draft of his famous poem, "Annabel Lee." In an upper room the series of surrealist illustrations made in the 1880's by James Carling for "The Raven" is on display. *Open daily except Christmas. Admission charged.*

14. Chippokes Plantation State Park. *Six miles east of Surry.* In 1612 Capt. William Powell of Jamestown was granted 1,400 acres on the James River, a tract within Indian territory. He named it Chippokes in honor of Chief Choupouke, an Indian who had befriended the settlers.

For more than 350 years Chippokes has been a working farm. Originally corn and other grains, tobacco, and apple trees were grown here, but in the 19th century peanuts became the principal crop. The last owners, Mr. and Mrs. Victor Stewart, introduced dairy farming. (The plantation was given to the state of Virginia by Mrs. Stewart in 1967.) Today the farm produces corn, peanuts, soybeans, rye, barley, and beef cattle. Exhibits of antique farm equipment on the grounds and displays at the visitor center illustrate the story of farming here.

Of the many buildings—rows of slaves' quarters, several barns, a large old river house—only the brick kitchen, built in the 18th century, and the mansion are open to the public. The handsome pale-hued brick house, constructed in 1854, is set in semiformal gardens with flowering trees, magnolias, holly, boxwood, and

crape myrtle, and is elegantly furnished in traditional colonial style.

Both walking and hiking trails wind through the farmland and meadows, and a picnic area sits on a bluff overlooking the James River. *Open daily early Apr.–late Oct. Admission charged.*

15. Great Dismal Swamp National Wildlife Refuge. *Suffolk.* The heavily forested lands and extensive waterways of the refuge, a quiet, tranquil landscape of some 100,000 acres, spill over from Virginia into North Carolina, providing habitats for black bears, bobcats, otters, white-tailed deer, and hundreds of bird species. Two unusual natives here, the Dismal Swamp log fern and the Dismal Swamp short-tailed shrew, are found almost nowhere else.

Lake Drummond, a large, round pond at the heart of the swamp, is fed by many creeks whose mirrorlike black waters are colored and purified by tannic acid from the bark of various trees in the area. Remnants of a great cypress forest can be seen in the many "knees" encircling the lake.

To enter the swamp by water, you can launch your boat at the public ramp on U.S. Route 17 at Dismal Swamp Canal, which leads to Feeder Ditch. At the Feeder Ditch Spillway boats are carried by tram to the other side, where the creek continues its course to the lake. Canoes can be rented at the entrance to Feeder Ditch; summer boat tours also begin here.

An interpretive boardwalk trail through the wilderness starts just beyond the parking lot at the entrance to Washington Ditch Road, south of Suffolk off Route 642. The ditch was named for our first president, who surveyed the area in 1768. Fishing, permitted only in Lake Drummond, is best in spring, when the bluegills, catfish, and speckles are plentiful. *Open year-round.*

15. *Dark, acid-stained waters double the scenic impact of this typical swamp.*

North Carolina

The remarkable diversity of its out-of-the-way places is a cordial invitation to explore the byways of this pleasant state.

The deep, dramatic gorge that attracts river-runners, hikers, and fishermen contrasts sharply with the serenity of the farm where Carl Sandburg, the "people's poet," spent his last years.

In two state-owned settings are colorful displays of native wildflowers and flowering trees. Museums here are dedicated to such subjects as 12,000 years of Indian cultures, a pre-Revolutionary battle, a Civil War fort, gold mining, the good works of country doctors and a progressive governor, and a village that time almost forgot.

1. Nantahala Gorge. *Along Rte. 19, 12 miles southwest of Bryson City.* Carved by the Nantahala River, this eight-mile gorge takes its name from the Cherokee word meaning "land of the noonday sun." The Indians found that the canyon here is so deep and narrow that only when the sun is directly overhead can its rays reach the bottom of the gorge. Indeed, the difference in elevation between the lowest point on the floor and the highest point on the rim is more than 1,800 feet, and at places the width is less than 100 yards.

The Nantahala River offers a variety of recreational opportunities along here. Water released from the Nantahala Power and Light Company dam, several miles upriver, rushes through the gorge for about 12 hours nearly every day, creating an inviting run for white-water enthusiasts. Rafts, canoes, and kayaks may be rented in the area, and the trip, though exhilarating, is not too challenging. There is easy access to the Appalachian Trail, which crosses the eastern end of the gorge. Picnic areas are maintained, and the river is stocked with trout; fishing is better in the calm evening waters than in the daytime torrents. *Open year-round.*

2. Carl Sandburg Home National Historic Site. *Flat Rock. Little River Rd., off Rte. 25.* Named Connemara by previous owners, who likened its view of the distant Blue Ridge Mountains to that of a mountainous region in western Ireland, this was Carl Sandburg's last home. Here at Connemara, in 1967, the poet and two-time Pulitzer prizewinner died.

Large but unpretentious, the 1830's clapboard structure stands as a memorial to the man and his work, and its interior reflects his life at the height of his career. In the living room his guitar leans against a favorite easy chair, and magazines from the 1940's lie in untidy stacks on tables and floor. Over the fireplace is a framed photograph of the Sandburgs taken by his brother-in-law, Edward Steichen.

A large office contains a typewriter surrounded by piles of books and cardboard boxes filled with research material and notes. On his desk, giving the impression that he has left only momentarily, lies one of the green eyeshades he invariably used.

A self-guiding walk leads to the farm area and its animals, and trails cross the pastures and woodlands of the 260-acre park, leading up Big Glassy Mountain (about 2½ miles round-trip), where bluebirds vie for attention with the many wildflowers. A small, wooded picnic area is near the visitor center. Crowded in late spring and foliage season. *Open daily except Thanksgiving Day, Christmas, and New Year's Day.*

3. Crabtree Meadows Recreation Area. *Mile 339.5, Blue Ridge Parkway.* Named for the cloudlike pink blossoms of the flowering trees that highlight the meadows in May, this is a most appealing 253-acre picnic and camping stop on the Blue Ridge Parkway. Columbines, crested dwarf iris, lady's slippers, and showy orchids also signal the spring season here, along with many songbirds. Raccoons, opossums, and white-tailed deer roam the meadows and adjacent forest. Also in resi-

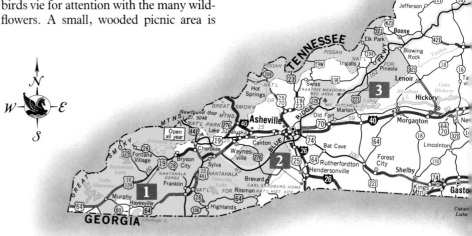

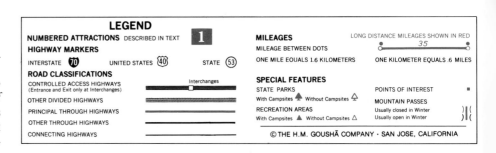

LEGEND

NUMBERED ATTRACTIONS DESCRIBED IN TEXT   **1**

HIGHWAY MARKERS

INTERSTATE **70**   UNITED STATES **40**   STATE **53**

ROAD CLASSIFICATIONS

CONTROLLED ACCESS HIGHWAYS (Entrance and Exit only at Interchanges)   Interchanges

OTHER DIVIDED HIGHWAYS

PRINCIPAL THROUGH HIGHWAYS

OTHER THROUGH HIGHWAYS

CONNECTING HIGHWAYS

MILEAGES   LONG DISTANCE MILEAGES SHOWN IN RED

MILEAGE BETWEEN DOTS   35

ONE MILE EQUALS 1.6 KILOMETERS   ONE KILOMETER EQUALS .6 MILES

SPECIAL FEATURES

STATE PARKS   POINTS OF INTEREST

With Campsites ▲ Without Campsites △   MOUNTAIN PASSES

RECREATION AREAS   Usually closed in Winter

With Campsites ▲ Without Campsites △   Usually open in Winter

© THE H.M. GOUSHA COMPANY · SAN JOSE, CALIFORNIA

dence are a few bobcats and black bears.

The picnic grounds are located in an area called "the loggy patch," a name it was given in the early 1800's by local farmers. At that time trees were killed by girdling so that crops could be grown underneath; the dead trunks were usually cut down later. In the loggy patch, however, the dead timber was left standing until it fell of its own accord, making the land more suitable to cattle raising than farming. Also dating from the early days are "the rye patch" and "the wheat patch."

A 40-minute walk along a trail shaded by birches and hemlocks leads from the picnic grounds down through a hollow to scenic Crabtree Meadows Falls.

The park offers naturalist programs, nature walks, hiking trails, and tent and trailer campgrounds. *Open May–Oct.*

4. Stone Mountain State Park. *West of Rte. 21.* Plunging waterfalls, granite outcroppings, narrow dirt roads, and trails

2. In this sylvan setting Lincoln biographer Carl Sandburg lived his last years.

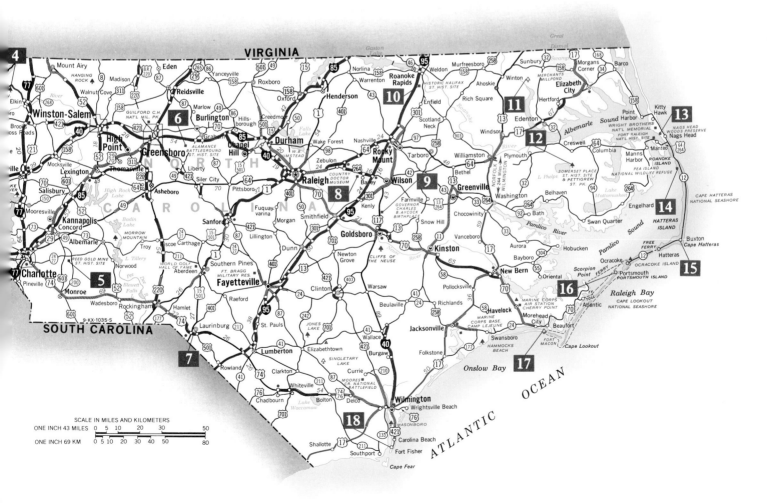

4. *One can hike to the top of this granite mass that rises to a height of 600 feet.*

of mine shafts, restored to memorialize the nation's first gold rush.

A large building near the mine contains a restored 1895 stamp mill, used today to demonstrate how, with several crushing blows, gold can be extracted from quartz. At the panning area, visitors are shown how to separate gold from soil. Lucky panners may keep their strikes. Gold objects serving monetary and other purposes are displayed in old bank and office safes at the visitor center.

A self-guiding nature trail winds through the fields and forests of this 840-acre historic site. A picnic area is across the road from the main entrance in a grove of tall pines and oaks. *Open year-round. Fee charged for panning.*

twisting through catawba rhododendrons and mountain laurel recommend this 11,285-acre park to lovers of the outdoors.

Creeks stocked with trout—rainbows, browns, and "brookies"—make this a fisherman's paradise. In Bullhead Creek (a "Fish for Fun" stream where fly-fishermen may practice their techniques but must toss back their catch) rainbows as long as 26 inches have been hooked; considerable expertise is required.

Trails lead to the 2,300-foot summit of rugged Stone Mountain, and to Stone Mountain Falls, Cedar Rock, and Wolf Rock. For mountain climbers there are 13 ascent routes, many of which are difficult and not recommended for beginners.

Throughout this densely forested area, lady's slippers, trilliums, bluets, and other wildflowers and ferns are often seen in settings that also harbor feathered populations of red-tailed hawks, ruffed grouse, black vultures, wild turkeys, and owls.

White-tailed deer, beavers, otters, minks, and foxes are occasionally glimpsed. Bears and even cougars have also been reported but are extremely rare. *Open year-round. Fish for Fun fee.*

5. Reed Gold Mine State Historic Site. *Rte. 200, west of Stanfield.* In 1799 the young son of John Reed, a German immigrant, found a shiny rock in Little Meadow Creek near his father's farm. Unable to

identify its composition, Reed used it as a doorstop until, in 1802, a jeweler offered him $3.50 and he sold it. The shiny rock was gold, and it weighed about 17 pounds—the first authenticated gold "find" in the United States.

Reed soon established a mining company, and in 1831 he expanded the operation from placer mining (creek panning) to underground mining, which continued under several ownerships until 1912.

Guided tours take you through a maze

6. Alamance Battleground State Historic Site. *Burlington.* On May 16, 1771, three years before the Boston Tea Party, a brief battle here ended in defeat for about 2,000 of North Carolina's independent western frontiersmen, who stood in armed rebellion against the royal governor and the colonial militia.

Known as "Regulators," these men and their families had voiced dissatisfaction with the corruption of British rule since 1768. For all their justifiable anger, the poorly trained and ineffectively led fron-

6. *Various primitive modes of construction are evident in these frontier structures.*

tiersmen were unable to prevail against the Crown. Their efforts, however, were not in vain. Their bold use of armed resistance set the stage for America's ultimate battle for independence.

Flags on the battlefield show where each side stood, and a bronze map explains the events that took place. A granite monument commemorates the battle. Another attraction on the grounds is the 1780 Allen House, an oak and ash log dwelling typical of those built by settlers on North Carolina's western frontier. A clock with wooden gears, a walnut desk, and other original furnishings evoke the homespun comforts of the past. The visitor center displays weapons and uniforms and presents a brief audiovisual show. Crowded during Colonial Living Week in mid-October. *Open year-round.*

7. Indian Museum of the Carolinas. *607 Turnpike Rd., Laurinburg.* The museum's emphasis is on the early Indians of the Carolinas, where, over a period of 12,000 years, 45 different Indian cultures have existed. Their present-day descendants include the tribes of the Cherokees, Coharies, Tuscaroras, Waccamaw-Siouans, and Catawbas. North Carolina, in fact, has the largest Indian population in the eastern United States. To compare these groups with other tribes, the museum includes exhibits of Indian artifacts and tribal customs from other parts of the United States and South America.

The permanent collection contains more than 200,000 artifacts, some more than 10,000 years old. In the 40 different exhibits are examples of pottery, stone tools and weapons, jewelry, and dugouts, including an unfinished craft still attached to a tree trunk. Contemporary paintings add a further dimension to the displays.

Tours of the museum and slide presentations are conducted by a staff archeologist. The excellent research library and the museum's collection are available to students and scholars.

Near the museum are the extensive Native American Gardens, which feature the various plants used by the Indians of the Carolinas for food, fibers, dyes, and medicines. A guide booklet for the gardens is available at the gift shop. *Open Wed., Thurs., and P.M. Sun. year-round.*

7. *Bowls, pipes, fabrics, and utensils are among the artifacts on display. The hut contains a family scene, and the dugout canoe is one of four in the collection.*

8. The Country Doctor Museum. *515 Vance St., Bailey.* In the rough and tumble environment of rural America's yesteryear, country doctors not only had to set bones, deliver babies, and combat disease, but prepare their own prescriptions as well. This museum demonstrates their multiple talents with a fine display of instruments, medical books, handwritten notes, and office equipment.

The collection is housed in two connected 19th-century buildings once used by two North Carolina country doctors. In the front room is a vast wooden cabinet displaying many apothecary jars and a large rolltop desk with cubbyholes for prescriptions and bills.

Civil War surgeons' amputation kits, a hinged leather artificial leg, turn-of-the-century obstetric instruments, and a model of a doctor's horse and buggy help to illustrate the history of medicine in the United States from about 1800 to the early 1900's. The instruments and equipment serve to enhance our appreciation of modern medical practice.

A small garden of medicinal plants separates the museum from a shed sheltering the doctors' buggies. The buggies poignantly confirm the importance of house calls in days (and nights) when they were not easy to make. *Open P.M. Sun.–Wed. year-round.*

9. Governor Charles B. Aycock Birthplace. *Off Rte. 117.* As governor of North Carolina from 1900 to 1904, Charles Ay-

cock modernized the state's public education system, in his eagerness to improve its quality, and built many new schools.

The youngest of ten children, Aycock was born in 1859 in the simple, unpainted frame house that is now the main attraction at this 19th-century farm complex. The restored structure contains a large fireplace with many early iron pots and pans. Among the furnishings and other articles only a pine chest, the family Bible, and an 1869 almanac are original family possessions. The two shed rooms flanking the front porch were once reserved for travelers in need of lodging.

A separate building, also reconstructed, houses the family kitchen and dining room. The original smokehouse, stables, and corncrib can be seen, and an 1870 one-room schoolhouse, which was moved to the site. The schoolhouse, furnished with desks and wooden chalk boards, characterizes the era when there was no effort to make school inviting.

Guided tours originate at the visitor center, where a small museum displays Aycock's gold-headed cane, law books, and replicas of his law office and the parlor of his home in Raleigh.

Demonstrations of candle dipping, butter churning, lye soap making, open-hearth cooking, and other home crafts are occasionally given on weekends. *Open Mon.–Sat. and P.M. Sun. year-round. Small charge for craft demonstrations.*

10. Historic Halifax State Historic Site.
The British general Lord Cornwallis stopped here in 1781 on his march north to Yorktown and to the defeat that was decisive in ending the Revolutionary War. Even then this was a busy commercial and social center; its restored area continues to reflect the aura of prosperity enjoyed here from 1760 through the late 1830's, at which time the railroad failed to make the town a major stop.

The area's colorful past is dramatized in an audiovisual show at the visitor center. Additional displays in an adjacent museum depict the early local tobacco and fur trade and the lifestyle of the planter gentry in the Roanoke Valley. Another exhibit shows the archeological methods used to unearth the site.

Guided tours include the Constitution-Burgess House, which, according to one tradition, is where the first constitution of North Carolina was framed. (It later became the property of Thomas Burgess, a local lawyer.) Also shown are two tavern-hotels, an early jail and town clerk's office,

and typical homes of the area's merchants and planters.

Special events are organized throughout the year to evoke the town's historic past and its important role as a recruiting center and weapons depot during the Revolution. *Open year-round.*

---

11. Merchants Millpond State Park.
Gatesville. Off Rte. 158. In 1811 a dam was built here to create a large pond and waterpower for a sawmill and gristmill. The activity attracted traders, which accounts for the name "merchants."

Today this 760-acre lake and the adjoining swamps—shadowed by towering bald cypresses and tupelo gums—are popular with fishermen. Many of the tupelo gums, distorted by the weight of parasitic mistletoe, have an eerie appearance.

Speckled perch, bream, jack, gars, catfish, and largemouth bass are caught here, while egrets, great horned owls, and ea-

gles are among the 180 species of birds seen in the area. The ingenious design of beaver dams up to six feet high may be admired, and hikers may encounter the garish but harmless white, pink, and black eastern mud snakes and hear the ringing calls of male green tree frogs that resound throughout the woods in spring and summer.

A tent and trailer campground is well situated in a remote setting of slash pines, American holly, and maples; there are also more primitive campsites deep within the swamp. The Chowan Swamp canoe trail, which begins at the millpond and proceeds south along a creek, offers an adventure of four or more days, round-trip. *Open year-round.*

---

12. Somerset Place State Historic Site and Pettigrew State Park. *Creswell.* History and recreation blend nicely in this 17,368-acre park, part of which was once

11. *The strange buttressed trunks of bald cypresses add to the mysterious aspect of the swamp adjoining the millpond.*

12. *This house proudly proclaims the position attained by a mid-19th-century planter.*

a coastal plantation named for the home county of its English owner, Josiah Collins. His grandson built a handsome clapboard mansion on his ancestral land around 1830 and filled it with fine Victorian mahogany furnishings, little of which remains. The mansion's distinguishing features include marble fireplaces, woodgrain painted doors, and wide porches. A rare 1850 Wilson sewing machine and a toy stagecoach with beeswax horses are further reminders of the past. Close by are the kitchen, dairy, icehouse, and other clapboard outbuildings, flanked by a formal garden of boxwood, holly, and crape myrtle, and several majestic trees.

The adjacent park is named for General James Pettigrew, who is buried here. Pettigrew played a major role in Gen. George E. Pickett's famous charge at the battle of Gettysburg on July 3, 1863.

More than five miles of trails penetrate the park's virgin forest of huge oaks, swamp chestnuts, and other hardwoods, which shelter red-shouldered hawks, pileated woodpeckers, and deer. A major attraction is Phelps Lake, second largest in the state and famous for the largemouth bass that entice anglers from near and far. Many ducks and geese can be seen on the lake in winter. The park has a picnic grove, trailer sites, and a boat ramp. *Open year-round.*

13. Nags Head Woods Preserve. *Kill Devil Hills. Ocean Acres Dr., west off Hwy. 158 Bypass.* An outstanding example of a mid-Atlantic maritime forest, this 640-acre preserve was created in 1978 through the cooperation of local citizens and the Nature Conservancy, a national organization. Over 60 different biotic communities are supported in the diverse environments here, from the wind-sculpted sands of Jockey Ridge and Run Hill—the two

largest dunes on America's east coast—to the more than 40 small woodland ponds containing duckweed and rare water violets. This rich ecological variety results from the protection the high dunes give delicate habitats from wind and salt spray and from the climatic effects generated by the converging of the southern Gulf Stream and the northern Labrador Current just offshore.

An unusual ecological mosaic is created here on the western shore where freshwater marshes, formed by water draining from the island ridges, adjoin saltwater marshes among the offshore hammocks. This is an ideal habitat for deer and river otters, as well as herons, egrets, geese, swans, and ducks. Some other feathered creatures seen along the nature trails are pileated woodpeckers, ospreys, and red-shouldered hawks. Guided tours of the preserve are given the second and fourth Saturdays of every month. *Open Tues., Thurs., Sat. year-round.*

14. Pea Island National Wildlife Refuge. *Rodanthe.* Each spring and fall, geese, ducks, and other migratory birds use the Atlantic Flyway for much the same reasons that travelers use the interstate highways—to get where they're going by the fastest route. This 5,915-acre island is one

13. *These pine trees are losing a struggle for survival as the moving sand dunes build up around them and keep needed moisture from reaching their roots.*

and one to Pamlico Sound attract bathers as well as fishermen, who may cast for sea trout, channel bass, pompano, and bluefish. The island is easily reached by road and heavily visited in spring and fall. *Open year-round.*

15. Buxton Woods Nature Trail. *Buxton. Exit from Rte. 12 at the road for Cape Hatteras Lighthouse and follow this to the intersection at its end; turn right here and continue to the parking lot.* Forests are rare on the Outer Banks, where wind and salt spray sweep the narrow land. But at Buxton, where the island broadens to a width of nearly four miles, the increased distance from the sea, combined with elevations up to 60 feet above sea level, creates a fascinating example of ecological interdependence. Here in the 2,000-acre forest, stunted trees form a protective canopy over the more fragile undergrowth, while the undergrowth stabilizes the soil that the trees need for their roots.

The three-quarter-mile loop of the pleasant self-guiding Buxton Woods Nature Trail offers an enlightening introduction to this symbiotic environment and its various inhabitants, many seldom found elsewhere on the islands. Woodland songbirds and wetland egrets, herons, and grebes make the forest and adjoining marsh their home. Ospreys may be seen overhead, and in the spring and fall the area is visited by the migratory birds of the Atlantic Flyway. Mammals, generally rare on the Outer Banks, live here too, including raccoons, otters, minks, nutrias, and white-tailed deer. During the summer mosquitoes are often a problem, so take a repellent. *Open year-round.*

14. *A freshwater marsh at an interval of particular loveliness. The flock of snow geese demonstrates all the subtle wing movements that sustain their flight.*

of the eastern seaboard's finest vantage points to observe the birds resting or en route. And beach lovers, fishermen, hikers, and photographers will also find much to enjoy here.

Extending for more than 12 miles along the shifting dunes of the Outer Banks, this complex of salt marshes and freshwater ponds supports otters, muskrats, and nutrias, as well as loggerhead, sea, and snapping turtles and diamondback terrapins. Ring-necked pheasants abound, while

egrets, herons, ibises, least terns, and black ducks are among the waterfowl and shorebirds that nest here. Peregrine falcons are often seen during spring and fall migrations, and more than 250 other bird species are occasionally observed.

The New Field Observation Area and two observation platforms facilitate sightings, while freshwater ponds supporting ducks, geese, and swans are easily observed from the car.

Five access points to Atlantic beaches

16. Portsmouth. For an adventure that's definitely off the beaten path, try this isolated island village, a 250-acre historic preserve administered by the National Park Service. In the 1850's and 1860's the village prospered as a port where cargo was transferred from seagoing ships to smaller boats for the journey inland. But shoaling of the inlet ended this enterprise, and by the 1890's most of the inhabitants had moved away. Today some 20 old buildings, including a schoolhouse, a

Methodist church, and a lifesaving complex, stand as weather-beaten reminders of the struggle between men and the sea on the Outer Banks. Although in general the picturesque village has not been restored, there are identifying signs to help visitors recapture the area's past.

Portsmouth can be reached by a small passenger ferry from Ocracoke, or by a car-carrying ferry from the town of Atlantic to the southern end of Portsmouth Island, some 20 miles below the village. There are no roads on the island, so keep in mind that only four-wheel over-sand vehicles can make the trip. *For a list of ferry operators and other information, contact park headquarters at Cape Lookout National Seashore, P.O. Box 690, Beaufort, N.C. 28516; phone (919) 728-2121. Usually accessible, weather permitting.*

16. *The shoaling that isolated this community can be seen in the distance.*

17. *Despite its sturdy façade, the fort surrendered when shelled by the Union.*

17. Fort Macon State Park. Since the early 1700's, when the pirate Blackbeard used Beaufort Inlet as a hideout, its strategic importance has been well recognized. After several unsuccessful attempts to fortify the island, the construction of Fort Macon was begun in 1826 and completed eight years later. But in the course of succeeding wars, the only action in this five-sided brick fort was on April 25, 1862, when it was shelled by Union forces and captured the next morning.

The fort, named for Nathaniel Macon, a North Carolina senator, is encircled by a moat that could be flooded with the tidewaters of Bogue Sound. From its impressive ramparts, which once overlooked the inlet, there are commanding views of the Beaufort region. Surrounding the fort's inner parade are quarters for the garrison, storerooms, and a kitchen and bakery. These are not furnished, but the commandant's quarters have been restored, and there is a small museum.

In addition to the fort, the park offers a protected ocean swimming area, picnic grounds with fireplaces and a shelter, and hiking. Fishermen will enjoy surf casting from the park's shores. *Open year-round.*

18. Fort Fisher State Historic Site and Marine Resources Center. Late in the Civil War the Union blockade of southern ports prevented the South from receiving essential war supplies. As a countermeasure, Confederate blockade runners made daring trips through fog and on moonless nights to land their precious cargoes.

Fort Fisher was built to provide cover for the Confederate seamen entering Cape Fear River on their way to the Confederacy's major port in Wilmington. Extending for one mile along the Atlantic Coast and across a sand peninsula, this series of redoubts was the South's largest earthwork fort. With a complement of 47 guns, it provided a mile of defense seaward and one-third mile inland.

Only a few mounds remain, carefully preserved from the eroding action of wind and rain. Exhibits in a small museum explain events that took place here from December 1864 to January 1865, when the fort finally fell to a determined Union action that employed some 58 warships and 8,000 infantrymen. Excavated artifacts, three outstanding dioramas, and a superb reproduction of a 10-pounder Parrot gun are among the displays.

On a more peaceful note, at the Marine Resources Center nearby, an aquarium displays several species of turtles and a nurse shark, plus fish and crustaceans common to the Atlantic.

Egrets, great blue herons, brown pelicans, and two species of ibises may be observed along the two short nature trails. Roseate spoonbills have also been sighted. *Fort open year-round except Christmas; center open year-round.*

South Carolina

The romance of the Old South blends with memories of the Confederacy and 19th-century enterprise—and the promise of the space age.

Consider these contrasting aspects of southern enterprise: On the nature trail in one state park are remnants of whiskey stills, and two other parks feature antebellum mansions built with profits from the cotton trade. The 19th century is further represented by a working gristmill, a hand-dug canal, and a pick-and-shovel goldfield.

An abiding interest in nature is confirmed in vast preserves set aside for local wildlife, and in another context, by an amazing collection of mounted African animals. The tragedy of war in the South is remembered in battlefields of both the Revolution and the Civil War.

1. Hagood Mill. *Pickens.* Benjamin Hagood was an enterprising miller who sought to capitalize on the traffic generated by the gristmill he built in 1825. On the same site he also operated a tannery and a general store. The mill still stands—good evidence of the workmanship that went into the two-story clapboard structure, with its heavy beams held in place by wooden pegs. The mill was active for more than 100 years; old-timers in the area recall that as late as the 1930's, crowds of farmers still gathered here to have their corn ground.

A descendant of Ben Hagood's donated the mill to Pickens County in 1972, and it was completely restored. Situated beside a narrow creek spanned by a wooden footbridge, in a quiet setting of oaks and mountain laurel, the mill is very photogenic. The huge wheel is still turned by water brought down from a mountain spring in a wooden sluice. On special occasions the sluice is opened, the wheel begins to turn, and with a great, rumbling racket of wooden cogs and gears, the mill again confirms the ingenuity of its builders. *Open year-round. To see the interior, reservations are required. Call (803) 872-9742.*

2. Pleasant Ridge State Park. It could be said that a whiskey still is as indigenous to the deep woods of the Southeast as the black pines, rhododendrons, azaleas, American holly, and mountain laurel. It

5. Among the natives that have made a comeback here is the carnivorous pitcher plant.

should therefore come as no surprise to see the abandoned stills of the clandestine moonshine industry along the nature trail in these scenic foothills of the Blue Ridge. For part of the way the foot trail follows a cool mountain stream edged with wildflowers in spring.

The 300-acre park is also the realm of white-tailed deer, raccoons, bobcats, hawks, and redheaded woodpeckers.

A popular feature here is the lake with a beach and supervised swimming. Pedal boats and rowboats are available for rent. This is not a choice spot for fishing, however. The park also provides fully equipped cabins, campsites with hookups, picnic shelters, a playground, a softball field, and gamecourts. Pleasant Ridge may be crowded on weekends in summer and fall. *Open year-round.*

3. Museum of York County. *4621 Mt. Gallant Rd., northwest of Rock Hill.* Here in the northern reaches of South Carolina

it is a pleasant surprise to come upon this fine museum of natural history, technology, and the arts, which so imaginatively presents aspects of the larger world and the universe.

A major attraction is the Stans African Hall, which contains the world's largest collection, by species, of mounted African hooved mammals, displayed in dioramas showing their natural setting. They are complemented by a collection of ceramics, tools, weapons, musical instruments, and other artifacts skillfully fashioned by African craftsmen. The Hall of the Western Hemisphere houses mounted specimens of North American wildlife, including the extremely rare wood bison. American Indian culture is reflected in pottery, baskets, ornaments, and stone tools.

In the Hall of Electrical Energy, an excellent illuminated diagram explains the mysteries of nuclear power. Children will enjoy pedaling a bicycle that generates enough power to project an image of the rider on a screen.

A 1908 two-horse carriage and a handsome Anderson 640 touring car, both pro-

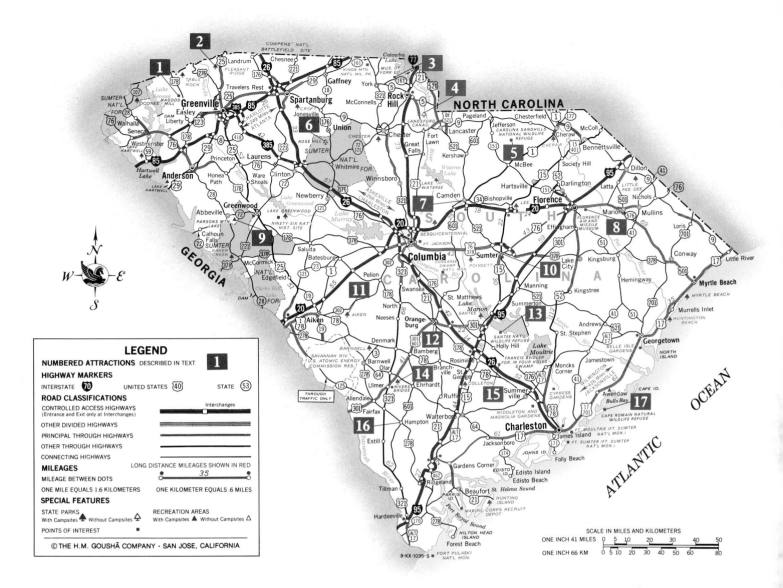

duced in nearby Rock Hill, are among the exhibits in the Hall of Yesteryear. The Settlemyre Planetarium invites both children and adults to explore the mysteries of time and space. The museum also offers an art gallery, lectures, and outdoor concerts. An active program concerned with the arts sponsors changing shows in all media. On some weekends craftsmen can be seen at their work.

Numbered stations on an adjacent half-mile nature trail are keyed to a booklet describing native trees, shrubs, and wildflowers. *Open Mon.–Fri. and P.M. weekends. Admission charged.*

4. Landsford Canal State Park.
Had the 19th-century canal promoters known how quickly the railroads would develop, many of them would probably never have started the laborious process of digging. By hindsight, the Landsford Canal could be an example. The Irish laborers started the job in 1820, working with picks and shovels, and took three years to create a two-mile stretch of navigable water. The canal was used primarily to bring cotton from the back country to the market at Charleston. After a few years the railroad put the canal out of business.

The park's remarkably well-preserved 200-foot section of locks built of cut stone blocks is the only remaining example in the state of the engineering techniques and fine masonry work required for the early-day canals. Note in particular the precise stonework on the arched bridge at the end of the locks.

The typical stone lockhouse was moved here from another site and will someday house a museum. A peaceful, pine-shaded area with tables and fireplaces beside the Catawba River provides a pleasant place to picnic, and the 1¾-mile towpath suggests an after-lunch stroll. Native birds can be identified along a nature trail leading through a handsome stand of hardwoods. *Open daily except Christmas.*

5. Carolina Sandhills National Wildlife Refuge.
Off Rte. 1, between McBee and Patrick. With American wildlife habitats steadily being destroyed by human encroachment, the 400 national wildlife preserves in the country have become key elements in sustaining the natural scene. The Carolina Sandhills Refuge is of particular interest because of its long history. Fifty-five million years ago the Atlantic Ocean's incessant pounding of the shores created the dunes that stand there today. Within a short span of time, settlers, in their struggle to survive, cut the timber

6. *Symmetry of the design helps to establish the mansion's timeless appeal.*

and overworked the land in this area. Eventually the soil was depleted and the farms were abandoned. In 1939 the Federal Government purchased 46,000 acres and established a wildlife refuge.

Now restored to its natural state, with forests of longleaf pines, pond pines, mockernut hickories, and persimmons, the land once again supports its original inhabitants. Beavers, deer, cougars, rare woodpeckers, owls, and wild turkeys are among the 42 species of mammals and 190 species of birds observed here. An 11-mile drive, hiking trails, observation towers and platforms, spring wildflower tours, and a photo blind provide extensive access to the wildlife. Several picnic tables with stone fireplaces are found at the Lake Bee Recreation Area. Seasonal fishing is allowed in designated lakes and creeks. *Open year-round.*

6. Rose Hill State Park. *Off Rte. 176, seven miles north of Whitmire.* Visitors to this magnificent stucco mansion, built between 1828 and 1832, will see evidence of the gracious and elegant life enjoyed by antebellum plantation owners and immortalized in Margaret Mitchell's classic *Gone with the Wind.* The owner of Rose Hill was Governor William Henry Gist. Known as the Secession Governor, Gist was elected in 1858; since South Carolina

had no official governor's residence at that time, he lived and worked here.

Furnished in authentic period style, the house contains several fine pieces that had belonged to the governor. An 1832 pianoforte and an 81-key piano stand in the second floor ballroom, which also features two fireplaces and a sliding partition used to divide the ballroom into two bedrooms. Gist's own bedroom contains his wardrobe and four-poster bed, which has three hinged steps with a chamber pot concealed in one of them.

A fine example of the Federal style, the mansion has graceful front and rear porches built in 1860, and a handsome front door flanked by sidelights and a fanlight. On the grounds, enclosed by the original black wrought iron fence, are boxwoods arranged in the pattern of two Confederate flags and several stately magnolias. Dogwoods line the entrance drive, but the roses for which the plantation was named are no longer grown.

A clapboard building houses exhibits of the local cotton culture and 19th-century plantation life. Picnic tables and a pleasant quarter-mile nature trail complete the amenities of this 44-acre park, where wild turkeys and deer may be seen. Sometimes crowded in May and August. *Park open year-round; mansion open P.M. daily. Admission charged for mansion tours.*

7. Historic Camden Revolutionary War Park. *Camden. Go east on U.S. Rte. 601 to Broad St. (Rte. 521). Turn right and proceed 1.9 miles to entrance on left.* More than

200 years ago Camden, the headquarters of Lord Cornwallis, was a hub of British activity, and owing to its strategic location, the focal point of two major Revolutionary War battles. Today the original buildings, restored and in some cases relocated, re-create the aura of the period.

Visitors can take a short self-guiding tour that includes the Drakeford House, an old log structure serving as a small museum of Revolutionary War artifacts excavated at the site. On a slightly longer loop, which can be walked or driven, information plaques explain several reconstructed points of interest, most notably the 1780 Kershaw-Cornwallis House, two British outer defense redoubts, and a 1777 powder magazine.

A hiking trail leads to unspoiled natural scenery observed by the region's first settlers. Children are drawn by a small farmyard they may enter with a tour guide to pet domesticated animals. Those with time to explore the streets of Camden will be surprised at the number of private homes of historic and architectural interest. *Open Tues.–Sat., P.M. Sun, and Mon. holidays. Admission charged.*

8. Florence Air and Missile Museum. *U.S. Rte. 301 at the Florence airport.* The undisputed heroes of our age, our astronauts have always given full credit to their predecessors, the aviators, and rightly so; for the space program was built upon a foundation of trial and error stretching back to the dawn of flight. That history of civil, commercial, military, and

8. *The birds of war peaceably assembled here are but part of the technology on display.*

naval aviation is preserved in the Florence Air and Missile Museum.

Dedicated to the Air Force and Air Corps personnel who fought and died in the service of their country, the museum is appropriately located on a World War II training base for fighter pilots. Exhibits include collections of aircraft, engines, weapons, insignia, uniforms, and equipment, as well as material relating to the space program. A display of photographs pays tribute to Amelia Earhart and other women in early aviation. Examples of space technology include a Gemini training capsule, instruments, launch computers, and Alan Shepard's space suit.

Set about the grounds are numerous aircraft, missiles, rockets, and tanks, including an A-26A bomber, a Grumman Albatross amphibian, and the 98-foot Titan intercontinental missile. *Open year-round. Admission charged.*

---

9. Parsons Mountain Lake Recreation Area. *From Abbeville go south on Rte. 72 to S. Main St.; turn left and watch for signs.* A quiet lake is the centerpiece of this fine wooded tract devoted to tent and trailer camping, picnicking, hiking, riding, and fishing. A large picnic grove flanks a supervised swimming area on the lakeshore, and a boat ramp invites fishermen to try for crappie, catfish, bass, and other species common to the region. The park also has a corral.

A trail to a nearby fire tower passes a series of pits dug in the mid-1800's by miners in a backbreaking search for gold.

From the top of the 80-foot tower one has a panoramic view of the mixed pine and hardwood forests of the Carolina piedmont. In the woods are deer and small mammals and a variety of birds to watch for. Indian paintbrush and lady's slipper are among the wildflowers that brighten the woodland trails. *Open year-round. Admission charged.*

---

10. Sumter County Historical Society Museum. *122 Washington St., Sumter.* As noted in its brochure, this relatively new museum is based on the classic concept that the more we know of the past, the better we know ourselves. The past is represented by structures ranging in time from a log house built in the mid-1700's to

10. *Azaleas and flowering trees characterize the inviting charm of the Old South.*

a 1920's garage. The James log house was moved here from a creekside location about 50 miles away, where it had been occupied by the James family for some 130 years. In the garage are various carriages, including a four-horse model and a classic surrey complete with fringe on top. A pole-barn contains an array of farm equipment used when mules were the primary motive power in the South. In one wing of an original carriage house is a railroad dispatcher's office and in the other wing, a turn-of-the-century kitchen.

The centerpiece is the Williams-Brice House, built in the late 1840's and extensively renovated (or replaced entirely) in 1916. But the grounds, designed by the landscape architect Robert E. Marvin and beautiful the year-round, are another reason for coming here.

The house is handsomely furnished with period pieces, including a fine grandfather clock. Old wedding gowns are displayed on mannequins, and there are many portraits, including one of Gen. Thomas Sumter by Rembrandt Peale. Also to be seen are household articles from the days before electricity, as well as toys and dolls, arms, and fossils from the area. *Open Tues.–Fri. and P.M. Sun.*

---

11. Aiken State Park. When places are named in honor of worthy citizens, the names are remembered, but their good works are often forgotten. This park and the county were named for William Aiken, Sr., president of the Charleston-Hamburg Railroad, which in the 1830's was the longest line in the world and a considerable engineering accomplishment. It deserves to be remembered.

The pleasant, hilly terrain of the 1,067-acre park provides lake and stream fishing, a spring-fed pond with a swimming area, boat rentals, campsites, and a shaded picnic ground, as well as a playground, softball field, and game areas.

A jungle nature trail about three miles long has markers identifying such native trees as red maple, water oak, persimmon, sweet gum, and sweet bay. Conducted walks in spring familiarize the visitor with the profusion of wildflowers that flourish here. The park, where more than 160 feathered species have been observed, is a favorite destination for birders in the spring and fall.

The three fishing ponds surrender bass and catfish. Anglers also favor the south fork of the Edisto River, which borders (and enters) the park. The area is apt to be crowded during the summer months, especially on weekends. *Open year-round.*

---

12. Orangeburg National Fish Hatchery. Fishermen—both young and old—are especially likely to enjoy this place. The aquarium gives one a close look at most of the species propagated here. Largemouth bass, striped bass, channel catfish, bluegills, and sunfish are bred for stocking federal waters; bluegills (and Asian mouthbreeders) are also used to control algae in the rearing ponds.

A major project now under way is the propagation of Atlantic sturgeon in an effort to keep them off the endangered list. Mature fish brought to the hatchery by commercial fishermen are kept in a holding house from their egg-laying stage until the fry—two or three months old—are ready for release in the ocean.

Visitors are unlikely to see much action in the hatchery's 20 ponds except when the fish are fed, on Mondays, Wednesdays, and Fridays at irregular hours. Although it is not part of the program, the hatchery offers a good vantage point for birders when hungry owls, egrets, and blue and white herons raid the ponds. *Open year-round.*

15. *The white ibis is an elegant presence in the watery world of a cypress swamp.*

13. Santee National Wildlife Refuge. Four separate units, all flanked by Lake Marion, make up this 15,095-acre tract where a vast array of bird, mammal, fish, reptile, and amphibian species thrive in a protected environment. The visitor center, on a cove called Scott's Lake, has a diorama, an aquarium, and other displays that help to acquaint nature lovers with some of the wildlife indigenous to the reserve, including American bald eagles, ospreys, river otters, cottonmouths, striped bass, and alligators.

Across Scott's Lake is the site of Fort

Watson, which was recaptured from the British in 1781 by Gen. Francis ("The Swamp Fox") Marion. Long ago a Santee Indian shell mound stood here.

This general area is ideal for hiking, bicycling, and fishing—Lake Marion is known for its Atlantic sturgeon, freshwater eels, chain pickerel, and bluegills. Each unit in the refuge has its own boat ramp. Birders can obtain a free printed checklist of the 293 species observed here. Among the permanent residents are pied-billed grebes, little blue herons, blue-winged teals, and Cooper's hawks. The many winged visitors include American woodcocks, barred owls, and rock doves. Picnicking is permitted, but neither grills nor tables are provided. *Open year-round.*

14. Rivers Bridge State Park. This is one of the many delightful recreation areas in the South that owe their existence to the tragedy of war.

It was here in February 1865 that a force of Confederate artillery, cavalry, and infantry under Gen. Lafayette McLaws fought in vain to stop Gen. William T. Sherman on his devastating march from Savannah north to Virginia. Outnumbered and outflanked, the Confederates were only able to delay Sherman for two days before he went on to burn McPhersonville and Columbia.

Years later the bodies of the Confederate soldiers who died then were brought

here for reburial and a monument was erected. Donations and purchases of land adjoining this hallowed ground brought the total acreage to 390, and in 1945 it was acquired by the state for a park.

Facilities now include campsites, picnic areas, a swimming pool, a wading pool for children, and a playground. A mile-long nature trail—beneath pines and live oaks draped with Spanish moss—is aglow in early April with the colorful blossoms of wisteria, dogwoods, and native azaleas. Observant hikers may see pileated woodpeckers, which are among the more unusual birds in this area. Fishing along the river and on a creek yields crappies, catfish, gar, and largemouth bass.

The war is recalled by a small brick museum containing a battle flag that was flown here, and other reminders of the conflict. The breastworks built by the Confederate troops are still clearly visible but softened by the years and lined with trees. *Park open year-round; museum open Mon.–Fri. and P.M. weekends.*

15. The Francis Beidler Forest in Four Holes Swamp. Ancient groves of bald cypresses taller than a 10-story building and up to 600 years old; virgin stands of loblolly pine and tupelo gum trees; alligators, cottonmouths, and fish-eating spiders hiding in a maze of swamp waters—all these contribute to the somber and mysterious majesty of this primeval sanctuary.

13. *This stretch of the Santee River is remarkably responsive to the setting sun.*

The forest preserve within the swamp was named for Francis Beidler, a remarkable lumberman and conservationist who allowed much of his timberland to stand untouched. In 1960 the National Audubon Society acquired 3,415 acres from the Beidler family for a sanctuary.

The swamp is a flooded forest and by its nature difficult to penetrate. Some sense of the inner character of this ecosystem is provided by the 1½-mile-long boardwalk with its 31 informative signs along the way. Experienced canoeists can take a half-day trip with a naturalist guide to reach the interior of the swamp.

Exhibits, photographs, and a slide show in the visitor center help one to understand and appreciate the swamp and the mammals, birds, and reptiles that abound here. *Open Tues.–Sun. year-round. Admission charged.*

16. Hampton Plantation State Park. In this wilderness dominated by loblolly pines and stands of other native trees, it is hard to visualize the orderly plantations of rice and cotton that thrived here from the early 1700's until 1860.

The sole reminder of those prosperous times is the plantation house, built in the mid-1700's. After slavery was abolished, the plantation system became unprofitable, and Hampton was farmed by sharecroppers, as were many other places.

The house was eventually left to Archibald Rutledge, a Hampton descendant and the state's first poet-laureate. In 1937 he undertook its restoration, a process he chronicled in the book *Home by the River.* Years later he sold the place to the state of South Carolina and remained as a tenant until his death in 1973.

The 15-room house, which had evolved over the years, now has a Greek Revival façade and two-story columns. It is left unfurnished to let its design speak for itself. In some areas a section of wall has been removed to show architectural and structural details of the past. The ceiling of the white ballroom is painted blue to give the impression of open sky. *Grounds open year-round; house open Sat. and P.M. Sun. Admission charged.*

17. Cape Romain Natural Wildlife Refuge. Except for changes brought about by erosion—acres of forest destroyed and the shoreline and islands rearranged—this area is virtually as it was in the days of the Sewee Indians, who fished and hunted here, and the pirates who found the maze of waterways to their occasional liking.

Most of the refuge's 20-mile stretch of coast, barrier reef, salt marshes, and open water are inaccessible by land. Its remoteness makes this a most likely environment for the preservation of such endangered species as the pelicans and loggerhead tur-

tles that nest here. The bird list available at the visitor center (at Moores Landing) includes 262 species, plus 76 that are considered rare. The greatest population here is during the spring and fall migrations and in the winter, although there are summer residents as well.

White-tailed deer are frequently seen. Southern fox squirrels are plentiful, and raccoons, though nocturnal, may be seen during the day. If you are lucky, you may spot a playful family of river otters or dolphins cruising the creeks and bays. Alligators are common and should be given a wide berth. Also keep an eye out for cottonmouths and copperheads, the poisonous snakes in the area.

Bull Island (named for an early settler) is the focal point for visitors. A two-mile trail, with informative plaques, leads through a lush forest of live oaks, magnolias, and loblolly pines, with such shrubs as cabbage palmetto, wax myrtle, and holly. A fine beach and excellent birding are other attractions on the island. Fishing is allowed in designated areas. Largemouth bass and bream are caught in the ponds, and surf fishermen try for channel bass.

Access to Bull Island is by ferry from Moores Landing. The ferry departs at 8 A.M. Fri.–Sun., and leaves Bull Island at 4:30 P.M. Round-trip fare at the time of writing was $10 for adults, and $5 for children under 12. *Refuge open year-round.*

17. *In a setting of dead trees, the osprey nest is a declaration of life. Almost unbelievable is the plumage of the wood duck.*

Georgia

The history of the Empire State of the South is a tapestry of colorful threads—some of which lead back to prehistoric times.

The Mound Builders left their mysteries, as they did elsewhere, and—not surprisingly—the war that weighed so heavily on the South is tellingly memorialized. Remarkable, however, is the variety of other highlights here. These include a gold-rush museum; state parks with great scenery, fishing, and birding; museums that recall the demands and pleasures of 19th-century life; a classic crossroads inn; and the plantation where, one might say, Brer Rabbit and Brer Fox were born.

The "trembling earth" of the Okefenokee Swamp is another world, as are the barrier islands that helped protect the Georgian colony from the fury of the Atlantic and the colonial ambitions of Spain.

1. Cloudland Canyon State Park. *Trenton. Off Rte. 136.* Over millions of years Sitton Gulch Creek has carved a large gorge through the western edge of Lookout Mountain, so that today the difference in elevation between the highest and lowest point is more than 1,000 feet. Spectacular scenic views of rugged rock faces, ridges, valleys, and waterfalls—including one that spills for almost 100 feet—await outdoor enthusiasts who visit this 2,000-acre area.

The forest is lush with hemlock, dogwood, holly, mountain laurel, and rhododendron. Hikers and nature lovers will enjoy the 4.7-mile Rim Loop Trail through thickly wooded mountain terrain frequented by cardinals, red-tailed hawks, barn owls, and pileated woodpeckers. Gray foxes and white-tailed deer are often seen, and occasionally a bobcat.

The park offers several picnic areas and a playground. Accommodations range from rustic cabins with fireplaces and screened porches to family camping areas and more remote primitive sites accesssible only by foot. *Open year-round.*

2. Dahlonega Courthouse Gold Museum. *Dahlonega.* The word that gold had been found here in Cherokee country in 1828 sparked a stampede of prospectors and soon led to the illegal annexation of much of the Indians' ancestral land. In less than 10 years more than $1.7 million in gold had been shipped to the Philadelphia mint alone, to say nothing of the ore and nuggets that were marketed in other ways. Among the new districts created from the Cherokee Territory, in Georgia's lovely mountains, was Lumpkin County. Dahlonega, which takes its name from a Cherokee word meaning "precious yellow," became the county seat.

Today a handsome 1836 brick building, which served for nearly 130 years as the courthouse here, contains many interesting reminders of the local quest for riches. A 12-minute slide show preceded by a short talk introduces visitors to the region's history. Exhibits and paintings trace the tragic removal of the Cherokees and illustrate the methods of gold mining, milling, and refining practiced in the area. Gold nuggets and coins, a working miniature model of a stamp mill, and a chart showing Georgia gold-production totals from 1832 to 1942 are among the many fascinating displays that reflect the days when gold was bought and sold for $15 per ounce. *Open Tues.–Sat. and P.M. Sun. Admission charged.*

3. Traveler's Rest. *Rte. 123, east of Toccoa.* In the early 1800's Georgia's Tugaloo River valley, once inhabited by the Cherokee Indians, became a busy crossroads for stagecoach and riverboat travelers. In 1833 Devereaux Jarrett, an enterprising local plantation owner, bought a small wayside inn, built around 1815, and expanded it into a long, rambling structure with eight rooms on the ground floor and five above—large enough to accommodate an inn, a store, a post office, and a home for the Jarrett family. It became known as Traveler's Rest and served as both an inn and home until 1877; it was held by the Jarrett family until 1955.

Now restored to its mid-19th-century appearance as a combined plantation hall and hostelry, it is paneled throughout with wide, unpainted pine planks and contains many original pieces, including a round table with a Georgia marble top, an

1. Lush growth in the mild climate has all but obscured the rocky canyon walls.

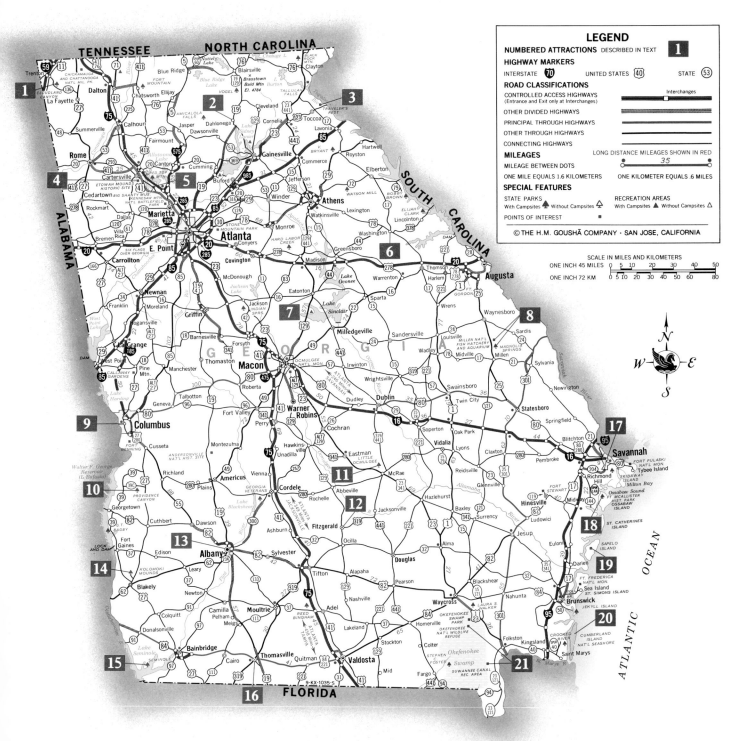

1840's cherry plantation desk, and a handsome 1840's walnut corner cupboard.

Also of interest in this colorful place are the original second-floor post office and a common bedroom with a tin tub and two beds (each large enough for three guests), reminders of the differences in the provisions for travelers then and now.

The outbuildings, among white oaks and American holly, include slave cabins and a loom house. *Open Tues.–Sat. and P.M. Sun. except Thanksgiving Day and Christmas. Admission charged.*

4. Etowah Mounds Historic Site. *Off Rte. 113.* For 500 years, from A.D. 1000 to 1500, Etowah Indians flourished on this 52-acre site. Here, along the river that now carries their name, they built a village with two public squares, or plazas, dominated by three great earthen mounds with flat platform tops and several lesser mounds. Encircling the village were deep ditches and a palisade with bastions.

As many as several thousand Indians may have lived here. The plazas, made of packed red clay, were gathering places for the villagers and other Indians from the valley, who came for commerce, important festivals, and burial ceremonies conducted by the priest-ruler. The largest of the platform mounds (63 feet high, with a platform ½ acre in extent) is believed to have supported a temple which may also have been the priest-ruler's residence. Excavations of one of the smaller platform mounds have revealed the burials of more than 500 of the tribal elite.

Today the great mounds loom in eerie silence above a plaza overgrown with field grasses. Traces of the moat and the borrow pits from which earth was taken for

113

mound construction can still be seen. If you climb the steps to the top of the highest mound, you will see on the eastern horizon a deep notch in the Allatoona mountain range. At the time of the summer solstice (about June 22) the sun rises through this notch, a phenomenon that may have figured in Etowah rituals.

Near the entrance to the site is the Etowah Archaeological Museum, which has artifacts, slides, and a diorama showing the lifestyle of the Etowah, who were of the widespread Mississippian culture. At a table containing chunks of marble and replicas of Etowah chisels and mallets, you are invited to try Etowah sculpting techniques. *Open Tues.–Sat. and P.M. Sun. except Thanksgiving Day and Christmas. Admission charged.*

---

5. Big Shanty Museum. *Kennesaw. Off Rte. 293 at Cherokee St.* Bearing the early railroaders' name for the community, this museum, housed in a former cotton gin, relates primarily to the history of its prized possession: an 1855 locomotive and tender. They were commandeered here in April 1862 by Union raiders led by a secret agent, James J. Andrews. Known as the *General*, the engine was stolen in a thrilling but unsuccessful attempt to cut the Confederacy's supply line between Atlanta and Chattanooga. Pursued north for 86 miles by Southerners manning a second engine, the Yankees eventually abandoned the locomotive near the Tennessee border. Of the 22 raiders, Andrews and 7 others were hanged. The rest escaped or were exchanged. In 1863 the Union, honoring the daring men, awarded the newly established Congressional Medal of Honor to 19 of the raiders. Andrews, as a civilian, did not qualify.

The museum's excellent diorama and a short slide show depict these historic events, while maps of the chase show the routes taken by several raiders who escaped after capture. Confederate money, envelopes bearing Confederate stamps, and Civil War weapons—including a British Enfield musket and a Spiller & Burr percussion revolver used by Confederate officers—are among the other displays. Special events include Civil War battle reenactments and such down-home pastimes as pie-eating contests and egg tosses. *Open daily Mar.–Nov.; P.M. Sun. Dec.–Feb. Admission charged.*

---

6. Washington-Wilkes Historical Museum. *308 E. Robert Toombs Ave., U.S. Rtes. 78 and 378, Washington.* In 1780 the Georgia legislature voted to set aside 100 acres in Wilkes County for a town to be named Washington in honor of the general. The little town prospered as cotton plantations and tobacco farms appeared, and the simple houses and log cabins were replaced by gracious antebellum homes.

The house that serves as the Washington-Wilkes Historical Museum was built in 1835 or 1836 and acquired 20 years later by Samuel Barnett, Georgia's first railroad commissioner, who added the front rooms, hallways, and the staircase. Now owned by the state of Georgia, the house has been restored to its mid-1800's condition. Elegant in its simplicity, this "upcountry" two-story white frame dwelling mainly reflects local events and customs from the cotton plantation era through the advent of the railroads in the period 1835–55. Many rare and unusual articles can be seen here, including a 1790's cotton gin and a number of 19th-century South Carolina pottery jars, some of which were made and signed by Dave the Slave. Also in the collection are feather-edged earthenware dishes carried as ballast by ships from England.

Many of the period furnishings in the museum were donated by residents of Washington; among the choice pieces are an 1855 Weber piano and Belter furniture of carved rosewood.

The Civil War collection on the second floor displays wartime memorabilia, including original newspapers, an 1861 Ballard breech-loading carbine, and Jefferson Davis's camp chest, sent to him by English sympathizers in 1865.

More recent history is represented by an illuminated, fully furnished dollhouse built in 1950. *Open Tues.–Sat. and P.M. Sun. Admission charged.*

---

7. Uncle Remus Museum. *Turner Park, Eatonton.* The fortuitous friendship of a talented young printer's apprentice on a plantation newspaper and the black slaves who shared with him their folktales has given us the classic characters of Brer Rabbit, Brer Fox, Sis Goose, and the other Critters of the Uncle Remus stories.

The author, Joel Chandler Harris, was born in Eatonton, and the slaves, "Uncle" George Terrell and "Uncle" Bob Capers, worked on the plantation of Joseph Addison Turner, lawyer, scholar, and the publisher of a small newspaper, who gave Harris his first job at age 13.

Two connected slave cabins house the museum. Here, in these simple log structures, the world of tar-baby, the laughing place, and the brier patch is brought to life by whimsical dioramas and other exhibits. At one end of the cabin is a replica of Uncle Remus's fireplace, around which are displayed the various 19th-century household articles mentioned in the tales. On one wall of the cabin hangs a large portrait of Uncle Remus and Joseph Sydney Turner, the Little Boy in the stories and the son of Joseph Addison Turner.

First editions of many of Mr. Harris's works, including his stories of the Old

5. Cowcatcher to tender, the steam-powered General *is a masterpiece of restoration.*

South and the Reconstruction days, are exhibited, and copies of his and other children's books are on sale. *Open Mon.–Sat. and P.M. Sun; closed Tues. Sept.–May. Admission charged.*

8. Magnolia Springs State Park and Millen National Fish Hatchery and Aquarium.

It is ironic that this delightful spring might not be so well known had it not been for one of the horrors of the Civil War. The notorious conditions at Andersonville Prison led to the construction of Camp Lawton, a 42-acre stockade, here where good water and plentiful timber were available. More than 10,000 Union troops were held in the camp in 1864, and vestiges of the fortifications can still be seen on a hill by the main entrance to Magnolia Springs State Park, a 948-acre recreation area that now includes the site.

The park is named for a spring with a prodigious flow of ice-cold water bubbling up to form a 15-foot-deep pool so clear that aquatic plants on the bottom are plainly visible. A large picnic area, with shelters, tables, and grills, is set among loblolly pines near the spring.

Two lakes, Upper and Lower, and two small ponds can be fished for bass, crappies, catfish, and bream. A launching ramp and boat dock are provided at Upper Lake, where water skiing is popular. The park also offers a supervised swimming pool, bicycle rentals, equipped rental cottages, and many tent and trailer sites with water and hookups.

On the Woodpecker Woods Nature Trail seven different species of resident woodpeckers may be observed. Highlights on the trail through extensive stands of dogwood, magnolias, live oaks, and pines are identified in a free booklet.

At the adjacent Millen National Fish Hatchery, the ponds are covered with plankton, a superior source of food for the fingerlings. The primary crop here is striped bass destined for the waters of Chesapeake Bay and Albemarle Sound. An aquarium displays various fish, turtles, and an alligator. *Open year-round.*

9. Confederate Naval Museum.

201 Fourth St., Columbus. The warships of the Confederate Navy, established in 1861 to defend the southern coasts and rivers,

7. The cabin recalls the setting that originally inspired young Joel Chandler Harris.

were built with limited funds and little skilled help; and there were few experienced sailors to man them. To preserve the history of this unlikely seagoing force, the museum was opened in 1970, featuring the remains of two important ships. The ironclad ram *Jackson* (named for the capital of Mississippi) was built at the Confederate navy yard here in Columbus. The 130-foot sail- and steam-powered gunboat *Chattahoochee* was built at Saffold, Georgia.

The ram *Jackson*, representing one of the new Civil War naval designs, was sheathed with four inches of iron plate and equipped with six Brooke rifles. But the 225-foot warship was still unfinished when the Union forces captured Columbus in 1865. Set on fire and cut loose from its moorings in the Chattahoochee River, the ill-fated ship burned to the waterline some 30 miles downriver.

The gunboat *Chattahoochee* began its career under the command of Lieut. Catesby Jones, who had been captain of the *Merrimack* in its famous battle with the *Monitor*. The ship was damaged by a boiler explosion in 1863 and when the war was over, was scuttled in the river.

Sections of these two ships, recovered from the Chattahoochee in the early 1900's, are displayed under cover on the lawn here. In the museum are artifacts from the two vessels, several ship models, weapons, and other Civil War memorabilia. *Open Tues.–Sat. and P.M. Sun. Admission free but donations encouraged.*

10. Providence Canyon State Park.

The farmers who scratched a hard living out of the soil here 150 years ago didn't know about contour plowing, cover crops, and crop rotation, and would be astounded today at the erosion they started with their mule-driven plows.

Under the grass and sod lies a deep deposit of sandy soil called the Providence formation by geologists. Its susceptibility to erosion is dramatically demonstrated by the gullies, some 150 feet deep, which began to form generations ago in the white, pink, and purple strata.

This scenic 200-acre canyon area dominates the 1,108-acre park and serves as a colorful backdrop for wild plants and shrubs, including the rare plumleaf azalea, whose flowers, ranging in color from orange to various shades of red, bloom from July to September. Other indigenous plants include verbena, maypop, wild ginger, and prickly pear.

A two-mile Canyon Rim Trail with 20 overlooks winds past clumps of sumac and stands of hickories and slash pines, where raccoons and opossums might be seen and hawks circle overhead. The park also has picnic groves, two short trails that lead to the canyon floor, and an eight-mile backpacking trail.

Geologists say that because of the clay-like, erosion-resistant soil underlying the Providence formation, the canyons will deepen less rapidly than before. But the sides of the gullies continue to erode. Visitors are warned not to walk close to the rim except at designated places.

10. *The Providence formation's susceptibility to erosion is dramatically revealed.*

On display at the interpretive center are samples of soil, chunks of iron, and primitive seashells, all found here. Also on exhibit is a glass-enclosed working beehive with a transparent tube through an exterior wall that allows bees to come and go. *Open daily except A.M. Sun.*

11. Little Ocmulgee State Park. This popular park is busy in the summer and especially so on weekends. But with 14,000 acres and a 265-acre lake to enjoy, one can usually find some areas that are off the beaten path; and in the off-season there's plenty of elbow room. The two hiking trails—one about two miles long and the other a little shorter—are not crowded at any time of year. They both loop through a scenic landscape of dogwood, pines, oaks, and hickories. In April the woods are spectacular with the dazzling bloom of wild azaleas.

Sharp-eyed observers may see bluebirds, cardinals, mockingbirds, and four species of woodpeckers. Among the other delights for birders are the brilliantly marked wood ducks and elegant egrets.

Raccoons, deer, squirrels, and alligators reside in the park; and on guided tours through the sandhills visitors can catch a glimpse of a gopher tortoise.

Boats and canoes are available for rent, and a launching ramp is provided. Fishing is popular in these waters, where largemouth bass, crappies, shellcrackers, and large bluegills abound. Near the beginning of a quarter-mile canoe trail a buzzard roost in a cypress swamp can be seen. Lakeside cottages, a large camping area with hookups, a swimming pool, which is likely to be crowded in good weather, a playground, two tennis courts, and an 18-hole golf course all contribute to the popularity of this outstanding recreational area. *Open year-round.*

12. Blue and Gray Museum. *Municipal Building, Fitzgerald.* With a collection that includes both northern and southern mementos of the Civil War period, this museum reflects the strange beginnings of the town of Fitzgerald.

In the early 1890's, when hostility between Yankees and Southerners was still deeply felt, P. H. Fitzgerald, an Indiana newspaperman and former Civil War drummer boy, became concerned about aging Civil War veterans, who found the cold northern winters difficult. Fitzgerald dreamed of a settlement in a pleasanter climate for these retired Union soldiers. In newspaper editorials he told of his hopes, and the response was so great that he began a campaign for funds.

In 1895, with the approval of Georgia's governor, Mr. Fitzgerald used the money he had raised to purchase 100,000 acres of pineland in the heart of Georgia. People began to arrive by wagon, train, steamboat, and on horseback; Confederate veterans also joined the colony. The town that quickly developed was named Fitzgerald. Some Southern antipathy to the project was diminished when streets were named in equal numbers for Confederate and Union generals.

In the ensuing years the families of the Blue and the Gray have donated many reminders of the Civil War period to the museum, which occupies a turn-of-the-century railroad depot. Among the items are a drum from a New York State regiment, a muzzle-loading rifle of the 4th Illinois Cavalry, an 1863 land grant signed by President Lincoln, a key to Andersonville Prison, a Confederate flag, and the mortar and pestle used by Jefferson Davis's physician. *Open P.M. Mon.–Fri., Apr.–Oct. Admission charged.*

13. Thronateeska Museum and Weatherbee Planetarium. *Albany. Driving west on Rte. 82, turn right onto Washington Ave.; continue to Roosevelt Ave., then turn right for the museum.* The museum, which takes its name from a Creek word meaning "place where flint is picked up," is devoted to artifacts that reveal both the history and the natural environment of southwest Georgia. It is housed in a 1913 railroad station that is now in *The National Register of Historic Places.*

The region's rich Indian heritage is reflected by prehistoric artifacts, including stone effigies and ceremonial pottery from the Mississippian culture.

The more recent past is represented by symbols of agriculture, industry, transportation, and other fields. Here are 19th century plows, harnesses, and machinery for processing pecans and weighing cotton. A 1908 Franklin and other antique automobiles are displayed along with horse-drawn vehicles. Parked on a siding by the station are a 1911 Georgia Northern locomotive, a boxcar, and a mail car containing model trains. A Children's Discovery Room has wheels and gears to turn and mystery items that children are invited to identify by touch.

Collections of shells and minerals and several aquariums and terrariums displaying local turtles, fish, and reptiles help to illustrate the natural environment. The small planetarium, in the old railway express office, has scheduled programs that are changed every few weeks. *Museum open P.M. Tues.–Sun. except major holidays. Planetarium open P.M. Wed., Sat., Sun. Admission charged for planetarium.*

14. Kolomoki Mounds State Park. *Six miles north of Blakely, off Rte. 27.* This 1,300-acre park is both a recreational area and a mystery-shrouded archeological site where seven 12th- and 13th-century mounds have been preserved. Kolomoki, with its mounds, plaza, and outlying villages, was an important population center for perhaps as many as 2,000 people.

The largest of the mounds, known as the Great Mound, rises from a base 325 feet by 200 feet to a height of 56 feet and is believed to have had two distinct platforms at the top, each with a structure, perhaps a temple. Two smaller mounds proved on excavation to be burial mounds. One excavated mound is now housed by the museum; from a platform you can look down into the archeological dig. The museum interprets events that took place at Kolomoki with dioramas and exhibits of artifacts.

The two lakes in the park, together with Kolomoki Creek, offer the fisherman ample opportunities for bass, crappies, bream, catfish, and trout. Rowboats may be rented, and there is a boat-launching ramp, but motors are limited to 10 horsepower. Hikers on the two short nature trails may see white-tailed deer, foxes, bluebirds, cardinals, hawks, and possibly an alligator. The park also has a swimming pool, two picnic areas, and a 35-site campground. *Park open year-round. Museum open Tues.–Sat. and P.M. Sun. Admission charged for museum.*

15. Seminole State Park. Named for the Indians who lived in this region before white settlers came, the 300-acre park is best known for water sports—boating, water skiing, canoeing, and swimming.

Seminole Lake, the main feature here, is a favorite with fishermen. Its shallow waters with beds of stumps and grass contain more species of fish than does any other lake in Georgia. The lake is also reputed to have the best largemouth bass fishing in the United States. Experienced anglers who come here maintain that live bait is the best for bass. Also caught here are crappies, jack, bream, catfish, and yellow perch. An encouraging note is the fish-cleaning table on the shore.

Picnic tables, some beneath shelters, are located along the lakefront. Rental cottages and tent and trailer campgrounds, shaded by longleaf pines, poplars, sweet gums, and cedars, also give a view of the lake. Pioneer camping is available in the more remote sections of the park, where the blossoming of dogwoods and wild blackberries signals the start of spring.

Birders will see several species of large hawks soaring over the stretches of marshy wire grass in search of the small mammals on which they prey. The gopher tortoise, an endangered species, is also found here.

Signs leading to the park are easily confused with signs for the Lake Seminole public launching ramp, which is not on park property. *Open year-round.*

16. Thomasville. The effect of the Civil War on this small town in southern Georgia was unpredictably beneficial. In 1861 the Atlantic and Gulf Railroad, with its terminus at Thomasville, was built to move men and supplies north to support the Confederate Army. The railroad's major contribution to the South, however, was the postwar transportation of wealthy Yankees, who came here to escape the rigors of northern winters. A number of luxurious resort hotels were established, and wealthy families from Chicago, Cleveland, Philadelphia, and New York built "winter cottages." Thus the town became a fashionable social center.

The northerners bestowed upon Thomasville a heritage of eclectic architecture that the local citizens have fortunately managed to preserve. The houses are a charming mélange of plantation, Greek Revival, Neoclassical, Georgian, Victorian, Queen Anne, and bungalow styles. A walking tour includes 35 interesting homes, a number of which are in *The National Register of Historic Places* and some open to the public.

In the heyday of the large resort hotels, a popular wooded area by the railroad tracks was called Yankee Paradise. Today the 26-acre area is more circumspectly called Paradise Park. A stately symbol of preservation here is the 300-year-old "Big Oak," some 70 feet high and twice as broad at the crown. Thomasville is also an agricultural center, and the farmers' market is the largest in the state.

The Thomas County Historical Society Museum displays artifacts and memorabilia from the area and has an on-site log cabin and an old-time bowling alley. *For tour information call the Chamber of Commerce at (912) 226-9600. Fee charged.*

17. Museum of Antique Dolls. *505 President St. East, Savannah.* The collecting of antique dolls and toys is a fast-growing hobby pursued by countless thousands, who search them out at country auctions and fairs, tag sales, antiques shops, and family attics. This charming collection, owned by Jo Elizabeth Gerken, a recognized doll historian and author, represents her lifelong interest in the subject.

The dolls range from a small Egyptian figurine, dated between 300 B.C. and A.D. 200, to a 1984 Annie, but most of the collection predates the 20th century. They are made of papier-mâché, cloth, wood,

16. *The Lapham-Patterson house is but one of many unusual homes in Thomasville.*

wax, and ceramics. Included is a group of unusual boy dolls, recognized as the best such collection in the United States, and an English poured-wax 1860's figure by Charles Marsh.

Several countries are represented, including the United States, Germany, Java, China, Japan, and India. Many excellent examples of doll furniture, doll clothes, magazine fashion plates, and beautifully designed dollhouses are also shown. A small Christmas tree decorated with rare 1880's Czechoslovak glass ornaments is on display year-round, surrounded by 19th-century playthings. Photography is permitted. *Open Tues.–Sat. except Sept., Thanksgiving Day, Christmas, and New Year's Day. Admission charged.*

---

18. Fort McAllister Historic Park. *Nine miles east of Richmond Hill on Spur 144.* An interesting blend of history and recreation is combined in the park's 1,600 acres of salt marsh, forest, and riverfront. The focal point, Fort McAllister, was built here at the mouth of the Great Ogeechee River in 1861 to protect Savannah during the Civil War.

The earthwork fort withstood half a dozen battles with Union gunboats from June 1862 to March 1863. It was finally taken from the landward side in hand-to-hand fighting by the troops of General Sherman at the end of their epic march to the sea. A walking tour with interpretive plaques encompasses the fortification, with its central parade ground, reconstructed magazine, and reproduction cannons. A printed tour guide describing 21 locations helps bring to life the drama and intensity of the action here.

A small museum displays dioramas of the final battle, early photographs of the fort, and Confederate uniforms. Machine parts and artifacts recovered from the wreck of a Confederate blockade runner contribute to an interesting collection. On summer weekends Civil War lectures and demonstrations in firing small arms are given by staff members.

A picnic area with tables, shelters, and a playground is located along the riverfront beneath tall slash pines.

Nearby Savage Island, accessible by a causeway, offers a camping area for tents and trailers and a nature trail among palmettos, water oaks, magnolias, and other native trees, some festooned with Spanish moss. A boat ramp is provided, and fishermen try for whiting, flounder, mullet, shrimp, and crabs. Care should be taken in the wooded areas to avoid poisonous snakes. *Open Tues.–Sat. and P.M. Sun. except Thanksgiving Day and Christmas.*

---

19. Sapelo Island. *Reached only by ferry from Darien. Tickets must be purchased at the McIntosh County Chamber of Commerce, Darien, on Rte. 17 at the north end of the Altamaha River bridge.* This small barrier island, with its uplands, wetlands, marshes, and combination of fresh and salt water, harbors an impressive array of birds, mammals, and fish. In the many marsh areas—carpeted with smooth cordgrass and black needlerush—green herons, clapper rails, and ruddy turnstones may be seen, as well as minks and raccoons. Purple marsh and fiddler crabs, oysters, white shrimp, mullet, and anchovies also find sanctuary here. In the higher elevations wild turkeys and deer roam the groves of loblolly pines and live oaks.

Indians had occupied the island for some 3,400 years before white settlers began to arrive in the 1500's. During the next few centuries the island changed hands repeatedly as the French, Spanish, and British fought for control. In 1934 R. J. Reynolds purchased most of the island and assisted in establishing the University of Georgia Marine Institute. After Reynolds' death the state acquired some 8,000 acres from his widow and created the Reynolds Wildlife Refuge.

A 30-minute ferry ride takes visitors to the island, where buses tour the marshland, dunes, and wildlife management areas. It is advisable to take insect repellent

20. Dunes reveal the eternal conflict of shifting sand and rooted plants. The wild horse (of Spanish descent) contemplates the bold advance of a cattle egret.

with you. Half-day trips are offered two or three times a week year-round. All-day tours, which include a nature walk, are scheduled once a month from March to October. Tour reservations should be made two to four weeks in advance. *For ferry schedule and further information, call (912) 437-6684. Fee charged.*

20. Cumberland Island National Seashore. *From Rte. 40 in St. Marys turn right at waterfront to visitor center.* This historic sandspit, the southernmost of Georgia's sea islands, has been inhabited for some 4,000 years. In the 16th century the Spanish built a fort to help protect their holdings in Florida. Their religious faith was buttressed also—by the establishment of a Franciscan mission and the conversion of many of the Timucan Indians. The Spanish called the island San Pedro.

In the 18th century, by an odd turn of events, the present name was proposed by a local Indian who had visited the Duke of Cumberland in England. Gen. James Oglethorpe, founder of England's Georgia colony, accepted the suggestion.

There were no further significant developments here until after the Revolutionary War, when Gen. Nathanael Greene bought a large tract of land on which his widow later built an imposing mansion. After the Civil War Andrew Carnegie's brother built a handsome home, which still stands. Two other homes built by Carnegie descendants can be seen today. One of them is open for tours.

This small island, about 18 miles long and 4 miles across at its widest point, supports a fascinating range of ecological zones, each with its own population of plants, birds, and animals. The beach, always uncrowded and fine for swimming, is spangled with shells and frequented by shorebirds that follow the tides. Sea oats help stabilize the grasses and the sand. Low-growing plants carpet the meadows between the dunes. Where the soil is deepest, a maritime forest of oaks, magnolias, red bay, and various pines is established, and a salt marsh sanctuary on the estuary side supports its own waving sea of cordgrass. The sloughs and ponds are home to alligators, otters, and minks; wild horses, said to be descended from those brought by the Spanish, may also be seen.

The island has walking trails and camps

21. For all the peaceful beauty of the lilies and calm waters of the Suwannee Canal, there lurks in the shallows a fearsome predator that has flourished since ancient times.

for backpackers (reservations required). A museum displays Indian artifacts and interprets the history of the island.

Access to the island is from St. Marys. The boat leaves at 9:15 A.M. and 1:45 P.M., and departs from the island at 12:15 and 4:45 P.M. Reservations are advisable. *Open daily Memorial Day–first Tues. in Oct.; then closed Tues. and Wed.,* Oct.–*May. For reservations call (912) 882-4335.*

21. Suwannee Canal Recreation Area, Okefenokee National Wildlife Refuge. Although a foothold has been established on the edge of this mysterious land, mankind comes as a stranger. This is the rightful realm of the alligator, black bear, and bobcat; the opossum, muskrat, and otter. It is home to lizards, turtles, and toads; snakes and salamanders. Some 40 kinds of fish and 230 species of birds are native to this region.

Many of the plants seen here are unique to the prairies, waterways, and forests of the Okefenokee Swamp. The tannic acid

in the vegetation stains the slow-moving water a rich brown. This does not affect the fish—bass, bluegills, catfish, and pickerel are regularly caught.

This fascinating environment can be enjoyed from a variety of perspectives on the hiking trails, the boardwalk over the bogs, the interpretive tram, and the guided after-dark tours, and from the observation towers and photo blinds. A restored homestead suggests the character of early-day life in the swamp.

To explore the 11-mile Suwannee Canal, one can rent a boat with outboard motor. For a wilderness canoe trip lasting up to six days, reservations must be made two months in advance. Precaution: insect repellent to fend off mosquitoes and deerflies is needed from April through October. The interpretive center provides an overview of the sights and activities to be savored and free folders on the plant and animal life. Picnic tables are also found here. *Open year-round. For canoe trip reservations call (912) 496-7156.*

Florida

The beaches and man-made wonders are all well known; among the surprises are wildlife preserves, battlefields, and archeological digs.

When one thinks about the Civil War, Florida does not readily come to mind. It was, however, the site of two hard-won victories for the Confederacy, and you can learn about the details at the Natural Bridge and Olustee battlefields.

The Sunshine State seems an unlikely place for the reestablishment of the buffalo—a prototypical symbol of the western plains. But at Paynes Prairie the living evidence can be seen on the hoof. At Bone Valley Museum another kind of evidence recalls animals that can't be reintroduced, such as the mastodon, the three-toed sloth, and the saber-toothed tiger. Among other highlights are some fine parks, wildlife preserves, and memorials to a prolific inventor and a much-loved writer.

1. Blackwater River State Park. This 590-acre preserve is a good example of Florida's enlightened policy of public-land management. The objective of the Florida Park Service is to maintain—and re-create where necessary—the plant communities and ecological systems that prevailed in the area before the first Europeans arrived in the early 16th century.

The Blackwater is one of the few remaining sand-bottom rivers in the Southeast, and despite the darkish color of the tannin-stained water, it is one of the cleanest. The water contrasts dramatically with the pristine white of the ever-changing sandbars deposited on the curves and oxbows of the meandering river.

The Blackwater, understandably, is a great favorite for both canoeing and swimming, with its fine sand beaches. Other features are the nature trails and a boardwalk across a swamp to a picnic area where you find the state's champion Atlantic white cedar, a noble tree indeed.

The ecological systems here include the river floodplain with swamps, sand levees, and small lakes; the pine flatwoods, dominated by slash pine with an understory of greenbrier, fetterbush, and gallberry; and the high pinelands that support longleaf pines, turkey oaks, and sweetleaf. White-tailed deer and turkeys may be seen in the woods, and the river otter roams the floodplain. *Open year-round.*

2. Grayton Beach Recreation Area. *County Rte. 30A, Grayton Beach.* A superb, mile-long beach of brilliant white sand awaits visitors to this interesting park. Behind the beach, high barrier dunes stabilized by sea oats and scrub overlook the clear green and azure waters where dolphins are sometimes seen. The appeal to swimmers is obvious.

Fishermen may surf cast, primarily for whiting and king mackerel. Western Lake, behind the dunes, is popular for boat fishing; its brackish water supports both fresh- and saltwater species. For those interested in wildlife there are the 15-minute Pine Woods Loop and the 40-minute Barrier Dune Nature Trail. The latter provides markers keyed to entries in a trail guide booklet explaining the many phenomena of the shoreline ecosystem, such as shifting sands, dune building, plant pruning by wind and salt spray, and decomposition and recycling. Elsewhere in the park plaques identify and explain the significance of various plant species.

Raccoons and alligators are common sights throughout this 356-acre expanse of salt marshes, slash pines, and palmettos. In the summer loggerhead turtle nests may be found on the beach. The park has two sheltered picnic areas and a campground. Although the sites are close together, dense scrub separates them and gives privacy. *Open year-round. Admission charged Memorial Day–Labor Day.*

3. T.H. Stone Memorial St. Joseph Peninsula State Park. *Port St. Joe.* A long barrier extending north between St. Joseph Bay and the Gulf of Mexico, this 2,516-acre park will appeal to a wide range of interests. Its miles of fine natural beach are good for swimming and fishing. The fall is best for catching large redfish, sharks, bluefish, and flounder, while spring is excellent for pompano, whiting, and speckled trout.

Three overlooks placed among the high palmetto-dotted dunes provide panoramic views of pristine terrain similar to that en-

2. Add to this the salt air and sounds of the surf by the silvery edge of the sea.

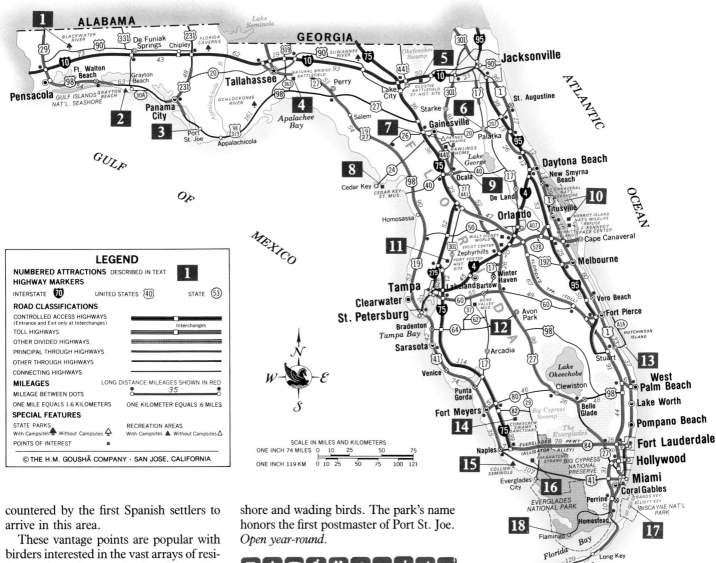

countered by the first Spanish settlers to arrive in this area.

These vantage points are popular with birders interested in the vast arrays of resident and transient species found here. Besides the many brown pelicans, willet, and great blue and green herons, more rarely seen species include white pelicans, magnificent frigate birds, American golden plovers, and Arcadian flycatchers, according to the season. In autumn this park is one of the best places in the country to observe migrating hawks, including the rare peregrine falcon.

On the bay side numerous salt marshes of needlerush and cordgrass nurture populations of fiddler and blue crabs, horse conchs, sea turtles, diamondback terrapins, and the inevitable alligators.

Near the Gulf beaches are two separate camping sites; more primitive camping is available in the 1,650-acre wilderness preserve at the northern end of the park. On the bay side are a marina and a launching ramp. The park also offers picnic grounds and two nature trails, which present chances to spot gray foxes plus many

shore and wading birds. The park's name honors the first postmaster of Port St. Joe. *Open year-round.*

4. Natural Bridge Battlefield. *Natural Bridge Rd., Woodville.* Of particular interest to Civil War buffs, this site illustrates the crucial role the lay of the land can play in military strategy. In early March 1865, Union Gen. John Newton and naval Comdr. William Gibson mounted a two-pronged advance toward Tallahassee. Newton landed his troops and headed north, but Gibson's gunboats ran aground in the St. Marks River. When word reached Tallahassee, the limited Confederate forces were quickly reinforced by volunteers—recuperating veterans, men of 70, and boys as young as 14.

When General Newton encountered stiff resistance at Newport Bridge, he opted for a surprise attack across a nearby natural bridge. This move had been anticipated by Confederate Gen. William

Miller, who entrenched his forces there. The Confederates repelled three Union attacks in 12 hours. Deciding the battle was lost, Newton retreated. Southern pride still warms to this moment of victory, for it left Tallahassee the only Confederate capital east of the Mississippi never to be occupied by Union armies.

Within a small, quiet area shaded by oaks and scrub pines, stone markers and a monument commemorate participating regiments and Confederate officers. Tablets provide battle details, and some of the original earth breastwork is still visible. A picnic grove contains tables and grills. *Open year-round.*

5. Olustee Battlefield State Historic Site. This site commemorates Florida's major Civil War battle. In February 1864, a Union force of 5,500 men, who were charged with severing enemy communications and food supplies between east and west Florida, clashed here in an open pine forest with nine Confederate regiments. The southern soldiers, although slightly outnumbered, forced their foes to retreat after a five-hour fight. The events of the day and other aspects of Florida's role in the Civil War are explained in a small interpretive center. A self-guiding trail through the 270-acre battle site begins with a recorded 10-minute "you-are-there" account by one "Private Bedley Jackson of the 28th Georgia Regiment." *Open year-round.*

6. Ravine State Gardens. *Twigg St., Palatka. From Rtes. U.S. 17 and State 100 going west, turn left on Mosely Ave.; go to the third traffic light. Turn left on Twigg to park entrance.* The ravine was formed by water flowing through the sandy ridges on the west shore of the St. John's River for hundreds of thousands of years. Grasses and shrubs slowly established themselves and stabilized the soil, retarding erosion. Trees followed, and the climax forest of mixed hardwoods and shrubs found here today gradually evolved—an interesting

range of loblolly pines, magnolias, dogwoods, cabbage palms, pignut hickories, laurel oaks, black cherries, sweet gums, the fernlike coontie, and the American beauty berry. The diversity of flora provides cover and sustenance for a variety of small mammals and birds. Peregrine falcons are known to visit here during their annual migrations.

The gardens in this 82-acre park were established in the 1930's, and camellias and azaleas were extensively planted to add their color in the spring, when the dogwoods also bloom. An annual azalea festival the first week in March features guided tours. Among the other attractions in this quiet, restful environment are a footbridge crossing the ravine, a water lily pond, two pure spring water boils, and five picnic areas. For views of the ravine you can drive through the park on a 1.8-mile loop, or walk or jog a fitness trail. In either case you will be close to the lush growth here. *Open year-round.*

7. Paynes Prairie State Preserve. If the Seminole Indian King Payne (who was killed in a battle with American settlers near the Georgia border in 1812) could have imagined that the white man would name a prairie in his honor, he would have been doubly surprised—because in his time this basin was a vast lake. It was

7. *Displays in this building feature Indian artifacts and local ecology.*

also a lake when Hernando de Soto saw it about 1540, and there was water here when naturalist William Bartram visited the site in 1774. But the water has had a way of coming and going in this huge, saucerlike basin because of a sinkhole in one corner. From time to time the sink would fill with debris, and the water would rise and remain. Years later the sinkhole would become "unplugged," the water would drain away, and the area would revert to savanna. In 1892 a small steamer plying the lake was stranded when the water disappeared. Since then the basin has been a treeless prairie.

In 1970 some 18,000 acres here were purchased by the state, and preservation of the prairie and its historic function as a habitat for wildlife was assured. A program is now in operation to perpetuate the ecosystem that Bartram observed and recorded. American buffalo have been reintroduced, and efforts are being made to breed native scrub cattle similar to the Andalusian stock brought to Florida by Spanish settlers.

A fine panoramic view of the prairie can be enjoyed from a 50-foot observation tower. The birding is superb. A list of 215 species seen here is available at the visitor center. Also listed are 27 mammals, 41 reptiles, and 20 amphibians native to the area. An audiovisual program explains the purpose and scope of the activity here, and Indian artifacts are on display. The region was inhabited as early as 10,000

5. *Mounted color guard honors the flag of Confederates who won a battle here.*

B.C. A recreation area at Lake Wauberg and Sawgrass Pond is popular for picnicking, swimming, boating, and fishing. In addition, the preserve has several miles of riding trails and a corral. Buffalo and other wildlife are best seen during guided observation walks conducted on Saturdays from November through March. Tours are free but reservations are required. *Call (904) 466-3397. Open year-round.*

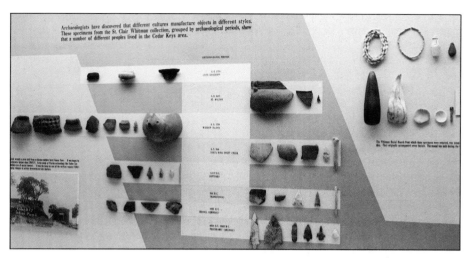

8. *Thoughtful presentation of its varied collections is a hallmark of this museum.*

8. Cedar Key State Museum. *Cedar Key.* Many small museums owe their existence to the energy and enthusiasm of just one individual, and this is an example. Much of the material here was assembled by the late Saint Clair Whitman, a dedicated naturalist, collector, and former resident of Cedar Key. Along with artifacts dating from 6000 B.C. to the colonial period, the museum houses a display of late 19th-century glassware, exhibits that chart local history, and Mr. Whitman's extensive collection of seashells.

Cedar Key has had its ups and downs. It was a bustling community in the 19th century and an important Confederate port during the Civil War. The lumbering industry boomed for a brief period, as did shipbuilding and associated activities. Today this is a quiet town to explore.

The museum documents the lumbering era in particular with an excellent collection of photographs and tools. Also on view: mementos of the fishing, oystering, and sponge industries, and the brushes and brooms of a palm fiber industry. The latter enterprise was swept away by the advent of plastics. *Open year-round. Admission charged.*

9. Marjorie Kinnan Rawlings State Historic Site. *Cross Creek. West on Rte. 325 from U.S. 301.* Readers of Mrs. Rawlings will recognize this setting as having pervaded much of her work. An unknown writer when she moved here in 1928, Mrs. Rawlings committed herself to this small, remote community and lived in poverty. Seven years passed before she sold her first story. But as the people and environs of Cross Creek fueled her creative fire, her reputation grew, and she eventually penned her most famous work, *The Yearling,* which won a Pulitzer Prize.

A typical Cracker homestead, designed for optimum cross-ventilation, the house consists of three clapboard units connected by porches and shaded by wide overhangs and the surrounding orange trees and magnolia. It is painted white with green trim and is modestly furnished. *Open year-round. Admission charged.*

9. *It was on this screened porch that Mrs. Rawlings did her writing. The manuscript in her old Royal typewriter is about the splendid isolation of her workplace.*

10. *This quiet setting of palms and grasses in the Black Point area is but one of the intriguing environments at Canaveral.*

10. Merritt Island National Wildlife Refuge and Canaveral National Seashore. The history of Merritt Island extends from prehistoric times to the space age. Inhabited by Indians since about 7000 B.C., the island in recent years has rocketed to renown as the site of the John F. Kennedy Space Center, with which the refuge and seashore share a border.

The seashore spans 13 miles of unspoiled golden sand between Apollo and Palyalinda beaches. You may hike this distance, stopping to swim and beachcomb, gathering such seashells as lightning whelks and angel wings. Other possibilities are shellfishing, crabbing, and surf casting for pompano, bluefish, and other species. Boating, canoeing, and fishing are also enjoyed at the adjacent Mosquito Lagoon. (Bring insect repellent.)

The refuge can be explored by car along two nature drives or by foot via two short hiking trails. Either way the range of wild-

life is stunning. Many of the 250 bird species that have been observed here make their nests on the refuge, including great blue and green herons, snowy egrets, turkey vultures, pie-billed grebes, and the rare anhingas and black skimmers. The refuge is also home to 19 endangered species, most notably the southern bald eagle and the brown pelican. Porpoises, manatees, and whales are occasionally glimpsed offshore, and the large tracks of sea turtles and other amphibians are frequently seen on the sands.

The Canaveral information center offers a slide show on the history of this tidal area and the wildlife it supports. Other programs include ranger-led weekend canoe trips for bird-watching, and excursions in June and July to watch the turtles nest and lay their eggs. *Open year-round.*

11. Fort Foster Historic Site. *U.S. Rte. 301, south of Zephyrhills.* The log fort and the wooden bridge spanning the Hillsborough River are reconstructions of the originals that were built here in 1836 during the Second Seminole War, said to be the most costly Indian war in U.S. history. The fort was to safeguard the bridge and thereby maintain communications along the Fort King Military Road from Tampa Bay to what is now Ocala. Twice the Seminoles attempted to burn the bridge and failed. The frontier bastion remained garrisoned until June 1838, and during the last few months its commander was Gen. Zachary Taylor, later the 12th U.S. president. The Second Seminole War officially ended in 1842, but seven years later the Seminoles threatened again, and the fort was briefly reactivated.

The fort may be visited only by one of the tours leaving hourly on weekends from adjacent Hillsborough River State

Park. A quarter-mile trip by van from the park's visitor center takes you to a shelter 900 feet from the site. From there you continue on foot along the old Fort King Military Road to the fort. Rangers in the uniforms of those 2nd Artillery soldiers who manned the fort in 1837 explain the events of that time and the life of the artillerymen posted there.

Hillsborough River State Park, which is noted for its beautiful, lush scenery, flanks 10 miles of riverfront, with some 3,000 acres of hardwood hammocks, pine flatwoods, and marsh. The river and its rapids attract fishermen, who catch bass, catfish, garfish, and other game fish. The park also has a swimming pond, a network of trails, and canoe rentals. *Historic site open weekends and major holidays; admission charged. Park open year-round.*

---

12. Bone Valley Museum. *Bradley.* The owner and curator of this museum, an amateur paleontologist, takes justifiable pride in his interesting assemblage of fossils. Most of the finds were unearthed in the Polk County phosphate deposits near the museum, and some date back before the age of man. They include giant barnacles 25 million years old, the cast of a skull

of a saber-toothed tiger, and the jaw of a mastodon, both of which grazed here 10 million years ago. A 150-pound leg bone confirms that a mammoth was also here.

Animated dioramas, murals, and three-dimensional models of various extinct animals—the three-toed sloth, saber-toothed tiger, and mastodon—help trace activity in the primeval environment of peninsular Florida and bring to life the moment of these animals on the stage of evolution. Among the other yields displayed here are petrified logs and Indian artifacts, including a 3,000-year-old dugout canoe. *Open year-round. Admission charged.*

---

13. Elliott Museum and Gilbert's Bar House of Refuge. *Hutchinson Island, Stuart.* These disparate museums are only about a five-minute drive apart, and both are worth seeing.

Among the fascinations at the Elliott Museum are the replicas of 19th-century shops—an ice cream parlor, tobacco and apothecary shops, shoe store, millinery, and a combination general store and post office—complete with display items and original fixtures. An elaborate four-ring toy circus with animals, performers, and even spectators will captivate children, as will a furnished dollhouse of the Revolutionary War period. Model trains, lead

soldiers, a collection of clocks and watches, classic automobiles, glassware, and Indian artifacts are some of the hundreds of other items to be admired.

These numerous theme exhibits reflect the interests of the late Harmon P. Elliott, who built the museum in memory of his father, Sterling. Both were prolific inventors; between them they obtained more than 220 patents. The father's knot-tying machine, patented in 1881, is one of the more intriguing innovations on view.

Named for the pirate Don Pedro Gilbert, who plagued this shore in the early 1800's, the Gilbert's Bar House of Refuge opened in 1876 and served until 1945 as a way station for seamen shipwrecked off the treacherous coastline here. Now completely restored and included in *The National Register of Historic Places*, the clapboard house contains some fine Victorian furniture and an array of antique nautical equipment, woodworking tools, and memorabilia. On display are such lifesaving devices as a Lyle gun, used to fire lines from shore to ship, and a breeches buoy. A surfboat recalls some of the hazards accepted by men who made sea rescues from this station. *Elliott Museum open P.M. daily; admission charged. House of Refuge open P.M. Tues.–Sun. except holidays; admission charged.*

13. The Elliott Museum faithfully recalls the nostalgic clutter of a country store. Reminders of dangerous shallows along this coastline are featured in the House of Refuge.

14. Corkscrew Swamp Sanctuary. Extending over an 11,000-acre wilderness of pine flatwoods, wet prairie, swampland, and typical hardwood hammocks, this haven for wildlife and native plants may be enjoyed on foot by means of an incredibly beautiful 1¾-mile-long boardwalk overhung by Spanish moss.

The sanctuary is the home of the nation's largest surviving stand of virgin bald cypress trees, many of which are now about 700 years old.

Among the many sights to be savored at close range are lettuce lakes, cypress knees, floating tussocks, water hemlock, ropes of strangler fig, ferns and lilies, brilliant hibiscus, royal palms, and various epiphytes (plants such as the tree-growing butterfly, cigar, and clamshell orchids that grow on other plants).

Cardinals, red-shouldered hawks, and rare birds known as limpkins are found here, and the country's largest colony of wood storks. There are also the familiar alligators, Florida water snakes, mosquito fish, and turtles.

A checklist of birds identified in recent sightings can be purchased, as can a 34-page booklet describing what you'll see on the self-guiding boardwalk tour. Displays in the visitor center include photos of the wildlife found in the swamp and a diorama of the ecological profile of a swamp. The sanctuary is managed by the National Audubon Society. *Open year-round.*

15. Collier-Seminole State Park. This 6,243-acre park is named for Barron Collier, an early settler in the area, and the Seminole Indians. Many Indians whose ancestors fought in the Second Seminole War still live in the area.

Self-guiding and conducted walks on the nature trail (nearly a mile long) reveal an interesting environment common to the coastal wilderness of Yucatán and the West Indies. Here too is the rare Florida royal palm with its distinctive lime-green upper trunk. The mangrove and cypress swamps, pine flatwoods, tidal creeks, and salt marshes shelter a broad range of wildlife. An observation platform permits an elevated view of ospreys, spoonbills, bald eagles, red-cockaded woodpeckers, wood storks, and other colorful birds. With patience and luck you might even glimpse the rare Florida panther, the Florida black bear, or the manatee, which are observed a few times a year.

Visitors may also explore the park on a 13½-mile round-trip canoe trail to the northernmost tip of the Ten Thousand Islands. The rivers and bays provide chances to fish for snook, mangrove snapper, and redfish.

A replica of an 1840's blockhouse serves as an interpretive center, with photo exhibits of native plants and animals and a review of Mr. Collier's achievements as a pioneering developer in the area. In the summer, campfire slide shows outline park activities. Canoes may be brought in or rented. A reminder: insects are a problem in summer. *Open year-round. Admission charged Dec.–May.*

16. Fakahatchee Strand State Preserve. A strand is a regional name for the long, narrow drainage channels, or sloughs, that develop in the mangrove swamps. The Fakahatchee is the largest of many such strands in the Big Cyprus Swamp.

This tract in southwest Florida, about 20 miles long and three to five miles wide, harbors some 44 species of orchids, the greatest such concentration in North America. One, the catopsis, is found only here. The preserve also contains the largest number of rare Florida palm trees, and the only known mix of bald cypresses and royal palms in the world.

In addition to bald eagles and American alligators, the strand is a home for mangrove fox squirrels, eastern indigo snakes, Everglades minks, black bears, and white-tailed deer. Infrequent sightings have been made of the rare wood stork and the fugitive Florida panther.

The preserve maintains a 2,000-foot boardwalk, seven miles to the west on U.S. Route 41; parking is limited to six cars. Booklets available from a box describe the highlights of the 19 suggested stops on the walkway, which is wide enough for wheelchairs.

A three-hour guided wade through swampland to see its rare plants can be arranged at the main office for parties of at least four; reservations must be made one week in advance. In January and February rangers also conduct canoe trips into the mangrove swamp and the estuary bordering the Ten Thousand Islands on the Gulf Coast. You can rent canoes or bring

14. *The boardwalk entering Corkscrew Swamp leads to the world of such fascinating creatures as the great blue heron.*

your own. Trips begin at 8:30 in the morning and usually last until late afternoon. *For guided-wade reservations, call (813) 695-4593. Open year-round.*

17. Biscayne National Park. *East of Leisure City, off U.S. Rte. 1.* This oceanic expanse of 175,000 acres encompasses the keys and living coral reefs of southern Biscayne Bay and is one of the largest marine preserves in the United States. The waters are turquoise and crystal clear, making it ideal for fishing, boating, snorkeling, scuba diving, and marine-gazing in general.

The obvious way to explore this watery paradise is by boat. Visitors can launch their own at Convoy Point, the mainland information center, or take one of the tours arranged there. A 1½-hour excursion in a glass-bottomed boat along the mangrove-fringed shoreline gives you a marvelously colorful view of the grassy seabeds and the shrimp, lobsters, green turtles, hawksbill turtles, sponges, and exotic tropical fish lurking there.

To savor the special appeal of a subtropical island, you can take a 50-foot excursion boat to Elliott Key seven miles offshore. The attractions here include a small swimming beach on the ocean side and the chance to snorkel or dive around living coral reefs. You can also stroll a boardwalk on a 1½-mile nature trail through a hardwood hammock and linger to enjoy an island sunset.

The visitor center on Elliott Key presents programs on the ecosystem of the wetlands and the plants and wildlife inhabiting them. At Convoy Information Center, exhibits similarly familiarize visitors with the local coral, sponges, and shellfish. Picnic tables with grills are located along the shore beside tree-high sea grapes and mahogany trees. Here you can watch brown pelicans, double-crested cormorants, white and blue herons, terns, and gulls seeking food offshore.

Bluefish, pompano, striped bass, and groupers are the fish most often snagged, but blue crabs and crayfish are also taken. Lobstering is not permitted: the preserve is a sanctuary for that prized shellfish. *To make reservations for a boat excursion call (305) 247-2400. Open year-round.*

18. *Ibis in the distant treetops overlook a waterscape typical of the Flamingo Area.*

18. Flamingo Area, Everglades National Park. Flamingo, on the shore of Florida Bay, is the center for sightseeing in the southern sector of the primeval Everglades. Visitors have their choice of foot trails, canoe trails, and privately operated cruises to take in the magical beauty of this environment.

Of the four walking trails suitable for families and children, Snake Bight Trail (four miles round-trip) is the most popular. You can walk it or ride the wilderness tram, which starts near the park ranger station. The trail unwinds beneath the umbrella of a hardwood forest inhabited by some 345 bird species and nearly 100 kinds of butterflies, including such rarities as the dingy purple wings, least Florida skippers, mimics, and byssus skippers.

Along with an interesting variety of amphibians and reptiles, the park is host to Seminole bats, nine-banded armadillos, black bears, Everglades minks, and bobcats. On the Rowdy Bend, Bear Lake, and Christian Point trails, you can see other facets of this unique ecological system.

Four cruises ply the local waterways, three of them along scenic Florida Bay, where at low tide you can expect to see brown pelicans, egrets, great blue herons, and other large birds scouting the shoreline for food. (The flamingo, however, is rarely seen.) For those more intrigued by the inland waterways and plant life, a pontoon boat makes sorties into the Everglades wilderness.

Canoeists can take any of five different trails. If time is no problem, you can tackle the 100-mile Wilderness Waterway, which takes you through the backcountry between Everglades City and Flamingo. Canoes, skiffs, outboard motors, pontoon boats, bicycles, and fishing gear may all be rented. Ranger-guided canoe tours can also be arranged. *For reservations call (813) 695-3101 no more than three days in advance. Open year-round. Admission charged.*

Michigan

Steeped in the history of mining and lumbering, the state is also influenced by the shoreline on three sides.

Note smaller scale in this portion of map.

SCALE IN MILES AND KILOMETERS
ONE INCH 58 MILES 0 5 10 20 30 40 50 60
ONE INCH 93 KM 0 5 10 20 30 50 70 96

The beaches and lighthouses featured here are reminders that the waters of three of the five Great Lakes wash the shores of Michigan. The early iron and copper mines and the lumber camps are recalled in a variety of museums and historic towns. Adaptive use of old buildings is exemplified in one historical museum in a former church whose stained glass windows are among the displays, and another in a handsome old public library. Nature lovers will not be disappointed in the variety of hiking trails, rivers and waterfalls, and a unique spring and garden.

1. Fort Wilkins Historic Complex and State Park. *Copper Harbor.*

When copper was discovered in Michigan's Upper Peninsula in 1841, that wild land suddenly loomed important enough to warrant military protection. In 1844 Fort Wilkins was built, and later on a lighthouse was put up as an aid to shipping. Today they vividly re-create the rigors and challenge of the age that made them.

Just outside Fort Wilkins are three log houses, once the quarters for married enlisted men. One house is furnished with a bearskin rug, a round table spread with Happy Families playing cards, a fireplace, and cozy domestic clutter. Within the stockade are 13 crisp white clapboard buildings. They include a bakery, fully equipped down to the barrels of flour and salt; a mess hall furnished with solid plank tables; the quartermaster's store, which sold both military and domestic items; and the sutler's store, where luxuries like champagne and peanuts were available.

In the company barracks, displays outline the history of the Upper Peninsula, from the discovery of copper and the United States–Chippewa Treaty of La Pointe, which opened the area to white settlement, to Fort Wilkins's eventual status as a state park.

The Copper Harbor lighthouse can be reached by ferry from the Copper Harbor marina mid-June through Labor Day. The 1866 lighthouse, with its keeper's dwelling, which replaced the original structure, is now refurbished as a museum and family home of the early 1900's. In the museum are several model ships, including the wooden side-wheeler *Sunbeam*, which sank off Eagle River in 1863.

Beyond the lighthouse is a rocky path to the tip of the point, where you can hear the sound of a bell buoy and enjoy the eroded shore and the small plants—labrador tea, cinquefoil, spruce, dwarf juniper, yellow-green lichen—clinging to the rocks. This is an idyllic place, well worth the ferry ride in its own right. *The ferry departs on the hour between 10:00 and 5:00, mid-June to Labor Day; book tickets in advance. Park and fort open daily year-round. Buildings open mid-May–mid-Oct.; admission charged.*

2. Coppertown U.S.A. and Old Red Jacket Downtown Historic District. *Calumet.*

By the early 1900's Calumet (formerly named Red Jacket) had become the principal trading town for the copper-mining communities of the Keweenaw Peninsula. It was rich, and part of its wealth went into its commercial and municipal buildings. Today the Old Red Jacket Downtown Historic District is a fascinating, nostalgic, and slightly melancholy place, best seen on foot with the help of an excellent brochure that's available at the mining museum, Coppertown U.S.A. Among the highlights are the frontier Gothic St. Anne's Church and the rococo Red Jacket Town Hall and Opera House.

Coppertown U.S.A. portrays the history and culture of Keweenaw Peninsula as one of the world's prime copper-producing regions. Exhibits include mining tools, heavy equipment, replicas of a mine captain's office, the 1915 Mohawk grade school, and a surgery. The surgery has mannequins of a nurse and patient and a collection of orthopedic devices—metal legs, hands, back braces, and so on—that are grim but pertinent reminders of the dangerous work of miners.

Railroad memorabilia include a pump handcar and a four-man gas-driven railcar. Outside is the Russell snowplow locomotive, whose plow is almost as high as a

1. *Canada geese take their ease at Lake Fanny Hooe in Fort Wilkins State Park.*

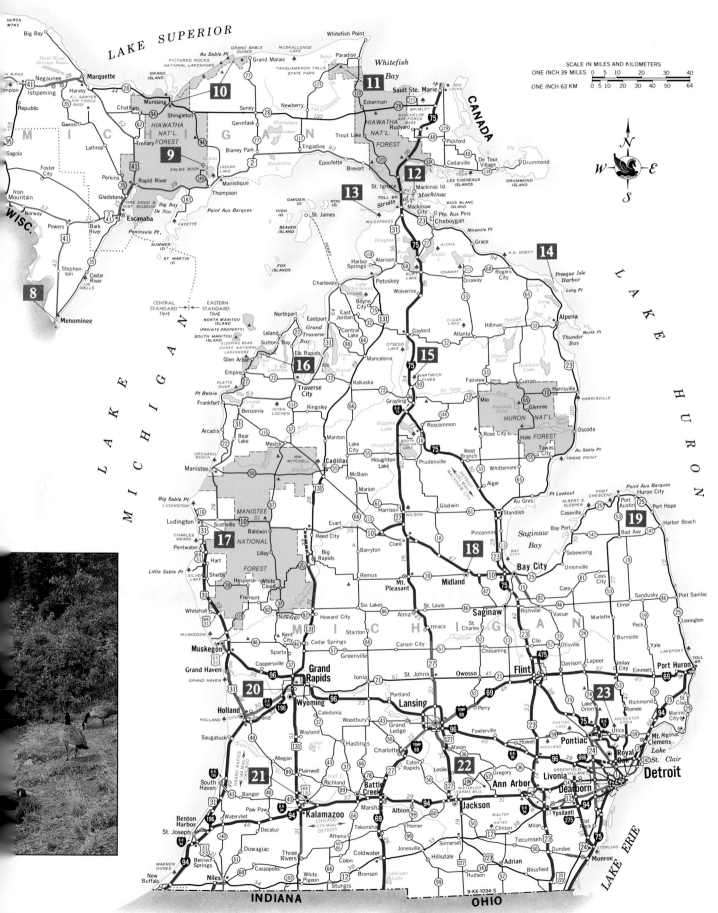

LAKE SUPERIOR

HURON MTNS.

Big Bay

Dead River Storage Basin

N RIPER

Negaunee   28   Marquette

Ishpeming   41

mpion   Harvey   K.I. SAWYER AIR FORCE BASE

Republic   35   ChatHam   Munising   Shingleton

35   Gwinn   FOREST   94

Lathrop   67   Seney   Newberry

Foster City   52   Trenary   Blaney Park   2

Iron Mountain   41   Perkins   Rapid River   149   Manistique

Norway   32   Gladstone   35   39   Thompson

Powers   21   2   41   Bark River   Escanaba

Stephenson   35   ORE DOCK & HIST. MUSEUM   Big Bay De Noc

Cedar River   J.W. WELLS   Fayette

Menominee   Point Aux Barques

10

GRAND SABLE DUNES   MUSKALLONGE LAKE   Whitefish Point

Au Sable Pt   Grand Marais   Paradise   Whitefish

PICTURED ROCKS NATIONAL LAKESHORE   TAHQUAMENON FALLS STATE PARK   Bay

GRAND ISLAND   77   123

11

Germfask   Eckerman   28   221   Sault Ste. Marie   SOO LOCKS

HIAWATHA NAT'L.   117   Trout Lake   KINCHELOE AIR FORCE BASE   75   48   Pickford

9   Engadine   FOREST   123   134   Cedarville   De Tour Village   Drummond

PALMS BOOK   INDIAN LAKE   Epoufette   Brevort   St. Ignace   MACKINAC Id.   LES CHENEAUX ISLANDS   DRUMMOND ISLAND

13   TOLL BR.   Mackinaw City   BOIS BLANC ISLAND

GARDEN ID.   12   Straits of Mackinac   Pte. Aux Pins   Cheboygan

HOG ID.   31   23

HIGH ID.   St. James   WILDERNESS   Ninemile Pt.

BEAVER ISLAND   75   27   Grace   P.H. HOEFT   Presque Isle Harbor   Long Pt.

FOX ISLANDS   Harbor Springs   68   ALOHA   14   Long L.

Charlevoix   Petoskey   ONAWAY   Onaway   Rogers City   65

Lake Charlevoix   Wolverine   33   68   Presque Isle Harbor

Northport   East Jordan   Boyne City   CLEAR LAKE   Hillman   Thunder Bay   Alpena

Leland   GRAND TRAVERSE BAY   Central Lake   Gaylord   Atlanta   North Pt.   Thunder Bay

Suttons Bay   31   Mancelona   15   OTSEGO LAKE   FLETCHER POND   HUBBARD LAKE   23

Glen Arbor   Elk Rapids   16   Torch L.   Fairview   Curran   Harrisville

Empire   72   Kalkaska   HARTWICK PINES   Mio   65   Glennie   HARRISVILLE

SLEEPING BEAR DUNES NATIONAL LAKESHORE   Traverse City   34   93   Grayling   144   BAMFIELD POND   HURON   Oscoda

Pt Betsie   Kingsley   72   Roscommon   Rose City L.   NAT'L   Au Sable Pt.

Frankfort   Benzonia   113   Higgins Lake   18   West Branch   Hale   FOREST   Tawas City   TAWAS POINT

Arcadia   31   INTERLOCHEN   Houghton Lake   75   Whittemore   65

22   Bear Lake   Manton   Lake City   Prudenville   Alger   Au Gres

Meslick   WM. MITCHELL   55   McBain   Gladwin   Standish   Pt Lookout

Manistee   LUDINGTON   131   Marion   61   Harrison   61   ALBERT E. SLEEPER   Port Austin   Huron City   Point Aux Barques

Big Sable Pt   29   MANISTEE   37   Evart   Clare   Pinconning   Caseville   PORT CRESCENT   142   Port Hope

Ludington   116   Scottville   10   Baldwin   Reed City   115   10   27   Wilson   18   Saginaw Bay   25   Bad Axe   19   Harbor Beach

CHARLES MEARS   31   17   NATIONAL   Lilley   Big Rapids   Barryton   Bay Port   142

Pentwater   Hart   FOREST   Remus   Mt. Pleasant   20   Midland   75   Unionville   19   Sandusky   46   Port Sanilac

Little Sable Pt   SILVER LAKE   Shelby   Hesperia   White Cloud   Six Lakes   Alma   St. Louis   Saginaw   Caro   53   Elmer   25

20   Fremont   Newaygo   Howard City   Stanton   Ithaca   St. Charles   Richville   81   Cass City   Marlette   Peck   Lexington

Whitehall   82   131   Cedar Springs   Carson City   57   Chesaning   23   Clio   Otisville   24   Burnside   Yale   LAKEPORT

MUSKEGON   Kent City   Sparta   46   Greenville   66   57   475   Davison   Lapeer   37   Imlay City   Port Huron

Muskegon   Coopersville   37   Ionia   21   St. Johns   Owosso   45   Flint   Emmett   69   TOLL BR.

Grand Haven   96   Grand Rapids   Portland   20   Perry   69   33   Lake Orion   Richmond   St. Clair   29

20   Wyoming   96   Lansing   TEMP 69   96   Fowlerville   Howell   59   Pontiac   Romeo   Marine City

Holland   196   Caledonia   Grand Ledge   127   Mason   48   Highland   696   Utica   Mt. Algonac

Saugatuck   40   Wayland   Woodbury   43   Charlotte   TEMP 69   Leslie   Gregory   106   Ann Arbor   Livonia   96   Royal Oak   St. Clair

21   Allegan   Plainwell   Hastings   78   Eaton Rapids   127   WATERLOO FARMS MUS.   Dearborn   Detroit   102

South Haven   43   131   Richland   89   Marshall   27   Homer   94   Jackson   WALTER J. HAYES   Ypsilanti   12   75

Bangor   40   Paw Paw   Gull L.   Battle Creek   Albion   60   19   Clinton   Milan   23   Flat Rock

Benton Harbor   195   Watervliet   94   Kalamazoo   66   69   Tekonsha   Jonesville   Somerset   Tecumseh   50   Dundee   24   STERLING

St. Joseph   46   Decatur   31   Athens   CHICAGO   Coldwater   Hillsdale   223   Adrian   Blissfield   223   Monroe   75

WARREN DUNES   140   Dowagiac   Three Rivers   Colon   223   Hudson   52

New Buffalo   94   Berrien Springs   51   Cassopolis   66   White Pigeon   12   Bronson   99

Niles   60   103   Sturgis   9-KX-1034-S

INDIANA   OHIO

LAKE ERIE

LAKE HURON

LAKE MICHIGAN

MICHIGAN

WISC.

CANADA

CENTRAL STANDARD TIME   EASTERN STANDARD TIME

8

23

22

19

18

17

SCALE IN MILES AND KILOMETERS

ONE INCH 39 MILES   0 5 10   20   30   40

ONE INCH 63 KM   0 5 10 20   30   40   50   64

N
W   E
S

house. But the museum's most unusual collection is perhaps the wooden pattern-shop models of cogs, valves, drive wheels, and other machine parts, which have a fine sculptural quality. *Open Mon.–Fri. year-round. Admission charged for museum.*

---

3. Little Girls Point County Park. *County Rd. 505.* The point is named in memory of a Chippewa girl who drowned here long ago. The sandy beach is very pebbly at the waterline, and the water is too cold for swimming until August. But swimming is not this park's main attraction.

The beach is celebrated for the agates that can easily be found among the waterline pebbles. Look for those with a translucent quality. They are most often white but can be other colors as well. A visit to the nearby agate shop will give beginning agate hunters a good idea of what to look for. When polished, the stones are remarkably transformed, frequently revealing veins and pockets of a second and third color—the result of impurities. Besides agates, there are attractive pebbles of all kinds and colors here—pink, gray, yellow, green, liver-colored, flecked with blue, red, and gold—most smooth and symmetrical, shaped by Lake Superior's stormy waters. *Open year-round.*

---

4. Lake Gogebic State Park. The park lies on the western shore of 15,000-acre Lake Gogebic (famous for its walleye and perch fishing) and is hemmed in by the Ottawa National Forest. For nonboaters and nonanglers there's a pleasant woodland trail, with a guide brochure and numbered points of interest; it passes through a northern evergreen swamp and forest of hemlock and spruce, fir and maple, past glacially deposited boulders and abundant signs of bird and animal life. The brochure notes that hungry deer do a good deal of plant pruning here in winter. You will see the evidence. The park offers a modern campground, a splendid swimming beach, play areas, and excellent snowmobile trails. *Open year-round. Admission charged.*

5. Agate Falls. The short trail to the falls begins in the Joseph F. Oravec Roadside Park on the south side of Route 28, passes under the highway, and then continues through woods above the broad Middle Branch of the Ontonagon River. At a point opposite a flat-topped rock above the falls you can either sit to rest on the massive roots of a white pine or, with a little care and agility, climb onto the rock for a much better view of the tumbling spate of lacy water.

But the best view of the falls is attained only by way of a not-quite-sheer scramble down an earthen bank with crumbling rock "steps" and slippery roots and a few necessary handholds. This route (dangerous in wet weather) leads to a ledge from which one has a fine view of the first plunge of the falls—enchanting even in the dry season—and a view of a second plunge that is not visible from above. Keep in mind that care and agility are indeed required for this part of the trail.

---

6. Iron County Museum. *Caspian.* This is an exemplary museum of mining, lumbering, and everyday life in Iron County. It occupies the former site of the Caspian Mine, and the gaunt old headframe, built in 1921, presides over the site like a somber guardian of times gone by.

In the onetime enginehouse is the Mining Hall, where ingenious maps using glass to indicate different levels dramatically convey the immense labor and skill of the old miners.

In the Lumbering Hall is the Monigal Miniature Logging Camp, said to be the largest of its kind in the world. It contains over 2,000 items, hand-carved from cedar telegraph poles over a period of eight years by William Monigal after he had a sawmill accident in 1931. It's an astonishing piece of work, full of vigor, color, and information and worth a visit in its own right. Among other exhibits are fine photographs, including one of a 20-sled logging train carrying a 900-ton load.

The Main Exhibition Hall houses numerous other exhibits, among them the Pioneer Hall (with oilpaper maps and surveying instruments), the Athletics Hall (note the photograph of the girls' 1911 basketball team), and the Pioneer Home. The Village Green, an extensive section of the exhibition hall, contains authentic

re-creations of local craft and trade shops. MacDonell's Blacksmith's Shop, for instance, has been rebuilt with the original timbers, bricks, and tools; even the ashes in the forge are original. Professor Faverio's Studio celebrates the area's heritage of Finnish, Swedish, and Croatian music.

On the grounds of the museum are the Transportation, Mining, and Farm complexes and the Logging Camp, all showing relevant tools and equipment. *Open Mon.–Fri. and P.M. Sun. Memorial Day–Sept. Admission charged.*

---

7. Menominee Range Historical Foundation Museum. *Iron Mountain.* The museum is housed in the old Carnegie Public Library, a distinguished neoclassical stone structure, built in 1901, with a massive porch and second-floor balcony. At the entrance is a reproduction of an old general store packed with goods of the late 19th century. There are exhibits of pioneer settlers, a diorama of Menominee Indians, and replicas of a trapper's cabin and a trading post. The cabin looks authentically uncomfortable; the trading post has whiskey and rum, bear grease and honey, knives, snowshoes, and bolts of cloth. Among the other displays are a saddle shop and memorabilia of one of Iron Mountain's professional itinerants, Foo-Foo the clown. Other occupations are detailed in exhibits of period office, banking, and brewing environments.

The passage of time and its ravages are also represented. A watchmaker's shop is complete with workbench and tools. A dentist's ledger shows that in May 1925 Harry Nead was charged $1 for an extraction. The optician has an eye-test chart for nonreaders. The reconstruction of a barbershop is endowed with a chair that looks as if it might easily be converted for electrocution. And the Morely Folding Bath Tub (1885) provided a convenience for cramped quarters at home. *Open Mon.–Sat. and P.M. Sun. June–mid-Oct.*

---

8. Menominee County Historical Museum. *Menominee.* The museum celebrates the spectrum of life in Menominee County from the earliest periods of Indian settlement to World War II, with emphasis on the mid-19th and early 20th centuries. The collections are housed in a former church, built in 1921 and notable for its stained glass windows.

10. *Primary colors—blue water over the yellow sandstone—create the lovely green.*

bling miniature volcanoes. Looking down on them and the contoured slopes of the springbed is similar to looking at a false color satellite photograph of the earth.

Large, slow brown trout cruise the pond, hemlock and arborvitae surround it, ducks and seagulls paddle its periphery. The outflow is a shallow, bubbling river. *Open year-round. Admission charged.*

---

10. Pictured Rocks National Lakeshore. *Munising.* The park is 40 spectacular miles long and no more than three miles wide; the Lakeshore Trail runs its length from the visitor center at Munising to Sable Falls; several roads run north into the park from Route H58.

Miners Castle Overlook, reached via Miners Castle Road, gives stunning views of a smoothly curved inlet of white cliffs above a submarine outcrop of yellow sandstone; the offshore water of Lake Superior is intensely blue, but above the yellow lakebed it becomes a rim of vivid green, and the shorescape is banded with white and yellow cliffs and green and blue water. At the northern tip of the inlet is Miners Castle, a double crag of cliff carved by erosion into the semblance of a medieval castle.

A side road from Miners Castle Road goes to Miners Falls, a high and narrow plummet between two massive cliffs; at their base are swirl holes, and the nearer face has been scooped out by erosion.

Three campgrounds in the park are accessible by car: at Little Beaver Lake, Twelvemile Beach, and Hurricane River. From Little Beaver Lake it's a short walk to Beaver Lake and the Lakeshore Trail. The campground at Twelvemile Beach provides access to an unbroken stretch of white sand. From Hurricane River one can walk (1½ miles) to the 1874 lighthouse at Au Sable Point, and beyond that to a 500-foot wooden log slide and the Grand Sable Banks and Dunes area.

Along the Lakeshore Trail there are 13 backcountry campgrounds. Scuba divers are catered to along the shore by the Alger Underwater Preserve. Late summer provides magnificent weather, but the park is also beautiful in winter and perfect for snowshoeing. *Open year-round.*

Menominee is named for a tribe of Indians whose name meant "wild rice," and the county's Indian heritage is displayed in stone and copper weapons, beadwork, and a dugout canoe said to be more than 1,000 years old, found buried in sand at the mouth of the Cedar River.

Menominee is in lumber country, and the museum has good photographs of logging camps, river drives, and timber trains, as well as a variety of lumbering tools. There are also re-creations of a law office, a photographer's studio, a cobbler's workshop, a music store, a railroad ticket office, and a dentist's surgery. Law and order are represented by leg-irons, handcuffs, a ball and chain, and early types of police radar.

A series of convincing tableaux indicates early-day home decor. Note the lampshade made from a mandarin's coat, sent by a young woman then living in Shanghai to her mother in Menominee— and the notice of its reception in the local

newspaper. In such details the museum gives local history a human face. *Open Mon.–Sat. and P.M. Sun. May–Labor Day; by appointment Sept.–Oct. Call (906)863-8465 or 863-6975.*

---

9. Big Springs–Palms Book State Park. *Manistique.* Here is a wide pool of eerily clear green water, 45 feet deep, fed by a cluster of springs flowing at a rate of 16,000 gallons per minute. The flow is such that the water never has time to freeze in winter or warm up in summer— it's always a steady 45°F.

One views the Big Spring (Michigan's largest) through observation holes in a raft that one personally hauls across the pond and back again by means of a cable. The sides of the pool are steep and white, delicately streaked with drifts of darker clay or sand. Bleached logs lie under the water like massive bones, and the several springs belch plumes of white silt resem-

11. Tahquamenon Falls State Park. The 36,000-acre park has three developed sections: the Upper Falls, the Lower Falls, and the Rivermouth unit.

The Upper Falls are among the largest east of the Mississippi and are most easily approached by way of the Brink stairs, an elaborate series of observation decks and steps that take one to river level. The 200-foot-wide lip of the falls, about 50 feet high, is a shallow S curve of ancient sandstone over which the soft brown Tahquamenon water, stained by its passage through cedar and hemlock swamps, pours at a rate of up to 50,000 gallons per second. The Gorge stairs downstream are steeper, longer, and offer less intimate but more comprehensive views.

The Lower Falls, actually a series of falls, lie on either side of an island (reached by renting a rowboat) and are seen either from there or from an easily walked half-mile trail that offers close-up views of the water boiling and fuming over the shallow falls. There are strong currents, undertows, whirlpools, and floating debris here, and understandably, swimming is forbidden.

The Rivermouth section of the park offers two campgrounds, swimming facilities, and boat access to Lake Superior's Whitefish Bay. A number of trails thread through the thick forest, the habitat of deer and bear, and they touch the river at several points. The Tahquamenon, which means "Marsh of the Blueberries," plays a part in the lore of Hiawatha. *Open year-round. Admission charged.*

---

12. Mackinac Island State Park. Fort Mackinac, the most important site in the park, occupies the crest of a hill overlooking the harbor and the charming old town. Within its stockade the original buildings re-create with the greatest fidelity the history of the fort and island, and life here during the 1860's and 1870's.

In the commissary, dioramas portray episodes in the War of 1812: the capture of the island by the British and their 350 Huron allies, the subsequent blockade by two American ships, and their capture by British boarding parties.

The island's nonmilitary history is recorded too: the curious story of Dr. Samuel Beaumont's pioneering experiments on the human digestive system, the lives of such sturdy Mackinac women as Madeleine La Framboise, who ran a trading post at Grand River, and Mrs. Bertha Palmer, "the undisputed queen of Chicago society," who graced the opening of the Grand Hotel during the island's most glamorous years as a resort. Other buildings vividly re-create the life of soldiers and officers here.

No motorized vehicles are allowed on the island, so if you want to travel extensively you walk, bring or rent a bicycle, take a guided tour in a horse-drawn carriage, or rent your own saddle horse at the Chambers Riding Stable on Market Street. The park also has hiking trails in the woodlands. *Park open year-round. Fort open late May–mid-Oct. Other buildings open June 15–Labor Day. Admission charged for fort includes admission to several nearby historic sites.*

---

13. Wilderness State Park. In general, the park lives up to its name: the woods are too thick for casual sightseeing, the beaches too pebbly, the lake water too cold for comfortable beach lounging or swimming; and much of the open terrain is too swampy for walking. The virtue of all this is that those who enjoy nature in its unmodified state will find this a rewarding place to be. The park lies on a peninsula of thick woodlands, marsh, and beaches. A dirt road leads from the campground and visitor center through woods toward the end of the peninsula; side roads lead from this central axis to beach and swamp areas on Sturgeon Bay and the southern side of the Straits of Mackinac.

The beaches are a mixture of sand and pebbles. The pebbles predominate at the waterline, and the lake-surge makes them rumble like distant thunder. The vegetation is patchy and dunelike near the water, and marshy with reedbeds near the inland woods. At its furthest point the road reaches a marsh-meadow with a view of Sturgeon Bay to the south and woods to the north and west. There is no way to cross the marsh except by boat or by wearing waders. (This is a favorite place for catching smallmouth bass.) No dogs are allowed in this area from May 1 to August 31 lest they disturb the endangered piping plovers that nest here during that season. Wood ducks, pintails, great horned owls, and pileated woodpeckers are also around. Information about the pleasant nature trails in the park is available at headquarters. *Open year-round.*

---

14. Old Lighthouse and Museum. *Presque Isle.* One hundred and fifty years ago, Presque Isle had the finest harbor in

12. Even a more forbidding cannon could not diminish the peaceful aspect of the town.

the Great Lakes, a cove protected from Lake Huron's fierce weather by headlands to the north and south. A busy port grew up there, and in 1838 $5,000 was appropriated from federal funds to build a lighthouse. In 1840 the light was lit, and for the next 30 years it served as a beacon to mariners up and down the coast.

In 1870 a taller lighthouse began service just a mile north, and the old light was left to weather the storms of time as best it might. Its four-foot-thick walls of hand-cut stone proved durable, and so did the keeper's small cottage. In the early 1900's the property passed into private hands and was gradually restored.

Today the cottage houses a museum crammed with curios, as a place on a trade route should be: a wine cabinet with hand-blown bottles, a crab-shaped incense burner, a saucy Indian statuette; best of all, one is urged to handle things, whether the torpedo-boat binnacle or the elephant trainer's hooked stick.

At the foot of the lighthouse is a bronze bell from Lansing city hall's old clock tower. It weighs 3,425 pounds, more than half as much again as the Liberty Bell, and you can make it ring out over the bay by pulling the bell hammer. You can also climb the hand-chiseled spiral stone staircase in the lighthouse to the catwalk for a fine view of the bay and of the garden with its cannon. *Open daily May 15–Oct. 15. Admission charged.*

---

15. Hartwick Pines State Park. When the first loggers came to Michigan, they found white pines of amazing size in the virgin woods. Legend has it that there were trees more than twice as high as those you'll see in Hartwick Pines State Park. These giants are remarkable in their own right. They tower more than 140 feet above the forest floor, each green pinnacle seeming to sway in the breeze to its own rhythm, as if the trees had acquired with age a kind of independence from the common wind. It's cool and shady in the forest, even on a hot day, and pleasant too, because the canopy of foliage limits the undergrowth.

Along the Virgin Pines Foot Trail is the reconstruction of a lumber camp that includes a camp store, a blacksmith's and carpenter's shop, a bunkhouse, cabin quarters for a married foreman, and the camp messroom, where the prodigious

16. *The Lake Michigan shoreline near Empire Bluff is prime territory for beachcombers.*

amount of food required to keep the loggers going is documented.

The interpretive center gives an excellent overview of lumbering during Michigan's white pine era, from 1840 to 1910. Perhaps the most intriguing exhibits are those describing the Shay locomotive. Patented in 1887 by William Ephraim Shay, it was designed to work in terrain impossible for conventional engines. It had flexible drive shafts, and if necessary could run on poles instead of rails. *Open year-round. Admission charged.*

---

16. Sleeping Bear Dunes National Lakeshore. The most spectacular feature of this spectacularly beautiful 71,000-acre park on the Lake Michigan shoreline is the Sleeping Bear Dunes area, readily seen from the 7.6-mile Pierce Stocking Scenic Drive, which overlooks South and North Manitou islands and the wonderfully complex unfoldings of wooded bays and headlands along the shore. At sunset, when the weather is calm, the lake, seen from the height of the dunes, is silvery, finely textured by small waves, and traced over by currents and windrows. The views inland, to the east, of ridges, val-

leys, and lakes, are hardly less beautiful. The drive is closed to all trailers and to motor homes more than 24 feet long.

A nine-mile hiking trail also crosses the dunes; it's easy to get lost here, and no drinking water is available. At Glen Lake, just west of the dune area, there are swimming and picnicking facilities. In the village of Glen Haven is the Coast Guard Station/Maritime Museum, which shows memorabilia of shipping on the Great Lakes and in particular along this shoal-ridden part of Lake Michigan.

In addition to the dunes section the park includes the Platte Bay and Pyramid Point sections to the north and south and North and South Manitou islands. Canoe rentals are available at the Platte River campground, and there are foot trails. In the Pyramid Point section there is a trail to Pyramid Point and beach access and picnicking at Good Harbor Bay. Both South Manitou Island (which has backcountry campgrounds) and the primitive wilderness of North Manitou Island can be reached mid-spring to mid-fall by a ferry from Leland. *Park open year-round. Pierce Stocking Scenic Drive open May–Nov., road conditions permitting.*

---

17. White Pine Village. *Ludington.* An extensive reconstruction of a small Michigan town in the late 1800's, the buildings are set in carefully tended grounds and are all authentically furnished.

The Abe Nelson Blacksmith Shop, for example, has a working smithy; Cole's General Store has an intriguing stock of goods, a countertop extended to accommodate hoopskirts, and a green pagoda-like tea chest painted with Oriental scenes.

Dwellings include the Quevillon trapper's cabin, built before 1850, where a hand-colored photograph of a severe-looking Catherine Quevillon presides over a single bed strewn with animal skins. The Burns farmhouse, built around 1880, is one of the most detailed reconstructions. In the kitchen is an elaborate flour and spice cabinet (The Portable Tin Pantry), in the dining room a portable home altar, and in the drawing room a 100-year-old Regina Music Machine that plays perforated metal discs and still produces a tuneful, mellow sound.

In the Abe Nelson Lumbering Museum are mementos of the old lumber camps, including excellent models of ox- and horse-drawn lumber wagons and good collections of lumbering tools, cowbells, and railroad lamps.

The Mason County Courthouse was built in 1849 from lake driftwood (lumber broken away from log booms) and is still on its original site. *Open daily Memorial Day–Labor Day. Admission charged.*

---

18. Dow Gardens. *Corner of Eastman and W. St. Andrews, Midland.* The gardens were developed in 1899 by Dr. Herbert Dow, founder of the Dow Chemical Corporation. They include massed plantings of annuals and perennials; a necklace of ponds; and collections of flowering crab apples, roses, rhododendrons, viburnums, junipers, and herbs.

Plantings are changed regularly; one can always expect to find the circular herb garden, for example, set with an intriguing variety of such plants as salad burnet, comfrey, scented geraniums, and nasturtiums. This and the three beds nearby, with candytuft, statice, heliotrope, strawflowers, carnations, and stock, are the sweetest-smelling part of the gardens—along with the rosebeds, with their superb show of All-American Selection winners.

Other attractions include the formal gardens; several magnificent old willow

18. *The water lilies and the shaded glen beyond are reminiscent of paintings by Monet.*

trees; the greenhouse full of bedding plants; the maze, shady and thickly planted with ground cover; and the rockery of dwarf evergreens near the entrance. *Open year-round except Thanksgiving Day, Christmas, and New Year's Day.*

---

19. Huron City Museums. *7930 Huron City Rd., Port Austin.* Huron City was founded in the 1850's by lumberman Langdon Hubbard; it prospered, suffered two major fires, and finally declined when its wells went dry. Today it's a museum town that reconstructs life here in the latter part of the 19th century.

Dogcarts, sleighs, and coaches are displayed in the carriage house. In Langdon Hubbard's barn is a collection of farm equipment that includes a forerunner of the forklift: a pulley-driven haybuck.

The ground floor of the Community House Inn (1877) is furnished in the busy style of the Victorian period, and the general store is provisioned with goods from toys to tea chests.

One of the most interesting buildings is the Point Aux Barques Life Saving Station, built in 1876 and moved here from its original site. Its lifeboat, which once saved 200 lives in a single mission, is on display in the Wreck Room.

Also worth seeing is the large, airy Huron City Church, where as many as 1,000 used to gather to hear the sermons of William Lyon Phelps, a Yale professor and one of the notable literary figures of his day. The William Lyon Phelps Museum contains his desk (made from a grand pi-

ano), a display of Staffordshire pottery, albums of calling cards, and other memorabilia. *Open Wed.–Mon., July 1–Labor Day. Admission charged.*

---

20. Blandford Nature Center. *Grand Rapids. From U.S. 131 take the Leonard St. exit, go west on Leonard and right on Hillburn.* The most unusual and appealing thing here is the animal hospital at the visitor center, where some of the patients are let out of their cages when they're on the mend. One of these is a perfectly healthy great horned owl, which made the

20. *Closeup of the Michigan lily proves the camera to be a means of seeing more.*

mistake when it was young of attacking a porcupine. Brought into the hospital, it recovered, but lost its nerve for hunting; so it now lives there, and if you do a passable owl-hoot imitation, it will answer.

There are several short trails in the center, including a 1½-mile cross-country ski trail, a half-mile pioneer plant trail, and a trail for "the perceptually handicapped." The Woodland Loop Trail passes through a forest of oak, beech, sugar maple, white ash, tulip, dogwood, and black cherry trees alongside Brandywine Creek, through secondary woodland, and through old meadow now slowly reverting to woods. The center's working farm is an especially good place for children. There are likely to be calves in the barn, a brooder of chickens, pens with goats, horses, sheep, and rabbits. With permission, children can help with simple farm chores. *Farm and grounds open year-round; visitor center open Mon.–Fri. and P.M. Sun.*

21. Kalamazoo Nature Center. *Kalamazoo. From I-94 take Exit 76 and go north on Westnedge; from U.S. 131 exit D Ave. east, then south on Westnedge.* This imaginative and attractive site includes an interpretive center, an arboretum and botanical garden, a farm, a period homestead, and nature trails. Learning can be fun here, and it's a fine place to take children.

The Sun and Rain Room in the interpretive center stretches from the basement to the glass roof and re-creates the environment needed by many exotic plants, with 600 tons of rock serving as the thermal mass in the naturalistic landscape.

A walkway spirals past this jungle to the basement, where there are displays of living snakes, fish, turtles, toads, a crow, and a screech owl.

The Growing Place is a greenhouse with orchids, cactus, an earthworm display, and suggestions for success with houseplants. Glen Vista Living Exhibit is a picture window on a tract of woodland; microphones bring wild sounds into the building, and remote sensors give indoor readings of temperatures at different levels of the wood. Outside the center are cages for predatory birds and access to the Beechwood and Marsh trails.

The young trees in the arboretum are spaciously set in a large meadow, which also includes the botanical garden, featuring rhododendrons, junipers, and plants adapted to arid conditions. Nearby is the

21. The girl in blue reveals a moment of rapture with her fuzzy yellow duckling.

Family Farm, with pettable horses, cows, pigs, goats, and sheep.

Just south of the center is the Delano Homestead. Built by a prosperous farmer in 1858, the main house and several outbuildings have been restored and furnished with period pieces. From the hand-painted stencils on the sitting room walls to the bed-warming stones in the upstairs bedrooms, the homestead vividly evokes farm life in the mid-19th century.

There are no picnic facilities, but carry-in lunches may be eaten on the grounds at designated spots. *Nature Center open Mon.–Sat. and P.M. Sun., Memorial Day, July 4, and Labor Day. Closed the two weeks after Labor Day and on Thanksgiving Day and Christmas. Delano Homestead open P.M. weekends. Admission charged.*

22. Waterloo Farm Museum. *Waterloo. Off Rte. 52.* This is a small but attractive and well-maintained mid-19th-century farm outside the peaceful village of Waterloo. The brick farmhouse was built in 1846–47 with decorative panels of fieldstone in the fashion then popular with German-American builders.

The kitchen pantry has an ingenious cabinet that forms a dividing wall with drawers accessible from the dining room.

The dining room itself, with rag rugs, wood stove, tea-leaf-pattern china, and a kerosene lamp with a painted glass shade, has an aura of period charm.

The parlor was kept for special occasions and used to display prized possessions: a horsehair settee, an arrangement of dried fruit in a big black oval frame, a piano, tables hung with heavy fringed cloths, and a curio/china stand.

Upstairs are a children's toy room with clothing and toys of the period, a bedroom with a trundle bed, and a device for tightening the ropes supporting the mattress so that one could "sleep tight."

The outbuildings include a granary, blacksmith's shop, barn, log cabin, windmill, and bakehouse. The blacksmith's shop has a full complement of tools, including a wheel-rimming machine. On Pioneer Day (the second Sunday in October) cookies are baked in a brick oven, and old-time crafts, including blacksmithing, are practiced. *Open P.M. Tues.–Sun., June–Aug.; P.M. weekends Sept.; second Sun. in Oct.; and first weekend in Dec. Admission charged.*

23. Rochester–Utica Recreation Area. There are actually two areas to explore here, the Utica and the Bloomer No. 2 units. The Utica Unit, signed on Rte. 59, has a picnic area close to the road, shooting ranges, and a foot trail.

The Bloomer No. 2 Unit on Bloomer Road is more pleasant and has two picnic spots. The first is by the bend of a stream and well shaded by willow and apple trees. However, this too is close to the road. The second and larger picnic area, with a shelter, is more secluded; nearby are horseshoe pits, slides, swings, and volleyball nets. Cross-country skiing is allowed, and equipment can be rented at the picnic shelter.

At the western end of the parking lot is a trail that leads down a wooded hill to what remains of the Clinton-Kalamazoo Canal, which would have connected Lake St. Clair with Lake Michigan if the money hadn't run out when the waterway got to Bloomer. Look for a canallike stretch of water covered with duckweed and the remains of a stone embankment, now half overgrown, near the Clinton River. *Open year-round. Admission charged.*

Ohio

The thousands of years represented by the attractions here are supplemented by the intriguing diversity of the subject matter.

The evidence of their art, pottery, mounds, and elaborate burial rituals confirms that advanced peoples lived here some 2,000 years ago. How incredulous those Indians would be to know that near their tribal lands would be born a man who would walk on the moon.

More believable, but nevertheless exciting in its time, was the iron horse, and a local museum exemplifies the caring relationship between a town and its railroad. The past is also recalled in the iron smelters, glassworks, potteries, and museums of midwestern America and the birthplaces of two United States presidents. A special treat is the amazing handiwork of a fabulous wood-carver who was a true American genius.

1. Magee Marsh Wildlife Area. The principal attractions in these seven acres of marsh and swamp forest edging Lake Erie are the bird trail, the beach, and the visitor center. The area is frequented by great numbers of small migrating birds hesitant to cross Lake Erie, as well as by larger waterfowl. The clearly marked bird trail loops around a large pond covered with water lilies and winds through the surrounding woodland. The trail is shady, overhung with viburnum, draped with wild grape, and punctuated by the ghostly white trunks of fallen trees; the early stage of the path is graveled, but the midsection is apt to be muddy. The wildlife is relatively tame, and quiet observers have an excellent chance of spotting many of the creatures, including muskrats and turtles, that inhabit the area. The spring migration lasts from late February to mid-June, when the goslings of Canada geese are showing signs of independence, and great blue herons and white egrets still linger. The best time for the fall migration is mid-October to mid-November.

The sandy beach is fringed with cottonwoods that shade the tables and grills in the picnic area. There are pleasant views of distant islands, and swimming is permitted during daylight hours.

In the visitor center mounted birds and mammals, antique wildfowl decoys and guns, and other displays graphically ex-

1. *Canada geese and goslings on a family outing benefit from official protection.*

plain the history and natural background of the marshland. A nearby observation tower provides a fine view of the area. *Area open daily; visitor center open Mon.–Sat. May–Aug., weekdays Sept.–Apr.*

2. Kelleys Island. *Take the ferry from Marblehead.* It is not known how long Kelleys Island was inhabited by people of the Erie or Cat nation before they were destroyed by the Iroquois in the late 1600's. But these first settlers are credited with leaving an enigmatic memorial: Inscription Rock, a large, flat-topped slab of limestone covered with Indian pictographs—of humanlike creatures, birds and animals, and smoking pipes—that have never been deciphered. The inscriptions, which are now nearly obliterated by the elements, were copied by U.S. Army Capt. Seth Eastman in 1850; a reproduction of his work is placed at the site.

Kelleys Island was resettled in the early 1800's. By 1910 it had a population of more than 1,000 and a thriving economy based on limestone quarrying, agriculture, winemaking, and fishing. Today only about 100 people inhabit the island year-round. Tourism is the major industry, and fishing, boating, swimming, and dining facilities are plentiful.

Visitors can ferry their cars over from Marblehead, but may prefer to rent bicycles or golf carts on the island to get about and see the sights. Just beyond a pretty lakeside campground about a 10-minute bike ride from the center of town is the 3½-acre site of Glacial Grooves, a state memorial. The limestone, scored to a depth of several inches by the irresistible force of a moving glacier, gives the appearance of smoothly rounded gray waves. One trough, some 400 feet long, 30 feet wide, and 10 to 15 feet deep, is thought to be the world's most spectacular example of glacial grooving. The glacier originated in the highlands of Labrador

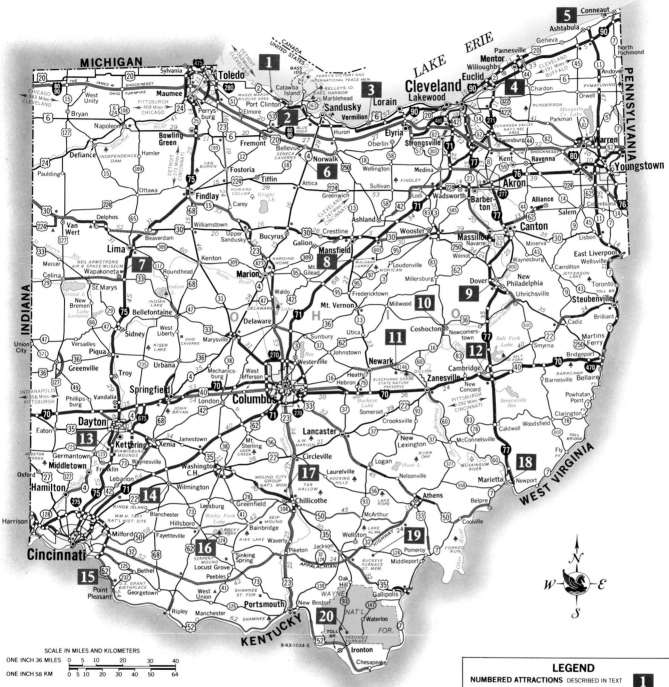

MICHIGAN

LAKE ERIE

INDIANA

PENNSYLVANIA

WEST VIRGINIA

KENTUCKY

9-KX-1034-S

and inched southward for 5,000 years to reach this point. It melted about 10,000 years ago. Best times to visit are spring and fall. *Accessible year-round.*

3. Great Lakes Historical Society Museum. *480 Main Street, Vermilion.* This waterfront museum contains an unusually well-displayed series of exhibits relating to the history of shipping and boating on the Great Lakes.

The introductory photographs and paintings depict wrecks in these waters, including the *275-foot Eastland,* "The Aristocrat of the Lakes," which suffered the worst accident in the history of lake shipping and transportation. Built in 1903 with 100 luxurious staterooms, the *Eastland* was taking on passengers in Chicago

8. *Weathered barn and silo and well-used tractor testify that Malabar is a working farm.*

for a pleasure cruise on July 24, 1915, when it capsized and sank at dockside in 10 feet of water; 812 people were trapped on board and drowned. A model of another famous wreck, the *Edmund Fitzgerald*, is shown lying on the floor of Whitefish Bay, her 26,000-ton cargo of iron pellets scattered about her.

Set before large picture windows and overlooking the lake as if from the prow of a ship is a collection of compass binnacles and steering wheels. A steam engine from the tugboat *Roger* and an engine-room console complete with brass dials and levers are also displayed. Here too are ship models, paintings, and murals relating to commerce on the lakes.

The theme of safety on the water is reinforced by collections of steam whistles, foghorns, shore beacons, and one of the most beautiful exhibits: the light from the Spectacle Reef lighthouse on Lake Huron. First used in 1874, this huge, precision-made Fresnel-type lens is made of brass with clear and ruby-red glass prisms. Admiral Perry's telescope is shown, along with a detailed map of the strategy that won him the battle of Lake Erie in 1812. *Open daily Apr.–Dec., weekends Jan.–Mar. Admission charged.*

---

4. Lawnfield. *Mentor.* The home of President James A. Garfield is a large white clapboard structure with a gambrel roof, brick chimney, large porch, and a porte cochere. Inside, the house is spacious, simply and elegantly furnished, and lovingly maintained, with fresh flowers in the vases and polished brass fire irons.

Visitors to the campaign office that stands near the house cannot help reflecting on how times have changed since 1880, when Garfield ran for president. It is no more than a simple one-story building with quarters for a secretary and a telegraph operator; a conference room and a library of leather-bound books complete the facilities. It was here that Garfield received the news of his election on the very telegraph equipment that stands on a table. His term of office was tragically short. After only a few months as president he was shot by a disappointed office seeker; he died 2½ months later.

The other outbuildings are a pump room of cut stone and a disused carriage house. Picnic tables are placed in the garden among tall trees, including a fine old weeping beech. *Open Tues.–Sat. and P.M. Sun. Admission charged.*

---

5. Conneaut Historical Railway Museum. *Conneaut. Watch for signs on Rte. 20.* Trains have long been powerful symbols of freedom, high adventure, and expansion; and since the 1880's the economy of Conneaut has been linked to the Nickel Plate Road, connecting Buffalo to Chicago with 513 miles of track. The railroad employed much of Conneaut's labor force, contributed substantially to town revenue, opened it to development, and became part of its folklore. That the bond between the railroad and the townspeople goes beyond economic factors is proved by the prodigious contributions of volunteer la-

bor and donated money that went into the creation of this excellent museum.

Housed in the old New York Central Railroad depot, the museum overflows with railroad memorabilia. One eye-catcher is a 19th-century advertisement showing a train in mother-of-pearl inlay, with mountains painted in watercolors in the background. There are also timetables, a chart of hobo codes, railway bonds, and travel permits, including that of Abraham Lincoln, signed by his own hand in 1857 when he was chief attorney for the Illinois Central Railroad.

Workaday exhibits include carmakers' and inspectors' tools, telegraph equipment, a fully equipped ticket office, and a working model of a boiler. And of course there are model trains, including an original cast-iron Lionel. Outside the depot children and buffs will enjoy climbing into the cab of a handsome 100-foot-long Berkshire steam locomotive built in 1944. A hopper car and a 1913 caboose complete with stove, washstand, and instructions for operating the air brakes are also intriguing. *Open P.M. daily Memorial Day–Labor Day. Admission free but donations encouraged.*

---

6. Seneca Caverns. In 1872 two boys were out hunting when their dog chased a rabbit into a brush-filled pit. When the dog did not return, the boys began searching through the brush. Toward the bottom of the pit they discovered a small hole with cool air streaming through it, and they could hear their dog barking below. As they dug to widen the opening, the limestone supporting them collapsed, and they tumbled some 10 or 12 feet down to the opening of a cave. The three companions climbed back out, and the caverns came to public notice.

Unlike most caves, the Seneca Caverns were not formed by erosion but rather by a great fracture in the limestone bedrock of the area. Its physical aspect differs accordingly from the norm: here one sees the bones of the earth—the tumbled strata of Columbus limestone—in their raw condition, not smoothed by the flow of water or the action of ancient seas.

The path through the cave is not easy. In some places it is impossible to stand upright, and the going is often steep and rough. The largest chamber is some 250 feet long and 10 or 12 feet high. At one end is Pie Rock, so called because it resembles a huge wedge of pie. Beyond it one descends to Old Mist'ry River, whose waters are so clear that they almost seem not to exist, but merely to be a light mist at the bottom of the cavern. The river's source is unknown, but it has been found that it slowly flows into Blue Hole Spring at Castalia, a few miles away.

The river's water level (which depends upon rainwater seeping down) determines how far one can descend into the cave. Twelve cave levels have been explored. In the dry season (late October) you may be able to reach the seventh level, more than 135 feet below the surface. On the return route one squeezes through the Needle's Eye and passes the Lock Stone, which is said to hold the jumbled and fractured strata in place; it's 150 feet long, 45 feet deep, and 60 feet wide, and is estimated to weigh 38 million pounds.

Emerging into the light again, one thinks of the underground landscape and the great monolith that holds the rocks in place, and with them the trees and peaceful Ohio fields. *Open daily Memorial Day– Labor Day; weekends only May, Sept., Oct. Admission charged.*

7. Neil Armstrong Air and Space Museum. *Wapakoneta.* "One small step for man, one giant leap for mankind": thus spoke the first man to set foot on the moon, astronaut Neil Armstrong. Armstrong's own first steps were taken in Wapakoneta, his childhood home, where this museum was established in his honor.

The museum building is a domed structure, half buried in a grassy mound, with two wings for galleries. The upper floor contains the Infinity Room and the Planetarium. In the Infinity Room, an 18-foot cube, one walks between ingeniously positioned rows of mirrors that reflect each other, oneself, and moving lights in numerous planes. In the Planetarium, pinpoints of revolving lights are thrown against the roof and walls to the accompaniment of electronic music. Both rooms seek to create a sense of being in infinite space, and both succeed quite well.

Other exhibits include a collection of photographs and models relating to the history of flight, in which Ohio has a proud role: Thomas Kirby, an Ohioan, made the state's first balloon ascent in 1834; the Wright brothers were Ohio boys; and the Goodyear dirigible RS1 was built at Akron in the 1930's. The story

continues with exhibits from Neil Armstrong's involvement with aviation, going back to a high school science project.

One of the most fascinating items found here is a genuine Gemini VIII spacecraft, with a panel cut away to reveal the interior: this was the world's first docking satellite, flown by Armstrong and Maj. David Scott in March 1966. Also displayed are the many honors bestowed upon the astronauts, including the Presidential Medal of Freedom. *Open daily Mar.–Nov. Admission charged.*

---

8. Malabar Farm. *Rte. 1, Lucas.* In 1939 the Pulitzer-prizewinning author Louis Bromfield bought four neglected farms, built a large, comfortable, and elegant home around one of the old farmhouses, and began to restore the fertility of his farmland. Since most of the money for the project came from the proceeds of a novel set on the Malabar Coast in India, he called the property Malabar Farm.

The "big house" is exceptionally attractive. The furnishings are predominantly French rural antiques highlighted by such striking objects as an Italian marble fireplace surmounted by ceramic Chinese horses set against a huge mirrored wall in the living room, a Steinway grand piano beside the floating double staircase in the hallway, and in the Red Room, paintings by Grandma Moses. An enormous curved desk with 28 drawers dominates the author's library despite the fact that it was too high for Bromfield to use comfortably.

Nine bedrooms upstairs include one where Humphrey Bogart and Lauren Bacall, who were friends of the author, stayed on their honeymoon.

The farm still supports a fine herd of purebred Holstein cattle, and the self-guiding tour of the barns, stables, meadows, and flower gardens allows visitors to see the farm animals and touch those in the petting barn.

About half of the acreage here is under cultivation; the rest is woodland, where there are hiking trails and a campsite for horse riders. A final appealing touch is the spring, supposedly once used by Johnny Appleseed, that wells up in its own enclosure at the edge of the property. *Open daily except Thanksgiving Day, Christmas, and Sun. in Dec. and Feb. Admission charged.*

---

9. Warther's. *331 Karl Ave., Dover.* Some artists languish all their lives for want of an appreciative market; others have fame and fortune thrust upon them; but Ernest Warther (1885-1973) was quite different. Although his wood carvings of trains, locomotives, and an old steel mill were immensely valued during his lifetime (the Smithsonian called the mill a "priceless work of art"), Warther never sold a single piece of his work, because, he said, "Our roof don't leak, we ain't hungry, and we don't owe anybody."

"Warther's" refers to the home the artist and his wife built in 1912, which now

9. *The master craftsman in 1965 with some of his creations and the tools he used.*

houses his remarkable collection of carvings in wood, bone, and ivory.

One's first introduction to these is a working model of the American Sheet and Tinplate Co., where Warther worked between 1899 and 1923. It is made of walnut and ivory and re-creates in detail the floor of the factory—not only the machines but his friends there. His best friend, for instance, is shown eating rhubarb pie and a piece of Swiss cheese complete with holes. The model was done from memory nearly 30 years after he left the factory.

His other work is even more extraordinary. What he set out to do, and accomplished, was to record the history of steam locomotion from 250 B.C. to the 20th century in a series of 64 accurately scaled, detailed working models.

Many of the carvings are large. The Great Northern Mountain type locomotive, carved in 1930, weighs over 60 pounds and contains 7,752 pieces, including bolts as small as an eighth of an inch and nuts to fit. The eight-foot-long model of the *Empire State Express* is shown crossing a bridge, which is made of 4,000 individually cut ebony bricks, with strips of ivory for the mortar. Warther's favorite was the Lincoln funeral train. A keyhole in the funeral coach has an ivory key that fits it, and the body in its draped coffin can be seen through a window.

Warther used only hand tools, and his quest for a knife that would hold its edge led to the establishment of his knife factory. Some models are sold in the gift shop. Also of interest is Mrs. Warther's collection of 50,000 buttons (no two alike), arranged in intricate patterns on the walls and ceiling of a separate small building. The gardens are pleasant, and a small picnic area is provided. *Open daily except major holidays.*

---

10. Johnson-Humrickhouse Museum. *300 N. Whitewoman St., Coshocton.* The museum is located in Roscoe Village, a restoration of an 1800's canal town. Most of its collections relate to Ohio's pioneering past, with exhibits of cornhusk dolls, domestic and farm implements, lamps and lanterns, early-day interior settings, and 19th-century weaponry, including Colt and Remington revolvers and the first rifle used by the U.S. military, the 1860 Spencer repeating carbine.

In addition, the museum has a high-quality collection of American Indian art and artifacts. Haida masks, Acoma pottery, Chippewa cradleboards, Eskimo animal effigies, a Crow headdress, distinctively patterned Apache basketry, and a Pomo mortuary basket are among the exhibits that exemplify Indian life.

Still another gallery features Oriental treasures. Inro and netsuke, 19th-century Japanese porcelain, vases and boxes of carved cinnabar lacquer, samurai swords and cases, antique stoneware bottles, and many other exquisite pieces are shown.

The museum also contains personal memorabilia of the Johnson and Humrickhouse families and an exhibit of French, Irish, Flemish, and American lace. All these collections are well lit and spaciously displayed.

Roscoe Village, a picturesque historic site, gives you an opportunity to become acquainted with the canal era. In addition to exploring the small village with its attractive shops, you can walk along the towpath and take rides on a trolley and a canal boat. *Museum open year-round. Admission free but donations encouraged.*

---

11. Blackhand Gorge State Nature Preserve. *Watch for signs on Rte. 146 near junction of Rte. 16.* About 10,000 years ago, the runoff of melting glaciers carved a gorge here in the sandstone bedrock known as Blackhand conglomerate. The preserve follows the course of the Licking River through this gorge, and a number of trails and a paved bicycle path invite exploration of the terrain.

The bike path passes a buttonbush swamp and then enters a woodland of sycamore, maple, sumac, and yellow poplar. In July the route is highlighted by the flowers of the wild phlox and bergamot.

Along the bike path one enjoys dramatic views of cliffs towering above the woods, with ferns, massive tree trunks, and roots delineating the weathered strata and fault lines. Across the gorge stands Blackhand Rock, a concave rock face above a bend and a wide pool in the river. Beyond this the path passes narrowly between two cliffs and then reenters the woodland, where one has intermittent views of the river and its dry-season sandpits and exposed boulders.

The railroad that crosses a bridge above the trail was originally used to carry sand from a nearby quarry to the glassworks of Newark, the nearest sizable town. One footpath traverses the rim of the old quarry; two others, the Owl Hollow and Chestnut trails, begin together with a steep climb up railed wooden steps to a small stream that descends the side of the gorge. Owl Hollow then loops through ferny hemlock woods, while the Chestnut ascends to higher woodlands before rejoining the bicycle path. *Open year-round.*

---

12. The Degenhart Paperweight and Glass Museum. *Cambridge. From I-77 take Rte. 22 west at Exit 47 and look for the museum on your right.* This part of Ohio was once a center of the art glass industry, in which John Degenhart, founder in 1947 of the Crystal Art Glass Company of Cambridge, was an eminent figure. The museum gives an excellent general account of commercial glassmaking in the Ohio Valley and of John Degenhart's work, in particular his craftsmanship and artistry as a maker of paperweights. The son of a glassmaker, Degenhart became a glassmaker himself at the age of nine.

As an introduction to the exhibits, the

11. *Retaining wall emphasizes stratification of the Blackhand conglomerate.*

museum offers a short videotape on glass-making. You can also ask to see a tape on the techniques of paperweight making.

The first displays give a broad survey of the major glassmakers of the region. This introduces you to a comprehensive display of pressed glass that shows the major trends and the wealth of patterns developed. In the 1870's most patterns were adapted from nature, while in the 1880's complex imitations of cut glass were in vogue. In 1900 there was a return to plainer, earlier styles.

Another exhibit shows collectors how to distinguish copies of old pressed glass from the originals. Technicolor arrays of glass owls, puppies, and dolls demonstrate the great variety of colors produced in glass by the addition of chemicals. The paperweight section of the museum shows the parts and steps in the making of a "five lily" weight and some of the major types of paperweights. Also shown are paperweights in the forms of lamps, doorstops, and even grave markers; these last are a tradition peculiar to the Guernsey County area of Ohio. Most of the glass was collected by Degenhart's wife, Elizabeth. One exhibit shows her dining room packed from floor to ceiling with pieces from her collection. *Open Mon.–Sat. and P.M. Sun. Apr.–Oct.; Wed.–Sat. and P.M. Sun. Mar. and Nov.; Sat. and P.M. Sun. Dec. and Feb.; closed Jan. and major holidays. Admission charged.*

---

13. Miamisburg Mound. *Mound Ave., Miamisburg.* This is the largest conical burial mound in Ohio, and like Grave Creek Mound in West Virginia (see p.86), it is attributed to the Adena Indians, who lived here probably between 500 B.C. and A.D. 200. The Ohio Valley was the heartland of the Adena culture, but its influence spread west into Indiana, south into Kentucky, and as far east as New York and Delaware. The Adena settled in small communities, practiced a limited horticulture, and buried their dead in conical earthen mounds. Within their orbit of influence there may be as many as 300 to 500 mound sites.

The Miamisburg Mound, built on a bluff, rises to a height of 65 feet from a base about 300 feet in diameter. But originally, before excavations, it was more than 70 feet high, and may have been the largest in the eastern United States. Eight feet from the top of the mound archeologists

15. *The 18th president of the United States was born in this sturdy clapboard house.*

discovered a bark-covered skeleton; 28 feet below that they found an empty vault surrounded by logs. Layers of ash and stone indicate that the mound had been built in stages over a period of time.

The slopes of the mound are shaggy with trees and vegetation. A flight of 116 stone steps leads to a paved circle on top, from which one can view the environs. A notice on the site gives some particulars of the excavations. The surrounding park has picnic tables and a playground. *Open year-round.*

---

14. The Clinton County Historical Society and Museum. *Rombach Place, 149 E. Locust St., Wilmington.* This most pleasant and unpredictable museum of local history is located in Rombach Place, an elegant town house built in 1830 by Gen. James William Denver, commissioner of Indian affairs under President Buchanan, governor of the Kansas Territory in the 1850's, and the man for whom the city of Denver, Colorado, was named. The house is listed in *The National Register of Historic Places* and is furnished throughout with handsome antiques.

To the right of the entrance hall is the Denver library, which contains the general's collection of Indian relics, his beaver top hat, the sand shaker used to dry the ink on his letters, and other memorabilia. Beyond this elegant room is a sitting room

containing a handsome horsehair settee and a luminous oil painting by Eli Harvey, a local Quaker famous for his animal bronzes. A number of these, including a sleek, recumbent greyhound, a "nervous puma," a stag, and an enraged elephant, may be seen in the Eli Harvey Room. A second sitting room is furnished with three pianos, violins by a local maker, and a wonderfully elaborate mirror. Porcelain dishes, toby jugs, and pewter sconces are displayed in the dining room.

Upstairs one finds a roomful of children's toys, a re-creation of an early 20th-century dentist's office with false teeth of that time, a collection of antique clothing, and a sewing room containing quilts. One of the most interesting items is a bathtub (with a built-in water heater) that folds up against the wall. In the barn behind the house are antique farm equipment, a storm buggy, and a very fine fire engine, circa 1876. *Open P.M. Tues.–Fri. Admission free but donations encouraged.*

---

15. U.S. Grant Birthplace. *Intersection of Rtes. 232 and 52 south of New Richmond.* The first home of Ulysses S. Grant, general of the Union Army during the Civil War and later president of the United States, is a typical small pioneer house: a white clapboard structure resting on a stone sill, with a brick chimney. Grant was born here in 1822, and the following year his family moved to Georgetown, where he spent his boyhood years.

From 1895 to 1936 the house stood as a historical exhibit in Columbus, Ohio, but in 1936 it was returned to its original site beside Big Indian Creek and facing the Ohio River. Simply furnished in the tradition of his time, the house contains Grant's cradle, the trunk he took to West Point, his Bible, and his cigar case.

Outside the house is a covered well of dressed sandstone. A cannon, set in concrete and bearing Grant's name and birth date on a plaque, points toward the river. Majestic chestnut trees grace the spacious lawn, which stretches down to the road, and behind the house is the Grant Memorial Church, an imposing structure with Ionic columns. *Open weekends and holidays May–Labor Day. Admission charged.*

17. Although now well tended, this burial mound withstood over 1,600 years of neglect.

16. Rocky Fork State Park. The major attraction of this 21,000-acre park is the seven-mile-long Rocky Fork Lake within its perimeter. Most of the park's facilities are oriented to the lake, which has several sandy beaches and an intricately interesting shoreline. Pedal boats, rowboats, pontoon boats, and motorboats can be rented at the marina, which also sells or rents fishing gear, live bait, water and snow ski equipment, and camping supplies. The fishing is particularly good for crappies, bluegills, and such game fish as bass, walleye, and muskies.

The country surrounding the lake is pleasant, with low hills, woodlands, and fields. Three short trails wind through the park—the Redbud, the Paw Paw, and the Deer Loop; the Deer Loop is the most heavily wooded and the most interesting. *Open year-round.*

17. Mound City. *Chillicothe.* This 2,000-year-old complex of mounds occupying 13 acres on the banks of the Scioto River is one of the most important sites of the Hopewell Indian culture, which blossomed and flourished in the Ohio Valley from about 100 B.C. to A.D. 400, overlapping the Adena culture. Their mound construction was especially intensive here in the Scioto River–Paint Creek area.

Mound City was apparently both a village and a burial site. The visitor center establishes what is currently known of the Hopewell lifestyle and displays some of the artifacts found in excavations of their burial mounds. The quantity and type of burial objects in particular mounds indicate the status and possibly the occupation of the deceased. They include shell beads, bear and shark teeth, pottery, ear spools of copper and silver, and—most remarkable for their stylized realism and exquisite workmanship—a series of effigy pipes bearing the likenesses of animals and birds: wildcat, beaver, great blue heron, and raven. The original pipes are now in the British Museum in London; replicas are on display here.

Other exhibits detail the remarkably extensive trade network of the Hopewell, their method of constructing the charnel mounds, and a reconstruction of the remarkable Great Mica Grave, in which the cremated remains of four bodies were laid on a bed of thin sheets of mica (brought here from the Blue Ridge Mountains), the whole then covered with earth, and overlaid with more mica.

The 23 mounds are spaciously placed but with no observable overall pattern. Beyond these parklike grounds the Scioto River flows, smooth, brown, and rapid. An interesting ¼-mile trail follows its

16. Near the state park this gravity-defying covered bridge spans Rocky Fork Creek.

banks (from which one can see the site of another Hopewell earthwork) and then turns back toward the visitor center. Along the way are plaques identifying plants and shrubs once important to the local Indians. *Grounds open daily; visitor center open daily except Thanksgiving Day, Christmas, and New Year's Day.*

18. Campus Martius Museum. *Marietta. Intersection of Washington and Second Sts.*

In April 1788, 48 New England men led by Gen. Rufus Putnam arrived here in the Northwest Territory to settle a tiny portion of the 1.8 million acres granted by Congress to the Ohio Land Company. On a bluff overlooking the confluence of the Ohio and Muskingum rivers they built a fort, which they named Campus Martius (literally, "field of Mars"). On the plains below they laid out their village, leaving undisturbed the strange prehistoric mound they had discovered.

Today Campus Martius is a museum that contains many relics of the early days of settlement here and includes the last standing portion of the fort. One wing of the museum encloses General Putnam's five-room house, which is restored and partially furnished. Many of the pieces belonged to the Putnam family. Most notable here is a black walnut table with a top cut from a single massive tree.

Other exhibits in the museum include a model of the flatboat used by the pioneers, early surveying instruments, and an extensive collection of frontier rifles, many made by J. Vincent, a local gunsmith whose workshop is displayed intact in the basement. A collection of Masonic memorabilia includes a ritual Masonic apron worn by George Washington. Behind the museum is the first office building in Ohio, the original log and clapboard headquarters of the Ohio Company.

Marietta's later development is represented by a fine collection of ecclesiastical silver, arrays of women's antique clothing, 18th-century furniture in the Hepplewhite and Chippendale styles, and a collection of dollhouses—to name but a few of the many historic objects on display. In Heritage Hall visitors can view reproductions of a cooper's shop and Richards Pharmacy, with rows of fascinating antique hand-labeled bottles, vials, and boxes. *Open Mon.–Sat. and P.M. Sun. year-round. Admission charged.*

20. *This early example of a blast furnace is a tribute to the skill of its masons.*

19. Buckeye Furnace State Memorial. In

the early 19th century one of the young nation's premier iron-producing regions was the Hanging Rock area of southern Ohio, a vast expanse of forest rich with deposits of ore and limestone. During the midcentury, 65 local furnaces were producing as much as 105,000 tons of pig iron each year, partly in response to a demand created by the Civil War.

But as coke began to replace charcoal in the smelters and the ore from the larger Lake Superior deposits began to reach Pittsburgh, Ohio's industry waned, and one by one the furnaces closed. Of those that still stand, Buckeye is one of the most completely restored.

Visitors to the site can see a replica of the office and company store where furnace workers, who were often paid as little as 65 cents in scrip for a 12-hour day, had to buy their food and other necessities. The store is now stocked with period items: axes, lunch pails, coffee makers and grinders, spittoons, and an elaborate tin spice cabinet.

A short walk from the office leads to the furnace, which is faced with massive blocks of local sandstone and somewhat resembles a Mayan temple. A series of signs along the way illustrates the lifestyle of the furnace workers. Other markers, in the bridge loft from which the furnace was charged with ore, charcoal, and limestone, describe the process of creating pig iron. Attached to the furnace is the casting shed. In its sand floor are the molds into which the molten iron flowed. The feeding channel was known as the sow, and

the ingot molds along its length were the pigs; hence the name pig iron. *Open Wed.–Sat. and P.M. Sun. Memorial Day–Labor Day. Admission charged.*

20. Lake Vesuvius Recreation Area. Set

among the rolling hills and scenic woodlands of the Wayne National Forest, this is a place of tranquil beauty. Lake Vesuvius, a long, narrow body of water curving sinuously through the hollows beneath embankments of trees and magnificent rock outcroppings, is ideal for canoeing and boating, and the sandy beach at Big Bend is inviting for swimmers. The fishing is also good for bass and catfish.

Several loop trails, ranging from a half-mile walk to a 16-mile path for backpackers, skirt the lake and cross a varied terrain. The facility also offers a 28-mile horse trail, campsites, picnic grounds, a boat dock, and rental boats and canoes.

The recreation area takes its name from the Vesuvius Furnace, located in one of the picnic spots. This truncated giant, built in 1833, was one of the first iron blast furnaces in the region, and it was one of the last to close, holding out against the prevailing economic winds until 1906. The structure has been partially restored by the U.S. Corps of Engineers. Though it lacks some of the ancillary buildings faithfully re-created at Buckeye Furnace, Vesuvius has the poignancy of a fallen hero. *Open year-round.*

Indiana

Augmenting the gentle beauty of the land are reminders of its early settlement and the hard labor and creative energy of the pioneers.

A river that gave its euphonic name to a famous nearby battlefield now borders a peaceful park; another inviting retreat pays tribute to a heroic frontiersman whose achievements were denigrated by his contemporaries. The engaging variety of the Indiana countryside is further revealed in parks and forests, and at Abraham Lincoln's boyhood home.

Restorations exemplify the life of the Amish and other pioneers who farmed here. American ingenuity is recalled in gristmills, canals, and museums of steamboats, phonographs, and other inventions; car fanciers will savor the collection of Cords, Auburns, and Duesenbergs, all built in Indiana and ranked among the finest automobiles ever made.

1. Bonneyville Mill. *Bristol.* In 1837 one Edward Bonney, a local tavern keeper and entrepreneur, constructed a mill on the wooded shores of Little Elkhart River. Now known as Bonneyville Mill, it is the oldest continuously operating gristmill with a horizontal waterwheel in the state of Indiana, and as it probably has from the beginning, it produces both flour and meal. In 1976 the mill was listed in *The National Register of Historic Places.*

Rather than standing upright, the waterwheel here is installed lying on its side and is enclosed in a steel case submerged in about seven feet of water. When the 12 doors on the sides of the case are opened, water flows through and drains out the bottom. The whirlpool thus created spins the wheel, which then turns the gears that drive the mill. Visitors enter the mill through the basement, where the gear system is visible, along with a display of old milling equipment.

The main floor contains the milling area with two sets of grindstones. On this floor the flour that is produced—wheat, rye, and buckwheat—is for sale.

On the second floor visitors can see a buckwheat flour sifter used to separate the flour from the hulls after it is ground. The third floor houses a grain cleaner composed of a series of screens for sifting and a fan for winnowing the grain before it is milled, as well as the gears and heavy

2. The plain structures and split-rail fence characterize the spare style of the Amish.

equipment that operate the mill's elevator.

On the mill grounds, which stretch along the river, shady picnic areas have been developed. Hiking trails wander through the property, and for those who like to fish, the river is stocked with trout. *Open daily May–Oct.*

2. Amish Acres. *1600 W. Market St., Nappanee.* In 1874 Christian Stahly, the first Amish settler in this area, built a farmhouse here for his son. Today the 80-acre restored farm provides not only a fascinating look at the old-fashioned ways of the German-speaking Plain People, but it also gives an overview of 19th-century American farm life in general.

The main house, its smokehouse and other outbuildings, and the nearby Grossdaadi Haus (Grandfather House) are visited in a group tour, which originates near the farm's main gate. The 12-room, white frame farmhouse, which was greatly expanded in the 1890's, is outfitted with peri-

od furniture, cookware, wood stoves, and equipment such as a sausage stuffer, spinning wheel, and rocker-action churn. After the tour visitors are free to roam the grounds and look at the other buildings, many of which were brought here from town and from other farms.

The sweet smell of hay fills a large barn containing threshing equipment and a hay wagon. Stables and milking stalls adjoin a barnyard and pasture. A horse-drawn school bus and an Amish church-bench wagon are among the old carriages in the wagon shed. Among the other buildings are a smithy, an icehouse, a sawmill, a

LEGEND		
NUMBERED ATTRACTIONS DESCRIBED IN TEXT		**1**
HIGHWAY MARKERS		
INTERSTATE **70**	UNITED STATES ⟨40⟩	STATE ⟨53⟩
ROAD CLASSIFICATIONS		
CONTROLLED ACCESS HIGHWAYS (Entrance and Exit only at Interchanges)		
TOLL HIGHWAYS		Interchanges
OTHER DIVIDED HIGHWAYS		
PRINCIPAL THROUGH HIGHWAYS		
OTHER THROUGH HIGHWAYS		
CONNECTING HIGHWAYS		

windmill, and a small 1870's town house. The farm has a sorghum press, a mint still where aromatic oil was distilled from mint plants, and a shop where brooms are still made from broom corn. The kitchen garden includes herbs and flowers, while mulberries and other old-time favorite fruit trees grow in the orchard. The farm is least crowded in spring and fall. *Open daily Apr.–Nov. Admission charged.*

3. Chain O' Lakes State Park.

The predominant feature in this 2,700-acre park is a series of 11 small lakes, all but three of which are strung together by natural channels of water. The lakes, called kettle lakes, were formed at the end of the last ice age. The weight of enormous blocks of ice left in the ground by a retreating glacier created the basins for the lakes. The subsequent meltwater filled the lakes and carved the connecting channels.

Not surprisingly, the principal activities here are swimming, fishing, and boating. Swimming is permitted only in summer, when a lifeguard is on duty, and the only motorized craft allowed are low-powered electric troll boats. Rowboats and canoes can be rented by the day, paddleboats by the hour. Anglers try for bluegills and bass. Wintertime activities include ice fishing, skating on the lakes, sledding, and cross-country skiing. Skis are available for rent.

The park also has some interesting trails circling the lakes and meandering through woodlands and meadows. In addition to more than 400 campsites, there is a small village of housekeeping cottages. *Park and campground open year-round, but facilities turned off Nov.–Mar. Admission charged.*

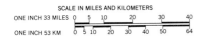

SCALE IN MILES AND KILOMETERS

ONE INCH 33 MILES 0 5 10   20   30   40

ONE INCH 53 KM 0 5 10   20   30   40   50   64

MILEAGES   LONG DISTANCE MILEAGES SHOWN IN RED
MILEAGE BETWEEN DOTS   ●━━━━━━●
ONE MILE EQUALS 1.6 KILOMETERS   35
                          ONE KILOMETER EQUALS .6 MILES

SPECIAL FEATURES

STATE PARKS
With Campsites ⬥ Without Campsites △

RECREATION AREAS
With Campsites ▲ Without Campsites △

■ POINTS OF INTEREST

© THE H.M. GOUSHA COMPANY · SAN JOSE, CALIFORNIA

4. *Auburns that are classics in every regard. Note rumble seat in the convertible.*

4. Auburn-Cord-Duesenberg Museum.

Auburn. Named for three noted producers of classic luxury cars, this museum is both a handsome showcase for automobiles and a celebration of the era between the first and second world wars when the luxury car was in its heyday. The creations of these three American makers are counted among the most beautiful automobiles ever made. The building itself is the Auburn Auto Company's former headquarters, a spacious structure now restored to its 1930 Art Deco splendor. The floor is geometrically patterned in pink, green, black, and cream marble, and the high ceiling beams are enriched with complementary designs.

The main exhibit on the ground floor contains some of the best engineered and most luxuriously appointed cars ever built, including a silver-and-black 265-horsepower Duesenberg speedster that oil tycoon J. Paul Getty paid $15,000 for in 1932 and a stunning 1936 Auburn boat-tail speedster that sold for $2,245. (Today it could cost $150,000.) Most of the automobiles are Auburns, Cords, and Duesenbergs from the 1920's and 1930's, when those manufacturers flourished. But other makers, such as Bentley, Bugatti, and Packard, are also represented. And in a gesture to the more recent past, the exhibit includes a psychedelically painted Bentley that John Lennon owned in the l960's, when the Beatles were riding high.

The cars exhibited on the second floor provide a more general overview of automotive history. A 1932 Ace motorcycle is shown, and an electric car that was on the road in 1888. Here too is a display of automobile-related items, including hood ornaments, hubcaps, and advertisements. The 1933 Chicago World's Fair is represented by various souvenirs, and the re-stored design studio and advertising office of the Auburn Company can be seen.

There are other exhibits tied primarily to the period between the two world wars, most notably the collection of 1920's jazz age fashions, and receivers and such from the golden era of radio broadcasting. *Open year-round.*

---

5. Tippecanoe River State Park.

Farther downstream, the river that borders this park gave its name to an 1811 battle, and thus to William Henry Harrison's presidential campaign slogan, "Tippecanoe and Tyler too," in 1840. Harrison led an armed force to victory against the Shawnees on Tippecanoe Creek, and John Tyler was his running mate.

But long before that, in the 1600's and 1700's, the river was a passageway for the canoes of intrepid French voyageurs from Canada who bartered for furs with this area's Potawatomi and Miami Indians.

Although the land was once cleared and cultivated, it was marginal for farming. It has since reverted to its natural state, with terrain that ranges from oak and pine woods to marsh and sandy scrub. Returned wildlife includes wood ducks, great blue herons, sandhill cranes, beavers, muskrats, and white-tailed deer. They can sometimes be spotted along the extensive network of hiking trails. About eight miles of the trails can also be used by riders who bring their own horses.

Tippecanoe is an Indian word for buffalofish, a sucker that was once plentiful here. But today bass and bluegills are dominant among the catches that lure anglers. Both boaters and canoeists use the river, but it is too hazardous for swimmers. The picnic ground on the riverbank is especially pleasant, with spaciously separated tables under fine old shade trees. *Park and campground open year-round. Admission charged.*

---

6. Elwood Haynes Museum.

1915 S. Webster St., Kokomo. Exit U.S. Rte. 31 at E. Markland St.; then turn left on Webster. Kokomo prides itself on being the City of Firsts, and the most outstanding of those firsts were the inventions of Elwood Haynes. In 1894 Haynes tested the proto-

5. *Imagine the sense of peace and quiet on this smooth stretch of sun-dappled water.*

8. *Harvesting herbs (left) at the doctor's house. Above are the appropriately trim carpenter's house and the widower's rough log cabin, complete with pensive widower.*

type for a horseless carriage with an engine fueled by gasoline, a substance then considered of little commercial value. Four years later he put it in production, and if it was not America's first commercially successful automobile, as Haynes advocates claim, it was certainly one of the earliest. Haynes also developed several metal alloys, most notably tungsten stainless steel and Stellite, an extra-hard blend of chromium, cobalt, and tungsten.

The museum, which is in Haynes's home, has four of his cars—the 1905 Haynes Model L and three from the early 1920's: the Haynes roadster, a touring car, and the Haynes-Apperson Jack Rabbit, called the Wizard of the Hills. It also contains photographs and documents relating to Haynes's life and inventions. Upstairs, local manufacturers have mounted exhibits of historic and contemporary products made in Kokomo. These range from crystal walkie-talkie radios and artillery shells to metal lifeboats, nonglare glass, pressed glass, marbles, and paperweights. Haynes's alloys are well represented. Products using them include not just rollers, bearings, and valves but also turbine blades, machine gun barrels, and surgical instruments. *Open P.M. Tues.– Sun. except holidays.*

---

7. **Amishville.** *Rte. 2, Geneva.* In this area of rolling farmland, Amish buggies are often seen on the road. They must be licensed and are required to carry a bright orange "slow-moving vehicle" plate. The Amish in this area consider the plate too gaudy and are pressing for a plain white sign. Amish homes can be identified by the absence of power lines, by the outdoor rack for canning jars, and in most cases by the nearby windmill.

Amishville itself is basically just a large campground. But the old Amish farmhouse here has the ring of truth. It looks as if simple, hardworking farm folk did indeed live here. And the visitor can learn a great deal about the Amish way of life from the group tour of the house and the informative talk given on the subject.

In keeping with Amish tradition, the house is sparsely furnished. The living room has little in it but chairs and a few plants, which the Amish allow to grow indoors. The large, functional kitchen has a wood- and coal-burning stove for winter and a kerosene cooker for summer. The pantry has large flour bins and hooks for hanging meat. The bedroom has a bed with a feather mattress and an Amish quilt, a small medicine chest, and surprisingly, a doll with a face on it. In very strict Amish communities children are not permitted to have such a doll because the face is considered a forbidden graven image.

Near the house is an outbuilding that was used for a variety of tasks ranging from washing to butchering. It contains such items as a hand-powered washing machine, a canning tub, and a lard press. A small smokehouse is nearby. The Grandfather House, not open to the public, typifies the practice of older parents' moving to a small house to make way for their children's growing families. *Open Apr.–Oct. Admission charged.*

---

8. **Conner Prairie Pioneer Settlement.** *Allisonville Rd., four miles south of Noblesville.* William Conner, who was raised by Indians, settled in this area in 1800. He lived as a trader and then as a farmer and became prominent in state politics. His Federal-style mansion of mellow red brick, built in 1823, still stands, and not only has it been restored but also an entire village duplicating a typical prairie settlement of the 1830's.

The village has more than a dozen buildings, mostly clapboard or log. Among them are an inn, a schoolhouse, a loom house, and a barn with bins of sweet-smelling grain. The houses include those of a doctor and a weaver, and homes and shops for a carpenter, a blacksmith, a potter, and a storekeeper. The furnishings throughout include period pieces or accurate reproductions.

The buildings also have occupants in period attire, and they take their roles to heart with the determination of dedicated Method actors. The carpenter, for example, hews wood and constructs items using authentic tools and materials. The doctor discourses on a then-popular medical notion of the four cardinal humors that affect one's health. And a talkative widower regales visitors with tales about his exploits as riverboatman and soldier.

The Conner house itself has been furnished simply but elegantly in the manner of the period. There are built-in cupboards and bookcases in the dining and drawing rooms; in the kitchen is a beehive oven that held 15 loaves of bread; on the stairs are rag-strip loomed carpets; and the main bedroom includes a four-poster bed with an 1858 patchwork quilt.

For youngsters and the young of heart, there is also Pioneer Adventure Center. Here the visitor can try playing such 19th-century games as quoits and stilt walking or crafts like candle dipping, preparing flax for spinning, and writing with a quill pen. *Open Tues.–Sat. and P.M. Sun. May–Oct.; Wed.–Sat. and P.M. Sun. Apr. and Nov. except Easter and Thanksgiving Day.*

---

9. Shades State Park. Early settlers called this area the Shades of Death, and there are various stories to explain the name. Some say it simply refers to the deep shade and the sometimes gloomy aspect of the forest. Others say it alludes to hostile Indians who took refuge here. Still others attribute it to the death of an early resident—either a settler slain by Indians or a husband axed by his wife. An Indian legend describes this as the site of a battle in which only 12 of 600 braves survived.

With its deep ravines overlooked by steep sandstone bluffs, this park has a spectacular, mysterious, rugged beauty that would understandably inspire tales of trouble and strife. It also boasts mature forests and virgin stands, since it was considered too rough and thin-soiled for homesteading. The area was later protected from loggers when converted into a health resort.

The park's major sites can be viewed along a series of moderate-to-rugged trails covering nearly 15 miles and leading to promontories, outcrops, streams, and waterfalls. Some trails may be impassable in wet weather. Sugar Creek, which flows through the center of the park, is very popular with canoeists. There is a canoe launch at the park's north edge at Deer's Mill Covered Bridge along Route 234.

About one-fifth of the 3,000-acre park has been set aside as the Pine Hills Nature

10. *Carved in the shoreline of the man-made lake is the record of its changing level.*

Preserve. Here two creeks running through a sandstone plateau have carved deep, steep-sided gorges with narrow, tree-topped hogback, or backbone, ridges rising above. Signs describe the trails as hazardous. But the trail to Turkey Backbone is broad, flat, and easily walked, and there are wonderful views from the ridge itself. *Open year-round. Admission charged.*

---

10. Raccoon State Recreation Area. *Rockville.* Located in the heart of Parke County's rolling farmlands, Cecil M. Harden Lake, often referred to as Raccoon Lake, was created by a dam on Big Raccoon Creek, a branch of the Wabash River. It provides an area for water sports as well as habitats for fish and wildlife.

Parke County, once the home of the Delaware, Shawnee, and Miami Indians, is known for its wealth of sugar maples, the source of a sweetener that was enjoyed by both the Indians and the pioneers who followed them. Maple sugaring is carried on today at several local sugar camps in Parke County.

The county is also known as the Covered Bridge Capital of America. Thirty-five such structures, built between 1856 and 1921, still remain on various streams and rivers. Two of them span Big Raccoon Creek.

The lake's sandy beach is surrounded by grassy bluffs set with picnic tables. The roped-off swimming area has a bathhouse,

a diving platform, and lifeguard stations. From the beach a road leads past several more picnic grounds, shaded by groves of hardwoods, to a campground; just beyond are a boat-launching ramp and a small marina for fishermen, who try for walleyes, crappies, bluegills, and catfish.

The quiet fields and the woodlands of oaks, walnuts, maples, and hickories harbor small mammals and birds, including the cardinal, the state bird. *Area and campground open year-round; water provided summer only. Admission charged.*

---

11. Midwest Phonograph Museum. *Junction of Rtes. 37 and 252, Martinsville.* Phonograph records, cassettes, and tapes are commonplace today, and we find ourselves immersed in recorded sound. But this is a relatively recent phenomenon. Until just over a century ago, sounds occurred and then vanished; even the most beautiful left only a memory.

The technical wizards whose genius finally captured sound are celebrated in an intriguing little museum packed with over 600 antique machines dating from the 1850's through the 1920's. The earliest piece in the collection is an 1858 phonautograph. Designed in France by Leon Scott, this machine, as the name suggests, enabled a sound to "write its autograph"—the sound's vibrations were recorded by brush bristles scraping over a piece of soot-covered paper, giving a printout much like an electrocardiogram. Although the reproduction of sound was still 20 years away, these mute graphic images proved to be the basis of modern sound-recording methods.

The collection also contains one of Thomas Edison's 1878 tinfoil phonographs, the first machines to reproduce sound, as well as an 1886 graphophone, designed by Alexander Graham Bell and Charles Sumner Tainter, and several of Emile Berliner's early hand-driven gramophones utilizing a recording disc, the forerunner of today's records. Among the most popular displays are jukeboxes dating from 1897 and a six-foot-high model of Nipper, the dog that listened to "His Master's Voice" and became the symbol of RCA. *Open P.M. weekends May–Oct. For further information and special appointments call (317)342-7666.*

12. Whitewater Canal Historic Site. *Metamora.*

So popular was the Whitewater Valley as a thoroughfare for pioneers making their way from Ohio to Indiana that by 1830 it was the most heavily populated area in the state. In 1836, seeking a means of shipping produce from the valley to distant markets, the Indiana legislature voted to build a 76-mile canal from Lawrenceburg to Hagerstown as part of a statewide transportation improvement program.

By 1847 the four-foot-deep Whitewater Canal was completed. It was fed by the west fork of the Whitewater River, and soon several mills, using tub wheels powered by water diverted through flumes, sprang up along its banks. However, because of floods and washouts, the canal deteriorated. The cost of maintenance and competition from the expanding railroad system led to its demise after less than 15 years of service.

Fourteen miles of the waterway have now been restored as the Whitewater Canal State Memorial, a project that includes the restoration of the Metamora Grist Mill. Built in 1845 on the bank of the canal, this two-story red brick mill, with a porch across the front and a museum on the second floor, has a waterwheel set in the spillway of one of the canal's locks.

Today the mill grinds whole-wheat cereal, white cornmeal, and grits, all for sale here. On the lower level one can see the elaborate system of slow-turning wheels and belts that power the grinding stones and sifters. A half-mile away is the restored wooden Duck Creek Aqueduct, which was built in 1843 to carry the canal 16 feet above the small stream. The *Ben Franklin*, a barge pulled by two draft horses, offers half-hour canal rides that include crossing the aqueduct.

Just below the mill a bridge crosses the canal to a picnic area with shade trees and a small bandstand. A stroll around the town of Metamora reveals some hand-some old buildings. *Gristmill open Wed.– Sat. and P.M. Sun. and Tues.; barge rides Tues.–Sun. in summer. Fee charged for barge rides.*

13. Hillforest. *213 Fifth St., Aurora.*

The Victorian mansion known as Hillforest was named Forest Hill by its builder, Thomas Gaff, a Scotsman who reached America at the age of three. Gaff grew up in the East, and in 1837, when that area was experiencing an economic decline, he journeyed west, finally settling in Aurora in 1843. There he found water that was especially well suited to the production of whiskey and began to manufacture his own brand, Thistledew.

Gaff's distillery flourished, and he soon owned much of Aurora, plus a fleet of steamboats. So enamored of his fleet was he that in 1856 he built a mansion overlooking the Ohio River with a façade reminiscent of a riverboat—broad eaves, a semicircular, two-story colonnaded porch, and a circular belvedere at the top resembling a riverboat's pilothouse.

The mansion, however, also reflects the influence of Italian Renaissance architecture so popular during that era. The main doorway, paneled with Venetian glass, opens onto an entrance hall with grain-painted Circassian walnut woodwork and parquet flooring in the Greek key design. The walls are decorated with *trompe l'oeil* painting of wood paneling and stylized lotus blossoms. Italian molds were used for the decorative plasterwork.

The suspended staircase, in steamboat style, has mahogany banisters and tiger maple spindles. Rosewood "brag" or "mortgage" buttons, traditionally installed when the house has been paid for, decorate the mahogany newel posts.

Arched walk-through windows open onto the porches, and a deliberately narrow doorway—too narrow for ladies' hoopskirts—leads to a stairway to the pilothouse, the gentlemen's retreat.

Now restored, the mansion, whose name was changed by a subsequent owner, is filled with handsome antiques—including a collection of rare blue milk glass, Meissen china, Bohemian glass candle holders, and a Pennsylvania Dutch weight-driven clock. *Open P.M. Tues.– Sun. May–Dec. 24. Admission charged.*

12. Although the canal is outmoded, the ingenuity of the locks is still appreciated.

14. Clifty Falls State Park. *Between Rtes. 56 and 62, Madison.* The highlight of this varied woodland park is a three-mile-long gorge, cut by Clifty Creek through layers of shale and limestone 425 million years old—some of the oldest exposed bedrock in the state. Five major waterfalls, ranging in height from 60 to 82 feet, give the area a rugged grandeur reminiscent of Alpine regions. Clifty Falls, located at the upper end of the gorge, cascades over a series of wide, shallow steps of rock jutting from the cliff before tumbling more than 70 feet into the pool below. Even in midsummer, when the flow of water is diminished, the falls are a dramatic sight. The strata of the cliff disappear into the woods on the other side of the falls like a bony shelf with a cargo of bonsai.

Ten hiking trails, of varying lengths and difficulty, run along the gorge and through surrounding woodlands, among them a mile-long, self-guiding nature trail. Other recreational facilities include a swimming pool, picnic areas, tennis courts, and a nature center containing exhibits of fossils from the gorge and a bird-watching room where a one-way window enables onlookers to view the winged visitors, leaving them undisturbed. An observation tower, just a short walk from the nature center, offers a panoramic view of the Ohio River half a mile to the south. The Hoosier Hills Bicycle Trail connects with park roads. *Open year-round. Admission charged.*

15. Jackson-Washington State Forest. *Rte. 250, Brownstown.* One of the most spectacular features of this primitive forest area is Skyline Drive, a five-mile auto loop running along the crest of a wooded ridge. Observation areas just off the road offer picturesque vistas of the surrounding woodlands and fertile plain, checkered with farm fields and the glinting roofs of silos and barns.

In addition, the forest is a key access point to the 60-mile Knobstone Trail for backpackers. There are also six hiking trails of varying difficulty within the forest's boundaries, including an eight-mile loop. Two trails are available for horseback riding, although horses are not available for rent. Fishing and boat-launching facilities are provided on Knob Lake and Spurgeon Hollow Lake, where likely catches include catfish and bass. Several picnic areas and a 72-site campground make this a pleasant and convenient resting place for travelers. *Open year-round.*

16. George Rogers Clark National Historical Park. *Vincennes.* The park commemorates a soldier who in his lifetime was one of our most neglected heroes. In 1772 the 20-year-old Virginian moved to the Kentucky wilderness. A born leader, he soon turned a small group of frontiersmen into a remarkably effective group of soldiers. In February 1779 Clark and some 175 of his troops crossed 180 miles of cold and flooded terrain to launch a surprise attack on the British contingent here at Fort Sackville. He had previously neutralized the British strongholds at Kaskaskia and Cahokia without firing a shot.

Clark's victories broke England's hold on the Old Northwest and helped secure it for the United States. The area now includes Ohio, Indiana, Illinois, Michigan, and Wisconsin. Yet this courageous leader spent most of his later life plagued by political rivals, unjustly accused of misusing funds, and on the verge of poverty. His great contribution to our nationhood was not fully appreciated until shortly before his death in 1818.

Today Clark is honored by an imposing granite rotunda built in the classical Greek style, with 16 massive columns and a skylight in the domed roof. In its limestone and marble interior are a bronze statue of Clark and murals depicting key episodes in his campaign. The memorial is the centerpiece of a small, graceful park built on the site of Fort Sackville, with formal lawns, steps, and a walk overlooking the Wabash River.

Other historic places in Vincennes include St. Francis Xavier Church, the territorial capitol, and Grouseland, the home of William Henry Harrison, the Indiana Territory's first governor and the ninth president of the United States. Nearby, a prehistoric Indian mound recalls the area's most ancient civilization. An open-air bus provides a tour past many of the town's historic sites. *Memorial and visitor center open daily.*

17. Lincoln Boyhood National Memorial. *Lincoln City.* Thomas Lincoln, the president's father, had moved three times in Kentucky because of land claim disputes. When he took his family across the Ohio River into Indiana in December 1816, he was searching for a more permanent homestead site. He found it near Little Pigeon Creek on a so-called quarter section (160 acres) of government-surveyed land, a plot he had laid claim to earlier. Here the family finally settled down and remained for 14 years.

It was at Little Pigeon Creek in 1818 that Nancy Hanks Lincoln died, succumbing to "milksick," an illness caused by milk from cattle that had eaten the poisonous snakeroot.

Today the site of the Lincoln cabin is marked by bronze castings of sill logs and a stone hearth. Just beyond this, behind a

16. *Better late than never, but better yet would have been to honor Clark while alive.*

19. *Eclectic exterior sets the stage for such interior delights as the Steamboat Gothic motif in the music room.*

split-rail fence, is a reconstruction of the little house. It contains the homely and convincing clutter of a log table and benches, a trundle bed, spinning wheels, a fireplace with iron pots, a broom, and bunches of dried herbs. In a shed behind the cabin the tobacco crop is dried. A few horses, sheep, and chickens complete the pleasant pioneer farm scene. Interpreters in period dress are at hand (tending the crops, flailing flax, and generally working the farm) to answer one's questions.

Five bas-relief panels depicting scenes from Abraham Lincoln's life decorate the visitor center, an impressive white building that contains the Abraham Lincoln and the Nancy Hanks Lincoln halls, which are used for meetings, lectures, and conferences, and a small museum of pioneer life. A walkway leads from the center to the small hill where the president's mother is buried. Another walk is the Trail of the Twelve Stones. Each stone is from a site that played an important part in Lincoln's life. *Open daily except Christmas and New Year's Day.*

18. Cannelton Locks and Dam. *Rte. 66.* Congress authorized the Corps of Engineers to start improving the navigability of the lower Ohio River in 1824. Since then improvements have constantly been made, and today shipping moves easily along this great waterway by virtue of a series of dams and locks along its length. Each dam backs up the water behind it, to create a long navigable "lake" that reaches

upstream to the next dam and lock. Seen in profile, the river resembles a staircase. The dams, in effect, are the risers and the lakes the treads.

The Cannelton Locks and Dam create a lake extending 114 miles to Louisville, Kentucky. The main lock chamber is 1,200 feet long, to accommodate tows; parallel to it is an auxiliary lock chamber 600 feet long. Both are 110 feet wide. The dam, which has 12 floodgates, reaches across the river from the locks to the Kentucky shore, a distance of 1,607 feet.

The whole structure cost nearly $100 million to build in the 1960's, and ample provisions have been made for the taxpayer to get a good view of the operation from a lockside walkway and an observation tower. From the tower the viewer sees not just the locks in operation but also the sandy banks on the Kentucky side of the river and the boiling water at the foot of the dam's massive gates. It is especially fascinating to watch a tug push a colorful, thousand-foot-long convoy of barges through the main lock chamber. The whole process takes about a half-hour. *Observation deck open daily until 7:00 P.M.*

19. Howard Steamboat Museum. *Jeffersonville. Exit Rte. 65 at Fourth St. Follow Fourth St. east to Spring St. Turn south on Spring to Market St. Continue on Market to the museum.* In 1834, 19-year-old James Howard borrowed $60,000 to open a shipyard: thus began one of the greatest steamboat-building companies in Ameri-

ca, a family enterprise that lasted over a century. Reportedly, at one time more that 80% of the steamboats docked in New Orleans were made in the Howard yards. The *J. M. White*, constructed there in the late 1870's at a cost of more than $300,000, was considered the most lavish and beautiful riverboat ever built in the Howard yards. The 1894 *City of Louisville* was the fastest in history.

Today the 22-room Howard mansion, built in the early 1890's by Howard's son, not only houses one of the country's best collections of riverboat memorabilia but is itself an intriguing architectural delight. The grand staircase is modeled on those that graced the great stern-wheelers and side-wheelers of the period, as are the house's 36 chandeliers and several of the hand-carved wooden archways. Among the furnishings, many of which were bought at the Columbian Exposition of 1893, are a brass bed recently valued at $35,000, an ingenious shower with both overhead and waist-level nozzles, and an armchair constructed from 13 pairs of perfectly matched cattle horns. Several of the upstairs rooms contain a superb collection of steamboat models, including one of the giant tugboat *Sprague*—longer than a football field, taller than a three-story building. There are also excellent historic photographs, tools of 19th-century shipbuilders, and relics from historic vessels, including a pilot's wheel 9½ feet in diameter. *Open Mon.–Sat. and P.M. Sun. except holidays. Admission charged.*

Kentucky

The emphasis on bluegrass, and all that it implies, may tend to obscure some of the other appealing aspects of our 15th state.

The prehistory of this area is recalled by Mississippian Indian mounds and the bones of beasts, now extinct, that came to the salt licks, mired down in the swamps, and left the only trace of their having been here.

In the days of the pioneers Daniel Boone explored the Appalachian Range, and evidence of his personal courage and wilderness skills still remains. Also preserved is a handsome tavern favored by Boone and his contemporaries.

In Kentucky you can see where Abraham Lincoln was born, where a country doctor performed a famous operation, a historic log meetinghouse, the world's largest cave system, and some lovely parks. A gristmill and an iron furnace are reminders of early industry; and a tiny, remote community still stands in tribute to a hardy breed of Kentuckians.

1. Wickliffe Mounds. *Rte. 51/60.* Between A.D. 800 and 1400 the bluffs at the confluence of the Ohio and Mississippi rivers were occupied by a mound-building people of the Mississippian culture. But like other mound centers of the central Mississippi Valley, it was abandoned by the time European explorers arrived, for reasons not yet understood. The site here at Wickliffe, administered by Murray State University, is today an active archeo-logical dig, offering visitors an intriguing glimpse not only of the way these people lived but of modern-day investigation of America's prehistoric past.

Of the three exhibit buildings here, each sheltering an excavation site, perhaps the most striking is the cemetery, where the complete remains of several skeletons with their grave ornaments may be seen. Another building displays an extensive collection of the coiled and paddle-smoothed pottery of the Mississippian culture. Among the exhibits here are both everyday utensils and ingeniously decorated formal and ceremonial ware, including animal effigy vessels. Placards and other displays explain the prehistory of the mounds and the story of the dig. *Open daily Mar.–Nov. Admission charged.*

4. *Although just behind the lodge, Lake Pennyrile maintains an aura of wilderness.*

2. The Market House Museum. *Paducah.* In 1827, some years after returning from his westward journey with Meriwether Lewis, Gen. William Clark came to western Kentucky and purchased 37,000 acres of land for five dollars. The tract included a small village called Pekin. Clark renamed it Paducah and set aside a riverfront area for a marketplace. The present Market House, built in 1905, is the third to exist here. A long, handsome structure of reddish-brown glazed brick, it is now a cultural center featuring the Market House Museum.

The major exhibit in the museum's collection is the complete interior of the hundred-year-old L.S. DuBois Drugstore, with its gingerbread oak paneling, soda fountain, and variety of pharmaceutical vials. Other treasures are a life-size painted-wood sculpture of Henry Clay carved with astonishing sophistication by a 12-year-old boy; Paducah's first motorized fire truck (1913 vintage); models of long-gone Paducah buildings; a sweet-toned bell forged from 400 silver dollars; vintage pianos and other antique musical instruments; and from the Civil War era, steamboat models and the brass rudder wheel and fog bell of the gunboat *Paducah.*

Mementos and photographs of Alben W. Barkley, vice president of the United States from 1949 to 1953, and the noted author and humorist Irvin S. Cobb, both prominent Paducans, are on display.

The building, whose old market-stall archways now serve as doorways, also houses the Paducah Art Guild Gallery and the Market House Theatre. *Museum open P.M. daily. Admission charged.*

---

3. Mayfield's Wooldridge Monuments. *Take Highway 45 overpass to N. Seventh St. extension, to Maplewood Cemetery.* This curious example of 19th-century eccentricity—a collection of 18 marble and sandstone figures—depicts the nearest and dearest of Henry G. Wooldridge, who as a 21-year-old moved to Kentucky in 1840. For the last 19 years of his life Wooldridge lived in Mayfield, and shortly before his death in 1899 he assembled his statuary entourage in a "strange procession which never moves," as it is called.

Wooldridge, a breeder of horses who according to Mayfield lore lost his only true love in a riding accident, never married. His widowed mother, seven brothers and sisters, and two young nieces are represented, as well as two hounds, a deer, and a fox (included to memorialize his interest in hunting), and two effigies of himself, one showing him astride his favorite horse, Fop, and the other standing at a lectern. The life-size figures surround his tomb, although only Henry G. Wooldridge himself is buried here.

The sandstone figures have now begun to erode, giving the faces of Wooldridge's entourage a bland, archaic look in sharp contrast to the more finely drawn and enduring detail of his own marble-sculpted features. The figures thus appear to distinguish between the man and his memories—or perhaps between his affections and his self-esteem. *Cemetery open daily.*

---

4. Pennyrile State Resort Park. Despite its many provisions for outdoor activities, this is a quiet, secluded resort pleasantly situated on a slope overlooking a small lake and beach. Its name comes from pennyroyal, an aromatic wildflower that

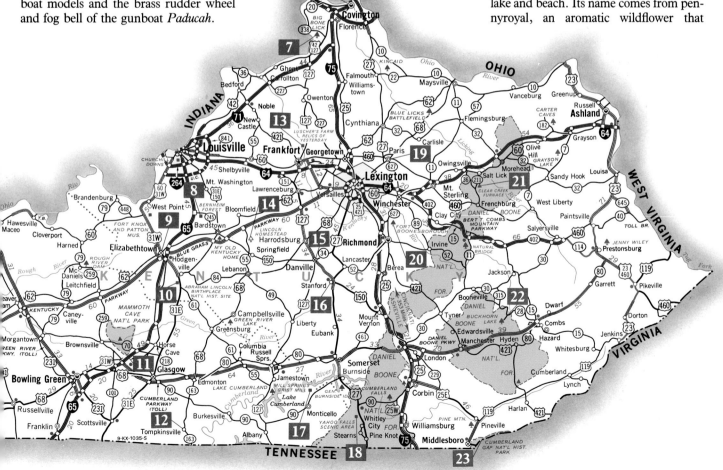

flourishes here, carpeting the hillsides with its small lilac-blue blossoms in May. The grounds of Pennyrile Lodge, which is built of native stone, are landscaped with flowering shrubs, including the delicately scented fringe tree.

With sandy beaches and a bathhouse complex, the 55-acre lake attracts many swimmers. Rowboats and pedal boats are available for rent. Lake Beshear, four miles from the park, is popular with fishermen, who try for crappies, largemouth bass, channel catfish, and bluegills.

Several trails, including one for horseback riders, wander through the park and the adjacent 15,000-acre forest, where white-tailed deer and wild turkeys are often seen. Bobcats also live here but rarely appear. Cardinals, wrens, and mourning doves fill the woods with their songs, particularly in spring.

Besides a riding stable, the park offers a nine-hole golf course, two tennis courts, and two playgrounds. The picnic area, overlooking the lake, is equipped with tables and grills. The campsites, situated in a more remote part of the grounds, offer the luxury of water and electricity hookups. *Open daily Feb.–Dec.*

5. Audubon State Park and Memorial Museum. *Rte. 41, Henderson.* This is a relatively small park of some 700 acres, but it contains a full range of camping and cottage facilities, a nine-hole golf course, several miles of hiking trails, a 325-acre nature preserve, and a lake with a beach and a boat-launching area. In addition, it is situated on one of the main migratory flyways and offers fine opportunities for observing many species of birds, especially the warblers that stop off here in the spring and fall. Native wildflowers put on a display in the spring.

The showpiece of the park is the John James Audubon Memorial Museum. The great painter of wildlife made his home in this area of Kentucky during the early 19th century, and it was here that he did much of the work from which his world-famous prints were made. The museum's superb collection of original Audubon paintings, prints, and memorabilia is remarkably comprehensive. It includes not only the familiar portraits of birds and animals, but also family portraits and a picture of Daniel Boone that Audubon did from memory many years after meeting him. The building itself, financed by the Works Progress Administration (WPA), was completed in 1938. The masonry structure, with its steep roofs and tower, suggests a French

château. *Park open year-round. Museum open daily Apr.–Oct.; weekends only, Nov.–Mar.; closed Jan. Admission charged for museum and beach.*

6. Main Strasse Village. *Covington.* Toward the end of the 18th century a group of German settlers came to the southern banks of the Ohio River and established the town of Covington. Today it is a bustling, modern metropolis with a population of some 50,000. Over the years the older neighborhoods had fallen into disrepair. In the 1970's a program was begun to restore a 30-block section of town dating from the 1830's, and the Carroll Chimes Tower was built.

Now called Main Strasse Village, its tall, narrow, closely clustered buildings reflecting the Germanic origins of its settlers, the area is filled with shops dealing in arts, crafts, and antiques. Strasse Haus, a publike cafe, serves traditional German and American dishes.

The Carroll Chimes Tower, a 100-foot brick structure built in traditional German medieval style with an illuminated clock on each of its four sides, stands opposite a mall with a center row of linden trees ending at a fountain decorated with a statue of a goosegirl. As the carillon of 43 bells strikes the hour, animated figures step out onto a balcony and reenact the story of the Pied Piper of Hamelin.

The village is not a museum; it is a busy, lived-in, restored area recalling the charm and appearance associated with the Old World in the 19th century.

7. Big Bone Lick State Park. *Rte. 338, Union.* Tens of thousands of years ago, when the glaciers of the last Ice Age blanketed northern Kentucky, this inviting 500-acre park was a marshland with a sulphur spring. Prehistoric mammals, including giant mammoths, mastodons, ground sloths, tapirs, and arctic bears, driven southward from their natural habitats, were attracted to the salt licks around the spring. Many became mired and perished in the bog, thus converting it into the vast prehistoric graveyard from which the park today takes its name.

A mile-long self-guiding nature trail through the area of the Ice Age swamp, complete with life-size models of a mam-

5. *Preserved snowy owl overlooks portrayal of stone terns in a first edition of Audubon prints. The artist's watch was probably purchased in London in 1826.*

6. *The clock shows that we missed hearing the 43-bell carillon by just 18 minutes.*

moth and a buffalo and other exhibits, explains the area's geological and ecological history. A small museum offers further educational displays and a slide show about the giant mammals.

Other enjoyable features include a 62-site campground with electrical and water hookups, a swimming pool, a small man-made lake stocked with bluegills, bass, and catfish for anglers, a playground, and a recreation area with facilities for tennis, volleyball, and basketball. A pleasant footpath meanders around the lake. *Park open year-round. Museum open daily Apr.–Oct.; weekends only, Nov.–Mar. Museum admission charged.*

8. Bernheim Forest. *Take Exit 112 from I-65 and follow signs to the forest.* In 1928 Isaac W. Bernheim, at one time a resident of Louisville, gave a tract of 10,000 acres to the state of Kentucky to be used as a recreation area and wildlife sanctuary. He

also generously established a foundation to provide for the development and care of the property.

The forest, a habitat for many kinds of animals and birds, is divided into two sections—an extensive wilderness and a parklike arboretum.

The entrance road, bordered with crab apple trees, ginkgoes, oaks, horse chestnuts, buckeyes, and other nut trees, takes you through the arboretum, a spectacular area in spring when the flowering trees are in bloom. On the left a meadow stretches toward three ponds, home to hundreds of waterfowl, including the elusive snow goose. To the right are formal gardens and plantings of azaleas, junipers, and Japanese maples extending to Lake Nevin, a pond much frequented by anglers trying for crappies and perch.

Several trails loop through the wilderness, including one that circles a 47-foot fire tower, which offers a superb view of the surrounding forested countryside. A self-guiding nature trail leads past a corral containing several deer and wild turkeys, and cages with barred owls and hawks.

The several picnic groves include tables and grills. A map of the forest is available at the nature center. *Open year-round.*

9. Schmidt's Coca-Cola Museum. *Rte. 31, Elizabethtown.* For more than 100 years the Coca-Cola Company has been quenching the thirst of America—and

that of the whole world—and reminding us just how thirsty we are with a barrage of brilliantly colored signs, coasters, dishes, glasses, ashtrays, posters, and a host of other objects, all dominated by a very familiar shade of red and carrying the admonition to "Drink Coca-Cola."

For most of those years the Schmidt family has been bottling Coca-Cola in Elizabethtown and collecting an astonishing assortment of Coca-Cola memorabilia. This assemblage, the private collection of Mr. and Mrs. W. B. Schmidt, said to be the largest in the world, is now on display here at the Schmidt bottling company, which welcomes visitors to both plant and museum. The collection spans more than 95 years of aggressive advertising.

From the reception hall (decorated with a large stained glass mural reflected in a pool containing Japanese carp) a ramp leads to a gallery overlooking the plant's high-speed conveyors and continues on to the museum. Arranged chronologically, the exhibits show the company's ingenious approach to advertising—from the turn-of-the-century trays picturing Victorian ladies dressed as for a garden party, to cigar bands, hand axes, children's toys, and the convenient packaging of the present-day six-pack. The range of items emblazoned with the familiar logo is nothing less than overwhelming. On the case of a clock, Coca-Cola is heralded as a brain tonic and a specific to relieve headaches and exhaustion.

The museum's centerpiece is a soda fountain created for the 1893 Columbian

7. *The real thing once walked where this replica of the woolly mammoth now stands.*

Exposition in Chicago. It includes an onyx and marble counter, Tiffany lampshades, wire ice cream parlor chairs, stained-glass dispensers, oak-framed mirrors behind the counter, and the parlor's original tin ceiling. *Open Mon.–Fri. except major holidays. Admission charged.*

---

10. Abraham Lincoln Birthplace National Historic Site. *Hodgenville.*

Kentucky abounds in log cabins, but none so enshrined as this. On a hill at the site of Sinking Springs Farm, a 300-acre tract bought by Nancy Hanks and Thomas Lincoln in 1808, stands a Doric-columned marble and granite memorial building with an impressive flight of 56 steps—one for each year of Abraham Lincoln's life. The memorial contains the simple one-room log cabin in which the 16th president of the United States was born on February 12, 1809.

Built of stout, squared, white oak beams with a wattle-and-clay chimney at one end, the cabin, unlike most dwellings of that day, has no half-loft and only one small square window, which perhaps was covered with oiled paper or an animal skin to keep out the winter cold. One wall of the memorial building displays photographs of President Lincoln in office.

Since the 1860's, as the Sinking Springs property changed hands, the cabin has been removed and later returned to the farm several times. This gave rise to a controversy as to its authenticity. In 1900 the Lincoln Farm Association was formed by several prominent Americans, including Mark Twain and William Jennings Bryan, to preserve Lincoln's birthplace. Ten years later President Theodore Roosevelt laid the cornerstone of the memorial building, and soon the cabin, if not the actual one, at least a fine facsimile, came to a permanent resting place. Original or not, it clearly captures the spirit of the time. And the contrast between the stark simplicity of the cabin and the grandeur of its protective covering seems both poignant and ironic.

The spring for which the farm was named is still there, rising from a grotto-like cave at the foot of the hillside. Several hiking trails wind through the fields and forests of the park, and picnic facilities are available. *Open daily except Christmas.*

11. Mammoth Cave National Park.

The main attraction at this 5,000-acre park is the extensive network of passageways and caverns in the cave itself. It is the world's longest cave system, and tours range from 1 ½ hours to a half-day tour that includes lunch in a fascinating underground dining room. There's also a strenuous six-hour Wild Cave tour, available by reservation.

Meanwhile, back on the surface, these hills and valleys along both sides of the Green River offer a wide range of opportunities for outdoor activities, including hiking, backpacking, camping, and horseback riding. Outings on a riverboat give views of the limestone cliffs edging Green River and occasionally of wildlife.

For many centuries this countryside was used for agriculture. Indians grew pumpkins, squash, and seed-producing plants here 2,000 years ago; during the 19th century the major crops on many small holdings were corn and tobacco. Since 1941, when the park was opened, the land has been allowed to revert to its original state as a deciduous forest. The changing patterns of vegetation are documented on a self-guiding motor nature trail that follows a one-way road along Joppa Ridge, one of the many wagon trails once connecting the farms that were formerly maintained in the area. A brochure keyed to the route is available at the park headquarters.

The park offers a course in orienteering, the skill of finding one's way with the aid of a map and a compass; many trails and backpacking routes, some through the primitive back country, wind through the countryside. Camping is permitted on designated sites. Permits, available at park headquarters, are required for camping in the wilderness area.

The forest is home to the Virginia white-tailed deer, raccoons, and other small mammals, as well as owls, warblers, and cardinals. Fishing and boating are permitted in the park. *Open year-round except Christmas.*

10. *There's little doubt that Abraham Lincoln would have been amazed and amused at the opulent setting created to house the humble one-room cabin in which he was born.*

11. *Impressionistic reflections add to the charm of this idyllic scene on Otter Pond.*

sister, is buried in the nearby cemetery along with other pioneers. Soldiers of the Revolutionary War and the War of 1812 are also interred here.

Picnic tables and grills, a playground, and a shelter, reminding visitors of the tradition of serving dinner on meeting-house grounds, are located under the trees. *Open year-round.*

13. Luscher's Farm Relics of Yesterday. *Two miles north of Frankfort on Manley Lewis Ferry Road, west off Rte. 127.* Farmers must know the characteristics of their land, their crops, their animals, and the cycle of seasons. These remain essentially the same, but the all-important tools and equipment they use are constantly changing. No one is more responsive to the importance of farm tools than the farmer himself, and this aspect of personal awareness is what makes this family-run museum so special.

The collection of antique farm tools and equipment here is one of the best in the country. It is a celebration not only of the American farmer but of the Luscher family's love of the land. Three generations of Luschers (descendants of a Swiss immigrant who settled in the Frankfort area after the Civil War) have devoted themselves to acquiring farm-related items, adding to the equipment in their own barns and sheds.

Displays here range from an 1840 wooden corn sheller and animal-driven plows and treadmills to gasoline-powered trucks and tractors built between 1914 and 1941—and all of this equipment is in working condition. Large sections of the walls are lined with antique hand tools, and one corner is devoted to household gadgets and kitchen implements, from antique washing machines to sausage grinders. Perhaps the pride of the collection is an early McCormick reaper, described on its museum placard as "the greatest machine of all time." A visit here is like a trip through America's past, an opportunity to experience the nation's growth as it was reflected in her developing machinery. The innumerable hand tools displayed are telling reminders of the never-ending manual labor involved in wresting a living from the soil. *Open Mon.–Sat. and P.M. Sun. Memorial Day–Labor Day.*

12. Old Mulkey Meeting House. *Tompkinsville.* Situated in a woodland near an ancient cemetery, the simple and austere log structure was built in 1804 by the Mill Creek Baptist Congregation, whose leader was John Mulkey, the son and grandson of Baptist preachers. Five years after the meetinghouse was completed, the congregation became divided, one faction accepting and the other rejecting the theory of predestination. John Mulkey, who rejected the doctrine, was followed by a majority of the members, and he continued for many years to espouse his beliefs in the area. The log building soon became

known as the Mulkey Meeting House. Brother Mulkey was a significant force in the religion of southern Kentucky and northern Tennessee. He delivered some 10,000 sermons and encouraged four of his six sons to become ministers.

The 30- by 50-foot building is designed with two shallow transepts, creating 12 corners to represent the 12 apostles; its three doors represent the Trinity. Instead of glass, the windows and doors are fitted with rough wooden shutters. Pictures of John Mulkey and his wife hang on the wall beside the preacher's stall.

Hannah Pennington, Daniel Boone's

14. Lincoln Homestead State Park.

Springfield. This is Lincoln country, and three buildings that were important in the life of Thomas Lincoln, the president's father, have been brought together in this 153-acre park. They include his childhood home, the girlhood home of his bride, Nancy Hanks, and the blacksmith and carpenter shop where he learned his trade. Of the three, only the Berry House, where Abraham's mother lived when she was courted by Thomas Lincoln, is original.

Although the 16- by 18-foot Lincoln homestead is a replica, it is constructed of hundred-year-old logs and stands on the same spot as the one built by the president's grandfather (for whom he was named), who was the first of the family to settle in Kentucky. Behind the cabin is the creek that became known as Lincoln's Run shortly after the family settled here. Several of the cabin's furnishings were made by the president's father.

The Berry House, a two-story structure built of massive yellow poplar beams and furnished in pioneer style, was moved to the park from its original site about a mile away. On display in the house is a copy of the marriage bond of Thomas Lincoln and Nancy Hanks.

A small covered bridge has been built across the creek, leading to a replica of the shop that belonged to Richard and Francis Berry, the master craftsmen who are said to have taught Thomas Lincoln his woodworking skill.

Something of an anomaly, which would have puzzled Thomas Lincoln no end, is the 18-hole golf course in the park. *Open daily May–Oct. Admission charged.*

---

15. McDowell House and Apothecary.

Danville. On South Second St. near Constitution Square State Shrine. The white clapboard Georgian house, dating from about 1789, was the home of Dr. Ephraim McDowell, known as the father of abdominal surgery, who lived here from 1795 until his death in 1830. It was in this house on Christmas Day, 1809, that Dr. McDowell performed the first laparotomy in America. Although the removal of the ovarian tumor was done without antisepsis or anesthetic, the patient, one Jane Crawford, survived and lived on for many years.

The house and the earlier small brick structure that served as the doctor's apothecary shop and office have been restored and furnished with period pieces, many of

14. *An excellent replica on the original site of Abraham Lincoln's childhood home.*

them belonging to the McDowells. A grandfather clock scarred by an arrow, hand-held fire screens (used by ladies to protect their complexions), fine handmade bedspreads, surgical instruments, candle molds, cooking utensils, and flatirons are reminders of the texture of pioneer life in this frontier town.

The apothecary shop collection of colorful 18th- and 19th-century jars and vials, accurately labeled and filled with herbs and simples of the period, are neatly arranged on the shelves; a fine old brass scale stands on the counter.

The gardens, too, have been restored and are included in the tour of the house and apothecary shop. *Open Mon.–Sat. and P.M. Sun. except Mon. in Nov.–Feb., Thanksgiving Day, and Christmas. Admission charged.*

---

16. William Whitley House State Shrine.

Rte. 150, Stanford. William Whitley, one of Kentucky's early pioneer settlers and hero of both the American Revolution and the War of 1812, completed his sturdy three-story brick dwelling in 1792. The

15. *The adjoining apothecary, though practical, does little justice to the handsome house.*

handsome structure, the first brick house in Kentucky, sits on a low eminence enhanced with stately shade trees. The walls are 23 inches thick, and the windows are set higher than usual to give protection against attack by Indians. A secret stairway leads from the kitchen to the second floor, providing an escape route and a hiding place. Among the period pieces on view are Whitley's rifle and powder horn, which he engraved with his own encouraging verse: "... fill me with the best of power I'le make your rifle crack the lowder." These possessions were returned to Mrs. Whitley after her husband's death in 1813 at the battle of Thames in Ontario. A soldier later claimed it was Whitley who killed the great Shawnee chief Tecumseh in that encounter.

There was, however, more to Whitley's life here than worry about the Indians. Nearby he built a horse-racing track, one of the first in a long Kentucky tradition. Whitley's pride in his home is perhaps most evident on the exterior walls, where glazed bricks prominently form his initials in front and those of his wife in back. A picnic shelter is on the grounds. *Open daily mid-Apr.–Labor Day; Tues.–Sun. the rest of the year. Admission charged.*

---

17. Mill Springs Grist Mill. *Off Rte. 90, seven miles north of Monticello. The entrance, easily missed, is set back from the road.* Since the early 1800's this steep, wooded hillside has been a mill site. The present mill, which dates from 1877, has a 40-foot iron overshot waterwheel, added in 1912 and believed to be one of the largest in the world. Power for the mill comes from 13 springs, which form a stream that cascades down the hillside into a large pipe leading to the waterwheel.

The building, a large white clapboard structure with a stone foundation, overlooks Lake Cumberland. A walkway takes you under the mill for a view of the wheel and the main drive shaft. Belts run from the shaft to the upper floor, where the corn is ground, usually on Saturday and Sunday afternoons. The cornmeal is sold at the nearby gift shop.

The opening battle of the Kentucky-Tennessee campaign in the Civil War was fought at Mill Springs on January 19, 1862, a conflict that resulted in a victory for the Union forces. Still standing on the hillside above the mill is Lanier House; once the home of an early mill owner, it served as the Confederate headquarters. A fortification also remains at Mill Springs.

From the mill a path leads to Mill Spring Park on Cumberland Lake, where picnic areas and a boat dock are located. Several scenic hiking trails wind through the park. *Park open Memorial Day–Sept.; mill open Memorial Day–Labor Day.*

---

18. Yahoo Falls Scenic Area. *Turn west off Rte. 27 onto Rte. 700. Go 3½ miles and turn north onto the gravel Forest Service road, Rte. 660. Continue one mile to the parking area.* As you turn onto Route 660, look for the grave of Jacob Troxel. During the American Revolution, "Big Jake" Troxel was sent by George Washington's staff to live among the Indians of Kentucky and prevent them from supporting the British. Welcomed by the Tsa-Waagan Cherokees, he lived happily in their village, eventually marrying the chief's daughter, Princess Cornblossom, and having a child by her, whom they named Little Jake.

For the next 30 years, however, relations between the Indians and the settlers were difficult. In 1810, Princess Cornblossom, then the head of her dwindling people, agreed to move the tribe to Tennessee. The Indians assembled for the journey near Yahoo Falls, but just before their departure they were massacred by a group of settlers. Arriving as the attack ended, Princess Cornblossom and her son shot and killed two of the three surviving whites. Grief-stricken for her people, the princess died soon afterward; two days later Big Jake followed her in death. Little Jake terrorized settlers in the area for several years before surrendering.

The Yahoo Falls Scenic Area, which lies within the Daniel Boone National Forest, has a picnic ground and shelter at the parking lot. Several trails are accessible here, including the 250-mile Sheltowee Trace for backpackers. The falls are reached by a signed ¼-mile path leading through the forest to the head of a steep gorge. There, from a walled observation platform, one looks down on Yahoo Creek as it plunges 113 feet from the Cumberland Plateau into the gorge below.

On the return to the parking lot a detour leads to a spot overlooking the confluence of the creek and South Fork River as it curves beneath a sandstone crag. This vantage point, surrounded by masses of mountain laurel, is a most pleasant place to linger and picnic. For volume of water, the best seasons for viewing the falls are spring and autumn. *Open year-round.*

18. *That man-made waterworks cannot equal those in nature is here confirmed.*

19. Duncan Tavern. *Paris.* The imposing three-story tavern of gray Kentucky limestone faces the Paris public square, a village plaza dating back to the days when this area was still part of Virginia. The tavern was built by Maj. Joseph Duncan in 1788 at a time when all the nearby structures were simple log houses.

Major Duncan died in the early 1800's, leaving his widow, Anne Duncan, with six small children. Unable to run the 20-room tavern herself, Mrs. Duncan leased the property and built an adjoining log and clapboard structure, now known as the Anne Duncan House, for herself and her family.

Because it was located near the Bourbon County courthouse, where thousands of lawsuits over land claims were presented, the Duncan Tavern was the scene of many gatherings of distinguished early Americans, including Daniel Boone and Michael Stoner.

In 1940, after serving as a public hostelry for more than 150 years, the tavern and the attached house were taken in trust by the Kentucky Society of the Daughters of the American Revolution. The elegant buildings are beautifully restored and furnished with an outstanding collection of antiques. The carpets, silver, china, paintings, carvings, and furniture all date before 1820. In recent years a formal garden of boxwood hedges and patterned brick walks has been established within the foundation walls of a third house that once stood on the property. *Open Tues.–Fri. year-round. Admission charged.*

---

20. Fort Boonesborough State Park. *Rte. 388, Boonesborough.* The fort that stands here today, evoking the period of Kentucky's early pioneer settlement, is a detailed reconstruction of one built nearby on the banks of the Kentucky River by Daniel Boone and about 30 fellow frontiersmen in 1775. These were the first settlers sent out by Col. Richard Henderson of North Carolina to establish a colony west of the Appalachians. Despite the fact that Henderson had purchased a vast tract of land from the Cherokees for the colony, the settlers immediately found themselves at odds with the Shawnees and other local tribes who were being encouraged by the British to attack American settlers during the Revolutionary War. Boone's daughter and two other girls were kidnapped by Indians. Boone and nine of his companions tracked the Indians and rescued the three captives.

About two years later Boone and a group of companions were captured by the Shawnees. Boone escaped, made his way to Boonesborough, and urged improvement in its defenses. The precautions were taken, and late in the summer of 1778 the little fort withstood a 10-day Indian siege, thus securing the survival and growth of the Kentucky settlements.

Upon entering the fort today, a visitor is taken back to the settler's world. Several of the cabins display furnishings typical of the period and the spartan circumstances, and in others frontier crafts are demonstrated, including weaving, carpentry, candlemaking, soapmaking, and blacksmithing. A small museum is devoted to Boone and the life of the pioneers.

The park also offers a large campground with hookups as well as primitive tenting sites, a recreation area with facilities for various activities, an inviting sandy beach along the river for swimming, and a boat-launching ramp. Fishermen usually catch bass, perch, bream, and catfish. The park is heavily visited on holidays and summer weekends. *Campground open year-round. Fort open May–Sept. Admission charged to fort.*

---

21. Clear Creek Furnace. *Salt Lick. Follow signs on Rte. 211 and enter at the first picnic area.* The competition for iron ore for this smelting furnace, located on a small stream called Clear Creek, culminated in a murder and a famous trial. The structure was built in 1839 by two partners, W. S. Allen and W. S. Lane. In January 1840, during a dispute between Mr. Lane and a Mr. Ewing, owner of a nearby furnace, over the rights to a local iron mine, gunfire broke out, and Mr. Ewing was killed.

Because of the prominence of the men involved, the trial drew wide attention. Conflicting opinions were formed, and rifts developed among families and friends. Mr. Lane pleaded self-defense and was acquitted.

The furnace, the last of its kind in this area, was fired for the last time in 1875. It is a pylonlike structure with a strong Mayan aspect and towers to some 40 feet. Massive cut stones were laid two deep to contain the fierce 2,000° temperature required for smelting iron ore.

The ruins are in a picnic ground sheltered by cedars at the southern end of the Clear Creek Recreation Area. The recreational facility also offers campsites and several foot trails. *Open year-round.*

---

22. Buckhorn Lake State Resort Park. *Rte. 28, Buckhorn.* This quiet mountain park takes excellent advantage of the lake created in 1961 by a 162-foot dam built several miles downstream on the middle fork of the Kentucky River. Primarily designed for secluded family holidays devoted to water sports, the park offers a sand beach, a boat-launching ramp, and a marina with 98 slips for water enthusiasts. In addition the park has a picnic area, a play-

20. *With few tools, splits of white oak, skill, and patience, baskets are made.*

23. *From Pinnacle Overlook one sees the forests, peaks, and valleys of three states, and the gap that beckoned settlers to the west.*

ground, tennis courts, and two self-guiding nature trails that wend through the woodlands. Anglers, either in boats or on the spacious fishing pier, are likely to catch largemouth and smallmouth bass, crappies, bluegills, channel catfish, and muskies. Rental boats are available.

The quiet park roads invite cyclists, and bikes may be rented. A modern 36-room lodge is operated by the park, and privately operated campgrounds are located nearby. Musical shows, square dancing, and other entertainments are offered occasionally in the lodge. *Open Apr.–Oct.*

23. Cumberland Gap National Historic Park. *Middlesboro.* It was the creek flowing north toward the Cumberland River that first showed the way through this section of the Appalachian Range. Herds of buffalo wandered along Yellow Creek;

then the Indians followed, creating the so-called Warriors Path, linking the Cherokees of the east with the Shawnees to the northwest. Fur traders, hunters, and pioneer farmers traveled the route. In 1775 Daniel Boone and a crew of axmen blazed the Wilderness Road for some 200 miles and opened a corridor that started the first migration to the west.

In the early 1800's faster and easier westward routes were developed, and the importance of Cumberland Gap declined. Today it is primarily interesting for its colorful history and stunning scenery.

A road (closed to trailers and vehicles more than 20 feet long) from the park's visitor center winds precipitously up to the 2,500-foot Pinnacle. A short footpath bordered with wild phlox and mountain laurel leads from the parking lot to an overlook with an astounding view of the gap and the valleys and peaks of three states. A mounted telescope brings intimate details of the panorama into sight.

Within the park is the Hensley Settlement, a wilderness community of 12 farmsteads established on Brush Mountain in the early 1900's by the Hensley and Gibbons families. It flourished for almost 50 years before it was abandoned in the 1950's. Now being restored, the community can be reached only by four-wheel-drive vehicles or a four-mile hike over rough terrain. Those who make the trip will gain some insight into the self-sufficient way of life that these stouthearted people chose to pursue.

Four primitive campsites, accessible only by foot, are located on the Ridge Trail, a route along the Kentucky-Virginia border. Picnic areas and hiking trails are scattered throughout the park. Maps and information are available at the visitor center in Middlesboro. *Park open year-round; visitor center open daily except Christmas.*

Tennessee

The superb state parks and the variety of other attractions might be predictable. Surprising is the dedication to preserving historic towns.

The varied communities to see include a treasure of Victorian architecture, a hamlet that recalls the stark realities of 19th-century life in the Tennessee hills, a charmingly naive experiment in gentlemanly colonization, and the oldest town west of the Appalachians. Here too is a reconstruction of an Indian village abandoned almost 500 years ago.

The Tennessee Valley Railroad is memorialized, as are the home, the locomotive, and the immortal story of Casey Jones. There are fine log structures to visit, a water-driven mill, a famous whiskey distillery (where they provide an excellent drink of lemonade), and a million-dollar collection of unusual teapots.

1. Chucalissa. *From I-55 take the Third St. South exit (Rte. 61) to Mitchell Rd. Go west on Mitchell Rd. about five miles to the entrance.* In the Choctaw language *Chucalissa* means "abandoned houses." Here at the edge of T.O. Fuller State Park, not far from the Mississippi River, lies the site of an Indian village that seems to have been abandoned in the 1500's, probably before the arrival in the area of the Spanish con-

quistador Hernando de Soto. De Soto may have visited the place in 1541, but his accounts are vague as to his exact location. It wasn't until the late 1930's, when excavation was under way for a swimming pool in T.O. Fuller State Park, that the modern world discovered the remains of the prehistoric village.

A full-time staff of archeologists and Choctaw Indians now maintains a reconstructed village and museum on the site. The village is reached via a passageway decorated with traditional snake images; a trench at the entrance reveals the strata that archeologists worked through to uncover the village and its history.

The reconstructed houses, set on a roughly circular plaza with a platform mound to the north, are rectangular, with conical thatched roofs resting on five-foot-high pole-and-mud walls. On the platform mound sits a much larger house, presumably that of the chief. Inside are tableaux of daily life in the village: women preparing meals, a shaman, or medicine man, performing a curing ceremony, the chief receiving a messenger from a neighboring tribe. The Burial Exhibit contains 37 skel-

etons lying as they were found, surrounded by burial objects. To see them in the dimly lit room is to experience simultaneously a vivid sense of the humanity of the people who lived here and sadness at their complete disappearance.

T. O. Fuller State Park, which encompasses 1,138 acres, offers equipped campsites (which are an easy half-mile walk from Chucalissa), picnic grounds, game fields, and trails. Trail guides are available in both type and braille for the Honeysuckle Nature Trail, which wends through woods inhabited by deer and wild turkeys. The park is heavily visited in summer. *Chucalissa open Tues.–Sat. and P.M. Sun. except Thanksgiving Day and the Christmas season; admission charged. Park open year-round.*

2. Reelfoot Lake State Resort Park. A cataclysmic earthquake on February 7, 1812—perhaps the most violent ever to strike the continental United States—caused an enormous area of land to sink as

2. Surreal is the only word for the cypress knees standing like cave-born stalagmites.

is a resting place for a large number of migrating waterfowl and therefore a favorite with birders. As many as 200 bald eagles have been observed wintering here before returning north. Between December 1 and mid-March the park conducts daily bus tours to look for these majestic birds. The tours depart from the Reelfoot Lake State Airpark Inn at 10:00 A.M. and take about two hours. Reservations are required. The varied plant life also draws botany enthusiasts. The visitor center, in Tiptonville, has a small museum of natural and local history. Among the exhibits are Indian artifacts and stuffed birds and animals. *For bald eagle tour information call (901) 253-7756. Park open year-round; visitor center and museum open Tues.–Sat. and P.M. Sun. Fee charged for tours and cruises.*

much as 10 feet. Water from the Mississippi River entered this depression, creating a 14-mile-long lake. Much of the lake's charm and strangeness is imparted by the venerable bald cypress trees that fringe its margins. They rise tall and ghostly from the dark water, and in spring and summer canopy the shoreline with delicate, fresh green foliage.

The shallow 18,000-acre lake is dotted with islands. The park includes a narrow strip around most of the shore, where

campgrounds, picnic and day-use areas, and boat launches are located. From April through October a cruise boat leaves from a jetty near the visitor center every morning at 9:00 for a 3½-hour cruise, stopping at Caney Island, where visitors can walk a nature trail and see Indian mounds. In midsummer the American lotus blooms abundantly in parts of the lake; when that happens the cruise boat stops to let people pick the flowers.

A sanctuary for wildlife, Lake Reelfoot

3. Teapot Museum. *Municipal building, Trenton.* Although known locally as the Teapot Museum, this exhibition's official title is "The World's Largest Collection of Rare Porcelain Veilleuses." A *veilleuse-théière* is hardly an ordinary teapot: it is also a night-light. The earliest veilleuses were food warmers, with a vessel in which a candle or oil was burned and a bowl above, on a stand. Eventually a teapot replaced the bowl. In 19th-century Europe these simple utensils for brewing tea and

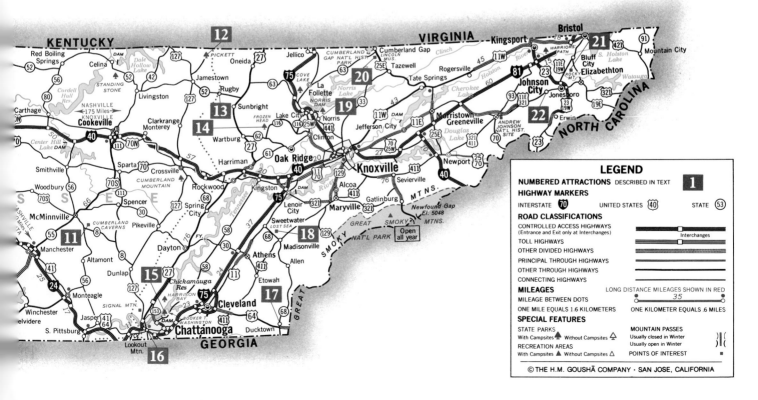

providing a night-light became, in the hands of master craftsmen, magnificent works of art.

This 19th-century collection—now valued at more than $1 million—was donated to Trenton by Dr. Frederick C. Freed, a local citizen. The town gave it a home in the local municipal hall. Housed in glass-fronted cases, the 525 teapots are decorated in varying degrees of sophistication and charming naivety with palm trees, Romeos and Juliets, birds, dogs, horses, flowers, vines, mermaids, cathedrals, and castles. The colors range from rich to delicate, from deep peacock blue and glowing gold to pale pink and white.

Seeing these ornamental objects, you can easily envision one glowing and flickering on a bedside table, offering comfort in an era before electricity. *Open Mon.–Fri., and A.M. Sat. year-round. When the museum is closed, the key is available from the dispatcher in the police department office in the municipal building.*

---

4. Casey Jones Home and Railroad Museum. *Jackson.* The legendary hero of the song "Casey Jones," the engineer died in the wreck of the *Cannonball Express* the night of April 30, 1900, in Vaughan, Mississippi. His speeding train had rounded a bend and come upon a freight train; Casey heroically stayed on the throttle to save the lives of his passengers.

Here is his house at the time of his death: a simple white clapboard with green shutters and wraparound porch. Two rooms are devoted to memorabilia and railroad history, including a model of the fatal accident scene complete with miniature trains. There is a small but interesting display of the evolution of railroad rails, from early strap rail through U and pear shapes to the current T shape.

In the rest of the house (only the ground floor is open to the public) there are also some lovely period touches—a lead tub, a marble sink, a straight-edge razor and strap, and a bottle of Nash's Laxative Syrup in the bathroom; a coal stove, a churn and dasher, and old green mason jars in the kitchen.

Outside the house is a replica of Illinois Central Railroad engine No. 382, the train in which Jones died. You can climb into the cab, handle the massive coal rake, and lean out of the window. *Open Mon.–Sat. and P.M. Sun. Admission charged.*

5. Fort Donelson National Battlefield. Early in the Civil War the Confederacy seemed to be invincible. But a Union reconnaissance in January 1862 indicated that the South's western line of defense was vulnerable at Fort Henry on the Tennessee River and Fort Donelson on the Cumberland. The North's expedition against the two forts was led by an obscure brigadier general, Ulysses S. Grant, whose strategy involved the first use of the Union's ironclad gunboats. Fort Henry quickly submitted, but the battle at Fort Donelson raged for three days. Gen. Simon Buckner was forced to surrender unconditionally to Grant on February 16, 1862, at the nearby Dover Hotel. It marked the North's first major victory in the Civil War and the emergence of a new hero, "Unconditional Surrender" Grant.

The visitor center displays relics of the battle—sabers, muskets, pistols, canteens, military maps—and portraits of the commanders. A short, evocative slide show explains the course of the battle.

An auto tour of the battlefield passes earthworks, trenches, and two reconstructed Confederate huts, as well as the Confederate Monument, honoring the Southern dead, who were refused burial in the nearby national cemetery.

Perhaps the most interesting features of the park are the two gun batteries overlooking a sweep of the Cumberland River. Near the lower battery are the barrels of

eight 32-pound guns as well as a columbiad, a cannon capable of firing a 10-inch cannonball a distance of three miles. It was fired at the Union ironclads at a distance of 1½ miles.

Visitors should be alert for poisonous snakes and ticks, and should also be cautious on approaching the Cumberland River, which is deep and swift in this area. Picnic grounds are located ½ mile past the visitor center in the direction of the river. *Open year-round except Christmas.*

---

6. Natural Bridge. *Waynesboro.* This double-span natural bridge, one of the few in the world, was formed over the last 4,000 years as a stream slowly eroded a cave into the rock below. When the center of the cave roof collapsed, the front and back portions of the ceiling remained in place, creating the twin spans of the stone bridge. The larger span is nearly 70 feet long and stands almost 50 feet above the streambed, and the second span is only a few feet shorter.

Before white settlers came, the Cherokee and Creek tribes used the shelter of the bridge and the nearby caves for council meetings. After the tribes were forced out of the area by the federal government in the 1830's, Natural Bridge became the preserve of outlaws in the Natchez Trace

8. The innate beauty of timbers wrought by ax and adze can't be duplicated by machine.

9. *It looks more like a sawmill than a distillery, but the wood yields the needed charcoal.*

area: the Younger Brothers, the Bloody Harpers, and later the Mason and Murrell Gang. In time the outlaw period passed, and until the Civil War, Natural Bridge served as a sort of courthouse for Harding and Wayne counties. David Crockett made one of his first speeches at the "Rock Courthouse" and was elected to the office of magistrate.

Years later Natural Bridge became a tourist attraction. The old trappings of commerce—including a honeymoon cottage—have since fallen into disrepair, and at this writing plans are being made by new owners to refurbish the area. A short, easy trail leads from the parking lot to Natural Bridge, which for now at least is back to being its natural self.

---

7. Franklin. Sitting sedately behind a perimeter of shopping malls and commercial enterprise, Franklin offers a treasure of Victorian architecture: dove-gray, plum, biscuit, and mustard-colored houses surrounded by neatly trimmed lawns and sheltered by the venerable maples lining its quiet streets. A 15-block section of the downtown area is listed in *The National Register of Historic Places.*

Most of the homes are privately owned, but the exteriors can be enjoyed from the car or on a leisurely stroll. One of the few open to the public—and also one of the best—is the Carter House, built in 1830 by Fountain Branch Carter and subsequently inhabited by three generations of his family. During the Civil War the

house served as a command post for Gen. Jacob D. Cox. A fierce battle that was waged nearby is commemorated in a museum attached to the house. The house itself is of brick—not large but well proportioned, of a pleasing step-ended design with a columned porch. The rooms are appointed with furnishings of the period. Outbuildings of the same era include a smokehouse, tool shed, family kitchen, and slave cabin.

The Carnton Mansion, which is outside the historic district, is also open to the public. Completed in 1826, it is a fine example of the palatial homes built by wealthy southern planters. It was a hospital during the Civil War; on the grounds is the only privately owned Confederate cemetery in the country.

A brochure with a map for self-guiding tours of the historic district is available at the Williamson County Courthouse, one of the landmarked buildings in Franklin. *Admission charged for house tours.*

---

8. Wynnewood. *Castalian Spring.* Built in 1828 as a stagecoach inn, this is the largest log structure in Tennessee and probably the largest ever built in the state. In 1834 the inn became the property of Alfred R. Wynne. It next served as a resort, then as a working farm, and remained in the Wynne family until 1971, when the state acquired it as a historic site.

Scrupulously maintained to preserve its authenticity, Wynnewood has qualities of coherence and tranquillity that make it a

pleasure to visit. You enter the house for a guided tour by way of a dogtrot, the local term for a hallway running through the building from front to back.

The room above the dogtrot functions as a small museum of diverse family souvenirs, mementos, and trophies. Adjacent rooms include a simply furnished "ladies' sleeping room" and two "sleeping rooms for gentlemen," in one of which you can inspect a loom, a cotton gin, and a weasel (used to wind yarn).

Outside you'll find a charming, well-tended old garden and a one-room log building. Formerly a doctor's office, it houses a collection of 19th-century medical equipment. At the far end of the main house is the old kitchen, equipped with a treasure of antique utensils. Farm buildings, including a handsome barn, add further authenticity and appeal. *Open daily May–Oct.; Mon.–Sat. Nov.–Apr.; closed Christmas. Admission charged.*

---

9. Jack Daniel Distillery. *Lynchburg.* Here's your chance for a spirited tour of one of America's most famous distilleries. From the moment you enter, the air is permeated by the pungent aroma of Tennessee sour mash, the company hallmark.

A brief introductory slide show explains the reasons for the distillery's location: the ready availability of good spring water, high-quality grain, and ample supplies of maple, from which the charcoal for filtering is made. This all-important material gives the whiskey its unique flavor.

You'll pass through 45 warehouses where the whiskey is aged in white oak barrels, made locally and used but once. Each warehouse holds 20,160 of the 60-gallon barrels (worth about $500 million in U.S. taxes alone).

In turn you'll see all the operations required for the production of this heady concoction: the yard where the charcoal is made, the grotto whence springs the water, the grain silos, the apparatus that mixes the raw ingredients (80 percent corn, 12 percent rye, 8 percent barley malt), the fermenting vats, stills, charcoal mellowing vats, and the bottling plant. The one-hour walking tour involves a good bit of climbing up and down steps and is not recommended for the infirm.

Along the way you visit the original company offices, which serve as a museum, and see the safe that led to the demise of Jack Daniel. Unable to open the safe,

10. *Form follows function to create the classic charm of a water-driven mill.*

he kicked it in a fit of rage, broke a toe, and developed a fatal case of gangrene. On a happier note: at the end of the tour coffee and excellent lemonade are served. *Open daily except Thanksgiving Day, Christmas, and New Year's Day.*

10. Falls Mill. *Four miles west of Belvidere on Rte. 64.* A good mill site must have a dependable flow of water for the raceway, a solid streamside foundation for the building, and easy road access to a nearby trading area. When these conditions are met, the turning wheels can be adapted to serve a variety of needs, as has been demonstrated here.

Beginning operation in 1873, Falls Mill produced cotton thread and wool for home spinning. In 1906 it became a cotton gin, and after World War II the structure served as a woodworking shop. In 1969 the mill was restored and, with equipment purchased from nearby mills that had closed, converted to a gristmill; it serves as such today. The 32-foot overshot wheel is said to be one of the largest in the country still in productive service.

The first floor of the building is given over to exhibits of tools and equipment related to power and industry. The second floor accommodates the working mill itself and a replicated old country store. Presently the third floor is closed to the public and used for storage.

The mill is attractively situated at the head of a wooded riverside dell. A short path brings you to a picnic area in a beautiful cove with a view of the milldam and falls. You may find yourself in the company of peacocks, ducks, and geese. *Open Mon.–Sat. and P.M. Sun. year-round. Admission charged.*

11. Cumberland Caverns. Rarely is nature's sculptural art more dramatically revealed than in these remarkable caverns. Three hundred feet below the surface of the ground, they were formed some 500 million years ago by the erosive action of a sea now known as the Gulf of Mexico, which then extended this far north.

A stream flows through the entrance gallery into a crystal-clear pool swarming with blind white crayfish. From the center of this pool rises a 4-million-year-old flowstone (formed by the conjunction of a stalactite and a stalagmite) named Moby Dick. Covering the ceilings is a wide and leaflike stalactite mass referred to as curtains. When lightly tapped they produce the bell-like tones of a pipe organ.

Subsequently you may contemplate the immense Volcano Room, from whose lofty ceiling hangs a giant chandelier of cut lead crystal. The natural rock terraces and balconies within the cave lend the chamber the look of a grand old theater. Equally mysterious caverns follow: the

Graveyard, the Popcorn Bowl, and the largest of the tour, the truly cavernous Hall of the Mountain King, 600 feet long, 140 feet high, and enhanced with curious formations called the Pagodas and the Chessmen. As you proceed through this enormous space—the largest cave in eastern America—the sensation of being at the bottom of the Grand Canyon gives way to the impresson of climbing through an archaic Italian hill town. *Open daily Memorial Day–Labor Day; then weekends only. Admission charged.*

12. Pickett State Rustic Park. Rolling hills and deep valleys, sparkling waterfalls, natural bridges and caves are but some of the discoveries to be made in this 11,572-acre wilderness nestled in the upper Cumberland Mountains. The park also includes some excellent runs for white-water canoeing.

The sinuous shoreline of a dark green lake, the centerpiece of Pickett, rewards boaters and hikers alike with an ever-changing view. The road to the lake sweeps past lightly wooded bluffs and dales set discreetly with cabins and campsites. The park is laced by a network of nine marked hiking trails. One of the most pleasing and accessible is the Lake View Trail, which is true to its name. Reaching

11. *They could be exotic flowers or denizens of a coral reef, but these fanciful shapes are formed by deposits of gypsum.*

12. A happy meeting of Natural Bridge and man-made lake created this idyllic scene.

clude an impressive 7,000-volume library of Victorian literature, Christ Church, built in the Carpenter Gothic style, and the Kingston Lisle House, which contains many of Hughes's own belongings. Other houses are open during the annual Rugby Pilgrimage on the first full weekend in August. Brochures and self-guiding maps for a stroll through the community are available at the visitor center.

A number of trails have been preserved here since Rugby was founded. Some of them are steep and rocky in places, and all are on private property. They lead to the Clear Fork River and what used to be the Gentlemen's Swimming Hole. *Tours daily Mar.–Oct. Admission charged.*

14. Frozen Head State Natural Area.

This is an out-and-out wilderness area for hikers and serious backpackers, with development confined to the trail system and one picnic area.

The region is crisscrossed by 10 blazed trails of varying difficulty, some of which are described on a trail map available at the headquarters. It is a 2.8-mile hike to the Frozen Head fire tower at an elevation of 3,324 ft. From the tower there's a fabulous view of the Cumberland Plateau and the Tennessee River valley.

The area is renowned for its wildflowers and flowering trees, and is especially popular in April, when they begin to bloom. On some weekends during that time the park sponsors guided flower walks. August is the time for a Folk Life Festival—dancing, arts, and crafts—while a horseback trail ride is featured in October. *Open year-round.*

15. Booker T. Washington State Park.

This congenial 350-acre park offers a variety of activities. Hikers can explore the area on several trails. Group sport possibilities include volleyball, basketball, croquet, shuffleboard, and badminton.

Boaters and anglers will be equally pleased by the park's scenic situation on Lake Chickamauga. The fish most commonly caught are bass, crappie, sauger, catfish, walleye, and buffalo.

The park honors Booker T. Washington, who was born a slave in 1856 at

this trail is a delight—first by a swinging bridge (which really swings), then a path winding above the laurel, dogwoods, and magnolias fringing the lake.

Another scenic excursion is Natural Bridge Trail. For a distance of about five miles the path wends upward through a forest of evergreens and hardwoods to higher altitudes and panoramic views of the surrounding hilltops before descending toward its terminus at Natural Bridge. *Open year-round.*

13. Rugby.

The 19th century bred a number of attempts at utopian living. Rugby, one of the more curious and colorful, was an English colony founded by Thomas Hughes, a social reformer, writer, and the author of *Tom Brown's Schooldays.*

In the model community he hoped to provide the younger sons of the English upper classes an opportunity to lead useful lives in areas of employment considered beneath them in England, where the law of primogeniture denied inheritance to all but the eldest son.

Named after the school Hughes had attended in England, Rugby was plagued by problems from its very beginnings in 1880. Its members were remarkably unequipped to wrest a living from the wilderness of the Cumberland Plateau. They took less to plowing than to tennis, croquet, the Dramatic Club, the Library and Reading Room Society, and putting out the newspaper, *The Rugbeian.* Although Hughes's experiment failed in 1893, it attracted a good deal of attention in both America and Europe.

Today the village, with its charming Victorian air and architecture, comes as a surprise in the rural countryside. Seventeen of the town's original 70 buildings have been preserved, and others have been authentically reconstructed. Three of the most important of the original structures are open for guided tours. These in-

Hale's Ford, Virginia. After the Civil War he worked as a laborer, studied at Hampton Institute, and became a teacher. He went on to become president of Tuskegee Institute, and is best remembered for his belief that working toward economic independence was the right way for his people to find equality. *Open year-round.*

16. Tennessee Valley Railroad and Museum. *East Chattanooga Station, 4119 Cromwell Rd.* This fine preservation of our colorful railroad history includes steam and diesel locomotives, Pullman cars, day coaches, mail cars, and all the other rolling stock that once made train travel such an exciting adventure. You'll see the *Maitland*, a drawing room Pullman built in 1926. In Office Car 98, the *Eden Isle*, you'll discover how executives traveled in the heyday of the steam trains. Built in 1917 for the president of the Baltimore & Ohio Railroad, it contains the original mahogany paneling, a sitting room, three bedrooms, a dining room with elegant glass-fronted cabinets, and a kitchen. A museum car contains such intriguing items as semaphore signals, pressure gauges, lanterns, and a massive wooden pattern for a driving wheel.

One of the museum's major attractions is a three-mile ride departing from East Chattanooga Station six times daily. On arrival at Grand Junction Station you'll find yourself in an exact copy of an old small-town southern railroad station.

Engine 4501 still proudly puffs its way from Chattanooga to Knoxville as part of a special annual Dogwood Arts Festival, held each April. Other excursions include an Autumn Leaf Special in October and several trips in the spring. *For information on special excursions and reservations call (615) 894-8028. Museum open daily June 10–Labor Day; weekends only Labor Day–Nov. Admission charged.*

17. Ducktown. *In Ducktown, follow signs to the Bura Bura Mine and the adjacent museum.* Picture this: from the edge of the museum parking lot you look down upon a desertlike area of red earth, undulating and rifted, with scant and scrubby vegetation, that extends into the distance. In the foreground of this landscape, far below you, is a chasm filled by a deep green

19. *The best shakes are split in this time-honored way—with ax, maul, and froe.*

lake. The colors in this stark landscape, from soft pastels to glowing reds and copper tones, constantly change with the seasons and time of day. The barren beauty of the 56-square-mile area has prompted comparison with the Dakota Badlands. But this is Tennessee's Copper Basin, and the vista is man-made.

Full-time copper mining began in 1851, and the early settlement grew into Ducktown, named for Chief Duck, a Cherokee Indian. Over the years a number of mines have flourished, and the creation of this surreal scene may be claimed jointly by timber stripping, erosion, sulphur dioxide fumes, and subterranean blasting done 20 years ago to crumple the network of exhausted mines. The green lake is said to be 4,100 feet deep.

At this writing, parts of the Bura Bura Mine are being renovated as a historic monument that visitors will be able to tour. The museum proper displays items of local history. *Site and museum open year-round. Admission charged for museum.*

18. Lost Sea. Although not exactly a sea, the underground lake in this cave system is said to be the world's largest. The lake itself was not discovered until 1905, but the caverns were known in pioneer times as a source of red clay, which when mixed with buttermilk produced a durable red paint. During the Civil War the Confederates mined saltpeter for gunpowder. Some of their mining tools are on display, as well as moonshine equipment.

Decending to the lake, you pass through a number of surreal chambers.

The 100-foot-long Keel Room is so rifted as to resemble a miniature canyon. The Sand Room was used by settlers to store food. (The cave has a steady temperature of 58°F and is free of insects.) If you take the longer "Wild Tour," you'll also visit the Cat Chamber, where the remains of a Pleistocene jaguar were found.

The lake occupies 4½ acres. So perfectly do the still, clear waters reflect the ceiling that at first glance there seems to be no lake at all. There are trips on glass-bottom boats, and the underwater lights show the undulating bottom to be grayish-white.

The lake has been stocked with trout. Regularly fed in an environment free of predators (and fishermen), many reach old age and great size. The largest to be recorded was a whopping 47 inches long and weighed 21 pounds.

Beyond this lake is another that is more than twice as large, but it can be reached only by divers with scuba gear. The regular tour lasts about an hour. To take the three- to five-hour Wild Tour, arrangements must be made in advance. *Open daily except Christmas. Admission charged.*

19. Museum of Appalachia. *Norris.* If through some time warp one could wander into an early 19th-century Appalachian village, it might well resemble this remarkable museum.

John Rice Irwin, the owner-operator-curator-restorer, has assembled a fascinating collection of 30 buildings. Log cabins, a log church, a schoolhouse, a smokehouse, a corn mill and cribs, an underground dairy, a loom house, a smithy—

these and similar structures were all acquired locally, moved to this 70-acre site, and when necessary, restored. They are all authentic for their time and function down to the smallest wooden hinge.

The main display barn also houses a comprehensive collection of frontier items: axes, boots, saddles and bits, a dog-powered treadmill, rifling machines and bullet molds, fishhooks, ox yokes, cowbells, looms, corn grinders, a varmint trap, dulcimers, and banjos. All this is but a small sampling of the more than 150,000 old-time articles to be seen here.

A number of artful details contribute to the illusion of a town temporarily abandoned. Dresses hang from the wall of a cabin. A wheel awaits completion in the wheelwright's shop. Someone has left an ax stuck in a stump, plates of dried beans and peppers on a table. Visitors often ask Irwin where the people have gone. *Open year-round. Admission charged.*

20. Lincoln Museum. *Lincoln Memorial University.* In 1863 President Abraham Lincoln expressed to Gen. Oliver Otis Howard (founder of Howard University) the hope that after the Civil War Howard would "do something for these people who have been shut out from the world all these years." He referred to the loyal mountain youth of East Tennessee.

Howard carried through, founding Lincoln Memorial University in 1896. The museum, opened a year later, is now the third largest devoted to the great president. It houses more than 250,000 objects and is still growing. The museum is remarkable in melding the dark and light sides of Lincoln's life and the period of history he helped to shape.

Arranged thematically, the exhibits trace the various periods and undertakings of Lincoln's life, from his days as a rail splitter to the fateful night in Ford's Theater. Among the many personal objects to be seen are Lincoln's favorite chair from his law days in Illinois, with the damaged leg he repaired; the carriage, restored, that Lincoln borrowed for his second inauguration; and the ebony cane he carried the night he was shot.

Those years are further documented by tableaux and holographs. Displays focusing on the Civil War period include uniforms, weaponry, and combat medicine

and surgery. The viewer is spared few aspects of the impact of bullet, cannonball, shell, and saber on human flesh and bone. Also on view are the original model of the Lincoln Memorial by Daniel Chester French and the bronze bust of the president by Gutzon Borglum. *Open Tues.– Sun. year-round. Admission charged.*

21. Rocky Mount. *On Rte. 11E, just north of Johnson City.* Rocky Mount, a handsome two-story house of hand-hewn, notched white oak logs, is one of the oldest territorial capitols in the United States standing on its original site. It was built in 1770 and served "the territory of the United States south of the river Ohio" from 1790 to 1792, when Territorial Governor William Blount used the building as his office. It later served as a stagecoach stop and as a post office. Since 1959 it has been a state historic site.

The house and outbuildings stand on a pleasant rocky bluff overlooking rolling farmland. Restored to its original appearance, the house is authentically furnished with a pre-1740 grandfather clock, a huntboard (a sideboard on which food was put for men returning from a hunt), old crockery, an ingenious swiveling cradle, and other quaintly colorful items.

A museum located in the visitor center houses historical exhibits, manuscripts, and memorabilia. Also chronicled are the development of an 18th-century pottery industry and the fashions worn by women during the late 19th century.

Rocky Mount is a living history museum: to carry this out, the guides are dressed in period costumes and play the part of historical characters related to the house. *Open daily except Thanksgiving Day, Dec. 21–Jan. 5, and weekends Jan.– Feb. Admission charged.*

22. Jonesborough Historic District. *Jonesboro.* The oldest American town west of the Appalachians, Jonesborough (today Jonesboro) was established in 1779 and became the portal to the southwest prior to the Louisiana Purchase in 1803. The picturesque community, listed in *The National Register of Historic Places*, is intent on preserving its 200-year-old legacy of history and architecture.

A tour of historic Jonesborough, the central part of the town, should begin in the visitor center at the History Museum,

where the community's development is charted by displays featuring pioneer tools and building techniques, early trades, commerce, transportation, religion, education, and recreation.

Leaving the museum, you can stroll down the brick sidewalks of the historic district and enjoy the rich variety of architectural styles. Victorian homes predominate; there are a dozen fine examples on and near Main Street. Among other highlights are the Chester Inn, the town's oldest building (1797), and the Christopher Taylor House, a two-story log cabin where President Andrew Jackson once resided as a young lawyer. You'll pass the Mail Pouch building, formerly a saloon, and the Salt House, where salt was rationed to the townspeople during the Civil War. Also to be seen are some very fine pre–Civil War churches. Home-made ice cream is featured in an inviting turn-of-the-century ice cream parlor.

The town also preserves its past with a succession of celebrations and old-fashioned observations of holidays. *Museum open daily Apr.–Oct.; weekdays only Nov.–Mar. Admission charged.*

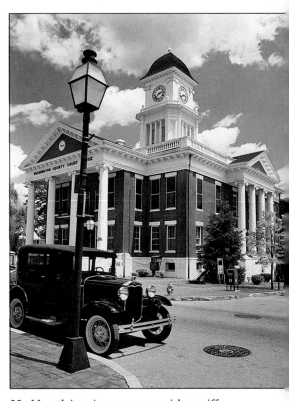

22. Nostalgia reigns supreme with a spiffy Model A Ford and the courthouse standing as a stately symbol of justice.

Alabama

It is still known as the Cotton State, but considering the scope of things a visitor may enjoy, the nickname can be misleading.

A favorite stopping place on the Natchez Trace in the early 1800's was Colbert Ferry. At an earlier date, say, 5000 B.C., bands of Indians were frequenting a rock shelter about 120 miles to the east. The sheltering cave is of geological interest, as are Rock Bridge Canyon, Dismals Garden, and Red Mountain.

Inviting hiking trails are to be explored in a number of parks, including one going over the highest point in the state. Pioneer times are represented by a covered bridge and a lively museum-village. Some surprising attractions are a fabulous display of mounted African wildlife and, at the headquarters of a paper company, an exceptional art collection and a lovely formal Japanese garden.

1. Colbert Ferry. *Natchez Trace Parkway.*
In the early 1800's a traveler bound for New Orleans and the Mississippi Territory had little choice but to take the Natchez Trace—a rugged, 450-mile road running from Nashville to Natchez. To cross the quarter-mile-wide Tennessee River, the traveler also had no choice but to pay George Colbert 50 cents for a ferry ride.

Colbert, a shrewd Chickasaw chief, is said to have exacted $75,000 from Maj. Gen. Andrew Jackson to ferry his Tennessee army during the War of 1812. In addition to the ferry, Colbert operated an inn, one of about 20 way stations along the trace where the traveler could stop for food, lodging, and companionship before venturing back on the hazardous trail, which was plagued by outlaws.

Today the heavily wooded site is still a congenial stopping place for the visitor. Its riverside location and the swimming and fishing make it one of the most pleasant of the recreational areas that the National Park Service maintains along the original trace. The honeysuckle grows tall around the clearing at the water's edge where Colbert's hostelry stood, and a short section of the old trail can still be seen, looking perhaps as it did in its heyday: a shallow path overhung with branches and creepers. Boating is permitted, but there are no rentals. Catfish and perch are the most common catches. *Open year-round.*

2. Madison County Nature Trail. *S. Shawdee Rd., Huntsville. Exit from U.S. Rte. 231 on Weatherly Rd. and follow signs.*
Set high above the city of Huntsville—atop aptly named Green Mountain—this network of paths in a charming 72-acre park offers a unique opportunity to observe nature in the southern Appalachians at first hand. The park's centerpiece is 17-acre, spring-fed Sky Lake; a traditional covered bridge with windowside benches spans a small cove, making a comfortable blind for viewing the mallards and Canada geese that live here year-round. In spring the shoreline is fringed with flowering mountain laurel, pink azalea, and crested iris. In fall the sourwoods, gums, maples, and dogwoods put on a spectacular show of foliage color.

Overall, about two miles of well-managed trails circle the lake and lead beyond into a woods filled with loblolly pines and such hardwoods as white oak, mockernut hickory, red maple, and black locust. Along the way some 500 species of trees and shrubs are labeled and identified. One side trail is marked in braille for the blind.

A simple A-frame chapel provides an opportunity for a few minutes of contemplation. But simply to walk here is to feel a sense of serenity and a pleasing intimacy with all those who have studied, named, and understood nature's handiwork. Mid-April to mid-May is best for seeing wildflowers; mid-October to mid-November for enjoying fall foliage. *Open year-round. Admission charged.*

3. Russell Cave National Monument. *Off Rte. 75.*
Discovered by amateur archeologists in 1953, this ballroom-size cavern is one of the oldest sites of human habitation in North America. Excavations here have revealed much about ancient Indian life and culture in the Southeast.

About 8,500 years ago a small band of nomadic Indians discovered the cave and took shelter in it. For about 6,000 years after that, it was used almost continuously as a winter refuge by Indians who sur-

4. *Rhododendrons play their role in this small masterpiece of nature's handiwork.*

vived by hunting and foraging. Later Indians, who had evolved a more complex lifestyle, used the cave as a winter hunting camp. From about A.D. 1000, however, when Indians had begun to practice agriculture and live in villages, the cave was only occasionally used as a shelter.

A small museum at the visitor center outlines the periods of Indian culture involved and displays weapons points, grinding stones, digging and stitching tools, pottery, and ornaments found at the site. A short, easily walked trail brings you to the cave entrance, a lip of gray rock jutting from a cliff overhung by trees and ferns. Below the entrance a small stream flows into the cave system. On entering the cave, you step down into a viewing gallery overlooking a five-foot-deep archeological excavation which has revealed the many layers of history.

With permission from park rangers, experienced, properly equipped spelunkers can also explore the adjacent cave system, which has several miles of passageways and caverns, including such attractions as Waterfall Passage. The park's 310 acres of natural terrain offer trails for hikers. *Open daily except Thanksgiving Day, Christmas, and New Year's Day.*

4. DeSoto State Park Resort. This elaborate complex of recreational and lodging facilities is the nucleus of a 4,990-acre park that stretches for 35 miles along the Little River, the only river in the country to flow its entire course on a mountaintop. The park is named for the Spanish conquistador Hernando de Soto, who in 1540 was the first European to explore the region. Situated on the wooded, undulating terrain of Lookout Mountain, the resort has cabins and camping areas as well as a lodge and an Olympic-size pool.

The area is magnificently scenic. Miles of hiking trails lead to mountain streams, miniature cliffs, mossy glens, and waterfalls. Among the most striking features to be encountered along the paths are huge, picturesquely weathered boulders. The most striking is Needle Eye Rock, which is split clear down the middle. The park is also noted for its flowering shrubs, and expanses of rhododendron and mountain laurel can be seen at their peak bloom from mid- to late May. A profusion of wild azaleas festoons the Azalea Cascade

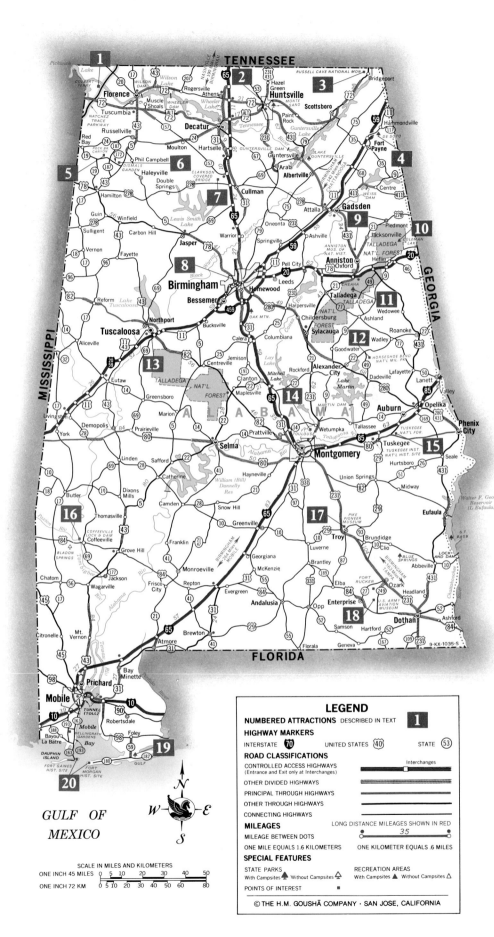

Trail with their delicate clusters of bloom.

Other parts of DeSoto Park also offer outstanding attractions. At DeSoto Falls, a few miles north of the resort, the Little River takes a 100-foot plunge into a large green lake before continuing its descent through a wide, leafy gorge. At Little River Canyon, the southern part of the park, the river makes another spectacular plummet. But the main attraction is the 16-mile-long canyon itself, which, with a depth of some 600 feet, is the deepest chasm east of the Rockies. A two-lane drive hugging the western edge of the rim provides good views. Legend holds that De Soto searched for gold in the caves along its cliffs. *Open year-round.*

5. Rock Bridge Canyon. This site takes its name from an impressive 80-foot-long, 100-foot-high natural rock bridge (one of the largest in the country) that spans a small, wooded box canyon with sheer sandstone walls. The best view of the bridge is from the canyon floor, which is reached by heading uphill from the parking area and turning right at the point where the trail forks. The canyon itself is littered with boulders, the debris of the rockfall that created the bridge. Picnic tables are set here, close to a waterfall cascading over a jumble of rocks.

The left fork of the uphill trail leads to the top of the bridge. The path wends through thick groves of mountain laurel, up steps cut in the rock, and then through a cleft in the rock to a high open place with eye-level views of the trees growing from the floor below. A short, somewhat precarious descent brings you onto the bridge. Along the path you pass a ladder reaching up to a cave.

An even more adventurous trail, steep and difficult in places and slippery when wet, leads from the parking area down to a small, dark green lake and then through woods and along the foot of cliffs to a waterfall and the remains of an old mill. Along the way are fine rockscapes and woodland scenery.

The best time to visit is in early to mid-May, when the mountain laurel and tulip trees bloom and the tall umbrella magnolias open their 12-inch flowers, filling the air with delicious fragrance. *Open year-round. Admission charged.*

6. Dismals Garden. Locally this site is known simply as The Dismals. But the visitor should not be put off by the gloomy-sounding name or the unimpressive entry area. In truth, the site is a small canyon with an imposing mixture of luxuriant vegetation and intricately eroded cliffs that have won it recognition as a registered natural landmark.

Starting at a waterfall, the mile-long walking trail follows a boulder-strewn stream and wanders through labyrinthine clefts and under natural bridges in the cliffs. Farther on, the canyon widens, and its sheer walls are pocked with hollows, marked with striations, and sometimes curiously rippled. Everywhere an exuberant, varied growth of trees, shrubs, and vines swarms over weathered, tumbled rocks. Even the stark rock walls of the canyon support pockets of ferns or dizzy ascents of vine.

A possible explanation for the chasm's odd name is that early settlers may have been struck by the subdued quality of the light, which is often blocked by the cliffs and filtered through a canopy of trees. (Among them are some of the country's tallest Canadian hemlocks.) In any case it is a place that leads one to observe the ways that the implacable canyon walls check the growth of vegetation. On every side there's evidence of nature's constant thrust for change.

The site also offers two camping areas, a picnic spot, and swimming in Dismal Spring, a natural pool. *Open May–Oct. Admission charged.*

7. Clarkson Covered Bridge. Built in 1904 and rebuilt in 1922 after a flood, this bridge was carefully restored in 1975 in preparation for America's bicentennial celebration the following year. One of the largest covered bridges in the state, it is 270 feet long, and it spans the 50-foot-deep gorge of Crooked Creek on a foundation of four cut stone piers. It has a cedar shingle roof and clapboard siding, but its most interesting architectural feature is the latticework of timbers that support the bridge. This design, the Town Lattice, named for its inventor, Ithiel Town, was sturdy, economical, and easy to build.

The bridge is set in a small, charming park with a millpond. The mill itself is now a private home. A quarter-mile trail

5. Relentless growth of trees, moss, and lichen will eventually overwhelm the rock.

7. *The partially covered bridge reveals the bare bones of Ithiel Town's famous truss.*

loops through a woodland of oak and mountain laurel and returns across a plank walk on top of the millpond dam. *Open year-round.*

8. Red Mountain Museum of Science.

1421 22nd St. S., Birmingham. From the Red Mountain Expressway, Rte. 31/280, take the Highland Ave. exit (if northbound) or the 21st Ave. S. exit (if southbound) and follow signs. Situated next to a highway that slices through Red Mountain, this unusual museum takes advantage of the site to provide a fascinating, on-the-spot outdoor exhibition of local geology and modern geological methods.

The highway cut, which is 210 feet deep, is seen from a ⅓-mile elevated walkway. The walls of the cut, which involved the removal of 190 million cubic yards of material, are labeled and signed at interesting points to help the visitor interpret 150 millon years of the earth's history revealed by the exposed strata. Alternating layers of shale and sandstone, for example, indicate that the area once fluctuated between being the seabed and the shoreline of an ancient ocean. Fossil deposits show the location of coral reefs. Layers formed by ash indicate volcanic activity in the region. Fault lines are also visible, and so are seams of iron ore—the mineral responsible for Birmingham's development.

In all, this display provides a rare op-

portunity for an intriguing journey through time. In the museum building itself are several small, well-designed displays pertaining to the sun and stars, the earth's geological development, ancient life forms, and local Indian culture. The exhibits are distinguished by their graphic boldness and dramatic use of sound effects. *Open Tues.–Sat. and P.M. Sun.*

9. Anniston Museum of Natural History.

Two miles north of Anniston at junction of U.S. Rte. 431 and State Hwy. 2. This re-

markable museum includes two outstanding private collections of mounted animal specimens—one of North American birds, the other of African animals.

Both collections are varied and extensive in scope and are distinguished by realistic mountings and ecologically accurate settings. Indeed, the bird collection was prepared by the 19th century ornithologist William Werner, who was a pioneer in the cyclorama style of presentation. Werner was a talented painter as well as a skilled taxidermist, and his backgrounds have a remarkable depth and artistry. The 600-specimen collection, which was assembled between 1870 and 1910, offers a rare opportunity to see now-extinct species such as the heath hen and the passenger pigeon. A recent addition to the collection is a model of a pteranodon, a prehistoric flying reptile with a 30-foot wingspan.

The even more striking African collection is the gift of a local resident who spent years hunting in Africa. Some exhibits concentrate on aspects of animal behavior. Others are panoramic re-creations of the continent's natural environments, such as a Sahara desert landscape complete with oryx, Barbary sheep, and desert snails and a marshland scene with hippos and egrets. The most outstanding display is a diorama of a grassland showing a giant baobab tree towering over an elephant, a rhino, a giraffe, and many smaller mammals and birds. *Open Tues.–Sat. and P.M. Sun. Admission charged.*

9. *Relative scale: baobab tree dwarfs the elephant, which in turn dwarfs the viewers.*

12. *Creek warriors on the peninsula had the best terrain but were too few in number.*

and led to statehood for Alabama in 1819.

The battle pitted two strong, shrewd leaders against each other: Andrew Jackson, commander of the Tennessee militia and future president, and Memewa, a powerful Creek chief. Memewa ("Great Warrior") had turned the small peninsula formed by this horseshoe-shaped loop in the Tallapoosa River into a village stronghold. With the river providing protection on three sides, he threw up a formidable log and earthen barricade across the fourth. But Jackson turned the tide of battle by having some 500 Cherokee allies make a surprise rear attack across the river while the general himself launched a full-scale frontal assault against the barricade. The wounded Chief Memewa escaped, but more than 800 of his 1,000 warriors died in battle. Jackson's force of 3,000 soldiers suffered about 200 casualties.

The small museum in the visitor center contains weapons, historic documents, a diorama showing the storming of the barricade, and an illuminated map tracing troop movements and battle phases. The three-mile drive through the battlefield (now a pleasing meadow) includes stops at the hill from which Jackson fired 70 cannon rounds at the barricade and at the site of Memewa's village. Another stop is at the mound on which the Creek prophets (medicine men) performed their prebattle dance and assured the Creek warriors that they would be immune to the effects of U.S. weapons.

The park has a picnic area at the edge of the river, a launching ramp, and several miles of walking trails. For weather the best times are spring and fall. *Open daily except Christmas and New Year's Day.*

10. Coleman Lake Recreation Area and the Pinhoti Trail. *Off Rte. 78.* Located near the northern tip of the Talladega National Forest, the Coleman Lake Recreation Area lies at the end of a long gravel road that winds through the woodland. A grove of tall pines is dotted with picnic tables set invitingly apart. A section of lakeshore is roped off for swimming, and a bathhouse with showers is on a nearby hill. Bass, shellcrackers, and bluegills are caught in many inlets, and trails circle the lake and lead across wooded hills.

The lake is also the current northern terminus of Alabama's longest hiking route, the Pinhoti Trail. In Creek, *pinhoti* means "turkey's home," and the hiker does indeed have a reasonable chance of seeing wild turkeys and white-tailed deer as well. The 80-mile trail, marked with a blaze that looks like a turkey track, runs mostly along a ridge system in the center of the Talladega National Forest, and it passes through some of the finest wild scenery in the South, skirting the shores of lakes and crossing mountains, including Cheaha Mountain. Since roads intersect the trail at several points, you can sample it without an overnight outing.

At the present time the Pinhoti Trail terminates near Clairmont Gap, south of Cheaha State Park, but it is planned to extend the trail nearly to Sylacaugus, making it more than 100 miles long.

Spring and fall offer the best weather and are generally free of crowds. *Coleman Lake Recreation Area open May–Jan. Pinhoti Trail open year-round.*

11. Cheaha State Park. This lovely 2,719-acre woodland park occupies the upper slopes of Cheaha Mountain, at 2,407 feet the highest point in Alabama. Although you can reach the summit via a short and scenic park road off Route 49, a main thoroughfare, you may find the longer, less-used access—Route 96 off Route 21—even more appealing. The narrow blacktop road crosses fields on the valley floor and then immerses you in pine-scented woods, passing small, rushing streams and miniature cascades in bosky dells. At the outset of the drive the climb is so gentle that one is unprepared for the sharp upward twists and turns that finally lead to the top.

A stone tower at the summit gives a fine view over the surrounding expanse of conifers to distant farmlands, mountain ridges, river valleys, and lakes.

At and near the crest of Cheaha are picnic areas, campsites with hookups and magnificent scenery, a lake with a white sand beach, cabins, a motel, game courts, and several hiking trails, both short and long. *Open year-round.*

12. Horseshoe Bend National Military Park. One of the early and crucial clashes between the United States and the American Indians took place on this site in March 1814. The battle of Horseshoe Bend not only ended the fighting in the year-long Creek War but also broke the power of the Creeks and forced them to give up a large portion of their territory. This opened the region to white settlers

13. Gulf States Paper Corporation National Headquarters. *1400 River Road, Tuscaloosa.* The corridors and conference rooms of this modern corporate headquarters are transformed into a rich museum by the varied and extensive art collection displayed on their walls, along with artifacts from various primitive cultures, bronze and porcelain sculptures, and Oriental artworks. The highlights of the exhibit are from the collection of American art gathered by the corporation's chairman, Jack W. Warner. The Warner Collection features several hundred paintings by a number of distinguished American

artists, including Carl Bodmer, Frederic Remington, Charles Russell, George Catlin, and Andrew Wyeth. A number of Basil Ede's wild-bird portraits are among the most popular pieces.

The headquarters also contains a serene and stately Japanese garden with pavilions and a pond. Designed by David Engel, one of America's foremost landscape architects, it is modeled on a garden in the Katsura Imperial Villa in Kyoto, Japan. Visitors are invited to view both the art collection and the garden in guided tours offered each hour on the hour; the last tour begins at 7 P.M. The complex is closed to the public during the business day. *Open 5–8 P.M. weekdays, 10 A.M.–8 P.M. Sat., and 1–8 P.M. Sun.*

14. Fort Toulouse–Jackson Park.

In 1717, when this region was part of French Louisiana, the French built a fort here near the strategically vital junction of the Tallapoosa and Coosa rivers. The fort—named for Louis XIV's son, the Count of Toulouse—was primarily a trading post where Indians exchanged fur pelts for guns and household items. The only serious conflict at this remote outpost came from within, when bored, ration-short soldiers mutinied. The fort was washed away, and in 1751 it was rebuilt and ringed by a palisade of pointed logs.

The French lost the French and Indian War—and the fort—in 1763. It was an overgrown ruin in 1814, when Maj. Gen. Andrew Jackson ordered a new, much larger fort to be built nearby. The Treaty of Fort Jackson, signed here that year, marked the formal end of the bitter and protracted Creek War. From the fort General Jackson began his campaign to protect the Gulf Coast from the British—a campaign that ended with their defeat in the battle of New Orleans.

Artifacts found on the site are displayed in the visitor center, and at this writing the two forts are undergoing reconstruction. The 164-acre park also offers a picnic area, a campground, and a launching ramp. Bass, bream, catfish, and crappies are among the fish that can be caught in the two rivers flanking the park. In a 30-acre arboretum the local shrubs and trees are labeled for identification along well-tended trails. Benches are placed along the way, offering welcome rest in this humid but lovely subtropical environment. The weather is most comfortable in spring and fall. *Park and visitor center open year-round; campground open Apr.–Oct.*

15. Tuskegee National Forest.

Watch for signs on Rte. 186. In the mid-1770's one of America's first artist-naturalists, William Bartram, passed through here on an epic

15. *Classic post-and-rail fence defines the pathway flanked by goldenrod.*

journey recording the flora and fauna of the Southeast. Today the 8½-mile Bartram National Recreation Trail is a major feature of this protected woodland.

It is fitting that the pathway was named for a naturalist, for this is terrain that has been beautifully and successfully reclaimed by nature. Most of it is former farmland that was purchased in the 1930's by the government in a program aimed at moving farmers away from their unprofitable, eroding land. The only signs of the former farmlands are peach, plum, and nut trees that are surprisingly encountered in the midst of the renewed wilderness.

With only 10,800 acres, this is the smallest of Alabama's national forests. But the Forest Service has deliberately avoided building extensive recreational facilities so that it can be enjoyed primarily as a wilderness. The Bartram Trail is easily accessible from two trailhead parking areas and at several in-between points where it crosses forest roads. Hikes of various lengths are possible, and the terrain is gentle and rolling.

Of particular interest is the 125-acre Tsinia wildlife viewing area, about a mile from the west end of Bartram Trail. A viewing tower and blind allow close-up observation of songbirds, rabbits, turtles, frogs, and waterfowl on the beaver pond.

Tuskegee National Forest has a sizable number of deer, turkeys, quail, and other wildlife, and they attract many hunters in

13. *The order, tranquillity, and meticulous care of Japanese gardens are duplicated here.*

season. The recreation area, just off Route 29, has picnic tables and grills and a replica of the log cabin birthplace of Booker T. Washington, founder of nearby Tuskegee Institute. Visitors are advised to bring drinking water. *Open year-round.*

16. Coffeeville Lock and Dam. Built by the U.S. Army Corps of Engineers in l961, this large lock-and-dam system permits shipping to go up and down the Tombigbee River between the gulf port city of Mobile and—via connecting canals and rivers—points as far north as Pittsburgh or Minneapolis. About 400 vessels per month use the lock.

Watching a tug with a chain of barges go through the lock is an impressive sight, and from a parking area on the embankment the visitor can get a good close view of the operation. The lock fills to raise northbound vessels to the level of the river above the lock, and it empties to lower southbound vessels to the level below. The lock gates operate with a hushed majesty, and when the lock fills, water rushing in from a hidden sluice wells up in a

silent, swirling eddy as if a river-spirit had been caught there, which in a sense it has. *Open year-round.*

17. Pike Pioneer Museum. *Rte. U.S. 231 N., Troy.* This remarkably lively folk museum is chock-full of items once used by this area's farmers and townspeople. The museum is a community undertaking, and its collection owes its striking variety and completeness to local citizens and merchants who scoured their attics, basements, stockrooms, barns, and outbuildings and donated their finds.

The museum has three main buildings. One is devoted to household items ranging from cookware, sewing goods, and spittoons to room tableaux complete with mannequins in period clothing. Another building contains newspaper typesetting and printing machines. The third structure concentrates on agricultural items. Besides field equipment and other farm implements, it has blacksmith and carpenter shop displays and a variety of horse-drawn vehicles. A local moonshine still and a portable boll weevil catcher are even found here.

The grounds are of equal interest with a

typical two-part log cabin with authentic furnishings, a windmill, a covered well with a pulley and bucket, and a country store fully stocked with period goods, including suits, shoes, patent medicines, bone buttons, penny candies, and plug tobacco. A shed for reducing syrup is in the picnic area. *Open Mon.–Sat. and P.M. Sun. Admission charged.*

18. U.S. Army Aviation Museum. *Fort Rucker.* The entrance of this army base declares it to be "The Heart of Air Assault," and some 90 aircraft have been put on display here to prove it. The exhibit includes not only attack aircraft but also planes that were used for such key support activities as observing the enemy, taking aerial military photographs, directing fire, illuminating battlefields, moving troops, delivering supplies, and evacuating the wounded.

In three hangarlike buildings and adjacent outdoor areas there are aircraft from many eras, dating back to Piper Cubs, called L-4's in the army and used as scout planes in World War II. The predominant

19. More in hope than conviction, fencing is designed to stabilize the dunes in the face of unpredictable Gulf Coast storms.

aircraft is the helicopter, which was first used in Korea in the 1950's and became the workhorse of the army in Vietnam.

The helicopter used by Presidents Eisenhower and Kennedy is also on display, as are a novel one-man backpack helicopter and a collapsible helicopter that fits in a crate. In addition to the aircraft, related photographs, documents, models, and flight suits are displayed. An Army Aviation Hall of Fame presents the stories of key commanders and daring combat heroes. *Open Mon.–Fri. and P.M. weekends except Christmas.*

19. Gulf State Park. In summer this park is usually crowded—and for good reason. The resort along the edge of the gulf not only has provisions for a large number of water sports and other activities but it also offers unusually pleasant campsites and a varied terrain that includes marsh, pleasant freshwater lakes, shrubby savanna, and sugary white beach. In spring and fall, however, the crowds disappear and visitors can enjoy all the park has to offer, as well as weather that is generally much more comfortable.

Alligator Trail leads through the palmettos, pines, ferns, and vines; Lakes Trail is flanked with reeds, blackberries, and water lilies. From the latter trail, following the shore of a lake and canal, one is more likely to see alligators, which should be given a wide berth. A small museum presents a survey of local wildlife.

Among the park's more unusual offerings are an 18-hole golf course and a fishing pier that projects some 800 feet into the gulf. April and October are the recommended months to visit. *Open year-round.*

20. *Fort Morgan (top), for all its forbidding ramparts and classic design, did not prevail in war. At Fort Gaines the gun now serves as an elegant piece of sculpture.*

20. Fort Gaines Historic Site and Fort Morgan Historic Site. "Damn the torpedoes! Full speed ahead!" shouted Adm. David Farragut as his Union fleet ran between the blazing gun batteries of these two forts and across the line of deadly torpedoes (mines) strung between them.

The twin forts, Fort Gaines on Dauphin Island and Fort Morgan on Mobile Point, guarded the neck of water that leads into Mobile Bay. By entering the bay and seizing control of it in August 1864, Farragut sealed off Mobile, the only remaining Confederate port on the Gulf.

The forts quickly fell to the Union forces.

Built in the early 1800's, the two thick-walled brick structures are constructed in the classic five-sided design with pointed bastions, or blockhouses, projecting from each corner. Walking on the ramparts and through the cryptlike, barrel-vaulted rooms below provides a good overview of the fortifications and their defenses, including the furnaces where cannonballs were heated red-hot so that they would set fire to wooden ships. The visitor can also see the sites of bakeries, blacksmith shops, and officers' quarters.

Fort Morgan has a museum with weapons, shells, uniforms, and other military relics and documents. At one site you can

also see the fort's own Eternal Flame, fed by natural gas from a deep well. Fort Gaines has a small collection of Civil War mementos and a display of seashells.

The peninsula on which Fort Morgan stands is popular with bird-watchers; more than 350 species have been sighted. Beaches, picnic areas, a fishing pier, and a nature trail are further attractions.

A ferry that runs regularly during the day permits both motorists and pedestrians to travel between the forts. The trip takes about half an hour. *Both sites open year-round; admission charged at each.*

Mississippi

A culture influenced by generations of agriculture on the rich soil of this gentle land is reflected in myriad ways.

The memorial plantations and the tribute to the Delta blues singers and to Jimmie Rodgers, the seminal country and western singer, are not unexpected. Although Casey Jones was not a singer, he is the well-remembered hero of a ballad about his train wreck near Vaughan.

Less well known features include artifacts from Mississippi's considerable Indian heritage, an impressive petrified forest, and an amazing model of the Holy Land.

The arts are splendidly represented. Holly Springs has a fine collection of paintings by a local artist; and a museum in Laurel features works of Sargent, Whistler, and other American masters, as well as a remarkable collection of Georgian silver. Literature is represented in the home of a famous local author and winner of the Pulitzer Prize.

1. Kate Freeman Clark Art Museum.
College Ave., Holly Springs. In the 1890's Kate Freeman Clark, a talented 16-year-old who grew up in Holly Springs, was taken to New York by her mother to study painting. During the next 30 or so years she produced more than 1,000 works, which she signed "Freeman Clark" to conceal the fact that she was a woman. Her paintings were widely shown, but she refused to sell any of them. Following her mother's death in 1923, Clark returned home, immersed herself in social activity, and abandoned her brushes. When she died in 1957 at age 81, she left her paintings and funds to the town for a gallery.

Today a modern single-story building houses her work: portraits, landscapes, and still lifes, which range from an academic treatment to a brighter, more contemporary style. One painting of a woman wearing a white dress in an impressionistic meadow seems to prefigure the advent of photo-realism. Most of the works are pleasing, and so is the small museum.

Anyone interested in antebellum architecture will enjoy exploring the streets of Holly Springs. A tour map is available at the Chamber of Commerce. *Museum open weekdays; obtain key from Holly Springs Bank or Chamber of Commerce.*

2. Rowan Oak.
Oxford. Take University Dr. exit from Rte. 7; turn left on Lamar, then right to Old Taylor Rd. This was the home of the famous writer William Faulkner (1897–1962). The scion of two old southern families, he incorporated into his novels and short stories the myths, traditions, and memories of his locale. He was awarded the 1949 Nobel Prize for Literature and two Pulitzer prizes.

A stately antebellum house with a columned portico, Rowan Oak is remarkable for its interior simplicity and for the sense it conveys of having been furnished by happenstance: Faulkner's work, not his home, was his object and his legacy.

To the left of the entrance is the library, in which the writer worked prior to 1952. His portrait as a young man hangs above two Chinese vases; copies of *Field and Stream* and a book about Switzerland lie on a small table beside a piece of abstract sculpture. To the right of the hall is a drab sitting room. The most interesting room is the one at the back, where he worked the last few years: on one wall is the outline of a short story written in his hand. Upstairs are four sparely furnished bedrooms. The grounds, by contrast, are lush with magnolia and cypress trees and climbing rose vines. *Open Mon.–Fri., A.M. Sat. and P.M. Sun. except major holidays.*

3. Delta Blues Museum.
Carnegie Public Library, 114 Delta Ave., Clarksdale. The birthplace of the blues, the heart of jazz, was here in the Mississippi Delta. Clarksdale and Coahama County were the home of such bluesmen as W.C. Handy, Charlie Patton, John Lee Hooker, and many others who gave musical expression to the sadness, despair, and cynicism they and other blacks felt. In the Delta Blues Museum visitors can listen to recordings, look at videotapes of great blues artists, and study an extensive collection of books, magazines, and memorabilia. These latter include classic blues instruments such as washboards, accordions, harmonicas, and a National Steel Duolian Guitar, as well as piano rolls, paintings, drawings, and photographs of the musicians.

For blues lovers this museum has obvi-

2. The architecture recalls the Old South as surely as Faulkner's evocative novels.

ous appeal, but even non-enthusiasts will be interested to know that from this small, impoverished area has come the soulful sound of a music that has echoed around the world. *Open Mon.–Fri. year-round.*

---

4. Great River Road State Park. *Rosedale.* Set between the Mississippi River and the levee, this pleasant and scenic park of some 200 acres centers around Perry Martin Lake, an oxbow of the great river. Fishing and boating are popular on the lake, but swimming is not allowed. The park boasts 61 concrete pads with water and electrical hookups for campers, as well as a primitive camping area.

From a 75-foot stockadelike observation tower there are splendid views of the Mississippi, its extensive sandbars, and the scrubland and cottonwoods that lie between the picnic area and the river.

The Deer Meadow Nature Trail winds through a woodland of pecan and mulberry trees and Virginia creeper. It's an easy trail to follow, although it is unsigned and its various forks and branches do not seem to coincide with the map provided. The path ends in a scrubby pastureland where deer are likely to be seen.

From the parking lot a narrow "fisherman's footpath" gives views of the lake, picturesque with dense stands of reed and the stark white trunks of dead trees. In early June the path is bordered by thickets of blackberry cane. The park has a boat launch and canoe and paddleboat rentals. *Open daily Apr. 15–Labor Day; Wed.–Sun. the rest of the year.*

---

5. Winterville Mounds State Historic Site. *On Rte. 1, north of Greenville.* This is one of the ceremonial mound complexes built in prehistoric America by Indians of the Mississippian culture. Although not as spectacular as the one at Etowah, Georgia (see p.113), it is nevertheless an impressive example of this strange way of life. Built about 1,000 years ago by an agricultural people who were the predecessors of the Choctaw, Chickasaw, and Tunica tribes, it was probably occupied for some 600 years before its populace was completely decimated by disease, drought, war, or famine.

The 40-acre park is said to contain 12 mounds, but only eight are readily dis-

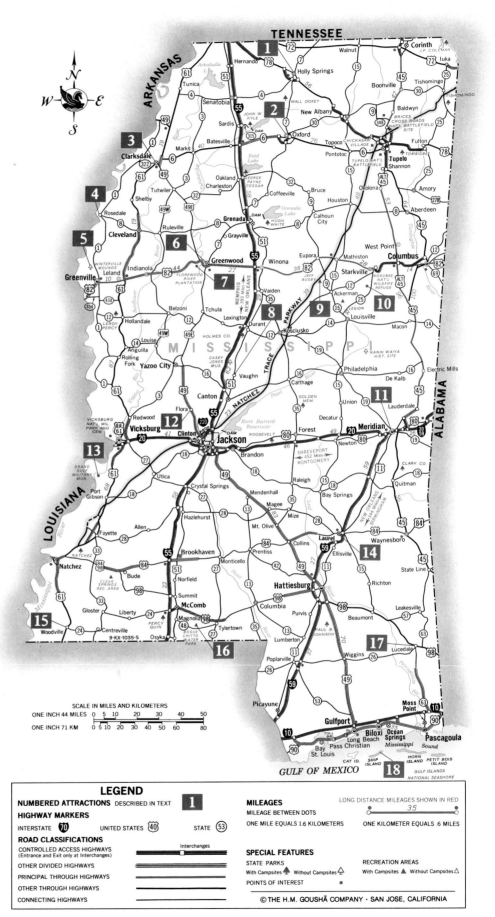

7. *The orderly buildings in their spacious setting speak silently of a bygone era.*

cerned. A flight of stairs leads to the top of the largest mound (about 55 feet high), where there is a roofless, windowless structure. The view is of pancake-flat Delta farmland, with a 360° horizon of woodland. One can see the pattern of other mounds and to the east, an open space called the Sacred Plaza, where dances and other ceremonies were held.

A museum in the visitor center gives an account of Indian mounds in the eastern United States and exhibits relics found at this site, including a collection of very small (one-inch) carved hands, jewelry, pots, pipes, arrowheads, and a dugout canoe. The park has a picnic ground with tables and grills. *Open Wed.–Sat. and P.M. Sun. Admission charged for museum.*

6. Cottonlandia Museum. *Greenwood.* Despite its name, this is far from being a one-crop museum. Cottonlandia offers a fascinating overview of the archeological, natural, economic, and social heritage of the Delta.

The museum's extensive collection of Indian artifacts includes some of the earliest dart and spear points made on this continent; a few are of the type used about 10,000 B.C. to kill mastodons. (On view are the locally unearthed bones of a mastodon that may have been killed in a hunt.) You can also see examples of the earliest ceramics produced in the New World: small, fire-hardened clay balls made and used as a source of heat for cooking food

by the people of the Poverty Point culture, which thrived in the lower Mississippi Valley some 3,000 years ago.

One of the most valuable—and exquisite—displays is the group of multicolored pottery effigy vessels, which depict a bobcat, deer, fish, opossum, and other creatures in a very naturalistic manner. The vessels date from sometime after A.D. 700. Some very fine pieces of Seneca pottery are also exhibited.

The enormous and colorful collection of beads alone makes a visit to this museum worthwhile. Various methods of manufacturing beads are described, along with fashions in beads from prehistoric times. Included are some 17th-century European beads of the kind that Peter Minuit used in trading for the island of Manhattan.

Relics of King Cotton include an Improved Eagle cotton gin, a McCormick Farmall tractor of the sort that retired mules from the cotton fields, an 1850 wooden harrow with hand-forged points made by slaves, and a boll weevil catcher. One case displays the various grades of cotton from "good middling" to "middling tinged" and "strict good ordinary."

Photos of steamboats and of Greenwood in its heyday, when docks, hotels, and saloons lined the Yazoo River waterfront, emphasize the importance of river transportation. *Open Tues.–Fri. and P.M. weekends year-round.*

7. Florewood River Plantation. *Greenwood.* This outstanding reconstruction of an 1850's Mississippi cotton plantation is

sited on 100 acres of land near the Yazoo River, just outside the town that describes itself as the cotton capital of the world.

The museum in the visitor center gives a vivid picture of the 19th-century cotton business. Two outstanding exhibits are the Whitney gin and the rare, shiny, red and yellow Lane and Bodley side-crank box-bed steamboat engine.

The mansion and other buildings are in parklike grounds attractively planted with southern wax myrtle, Japanese boxwood, crape myrtle, live oak, peach, Callery pear, and dwarf plum trees. Costumed guides give tours of the mansion, which is decorated in strikingly elegant antebellum style. The period furnishings include the indispensable wig-dresser in the master bedroom and a "petticoat table" with a floor-level mirror, for a lady to make sure that her ankles were decently covered.

Among the many outbuildings are the potter's and candlemaker's shops, where scheduled demonstrations are given. The use of the land on a Delta cotton plantation of the period is also well represented, with a vegetable garden and fields of cotton, corn, sorghum, and peas. In the fall you may help pick the cotton balls. Mules and horses graze in one pasture, goats in another. *Plantation open Tues.–Sat. and P.M. Sun., Mar.–Nov.; admission charged. Museum open Tues.–Sat. and P.M. Sun. year-round. Entire park closed Thanksgiving Day, Christmas, and New Year's Day.*

8. Casey Jones Museum. *Vaughan.* The famous train wreck in 1900 that sent the brave engineer Casey Jones on a "one-way trip to the promised land," as the ballad goes (see p.164), occurred at Vaughan not far from this museum. The building is a turn-of-the-century train station brought from the nearby town of Pickens.

The exhibits include rail station telephones and telegraphs, trainmen's uniforms, track maintenance tools, flagmen's signal kits, scale models of trains, and an Illinois Central engine bell to which 20 silver dollars were reportedly added to produce its distinctive tone. Among the exhibits devoted to Jones are commemorative depictions of the wreck, and the bell from engine No. 382 of the *Cannonball Express* that Casey drove that fatal night. *Open Mon.–Sat. and P.M. Sun. year-round. Admission charged.*

9. Jeff Busby Campground. *Natchez Trace Parkway.* This small, pleasant recreation area offers an agreeable place to camp and the opportunity to drive up Little Mountain, at 605 feet the highest point on the Natchez Trace. The view of forest all around, dotted with pockets of cultivated land and even fewer habitations, provides a refreshing sense of wilderness.

An exhibit in the shelter at the top of the hill is concerned with the past glory, recent tribulations, and current partial recovery of the great eastern hardwood forest (once the greatest hardwood forest in the world), of which it was said that "a squirrel could have gone from Maine to Texas without touching ground." But to the white settlers the forest was an enemy to be beaten back. Today the salutary effects of proper land management can be seen along the Natchez Trace.

From the top of Little Mountain a short trail descends the hill in wide, easy loops. Over two dozen kinds of wild plants, including sweet gum, greenbrier, American linden, and blackjack oak, are labeled according to their use in Indian cooking and pharmacopeia. *Open year-round.*

10. Noxubee National Wildlife Refuge. *Reached from either Rte. 25 or Alt. 45; watch for signs.* Surprisingly, only 3,000 of the more than 46,000 acres in the refuge are designated as a sanctuary. Anglers enjoy Loakfoma Lake and Bluff Lake and take good catches of largemouth bass, bluegills, and crappies from their waters.

For birders the best place is Canada Goose Overlook, a wooden walkway and viewing platform that juts out high above Bluff Lake. It's well worthwhile to bring binoculars. From this elevation one can see grassy meadows studded with giant nesting boxes. From November through January tens of thousands of waterfowl, primarily wood ducks, green-winged teals, Canada geese, and American widgeons, visit the refuge. In late winter and early spring a variety of songbirds add their grace notes. Wood storks and wild turkeys may be seen, and occasionally the endangered red-cockaded woodpecker and the bald eagle. The American alligator is also present.

The refuge is crisscrossed with narrow gravel roads; a map may be obtained at refuge headquarters. Visitors entering the woods during the gun-hunting season in November and December are required to wear hunter-orange. *Open year-round.*

11. Jimmie Rodgers Museum. *Off 39th Ave., Meridian.* The blue yodels and simple melodies of Jimmie Rodgers, "The Singing Brakeman," may sound hopelessly dated when you hear them in the museum. But without this beginning in the late 1920's, the phenomenon of country music might never have evolved in its present directions. Rodgers, who died in 1933, is rightly remembered as the progenitor of this unique form of musical expression. And he was indeed a brakeman, as well as a baggageman and switchman, during the era of the steam engine. Many of the items featured here, including brake shoes, ticket stamps, flares, torpedoes, and lamps, relate to his work. The museum building resembles a train station, complete with an engine and caboose outside.

Rodgers's popularity is demonstrated by fan mail from as far away as Japan, honorary citizenship papers from the city of New Orleans, and first-day covers of the postage stamp acclaiming him as the Father of Country Music. Original recordings and sheet music of his songs are displayed, as well as his denim jacket and other belongings. At the end of May, Meridian sponsors a Jimmie Rodgers Memorial Festival. *Open Mon.–Sat. and P.M. Sun. year-round. Admission charged.*

12. Mississippi Petrified Forest. *Flora.* Considering the comparatively short span of time allotted the human record, the scope of the geological record here is almost impossible to comprehend. The fossilized logs in this small forest (the only petrified forest east of the Rockies) are some 36 million years old. The remains of living denizens of primeval forests, they were deposited here as driftwood and buried in and preserved by the sand and silt. A smooth path traverses the site, a lush woodland of loblolly pines, sweet gums, elms, wild plums, and occasional clumps of yucca and pear cactus.

The most striking feature found here is

12. After 36 million years of weathering, the fallen tree and sandstone are almost as one.

a curiously anomalous section of deeply eroded red and pink cliffs, studded with extruding petrified logs, that resembles a miniature badlands. These exposed cliff walls are a fascinating cross section of natural history. The red sands in their lower parts were the river deposit in which the petrifaction process originally began.

Markers along the path are keyed to a descriptive leaflet available at the entrance to the site. The 40-minute walk terminates at a small but interesting museum devoted to petrified wood. The displays also include some vertebrate fossils and an array of gems and minerals. *Open daily except Christmas. Admission charged.*

---

13. Grand Gulf Military Monument. *Port Gibson.* The restored buildings here are reminders that this was once a thriving river port nurtured by the cotton boom and so prosperous that it was a candidate to become the state capital. But in 1843 a yellow fever epidemic struck. Ten years later many who survived the epidemic were killed by a major tornado. Then in 1855 the Mississippi River began to shift its course, and in the next five years it destroyed 55 city blocks, including the entire business area. In 1862 the final blow came when attacking Union forces led by Gen. U.S. Grant outflanked Confederate troops established here and forced them to

abandon Grand Gulf. Nothing remains of Fort Wade and Fort Cobun but some remnants of earthworks.

Today the park commemorates both the battle and Grand Gulf's heyday. The museum here has a detailed map of that battle and photos of the Union ironclads that were involved, along with swords, rifles, muskets, cannonballs, flags, and war-related documents.

On the handsome park grounds are a few hand-hewn log houses, a lovely Carpenter Gothic chapel, and an atmospheric graveyard overhung with Spanish moss. Probably unique in the world is the home-made submarine, powered by a Model-T Ford engine, which was used to run whiskey during Prohibition. A boardwalk leads to the edge of the river, and a hilltop observation tower provides an overview of this instrument of Grand Gulf's rise and fall. *Open year-round.*

---

14. Lauren Rogers Museum of Art. *Fifth Ave. at Seventh St., Laurel.* The emphasis here is on 19th- and 20th-century painting, and indisputably this distinguished museum houses one of the most outstanding collections in the South. Seven elegant galleries invite one to linger with masterpieces by James McNeill Whistler, John Singer Sargent, Winslow Homer, and Mary Cassatt, among other notable artists.

There is a rich collection of landscape paintings, from dramatic renderings of the American wilderness by Albert Bierstadt to Thomas Moran's grandiose sunset scene and the moody impressionism of George Inness's later works.

In addition, the museum contains an excellent exhibit of Georgian silver. Highlights include a classic 1785 George III teapot by Hester Bateman, one of the few female silversmiths of her time; William Plummer's celebrated cake baskets; and plates by Paul Lamerie, acclaimed in the early 1700's as the finest of England's craftsmen in silver and gold.

Another of the museum's displays provides a fascinating insight into the subtle relationship between art and archeology. The Catherine Marshall Gardiner Basket Collection features the superb work of North American Indians and Pacific islanders, as well as pieces from Africa and the Orient. The craftsmanship in one set of miniature baskets is so fine that it is displayed under a magnifying glass.

The Georgian Revival building, with its handsome brick exterior, golden oak hallways, and elaborate ironwork, is itself an elegant tribute to the admirable architecture of the Old South. *Open Tues.–Sat. and P.M. Sun. year-round.*

---

15. Rosemont Plantation. *Woodville.* Jefferson Davis grew up on this gracious plantation, reached from the highway by a long, shady lane. Though best known as the president of the Confederate States of America during the Civil War, Jefferson Davis had already made his mark as a soldier, congressman, senator, a founder of the Smithsonian Institution, and a U.S. secretary of war.

The pastures and gardens of the plantation are bordered by hand-split rail fences, and the roses that gave the plantation its name still grow in profusion. Even in summer the grounds can be surprisingly cool, shaded by evergreen magnolias and immense live oaks festooned with Spanish moss. One can readily believe the roadside sign that reads: "Quiet, you are entering the early 19th century."

The inviting white manor house, built in 1810 by Jefferson Davis's father in the Federal "planter's cottage" style, has been well preserved. A porch with square pillars runs the width of the building, and a roof of multiple peaks rises high above the first story. Dormer windows and white

13. This dumpy-looking mortar could hurl a 200-pound explosive bomb 2½ miles.

15. *The symmetry of the Federal-style exterior is echoed by the window treatment and arrangement of the furniture in the living room.*

latticework add their appeal. At the end of the porch the lattice supports a bush of tiny magenta roses. Among the furnishings of the Davis family are a whale-oil chandelier and a spinning wheel that belonged to Davis's mother.

Near the house are former slave quarters, an office, and a kitchen. *Open weekdays Mar.–Dec. 15. Admission charged.*

16. Bogue Chitto Water Park. *McComb.*

Silvery canoes stacked like sardines and piles of black inner tubes near the entrance indicate the primary interests here. This access point to the Bogue Chitto Float Trail is part of an extensive system of parks and boat-launching sites along the Pearl River and its major tributaries.

The river here is wide and yellow, flowing swiftly between steep banks whose overhanging oaks and willows provide boaters with welcome shade on hot days. A paved road leads through the park to the boat ramp, designed to accommodate larger boats as well as the canoes available for rent. Fishermen come here especially for outsize catfish. Those who ply the river quietly may see the deer, opossums, beavers, turkeys, armadillos, raccoons, or small black bears that live here.

The park's unspoiled, densely wooded landscape is crossed by well-marked trails that lead to the banks of the Bogue Chitto, where one can peer through the trees on the 30-foot cliff to the river below. Along the hiking trail birds are noticeably plentiful, and the woods resound with the rhythmic rat-a-tat-tat of woodpeckers mingled with the symphonic choruses of tree frogs. The park's campsites offer privacy along with modern conveniences. Additional facilities include primitive camping areas, playgrounds, and a picnic area with grills. *Open year-round.*

17. Palestinian Gardens. *Lucedale.* In setting out to create this scale model of the Holy Land, Harvell Jackson was inspired by the idea that to understand the Bible, one should have some sense of the places central to its narrative.

Depicting the Holy Land (scaled at one yard to the mile) on these 20 acres of Mississippi woodland was a labor of love that took him and his wife many years. The Dead Sea and the Mediterranean are represented by ponds, and the towns and villages are mostly made of concrete, domed and pillared with white plaster and carved with doors, windows, and niches. Many of the plants surrounding the models are species mentioned in the Bible.

The Reverend Mr. Jackson himself conducts tours of the gardens. His informative discourse adds to the appeal of his model of Palestine during the time of Jesus, and enables one to conjure up the image of Mount Hebron clad in eternal snows upon a little hillock whitened with marble chips. *Open daily Mar.–Nov. Admission free but donations encouraged.*

18. Ship Island. *Biloxi.* From a pier just behind the Buena Vista Motel in Biloxi, the bright turquoise and orange excursion boat sets out on its 1½-hour, 12-nautical-mile trip through the Mississippi Sound to Ship Island, part of the Gulf Islands National Seashore. For most of the voyage the shore is out of sight, and one has the sense of being truly at sea. Only leaping dolphins and an occasional fleet of shrimp boats, their nets outstretched like wings, break the flat expanse of blue.

The ferry lands at a wooden pier to the left of which stands Fort Massachusetts, a grand and elegant red brick structure with rows of arched doorways and waves of vault-ceilinged chambers that give one the impression of walking through a Renaissance painting. Designed by the French engineer Simone Bernard, the fort was begun in 1859 as part of a coastal defense system. It was first occupied by the Confederates, and then by Union forces in the Civil War and named for the Union ship *Massachusetts*, which was involved in a minor engagement here. Free tours of the fort are conducted twice a day.

A boardwalk bisects the island, leading to a long white beach staffed by lifeguards and dotted with grass-roofed cabanas and bright beach umbrellas. Body- and windsurfing are popular. Along the boardwalk are bathhouses and a snack bar. The walkway's purpose is expressed in a sign: "For want of grass the sand is lost, for want of sand the dune is lost, for want of dune the island is lost, for want of the island the harbor is lost." Best in spring and fall to avoid mosquitoes and fierce heat. *Open year-round. Fare charged for boat.*

Minnesota

The Ice Age glaciers left this magnificent legacy of lakes, streams, valleys, hills, and rolling plains, an ideal land for touring and camping.

The exploits of Minnesota's Indians, French voyageurs, and fur trappers are recalled in scenic and historic places and in place-names throughout the state.

In the mining area one can descend almost half a mile underground to experience the unique world of the workers there. And at Pipestone National Monument one can visit the quarries of catlinite reserved for use by Indians in fashioning their traditional ceremonial pipes. Museums feature distinctive architecture, collections of tools, utensils, and equipment used by pioneers, and artifacts reaching far back into our past.

1. Zippel Bay State Park. These 2,800 acres of wilderness parklands are situated along the shores of Lake of the Woods, a 950,000-acre body of water that forms part of the border between Minnesota and Canada. As early as 1700 the voyageurs—those French fur traders who plied the waters of the Northwest—traveled along this great waterway.

Zippel Bay, a reedy inlet running almost at right angles from the lake, borders the park on the west. It is a pleasant, quiet stretch of water with a small marina, a boat ramp, and a fish-cleaning station.

Along the lakeshore, reached from the park entrance by a straight gravel road, is the swimming beach—three miles of sand considered to be the finest in the state. The nearby picnic area, with tables and a shelter, is set in a mown meadow surrounded by woodlands. Sixty primitive campsites are available, located in remote areas of the park. Trails through woodlands of white birches are excellent for skiing and snowshoeing in winter.

Many visitors come just to pick blueberries in midsummer, when a plentiful wild crop borders the roadways, or for the excellent fishing. For others, the anticipation of seeing a moose or black bear, which roam the park freely, or the likelihood of hearing the forlorn call of the timber wolf, is the appeal. Other attractions are the white pelicans, which nest around the lake, the sandhill cranes, and the common loon, the state bird, whose haunting cry often breaks the stillness of the woods. *Open year-round. Admission charged.*

2. Voyageurs National Park. The trappers and traders who canoed the waters of this scenic wilderness in the 1700's would be surprised to know that their legacy is not in furs or dollars but in a 217,000-acre park named in their memory. Within the bounds of the park are countless streams and ponds and more than 30 lakes, interspersed by islands of bog, marsh, water meadow, and forest, forming many hundreds of miles of waterways. The only way to see the entire area up close is by boat, or by snowmobile after January 1, when roadways are plowed on the frozen waters. Thirty-two miles of hiking trails are maintained and are accessible only by water.

Wildlife abounds here. Black bears are common, and in the winter of 1984–85 the park was home to 26 timber wolves. Beavers and white-tailed deer are also plentiful, and moose are sometimes seen. Among the birds that nest here are the osprey, eagle, and great blue heron; bird-watchers also frequently observe kingfishers, loons, and cormorants.

From both Rainy Lake and Kabetogama Lake visitor centers, park naturalists lead guided canoe trips, providing canoes, life jackets, and instructions. Less strenuous boating is also available on both lakes. Telephone Rainy Lake at (218) 283-9821 or Kabetogama Lake at (218) 875-2111 for information and reservations.

Fishing is allowed throughout the park, and catches include black crappies, lake trout, muskellunge, northern pike, rock bass, and walleye. Several fine beaches offer excellent swimming.

During the winter, snowmobiling, ice fishing, cross-country skiing (races take place in January), and snowshoeing are

2. The trees manage to find a footing on every piece of land that isn't under water.

popular. Snowmobiles, skis, food, and fuel supplies are available in the business communities located by the entrances of the lakes. *Open year-round. Fee charged for trips and cruises.*

3. Grand Portage National Monument. *Grand Portage.* Long before the arrival of whites, Indians had been bypassing an unnavigable stretch of the Pigeon River by an overland route they called Great Carrying Place. French voyageurs, translating the title literally, named it Grand Portage. In 1778 the North West Company, formed by a group of Canadian traders, established its headquarters at the start of the trail on the shore of Lake Superior. At the time this was a crossroads for

hundreds of fur trappers and traders. The headquarters was abandoned in 1803 and fell into disrepair. The general area became an Indian reservation in 1854.

In 1958 the Grand Portage Band of Minnesota Chippewa Indians donated the site of the Grand Portage National Monument to the U.S. government. The monument now features a carefully re-created complex of North West Company buildings. The principal structure is the Great Hall, an impressive log and post structure originally chinked with river clay and bear grease—and now with concrete. Also on the grounds are a kitchen fully equipped with period utensils, a fur press for pack-

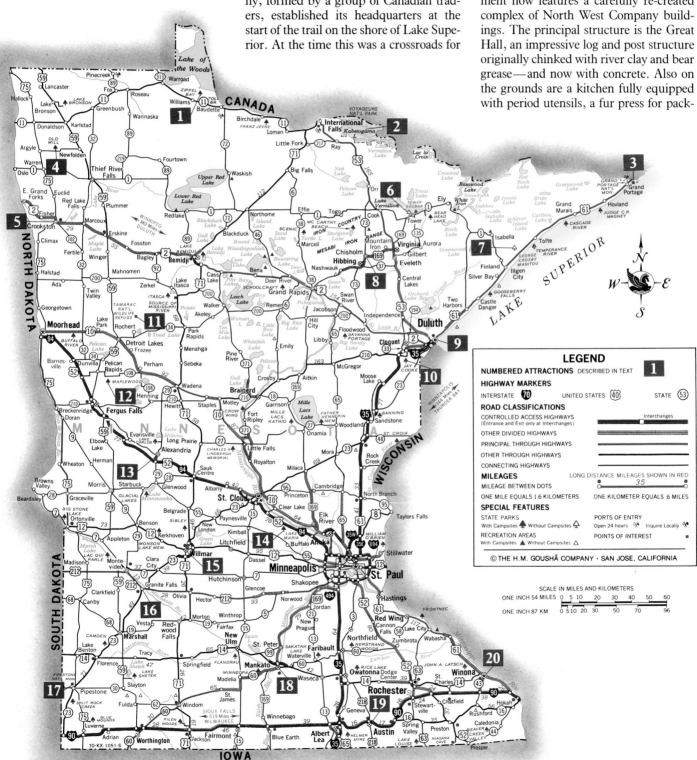

LEGEND

NUMBERED ATTRACTIONS DESCRIBED IN TEXT

HIGHWAY MARKERS

INTERSTATE **70**   UNITED STATES **40**   STATE **53**

ROAD CLASSIFICATIONS

CONTROLLED ACCESS HIGHWAYS (Entrance and Exit only at Interchanges)   Interchanges

OTHER DIVIDED HIGHWAYS

PRINCIPAL THROUGH HIGHWAYS

OTHER THROUGH HIGHWAYS

CONNECTING HIGHWAYS

MILEAGES   LONG DISTANCE MILEAGES SHOWN IN RED

MILEAGE BETWEEN DOTS   35

ONE MILE EQUALS 1.6 KILOMETERS   ONE KILOMETER EQUALS .6 MILES

SPECIAL FEATURES

STATE PARKS   PORTS OF ENTRY

With Campsites ▲ Without Campsites △   Open 24 hours ⚲ Inquire Locally ⚲

RECREATION AREAS   POINTS OF INTEREST

With Campsites ▲ Without Campsites △   ■

© THE H.M. GOUSHĀ COMPANY · SAN JOSE, CALIFORNIA

SCALE IN MILES AND KILOMETERS

ONE INCH 54 MILES 0 5 10 20 30 40 50 60

ONE INCH 87 KM 0 5 10 20 30 50 70 96

ing furs into bundles, a warehouse with birchbark canoes, and a cabin built in 1900 that is now a gift shop. Part of the complex is enclosed in a stockade built to create a sense of order during the Rendez-vous, the trappers' hectic annual meeting.

The site also has two trails: the original 8½-mile Grand Portage Trail, which cuts through the reservation to Fort Charlotte, where you will find primitive backpacking campsites, and the half-mile Mount Rose Trail, which offers a fine view of Lake Superior. *Open May 15–Oct. 15.*

4. Old Mill State Park. As you cross the seemingly endless open acres of the Red River valley's well-kept cropland, it is difficult to believe that the homesteaders who settled this region just over a century ago encountered prairies and riverine forests much like the ones found in this 287-acre park today. Beavers, raccoons, deer, and an occasional moose may be seen here, along with many of the area's native plants. Inviting paths, including a three-quarter-mile self-guiding nature trail, weave across the varied terrain. Many of these trails are groomed for snowmobiling and cross-country skiing in the winter. In addition the park offers picnic and camping sites, a swimming pond, and winter ice-skating and sledding areas. Fishermen try for pike and bullheads.

The park's centerpiece, as the name suggests, is an old mill. Built in 1889, it is powered by an eight-horsepower steam engine, and grinding demonstrations are given on several summer weekends. A restored one-room log cabin, evoking the rugged life of the area's early homesteaders, may be seen nearby. *Open year-round. Admission charged.*

5. Polk County Museum. *Crookston.* Many intriguing aspects of the 19th and early 20th century seem alive and well in this excellent museum, which is run by the Polk County Historical Society and a well-informed curatorial staff. The buildings and hundreds of artifacts are well displayed. Engaging in their variety, they represent all aspects of life in this region.

The buildings include an 1890 school-house that was used until the 1930's, a log

7. *Imagine the rustle of leaves while walking along Yellow Birch Trail in the fall.*

cabin built in 1872 by a Norwegian settler, and a reconstruction of a blacksmith's shop. Several early automobiles, a five-foot Minnesota binder, a thresher, a tractor, an 1898 fire engine, a one-horse sleigh, and a variety of small farm implements are displayed in a pole barn.

The main building, a large, modern structure, contains well-furnished period rooms and a general store, doctor's office, barbershop, editor's office, a 60-year-old model electric train, and a carousel layout with horses that "gallop." Here too are a square piano made in Boston and an amusing assortment of ladies' hats.

A chapel with a composite of furnishings from several local denominations displays vestments, altar silver, a font, and on the walls the Stations of the Cross.

The local people who acquired the objects on display here are shown with their farms, their animals, their industries, and their countryside in an excellent collection of photographs. *Open P.M. Tues.–Sun. June–Sept. Admission charged.*

6. Tower–Soudan State Park. The unusual centerpiece of this splendid park is 2,341 feet underground and is reached by a three-minute elevator descent, a three-

quarter-mile subterranean train ride, and a climb up a short flight of stairs. This is the 27th and lowest level of the Soudan Iron Mine, sometimes called "the Cadillac of mines" because of its outstanding methods of operation and safety record during its 80-year history.

The rock here is ancient and stable, relatively dry, and does not produce toxic or explosive gases. The fine red dust that clings to some of the machinery and structure is a silent reminder of the ore crusher, whose voice was a constant assurance that all was well when the mine was operating. The tunnel, part of some 55 miles of underground access, is spacious, well lit, and a steady 50° year-round. Fresh air circulates naturally down from the surface, and knowledgeable guides make one's visit enjoyable and informative. Sturdy shoes and a sweater or jacket are recommended.

The park visitor center offers displays explaining the geology of the area and the mining process. In addition, various pieces of specialized mining machinery may be seen, including the hoist, the giant ore crusher, and the 500-horsepower air compressor used to operate the drilling equipment. Last worked in the early 1960's, the mine today serves as a tribute to the herculean efforts that humans have made to wrest a living from the earth.

The 1,200-acre park offers five miles of surface trails for hikers and about 50 miles of trails for cross-country skiing and snowmobiling. A wildlife habitat, the park is home to timber wolves, deer, hawks, and other creatures. *Park open year-round. Mine tours daily, Memorial Day–Labor Day; admission charged.*

7. George W. Crosby Manitou State Park.
Dramatically highlighting the wild beauty of the rugged Manitou River valley is the rocky gorge shaped by ancient volcanic and glacial action and the river itself, tumbling through the forested landscape to Lake Superior.

At the cascades the river moves down through a series of branching waterfalls to a peat-dark pool. Along the edge, boulders, some convenient for sitting, show high-water marks, indicating the water level during the spring melt. But even in August there is a quick, substantial flow between the conifer-shaded banks.

Twenty-three miles of wilderness trails follow the river and wind through the park's stands of birch, aspen, and hemlock. Some of the trails are difficult, but an easy quarter-mile path leads from the parking area to a picnic site beside Benson Lake in the center of the 3,400-acre park. The topographic trail map shows the relative steepness of the routes.

Along the river and by the lake 21 primitive campsites have been cleared for backpackers. Water must be carried in or boiled, and fire rings are provided.

Moose come here to browse on the fast-growing conifers, black bears are common, and timber wolves prey on the large population of white-tailed deer. Hikers often see the ruffed and spruce grouse. If you can get close enough, you can tell them apart by their markings. The tail of the spruce is dark, with a single band at the edge; that of the ruffed is striped white, brown, and black. Trout fishing is permitted in both stream and lake.

Snow frequently stays from November through April, and although the trails are rough, the campsites are open. Experienced skiers can enjoy 11 miles of cross-country trails. *Open year-round.*

8. Minnesota Museum of Mining.
Chisholm. When Minnesotans speak of "the range," they are not referring to a string of mountains or to vast grasslands; they are talking about the Mesabi, Vermilion, and Cuyuna—some of the richest iron ore ranges in the United States. Located in the heart of this area is a sprawling museum that rewards visitors with a remarkably vivid sense of the sheer magnitude and ruggedness of iron mining.

Fascinating exhibits of antique miner's equipment, old photographs, and models of ore-processing operations are just the beginning. On the museum grounds visitors can tour a variety of heavy mining machines, some of truly astounding size. One of these is a piercing machine that uses a high-velocity 5000° F flame to drill through rock. Dominating the area like some great mechanical dinosaur is a 1910 Atlantic steam shovel weighing 110 tons. But perhaps the awesome scale of iron mining is made clearest in a simple exhibit of ore truck tires, some 10 feet in diameter and weighing nearly three tons, each more costly than today's average automobile.

The most moving display is a life-size underground replica of a 150-foot turn-of-the-century mine drift. Visitors descend a short stairway to enter the miners' daily world, where well-worn picks and drills, electric pit-mule carts, water pumps, columns of carefully placed support timbers, and wire-covered rescue stretchers make it easy to imagine the courage and determination and backbreaking labor demanded of these early diggers of ore. *Open daily mid-May–Sept. Admission charged.*

9. Glensheen.
3300 London Rd., Duluth. Among the welcome by-products of Minnesota's prosperous iron industry in the early 1900's are the stately homes built in the Duluth area. One such sumptuous manor house is Glensheen, the 39-room Jacobean-style home of millionaire attorney and iron mine owner Chester Congdon, built in 1905–08 on the shore of Lake Superior. Named for the soft shimmer of the sun on a brook flowing through a small glen, the 7½-acre estate includes a carriage house, boathouse, bowling green, and well-tended gardens.

Glensheen is noted for its hand-carved woodwork, elaborate ceiling plasterwork, and stained glass windows. The entrance hall, oak-paneled in a 16th-century English pattern, is lighted by brass chandeliers incorporating the motif of the British lion. A red marble fireplace sets the color scheme of the mahogany-paneled drawing room, which is considered to be the most beautiful room in the house. The living room, which has a brick fireplace, burlap wallpaper, and a canvas ceiling, contains "the Little Museum," where mementos of the family's travels are displayed.

The reception room features a ceiling of

9. *Of brick and tile and built to last, in tribute to iron, another of earth's vital products.*

gold leaf, and the billiard room has walls paneled of oak and "Japanese leather" (made of paper). For all the elegance and fine materials, an inviting sense of human scale is sustained throughout. A series of terraces with balustrades and a small pond lead from the house to the lakeshore.

Visitors are guided through the mansion but may tour the gardens and outbuildings on their own. *Open daily except Wed., mid-May–mid-Oct.; P.M. daily except Wed., Feb.–mid-May and mid-Oct.–Dec.; P.M. weekends in Jan. Closed Easter, Thanksgiving Day, Christmas, and New Year's Day. Admission charged.*

---

10. Jay Cooke State Park. The importance of railroads in the 19th century is easy to forget in this era of superhighways and jet planes. A reminder is the fact that this 8,715-acre park is named for Jay Cooke, who was instrumental in establishing Duluth as the eastern terminus of the Central Pacific Railroad's route to the West Coast. The park comprises the rugged countryside flanking both sides of the St. Louis River as it flows through massive rock formations toward Lake Superior. The hills, forested with hardwoods, harbor 46 species of animals, including timber wolves, black bears, and coyotes.

Fifty miles of trails wander through the woodlands and along the river. There are some easy hikes in the park, but the Lost Lake and Silver Creek trails, traversing swamps, steep hills, and ridges, are best left to the well conditioned. Trout fishing is popular in Silver Creek.

The Grand Portage Trail, part of which lies within the park, was used by travelers 300 years ago to avoid an impassable section of the St. Louis River cutting through this area. Several trails are shared by hikers and horseback riders, and some lead to overlooks with fine views of the river valley. The Carlton Trail begins near the park nature center and crosses the river by means of a swinging bridge.

Modern campsites are located near the river; backpacking and group camps are found in wilderness areas. Two picnic grounds, one by the river and the other on Oldenburg Point, are invitingly set among birch trees. In the springtime one should ask about the superb display of trilliums and other wildflowers.

In winter, the park is popular with cross-country skiers as well as snowmobilers. *Open year-round. Admission charged.*

---

11. Tamarac National Wildlife Refuge. *Headquarters at junction of Rtes. 26 and 29, Rochert.* Crisscrossed with quiet roads and gently sloping hiking trails, the 43,000 acres of these woodlands and wetlands offer the solitude of unspoiled nature. More than 20 lakes dot the refuge, their shores providing nesting sites favored by loons, herons, Canada geese, wood ducks, mallards, and teals. Bald eagles also nest here, and golden eagles sometimes may be seen during their fall migration. In all, more than 200 bird species have been observed within the refuge, along with deer, black

bears, beavers, and occasionally moose.

Berry picking and mushrooming are allowed in the lower third of the refuge, where in a good season chokecherries, pin cherries, raspberries, and morel mushrooms are abundant. Fishermen are likely to catch northern pike, walleye, bluegills, and yellow perch, and boat-launching areas are provided on several of the lakes. Nearly eight miles of trails are groomed for skiing in the winter.

Two of the most popular ways to enjoy the preserve are the Blackbird Auto Tour and the Old Indian Hiking Trail. The auto tour makes a 10-mile loop along refuge roads and passes many areas of geological and ecological interest. A printed guide to the tour is available at the visitor center. The hiking trail, about a one-mile loop, leaves Route 29 at the shore of Tamarac Lake and leads past an ancient Sioux burial ground to a camp area used as late as the 1930's by Indians gathering wild rice and sap for maple sugar. Harvesting the wild rice today is allowed only by special permit. *Open daily year-round.*

---

12. Maplewood State Park. This exceptionally beautiful park—some 9,000 acres of hills, valleys, woodlands, and small lakes—lies between Minnesota's eastern forests and western prairies, and it has plants and animals native to each of the ecological zones. Archeological evidence indicates that the area was inhabited by Indians at least 6,000 years ago.

10. *The St. Louis River carves its turbulent way through a rocky gorge. With a steady gaze, the black bear suggests that this territory is his.*

12. *The abandon of wild lettuce and Canada thistle enlivens the lake's sunny shore.*

Lida, the largest of the lakes, features a swimming beach and a picnic area nearby. Family campgrounds overlook Grass Lake, and smaller ponds in remote areas have primitive campsites. Miles of trails for hiking, horseback riding, skiing, and snowmobiling wander through the parklands; many lead to overlooks with superb views of the surrounding hills and valleys.

Two ramps are provided for boaters—one at South Lake Lida and one at Beers Lake. Fishing is excellent at both lakes, with walleye, northern pike, and panfish the likely catches.

Forty acres have been set aside as a demonstration woodland. Trees here are labeled with botanical notes and information as to their usefulness to man. Basswood, for instance, is good for beekeepers and cabinet- and toymakers. Paper birch, black cherry, sugar maple, ironwood (including the largest such tree in Minnesota), slippery elm, and various oak species are included. Experiments here show that shrubs and trees increase dramatically in

size, number, and variety when browsing deer and rabbits are excluded from the area. *Open year-round.*

13. Runestone Museum. *206 Broadway, Alexandria.* Visitors at this comprehensive museum of local history are rewarded with an intriguing glimpse of Minnesota's Scandinavian heritage. Harnesses and sleighs, ladies' fashions, razors, mustache cups, Indian artifacts, an impressive group of carved figures depicting the logging industry, and stuffed animals (including a bear and timber wolves) are but a few of the countless wonders here.

The museum's prize, however, is the runestone itself. Discovered in Kensington by a Swedish immigrant farmer in 1898, the three-foot-high stone bears an ornate inscription in the runic alphabet of medieval northern Europe. Some investigators claim it was carved in 1362 by

Scandinavian explorers of the American wilderness, and the arcane debate over the stone's authenticity is eloquently depicted in various displays.

On the museum grounds a blacksmith's shop, general store, church, and schoolhouse have been arranged to resemble a late 19th-century village, and there is a large exhibit featuring antique boats, farm equipment, fire engines, and automobiles, including a 1925 Model T and a 1941 Buick. *Museum open daily mid-May–mid-Oct.; weekdays mid-Oct.–mid-May. Other buildings open daily mid-May–mid-Oct. only. Admission charged.*

14. Lake Maria State Park. This hilly, forested land, with two lakes and numerous marshes and ponds, is a surviving 1,312-acre fragment of the Big Woods, a mighty primeval forest that covered 3,000 square miles of south-central Minnesota. Glaciers advanced and receded here three times. The last incursion, during the Wisconsin Ice Age, which ended 10,000 years ago, deposited boulders and rocky debris along with till and loam from the Lake Superior and Red River valley regions.

The landscape is a superb habitat for wildlife. Popular with birders, it harbors more than 200 species, including goldfinches, meadowlarks, gulls, bald eagles, Cooper's hawks, and several species of owls—screech, great horned, snowy, and short-eared. White-tailed deer and many small animals are also at home here.

Lake Maria, fringed with tall reeds and water lilies and encircled by dense woods of maple, birch, and red oak, brings fishermen, who try for walleye, perch, sunfish, carp, bullhead, and bass. A boat ramp is provided.

A large, primitive group campground has a parking lot; several other primitive campsites must be reached by foot. Opposite a small wooded island in Lake Maria is a shady picnic ground.

The park has seven miles of hiking and horseback riding trails, and for winter sportsmen, 12 miles of ski trails. Nature walks are conducted by the park's naturalist. *Open year-round.*

15. Kandiyohi County Historical Society Center. *610 NE Old Hwy. 71, Willmar.* Here is an enticing little museum with the

17. *These granite boulders were considered to be guardian spirits. Offerings of tobacco and food were left here for good luck.*

eclectic charm of grandmother's attic. Its well-organized displays feature everything from Indian artifacts and a Red River ox-cart, used by early settlers on Minnesota's western frontier, to old cars and antique dental and printing equipment.

Other buildings on the grounds add to the vivid sense of a varied and lively local history. The Dakota Sioux and the history of their conflict with settlers are included. In the restored Sperry House, built in 1893, the pump organ and cylinder pho-nograph in the parlor, the curling irons heated by a kerosene lamp, the carved oak

19. *An elegant world—seen by hikers and venturers on cross-country skis.*

woodwork, stained glass windows, and period furnishings create with remarkable authenticity the atmosphere of a prosper-ous turn-of-the-century farmer's home. A fully equipped 1880 schoolhouse stands nearby, with an 1895 riddle scrawled on the blackboard. The agriculture building has an extensive collection of antique farm tools. Many professions, trades, and in-dustries, including transportation, are in-terestingly presented. You can climb into the cab of a steam locomotive, put your hand on the throttle, and wish the great whistle would really work. *Open P.M. dai-ly Memorial Day–Labor Day; P.M. Sun. the rest of the year.*

---

16. Upper Sioux Agency State Park. The land in this 1,280-acre park is much as it was more than a century ago, when the Dakota Sioux Indians freely roamed the wooded ridges and the open prairie knolls and fished the rivers here. Yet it is one of history's ironies that this idyllic setting was the scene of a tragic confrontation.

In 1857 the Dakotas were compelled to relinquish their vast lands in Minnesota and settle on a 10-mile strip on either side of the Minnesota River. Their resentment grew, partly because of abuses they suf-fered from government agents, and in the summer of 1862 the Sioux War erupted. The conflict lasted only six weeks, but it took the lives of some 500 whites and an untold number of Dakotas. Even though many members of the tribe had refused to

join the war parties and instead led a large group of settlers to safety, the government disbanded the Dakotas and parceled out the reservation land to white settlers.

Today both the Minnesota and Yellow Medicine rivers invite canoeing, hiking, horseback riding, fishing, camping, and a variety of winter sports. Park roads and trails offer spectacular views. Herons, pel-icans, and wood ducks may be seen in the river shallows, accompanied by a sympho-ny of songbirds among the grasses and shrubs. In September vast numbers of monarch butterflies visit the park to feed on the prairie wildflowers.

Only one of the old agency buildings remains, and it serves as a visitor center, where an informative slide show explains the history of the site. Outside, one can wander among the ruined foundations of the agency buildings, leveled monuments to a time of infamy and disillusionment. *Park open year-round. Admission charged. Historic-site visitor center open daily May–Labor Day; weekends Sept.–Oct.*

---

17. Pipestone National Monument. *Pipe-stone.* The quarries of soft red stone found here were probably first worked by Indi-ans more than 400 years ago and for many years were open to all. Legend holds that when the different tribes were at war with each other, the Great Spirit called them together here and fashioned a pipe from

190

the stone. As he smoked the pipe, he told the tribes that this place belonged to them all, that they must make their ceremonial pipes of the stone, and that they must meet in this honored place as friends.

But in the 19th century the Yankton-Dakota Indians took over the quarries and made other tribes trade to obtain the pipestone. The U.S. government seized the site in 1893 and in 1937 established the Pipestone National Monument (a 283-acre park) by an act of Congress, which gives all Indians once again the right to quarry pipestone (also known as catlinite).

A short loop trail leads from the visitor center to the quarries through a tract of prairie where plants are identified and their use by the Indians explained.

At the historic area you can see an exposed quartzite cliff and several pits that are still quarried, and near the visitor center you can enter a pit in which the floor and lower wall are pipestone.

The visitor center has displays of pipes and various smoking equipment. A nearby cultural center, where craftsmen can be seen at work, sells mementos, pipes, and other carved articles. *Open daily except Christmas and New Year's Day.*

---

18. Blue Earth County Historical Museum. *Mankato.* Rensselaer D. Hubbard, founder of the Hubbard Milling Company, built this elegant white brick two-story house in 1871, only 19 years after the town was first settled. Its handsome pro-

portions, pillared porches, mansard roof patterned with different colors of slate, and stained glass windows set the style for local mansions yet to come. In 1890 he added a splendid carriage house next door. The buildings, now in *The National Register of Historic Places*, serve as the museum and headquarters of the Blue Earth County Historical Society.

The house also has a notably rich interior, with carved cherry and oak woodwork and three unusual fireplaces (one of Brazilian white onyx and Italian black marble, another of Spanish marble, and a third of Georgia marble). Displayed in the rooms are 19th- and early 20th-century furniture, costumes (including those of Plains and Woodland Indian tribes), pottery, china, kitchen equipment, and other memorabilia from the early days of Mankato. Among the vehicles in the carriage house are a real Concord stagecoach and an 1895 Haynes-Apperson auto in perfect running condition. *Open P.M. Tues.–Sun. except holidays. Donations welcomed.*

---

19. Jay C. Hormel Nature Center. *Austin. Take Exit 180A from I-90 and drive half a mile north on 21st St. NE.* Three environments—a forest of hardwoods and pines, a floodplain, and a prairie—make up the center's 278 acres, offering refuge to a variety of birds and animals. Some of these inhabitants, including live snakes, frogs, turtles, and salamanders, can be seen up close at the Interpretive Building.

Also shown are the furs, skins, and antlers of other local wildlife.

Pleasant trails covered with wood chips crisscross the area and bridge Dobbins Creek, a stream that meanders through the grounds. The North Trail, for instance, skirts a prairie colorful with milkweed, bergamot, and rudbeckia and then passes a pond ringed with tall cattails before it swings south into the hardwoods to connect with the Pine Loop, which circles a stand of red pines. A tree-walk guide is available at the Interpretive Building.

Among the programs offered are nature walks, bird-watching, orienteering, snowshoeing, night hiking, and maple sugaring. Equipment and lessons are available for cross-country skiing. The center has lecture and film programs and a research library. *Open Tues.–Sat. and P.M. Sun.*

---

20. Julius C. Wilkie Steamboat Center. *Levee Park, end of Main St., Winona.* The riverboat ranks with the locomotive as a stirring reminder of the glorious age of steam in America. The housing for this trove of riverboat memorabilia is a reconstruction of the stern-wheeler *Julius C. Wilkie* (which burned in 1981), and it captures the essence of the real thing. The pilothouse has a wheel that could require the combined efforts of three men to turn. And the sumptuous atmosphere of the grand salon, decorated in pink, white, and burgundy, with gilt chairs from Spain, plush curtains, chandeliers, and a floral carpet, is vividly re-created.

The lower "deck" is a museum containing manuscripts by paddleboat inventor Robert Fulton, a "doctor" pump (used to prevent the ship's boiler from running dry and exploding), and the *Wilkie's* carbon-filament spotlight, capable of throwing a 500-foot beam—a crucial piece of equipment for travel at night along the ever-changing river channels.

There are also a number of riverboat models. Among them are ones of the *War Eagle*, which carried Civil War troops, and of the stern-wheeler *Buckeye.* Stern-wheelers had an advantage in the shallow waters of the upper Mississippi River. The wheel could be put in reverse to force water under the boat and lift it clear of shoals. *Open daily May–mid-Oct.; variable schedule mid-Oct.–Apr. Admission charged.*

20. This replica suggests the charm of sailing on an ornate Mississippi riverboat.

Wisconsin

Variety abounds in the Badger State—in the superb parks and wildlife areas, in the arts and architecture, and in historic places.

The hard-working pioneers who laid the foundation for a prosperous state are honored here. A logging museum, exhibition farm, gristmill, old inn, and the re-creation of a typical small town provide the honest flavor of a vigorous past.

Nature lovers will find good birding, hiking in a blessedly quiet wilderness, a refuge with spectacular visitations of waterfowl, and a superb bike trail. Other attractions include folk art cast in concrete, art inspired by nature, Victorian furnishings and 19th- and 20th-century art all under one roof, a world-class paperweight collection, and unusual period homes.

1. Big Bay State Park. As quiet and beautiful as it is remote, this waterside retreat is located on Madeline Island, the largest of the pancake-flat Apostle Islands in Lake Superior. The park is reached by taking a half-hour ferry ride from Bayfield harbor on the mainland and then driving another five miles or so across the island. It is well worth the trip. Trails run along the edge of a sheltered blue bay, traversing woodlands and dry, sandy heaths. There are areas of rocky shoreline as well as dunes and a long beach of fine white sand. For much of the way, the main hiking trail runs along a needle of land separating the bay from a calm lagoon fringed with cattails and water lilies.

The park has a few rustic campsites, but there are other sites on adjacent village land. Weather is best in spring and fall. The ferry runs from Ice-Out in April through December. In winter—when the park offers snowmobiling, cross-country skiing, and ice fishing—the island is reached by a power-driven windsled, a sort of toboggan. And when the ice becomes strong enough, a road for vehicles is plowed across the channel. *Park open year-round; campgrounds open May–Sept. Admission charged.*

2. Amnicon State Park. The Amnicon River, which courses through this pleasant park, has a dramatic series of waterfalls and cascades. And surprisingly, the water rushing over them is a rich, creamy, root-beer brown—a color imparted by tannic acid from vegetation. But the waterfalls are more than a scenic attraction. They also make it possible to see the park's other interesting feature, a geological fault line running through the area.

The Douglas Fault, visible at the foot of the falls, was created about a million years ago, when a deep layer of volcanic basalt rock began to push its way through the thick sandstone bed on which the park rests. Today at the falls the river flows through a smooth channel in an upthrust cliff of dark basalt before tumbling into a plunge pool and proceeding on to pink sandstone cliffs even more eroded and smoothed by the water. Just below the falls, a 12-foot-wide zone of reddish rocks and pebbles (fault breccia) marks the point where the basalt and sandstone ground against each other.

A covered bridge leading to a charming, pine-covered island in the river offers excellent views of the falls. The river can be followed on trails that extend along its bank and circle the island. Canoeing—in areas away from the falls—is particularly good in spring, when the water is high. During the long Wisconsin winter, trails are maintained for snowmobiling and cross-country skiing. *Open year-round. Admission charged.*

3. Lucius Woods Park. *U.S. Rte. 53, Solon Springs.* Tucked compactly between U.S. Highway 53 and St. Croix Lake, this park has only 41 acres. But it is enjoyable to visit for its pleasant swimming beach and its tall stands of ancient red and white pines—and in winter, for winter sports.

The beach is a small half-moon of sand nestled in the wooded shoreline of the invitingly spacious lake. A lifeguard is in attendance in season, and a bathhouse, a picnic area, and a playground are nearby. The lake also offers fishing and boating, and there are paddleboats for rent.

The white pines with their deeply furrowed bark and the red pines with their scaly plates of ruddy bark are best seen along the hiking trail that follows the creek through the grounds. The park also boasts a 115-foot white spruce, the largest in the state.

Winter activities center on snowmobiling, ice skating on the lake, and tube sledding on a run lined with hay bales to keep you on course. Cross-country skiing is also permitted, but trails are not cleared. *Open mid-May–Sept. and during snow. Admission charged.*

4. Crex Meadows Wildlife Area. Uncommonly beautiful and richly endowed with wildlife, this nature preserve ranks among the most appealing in the country. Its open landscape encompasses 30,000 acres of grassy meadows, prairie and heathlike terrain, open pools and lakes, and reedy marshes. There are small stands of scrubby oak and willow as well.

Sandhill cranes and white-tailed deer are often sighted in the areas planted with corn to feed wildlife, and one might see a black bear wandering in the marsh grass. Over 100 species of birds nest here, and some 250 species have been observed. Spring and fall are the best viewing times, but bald eagles, ospreys, and sharp-tailed grouse can be seen from April to October.

Gravel roads provide excellent access, but they are not suitable for bicycles with narrow racing tires. In winter cross-country skiers have free run of the trails, and snowmobilers can swoosh along a 15-mile groomed trail. To avoid disturbing birds during their crucial nesting period, camping is permitted only from September through December. *Open year-round.*

5. Wisconsin Concrete Park. *Rte. 13 south of Phillips.* Fred Smith and his amazing, colorful concrete sculptures are a part of the lore and legend of this part of Wisconsin. A lumberman, Smith retired at

1. Girded by rock and topped with trees, this is truly a golden island—at break of day in the fall of the year.

the age of 64 in l950 and immediately began to make his folk-art sculptures—an impulse that, he said, "just comes to me naturally." By the time a stroke disabled him 15 years later, he had created more than 200 figures. And he steadfastly refused to sell to collectors, choosing to leave his work "for the American people."

Smith's farm is now a public park, and his artistic endeavor preserved there is a strange but delightful collection of concrete figures: giant Indians, folk heroes, scenes from movies and history, life-sized deer, bears, and other animals, and local characters whom Smith knew, such as Mabel the Milker milking a cow. Some pieces incorporate real buggies and wagons. His last work portrayed a beer wagon drawn by a team of eight Clydesdale horses.

Smith applied his concrete over a frame of wood and chicken wire, and then embedded bits of glass and other materials in the surface for decoration. The resulting figures are storybook primitives with a rigid, straight-armed stance. The effect is at once outrageous, touching, funny, and charming. *Open year-round, but partly inaccessible when snow is deep. Admission free but donations encouraged.*

---

6. Rhinelander Logging Museum. *Off Rte. 8 in Pioneer Park, Rhinelander.* In the l870's the town of Rhinelander was established as a supply center for the logging camps that were clearing the last of northern Wisconsin's virgin wilderness. This museum, with its reconstructed log cookhouse and bunkhouse, re-creates a logging camp of that era.

In the authentically furnished cookhouse are a period stove, sink, cookware, and long tables set with enamel plates and cups. Here too is the horn used to call the men to dinner. The rest of the museum displays ox yokes, pulleys, saws, axes, peaveys, pike poles, and the spiked shoes lumbermen wore when they were floating logs downstream.

The exhibits continue outdoors under tall pines, with a combination blacksmith's and carpenter's shop, a boat shed, and a rural schoolhouse. Most notable, however, is the collection of heavy equipment, which includes vintage fire engines, locomotives, log-hauling equipment, a water truck used to ice roads for log sleds, and boom sticks, the huge, chain-linked logs used to raft pulpwood across Lake Superior. *Open daily mid-May–mid-Sept. Donations accepted.*

---

7. Newport State Park. In the late l9th century the village of Newport was a thriving logging town complete with its own dock on Lake Michigan. Today all that remains of Newport are lilac bushes, crumbling traces of the store and post office, and pieces of driftwood from the old pier. The 2,200-acre park that encompasses the site has been allowed to revert to wilderness. No vehicles are permitted beyond the short stretch of blacktop, and snowmobiles are banned.

The wilderness is crossed by nearly 28 miles of hiking trails kept open in winter for cross-country skiers. Some trails hug the northern shoreline, passing rocky cliffs and sandy coves. There are good vistas of Lake Michigan's bright, clear water and plenty of flat lakeside rocks from which to view them. Other trails head south along the water, then cut inland through mixed conifer and hardwood forests or through abandoned farmland now reverting to wilderness.

Deer, coyotes, and porcupines are common. Many birds nest along the shore of the park's large freshwater lake. Wilderness campsites are scattered along the trails. In warm weather the park can also be enjoyed for its half-mile-long beach and adjoining picnic areas, easily reached from the parking lots. *Open year-round. Admission and use fees charged.*

---

8. The Farm. *Rte. 57, four miles north of Sturgeon Bay.* On the signs for The Farm, the word *The* is underlined, and rightfully so, for this sample of American rural life is as close to the real thing as any re-created homestead can be. The emphasis here is on animals, especially young ones that can easily be petted. Children, and adults as well, are likely to be charmed, entertained, and educated.

Breeding is scheduled so that various animals will be born throughout the summer, when the farm is open. Although the cast of animals is ever-changing, the visitor is likely to encounter calves, kids, kittens, puppies, chicks, lambs, rabbits, and piglets. Bottles of milk to feed to the animals are on sale. Chickens, ducks, and turkeys await a handout of corn. There are nanny goats to milk, and many larger animals, such as horses, donkeys, and cows.

Besides the hutches, coops, stables, barn, paddock, and pastures for animals, the 40-acre farmstead has about half a dozen century-old log cabins and outbuildings that were relocated here. Most of them contain antique farm tools, equipment, and domestic utensils.

For visitors interested in plant life, the farm has a well-kept, sweet-smelling herb

7. *Trilliums are among the woodland delights that are looked forward to in spring.*

8. *This orchard, photographed in late May, is but one in an area where thousands of acres of cherries burst into glorious bloom.*

garden, a kitchen garden, and a corn walk where several kinds of corn and the important grains rye, wheat, and barley are grown. All the garden plants are labeled, and many wild plants along a pleasant nature trail are identified. *Open daily Memorial Day–Labor Day. Admission charged.*

9. Leigh Yawkey Woodson Art Museum. *Franklin and 12th Sts., Wausau.* Artwork inspired by nature is the specialty of this museum, which is housed in a gabled brick mansion resembling a comfortable country house in England's Cotswolds.

Prominent among the museum's permanent displays are the Royal Worcester porcelain birds collected by Leigh Yawkey Woodson, whose daughters established the museum as a memorial to their mother. The collection contains complete sets of both American and English birds, all delicately detailed by the artist Dorothy Doughty. Other ceramics include 18th-century Worcester lusterware by Leeds and Wedgwood. A glass collection features Victorian glass baskets as well as Art Nouveau and modern pieces.

The museum's wildlife art collection concentrates on birds, ranging from 18th- and 19-century prints by Mark Catesby and John James Audubon to more recent paintings by Roger Tory Peterson. It also

includes duck decoys and bronze sculptures. The museum has changing exhibits as well; nature is usually—but not always—the theme. *Open Tues.–Fri. and P.M. weekends except holidays.*

10. Dells Mill. *Off Rte. 27, three miles north of Augusta.* Today Wisconsin is famed as the dairy state, but during the second half of the 19th century the chief agricultural product was wheat, and it was an important part of the nation's breadbasket. Dells Mill, opened in 1864, was one of hundreds of gristmills that sprang up to grind the grain into flour and feed.

Rising high above a rocky streambed (terrain called dells in Wisconsin), the mill is an impressive five-story structure built by German millwrights with hand-hewn

10. *The calm and quiet millpond belies the racket of the machinery it drives.*

195

11. *The octagon may not induce spiritual power, but the beauty is undeniable.*

pine timbers secured with pegs of oak. The well-preserved mill is still capable of processing about 2¼ tons of grain an hour, but it is now primarily a museum reflecting country life in bygone days. The exhibits include plows, scythes, harnesses, a ropemaking machine, sleighs, buggies, a reconstructed prairie schooner, and even a century-old funeral coach complete with drapes and silver angels.

The most intriguing exhibit, however, is the mill itself, with its old overshot waterwheel, its drive shaft and cogged wheels with hard maple teeth, its grain bins, and its complexities of beams, pipes, and more than a half-mile of leather belts that drive the roller mills. *Open daily May–Oct. Admission charged.*

---

11. Octagon House. *1004 Third St., Hudson.* In 1855, when this distinctive eight-sided, stuccoed dwelling was built, such structures were in vogue partly because the octagonal shape was believed to endow the building with certain beneficial spiritual powers. Most such houses were built in the Northeast by followers of the phrenologist Orson Fuller, who published a book on the subject. A former New Yorker, John Shaw Moffat, brought the idea with him and built this house with a commanding view of the Mississippi.

Today that vista is blocked by surrounding structures. But the house, which can be seen by guided tour, has been lovingly restored and furnished with heirlooms from local families. Many items, such as the black walnut dining set,

came to the area by riverboat. The piano in the lace-curtained parlor survived two river dunkings but still plays. Other items are of local origin, such as the parlor's cherry log table and the kitchen's Civil War–era pot holder, boldly embroidered "Any Holder But A Slave Holder."

The upstairs porch displays a collection of dolls with examples from the 1830's through the Shirley Temple era. The Garden House and the Carriage House also contain collections of miscellaneous memorabilia. *Open Tues.–Sat. and P.M. Sun. May–Oct. Admission charged.*

---

12. Bergstrom-Mahler Museum. *165 N. Park Ave., Neenah.* Evangeline Bergstrom, who lived in this lakeside Tudor-style house until her death in 1958, was one of the world's leading collectors of glass paperweights. Indeed, her 1940 book on the subject did much to spark renewed interest in this form of art glass.

The 1,500 weights and other glass pieces that Mrs. Bergstrom gathered form the museum's primary permanent collection. The display is so wide-ranging and comprehensive that it is hard to imagine any style, period, or major maker of paperweights that is not included. Not only do the paperweights vary enormously in decorative motifs, but many are embedded with items ranging from delicate glass flowers and fruits to working compasses.

The museum also includes mantel ornaments, doorknobs, vases, and prize marbles. And it has been augmented by some modern French portrait pieces by Baccarat, Cristal d'Albret, and St. Louis.

Another permanent exhibit is the Mahler Germanic Glass Collection, which consists primarily of drinking vessels made in central Europe from the 16th through the 19th century. These elaborately decorated tumblers, beakers, decanters, and goblets encompass a wide array of glass types, and many are colorfully enameled with heraldic crests, scenes, and sovereigns' portraits. Some have gold and ruby overlay, delicate scrollwork, and cut ornaments.

The museum also shows traveling ex-

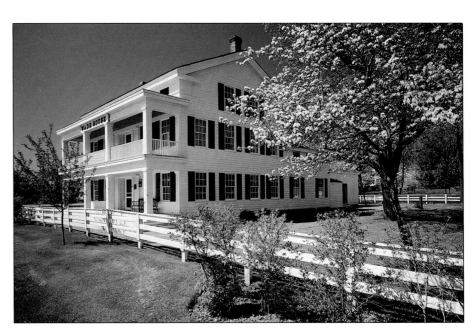

14. *Imagine the relief of weary 19th-century travelers as this inn came into view.*

hibits of glassware and other artwork. *Open Tues.–Fri. and P.M. weekends. Closed holidays except Easter.*

13. Rahr–West Museum. *Park St. at N. Eighth St., Manitowoc.* Consistent with its two-part name, this museum has a split personality. The original building, given by the Rahr family, is a shingled Queen Anne–style mansion built by Joseph Vilaf in 1891. It is filled with authentic Victorian furnishings and 19th-century art, including works by such noted painters as Rembrandt Peale, Adolphe Bouguereau, and George Paxton. The mansion also has

collections of contemporary porcelain, American Indian artifacts, antique dolls, and most notably, rare Chinese ivories.

In striking contrast, the museum's sleek, modern exhibition wing, a gift of John and Ruth West, is home to a collection of 20th-century art with more than 150 canvases. Most of the painters are Americans, ranging from abstractionists such as Frank Stella, Joseph Raphael, and Sam Francis to more representational artists such as Neil Welliver, Milton Avery, and Jane Freilicher. The new wing also devotes a large space to traveling exhibits. *Open Mon.–Fri. and P.M. weekends.*

14. Old Wade House. *Rte. 23, Greenbush.* This attractive Greek Revival inn, built in 1851 by Sylvanus Wade, is part of a group of preserved buildings here that give an intriguing insight into life and travel in 19th-century America.

Wade, an optimistic entrepreneur from the East, built the inn in the Wisconsin wilderness to cater to travelers making the bone-rattling stagecoach journey along the plank road between Sheboygan and Fond du Lac. Tours of the 27-room structure reveal that Wade entertained his guests in a simple barroom and a parlor with a pump organ. He fed them family style on long pine tables in the dining room, with

---

ADVENTURE—Off the Beaten Path

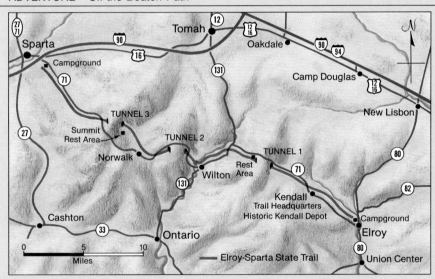

The Elroy–Sparta Bike Trail

Thirty-two miles along an abandoned railroad bed, through three dark tunnels and across 33 trestles...by bike! A family outing? With two kids, ages 12 and 14? Surely my wife, Kate, wasn't serious—well, as it turned out, she was.

We camped in Sparta, where we had arranged to rent bikes, purchase the $1 trail tickets, and have a shuttle service pick us up at journey's end. The morning sparkled with all the contagious cheerfulness of early autumn—the exhilaration of pedaling freely through open, rolling farmland, the foliage a blaze of color, the trail's crushed-limestone surface crunching under our tires.

After only a few miles we began to appreciate the 1870's trestle builders, whose restored structures, now resur-

faced with solid diagonal planking and equipped with sturdy guard rails, carried us over the hilly countryside. Near Norwalk we reached the first tunnel, a three-quarter-mile cavern, the longest on the trail. The darkness inside made us feel as though we were entering a spooky funhouse—an illusion our 12-year-old enhanced with his own eerie sound effects. Dismounting, as the sign advised, we bunched up apprehensively and followed the bright beams of our flashlights. Our confidence began to return as we became accustomed to the thrill of the unknown.

We filled our canteens at the Summit Rest Area—a slight misnomer, since the steepest grade on the entire trail is 3 percent—and paused to talk with some

serious cyclists on a much longer tour along the National Bicycle Trail. Then before we knew it, we were stopping for lunch at a restaurant in Wilton, after which we moved on to Kendall and visited the historic Chicago & Northwestern depot. Arriving in Elroy, the last stop, we were slightly sore in strategic places but firmly convinced that the bicycle—faster than a walk and slower than a drive—is one of mankind's most delightful inventions. —*Ned Hall*

Information: (608) 463-7109 or 337-4775

dishes prepared in a large winter kitchen.

Upstairs, the Wade family lived in rooms furnished with washstands, chests, and trundle beds, while the servants got by in more modest quarters near the back stairs. Resident guests also lived modestly in eight tiny rooms squeezed onto the third floor, sleeping on corn-husk mattresses with sheets that were changed once a month. Amazingly, 60 percent of the inn's original furnishings remains intact.

Also located here are a re-created blacksmith's shop with a working forge and another restored and refurbished house in the Greek Revival style that is particularly handsome. Even more interesting is the Wesley W. Jung Carriage Museum, which has an outstanding collection of more than 100 antique horse-drawn vehicles, all gleamingly restored. Among them are farm wagons, a butcher's wagon, a self-unloading coal wagon, fire engine pumpers, a 10-passenger sleigh, public omnibuses, a circus calliope, and children's play carriages, as well as elegant carriages and everyday buckboards.

For a small extra fee you can ride a horse-drawn carriage from the visitor center to the inn and the carriage museum. *Open daily July–Aug.; weekdays only, May, June, Sept., Oct. Admission charged.*

---

15. Horicon National Wildlife Refuge.
Millions of waterfowl migrate along the great Mississippi Flyway, and this federal wildlife preserve of 21,000 acres and an adjoining state wildlife area with 10,000 acres were established primarily to provide them with a refuge. Careful management has turned this into one of the nation's greatest areas for wildfowl—and for people who enjoy seeing them.

The marsh is best known for the big black-necked Canada geese that touch down here by the tens of thousands in the fall—and unfortunately attract thousands of viewers. But at other times of the year the marsh is a quiet refuge for the visitor as well as for the plentiful wildlife. In the spring northbound geese and ducks stage a smaller migratory show. And during the summer the marsh teems with nesting egrets, blue-winged teals, coots, great blue herons, mallards, wood ducks, and redheads. An occasional white-tailed deer and marsh fox may be seen as well.

Six miles of interconnecting trails wind through the marsh and along the impoundments around the edges. They tra-

15. *Although less elegant than when in flight, this gaggle of geese is still impressive.*

verse a beautifully austere landscape of lush reeds and rough marshlands mingled with clear lakes, sparse pockets of brush, and small stands of trees. Some areas can be seen by car along perimeter roads. Fishing is allowed from the banks of the lakes and ditches. Northerns, bullheads, and crappies are likely catches. *Most areas open and accessible mid-May–mid-Nov.*

---

16. Stonefield. *Cassville. On Hwy. VV off Rte. 133.* Centered around a classic village square with bandstand and apple trees, Stonefield re-creates the small-town Wisconsin of nearly a century ago. The 30-odd mostly clapboard structures are new, but they are constructed in a turn-of-the-century style, and most are filled with authentic period furnishings.

The law office has leather volumes and wooden file cabinets; the doctor's office, an examination table and surgical tools. The butcher shop has a marble counter and scales, while the ladies' hat shop is an oasis of feathers, lace, and satin. The goods in the Farmers' Store include corsets, shirt collars, and chewing tobacco. A wonderful array of patent medicines and toiletries line the drugstore's shelves. The cheese factory, newspaper printing shop, cigar factory, and photography studio all display period equipment. Other buildings include a train station, bank, church, creamery, stables, school, firehouse, and

saloon. There is even a furniture–undertaker's shop (a common combination at the time) with cabinetmaking tools in front and embalming equipment in back.

A visit to the village should include the adjoining State Farm Museum, which has displays devoted to the settlement of Wisconsin and the evolution of agriculture here. Especially interesting are the beautifully crafted scale models of reaping machines complete with horses and humans.

The ticket to the village also admits the visitor to another Stonefield, the mansion which gave its name to the village. The restored brick structure, which stands just across the highway in the Nelson Dewey State Park, was the home of Wisconsin's first governor, Nelson Dewey.

The 739-acre park, which is open year-round, offers quiet beauty, camping sites, nature trails, and excellent bird-watching. More than 85 species nest here in summer. The overlook on the bluffs above the village provides fine views of the Mississippi meandering through a wide valley. *Stonefield open daily Memorial Day–Labor Day. Admission charged.*

---

17. Dickeyville Grotto. *U.S. Rte. 151 and W. Main St., Dickeyville.* One does not have to be religious to be awed by the painstaking work that went into making the small collection of shrines here on the grounds of Holy Ghost Church. Built by

Father Mathias Wernerus between 1925 and 1930, the concrete structures are embellished with a bewildering array of stones, shells, tiles, and glass. Completely covering the shrines' columns, arches, niches, and walls, these bits and pieces create intricate, mosaiclike designs—of flowers and abstract patterns as well as crosses and other religious symbols.

The main grotto is a small chapel flanked by mosaic flags. Inside, a statue of the Virgin Mary with the infant Jesus rises above an elaborate altar. Appropriately, the ceiling is a heavenly blue, every inch encrusted with cowrie shells, quartz, colored glass, mosaic tiles, and stones.

The other heavily decorated shrines are dedicated to Christ, the saints, the Eucharist, and on a secular, patriotic note, to Christopher Columbus. *Open year-round. Admission free but donations appreciated.*

18. Tallman Restorations. *440 N. Jackson St., Janesville. From I-90 take Business Exit 14; follow signs.* In the late 1850's land speculator William Tallman paid the princely sum of $42,000 in gold to build the house and barn here. Styled after an Italian villa, the house has 26 rooms on five levels: a basement, three main stories, and a small rooftop observatory. No effort has been spared to make the rooms look not only authentic but lived in.

In the brick-floored basement, the kitchen has a stone fireplace and a dumbwaiter and is outfitted with cutting boards, meat grinder, and period utensils. The adjoining pantries are equipped for canning, churning, and butchering, and the laundry has a cradle washer and a coal-heated steam iron.

The ground floor has both a formal parlor and dining room (with the table set for a meal) and more comfortable smoking, sewing, and breakfast rooms. When Tallman entertained Abraham Lincoln here in 1859, the future president reportedly found the parlor too fancy for his taste and moved to the sewing room.

Upstairs, the second floor contains bedrooms, servants' quarters, and an office with Tallman's pigeonhole desk. The third floor has large, gallerylike rooms where children played and the visiting seamstress prepared new spring and fall wardrobes. The observatory looks out across the lead roof to the leafy grounds.

Another, smaller restored and refurbished home can also be visited. It is an 1842 Greek Revival stone house that was moved here to save it from demolition. A museum in the former barn displays local police memorabilia, dolls, paper toys, and Lincolniana. *Open Tues.–Sun., June–Aug.; weekends only, May, Sept., and Oct.*

19. Kenosha Public Museum. *5608 10th Ave., Kenosha.* In 1933 Kenosha's city fathers paid just $1 for this stately turn-of-the-century building, once used as the main post office. But then they had the formidable task of moving the 1,200-ton masonry structure two city blocks to its present site on the edge of the civic center.

The museum's purpose is primarily educational, and its main exhibits on the ground floor focus on the study of nature and artifacts from various cultures. A collection of preserved wildlife specimens includes a black bear, otter, and badger as well as mounted fish and birds and drawers of butterflies. Dioramas show fighting dinosaurs, ancient tar pits, a coal age forest swamp, and Chippewas fashioning a canoe. Representing American Indian cultures are such items as feather necklaces from Peru, a totem pole from the Pacific Northwest, carved ivory and soapstone from northern Canada, and beads, baskets, and pottery from the Southwest. There are also artifacts from Africa, New Guinea, and China.

In the basement an unusual collection of small dioramas presents the studios and works of the world's greatest sculptors. One shows Michelangelo with the Pietà and his statues of Moses and David. The stairway leading to the basement has four window panels of 18th-century enameled glass emblazoned with British and Swiss coats of arms. *Open Mon.–Fri., A.M. Sat., and P.M. Sun. except holidays.*

16. *With progress came the loss of charming villages such as the one replicated here.*

Iowa

The natural wonders and appealing historic and scenic places provide another perspective on the state "where the tall corn grows."

One of the many state parks is enjoyable both under and above the ground; another is named for the astonishing rocks found there; and a national monument preserves the mysterious legacy of prehistoric Indians. The farm where one family lived for 100 years is now a museum and crafts center. A second Iowa family has bequeathed an amazing assortment of musical instruments, which are now on display.

A museum village recalls life at the turn of the century. Nostalgia is further reinforced in an old-time drugstore and a collection of early telephone equipment. A replica of a village street includes a bank robbed by Jesse James, while a popular American artist is remembered in a town of rural charm. Early transportation is represented in a museum of antique aircraft. Ardent birders come to Iowa to see waterfowl by the hundreds of thousands.

1. Plymouth County Historical Museum.
335 First Ave. SW, Le Mars. This intriguing museum's split personality adds to its interest. One part of the collection is devoted to local history. Several rooms have been furnished in the style of an 1890's middle-class home, and there are plans to refurbish other rooms as replicas of period business offices. Antique farm machinery and a "Hall of Fame" of people associated with the county may also be seen. A large one-room log cabin from the Civil War era in Plymouth stands nearby.

The other, more surprising dimension of the museum is the Parkinson Collection of antique and exotic musical instruments. Started in 1855, the collection has now been continued for five generations by the Parkinson family, and today it includes several hundred pieces. The oldest is an Egyptian cradle harp estimated to date from 1450 B.C. Other exotica are nose flutes from Fiji, Irish battle harps, two-string Asian violins with resonators made from coconut shells, a violin made from bones by Spanish pirates, and giant African prayer drums 2½ feet in diameter. Among the most popular pieces are late 19th-century pump organs, a handsome collection of Swiss and American music

boxes, and a European military horn with the bell extending back to allow its user to face the enemy while sounding calls to the troops behind him. *Open P.M. daily Memorial Day–Labor Day; P.M. Tues–Sun. the rest of the year.*

---

2. Drug Store Exhibition.
The Druggists Mutual Companies, Rte. 18W, Algona. In 1902 a druggist in Titonka was burned out of his store. Unhappy with the settlement for his loss, he established his own insurance company. That company sells primarily to pharmacists, and over the years policyholders have donated early cabinets, scales, mortars and pestles, patent medicine bottles with embossed lettering, and similar objects to this museum, which successfully recaptures the atmosphere of an early 1900's drugstore.

A container once holding heroin and terpin hydrate for coughs, plus boxes of Gastrotone, Hollister's Golden Nugget Tablets, and Mother Gray's Sweet Powders, are reminders of the days when almost any compound could be sold over the counter. A 1910 crude drug-sample

case once used by medical students, an optometrist's kit with lenses, and a dispensing counter with an early Oliver typewriter and handwritten prescriptions are among the rarities displayed.

A fully equipped soda fountain circa 1890 brings back to life the gentle years when a root beer was often placed on the marble counter with two straws. *Open weekdays except holidays year-round.*

---

3. Old Bradford Pioneer Village.
Rte. 346, east of Nashua. The village of Bradford, founded in the 1840's as an Indian trading post, was named for a Winnebago chief. It continued to thrive for many years as a supply center on the wagon route west. But in the late 1800's the village was bypassed by the railroad, and eventually it was nearly abandoned.

Today 12 buildings, many moved to the village from nearby towns, re-create the atmosphere of the plains in the 19th and early 20th centuries. Two log cabins built in the 1850's and appropriately furnished may be seen, together with a one-room schoolhouse, a doctor's office, an 1860's

5. Prehistoric Mound Builders may also have been inspired by the mighty Mississippi.

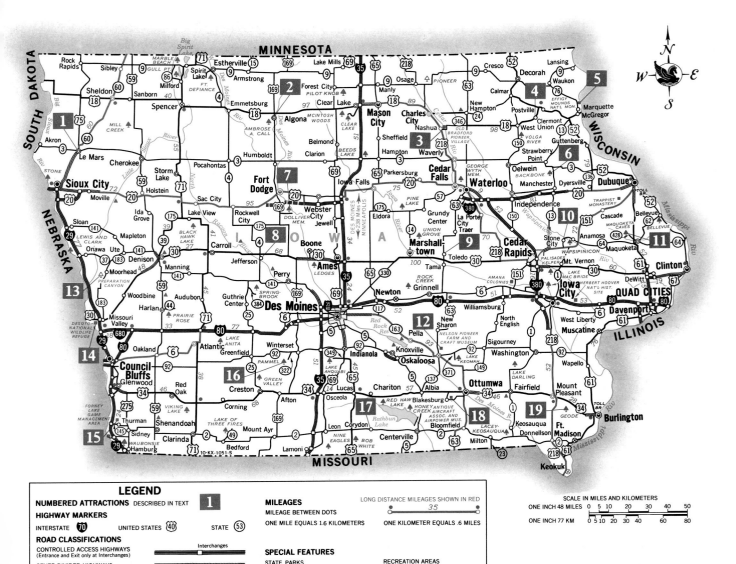

LEGEND

NUMBERED ATTRACTIONS DESCRIBED IN TEXT **1**

HIGHWAY MARKERS

INTERSTATE **70**　　UNITED STATES **40**　　STATE **53**

ROAD CLASSIFICATIONS

CONTROLLED ACCESS HIGHWAYS　　Interchanges
(Entrance and Exit only at Interchanges)

OTHER DIVIDED HIGHWAYS

PRINCIPAL THROUGH HIGHWAYS

OTHER THROUGH HIGHWAYS

CONNECTING HIGHWAYS

MILEAGES　　LONG DISTANCE MILEAGES SHOWN IN RED

MILEAGE BETWEEN DOTS　　35

ONE MILE EQUALS 1.6 KILOMETERS　　ONE KILOMETER EQUALS .6 MILES

SPECIAL FEATURES

STATE PARKS　　RECREATION AREAS

With Campsites ▲ Without Campsites △　　With Campsites ▲ Without Campsites △

POINTS OF INTEREST ■

SCALE IN MILES AND KILOMETERS

ONE INCH 48 MILES　0　5　10　20　30　40　50

ONE INCH 77 KM　0　5 10　20　30 40　60　80

---

blacksmith's shop, and a general store where the 1902 price list shows hamburger for seven cents a pound and a 49-pound bag of flour for a mere $1.05.

The Chicago Great Western Railroad depot, brought from Fredericksburg, is especially interesting with its potbellied wood stove, rack of old timetables, Western Union office, and attached baggage room. The Heritage House, formerly a school, displays pioneer arts and crafts. *Open daily May–Oct. Admission charged.*

---

4. Montauk. *Clermont.*

It is odd to find a house in Iowa named for a lighthouse far away on New York's Long Island. But William Larrabee was an easterner for whom Montauk Lighthouse was a symbol of safety, steering ships through perilous waters, and he felt that his home should serve the same function for his family. Larrabee, a wealthy miller and landowner who later became Iowa's governor, built this fine Italianate home in 1874.

The Larrabees, with their four daughters and three sons, were the only people ever to live in the house, and when the daughter, Anna, died in 1965 at age 97, the house and everything in it was left to the state. All the furnishings, silver, china, toys, musical instruments, books, paintings, statuettes, photographs, and bric-a-brac belonged to the Larrabees. Seldom does a house-museum so accurately reveal the taste and activities of one specific household. In any of the nine rooms on display, one rather expects a family member to come walking in.

The outbuildings on the 80-acre estate include a laundry, creamery, well house, windmill, and workshop. *Open P.M. daily Memorial Day–Oct. Admission charged.*

---

5. Effigy Mounds National Monument.

Dart points found locally attest to the presence of a primitive hunting people on these lands as long ago as 12,000 years. But the tremendous fascination of this 1,475-acre national monument dates from much more recent times.

Found here is an exceptionally large number of mounds (191 all together) of several types—linear, conical, and effigy—and from several periods. The mounds shed light on a succession of cultures in this area from around 500 B.C. almost to historic times. The oldest (which include both linear and conical mounds) were created by Indians of the Red Ocher culture, so called because they put their burials on a floor first sprinkled with red ocher (iron ore dust).

Excavations of other mounds have revealed an assortment of elaborate grave goods fashioned from seashells, obsidian, and other unexpected materials obtained by far-reaching trade. The artifacts show the influence of the Hopewell culture, which centered in Ohio around 100 B.C. to about A.D. 400 (see p.142).

The most intriguing formations to see, however, are the 29 effigy mounds in the shapes of bears and birds in flight built by Indians who farmed this land until about 1350. The Great Bear Mound is especially impressive, being 137 feet long, 70 feet wide from shoulder to foreleg, and more than 3 feet high.

A network of hiking trails connects the mound sites with scenic river overlooks. Ferns and wildflowers (many with identification stakes) and an abundance of birds following the Mississippi Flyway add to the pleasures of the outing. A 14-minute orientation film is shown in the visitor center, where displays illustrate mound-building techniques and the coming of the white man. Ranger-guided tours of the mounds leave the visitor center on a regular schedule each day and take 1½ hours. *Open daily except Christmas.*

6. Backbone State Park. A high quarter-mile "spine" of rock runs through the center of this scenic 1,800-acre state park, where some 12 miles of hiking trails offer excellent opportunities to explore caverns, climb natural rock stairways, and admire the tall white pines overhanging the cliffs. Deer, wild turkeys, raccoons, and an occasional coyote roam the land, and songbirds, including bluebirds and a few wild canaries, flit through the woods.

A lake offers swimming, and the South Fork of the Maquoketa River is stocked with trout. Paddleboats, canoes, and rowboats may be rented. An old trout hatchery is now a fishing exhibit where trout of various sizes may be seen and fed; a fishing clinic is given every Saturday from Memorial Day to Labor Day.

In winter the roads are not plowed out, and campers must either backpack in or use a snowmobile. A winter carnival, held the last weekend in January, features dogsled, ski, and snowmobile races. *Open year-round. Admission charged.*

7. Dolliver Memorial State Park. Creeks, ravines, forested hills, sandstone bluffs and outcroppings, and small patches of prairie make this 583-acre park a beautiful and varied place to explore. Especially intriguing is Boneyard Hollow at the park's northern end. A ravine about a quarter-mile long and 50 to 65 or more feet deep, it narrows down to a gash about 10 feet wide. Settlers reported finding many bones in the ravine, the remains of buffalo driven over the edge by Indian hunters.

The sandstone bluffs, which are about 250 million years old, hold deposits of copperas, a sulfur-and-iron substance that was once prized by Indians for use in mixing face paint. You can get a good view of the copperas beds from the footbridge crossing Prairie Creek. The creek, which meanders through the hills to join the Des Moines River, passes beneath three Indian mounds—a linear ceremonial mound flanked by conical mounds—dating from about A.D. 1100.

Several rather steep hiking trails traverse the park beneath dense canopies of oak, maple, and other hardwoods, and lead along the Des Moines, which forms the park's eastern border. A boat ramp is provided for fishermen, who can expect to catch smallmouth bass plus channel, blue,

and flathead catfish; flatheads weighing up to 40 pounds have been taken.

A campground stretches along a bluff above the river, and picnic tables are set on attractive grassy areas beside the park road. The park is named in honor of Jonathan P. Dolliver, an Iowan who served in Congress from 1888 until his death in 1910. *Open year-round. Admission charged.*

8. Jefferson Telephone Company Museum. *105 W. Harrison St., Jefferson.* The imaginative precursors of the sleek, standardized telephone equipment we use today can be seen in this small museum in the basement of an independent telephone company building. Here you will see an 1880's voice box (the voice was transmitted by a string to a person not more than 100 feet away in the same building), a circa 1910 secretarial desk with a telephone mouthpiece, and a Gray Telephone Pay Station Company wall unit with slots for silver dollars, half-dollars, and three other coin denominations. An oak board with switches used to test circuits is another example of the early-day telephone equipment on display. These pieces, made be-

6. *Views from the rocky ridge reveal the wayward course of the Maquoketa River.*

fore the dominance of anonymous design, have the engaging variety and informal character of handmade objects whose mechanics one can almost understand.

Also worth seeing in Jefferson is the Greene County Courthouse, a magnificent Beaux Arts structure built in 1917 and listed in *The National Register of Historic Places*. Standing beside the courthouse is the modern 162-foot Mahanay Memorial Carillon Tower, whose 32 bells play musical selections several times daily. In summer you can take an elevator to the tower's observation deck, where the view extends for 25 miles. *Museum open weekdays except holidays. Admission charged.*

12. *Voting house, beside the general store, proclaims its function with a flying flag.*

9. Tama County Historical Museum.
State St. at N. Broadway, Toledo. Constructed in 1869, the solid brick building now housing this museum of local history served as the county jail for more than 100 years before being converted to its present use. It was placed in *The National Register of Historic Places* in 1981.

The first floor now houses artifacts from the local Mesquakie Indians and implements used by early settlers. The second floor, however, preserves the mood and interior of the old jail. Four cells may be visited: two women's cells, a maximum-security cell, and one that dramatizes the chilling isolation of solitary confinement.

Displays of military uniforms, historical photographs, and memorabilia from the offices of early doctors, dentists, lawyers, and bankers are also on view. One room is devoted to the finery of prairie life, such as china, ladies' fashions, and the prized beaver hats that men wore for dress. *Open P.M. Wed.–Sat. except holidays.*

10. Stone City.
Once a thriving center for limestone quarrying, as the name implies, this community started to decline around the turn of the century when cement began to replace stone as a favored construction material. But the artist Grant Wood (1892–1942) brought a brief moment of renewal when he chose the village as the site of the Stone City Colony and Art School in 1932–33. Wood was widely known for his canvases "American Gothic" and "Stone City," and other stylized renderings of rural Midwest life.

Nestled in the valley of the Wapsipinicon River, the town has several imposing structures built by the quarry owners. On a hill overlooking the village and the pastoral countryside stands the shell of the huge Victorian mansion which served as the colony's headquarters. Eight-week courses in sculpture, figure drawing, and other subjects were given here for a mere $36, and dormitory lodging was provided for $1.50 a week. The mansion served as a summer camp and as a part-time residence until 1963, when the interior was gutted by fire.

Today Stone City's past is softly echoed by its handsome 19th-century stone residences. Time, in these environs, seems to slow down, and there is little to disturb the pervading calm. All together, this is a picturesque place to see.

On the second Sunday in June each year the Grant Wood Art Festival attracts many artists and craftsmen who display their creations outside a splendid 1880's stone horse barn. During the festival a collection of early photographs, tools, and other memorabilia may be viewed in an 1860's stone blacksmith's shop that is not otherwise open to the public. Nostalgia is further summoned by the replicated ice wagons parked on the hillside. Colorful vehicles such as these (reminiscent of gypsy caravans) were once used to house the art students. *Admission charged for festival.*

11. Maquoketa Caves State Park.
A network of 13 caves runs beneath the eastern section of this park, and as early as 1835 explorers cut their names into the dripping limestone walls. These natural chambers range from 30 feet to more than 800 feet in length. Some are lighted and have walkways, but experienced spelunkers using flashlights may enjoy the challenge of penetrating several unlighted caves, which can be demanding—and muddy. The temperature stays at about 50° F.

For visitors more interested in aboveground activities, there are birds, wildflowers, shady forests, and scenic views to enjoy. Great horned and barred owls, red-tailed hawks, and hummingbirds can be found in the stands of oak, ash, hickory, and maple. Columbines, bloodroot, mayapples, hepaticas, and the endangered monkshood share ground space with morels. Picking the mushrooms is allowed.

Hikers in all seasons can enjoy some five miles of trails in the park, leading to overlooks with views of the steep ravine that is a dominant feature here, and to a natural bridge. The wind-twisted cedars growing out of cracks in cliff surfaces create a magic of their own. *Open daily year-round. Admission charged.*

12. Nelson Pioneer Farm and Craft Museum.
Glendale Rd. E., off Rte. 63, Oskaloosa. The Nelson family farmed this land for 114 years. The sturdy brick house, furnished as it was in the mid-1800's, and the big barn with all its equipment are the nucleus of this memorial to 19th-century farm and community life.

A charming country store displays a typical selection of early-day merchandise. The small voting house with its curtained booth and kerosene lamps is believed to be the first built west of the Mississippi solely for voting purposes. There's a furnished 1867 log cabin, and a post office with several names still visible on the back of combination lockboxes. A 19th-century one-room school, furnished as it was in 1911, has a slate on every desk and a corner stool with a dunce cap awaiting the reluctant scholar. The museum building contains early coal-mining tools, a superb 1874 round table made from 3,000 pieces of 50 different Iowa woods, vintage toy trains, and Indian artifacts. In a plot near the museum is a touching tribute to faithful animals: the headstones marking the graves of Becky and Jenny, two mules that served in the Civil War and then came to the farm. *Open Tues.–Sat. and P.M. Sun. mid-May–mid-Oct.*

13. Preparation Canyon State Park. Under the leadership of Charles B. Thompson in 1853, 60 Mormon families took leave of a wagon train on its way to Utah to farm this fertile hill country. Guided by Thompson, they set up the town of Preparation and began a "School of Preparation for the Life Beyond." Actually, they were preparing for a swindle by their leader, to whom they had deeded all their property. For three years Thompson grew wealthy on the labor of his followers, until finally they lost faith in his religious purity and demanded their property back. Thompson refused, was driven out, and disappeared, leaving confusion over the land titles that took ten years to resolve. For a while the settlement thrived, but by the turn of the century it was dead.

The park now has more than 300 acres, including the site of Preparation, much of it sold to the state by descendants of the original settlers. The canyon is in a secluded part of the park, which is enclosed by a scallop of ridges. Its glacial formation invites nature studies along several steep hiking trails. Red foxes, deer, wild turkeys, and coyotes make their homes on the forested slopes. Red-tailed and Cooper's hawks, quails, great horned owls, and many songbirds may also be seen. *Accessible year-round. Park roads open Apr.– Nov. Use-fee charged.*

14. DeSoto National Wildlife Refuge. This inviting refuge flanks DeSoto Lake, actually a seven-mile-long oxbow of the Missouri River isolated in 1960 by a levee and a new channel cut across the bend by

14. *The Missouri Valley abounds with gentle waterscapes and exquisite scenery.*

the U.S. Army Corps of Engineers. The refuge is a popular destination for birders during spring and autumn, when more than half a million geese and ducks may stop over. Much of the acreage is planted with alfalfa, native grasses, winter wheat, and milo so that migratory birds can nest and feed undisturbed.

Sandhill cranes, quails, pheasants, eastern meadowlarks, American woodcock, and many songbirds are also drawn to this peaceful setting amid cottonwoods, dogwoods, and multiflora roses. Deer, coyotes, and fox squirrels are residents as well. Among the wildflowers to be seen are great lobelia, blue vervain, American lotus, and wild lettuce. From mid-April through May the delicious morels may be picked in some areas. Anglers are likely to catch largemouth bass, channel catfish, crappies, northern pike, and bluegills.

A 12-stop auto tour of the refuge (detailed in a free interpretive folder) begins at the visitor center, where a windowed gallery on the lake offers a marvelous vantage point for viewing great numbers of migratory waterfowl.

The center also has a veritable warehouse of well-preserved objects recovered in 1968–69 from the stern-wheeler *Bertrand*, which sank in the Missouri in 1865 and became entombed in silt and sand as the river shifted course. Her 150-ton cargo included blasting fuses for the Montana goldfields, bottles of schnapps, brandy, and champagne, plus Indian trade goods, dinnerware, glass tumblers, and clothing.

At the last stop on this route a short trail brings you to a platform overlooking the location where the *Bertrand* was excavated and, after the removal of her cargo, reburied. *Refuge open daily mid-Apr.–Sept. and mid-Oct.–first week in Nov.; visitor center open daily except Easter, Thanksgiving Day, Christmas, and New Year's Day.*

15. Forney Lake Game Management Area. *Off Rte. L44, 2.3 miles north of Thurman.* Covering a shallow marsh in the Missouri River floodplain, this 1,000-acre area is a nesting and breeding ground for pheasants, coots, and grebes as well as a refuge for migratory birds. The wetlands attract white pelicans, great blue herons, egrets, mallards, and teals. Over 100,000 geese visit during their seasonal migrations, primarily snow geese and blues, but Canada geese and whitefronts may also be seen. Other visitors include bald eagles, red-tailed hawks, and warblers.

Turnouts along the 1½-mile gravel road offer limited parking but splendid views. Be sure to bring binoculars and telephoto lenses, since the expanse of open marsh makes it difficult to get close to the birds. *Open year-round.*

16. Pammel State Park.

Set in hilly upland country, this tranquil 280-acre park has two major features: a long limestone ridge called Devil's Backbone and Middle River, which flows north along one side of the ridge, makes a sharp turn, and then reenters the park on the other side of the ridge, flowing in a southeasterly direction. A picturesque tunnel burrowing through the ridge once carried water to a nearby gristmill. It has since become Iowa's only road tunnel. The road leads past a pleasant picnic area at the riverside. The park has three other picnic areas as well, including one on top of the ridge.

Foot trails and snowmobile trails circle through the woods, which harbor wild

18. *Limited space allows close inspection. In foreground: a 1934 Rose Parakeet.*

turkeys, hawks, deer, foxes, coyotes, and many rabbits. Fishing, mushroom picking, and primitive camping are the other attractions here.

The park is in Madison County, which has six covered bridges. The best preserved is the 1870 Donahoe Bridge in Winterset's city park. Two more of these timbered spans are nearby. All bear a striking resemblance to their counterparts in New England. *Open year-round.*

17. Wayne County Historical Museum.

Rte. 2, Corydon. Although the exterior of this museum is rather austere, it is full of delightful surprises. Primarily devoted to local history, it contains more than 80,000 items, almost all from Wayne County. The major attraction, perhaps, is the recreation of Main Street in a typical Wayne County village of the late 19th century, with a general store, doctor's office, barbershop, jail, courtroom, dentist's office, beauty salon, and post office and life-size models of shopkeepers and customers. There's even a replica of the Corydon bank that Jesse James robbed, including the safe actually involved in the robbery. At the south end of "Main Street" is a collection of some 300 mounted birds and animals from Wayne County.

Toys, textiles, and musical instruments are also exhibited. Another section of the museum has a bedroom, a living room, and a kitchen with period furnishings. A highlight of the historical collection is a life-size diorama showing a Mormon family heading west in a covered wagon drawn by two oxen. Outside, a small park contains a one-room log cabin with a loft, one of the first dwellings in the county. An exhibit of antique farm equipment and vehicles includes a charming horse-drawn yellow school bus. *Open P.M. daily June–Oct. Admission charged.*

18. Antique Aircraft Association and Airpower Museum.

Bluegrass Rd. northeast of Blakesburg. The aircraft made before the advent of the retractable landing gear, ultimate streamlining, and jet engines have a special sculptural beauty. Flying them, especially in an open cockpit, is in a class by itself, and so—with the motto "Keep the antiques flying"—devoted pilots started an association in 1953. This field, with its

two grass landing strips and row of hangars, has become headquarters for over 40 chapters of the nationwide association.

Several "type club" fly-ins are scheduled each year at which owners of a particular make of aircraft, such as Fairchild, Luscombe, and Cessna, converge on the field for a weekend of tall tales and shared admiration of the aircraft.

The adjacent Airpower Museum presents a history of aviation and includes miniature models of combat aircraft up through World War II. In the collection of 25 operational aircraft are a 1931 Stinson Junior S. monoplane, a 1925 Anderson biplane, and a 1929 Fairchild 71 Pan Am airliner. Often crowded during special events. *Open weekdays and P.M. weekends except Thanksgiving Day, Christmas, and New Year's Day. Admission free but donations encouraged.*

19. Geode State Park.

The park and 205-acre lake are named for the curious rocks formerly discovered in abundance here. Geodes are found in many places and can be purchased in most rock shops. But how amazing it must have been for the first person to break open one of these dull-looking spherical rocks and see the colorful crystalline formations inside.

The 1,640-acre park is popular with fishermen, who try for large- and smallmouth bass, bluegills, crappies, and tiger muskies up to three feet long. A 300-foot beach with an offshore float attracts swimmers, and there are puffy winds to challenge small-boat sailors.

Good camping facilities and nice hiking trails recommend this quiet area to anyone interested in nature. The walk on the one-mile interpretive trail is enhanced by the excellent brochure that explains the forest ecosystem and indicates the likely animal dens and food sources favored by the raccoons, deer, and other wildlife. Hickory, hornbeam, oak, American elm, and black walnut are prevalent in the woods.

In winter, cross-country skiers use the hiking trails and are often able to cross the frozen lake. Sledding, snowmobiling, and ice fishing are other cold weather activities to be enjoyed. Crowds may be a problem on holiday weekends. *Open year-round.*

Illinois

The appreciation of nature is obvious here, along with the imprint of the region's first inhabitants, early settlers, and young Abe Lincoln.

When Abraham Lincoln was a state legislator, he was influential in the development of canals and railroads, and a preserved section of each is now used for recreation. At the reconstruction of his father's farm, where Lincoln often visited, you'll see and hear the dress and dialect of the 1840's. Another reconstruction of log cabins, a restored Mormon community, a little-changed Victorian village, and an American Indian ghost town provide further historical insight.

Historical collections are housed in two handsome mansions, and there's a world-famous museum of various kinds of timepieces. Other places are dedicated to the fascination of nature.

1. Apple River Canyon State Park.

The cool, clear waters of Apple River flow through the center of this lovely park, gently but steadily cutting through masses of limestone, dolomite, and shale as they have done for thousands of years. In the canyon, vertical cliffs now rise 250 feet above the small stream. Flowering plants, shrubs, and some 14 different kinds of ferns grow in the crevices of the rock face, transforming it into a hanging garden. Elsewhere the river eddies between sloping banks canopied by cottonwoods, black willows, hackberry, and sycamores.

For nature lovers and amateur geologists the 296-acre park has special interest. It is in a small region that was untouched by glaciation, and it apparently served as a refuge for many plants that did not survive the glacial period in most parts of Illinois. As a result, several exquisite relict plants are found here, including the bird's-eye primrose, the flower-of-an-hour, and the jeweled shooting star.

In more recent times the region was prized for its deposits of lead. Indians dug it out for exchange with French traders 300 years ago, and in the 19th century settlers established profitable mines here.

Five hiking trails wind among the wooded hills, providing opportunities to enjoy the lush vegetation, the cliffs, streams, and springs, and perhaps to spot deer, small mammals, hawks, pileated woodpeckers, and occasional bald eagles.

Wildflowers splash the park roadsides from spring into fall. The river is stocked with smallmouth bass, crappies, and other game fish. Cross-country skiing, tobogganing, and camping are popular in winter. *Open year-round.*

2. Time Museum.

At the Clock Tower Inn, Business Rte. 20 and I-90, Rockford. Time does march on, and the steps have been measured not merely by ticks and tocks but by the drip of water clocks, the sands of hourglasses, and the silent shadows of the sundial. Such is the stuff of this unique, world-famous museum.

Numbering nearly 4,000 timekeeping devices, this superb collection traces the state of the art from the earliest instruments, dating as far back as 3000 B.C., to the atomic clocks of today.

Among the many rare and remarkable timetellers are one of the earliest spring-driven French table clocks (about 1520), one of the first pendulum clocks made in Holland (1657), an early long-case clock constructed to automatically show both sun and mean time, and the most complicated astronomical clock in the world, made between 1958 and 1964 by Rasmus Sornes of Norway.

A chariot clock from about 1600, decorated with gold on copper, depicts the mythical, gluttonous King Gambrinus, who is credited with the first brewing of beer. At the hour, the charioteer strikes the elephants drawing his cart, while the thirsty king rolls his eyes and raises a tankard to his lips.

Anyone who admires craftsmanship in general, including jewelry and fine woodworking, will be intrigued by the quality of this most comprehensive collection. *Open daily except Mon., Thanksgiving Day, and Christmas. Admission charged.*

3. Illinois Railway Museum.

Olson Road, Union. Railroad buffs can steam into the past aboard old coaches pulled by locomotives along some four miles of track. Vin-

tage streetcars also make a loop, stopping at the carbarns that house elevated trains, mail and baggage cars, and a wide range of antique trolleys.

More than 200 engines and cars recall the charm and excitement of railroading in days gone by. Much of the equipment has been restored and is fully operational. Of special interest is the 1889 Nevada Northern private car *Ely*, with paneled and mirrored bedrooms and a plush sitting room. An elevated railroad car from Chicago still displays 1907 advertisements for chewing gum, while another veteran of Chicago's busy traffic—a "Green Hornet" streetcar—harks back to the 1940's, when there was a popular radio program of the same name.

Frequent departures from an authentic depot are announced by stationmasters, and the trains are staffed by uniformed engineers, conductors, and trainmen. One of the interpretive charts translates the intriguing code of "whistle talk," while another explains why the expansion of the railroads had created a need by 1883 to divide the country into standardized time zones. Special events include a Fourth of July Trolley Pageant. The museum is usually crowded on Sundays. *Open daily Memorial Day–Labor Day, Sun. in Apr. and Oct., weekends in May and in Sept. after Labor Day. Trolleys run when museum is open; steam trains only on weekends and holidays, Memorial Day–Labor Day. Admission charged.*

4. Volo Bog State Natural Area.

Visitors to this 869-acre wilderness area can find themselves on shaky ground: the main attraction here is a so-called quaking bog about 50 acres in extent, designated a national natural landmark. The bog is a deep, spongy mat of vegetation and roots, and if you were to tread directly on it, the sensation would be similar to that of walking on a water bed. To preserve it, visitors are required, however, to stay on the half-mile loop trail, which starts at the visitor center near the parking lot. The wet areas

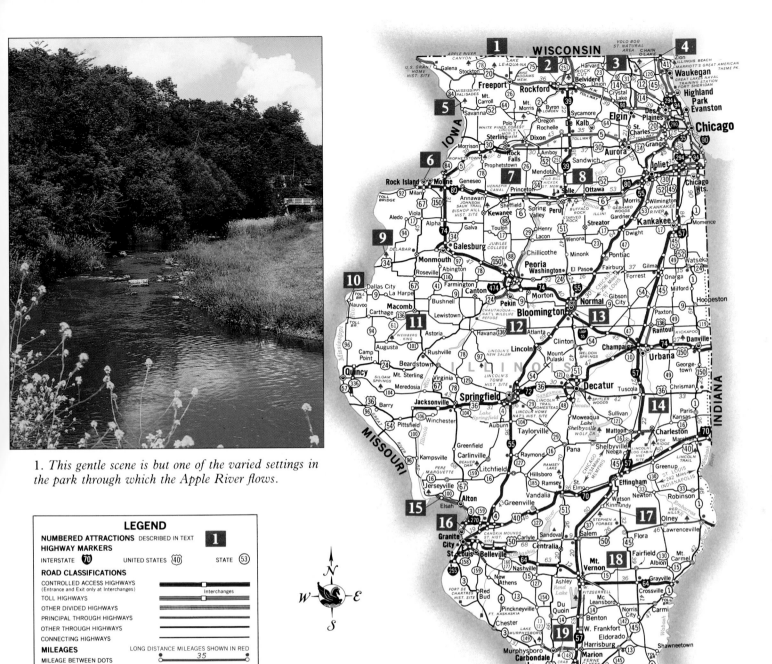

1. *This gentle scene is but one of the varied settings in the park through which the Apple River flows.*

LEGEND

NUMBERED ATTRACTIONS DESCRIBED IN TEXT   `1`
HIGHWAY MARKERS

INTERSTATE `70`   UNITED STATES `40`   STATE `53`

ROAD CLASSIFICATIONS

CONTROLLED ACCESS HIGHWAYS
(Entrance and Exit only at Interchanges)
    Interchanges
TOLL HIGHWAYS
OTHER DIVIDED HIGHWAYS
PRINCIPAL THROUGH HIGHWAYS
OTHER THROUGH HIGHWAYS
CONNECTING HIGHWAYS

MILEAGES

LONG DISTANCE MILEAGES SHOWN IN RED
MILEAGE BETWEEN DOTS   35
ONE MILE EQUALS 1.6 KILOMETERS   ONE KILOMETER EQUALS .6 MILES

SPECIAL FEATURES

STATE PARKS   RECREATION AREAS
With Campsites ▲ Without Campsites △   With Campsites ▲ Without Campsites △
POINTS OF INTEREST ■

© THE H.M. GOUSHA COMPANY · SAN JOSE, CALIFORNIA

SCALE IN MILES AND KILOMETERS
ONE INCH 53 MILES   0 5 10   20   30   40   50   60
ONE INCH 85 KM   0 5 10 20 30   50   70   96

are crossed by a boardwalk resting on Styrofoam pontoons.

Fourteen stops along the trail permit close-up inspection of an unusually rich plant life which changes from area to area because of the changing light, temperature, and humidity. In the tamarack forest you'll find buckthorn, quaking aspen, winterberry, and several types of fern. As for the stinging nettle and poison sumac, look but don't touch. Both are illustrated in the seasonal trail guides.

Rose pogonias and bog twayblades are among the six kinds of wild orchids thriving here, along with marsh cinquefoils, starflowers, Indian pipes, and other wildlings. Among birds frequently seen are cranes, herons, white-winged crossbills, yellow-headed blackbirds, ruby-crowned kinglets, and almost 200 other species.

Summer programs include guided bird and wildflower excursions and a "Bats Are Beautiful" walk to an old barn, where hundreds of these mosquito-eaters literally hang out. *Trail open year-round. Visitor center open Wed.–Sun., Memorial Day–* *Labor Day; weekends and state holidays remainder of year. Entire area closed Christmas and New Year's Day.*

5. Mississippi Palisades State Park. This hilly, 2,550-acre park was named for the Hudson River Palisades, and the resemblance is striking, with a dramatic limestone bluff dominating the region and overlooking the Mississippi.

The recreation area offers 11 miles of hiking trails, some with steep climbs from river level to overlooks on the bluffs that reward you with sweeping views, especially magnificent at sunset. There are also less demanding trails, and if you don't want to hike, you can drive to Lookout Point to enjoy the scenery.

Thick growths of oak, ash, and white pine provide a fertile haven for wild turkeys, deer, and many kinds of songbirds. In spring and summer, violets, lobelias, and other wildflowers carpet the valleys and slopes, and many kinds of ferns grow rampant in the ravines.

Of particular note among the unusual rock formations are Indian Head, etched by ages of erosion, and Twin Sisters, two rock columns suggestive of their name. In all, this majestic setting encourages climbers to challenge the many limestone walls, seamed by centuries of wind and rain.

An adjacent private concession provides river access to boating and fishing. Anglers here try for walleye and northern pike. In winter the slopes and trails are used for cross-country skiing and sledding. *Open year-round.*

8. *From this vantage point in the park one sees Starved Rock Lock and Dam.*

6. Black Hawk State Park. *Off Rte. 5, Rock Island.* Those who fish the creeks and hike the trails of this 207-acre park follow the footsteps of the Sauk and Mesquakie Indians, to whom this region was once home. The park is named for one of the Sauks' greatest leaders.

You'll find an activities center in the limestone lodge, one of those many built-to-last structures erected by the CCC during the Great Depression. The park itself occupies the site of a former recreation and amusement area. Highly popular at the turn of the century, it boasted the first figure-eight roller coaster west of Chicago.

The essence of that era is captured by a photo display in the Hauberg Museum, a part of the lodge. The museum is otherwise devoted to portraying the lifestyle of the Sauk and Mesquakie Indians. Among the objects on view are a bark house, containing articles of everyday use, and a bust of Black Hawk copied from a life mask.

About half the park is a nature preserve wherein hackberry, hickory, and oak trees provide a canopy for rue anemone, wild orchids, trilliums, and some 30 other kinds of wildflowers. More than 100 bird species have been identified, and migrations fill the sky in spring and autumn.

Annual events include bird and wildflower walks in the spring, and geology and archeology outings in October. Various programs are periodically given in the amphitheater. Cross-country skiing is also popular. *Open daily except Thanksgiving Day, Christmas, and New Year's Day.*

7. Hennepin Canal Parkway. Completed in 1907, this canal linked the Mississippi and Illinois rivers as part of an interstate waterway connecting the East Coast with the Upper Mississippi Valley. It was a project that would have won the approval of Father Louis Hennepin, the French cleric who explored this region in the late 1600's. But although the canal embodied a number of innovative designs, it was never the right size for commercial traffic. In 1951 the U.S. Army Corps of Engineers finally closed it to commerce but left it open for recreational use.

The main part of the canal runs between Rock Island on the Mississippi River and Bureau Junction on the Illinois, while a feeder canal about 30 miles long links it with Rock Falls to the north. The canal corridor—which extends for about 100 miles and ranges from 380 feet to a mile in width—offers a pleasant venue for hikers, bikers, and horseback riders as well as boaters and canoers, fishermen, campers, and picnickers.

Marked trails along the old towpath run for more than 70 miles from the region of Tiskilwa to a point near Rock Falls, and several boat ramps and campsites are available at intervals between. Bass, bullheads, channel catfish, and bluegills are caught in the waters of the canal, which are never deeper than five feet.

The entire parkway offers 264 points of access, so if you don't want to hike you need not walk very far to reach the canal's banks. In winter the towpath is used for snowmobiling, and a 4½-mile trail in the visitor center area (near Sheffield) is groomed for cross-country skiing. Exhibits in the visitor center include a photographic display of the canal's construction and its early use. *Park open year-round; visitor center open daily except Christmas and New Year's Day.*

8. Starved Rock State Park. According to a legend from the 1760's, the Illiniwek Indians, one of whom had murdered the Ottawa chief, Pontiac, sought safety from the avenging Ottawas atop a high sandstone butte. Surrounded by their opponents, they eventually starved to death.

The appeal of this 2,630-acre park, which stretches along the southern edge of the Illinois River, is primarily in the 18 canyons cut in the sandstone bluffs by feeder streams and in the enormous variety of plant life found here, all of which can be enjoyed from the 20 miles of well-marked hiking trails.

The Interior Canyon Trail penetrates the cool, damp canyon recesses, wonderfully beautiful, with rugged rock formations, waterfalls, and a lush growth of ferns, mosses, and delicate flowering plants. The Bluff Trail takes you along slopes where oaks and sugar maples shade an understory of witch hazel, wild hydrangeas, and trilliums, and skims the bluff tops crowned by oaks, cedars, white pines, and shrubs preferring a drier soil. Along the River Trail one walks beneath a light canopy of cottonwoods and black willows and enters the forested floodplain, where the deeper soil nurtures hickories and bur oaks, blueberries, jack-in-the-pulpits, and many other nut-, fruit-, and flower-bearing plants. The River Trail also leads to Starvation Rock.

The park harbors small water-loving animals, flying squirrels, deer, and many species of birds—bluebirds, indigo buntings, scarlet tanagers, chickadees, and cedar waxwings, to name a few.

If you would like to try the bridle trail through this pretty park, there are horses for rent. Boats are available for those lured by white bass, bullheads, channel catfish, and walleye. There is also a fishing area accessible to wheelchairs. Playgrounds, picnic sites, campgrounds, an archery range, and a skating pond further the wide appeal. Snowshoeing and cross-country skiing are also popular in winter. *Open year-round.*

9. Delbar State Park. Stretching along the Mississippi River, these 89 acres constitute a well-planned recreation area with two nature trails, a campground, and several inviting picnic areas. The park is named for the brothers who donated the land for public use.

Most of the park is densely shaded by tall blackjack oaks, but birch trees and the stately shagbark hickory also cast their shadows. Within this limited space deer as well as smaller woodland mammals are sometimes seen, and more than 50 bird species have been counted, among them wild canaries and white-tailed hawks.

Fishermen may launch boats at the river ramp or use the two boat docks to try for channel catfish, buffaloes, walleye, and crappies, as well as large- and smallmouth bass. In the Mississippi backwaters ice fishing and ice skating are winter possibilities. *Open daily except Christmas and New Year's Day.*

10. Nauvoo Restoration. *Off Rte. 96, Nauvoo.* Joseph Smith, the Mormon leader, brought his people here after they had been driven from Missouri in 1839. Buying land that was then partly swamp, he named it Nauvoo, the Hebrew word for "beautiful place." His followers were quick to make it so, building a community with stately brick homes, a school, shops, farms, and orchards, and commencing an Olympian temple. But in June 1844 Joseph Smith and his brother were murdered in Carthage, 24 miles away. Two years later, shortly after completion of their temple, the Mormons were again forced to move, this time under the leadership of Brigham Young.

In the autumn of 1846 a U.S. Army

10. *It's quite evident that the brick for the front of the house was hand-picked. In the printshop the smell of ink and beauty of the old press can be savored.*

officer, Col. Thomas L. Kane, visited Nauvoo while traveling through the area, which he found generally marred by careless settlers. "I was descending the last hillside upon my journey," he later wrote, "when a landscape in delightful contrast broke upon my view. Half encircled by a bend of the river, a beautiful city lay glittering in the fresh morning sun; its bright new dwellings, set in cool green gardens, ranging up around a stately dome-shaped hill, which was crowned by a noble marble edifice. . . ."

Many of the original buildings remain. Among the more interesting are the two houses once occupied by Smith (whose grave can also be seen) and Brigham Young's house, often used for church council meetings.

Other attractions include the magnificent home of Heber Kimball, a Vermont blacksmith, with its delicate hand-carved porch railings, and the elegant Federal-style house of Wilford Woodruff, who hand-picked the front-wall bricks for uniform texture and color.

Displays in the large visitor center include paintings of key episodes in Smith's life and a model of the temple, which was later partially destroyed by fire. A film depicting major events in the history of Nauvoo is also shown. Near the center is the Monument to Women, a group of bronze statues honoring the many roles of women in society. *Open year-round.*

11. Weinberg King State Park. People with horses quite understandably favor this 772-acre park, with its 15 miles of riding trails and a horse-camping area lightly shaded by tall honey locusts. In winter these trails are used for snowmobiling. One doesn't need a mount to explore the four miles of nature trails in this quietly lovely setting of small hills, grassy meadows, and groves of locust, Osage orange, walnut, oak, and olive trees. Deer, rabbits, owls, doves, and quail are frequently seen, and coyotes and red and gray foxes are sometimes glimpsed when the sun is low. Wildflowers abound, especially along William Creek, which wanders for two miles through the park.

A small pond with a fishing dock is fed by the shallow creek. Both pond and stream yield channel catfish, bluegills, and bass. Tables and stoves are provided in three picnic areas. *Open year-round.*

12. Chautauqua National Wildlife Refuge. In the fall and winter enormous concentrations of migrating waterfowl settle down for rest and replenishment at this 4,500-acre refuge. A major stop on the Mississippi Flyway, it comprises Lake Chautauqua and a narrow rim of timber, sandy bluffs, and marsh. More than 100,000 mallards, northern pintails, wood ducks, shovelers, mergansers, and other duck species stop here, and some 40,000 geese can also be expected to pay a call.

In all, nearly 300 kinds of birds frequent this area. Bald eagles claim it as a winter home. In the summer visiting herons can be seen along the shores as they patiently wait for unsuspecting fish to come within range.

In addition to birding, wildlife enthusiasts are likely to observe deer and a wide assortment of small mammals. Badgers, muskrats, and minks, however, are elusive and rarely seen. Since the refuge includes several distinct environments, a great variety of trees, grasses, and wildflowers grow here. Along the interpretive trail near the refuge headquarters you may find showy lady's slippers, prairie dandelions, and other endangered plants.

Boats may be launched at the recreation area. The fishing is good, especially between April and June, when water levels are kept high. Visitors are also permitted to gather nuts and mushrooms and pick the wild raspberries and blackberries. *Open year-round.*

13. David Davis Mansion. *1000 E. Monroe St., Bloomington.* The opulent, 15-room yellow brick mansion is a Victorian gem inside and out. Designed by architect Alfred Picquenard for U.S. Supreme Court Justice David Davis and completed

13. *Varied window details on the symmetrical façade are an interesting touch. The sitting room is purely Victorian.*

14. *Replica of a cabin where Abraham Lincoln visited his father and stepmother.*

in 1872, it incorporates several features then unheard of in an average home, with flush toilets fed by an attic water tank, a central hot-air coal furnace, and closets with built-in drawers.

Davis actually spent little time here, leaving his wife to furnish the rooms with ornate sideboards and other fancy pieces, some of which were purchased from a furniture maker in New York.

Of the eight marble fireplaces, the one in the parlor—of dazzling white Carrara—is the most impressive. Hallway walls, seemingly covered with patterned paper, are in fact hand-painted. In the family sitting room the width of the judge's favorite maple rocking chair attests to his love of food, which was prepared on a cast-iron coal-burning stove.

Certain details of the design reflect the Victorian inclination toward an asymmetry that related to the variation found in nature. Thus the paired windows are all different in design, as are the iron porch and roof railings and six chimneys.

The visitor center in an adjacent early-1800's horse barn displays photos of the Davis family in settings that portray their lifestyle. *Open Thurs.–Mon. year-round except Thanksgiving Day, Christmas, and New Year's Day.*

---

14. Lincoln Log Cabin State Historic Site. *S. Fourth St. Rd., south of Charleston.* This is a reconstruction of the two-room log cabin Abraham Lincoln's father Thomas and stepmother Sarah Bush Lincoln moved into in 1840. At the time the future president was a circuit-riding lawyer living in Springfield, and he often visited here while making his rounds.

Visitors are immediately immersed in the mid-19th century as costumed men and women assume the roles of Lincoln family members and neighbors and go about their daily chores. They also answer questions. If something strikes you as strange about their speech, remember that they're talking in an 1840's dialect. Such is the authentic aura imparted here. You'll be interested to know that 18 persons once shared these cramped quarters.

The 86-acre site also includes a reconstruction of an 1840's farm with a barn, smokehouse, and corncrib built from hand-hewn logs, a kitchen garden, an orchard, and pastures.

Special summer programs include an 1845 Fourth of July sparked by speechifying, politicking, and flag raising while craftsmen hawk their wares. Other events of note: square dances, a bluegrass music festival, and a militia muster (with flintlock shooting competitions).

A short distance to the north stands the stark, unpainted Moore house, where President-elect Lincoln visited his stepmother and her daughter the day before he left for his inauguration. *Site and buildings open daily June–Aug.; weekends only, Sept. Tours given on request Oct.–Apr.*

---

15. Elsah and the Senator Vadalabene Bike Trail. Elsah is a town that time forgot, leaving visitors all the richer. It courted prominence in 1883, when it was thought that railroad magnate Jay Gould might build a bridge there. He did not, and by the 1890's Elsah had settled into its role as a sleepy Mississippi River port.

The town, a small community with two parallel main streets, has changed little since the 1850's. As a charming result, limestone, frame, and brick buildings peer modestly through leafy branches and picket fences. The houses, privately owned, cannot be visited. No matter. A

15. *No pretension in Elsah, where the village hall cost $645 to build in 1887.*

16. *Reconstruction, left, is of a circa A.D. 700 Woodland Indian pit house. The Mississippians later built ground-level "wall trench" houses, right.*

The most precise of these has been dubbed Woodhenge because of its similarity to England's Stonehenge; it may possibly have been a horizon calendar.

Artifacts in the museum portray life at Cahokia, while a slide show charts local Indian history and archeological techniques. A guided trip lasting 1½ to 2 hours takes you to the top of Monks Mound. *Open daily except Thanksgiving Day, Christmas, and New Year's Day.*

17. Ingram's Pioneer Log Cabin Village.

Kinmundy. If you are curious about frontier life, you'll find some answers here. For one thing, the dollar—and the penny—went a lot farther. A meal could set you back a nickel, while the price of a night's lodging at Jacob's Well Inn was six cents (if you had to share your bed with a stranger, the cost was shared).

Jacob's Well was formerly a stagecoach stop on the old Egyptian Trail between Terre Haute and St. Louis. Travelers on this route who were guests here include, in their different eras and professions, Abraham Lincoln and Jesse James.

Today the building is one of 15 log structures in this replication of a pre-Civil War frontier village. The log cabins are furnished with period pieces. The 1828 Strullmeyer Cabin contains a fine cradle, and the Preacher's Cabin (circa 1860), built for a Methodist circuit rider, displays a handsome, roughly built corner cupboard. The rarest item is the immigrant's chest at the inn. Such chests were often used as coffins, and few of them have survived their owners.

During weekends in late September and mid-October, craftspeople demonstrate weaving, leather tooling, coopering, and other old-time skills. The sounds of a country fiddler are also heard. *Open daily mid-Apr.–mid-Nov. Admission charged.*

18. McCoy Memorial Library. *Rte. 142 (Washington St.), McLeansboro.* An elegant mansion with gingerbread, columned porch, cupolas, and ornate iron trim, built in 1883 as the residence of a local merchant, now serves as the home of the McCoy Memorial Library and the Hamilton County Historical Society Museum. The original furnishings attest to the first owner's taste for gracious living.

sidewalk stroll transports you back to mid-Victorian times with flower gardens, decorative porch railings and pillars, and the pervading sense that tomorrow here will be much like today.

Among the many places to see are the Bates-Mack house, with its carved gingerbread eaves, the late 1850's brick Bradley house, and the Riverview House, a rambling clapboard that was once a hotel. The town school, circa 1857, is now the civic center, housing a museum with displays of local history. Little wonder that the entire town of Elsah has been entered in *The National Register of Historic Places.*

A restaurant on La Salle Street has two walls lined with jellies, jams, homemade bread, and other things you'll swear you'll resist but can't. This is a good stopping point when biking the Vadalabene Bike Trail, a 15-mile macadam artery that runs between Alton and Grafton and offers fine views of the Mississippi.

16. Cahokia Mounds State Historic Site.

Rte. 7850 (Collinsville Rd.), near Fairmont City. One of the first—and largest—of the hundreds of towns built by Indians of the remarkable Mississippian culture, Cahokia once covered nearly six square miles on the now-extinct meander channel of the Mississippi River. Like St. Louis today, it was at the crossroads of America, well located for trade as well as farming. At its peak Cahokia may have had a population of 40,000, although some archeologists doubt that it ever exceeded 5,000 to 8,000. Whichever, it was the largest prehistoric center north of Mexico, with a "central city," suburbs (including one in present-day downtown St. Louis), and outlying farm communities.

Of the hundred or so earthen mounds constructed here between 900 and 1250, the centerpiece is Monks Mound. Covering 14 acres of land and rising in terraces 100 feet above the plain, it dominated several plazas and avenues. On its uppermost platform loomed a stockaded building about 104 by 48 feet—the "White House"—where the ruler was ensconced.

For reasons that may never be known, Cahokia eventually went into a decline, and by 1500 it was nothing but a ghost town. Advancing white civilization has destroyed many of the mounds, but 40 or so are found on this site. Of particular interest in addition to Monks Mound is Mound 72. Its excavation has disclosed the grave of a chief (buried with a rich hoard of ornaments) and the remains of some 300 sacrificial victims, more than half of them young women.

Other excavations have revealed several circular arrangements of wooden posts.

17. *Utensils in this replicated 19th-century cabin are typical of the time.*

Visitors may admire among other things a handsome fireplace of African mahogany, a French *vernis Martin* cabinet, a Steinway piano, various art objects, examples of finely crafted woodwork, and a stairway of carved walnut.

The museum occupies the second floor in rooms that still preserve their original paneling of carved walnut, chestnut, and cherry, along with some handsome pieces of furniture. Objects in the museum, including photographs of street scenes and shop interiors, trace the development of this typically midwestern county. Also featured are Indian stone artifacts and several of the celebrated plaster groups executed by John Rogers in the 1870's. Of special interest is a huge desk with hinged sides revealing mailboxes and a letter slot. *Library open Mon.–Sat. except holidays; museum open P.M. Mon., Wed., Fri. Admission charged for museum.*

19. Crab Orchard National Wildlife Refuge. At this extensive, watery refuge (43,000 acres), a stopping place for migratory waterfowl on the Mississippi Flyway, sharecropping arrangements with local farmers specify that certain amounts of milo, corn, soybeans, and clover be left in the fields for the vast flights of Canada geese and ducks alighting here.

Common loons, green herons, turkey vultures, and yellow-crowned night herons can usually be found here as well, and the refuge is a nesting site for bald eagles and many kinds of songbirds. Two observation towers on Crab Orchard Lake offer excellent views of waterfowl and occasionally of other wildlife.

Gravel and blacktop roads lead to three lakes, which have lovely swimming beaches, boat docks, and boat-launching sites. In addition the refuge has 44 miles of trail. Of particular interest is the Chammestown School Trail, which makes a loop into an area otherwise closed to the public. Highlights of the route are explained in a free booklet available at the visitor center. The refuge also has three campgrounds with some 400 campsites.

In the southern sector of the refuge a 4,050-acre wilderness area has been established. Dramatic sandstone outcroppings and woodland creeks make this an exhilarating place for hiking and backpacking; but fires and camping are not permitted.

Bellwort, white trilliums, showy orchids, lady's tresses, and butterfly weed are among the many wildflowers that brighten the spring and summer scene. In August marshmallows, with their huge white blossoms, add magic along the lakefronts. *Open year-round.*

20. Heron Pond–Little Black Slough Nature Preserve. *Off Rte. 45, seven miles south of Vienna.* In a setting of natural wetlands, forests, and bluffs along the Cache River, this picturesque preserve provides a variety of habitats for many plants and animals not usually found this far north. The large pileated woodpecker is common, along with a host of songbirds whose mellifluous chorus includes the golden-colored prothonotary warbler, a species closely associated with the cypress swamps. The inconspicuous Swainson's warbler, a rare bird in Illinois, nests in the thickets of giant cane that grow along the swamp's shore. Occasionally river otters and bobcats are seen, as well as poisonous cottonmouth snakes that must be watched for and avoided.

Hiking trails have been marked in parts of the area's nearly 4,000 acres, and a floating boardwalk provides visitors with an intimate view of the swamp environment. The northern edge of the preserve is bordered by steep slopes and sheer rock cliffs over 50 feet high. Visitors may find delicate prairie plants in the small glades, and from the high bluffs they are rewarded with an inspiring view across almost five miles of the forest-swamp mosaic below. *Open year-round.*

18. *The same architects were used by the owner for both his mansion and his bank.*

Missouri

The two great waterways that border and divide this state brought early explorers and settlers whose influence can still be appreciated.

The most dramatic evidence of early settlement is the town of Ste. Genevieve, established on the Mississippi River more than 250 years ago, when France claimed this area. An attractive legacy is the French-Creole architecture that evolved. Another charming river town is Arrow Rock on the Missouri. Settled in 1815, it reflects the character of the frontier. The influence of early 19th-century German immigrants in the Midwest is apparent in the village of Hermann.

Three water-driven mills are reminders of the time when every farmer's daily bread was made from grain that he grew himself. Among the eight recreation and wildlife areas included here is one that preserves a magnificent section of the "sea of grass" that seemed so endless to the pioneers headed west. Some impressively famous people are honored in Missouri. They include such diverse personalities as a universally celebrated writer, a great scientist who was born a slave, and an unforgettable British prime minister.

1. Squaw Creek Wildlife Refuge. This is the kind of spacious landscape that encourages one to linger and look. The sizable refuge—an expanse of almost 7,000 acres of marsh, pond, meadow, and wooded bluffs—provides a year-round haven for birds of many kinds. Pheasants and hawks are best seen in January and February; a variety of waterfowl stop off in spring; May is the month for warblers; and in late summer the avocets and other shorebirds arrive. Come October and the fall migration, legions of snow geese and ducks descend. In the winter months one of the largest concentrations of bald eagles in America—up to 3,000 at peak—makes this refuge a temporary home.

Squaw Creek also shelters a goodly population of white-tailed deer, minks, foxes, southern lemmings, and mule deer (a few stragglers from the west). And along the refuge roads early in the morning, the wary coyote is often seen.

The extensive gravel roads and a number of trails offer a choice of driving, bicycling, or hiking; the Bluff Trail, starting behind the visitor center, gives panoramic views of the ponds and marshes. In spring the area blushes with wildflowers, and the end of July finds the American lotus in spectacular flower. *Open year-round.*

---

2. St. Joseph Museum. *Eleventh and Charles Sts., St. Joseph.* Known as the city "where southern hospitality meets western democracy," St. Joseph played a vital role in 19th-century westward expansion, as railroads and the Pony Express augmented the steamboat, and became quite prosperous in the post-Civil War decades. Homes constructed in that period include this museum building, an impressive, 43-room Gothic-style mansion erected in 1879 and decorated by Tiffany of New York for its second owner, Mrs. Kate Tootle, in 1887.

The St. Joseph Museum, established in 1926, is dedicated primarily to the preservation of diverse cultures, especially that of the North American Indian. Several items are of particular note: a beautiful birchbark canoe, Navajo baskets, colorful Pomo basketry, Iroquois masks, and Seminole costumes. In the Eskimo collection you'll see clothing, domestic and hunting utensils, masks, and exquisite walrus carving.

Various mounted animals haunt the natural history section, while local history devotes one room to Jesse James, who lived in St. Joseph and was shot down on the corner of 13th and Lafayette streets on April 3, 1882. Other exhibits in this potpourri of a museum include Tiffany windows, military equipment, 19th-century women's fashions, dolls and dollhouses, mannequins, and miscellanea from foreign cultures. *Open Tues.–Sun., Oct.–Mar. Admission charged.*

---

3. McCormick Distilling Company. *Highway JJ, Weston.* The explorers Lewis and Clark stopped at this limestone spring for its refreshing water on their way west in 1804. By the 1830's the spring was supplying an ever-increasing number of wagon trains. Most people were just tasting water, but Ben Holladay recognized in it something more. He knew that limestone water, being both iron-free and acid-free, was especially good for making whiskey.

1. Snow geese, on their fall migration, are resting here before heading on south.

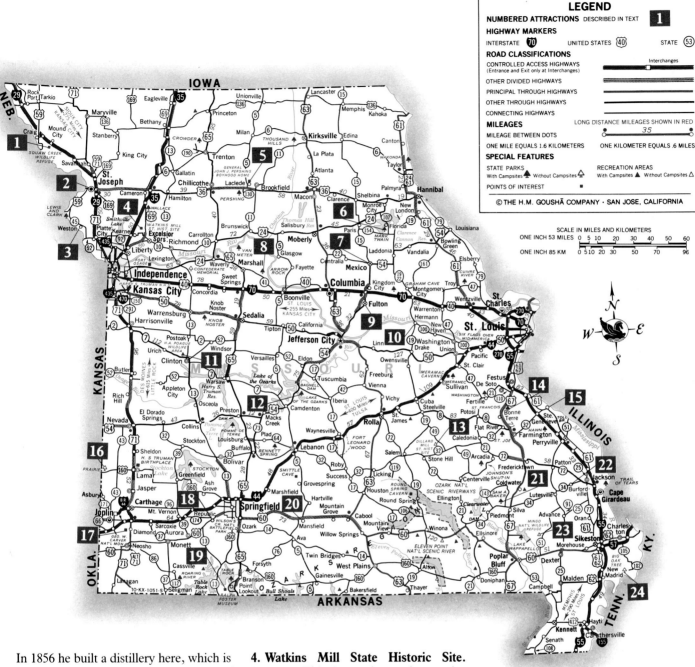

In 1856 he built a distillery here, which is now included in *The National Register of Historic Places.*

Guided tours visit all stages of whiskey making by the sour-mash process, which involves adding to a batch of fermented mash some of a previous batch (as when making sourdough bread) for smoothness and continuity of flavor. The colorless alcohol distilled from the mash is aged for 5 to 10 years in white oak barrels that are custom-charred on the inside to create the characteristic flavor and golden hue. The six-story warehouses here contain 24,000 barrels—"the world's entire supply of Missouri whiskey." *Tours available Mon.– Sat. and P.M. Sun., Mar.–mid-Dec.*

4. Watkins Mill State Historic Site.

Kearney. This interesting and attractive 19th-century complex includes the woolen mill and family home of Waltus Watkins and his wife, Maryann. Built in 1850, the house has a simple but elegant brick façade and 20 rooms to accommodate the family of 11 children. Most of the place is unfurnished but nonetheless pleasing, with its walnut trim and cherry doors.

Watkins's first venture was a cotton mill, which was unsuccessful, but he had a flair for farming and expanded a holding of 80 acres into a property of more than 3,000—the Bethany Plantation. In 1860 Watkins turned again to the textile business and began to build his woolen mill. Like the house, the mill was made from

his own timber and bricks. Deer tracks made on the bricks before they dried can be seen in the floor of the storage shed. More than 50 textile machines, valued at $20,000, were shipped in by river and hauled the final 20 miles by oxen. Eventually the Bethany Plantation became a self-sustaining community.

The three-storied textile mill is the only one in the country with its original machinery. The various hankers, pickers, twisters, and looms stand lean and elegant in design in silent tribute to a prosperous

6. *Imagine what Mark Twain would have to say about the fuss made over his birthplace. The small cabin, with only two rooms, housed the seven members of the Clemens family.*

first editions of his books and a manuscript copy of *The Adventures of Tom Sawyer*. Other displays offer a colorful view of Mark Twain's adventurous life as a steamboat pilot, printer's apprentice, soldier, gold and silver prospector, laborer, newspaper reporter, and one of America's best-loved writers.

An oak-shaded picnic area overlooks the south fork of Mark Twain Lake, a large, sprawling body of water partly bounded by the Mark Twain State Park. Fishing and swimming are permitted in Tom Sawyer Lake, a pond nearby. From the picnic ground you can take a short, rugged path to the observation platforms on the sheer cliffs of Buzzard's Roost for excellent views of the surrounds. *Birthplace and museum open daily except Easter, Thanksgiving Day, Christmas, and New Year's Day; admission charged. Park open year-round.*

7. Audrain Historical and American Saddle Horse Museum. *501 S. Muldrow St., Mexico.* The Ross House, an imposing mansion built in 1857, was bought in 1868 by Colby T. Quisenberry, who introduced Kentucky saddlebreds to the area. Since then, the town of Mexico has been pleased to call itself the Saddle Horse Center of the World. It is therefore appropriate that the Saddle Horse Museum adjoins the Ross House, which has been restored as a museum by the Audrain County Historical Society.

The Saddle Horse Museum features trophies and other mementos of the superhorse Rex McDonald and the famous trainer and equestrian Thomas Bass. Rex McDonald (1890–1913), a black stallion, was considered the "champion of champions and sire of champions." Other exhibits include riding habits, the saddles of famous riders, and paintings of saddle horses by George Ford Morris.

The historical museum contains Currier and Ives prints, mostly of landscapes and Civil War scenes, a wardrobe of late-19th-century clothing, complete with wedding gowns and ostrich-feather hats, and local historical items. The house is named for County Judge James E. Ross, a former owner. *Open P.M. Tues.–Sat., Feb.–Dec.; P.M. Sun., Mar.–Nov. except major holidays. Admission charged.*

business that finally succumbed to new techniques of mass production at the turn of the century. It might be noted that loom tenders made $1.50 a day. The person who operated the mechanical sheep-shearer earned $2.50 a day and paid 50¢ of this to the boy who turned the crank.

Adjacent to the historic site is a recreation area with a pretty lake, campsites with hookups, and trails. *Open daily except Easter, Thanksgiving Day, Christmas, and New Year's Day. Admission charged.*

5. General John J. Pershing Boyhood Home State Historic Site. *Laclede.* Graduated from West Point in 1886, Pershing underwent his baptism of fire against Geronimo's Apache Indians and completed his career as commander in chief of American forces in World War I.

Pershing's boyhood home is an unpretentious but attractive two-story white clapboard with restrained Gothic trim. While the furnishings are not those of his family, they are of the period. There are Pershing memorabilia throughout. An upstairs room serves specifically as a small museum for Pershing's many medals, among them the Silver Star for gallantry. Also on view are photos of some of his early campaigns, and the bejeweled sword given him by the city of London in 1919.

From a tape recording that outlines his life, you'll learn that Pershing favored Gary Cooper for the starring role in a projected movie about his life, and that his nickname, "Black Jack," was a reference to his onetime command of the 10th (black) Cavalry.

Relocated on the site is the small school where Pershing once taught for $35 a month. A bronze statue of Black Jack Pershing also stands on the grounds before a Wall of Honor inscribed with the names of several hundred war veterans. *Open year-round. Admission charged.*

6. Mark Twain Birthplace and Museum State Historic Site. *Florida.* Mark Twain was born November 30, 1835, in what he later described as ". . . the almost invisible village of Florida, Monroe County, Missouri. . . ." On another occasion he noted that "recently someone. . . sent me a picture of the house I was born in. Heretofore I always stated that it was a palace, but I shall be more guarded now." The small two-room plank cabin is modest, to say the least.

Moved to its present site in 1930, the house is now enclosed by the striking Mark Twain Museum. Here you will see

8. Arrow Rock State Historic Site. *Arrow Rock.* Arrow Rock was first settled in 1815, 11 years after Lewis and Clark deemed the area "a handsome spot for a town." Established as a town in 1829, it became an important stop on the Santa Fe Trail, and in the 1860's its population peaked at more than 1,000. Then the railroads bypassed the town and it began to decline. Today it has about 80 residents.

The most interesting buildings can be seen on a guided walking tour that starts at the visitor center on Main Street. Among them is the restored house of the portrait painter John Caleb Bingham, a two-room log cabin built by the artist himself in 1837 on land that he bought for $50. The furnishings are of the period, but the only piece that belonged to Bingham is his easel. The courthouse, built in 1839 of clapboard with handworked beading, contains Bingham's engravings of it.

Another famous resident was Dr. John Sappington, who brought quinine to Arrow Rock to combat outbreaks of malaria. The museum in his name contains first editions of his medical book and memorabilia of his practice.

The John Sites Gun Shop (1844), with its bullet molds and powder horns, and the medicinal herb garden of the Country Doctor Museum illustrate various aspects of 19th-century self-preservation. The Tavern, built in 1834, still serves meals. *Tours daily Memorial Day–Labor Day. Admission charged.*

9. The Winston Churchill Memorial and Library. *Westminster College, Fulton.* In 1946 Britain's wartime prime minister, Winston Churchill, accepted an invitation from his Missouri-born friend President Harry Truman to speak at Westminster College. In that historic address Churchill described the Soviet grip on eastern Europe: "From Stettin in the Baltic to Trieste in the Adriatic, an iron curtain has descended across the continent."

In the early 1960's it was decided to honor the great British leader by reconstructing at the college a London landmark that had been destroyed in World War II by enemy action. The chosen structure was St. Mary Aldermanbury, a 12th-century London church demolished by the great fire of London in 1666 and rebuilt by Sir Christopher Wren. In 1940

the church had been struck by bombs and it still lay in ruins.

Dismantling began in 1965. Seven thousand stones weighing a total of 700 tons were cleaned, numbered, and shipped to Fulton, with new stones hand-cut as necessary. Wood carvings, plasterwork, windows, and brass chandeliers were all re-created from Wren's designs. A new organ was built in London, five new bronze bells were cast in Holland, windows were copied by a glass company in West Virginia, and a London wood carver duplicated the original pulpit.

Dedicated in 1969, the white church radiates an elegant simplicity. The interior is light and spacious, the decor rich but unobtrusive. A library and a museum in the undercroft relate to the life and long public service of the prime minister. *Open daily except Thanksgiving Day, Christmas, and New Year's Day. Admission charged.*

---

10. Historic Hermann Museum. *Hermann.* The German school building with its clock tower recalls an era when German immigrants established a number of midwestern towns like Hermann, which

was founded in 1836. The school was built in 1870 and functioned as such until 1955. It now houses some town offices and a four-room museum.

The *Kinder* Room, with its German readers, dolls and dollhouses, and toy carousel, reminds us of the origin of our own kindergarten. In the Heritage Room you'll see a collection of long-stemmed Dresden pipes painted with every kind of subject. Wine labels attest to Hermann's once flourishing, then moribund, and now reviving wine industry. Redware from the Hoefel Pottery (about 1860) records yet another local industry. These and numerous other items—such as old German newspapers, Bibles, and language primers—document the roots of the settlement.

The River Room, with its steamboat memorabilia and old photos of riverboat personalities, underscores Hermann's location on the Missouri River. Among timbers salvaged from historic boats are some from the *General Meade*, which was once surrounded by a herd of swimming buffalo in the Yellowstone River. *Open daily Apr.–Oct. Admission charged.*

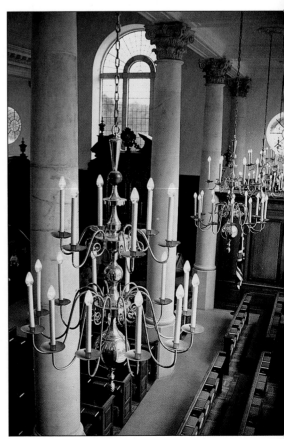

9. *Solid and straightforward, the church is a fitting memorial to England's wartime prime minister. The church's interior is in the ornate English baroque style.*

11. Haysler A. Poague Wildlife Area. Formerly devastated by strip mining, this 879-acre setting with its irregular necklace of some 14 ponds and lakes is primarily a site for anglers and hunters.

There are no trails, but gravel roads wind among the ponds, which are attractive and worth seeing, although quite small for pleasure boating. The renewed landscape is now lush with oaks, cottonwoods, sumacs, willows, Osage orange trees, and a profusion of wildflowers, such as white and yellow water lilies and black-eyed Susans. Fishermen, who try mostly for channel catfish and largemouth bass, may use outboard motors up to 10 horsepower. *Open year-round.*

12. Lake of the Ozarks State Park. Created in the 1930's by the damming of the Osage River, the Lake of the Ozarks is the largest man-made lake in Missouri, with a main channel 120 miles long. The park's 17,087 acres embrace the Grand Glaize arm of the lake and the surrounding Osage River hills—a landscape of dense oak and hickory forests, stretches of prairielike savannas, caves, bluffs eroded by the Grand Glaize Creek, and open, rocky areas like miniature deserts with temperature extremes, known locally as glades.

In addition to the pleasures of the lakeshore, the park offers 10 trails of varying lengths for horseback riders (horses can be rented at a stable on Route 134 near the campground), hikers, and backpackers. The trail through the Bluestem Knoll Savanna gives you a view of the kind of prairie landscape that greeted the first settlers, while the Woodland Trail offers the peacefulness of Patterson Hollow Wild Area, an untouched wilderness of old meadows and oak and sassafras woodland. You'll especially enjoy this path, and the Trail of the Four Winds, if you're interested in butterflies. Spring wildflowers, on the other hand, are best observed along the Lake View, Swinging Bridges, and Rocky Top trails.

Missouri claims more caves than any other state, some 4,000 in all. The park's Ozark Caverns, a feature unto themselves, are reached by taking Routes A and C off Route 54. Main attractions: the stalactite formations and Angel's Shower, a waterfall descending from apparently solid rock. A guided one-hour tour covers 1½ miles. *Open year-round. Charge for tours.*

12. Among the probing fingers of forested land there's many a cove to explore.

13. Dillard Mill State Historic Site. *Dillard.* Situated by a green lake surrounded by grassy bluffs, Dillard Mill is unusually picturesque and beautifully restored.

During the heyday of waterpower, Dillard was one of 20 mills within a 40-mile radius. At full summertime capacity, this one produced 60 196-pound barrels of flour a day in an 18-hour shift. At the height of the season farmers camped nearby for as long as four days, waiting to get their harvest of grain converted to flour.

The roller mills, grain elevators, sifting machines, and other equipment were powered by a 24.2-horsepower Samson turbine. The original leather drive belts are still in use. The main drive wheel inside the mill has wooden teeth of hard maple so that if anything goes wrong the teeth break, not the wheel or belts. And the turbine, which sits under water in the flume, runs on wooden bearings to avoid the problem of rust. One leaves the mill with a newfound respect for the skills of the old millwrights and engineers.

The 132-acre site offers trails, picnic areas, and fishing in a clear Ozark creek. Spring and fall are the best for weather. *Open Mon.–Sat. and P.M. Sun. year-round except Easter, Thanksgiving Day, Christmas, and New Year's Day. Admission charged for mill.*

14. St. Francois State Park. Moonshiners and outlaws once made this wilderness in the Pike Run Hills their own. Today it is a park with 2,616 acres of meadow and hill, creek, bluff, glade, forest, and lush bottomland, plus a well-tended camping area, picnic sites, and several trails.

Beginners and families can canoe the lazy, meandering Big River, and one can float 24 miles downstream to Washington State Park. Anglers favor the stream for its bass and catfish.

Both horseback riders and hikers use the 11-mile Pike Run, which starts in a meadow dotted with juniper (and in June and July bright with yarrow and black-eyed Susans), and then enters woodland, crossing creekbeds and clearings as it follows an old logging road through some of the wildest parts of the park.

The Mooner's Hollow Trail, which is for hikers only, makes a 2.7-mile loop in the Coonville Creek Wild Area, once a favorite haunt of illicit whiskey makers

15. *Symmetrical roof and supporting posts add distinction to the Bolduc house.*

who used the clear, cold creek water to make moonshine. This path runs through some idyllically attractive countryside, mostly beside or within earshot of the bubbling creek in a forest of white and red oaks, cedars, and shagbark hickory trees with an understory of dogwood. *Open year-round. No water at campsite in winter.*

15. Ste. Genevieve. The oldest town west of the Mississippi, this charming community was settled by the French more than 250 years ago, when the area was still part of Upper Louisiana, claimed by France. A walk through the streets reveals a rich architectural heritage: the unique appeal here is the survival of so many of the old French-Creole buildings. A remarkable feature is that their walls are constructed with logs set vertically—not horizontally—on the ground or on a foundation.

Tours from the visitor center at 3rd and Merchant streets take in a number of historic buildings. One of the more prominent is the Guibourd-Valle House, built in 1785. In the attic take note of the handsomely pegged oak beams and fine Norman trusswork. Another is the Bolduc House, which dates back to 1770 and is considered to be the most authentically restored French colonial house in America.

You'll also see the Old Academy, chartered in 1808 as Missouri's first institution of higher learning. In 1854 one could get six months' schooling in reading, writing, arithmetic, history, and other standard subjects for $12.50. Greek and Latin cost $10 extra. Along the south side of the square runs the Plank Road; formerly surfaced with logs, it was built to transport ore and was 42 miles long, the longest of its kind in the United States. *Visitor center open daily. Charge for tours.*

16. Prairie State Park. *From Rte. 43, take Rte. K west to Rte. P; watch for signs to the park.* Two hundred years ago, one-third of Missouri—some 13 million acres—was prairie, a level or rolling expanse of tall grasses and wildflowers and few trees. With settlement and farming, there are now fewer than 75,000 acres of prairie in Missouri, and 2,240 of these are protected in Prairie State Park.

A number of interlinked trails traverse open prairie, bluff, and stream valleys. Along the three-mile Coyote Trail you'll be struck by the spaciousness of the land- and skyscape and the endless horizon with the sealike expanse of grass melting into the blue of the sky. It is easy to understand why the pioneers called their wagons prairie schooners. Striding freely along the mown path in the sweet-scented air, you'll also notice how this vast tableau is balanced by minute natural detail—petal, leaf, grass blade, and seedpod—calling for close-up scrutiny.

Buffalo roam in some areas. For safety, stay in your car until you have learned from the park office where the animals are located. Nature programs include films and guided walks. The favored time to visit is spring, for the wildflowers. *Open year-round.*

17. George Washington Carver National Monument. *Diamond.* Educator, scientist, and humanitarian, George Washington Carver was born a slave in the early 1860's on the Moses Carver farm, located here. Shortly afterward he and his mother were kidnapped by Confederate bushwhackers and taken to Arkansas. The young child was later returned to the Carvers, who reared him as their own. Though George left when he was about 12, the love of nature he gained on this site stood the future botanist in good stead.

On view in the museum are many tributes paid this remarkable man: a model of the submarine named for him, stamps issued in his honor, a commemorative half-dollar, and a letter from Albert Einstein referring to him as "the great scientist."

Collections of his publications, together with scientific exhibits, dramatize his impact on agricultural methods. He derived more than 300 products from the peanut, 100 from the sweet potato (including ersatz coffee, shoeblacking, and ink), and scores of products from Alabama clay.

From the birthplace site a short trail

17. *Carver as an aspiring youth, rendered by sculptor Robert Amendola.*

219

leads to the restored two-room clapboard house built by Moses Carver in 1881, where George often visited. The path runs through light woodland, passing a bronze statue of the scientist as a boy and a pond with a picnic area. *Open year-round.*

18. Wilson's Creek National Battlefield.
Republic. The battle fought here on August 10, 1861, largely determined the side Missouri would be on for the ensuing years of the Civil War. Many Missourians favored neutrality, but some, including the governor, championed the South.

After pro-Union forces seized the state capitol at Jefferson City, installing their own government, Confederate efforts to gain control led to the bloody confrontation at Wilson's Creek. Though the Confederates drove the Union forces from the field, they were unable to follow up and recapture the capitol, and Missouri remained in Union hands.

The visitor center has excellent displays whose very titles provide a minihistory of events: "Missouri's Dilemma: Union or Confederate?"; "Why Wilson's Creek?"; "Uniform Confusion" (battle dress was confusingly similar for a time); "Unready but Willing" (about the volunteers).

The highlight, however, is the topographic battlefield model in the small theater: computer-controlled points of light reconstruct troop movements and artillery fire, with commentary and realistic effects on the sound track.

Other places of interest are the Ray House, used as a Confederate field hospital, and Bloody Hill, the site of some of the fiercest fighting, where a marker honors "the hundreds of brave men, North and South, who, on this field, died for the right as God gave them to see right." *Open daily except Thanksgiving Day, Christmas, and New Year's Day.*

19. Ralph Foster Museum. *The School of the Ozarks, Point Lookout. Take Hwy. V west off Rte. 65, south of Branson.* Ralph Foster, a pioneer radio broadcaster and a local luminary, was also a philanthropist whose donation of Indian artifacts to the museum of the liberal arts college accounts for its name.

18. *Here, in the misty dawn, is the last landscape that many brave men would see as*

"Everything under the sun" aptly describes the 750,000 items displayed here. A single glance may take in meerschaum pipes, President Grant's rolltop desk, a 1930 telephone exchange, as large a collection of oyster plates as you'd ever hope to see, whiskey decanters in the shapes of speedboats and covered wagons, a huge model of the Hoxie Bros. circus, a tribute to the Kewpie doll craze, and a potpourri of other improbable, delightful objects.

For instance, to see Cicero Weaver's vaudeville suit in the Si Siman (country) Music Room, you'll pass the original truck used in the *Beverly Hillbillies* show and the life-size plastic model of Tom Mix's horse, Tony, with Tom's hand-tooled saddle with silver conchas.

A display you may not want your children to see portrays the grimmer side of life: items relating to law enforcement and outlaws, with handcuffs, leg irons, the last suit worn by Doc Holliday, a Jesse James Colt .44, Pancho Villa's dagger, Bat Masterson's gold-handled sword cane. The Hall of Weapons contains a parade of Colt firearms, and the archery collection includes blowguns and poison arrows. In contrast, the Rose O'Neill Room has a beguiling collection of her Kewpie dolls, enormously popular for decades.

By and large this is a fascinating place, and except for the instruments of destruction and mementos of death, fun for kids. *Open Mon.–Sat. and P.M. Sun., Mar.–*

Nov.; weekdays in Feb. and early Dec.; closed Thanksgiving weekend and mid-Dec. –Jan. Admission charged.

20. Laura Ingalls Wilder–Rose Wilder Lane Home and Museum. *Mansfield.* This is a required visit for dedicated admirers of *The Little House on the Prairie.* It was here that author Laura Ingalls Wilder penned that beloved portrait of rural America, published in some 40 languages.

Museum displays include foreign and domestic editions of her various books, press clippings, and worldwide fan mail, much of it from children. Among personal belongings are the 1889 lap desk Laura brought here by covered wagon from her home in De Smet, South Dakota, the pens she used all her life, her sewing machine, and samples of her needlework.

Half of the museum is devoted to the mementos of her daughter, Rose Wilder Lane, an author as well.

Laura and her husband, Almanzo, moved to Mansfield in 1894 and into their house in 1897. Laura thought it best "to be happy with simple pleasures," and the house is small and rather undistinguished. It is next door to the museum and may be seen only by a guided tour. One may note the Currier and Ives prints, a Western Cottage organ, and a Victrola in the drawing room, some throw pillows made by Laura, and several tables crafted by Al-

they fell while defending their beliefs.

manzo, a carpenter. His workshop contains the tools of his trade as well as some leather and lasts, for he also made his own shoes. *Open Mon.–Sat., May–mid-Oct. Admission charged.*

---

21. Sam A. Baker State Park. Geologically interesting and scenically wild, this 5,000-acre park, with its many domes of igneous rock, contains some of the oldest exposed formations in North America. The highest of these is Mudlick Mountain. At 1,313 feet, its summit is battered by high winds, ice storms, and lightning, which have bent, stunted, and generally shaped the trees here into bizarre and fascinating forms. You can reach the fire tower at the summit by car, or by foot or horseback on Mudlick Trail.

You can also hike the 1½-mile Shut-Ins Trail. From its start in an oak woodland, it crosses a number of clearings, colorful with black-eyed Susans and other meadow flowers, as it follows Big Creek Valley. Past the sharp outcrops of rock jutting through the trees, you reach the Shut-Ins area, where the creek has swung wide of an imposing granite cliff, creating a large pool. You can swim here in a setting that is a natural sun-trap.

From this trail you can scramble to the top of the ridge to connect with Mudlick Trail. Along the way the view over the valley to the distant hills is spectacular,

and there's a convenient stone shelter, with a fireplace, for resting or picnicking. The remaining climb to the ridge is a real challenge. Take it if you're in good shape and not daunted by steep slopes.

Both Big Creek and the St. Francois River can be canoed and fished, the latter stream being the better one in summer for the flow of water. The park has an extensive modern campsite and a lodge that's open May to September. *Open year-round.*

---

22. Bollinger Mill State Historic Site. *Burfordville.* A picturesque scene from America's past is captured here. The four-story mill stands by a wide millpond and weir, and just beyond is one of Missouri's four covered bridges.

Dating from 1867, the mill was built by Solomon Burford, Burfordville's first postmaster. Powered by a turbine, it is beautifully restored and in working order. As a feature of the tour a valve is turned to open the turbine louvers: the drive shaft and belts begin to turn, the elevators move, and the massive buhrstones begin to grind. The staff is not only enthusiastic but well-informed.

The 140-foot-long Howe-truss bridge, originally built of yellow poplar, was begun in 1859, delayed by the Civil War, and finished 10 years later. Restored in 1950, it is one of two covered bridges in Missouri still open to traffic. *Mill open Tues.–Sat. and P.M. Sun. except Easter, Thanksgiving Day, Christmas, and New Year's Day. Admission charged.*

---

23. Mingo National Wildlife Refuge. The vast area of marsh, dike, and river (21,676 acres) here supports large numbers of wildlife but is maintained primarily as a feeding ground for migratory waterfowl on the Mississippi Flyway.

A gravel loop road skirting most of the refuge allows leisurely walking, horseback riding, and driving. The diked waterways, and the Mingo River itself, are open to canoeing, an ideal way to see this region. Motorboats are not allowed.

The Flat Banks Road, which gives access to the river and an 8,000-acre wilderness preserve, runs through verdant marsh meadows and woodland and past acres of yellow water lilies couched on flat blue-green leaves. The Mingo River is

lovely, with ghostly cypress stumps and flat, lightly wooded banks.

The mile-long Boardwalk Nature Trail loops through the woodland swamp, hung with vines and rich with sycamores, sweet gums, pin oaks, sugar maples, and some water tupelos and bald cypresses. It's an easy trail and has benches along the way. An annotated guide describes aspects of the natural scene at 15 stops.

The Bluff Overlook Trail, starting at the visitor center, is enchanting when spring wildflowers bloom, and affords splendid views across the marsh.

From September 30 to March 15 visitors are asked to stop at the visitor center before venturing into the refuge. Limited picnic facilities are available. *Refuge open year-round. Visitor center open daily, mid-Mar.–Nov.; weekdays Dec.–mid-Mar.*

---

24. Big Oak Tree State Park. This 1,007-acre preserve is part of the virgin forest and swampland that once covered much of Missouri's Boot Heel region.

The park, noted for state and national champion trees of dramatic size, was named for a bur oak that started to grow in 1620, the year the Pilgrims landed at Plymouth Rock. Felled in 1954 at the age of 334 years, it was 143 feet tall with a spread of 114 feet. Its sawn-off trunk stands at the head of a 1¼-mile boardwalk that runs to a grassy swamp and passes some of the most magnificent trees in the forest. Among these is the state champion bur oak (height 142 feet) and the national champion slippery elm (115 feet), which died in 1986 but at this writing still stands.

The swamp was created by an earthquake in 1811, which caused the earth to sink from 10 to 50 feet. Today parts of it look like a giant bowling green planted with dead trees. The "green" is actually duckweed, and among the trees are some living bald cypresses. The loud plops you hear along the boardwalk are slider turtles dropping into the water from the logs where they have been sunning, or perhaps a jumping buffalofish, which can weigh as much as 20 pounds. The swamp is also home to the ruddy duck, the hooded merganser, and the harmless banded water snake. *Open year-round.*

Arkansas

In addition to the expected pleasures to be found in the Ozarks and along the rivers, there are further delights—historic and otherwise.

Most surprising—and possibly rewarding—is a state park where you can dig for diamonds and keep what you find. Oil is another treasure rendered from Arkansan earth, and a new museum provides its fascinating story.

Two historic towns offer such highlights as superb antebellum homes, the place where the notorious bowie knife was forged, and a fine stern-wheeler steamboat. The age of steam is also represented by a scenic train ride through piney woods. The courthouse of the famous Hanging Judge Parker, battlegrounds, an incredible cavern, and a magnificent wilderness river are further attractions.

1. Pea Ridge National Military Park. In the early phase of the Civil War the Union forces in Missouri, intent on controlling that state, an important link to the West, drove the pro-Confederate troops there into neighboring Arkansas. Inevitably, when the southern forces attempted to move back into Missouri to capture the vital crossroads city of St. Louis, the two armies clashed. After a raging battle at Pea Ridge, the Confederate soldiers, low on ammunition, were forced to retreat, and Missouri was "saved" for the Union.

A seven-mile self-guiding automobile tour on an excellent paved road takes you to the scenes of that struggle, including Pea Ridge, which overlooks the battlefield, and the restored Elkhorn Tavern, a focal point of much of the fighting. A 10-mile hiking trail also makes a loop of the region. An outstanding slide program depicting the famous battle is presented at the visitor center.

Apart from its historic interest, the park is a scenically inviting place to explore, with rugged bluffs, valleys, the meandering Little Sugar Creek, and woods filled with maidenhair ferns and massive wild grapevines. The park, a wildlife sanctuary, is home to deer, coyotes, and bears, which have been reintroduced to the area. *Open year-round except Thanksgiving Day, Christmas, and New Year's Day.*

3. *Water so clear that the surface disappears—a quality shared by too few rivers.*

2. Withrow Springs State Park. Bordered by the towering bluffs along the War Eagle River, this secluded 786-acre retreat contains everything associated with the Ozark mountain region: a magnificent wilderness of ridges and valleys, plentiful wildlife, woodlands, and a small creek fed by clear springs.

The sparkling waters of the War Eagle River nourish the life of the park, providing an excellent canoe run and fine fishing for catfish, bream, perch, bass, and goggle-eye. Hikers have three scenic trails to explore. The three-quarter-mile Dogwood Trail, named for the area's most prevalent tree, makes a loop along ravines and ridges in heavily wooded terrain. The moderately difficult War Eagle Trail begins at a bridge, climbs up a 150-foot bluff overlooking the river, and then continues on to a large cave with an underground stream. The trail is about a mile long and requires backtracking. The Forest Trail follows an old roadway through a hardwood forest and connects with a gravel road that leads back to the campground, a trip of about 2½ miles.

Canoes can be rented, and a swimming pool, tree-shaded picnic grounds, and several camping sites are provided. *Open year-round.*

3. Buffalo National River. One of the most scenic rivers in the United States, the Buffalo has miraculously escaped alteration or impairment by civilization. To keep it that way it has been designated a national river, and its entire 132-mile length is protected by the National Park Service, which also administers a 95,000-acre strip of wilderness bordering its serpentine course. As it winds through peaceful valleys and beneath huge limestone cliffs, rushing over rapids and slipping through placid pools in its journey from headwaters in the Boston Mountains to its junction with the White River, the river tumbles 1,900 feet.

The Buffalo is especially popular with canoists and kayakers, who can enjoy a half-day trip or a 10-day, 120-mile expedi-

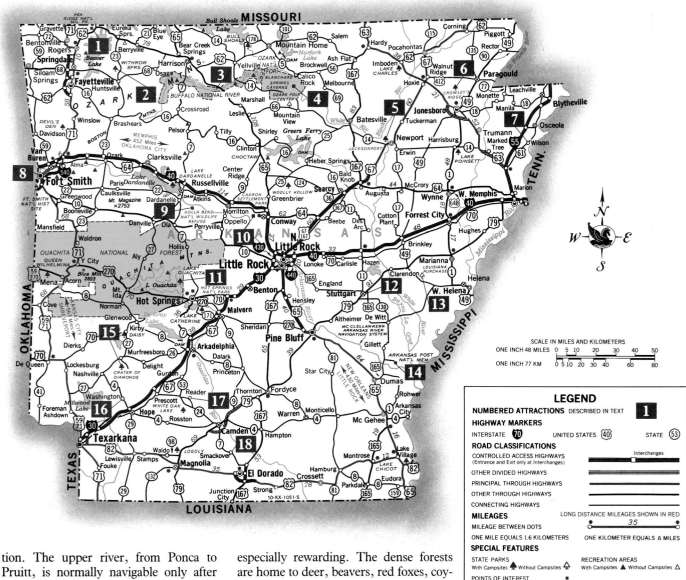

LEGEND

NUMBERED ATTRACTIONS DESCRIBED IN TEXT **1**

HIGHWAY MARKERS

INTERSTATE **70**   UNITED STATES **40**   STATE (53)

ROAD CLASSIFICATIONS

CONTROLLED ACCESS HIGHWAYS   Interchanges
(Entrance and Exit only at Interchanges)

OTHER DIVIDED HIGHWAYS

PRINCIPAL THROUGH HIGHWAYS

OTHER THROUGH HIGHWAYS

CONNECTING HIGHWAYS

MILEAGES   LONG DISTANCE MILEAGES SHOWN IN RED

MILEAGE BETWEEN DOTS   35

ONE MILE EQUALS 1.6 KILOMETERS   ONE KILOMETER EQUALS .6 MILES

SPECIAL FEATURES

STATE PARKS   RECREATION AREAS
With Campsites ▲ Without Campsites △   With Campsites ▲ Without Campsites △

POINTS OF INTEREST ■

SCALE IN MILES AND KILOMETERS

ONE INCH 48 MILES   0   5   10   20   30   40   50

ONE INCH 77 KM   0   5 10   20   30   40   60   80

---

tion. The upper river, from Ponca to Pruitt, is normally navigable only after substantial rainfalls.

Canoes and kayaks can be rented, with transportation provided to and from any of the 19 access points. Picnic areas and campsites are scattered along the river. Some 160 kinds of fish have been found in the Buffalo, the most abundant of which are smallmouth bass, goggle-eye, perch, bream, and catfish.

Several hiking trails and old abandoned roads give access to the canyons, hollows, bluffs, forests, and meadows of the surrounding Ozark wilderness, which has changed little in character in the last century. In this richly varied environment some 800 different plant species come into flower between late January and late autumn. The Lost Valley Self-Guiding Nature Trail, which follows Clark Creek as it skirts waterfalls, towering fern-clad cliffs, a natural bridge, and a 200-foot cave, is

especially rewarding. The dense forests are home to deer, beavers, red foxes, coyotes, and a great variety of native birds. River guides and other information may be obtained at the Pruitt, Silver Hill, and Buffalo Point information centers and at the park headquarters in Harrrison. *Open year-round.*

4. Blanchard Springs Caverns. *Mountain View.* Because some of the more enchanting caves here were not discovered until the 1960's, this magnificent underworld system isn't yet as well known as New Mexico's Carlsbad Caverns, though it is in many ways as spectacular.

Visitors to this subterranean marvel have a choice of two tours. Along the easier, the Dripstone Trail, you pass through the aptly named Cathedral Room, an

enormous chamber whose size is accentuated by a play of light on a number of dazzling rock formations. You'll see the stunning Coral Room, found in 1963 and considered "the cave find of the century."

The Discovery Trail is a taxing 1⅔-hour walk, including 700 steps, and is available only from the first of April through October. Commensurate rewards include seeing the bubbling origin of Blanchard Springs and the haunting Ghost Room.

The caverns are located in an unspoiled area of the Ozark National Forest near Sylamore Creek, a pristine white-water stream claiming one of the few old-fashioned swimming holes left in this part of the country. A recreation area at the cavern site offers camping and a variety of outdoor activities. *Open year-round. Admission charged.*

5. Jacksonport State Park. The romance of the Old South and the boisterous steamboat days lives on in this small, pretty park along a sweeping bend of the White River. Jacksonport began as a shipping point in the early 1800's and later became a busy steamboat port. Its glory days came to an end in 1891, when a new railroad line made nearby Newport the center of commerce and the county seat. From that time Jacksonport steadily declined. All of its buildings have vanished, many destroyed by floodwaters, except for the old Jacksonport Courthouse.

The stately courthouse, built in 1869 on a high, sturdy foundation of Arkansas limestone, has been restored and included in *The National Register of Historic Places.* It is now the focal point of the park, housing a museum of memorabilia and relics that trace the history of the community through the steamboat era. Other exhibits show the harvesting of freshwater pearls from the river and the manufacture of pearl buttons from mussel shells with the use of a button-cutting machine.

Moored at the steamboat landing across the levee from the courthouse—and maintained as though ready for a week's cruise—is the *Mary Woods II,* a white double-deck stern-wheeler.

Campsites and picnic tables are pleasingly situated on an open, grassy expanse along the river beneath a scattering of shade trees. The 154-acre park also has a sandy swimming beach, a boat ramp, a small woodland, and a lovely pecan grove.

An annual Riverboat Festival is held during the last weekend of July. *Park open year-round. Courthouse open Tues.–Sun. except Thanksgiving Day, Christmas, and New Year's Day. Steamboat open Tues.– Sun., May–Labor Day; weekends Apr. and Sept.–Oct.; admission charged.*

6. Crowley's Ridge State Park. Crowley's Ridge, a geological curiosity, is an erosional remnant left when the Mississippi and Ohio rivers retreated westward, probably at the end of the last ice age. Rising like an island 100 to 200 feet above the flatlands, the sandy ridge is from 1 to 10 miles wide and runs for 210 miles from Helena, Arkansas, to Cape Girardeau in Missouri. Built on the slopes of the ridge, where once the Quapaw Indians camped, this 270-acre park is an old-fashioned summer getaway with a great spring-fed swimming hole, a productive fishing lake (bass, catfish, crappie, bream), a network of leafy trails, and plenty of places to pic-

nic, camp, watch birds, and play ball. Along the Dancing Rabbit Trail, a name of Quapaw origin, you'll sway your way over two swinging bridges.

Depending on the season, the lake is home to such waterfowl as scaups, mallards, and Canada geese. Whistling swans also make an occasional appearance. Chances are good that you'll spot some deer. Benjamin Crowley, for whom the park is named, settled here following his participation in the War of 1812 because of the plentiful wildlife. *Open year-round.*

7. Hampson Museum State Park. *Wilson.* Persons interested in America's past, and in particular the ancestors of the American Indian, will find the Hampson Museum an especially rewarding one. Its enormous collection of artifacts—some 41,000 items including remarkably beautiful ceramics, stone tools, weapons, human and animal effigies, and skeletal remains—serve to portray the culture of the farming and mound-building people who lived in this area from about 1350 to 1700 and then seemed to disappear.

Many of the exhibits were excavated by Dr. James K. Hampson in the 1920's on his family plantation, Nodena (five miles from Wilson), where a palisaded village with two pyramid mounds once existed.

The small park, which is right in the village of Wilson, also offers a pleasant picnic area and a playground. *Open Tues.–Sat. year-round, and P.M. Sun. mid-March–mid-Nov. except Thanksgiving Day, Dec. 24, Christmas, and New Year's Day. Admission charged for museum.*

8. Old Fort Museum. *320 Rogers Ave., Fort Smith.* Fort Smith's colorful frontier saga began when it was established by the U.S. Army in 1817 as a border post between Arkansas and Indian Territory. The area's dramatic events of that time are highlighted in the museum, which also displays pioneer relics, Indian beadwork, ponchos, stone tools, and weapons. Large murals depict the fort in its heyday. A well-equipped drugstore with an operating soda fountain of 1920–40 vintage serves up a fine scoop of nostalgia.

On the Old Fort property a well-pre-

5. The riverboats could not compete economically, but their charm is unsurpassed.

9. *The platform provides a semi-bird's-eye view of the vast numbers of geese, ducks, and other species that stop here to feed and rest.*

served courthouse and jail and a reconstructed gallows recall the reputation of a famous resident, U.S. Judge Isaac C. Parker. In sentencing 160 outlaws to death, Parker became known as the Hanging Judge, earning credit in the process for bringing law and order to this freewheeling frontier. *Open daily June–Aug.; Tues.–Sat. and P.M. Sun., Sept.–May. Admission charged.*

9. Holla Bend National Wildlife Refuge. *From Dardanelle take Rte. 7S and turn left on Cty. Rte. 155.* This 6,367-acre sanctuary is actually an island formed in 1954 when the U.S. Army Corps of Engineers cut a new channel for the Arkansas River across a deep bend in the old channel.

Located on a main flyway of migrating birds, the refuge with its ponds and lakes is a winter home for some 5,000 Canada geese and as many as 35,000 ducks of various species. Up to 40 bald eagles can be seen sojourning here from November to March. Permanent residents include herons, egrets, gulls, and terns. Alligators are numerous in these waters, which mark the creature's northernmost range.

More than a third of the refuge is farmed, and a portion of each year's crop of corn, milo, and other grains is left in the fields for the birds. Quiet timberlands of cottonwoods, box elders, and pecans occupy the higher ground, and black willows edge the old river channel.

You can observe the entire sanctuary by following the eight-mile self-guiding, all-weather drive. Picnic tables are provided along the route. Fishing is good, primarily for bream, crappie, bass, and catfish. A boat ramp is located on Lake Lodge. *Open year-round.*

10. Cadron Settlement Park. *Rte. 319 west of Conway.* This site, blessed with good spring water, forest cover, and a natural harbor where Cadron Creek flows into the Arkansas River, was first used in the late 1770's as a trading post by Spaniards bartering with the local Osage Indians. With the Louisiana Purchase of 1803 the United States acquired Arkansas, and several years later a number of families settled here. Gristmills and a tannery were built, and a general store was opened. In 1820–21 Cadron vied with Little Rock in a contest to become the territorial capital, and lost. When the railroad passed it by, the little river town finally died.

In 1972 the U.S. Army Corps of Engineers undertook the restoration of Cadron as a recreation area. An imposing two-story blockhouse of sawed cypress logs has been reconstructed on the hilltop site of the orginal building overlooking a bend in the Arkansas.

An easy-to-moderate hiking trail wends through this quiet region of hills and bluffs. Named for the Cherokee leader Tollantusky, who lived at Cadron from 1809 until his death in 1818, the trail underlines the former importance of the settlement as it follows at various points the Butterfield Stagecoach Road, the Toad Suck Ferry Road, and the Old Military Road. Two overlooks atop bluffs more than 100 feet high offer an excellent view of the half-mile-wide river. The park has a boat-launching ramp and picnic areas. *Open year-round.*

11. Lake Ouachita State Park. The park is nestled in the pine-covered hills bordering the eastern end of Lake Ouachita (pronounced *Wash*-i-taw) and offers camping, boating, waterskiing, swimming, and fishing along the lake's 975 miles of picturesque shoreline. Fishermen come for bass, bream, rainbow trout, and pike.

At the park's full-service marina you can rent an 80-horsepower barge, large enough to accommodate a recreation vehicle up to 31 feet long (and weighing no more than 11,000 pounds with all your gear and supplies), and cruise the lake in your own "home." There are also barges with permanently attached trailers, rental boats, and free launch ramps.

Boaters taking the Geo-Float Trail can examine a number of the area's unusual geologic features, including minicaves and earthquake remains, while landlubbers can strike out on two hiking trails that wander through the lush woodlands of the 365-acre park to see the native plants, birds, and animals.

Since the late 1800's vacationers have

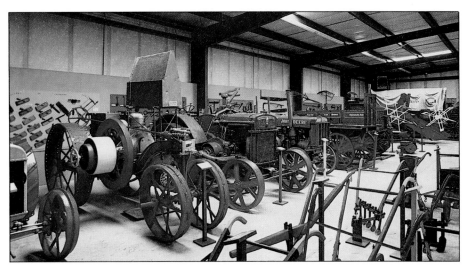

12. *These machines were built to last—and here they are. Note hand tools on wall.*

been lured by the Three Sisters—natural springs that are said to have curative powers. Today these springs, located near the north end of the lake, have been tapped to supply water for the park. *Open year-round. Barges not available in Jan.*

🚻🏕️🚐🚶🥾🔭🏊🛶

12. Stuttgart Agricultural Museum. *921 E. Fourth St., Stuttgart.* From the name, one could accurately surmise that the town was founded by German immigrants. This fascinating museum complex preserves the farm equipment, household antiques, and other relics of the prairie farm culture that they developed here in the years after the Civil War.

Funds to build the museum were donated by local farm families, who also contributed all the items on display, among them some impressive 19th-century steam-powered farm machinery. Local craftsmen have also built replicas of a 1914 schoolhouse, the old community firehouse, complete with the refurbished 1926 fire engine, a fully furnished 1880 prairie home, a scaled-down model of an 1896 Lutheran church, and the façades of stores that once existed here.

Among the charming and unexpected exhibits is a collection of musical instruments and music boxes that entertained the great-grandparents of the women who run the museum today. *Open Tues.–Sun. except major holidays. Admission free but donations encouraged.*

13. Louisiana Purchase State Park. *Rte. 49S.* In 1815, 12 years after the Louisiana Purchase, a team of government surveyors blazed two big sweet gum trees in a trackless swamp in eastern Arkansas. Those marks were the starting point for the monumental task of determining the bounds of that addition to the United States.

Though the blazed trees are gone, 37.5 acres of the headwater swamp have been preserved as a state park. A 950-foot-long boardwalk leads through the area to a marker designating the initial point for the entire survey. The stroll offers a close-up view of this natural environment, where you can find the uncommon swamp cottonwood tree, the golden prothonotary warbler, and the little brown-and-green amphibian called the tree frog.

Much of the lower Mississippi River valley was once wooded swampland like this, and you get a fleeting sense, without having to get your feet wet, of how overpowering this landscape must have seemed to those surveyors who came to chart it. Mosquitoes are intermittently pesky, so bring along some repellent. *Open year-round.*

🥾🚶🚻

14. Arkansas Post National Memorial. *Gillett.* Called the birthplace of Arkansas, the small settlement of Arkansas Post was established in 1686 by Henri de Tonti on a grant given him four years earlier by his chief, the great French explorer La Salle. The trading post was probably abandoned

a few years later, but in the early 1700's profitable trade with the Indians revived interest in the region, and Arkansas Post was rebuilt.

Becoming an American village in 1803, Arkansas Post grew into a bustling frontier town, and in 1819 it was made the first territorial capital of Arkansas. But it faded away when the government moved to Little Rock in 1821.

During the 1700's and 1800's Arkansas Post was relocated within a 35-mile area numerous times because of floods and the river's instability. Several of these sites are within today's 221-acre memorial park. A setting of quiet beauty at the meeting point of the White, Arkansas, and Mississippi rivers, it probably looks much as it did in Tonti's time. Self-guiding trails help re-create the past.

The park is also a fine wildlife preserve and a magnificent spot for bird-watching, as it was for John James Audubon. A fishing lake yields 10-pound bass and catfish, and a boat-launching ramp just beyond the park gives access to both the White and Arkansas rivers. The visitor center has some first-rate archeological, historical, and wildlife exhibits. Picnic areas abound. *Open year-round.*

🚻🚶🚻🛶

15. Crater of Diamonds State Park. *Murfreesboro.* Here's a unique chance to combine fun and profit by prospecting in the only significant diamond deposit in the North American continent. You get to keep any stones you find.

Best known for diamonds, the area (an eroded volcanic pipe) also yields amethyst, agate, jasper, quartz, and other semiprecious stones. A 40-acre field is deep-plowed regularly to expose new earth. Though generally you must dig for stones, diamonds are occasionally found lying on the surface, sparkling in the sun.

Many of the diamonds are of an industrial quality, but every year visitors turn up hundreds of gems of significant quality and value, and some lucky prospectors carry away diamonds ranging from two to five carats. The largest ever found, the Uncle Sam, was 40.23 carats.

The first diamond from this area was found in 1906, but for various reasons commercial mining has never been successful here, and in 1972 the field was made part of an 888-acre park along the piney banks of the Little Missouri River.

Some tips: wear a hat because there's little shade. Bring boots or overshoes because the plowed earth is usually muddy. The park visitor center provides digging equipment and advice on diamond "mining" methods, and will identify and certify any stones you unearth. Diamonds are most often found a few days after a heavy rain, so the best time to look for them is during the rainy season from February through June. *Park open year-round. Admission charged for diamond field.*

16. Old Washington Historic State Park.
Washington. The town of Washington was a frontier jumping-off place for people streaming into Texas and the Great Southwest in the first half of the 19th century, but after the Civil War it declined and today has fewer than 300 people.

In 1958 a few residents began restoring some of the beautiful antebellum homes. That project has expanded to cover practically the entire town and to include a variety of public buildings. Highlights here now include the village smithy, where the knife used by Col. James Bowie was designed (a resident knifemaker gives demonstrations); the tavern frequented by Houston, Austin, Bowie, Crockett, and the grandiloquent frontier poet Albert Pike; a cotton gin; the old county jail, now a restaurant and inn; and the 1836 courthouse, now a museum.

All of this is today a historic state park. An interesting two-hour tour of the restored area conducted by guides in period costumes gives you an overall sense of strolling back into the 19th century. The streets are still shaded by great catalpa trees, and in mid-March the village is aglow with the bloom of jonquils. During the Frontier Days Festival—in late October or early November—the townspeople dress in old-time garb, and 19th-century crafts, music, and food are featured. One can picnic here under trees that are nearly as old as the U.S. *Historic buildings open Mon., Wed.–Sat., and P.M. Sun., except major holidays. Charge for tours.*

17. Reader Railroad. *Reader.* This is the oldest all-steam standard-gauge railroad company still operating in the United States. Burning wood and throwing sparks, it makes two round-trips daily through the bucolic countryside and piney woodlands of southwest Arkansas between the old mill town of Reader and a logging site, Camp DeWoody.

The 1½-hour ride aboard the railroad—nicknamed the Possum Trot Line—is a leisurely one. A possum moving at a fast trot probably could keep up, and you might see just such a critter lazing along the right-of-way. The passenger cars are not air-conditioned, and on summer days this excursion can be hot and sticky.

Once a month, from June through October, the train makes a sunset run that includes live bluegrass and country music and dinner featuring locally popular foods. When the weather is cool, oil lamps and heat from stoves add to the ambiance of the 2½-hour excursion.

You can picnic at the station-house pavilion at Adams Crossing, but White Oak Lake Park, only six miles away on Route 24, is a much more pleasant picnic spot—a quiet wooded retreat with fishing, camping, swimming, and trails. Trains usually run weekends in May, and Thursday–Sunday in June–mid-August, with departures at 11 A.M. and 2 P.M., but schedules may change. *For information and reservations (which are required) call the Reader Line General Offices in Malvern (501) 337-9591 or the train station in Reader (501) 685-2692. Fare charged.*

18. Arkansas Oil and Brine Museum.
Smackover. The French called the area *sumac couvert*—"covered with sumac." To American ears those words sounded like "Smackover," though its history has less to do with sumac than petroleum.

Smackover was the scene of a wild and woolly oil boom during the World War I era, when great oil strikes were made in the Texarkana region. After that it faded to a kind of uneventful small-town respectability. You'll see no evidence of the old shoot-'em-up, strike-it-rich excitement, and though just about every cow pasture and vacant lot in this area has one of those woodpecker-looking oil rigs silently pumping away, few local residents know much about the colorful history of the petroleum industry or all the nuts and bolts of how it works.

This brand-new museum essays to give visitors a historical view and practical understanding of the oil business. Giant antique derricks and a working well are among the outdoor exhibits tucked into a pretty section of pinewoods along scenic Route 7, just north of town. Another is a replica of a Roaring Twenties gas station. And in the impressive visitor center you'll find a gift shop, archives, and some excellent exhibits documenting those hectic boom times. *Open Mon.–Sat. and P.M. Sun. year-round.*

17. *Man-powered turntable is used to head old* **Number 7** *back toward its starting point.*

Louisiana

Mysterious bayous, dazzling camellias and azaleas, and stately plantation houses are here—along with some unexpected pleasures.

One of the richest archeological sites in North America is Poverty Point, in north-central Louisiana, where prehistoric hunters built vast earthworks. On another site, once a fortress and capital of the Spanish province of Texas, one is introduced to the painstaking methods of archeological research. A former World War II training camp is now a museum of American military history.

One plantation has the prototypical antebellum mansion. Another, developed by a woman who was once a slave, became a popular center for local writers, artists, and crafts people.

Flowers, for which the South is famous, can be enjoyed on a hiking trail, in an arboretum, a state park, and a garden. One bayou combines a recreational park with a wildlife preserve, and another is home to Spanish-speaking trappers whose forebears came here in the late 1700's.

1. Cypress Black Bayou Recreation Area.
This 340-acre piney park is perched at the junction of two large bayou-fed reservoirs. Here one can fish from several of the piers, launch a boat or rent one, swim at a sandy beach, walk for more than four miles along wood-chip-paved nature trails, rent a cabin, camp with all amenities, pitch a tent, or enjoy a picnic.

The park's nature center has facilities for the study of plants and animals native to these woods. It was established with the help of the local school board and welcomes students and researchers from all parts of the country.

The park is popular with birders, who often come to observe the many kinds of songbirds and waterfowl that inhabit the towering pine forest and the quiet waterways. The park is usually crowded from July to Labor Day. *Open year-round. Admission charged.*

2. Lake Claiborne State Park.
Some 600 well-wooded acres touch the shores of Lake Claiborne here, bringing outdoor enjoyment to visitors who come to spend the day as well as to overnight campers.

The lake was formed in the late 1960's, when Bayou d'Arbonne was dammed and its waters flooded more than 6,000 acres of cleared woodland. A sandy beach has been created at one end of the lake, whose pure, clear water is excellent for swimming. There are boats for rent and a launching ramp where you can put in your own. The lake is stocked with walleye, largemouth bass, black crappies, bream, and other local species. Waterskiing is also a popular pursuit.

More than 80 campsites provide both water and electricity hookups, picnic tables, and barbecue grills. Summer weekends can be crowded. *Open year-round. Admission charged.*

3. Poverty Point State Commemorative Area.
On Rte. 577. Just how Poverty Point got its name is not known for sure. One theory holds that repeated crop failures in the 19th century left the area destitute. Despite its name, however, Poverty Point is one of America's richest archeological sites.

The lower Mississippi Valley was inhabited from 3,500 to 2,500 years ago by Indian tribes who developed a culture sufficiently organized and enduring to construct massive earthworks here on a bluff along Bayou Macon. It is estimated that 5 million man-hours were required to build the complex, which consists of six semicircular rows of long, low ridges (divided into sections by aisles) and four mounds, the largest of which is bird-shaped and rises to a height of 70 feet.

These ridges and mounds were assumed to be part of the natural landscape, but when they were viewed from an airplane, it became obvious from the striking symmetry of their design that they were the work of man.

The largest of several centers of the Poverty Point people, the complex is shrouded in mystery, and scholars still ponder the purpose for which it was built. Although one of the mounds was located over a crematory, archeologists do not interpret the place as an ancient burial site. Conjectures about the use of the concentric ridges range from building foundations to an astronomical observatory.

An observation tower provides an overview, and a guided tram tour loops through the 400-acre site. The museum in the information center displays an impressive collection of effigies, jewelry, tools, weapons, and other artifacts from the site. Some of the materials were obtained by trade with people far away. The ingenuity of the residents of this rock-free terrain can be seen in their production of fire-hardened clay balls to use as cooking stones. They also made stone beads with perfectly cylindrical holes, a feat that has long puzzled experts; it is now believed that they used a reed at the end of a stick for a drill, with sand as an abrasive. *Open daily except Christmas and New Year's Day. Admission charged.*

4. Mansfield State Commemorative Area.
On Rte. 175. The three-day battle of Mansfield in April 1864 was an important victory for Confederate forces, who stopped a major Union advance aimed at cutting off and reannexing Texas. The site of the conflict, now maintained as a commemorative area, extends across 44 acres of flat farmland about four miles south of the town of Mansfield.

The battle was fought on both sides of what is today Highway 175, known then as the Old Stage Road. The trenches and remnants of the lines of battle have been restored, and signs along a quarter-mile walking trail through the area tell the story of the conflict. A small museum displays weapons, uniforms, riverboat models, and two dioramas—one depicts Gen. Richard Taylor's Confederate forces routing the northerners; the other shows how retreating Union navy engineers ingeniously refloated their vessels trapped in the Red River by building dams to raise the water level. *Open year-round. Admission charged.*

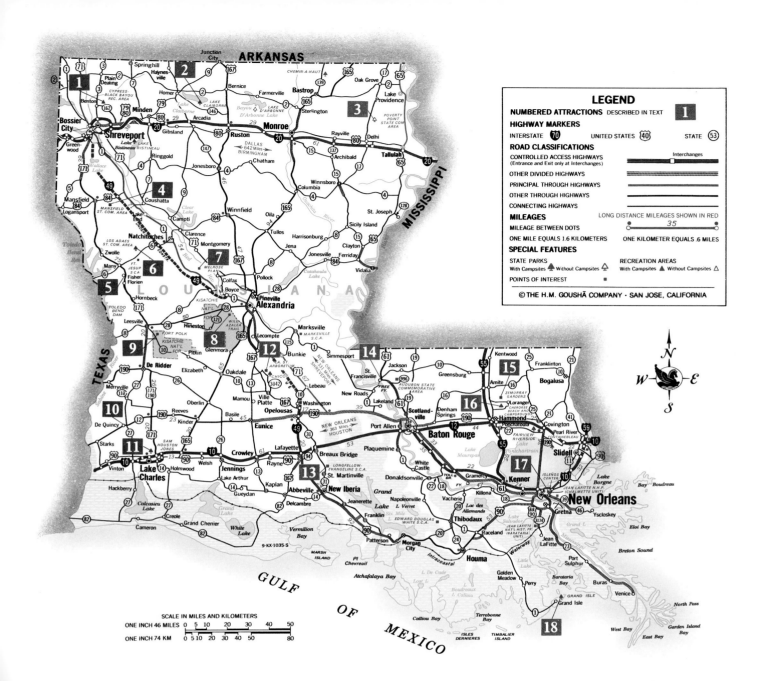

LEGEND

NUMBERED ATTRACTIONS DESCRIBED IN TEXT [1]

HIGHWAY MARKERS

INTERSTATE (70)   UNITED STATES (40)   STATE (53)

ROAD CLASSIFICATIONS

CONTROLLED ACCESS HIGHWAYS   Interchanges
(Entrance and Exit only at Interchanges)

OTHER DIVIDED HIGHWAYS

PRINCIPAL THROUGH HIGHWAYS

OTHER THROUGH HIGHWAYS

CONNECTING HIGHWAYS

MILEAGES   LONG DISTANCE MILEAGES SHOWN IN RED

MILEAGE BETWEEN DOTS   35

ONE MILE EQUALS 1.6 KILOMETERS   ONE KILOMETER EQUALS .6 MILES

SPECIAL FEATURES

STATE PARKS   RECREATION AREAS
With Campsites ⛺ Without Campsites △   With Campsites ▲ Without Campsites △

POINTS OF INTEREST ■

© THE H.M. GOUSHA COMPANY · SAN JOSE, CALIFORNIA

SCALE IN MILES AND KILOMETERS

ONE INCH 46 MILES   0 5 10   20   30   40   50

ONE INCH 74 KM   0 5 10 20 30 40 50   80

9-KX-1035-S

GULF OF MEXICO

3. Trees tend to naturalize a mound created with 10 million baskets of earth.

5. Fisher: Historic Sawmill Town. *Off U.S. Rte. 171 four miles north of Florien; turn west at the blinker.* Shaded by the longleaf pines that once brought wealth to its citizens, this almost completely deserted turn-of-the-century sawmill town lies at the end of a quiet road a half-mile downhill from the First Baptist Church.

As you approach the town, which is in the process of being restored, the long, low, white commissary faces you across a square, its porch stretching the entire width of the building. Off to one side, with a white picket fence in front, stands the old opera house, a hall that served as the center of the town's activities. Its ticket window, with a little rounded shelf, opens onto the front porch. Alongside the old railroad tracks, now almost hidden by patches of weeds, is the railroad station, with its paneling, benches, and ticket office still intact. The interiors can be visited by appointment. Call (318) 156-2913.

The town comes to life once a year during the fourth weekend in May, when the annual Sawmill Days Festival is held.

---

6. Los Adaes State Commemorative Area. *On Rte. 485 off Rte. 6.* The fortress and village known as Los Adaes, which under Spanish rule served as the capital of the province of Texas, was built in 1719 as a stronghold against the threat of the French, who had begun colonizing the area to the east. Its reign as the center of the Texas government ended a half-century later, when France gave the unprofitable Louisiana colony to Spain and the fort was closed as unnecessary.

In the 18th century, when it flourished, the town was inhabited by Mexican soldiers and Los Adaes Indians; it included a blacksmith's shop, a small chapel, and soldiers' barracks. All the buildings have disappeared, and the 14-acre site is now being excavated and reconstructed.

The information center displays a collection of tools, weapons, and other artifacts found on the grounds. The site of the fort itself is marked by a flag and an ancient cannon. The articles that have been recovered and the rebuilding of the fort offer an introduction to the painstaking procedures of responsible archeology. *Grounds open daily except holidays.*

---

7. Melrose Plantation. *Junction of Rtes. 493 and 119.* The tales this fascinating early Louisiana property has to tell revolve around two remarkable women who held sway here a century apart. The first was a determined and enterprising slave named Marie Therese Coincoin, who in 1778 was freed along with several of her 14 children. She obtained a land grant on the Cane River from the Spanish colonial authorities, and aided by her sons, she cleared the land and established a successful tobacco and corn farm that eventually became known as Melrose Plantation.

The other woman was Mrs. Cammie Garrett Henry, known simply as Miss Cammie, who came into possession of the plantation at the turn of the century. She carefully restored the original two-room cypress-timbered house called Yucca that Marie Therese built in 1796, as well as the imposing white clapboard Big House that Marie Therese's grandson completed in 1833, and turned Melrose into a center for local arts, crafts, history, and folklore.

Miss Cammie invited artists and writers to come and work in Yucca House, and over the years the little structure probably housed more notable writers than any other in the South. The renowned hospitality of Melrose was convincingly confirmed by one writer who came for a six weeks' visit and stayed for 32 years.

Yet another remarkable woman came out of Melrose. In the 1940's the plantation's onetime cook, Clementine Hunter, began to paint colorful and charming primitive works; she became known as the black Grandma Moses. Some of her murals can be seen upstairs in Yucca House.

Other buildings on the grounds include the African House, the Weaving House, and the Bindery, which serves as a visitor center. *Open Tues.–Thurs. except Thanksgiving Day, Christmas, and New Year's Day. Admission charged.*

---

8. Wild Azalea Trail. *Kisatchie National Forest, Evangeline Ranger District.* This is the place to be if you want to walk. Here you can settle for an hour or two of ambling in the woods or devote two days to hiking the full 31 miles from end to end. The trail, named for the wild azaleas that bloom in the forest in early spring, winds through great stands of hardwoods and pines, skirts a bog, and crosses open meadows and several creeks as it makes its way from Valentine Lake, west of Alexandria, to Route 165, south of the city.

Well marked with yellow blazes, the trail goes through woodlands that the Forest Service keeps in top condition by constantly clearing underbrush and thinning trees, a procedure that improves the soil and promotes new growth. The route also takes hikers through the Castor Creek Scenic Area, a part of the forest that has remained untouched for years.

At several places the trail crosses Forest Service roads, where hikers who want to walk only a part can park cars or arrange to be picked up. Tent camping is permitted along the trail. *Open year-round.*

9. Fort Polk Military Museum. *Off Rte. 171.* Named for Louisiana's famed "Fighting Bishop," Leonidas Polk, an Episcopal prelate who became a Confederate general, this post was established on the eve of World War II to support the famous Louisiana Maneuvers. Dwight D. Eisenhower, Omar Bradley, and George S. Patton, Jr., were among the key future war leaders who took part in the crucial, grand-scale exercises, which tested the army's ability to use tactics, weapons, and support equipment that had been developed since World War I. For instance, the importance of cub planes for reconnaissance was proved here.

The post came alive again during the Vietnam years. At what became known as Fort Swampy, more than a million men

7. Lush southern growth softens the strong architectural lines of the Big House.

got a foretaste of Southeast Asia in the dense, mosquito-ridden areas of junglelike growth that are part of the varied terrain here. The fort is now the home of the army's 5th Division.

The museum illustrates the history of the base and the units that have served here. Its collection encompasses posters, uniforms, insignia, weapons, and other military memorabilia, some dating back to the Civil War. A 2½-acre park contains more than 100 military vehicles and other equipment. *Open daily except Thanksgiving Day, Christmas, and New Year's Day.*

---

10. DeQuincy Railroad Museum. *DeQuincy.*

This is indeed an appropriate site for a railroad museum. DeQuincy was settled in 1895 at the juncture of the Kansas City Southern and the old Missouri Pacific railroads, and the imposing, tile-roofed Spanish Colonial Kansas City Southern depot, which houses the museum and is in *The National Register of Historic Places,* was once the pride of DeQuincy.

The museum provides a view of railroading here at the turn of the century. On display are the tickets and timetables of the early 1900's, the old-fashioned mail pouch that the engineer of a passing express train caught with a hook, and memorabilia of the town's railroad men. The mannequin of a ticket agent, sitting in his office with his back to the door, is so real that visitors sometimes whisper for fear of disturbing him as he works at his desk, complete with antique typewriter and telegrapher's key.

On the grounds are a 1913 steam locomotive with coal car and vintage caboose attached. An annual Railroad Festival is held here the second weekend of April. *Open P.M. Wed.–Sun.*

---

11. Sam Houston Jones State Park.

Named originally for the hero of the Alamo, who according to legend often stayed in this area, the 1,068-acre park now carries the name of the 1940's Louisiana governor who was responsible for preserving these grounds. Here you will find some of the loveliest landscape in Louisiana—towering pines, dense woodlands, gentle streams, lakes, and cypress-bordered lagoons.

The quiet, scenic waters are ideal for

8. *Rising mist above silvery rapids defines a moment of morning on Kisatchie Bayou.*

boating, and boats are available for rent. A launch ramp and two docks are provided for those who bring their own. Fishing from a boat or along the banks can produce a catch of white perch, bream, or bass. The park has several campsites, picnic grounds, and nature trails.

Wildlife is abundant, and a herd of 20 deer is kept in a special fenced-off section of the woods. Some birds, such as the flock of Muscovy ducks that waddle along the paths greeting the visitors, are domesticated. Another tame resident is a brown pelican that arrived with a broken wing and decided to stay. During the migrating season birders come here for a tally of the species that stop to rest and feed on their way across Louisiana. *Open year-round. Admission charged.*

---

12. Louisiana State Arboretum. *On Rte. 3042.*

In this unexpectedly hilly region of Louisiana the state has established an arboretum where native plants can be studied and enjoyed. Two and a half miles of good, well-marked trails traverse woodlands and wander down into a ravine, with plants identified along the way.

Because of the variations in topography and microclimates, almost every kind of Louisiana plant life can be found here. Most of the 600 acres have been left completely wild. Among the trees in the forest are catalpas, live oaks, persimmons, and the unusual big-leaf magnolia. The animal life that flourishes here includes raccoons, white-tailed deer, opossums, wild turkeys, and great barred owls.

The interpretive center contains exhibits of a few unusual plant species that grow here and pictorial displays of native fauna. For birders, who come mainly in spring, a

Introduction to the Bayou

In this trackless, watery forest of mangrove and moss-laden cypress—the vast, unchanging realm of the alligator, egret, and heron—mankind will ever be a stranger. This stranger boarded a Cypress Bayou Swamp Tour pontoon boat near Houma to experience, if only briefly, a truly unique environment.

Along the waters of Bayou Grand Caillou, the only sound is the engine of the 12-passenger craft, accompanied by the distant rat-a-tat of a woodpecker. Edging the bayou is an impenetrable jungle of cypress, willow, hackberry, wild hibiscus, elephant ears, and lotus. The undisputed master here is the alligator, which has survived unchanged for 100 million years or more.

We are treated to an unusual view of this fearsome predator when our guide puts half a raw chicken on a long pole and holds it over the water at an appointed place. A waiting gator (conditioned by the engine sound) shoots straight up out of the water with its giant pink, tooth-studded jaws wide open. The meat—and part of the stick—is gone with a bone-crushing snap. We tie up at a nearby wooden dock and a bit apprehensively start on a walk beside the primeval swamp.

Extending for a few hundred yards just inches above water level, the trail follows a narrow ridge between the slow-moving waters of the bayou and the still vastness of the swamp. Along it we see an early-blooming stand of spider lilies—in mid-March—savor leaves of the aromatic bayberry, inspect woodpecker holes in the soft, yellowish wood of the hackberry tree, and spy hawks' nests high in the cypress grove. Our guide identifies the tracks of the mink, armadillo, and nutria. On the ride back he also points out a floating log, and as we draw closer we see that it's swarming with water moccasins, observing the springtime rite that assures the species' preservation.

As we leave the boat and re-enter the noise and clutter of roadside America, we share a feeling of change and impermanence after experiencing a world of still waters and wild creatures that could prevail forever.   —*M. Perry.*

For reservations call (504) 873-8005.

---

checklist of both migratory and native species is available at the center.

Walking and looking are the only activities allowed here. But adjoining Chicot State Park has full facilities; its entrance is 1½ miles to the south on Highway 3042. *Open year-round.*

---

13. Longfellow–Evangeline State Commemorative Area. *Rte. 31, St. Martinsville.* Like many other sites here in the heart of Cajun country, this 157-acre park, tucked behind an iron fence on St. Martinsville's main street, commemorates the original French Acadian settlers who came to the area in the mid-1700's after being expelled from Canada by the conquering British.

It also commemorates one of America's most popular and beloved poems, Long-

fellow's epic "Evangeline," the tale of two star-crossed lovers separated by the expulsion. Tradition holds that the poem, which ends differently, was inspired by the story of Emmeline Labiche, who died brokenhearted after discovering her long-lost beau had married someone else. A statue of Evangeline, sculpted in 1927, rests over the grave that is thought to be Emmeline's in the yard of nearby St. Martin's Church.

The main attraction in the park itself is Acadian House Museum. Built of adobe and brick in 1780, the two-story structure is typical of French plantation architecture. It has been carefully restored and filled with early Louisiana pieces. A visitor center has other exhibits, and a crafts shop is an exact reproduction of a small 18th-century Acadian cottage.

The park backs onto Bayou Teche, and by a little lagoon you will find an exceptionally inviting picnic area filled with

trees curtained with Spanish moss. *Open daily except Thanksgiving Day, Christmas, and New Year's Day. Admission charged.*

---

14. Greenwood Plantation. *Just off Rte. 66, St. Francisville.* This handsome, two-story mansion is one of the loveliest antebellum plantation homes in the South. Colonnaded on all four sides, the pristine Greek Revival structure stands on a slight rise overlooking a reflecting pool edged with azaleas, willows, and moss-draped live oaks. Lavishly furnished with Victorian antiques, it is such a perfect-looking Southern mansion that it has been used as the setting for a motion picture and two television miniseries.

Surprisingly, however, the building is a reconstruction. The original mansion, built by cotton and sugarcane planter Ruffin Barrow in 1830, was completely destroyed by fire in 1960 except for the 28 columns surrounding it. The rebuilding was the dedicated undertaking of Carolyn and Richard Barnes, who also farm the plantation, now reduced in size from 12,000 acres to 278. To make it look as much like the original as possible, they used old photographs and information from Barrow's descendants for reference. Even some of the furniture and paintings are original. *Open Wed.–Sat. and P.M. Sun. except Thanksgiving Day, Christmas, and New Year's Day. Admission charged.*

15. Zemurray Gardens. *Rte. 40, about 12 miles east of I-55.* Mr. and Mrs. Sam Zemurray, who purchased this property in 1928, were so impressed with its natural beauty that they decided to create a woodland park. They repaired a dam and spillway on a stream that flows through the grounds to form tranquil 20-acre Mirror Lake. And since they were fond of spring-blooming shrubs, they planted the shoreline with camellias, redbuds, dogwoods, and especially azaleas.

While the rest of this pleasant 150-acre park can be visited any time, the garden area around the lake is open only in the spring, when it is abloom with flowers. And it is the gardens that make this park so special. A trail takes visitors completely around the lake and through the landscaped grounds. It crosses several streams and passes vistas with statuary brought from Europe by the Zemurrays.

Since the exact months when the gardens are open can vary, it's best to check with the Baton Rouge tourist office before driving here. *Gardens open daily, usually Mar.–May. Admission charged.*

16. Cherokee Beach and Campgrounds. *Four miles east of Tickfaw on Rte. 442.* Tubing is the main attraction here. The gentle Tangipahoa River, which flows southward to Lake Pontchartrain, is protected by the state Scenic Rivers Act and is ideal for tubing. Its slow pace, less than a mile an hour, provides a quiet, carefree ride as the river curves its way between bluffs clad with hardwoods and white, sandy shores.

Cherokee Beach and Campgrounds, a wooded area that extends for three miles along the river, is headquarters for float trips of one hour and four hours. On weekends, when buses are available to take tubers a mile upstream for the start of their run, five-hour trips are offered. Shuttle buses meet all trips and return the tubers to Cherokee.

Tubes and life jackets are available for rent, or visitors may bring their own. During the summer, when lifeguards are on duty, swimming is also popular.

Campsites and picnic areas are located along the river and in the surrounding woodlands; fishermen can try their luck for catfish, perch, and bass. Several miles of marked nature trails range through the 200 acres. Summer and holiday weekends can be crowded and are best avoided. *Park open year-round; tubing Apr.–Sept. Admission charged.*

17. Isleños Center. *Rte. 46, 6½ miles east of Chalmette.* In 1778 the Spanish king sent a group of Canary Islanders to Louisiana to colonize this isolated delta area east of New Orleans and protect it from the British. The descendants of these people, called Isleños ("Islanders"), still speak Spanish and continue to live as they did 200 years ago. Known for their skill as trappers and fishermen, the Isleños have stayed on the bayous, where they find an abundance of game such as opossums, raccoons, and nutrias.

The Isleños Center is maintained by the National Park Service as a unit of the Jean Lafitte National Historic Park. Located in a 19th-century white house with a wide lawn shaded by pecan trees, it displays many of the crafts of these people, their trapping and fishing devices, the ancient skin-curing methods that they still use, as well as vintage photographs and other memorabilia. Since the center occasionally closes because of lack of staff, it is best to phone ahead. Call (504) 682-0862. *Open Sat.–Thurs.*

18. Grand Isle State Park. For those who enjoy sun, sand, and saltwater sports, Grand Isle is the epitome of a park. It stretches for more than a mile along the Gulf of Mexico at the tip of a narrow eight-mile barrier island connected to the mainland by a bridge. This wild place of wind and waves can seem to be the very end of the world.

The 400-foot fishing pier (with a fish-cleaning station) gives visitors a chance to try their luck here, where almost 300 different species of fish are found.

Between the beach and the camping areas a wide protective levee has been built with sand dredged from just offshore. Because this created a strong undertow, swimming is allowed only at one's own risk.

Birders gather during the spring and fall to watch the migrating flocks on the flyway that crosses the island. Campsites do not have utilities, but there's running water at the boathouse. Summer and holiday weekends can be crowded. And a three-day Tarpon Rodeo, held each August, attracts thousands of competitors. *Open year-round. Admission charged.*

15. Mirror Lake performs its function as do the azaleas in the piney woods.

North Dakota

Here in the geographical center of North America are some fabulous landforms and bittersweet recollections of pioneer times.

Dramatic sections of badlands terrain can be seen in three different parks, and the pioneer era is memorialized by a fine old wind-driven gristmill, a museum of impressive early-day farm machinery, and a reconstructed pioneer village with an extensive collection of memorabilia. The history of the inevitable and tragic conflict between the Indians, whose land this was, and the settlers, who claimed it as their own, is recalled in the forts and Indian villages.

On a peaceful note are an international garden, sanctuaries for game and waterfowl, and a couple of good places to fish.

1. Writing Rock State Historic Site. *On Rte. 5 north of Grenora.* No one knows who etched the mysterious maplike network of lines, circles, and dots on the five-foot-high gray granite rock found at this site. And although the imaginative viewer can discern a bird in flight and other possible figures, no one is really sure what the ancient pictographs represent. Scholars speculate that the markings are the handiwork of a prehistoric people who were later driven away by repeated droughts.

The Plains Indians who settled in this region some 700 years ago held the markings in awe, and one of their many legends about the symbols contended that they changed from time to time to foretell the future. Some Indians continued to make pilgrimages here even after being resettled in other states.

Today the rock, together with a smaller, similarly etched specimen found about a mile away, is in a simple fieldstone building for protection from erosion by the harsh North Dakota weather. Here they stand as reminders of an ancient urge to communicate. *Open year-round.*

2. Danish Mill. *Kenmare.* The two 1,800-pound grinding stones in this three-story windmill are the only originals in any of the six similar mills surviving in the United States. Built in 1902 by Christian Jensen, a Danish immigrant, the picturesque

4. *Evocative of the locale—in another time—are these and other buildings here.*

red-shingled mill ground up to 200 sacks of grain per day at its original site 11 miles to the north. It ceased operation in 1918 and is now a respected fixture in Kenmare's town square.

Visitors willing to climb the cramped stairway can inspect the heart of the great machine—hand-hewn maple gears. The speed of the gears, and thus of the grinding, was regulated by turning and trimming the four canvas sails that powered the mill. *Open year-round.*

3. International Peace Garden. This 2,300-acre wooded garden commemorates the heartening fact that the boundary between the United States and Canada is the longest undefended international border in the world. On a monument marking the line the two nations pledge that ". . . as long as men shall live, we will not take up arms against one another."

The garden, on land donated by North Dakota and the Canadian province of Manitoba and dedicated in 1932, was the inspiration of Henry Moore, a Canadian horticulturist who believed that those who love flowers, trees, and the outdoors could be a powerful force for peace between nations. Moore's dream of a garden symbolizing the human yearning for peace is beautifully realized here on the rolling foothills of the Turtle Mountains.

Two automobile tours—one in the Canadian half and the other in the United States—are each about 3½ miles long and have several stopping places for sightseeing and picnicking. The Canadian Natural Drive winds past Lake Stormon through groves of birches, maples, and oaks. An arboretum along the way contains more than 100 labeled trees and shrubs. To enjoy the natural beauty more closely, one can take the 1½-mile Lake View Hiking Trail, where beavers may be seen at work. Another walk of the same length goes through the well-tended formal gardens marking the nations' boundary line in the center of the park. It continues on past several lovely fountains, reflecting pools, and cascades to the 120-foot Peace Tower.

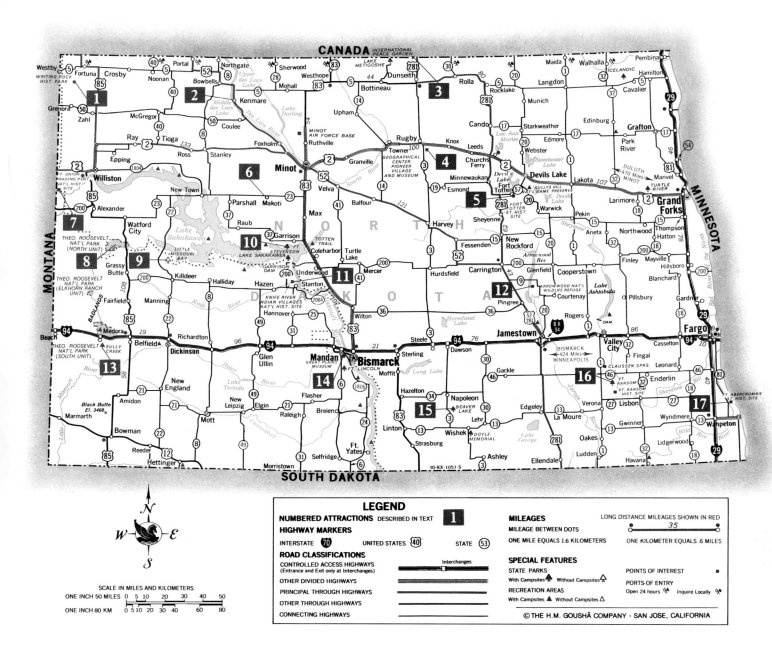

At the start of the United States Cultural Drive is an 18-foot floral clock, which is one of the park's most photographed features. This drive also leads to the park's campground and lodge, and passes the International Music Camp, which sponsors a variety of educational programs, an old-time fiddlers' contest, and a festival of the arts in summer. *Open daily year-round. Admission charged.*

4. Geographical Center Pioneer Village and Museum. *Rte. 2, Rugby.* When you visit this 20-acre park, you are halfway "from sea to shining sea." Nearby is a

cairn marking the exact geographical center of the North American continent. The Atlantic, Pacific, and Arctic oceans and the Gulf of Mexico are all about 1,500 miles away. You can even buy a square inch of the continent, complete with deed, at the Pioneer Village for a few dollars.

The village consists of some 30 authentic North Dakota frontier homes, offices, a general store, livery stable, saloon, church, home-operated telephone exchange, and the stately windmill—that lonely sentinel of the prairie farmstead before the advent of modern power. Most were donated, moved to the site, restored, and furnished by local people and businesses. Walking down the town's main street, you are transported back to the re-

gion's tempestuous past as part of the Dakota Territory. In the extensive collections of frontier memorabilia are reminders of the conflicts between the Indians and the first settlers, who included many Scandinavians, Germans, and Russians.

A fascinating railroad exhibit features an 1886 Great Northern Railroad depot and, on the other side of the tracks, a typical hobo jungle.

The museum houses a colorful array of frontier artifacts that include feathered Indian headdresses, a fine beaded vest once worn by a Chippewa medicine man, and old photographs and postcards showing how towns in the area looked in the early days. Among other collections are old clocks, lamps, firearms, and mounted specimens of native birds and animals. The museum also has records of a local youth reputed to be the world's tallest man. *Open Mon.–Sat. and P.M. Sun., May–Sept. Admission charged.*

---

5. Fort Totten State Historic Site and Sullys Hill National Game Preserve. In the summer of 1876 troopers of the U.S. 7th Cavalry rode from the fort into the pages of history. They were assigned to join another cavalry unit commanded by the flamboyant Lt. Col. George A. Custer in a punitive expedition against the Indians led by chiefs Sitting Bull and Crazy Horse. The confrontation at the Little Bighorn region of Montana is recalled today as Custer's last stand.

Fort Totten is the best preserved of all forts built during the turbulent days of the Plains Indian wars, and Cavalry Square looks much as it did on that fateful day more than a century ago. Restored officers' and enlisted men's quarters, the commanding officer's house, and other buildings still look out onto the broad square. A display of photos at the visitor center in the old commissary traces the history of the fort, first as a military outpost. Then, as part of the surrounding Fort Totten Sioux Indian Reservation, it became a school, a tuberculosis sanatorium, and from 1940 to 1959 a community school. In the former hospital are excellent displays of Indian and pioneer clothing and other artifacts.

Almost next door is the Sullys Hill National Game Preserve, a 1,600-acre home for grazing herds of buffalo, elk, and white-tailed deer, a well-populated community of animated black-tailed prairie dogs, birds, and waterfowl that seek out the two lakes. A four-mile auto tour leads to a scenic overlook and to Sullys Hill, where there is an observation tower and three Indian burial mounds. A short hiking trail and a 1¼-mile ski trail are other attractions. *Historic site and preserve open year-round. Fort Totten visitor center open daily mid-May–mid-Sept. An auto tour available May–Oct., weather permitting.*

---

6. Makoti Threshers Museum. The era when four-footed horsepower was first being replaced by four-wheeled machines has not been forgotten in the small agri-

cultural community of Makoti. The Threshers Association boasts a remarkable museum of antique and classic threshers, farm tractors, and stationary engines. Housed in six buildings, this impressive collection includes a number of very rare pieces of farm equipment. Most of the machines are operational, and some are lovingly restored. You don't have to be a tractor buff to be fascinated by a 1909 Hart Parr, a 1917 Plow Boy, a 1920 Titon, and a wood-body thresher made by International Harvester in 1920. One prize exhibit is the massive 110-horsepower Case steam traction engine built in the early 1900's—about 14 feet high with iron rear wheels 7 feet in diameter.

The first weekend in October is the highlight of the year. That's when crowds of enthusiasts arrive for the annual Makoti Threshing Show, and the steam and gas tractors, antique cars and trucks are paraded down Main Street by their owners. Also featured are a horseshoe tournament and the John Deere Two-Cylinder Slow Race. A pancake breakfast and luncheon are served from the so-called cook cars that were hauled into the fields to feed farmhands. *Open year-round by appointment. Admission free but donations encouraged. For information call (701) 726-5693 or (701) 726-5649 (weekends).*

---

7. Fort Union Trading Post National Historic Site. On a typical busy day some 150 years ago, this fortified trading post on the banks of the upper Missouri River would have been surrounded by Indians grouped according to tribe, all eager to trade beaver and buffalo hides for guns, powder, beads, and blankets.

Fort Union was built by John Jacob Astor's American Fur Company about 1829 to buy and ship beaver pelts to the eastern market. When silk top hats became more fashionable than ones made from beaver, the trade declined, and was supplanted by the demand for buffalo robes.

As one of the most remote and luxurious large western outposts of the period, the fort was visited by many prominent travelers and adventurers, including the artists John James Audubon, Karl Bodmer, and George Catlin, who traveled by steamboat 1,900 miles from St. Louis.

The fort was largely dismantled in 1867. The National Park Service acquired the site in 1966 and began the excavations that are now open to visitors. Outlines of

foundations are visible, and signs identify the various building sites. The staff of the visitor center, dressed as trappers and traders, will explain the displays of Indian clubs, military buttons, and other relics. *Open year-round, weather permitting.*

---

8. Theodore Roosevelt National Memorial Park, North Unit. In 1883 a young politician from New York came to the North Dakota badlands to hunt buffalo and was inspired by the beauty of the place. A few months after his return to New York, his wife and his mother died, both on the same day, whereupon he returned to this haunting wilderness for comfort and solace. Later, as president, Theodore Roosevelt championed the idea of a National Park Service, and this, the only national park honoring an individual, is dedicated to his memory.

The dramatic landscape that so influenced Roosevelt is still impressing visitors. The badlands' configurations tell the history of this part of the continent. Some 60 million years ago, runoff from the Rocky Mountains deposited the debris

8. *Layers of soil and volcanic ash have been building for 60 million years here where the black-tailed prairie dog thrives.*

that forms the badlands' distinctive multi-colored layers. Ash from volcanoes in the west added the layers of blue. Bolts of lightning ignited seams of soft coal, baking the sand and clay and adding red hues. In time swift-running streams cut through the layers, sculpting the terrain.

This moonlike landscape can be enjoyed along a 13-mile scenic drive or experienced on foot or horseback along several well-marked trails that include 11-mile routes through the rugged backcountry as well as a half-mile nature walk. Either way, the chances are good you will see some of the park's abundant wildlife, such as coyotes, golden eagles, buffalo, mule deer, and prairie dogs. There is good canoeing when the water is high in the Little Missouri after the ice melts in early April. *Open year-round; part of scenic drive closed Dec.–Mar. Admission charged.*

9. Little Missouri Bay Primitive State Park. *Off Rte. 22 north of Killdeer.* Few places in North Dakota offer visitors a bet-

ter opportunity for a firsthand experience of the badlands wilderness than this remote 5,300-acre park. A campground at the end of a three-mile gravel road has no electricity, but there is running water. Some 75 miles of trails for hiking and riding offer unexcelled views of the dramatically eroded landscape and Little Missouri Bay in the distance. Some of the trails are steep and call for excellent balance, plenty of stamina, and sturdy hiking boots. There is a corral where you can keep a horse, and a concession that rents horses from mid-May through September. *Open year-round.*

10. Fort Stevenson State Park. Fort Stevenson, a frontier post, was built in 1867 and named for Union Brig. Gen. Thomas G. Stevenson, who died in the Civil War. It was abandoned in 1883 after the Sioux surrendered and now lies beneath the waters of man-made Lake Sakakawea. But the wooded 437-acre park, which is located on a triangle of land projecting into the

lake, offers many attractions. Fishing for northern pike, bass, and crappies is excellent. In July the Governor's Cup Walleye Derby attracts many contestants, and in October king salmon fishing is good.

The campground, with over 100 units, offers beautiful views from the bluffs overlooking the lake. Near one of the park's two boat ramps a busy prairie dog town will charm children. A jogging trail and a quarter-mile nature trail offer opportunities to see great horned owls, pheasants, migrating eagles, songbirds, and deer. Campfire programs on wildflowers, frontier schoolteaching, geology, and other topics are scheduled. Winter sports include cross-country skiing, snowmobiling, snowshoeing, and ice fishing. July and August offer the best weather, and holidays are likely to be crowded. Houseboats, sailboats, and fishing boats are available for rent at the park's full-service marina. There are separate launch ramps for those who bring their own boats. *Open year-round; water and electricity shut off Labor Day–mid-May. Admission charged.*

11. Knife River Indian Villages National Historic Site. Centuries before Lewis and Clark wintered here in 1804–05, Hidatsa, Arikara, and Mandan Indians established themselves productively along the Missouri River in this area of prairies and rich

237

13. *The Little Missouri River brings water to a harsh land.*

14. *Mannequins portray Custer and his wife at Fort Lincoln.*

bottomland. They lived in round earthen lodges supported by wood frames. Excellent gardeners, they grew corn, squash, tobacco, beans, and sunflowers, and they hunted buffalo, deer, and elk.

As European trappers and traders pushed west, these tribes became middlemen between other Indian peoples such as the Crow, Cheyenne, Arapaho, Cree, and Dakota. Trade and prosperity increased until 1837–38, when a smallpox epidemic killed as many as 80 percent of the Indians living in this area.

In the present 1,294-acre park, an auto tour passes the remains of the largest Hidatsa village. Vestiges of lodge foundations, an entrenchment, and travois trails remain. A half-size reproduction of a lodge stands near the visitor center, where colorful beads, iron hatchets, and other trade items are displayed. Weekend guided canoe tours are popular. A checklist of birds to be seen here is available for use along the short nature trail. Cross-country skiing is popular in winter. Summertime programs include demonstrations of such tribal activities as flint shaping, hide tanning, gardening, games, and dances. *Open year-round except Thanksgiving Day, Christmas, and New Year's Day. For canoe tour reservations call (701) 745-3300.*

12 Arrowwood National Wildlife Refuge. During the dawn of life in this region, glaciers scoured out the potholes and shaped the gentle slopes that now provide a remarkably beneficial environment for a variety of wildlife—a mixture of watery marshes, wooded ravines, cropland, and extensive grassland.

Encompassing almost 16,000 acres on which 250 species of birds have been observed, this serene, uncrowded refuge also harbors a herd of about 300 deer. These shy and graceful animals are often seen along the 5½-mile Whitetail Trail, a self-guiding auto route. Colonies of inquisitive prairie dogs inhabit this route, as do mourning doves, minks, and raccoons.

In spring there are outings to a blind from which the intricate and artistic mating dances of male sharp-tailed grouse may be seen at close range. The 16-mile-long James River valley is an excellent site for observing white pelicans, Canada geese, and many duck species, including shovelers, canvasbacks, redheads, and coots. Boating and canoeing are permitted on selected waterways. Other popular activities are picking chokecherries and Juneberries and picnicking. In winter this peaceful place is ideal for cross-country skiing and ice fishing. *Open daily. For grouse-blind reservations call (701) 285-3341, mid-Mar.–mid-May only.*

13. Sully Creek State Park. This scenic, 80-acre primitive park of dramatic, sculptural landforms and the creek that runs through it are named for Gen. Alfred Sully, who came to the Dakotas in the 1860's to battle the Sioux. But the Indian fighter most associated with the area is Lt. Col. George A. Custer, who camped just south of this area with his 7th Cavalry on his way to a fateful encounter with Crazy Horse and Sitting Bull at the Little Bighorn River.

The stark and compelling beauty of this land was created by silt, sand, and clay deposited by runoff from the rising Rocky Mountains some 60 millon years ago. The colorful layers of sediment have since been revealed by the erosion of wind and water, including such watercourses as the Little Missouri River and Sully Creek. In a setting of cottonwoods and sagebrush are 30 primitive vehicle and tent sites with picnic tables and fire rings, a well house with water, and a corral where visitors can keep horses. *Open year-round.*

14. Great Plains Museum. *On Rte. 1806, 2½ miles south of Mandan.* The absorbing and imaginative collection found here is almost entirely devoted to the bitter confrontation between the Indians and white settlers that culminated in the great battles of the Little Bighorn, 1876, and Wounded Knee, 1890.

What comes across most strongly is the extraordinary contrast between the opposing nations—factory-made uniforms versus Sioux ghost-dance shirts trimmed with mink cuffs; the whole range of U.S. Army paraphernalia versus a few rifles used by the Indians; scenes of Lt. Col. George A. Custer and his wife Libbie at their Fort Lincoln home juxtaposed with the great Sioux leader Sitting Bull emerging from a lodge built of logs.

The life-size dioramas are the museum's most impressive feature. Additional dioramas, which show Blackfoot, Yankton Sioux, Mandan, and other warriors, were carefully derived from the paintings of the Swiss artist Karl Bodmer. Particularly striking is a figure of a Hidatsa brave wearing an ornate headdress of magpie and wild turkey feathers with horsehair embellishments. In all, this is a complete, clearly explained, and thoroughly interesting exposition of the subject matter. *Open daily Apr.–Oct. Admission charged.*

15. Beaver Lake State Park. This 290-acre park on the west bank of Beaver Lake preserves a fragment of the landscape as it must have looked since time immemorial—a setting of water fringed by box elder, chokecherry, and Juneberry giving way to prairie uplands.

The park, created with the help of a WPA work force during the arduous times of drought and depression in the 1930's, has over the years developed into an attractive secluded site.

Apart from providing opportunities for general outdoor activities, Beaver Lake Park is an excellent place to observe a surprisingly large variety of birds—whistling swans, pelicans, grebes, and cormorants can be seen here, as well as throngs of warblers, finches, and migratory waterfowl. Other wildlife and geological features are signed along a nature trail.

There are 25 trailer campsites with water and electricity situated around an oval that used to be a popular local racetrack, and 17 primitive sites as well. For anglers there are pike and carp to be had in the lake, and an area is set aside for swimmers. On summer weekends campfire programs are held in the evening in a natural amphitheater overlooking the water. But holiday weekends are best avoided. The winter sports are ice fishing, cross-country skiing, and snowmobiling. *Open year-round; campground open Apr.–Sept. Admission charged.*

16. Fort Ransom State Park. Indians and Norwegian settlers once fought bitterly for control of this region of hilly grassland and wooded slopes. Today a 900-acre park that sits along the Sheyenne River preserves much of the scenic beauty that was noted by the area's first farmers.

A road leads to a centrally located vantage point with a fine view of the park and surrounding farmland. For further explorations there are facilities for canoeing, horseback riding, and hiking. Wildlife is plentiful, particularly white-tailed deer, and bird-watching is exceptionally rewarding, not only for such fowl as pheasants, partridges, and wild turkeys but also many species of songbirds, shorebirds, and raptors. The river is lined with American elm, bur oak, and green ash, and there is an ongoing project in the northwestern part of the park to reestablish the native prairie grasses.

The park's camping facilities are still limited and primitive, but they do include a canoe campsite and, for those who bring their own horses, a corral with stables. In winter there are 50 miles of groomed snowmobile trails. *Open year-round. Admission charged.*

17. Fort Abercrombie State Historic Site. *On Rte. 81.* Established in 1858 at the approximate head of navigation on the Red River of the North, this outpost served to protect the northwestern frontier and guard the Montana gold fields. In 1862 its soldiers and more than 150 homesteaders withstood a six-week siege by Sioux Indians. Afterwards the post was strengthened with log blockhouses and palisades. As the Indians were pushed farther west the fort's importance diminished, and it was abandoned in 1877.

The only surviving original building is a guardhouse. But three new blockhouses and a palisade have been reconstructed on the site, and signs indicate where officers' quarters, storehouses, traders' post, and other structures once stood. Cassette players can be rented for a detailed account of the fort's history.

A small museum nearby displays objects of local significance, including an outstanding collection of articles brought to the region by the Norwegian settlers. Among them are decorated wooden trunks and other household items. The violence of frontier life is represented by stone tomahawks, arrowheads, padlocks, and pistols found at the site along with bullets fired into the fort by Indians. Of particular interest are an 1872 Remington-Rider rolling block rifle with bayonet, a rare 1861 Red River oxcart, and a leather mail pouch used by Pony Express riders.

Ceremonial ornaments and a buffalo robe recall the Indian way of life. Items from the Civil War and both world wars round off the collection, together with such engaging oddments as a chair saved from the Great Chicago Fire and a vintage Zenith movie projector. *Open mid-May–mid-Sept. Admission charged.*

17. *Blockhouses and palisade (since reconstructed) fortified the old trading post.*

South Dakota

Inviting parks and forbidding Badlands merge here with memories of trappers, traders, homesteaders, and the indomitable Sioux.

The many parks include shady retreats, lakes, and a variety of hiking trails. A vast wildlife refuge offers prairies, marshlands, streams, and ponds where the birding is unexcelled.

In the Badlands, wind, water, and time have created some 240,000 acres of colorful buttes, pinnacles, plateaus, valleys, and ridges; the distant geological past is further recalled in a petrified forest and two ancient caves. More recent human history is represented by artifacts of the Indians whose territory this was, and the buildings, tools, utensils, and weapons of the soldiers, traders, and homesteaders who ultimately prevailed on the prairie.

1. Petrified Park. *500 Main St., Lemmon.* Long ago tropical swamps covered the region around Lemmon. Gradual climatic and chemical changes and the passage of time turned the remnants of that distant era—trees, grasses, plants, and marine and animal life—into stone. In the 1930's O.S. Quammen, an amateur geologist, collected some of the best specimens of the petrified material for an artistic outdoor display.

The small park is studded with 100 cone-shaped pyramids ranging up to 32 feet in height and piles of "cannonballs" in graduated sizes. A grotto constructed of petrified wood contains the fossils of enormous animals, while a circular museum built of petrified logs and slabs of petrified grass houses Indian and pioneer artifacts. A turreted fairy-tale castle, built with more than 300 tons of petrified material, including tree trunks more than 30 feet tall, is especially intriguing. Teeth marks, petrified snakes, and fossilized marine life are eerily recognizable in many surfaces. All together, the multiplicity of forms and the incredible range of colors in the petrified materials make this a fascinating place to see. *Park open year-round; museum open mid-May–mid-Sept.*

2. Klein Museum. *West of Mobridge on Rte. 12.* This museum, with its excellent collection of artifacts from the area's pioneer days, was the inspiration of Jake

4. This gurgling stream adds its muted voice to the mysterious character of the park.

Klein, an early South Dakota homesteader. One of the more colorful features is the trapper's shack, complete with a skillet and coffeepot on a wood-burning stove and a life-size model of a bundled-up trapper standing as if to greet you. You can also explore the old-time offices of a dentist and a doctor, and Jake's Room, which displays items from Klein's own homesteading days.

In addition the museum has a good assortment of pioneer tools and an exhibit of Indian artifacts, including headdresses and beaded bags. Vintage vehicles and heavy machinery are on view in another building, and a little white one-room schoolhouse is open for inspection.

Just west of Mobridge, on Highway 20, you'll find the grave of Sitting Bull, marked by a huge stone sculpture of this Sioux medicine man and leader. Nearby, overlooking Lake Oahe, is a monument to Sacajawea, the young Shoshone woman who in 1804–06 served as a guide and interpreter for Lewis and Clark on their expedition to the Pacific Coast. *Museum open Mon.–Fri. and P.M. weekends, May–Sept.; Mon., Wed.–Fri. and P.M. weekends Apr., May, Oct. Admission charged.*

3. Fort Sisseton State Park. The establishment of Fort Sisseton in 1864 followed the Sioux rebellion against broken treaties and the influx of settlers on their lands. In service for 25 years, the fort was finally closed in June 1889, just a few months before South Dakota became a state.

On the spacious, grassy grounds dotted with shade trees are 17 major buildings, including officers' quarters, a bakery, stable, library-schoolhouse, and adjutant's office—some inside the sod ramparts and some outside. Many of the structures have now been restored, and you can take a self-guiding tour through the entire park.

The visitor center and a museum are housed in the North Barracks, designed as living quarters for 150 soldiers. Picnic areas and primitive camping facilities are provided. *Park open year-round; visitor center open P.M. daily, May–Labor Day.*

4. Sica Hollow State Park. This peaceful park is in a deep, 1¼-mile-long winding hollow almost invisible from the surrounding hills and prairies and sheltered from winter winds. The hollow was a special place to the Sisseton Indians, and its entrance was a guarded secret. According to their legend, North Wind "tried every opening into the Hollow, but the great trees held back his white breath." Deer and antelope, the story goes on, "slipped into the folds of the hollow...where they found open water and salt when all the earth above was hard with ice."

To the Indians there was also something sinister about the place, and they named it *sica*, or evil. Along the half-mile Trail of the Spirits, a registered national recreation walking trail, you will see murmuring, cascading streams, reddish bogs, and the glow of swamp gas, all of which suggested to the Indians the presence of

spirits. A viewpoint and parking area near the west entrance provides an excellent trailhead for a hiking or horseback-riding trip down into the hollow. A picnic ground is equipped with tables and grills. Primitive camping is allowed for groups only; for permission call (605) 448-5701. *Open year-round.*

5. Blue Cloud Abbey. *Twelve miles west of Milbank off Rte. 12.* The doors are never locked at this quiet, peaceful abbey, a Benedictine monastery founded in 1950. Guests are welcome to come here for rest

and contemplation and, with reservations, may stay the night or longer. The monks have vowed to live by the rule of St. Benedict, written by the saint in the sixth century and emphasizing the importance of prayer and work in the monastic life.

The monks labored for 17 years in building the abbey. Today they are involved in making candles, keeping bees (honey is sold at the abbey), and tending the gardens that provide much of their food. In a workshop open to visitors, they create ornate and colorful vestments for churches of many different denominations throughout the world.

On the outside wall of the monastery is an excellent mosaic of the Virgin Mary.

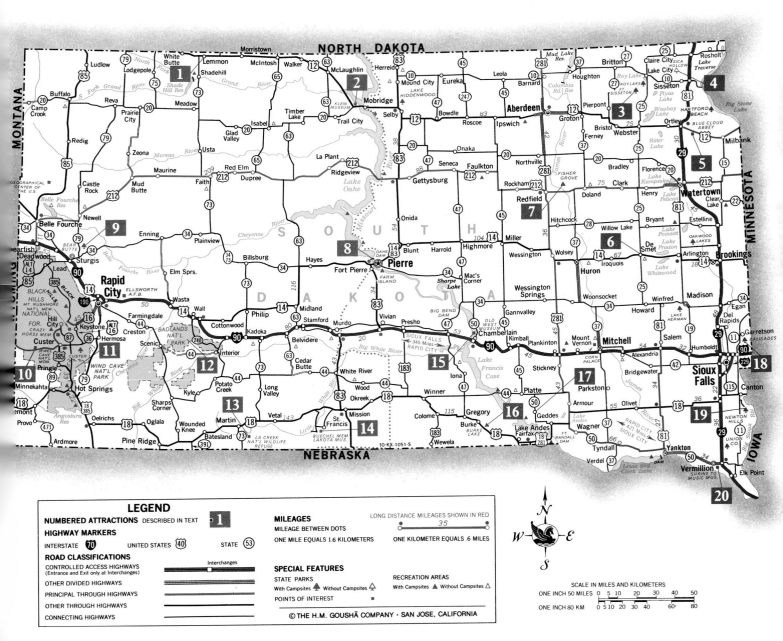

Contemporary stained glass enhances the church's sanctuary, and current artwork hangs in the lower lounge. A room has been adapted as a chapel for Protestants; however, everyone is welcome in the abbey church. The abbey also houses the American Indian Culture Research Center, created by members of 14 midwestern reservations to preserve the heritage and beliefs of the first Americans.

The home cooking provided here, the absence of television and radio, and the caring atmosphere make even a short visit memorable. *Open year-round.*

6. De Smet. This is the *Little Town on the Prairie* made famous by Laura Ingalls Wilder in the *Little House* books describing her childhood here in the 1880's. For a self-guiding map of the town locating the places she wrote about, go to the Laura Ingalls Wilder Memorial Society, which is headquartered in the Surveyor's House (at the corner of First Street and Olivet Avenue) and has a receptionist present from the first of June through September. The map leads you to 16 restored places and sites, including the Loftus store, the church that "Pa helped build," the home where Laura and Almanzo Ingalls lived in 1894, and the family homestead site 1½ miles out of town.

The society gives guided tours of the Surveyor's House, where the family lived for a while, and the Ingalls House, which was built by Laura's father in 1887 after she married. It is furnished with many original pieces, including the "chest that Pa made," and displays family memorabilia. *Tours given May 30–Sept. 15; in May by appointment. Admission charged.*

7. Fisher Grove State Park. Along the banks of the winding James River, this pleasant grove is a welcome oasis in the midst of the seemingly endless prairies, its cottonwoods, willows, and box elders fringing the riverbanks and sheltering the picnic and camping grounds.

The 360-acre park honors Frank I. Fisher, an early settler who in 1878 purchased 80 acres of land here along the James for 40 cents an acre with the intention of establishing a settlement. Shortly afterward, however, the railroad bypassed the area, and the few buildings that had

been constructed were torn down and used for firewood. A three-quarter-mile nature trail winds through the park and leads to the location of the original settlement. An 1884 schoolhouse, fully restored, serves as the visitor center. A boat ramp is provided for canoeists. *Open year-round. Admission charged May–Sept.*

8. Robinson State Museum. *500 E. Capitol Ave., Pierre.* For a sweeping view of South Dakota history—from the times of its early Indian cultures up through World War II—this small museum is splendid. The most important displays are those of the Sioux culture; among them are a life-size diorama of a campsite with tepees and a magnificent streamlined wood carving of a galloping horse (circa 1875). The carving was included in an American Indian art show sent to England in 1976. An exhibit of special historic interest is the lead plate that was placed on a bluff overlooking the Missouri River by the Verendrye brothers in 1743, claiming this area for France.

Other displays graphically show how the lives of South Dakota's people have been affected by the fur trade, the gold rush, the coming of the railroad, and military service. *Open Mon.–Sat. and P.M. Sun. except legal holidays.*

9. Bear Butte State Park. The centerpiece of this park is a solitary, cone-shaped mountain that rises 1,200 feet above the plains. Named Bear Mountain by the Sioux, it was regarded as a holy place by both the Sioux and the Cheyennes. Red Cloud, Sitting Bull, and other Indian leaders paid visits here, and an Indian conference was held at Bear Butte in 1857 to discuss the encroachment of white settlers and gold prospectors in the region.

For more than a century the mountain has also drawn scientists from far and wide. Among geologists it is a famous example of a laccolith. Formed millions of years ago by a great upheaval of molten rock, it is a volcano that never erupted. The mountain, also a prominent landmark for pioneers, was registered as a national natural landmark in 1965.

For ambitious hikers, a national recreation trail leads from the parking lot to the summit. A less strenuous trail crosses the

10. As is the case with snowflakes, no two calcite crystals are identical in form.

grassy lower slopes. You can see a few buffalo grazing in a pasture near the base. A printed trail guide for the 1,845-acre park is available at the visitor center, which has displays of homesteader and Indian artifacts. Camping and boating facilities are found at Bear Butte Lake just across the highway. *Open May–mid-Sept.*

10. Jewel Cave National Monument.

The star attraction in this 1,275-acre park is the dazzlingly beautiful cave filled with colorful, jewellike calcite crystals. Located in Hell's Canyon, it was discovered by prospectors in 1900 and declared a national monument in 1908. Exploration has proved it to be the nation's second largest cave system: more than 73 miles of passageways have been mapped so far.

Visitors to the cave have a choice of three tours. The popular hour-long Scenic Tour follows a paved half-mile route, with aluminum stairways and handrails, and is specially illuminated to show the rich colors of the crystals. The more difficult Historic Tour is unpaved, with ladderlike steps and no lighting (visitors carry lanterns), and takes almost two hours. Reservations are required for the Spelunking Tour, part of which is covered on hands and knees. But it is carefully supervised, and no previous caving experience is needed. To avoid long waits, arrive first thing in the morning or visit early or late in the season. Wear low-heeled walking shoes and a sweater.

The visitor center has an exhibit room displaying the incredible types of crystal formations found in the cavern.

Few people stop to explore the terrain of this ruggedly magnificent park, which enjoys moderate winters and cool summers. In addition to Hell's Canyon and Lithograph Canyon, the landscape includes hills and ravines, springs and meadows, and stands of ponderosa pines. Wildflowers are rampant in spring and early summer, and wildlife is abundant. *Monument and visitor center open daily year-round. Cave tours May–Sept.; spelunking June–Aug.; admission charged for cave.*

11. Wind Cave National Park.

The cave here, named for the strong breeze created by the difference in atmospheric pressure inside and out, is a 40-mile maze of chambers and passageways. It is noted for the excellent examples of boxwork, a strange, honeycomblike formation of limestone, and for other decorative deposits such as frostwork, flowstone, popcorn, and delicate helictite bushes.

Cave tours of varying difficulty and length are possible. Wear good walking shoes and a jacket. Reservations are recommended for the special Candlelight Tour, which ventures through unpaved and unlighted parts of the cave, and they are required for the strenuous four-hour spelunking tour.

The 28,000-acre park is a wildlife refuge, with great stretches of open prairie grassland interspersed with mixed hardwood and ponderosa pine forests. One might see buffalo, elk, pronghorn antelope, coyotes, mule deer, badgers, and prairie dogs. Birds that find refuge here include owls, grouse, magpies, and golden eagles.

The park has a large campground and amphitheater, two self-guiding nature trails, and a picnic area. Bicycles are permitted on the roadways. *Park open year-round. No cave tours on Thanksgiving Day, Christmas, and New Year's Day; admission charged for tours.*

12. Badlands National Park.

One can imagine the dismay with which travelers eyed this 50-mile stretch of seeming moonscape that appears so abruptly on the grassy plain. The cliffs, gorges, soaring spires, knife-edged ridges, flat-topped mesas, and fossil-filled canyons, carved and etched by millions of years of rain, wind, and frost, stand as a classic example of the effects of erosion.

Most visitors to the Badlands simply drive the scenic 40-mile loop along Highway 240. But for those willing to venture off this well-worn path there are many little-known spots to enjoy. The park encompasses nearly a quarter-million acres, and some 64,000 acres of the most spectacular landscape are a roadless wilderness

12. Here's dramatic testimony to the eternal forces of erosion. Colorful viewpoints (left) are abundant and varied in this landscape.

area open only to hikers and backpackers.

The Cedar Pass Visitor Center, at the eastern end of the park, schedules several ranger-guided nature walks, evening slide lectures, and stargazing programs. Guided tours and other programs are also offered at the White River Visitor Center, located in the South Unit of the park, which includes part of the Pine Ridge Indian Reservation. Bighorn sheep, buffalo, pronghorn antelope, and mule deer roam the Badlands. White-throated swifts and cliff swallows nest in the cliff faces, and golden eagles build on the buttes. Junipers, cottonwoods, and wildflowers manage to survive the extremes of weather. There are two campgrounds with limited facilities; water is available at only one of them. *Park open year-round; Cedar Pass Visitor Center open daily except Christmas and New Year's Day; White River Visitor Center open mid-June–Labor Day. Admission charged in summer.*

13. Lacreek National Wildlife Refuge.

Off Rte. 73. This 16,250-acre refuge, a mixture of sand-covered dunes, marshland, streams, and ponds, offers protection to some 260 species of birds, many of them migrating and nesting waterfowl, and more than 50 kinds of mammals. Its name was derived from Lake Creek, the spring-fed stream that provides much of the water for the refuge.

Trumpeter swans, white pelicans, cor-

morants, Canada geese, and many kinds of ducks nest here annually, along with sandpipers, pied-billed grebes, coots, and long-billed curlews. From early March to the end of May, migrating birds gather here by the thousands, and again from late August until the middle of November.

Visitors can drive through the refuge on the gravel roadway. There is also a short bird walk. Mosquitoes are numerous in summer, so bring along insect repellent. Adjacent to the refuge is the White River Recreation Area, which offers fishing, boating, swimming, camping, and picnicking facilities. Fishing is also permitted within the refuge at Pond 10 and Cedar Creek Pond. *Open year-round.*

14. Buechel Memorial Lakota Museum.

350 S. Oak St., St. Francis. The small but fascinating museum is part of St. Francis Mission on the Rosebud Indian Reservation. The museum was established as a memorial to Father Eugene Buechel, a Jesuit missionary who spent a great deal of his life among the Dakota (or Lakota) Sioux and died in 1954. In addition to collecting and preserving the artifacts of their culture, he helped to preserve their language, writing three books and compiling 30,000 entries of Dakota words that formed the basis for a dictionary.

The museum's collection includes elaborate tribal robes, headdresses, jewelry, tools, hunting knives, bows and arrows

and other weapons, musical instruments, horse gear, and games. Some of the pieces date back to the 1850's.

Father Buechel left two other valuable legacies: 2,300 photographs that he took during his years among the Sioux and a collection of Plains plant specimens that he gathered, mounted, and cataloged, noting the Dakotas' use of them. *Open daily Memorial Day–Labor Day.*

15. Old West Museum. *Chamberlain.*

Take Exit 260 off I-90; follow sign. An enormous range of items from the 1860's to the 1930's fills this six-building museum, all of it collected by Gene and Alice Olson with the help of their son, Greg.

Represented in one building is a typical old-time main street: here you'll see a barbershop, a telephone and telegraph office, a blacksmith's shop, dry goods store, veterinarian's office, apothecary's shop, and post office, with all their accoutrements. Also shown are dolls, toys, household items, firearms, a variety of jukeboxes, two Seeburg pianos and other coin-operated melody makers, and hundreds of old photographs, postcards, posters, and related ephemera.

Examples of Sioux beadwork, stone implements, and buckskin garments are among the Indian artifacts on display.

Exhibits in separate buildings include automobiles, tractors, farm tools, carriages, sleighs, and an old schoolroom. Further reminders of early days on the prairie are a buffalo and a Texas longhorn steer that share a sturdy corral. *Open daily Apr.–Oct. Admission charged.*

16. Burke Lake Recreation Area. *Two miles east of Burke off Rte. 18.* This quiet, pleasant 206-acre park centering around a small, tree-fringed lake offers a welcome respite from the surrounding prairie. Although primarily a recreation site, it accommodates wildlife as well, and visitors here will see many species of resident and migratory birds, including partridges, turkeys, pheasants, and grouse.

The lake has a sandy swimming beach and is ideal for boating, sailing, and canoeing. Picnic tables and stone fireplaces are set under the trees along the shore, and shady campgrounds are within easy walking distance. A hiking trail follows the shoreline and wanders through the woodlands. In winter, hardy sportsmen

15. *If you don't see it here, try one of the other five buildings of memorabilia.*

fish for perch through the ice, and cross-country skiers enjoy the heavy snows. *Open year-round. Admission charged.*

17. Papineau Trading Post. *Geddes.* The trading post, a 20- by 30-foot log cabin, was built in 1857 by Cuthbert Ducharme, a French-Canadian fur trader, on the bank of the Missouri River a few miles from Geddes. It was relocated at this small turn-of-the-century railroad town when the first site was flooded by the construction of a dam. The room now serving as a lobby was a later addition.

Soldiers, cowboys, boatmen, and westward-bound travelers stopped at the post for supplies, including liquor. Legend has it that Ducharme, who was nicknamed Papineau (meaning pap water, or whiskey), poured the whiskey into a dishpan and tied a tin cup to it, allowing his customers to help themselves—a full cup for 25 cents. Ducharme was also known for his skill at handling a gun, and the records of the U.S. Army Corps of Engineers state that the original Ducharme cemetery contained 27 graves, 14 of which were unidentified. Several of the tombstones have been removed to the trading post in Geddes; they are considered fine examples of 19th-century mortuary art.

The original log structure contains the accoutrements of a fur trader's life in the second half of the 19th century: traps, knives, guns, a kerosene lamp, dishes, pots and pans, a table, some rawhide chairs, and a liquor barrel, plus Indian relics. *Open daily mid-May–mid-Sept. Admission free but donations encouraged.*

18. Palisades State Park. This strikingly beautiful park of gorges, vertical cliffs, and dramatic rock formations borders both sides of Split Rock Creek. According to Indian legend, the sheer-walled canyon through which the stream flows was created when a god from the spirit world threw a tomahawk to earth.

The massive layers of quartzite in the cliffs, formed some 1,200 million years ago, are interspersed with beds of pipestone, or catlinite, a soft red stone held sacred by the Indians. There are shallow diggings here where Indians once quarried the stone to fashion into pipe bowls.

The creek, which has several rapids and

18. *Here are rock, water, and growing plants as only nature could arrange them.*

quiet pools, provides excellent swimming, fishing, and canoeing. The 111-acre park has a tree-shaded campground and two picnic areas overlooking the picturesque stream. Hiking trails follow its course, wandering along 80-foot-high cliffs, which are sometimes used as training areas for rappellers. During the summer a park naturalist offers a junior ranger program for youngsters, outdoor cooking classes, nature walks, and evening hikes. *Open year-round. Admission charged.*

19. Newton Hills State Park. Newton Hills is the southern end of a chain of hills named Coteau des Prairies (Hills of the Prairies) by early French explorers. Stretching for some 200 miles and rising more than 2,000 feet above sea level, the ridge was formed by glacial deposits.

The park, in a beautiful wooded setting, has a bridle trail and several hiking trails, some with swinging bridges spanning small ravines. Many of the trees and shrubs are identified along the Coteau and Woodland trails.

More than 200 species of birds have been observed in the park, whose 948 acres also harbor white-tailed deer, marmots, and other wildlings. Pine-shaded campgrounds, picnic shelters, and hand-built stone fireplaces are provided, as well as game courts. Man-made Lake Lakota, at the southeast border of the park, has a

sandy swimming beach, a boat ramp, and an adjacent picnic ground. *Open year-round. Admission charged.*

20. The Shrine to Music Museum. *On the University of South Dakota campus, Vermillion.* Professor Arne B. Larson has gathered more than 2,500 musical instruments from around the world and donated them to the university. They include instruments of all kinds—American, European, and also nonwestern—thoughtfully grouped and handsomely displayed.

There are some marvelous oddities, such as a zither in the shape of a crocodile, a trombone whose bell is a dragon's head, and an ancient harp so elegantly arched that one wonders how it could be plucked. These instruments, both ancient and modern, are valued not only for documenting the history of music in various cultures of the world, but also for revealing the imagination and superb craftsmanship of those who created them.

The teaching collection on the first floor is also open to the public. Visitors to this gallery might be fortunate enough to meet Professor Larson, who often comes to this section, and with luck, hear him demonstrate some of the more unusual instruments in the collection. *Open Mon.–Sat. and P.M. Sun. except major holidays. Admission free but donations requested.*

Nebraska

Indians, pioneers, and some wondrous animals—now extinct—have left their mark on the broad plains and sculptured landscapes here.

A state park reveals a rock shelter where Indians lived for some 3,000 years, and a national monument discloses the remains of incredible animals long vanished from the earth; elsewhere are images incised on stone by prehistoric artists. Fort Hartsuff, built to protect settlers, is a reminder of more recent history.

More heartening are the honors bestowed on a chief who won major legal rights for his people, and an impressive reproduction of the Sioux prayer circle created by an enlightened white poet.

One can see a section of the Oregon Trail and some of nature's mighty sculpture that beguiled pioneers on their westward course. A restored pioneer village, a community made famous by a Pulitzer Prize-winning author, and a great old mansion invite inspection. The days of waterpower are splendidly represented by two historic mills. Here too are some beautiful and refreshing recreation areas.

1. Toadstool Park. *From Rte. 2 go west two miles on gravel road to railroad track; turn north and continue eight miles.* Historically called Little Badlands, this remote, unstaffed area is one of the most spectacular such settings outside of Badlands National Park. Dramatic cliffs and gullies plunge among domes of clay some 100 feet high, creating the illusion that you are standing amid a toy model of a vast mountain range. Even more intriguing are the rock toadstools that give the park its name. Hard, rocky material was left balanced on slender columns when the soft clay beneath eroded more quickly. Several are over 20 feet high.

These clay beds were deposited here by ancient rivers as much as 40 million years ago. The erosion that sculpted them has been going on for nearly a million years—since the beginning of the Ice Age—and the relentless process continues.

A sod house stands near the picnic area, and a mile-long hiking trail leads across the Badlands, where you have a good chance of seeing elk and hawks. The ground is loose and steep in places, but walking is not too difficult. Sturdy shoes are recommended. You can camp here,

but be warned it's rough and primitive, with no amenities at all. *Open year-round but may be inaccessible in wet weather.*

2. Chadron State Park. With a mixture of prairie, broken ridges, sandstone buttes, stands of ponderosa pine, and occasional small streams, the scenery here in the Pine Ridge region has a variety and beauty unlike any other part of Nebraska. At an altitude of 4,000 feet the relatively low temperature and humidity are also pleasantly atypical—particularly in summer.

The approach to the park, a divided road passing through a gate flanked with serpentine brick walls, suggests an environment much too formal to be off the beaten path. The literature handed out at the gate furthers the impression, listing activities that include paddleboating, horseback riding, film programs, archery and tomahawk-throwing lessons, craft classes, "trapper's stew" campfire cookouts, swimming in a large, man-made pool, and in winter, cross-country skiing. But this park is indeed far from well-traveled highways, and the only part that receives heavy use is the campground area in midsummer. Otherwise, solitude is always a short walk away in the 840 acres here. A hiking trail winds through the park and extends for some nine miles into the surrounding national forest. The park also has five miles of scenic roads with picnic areas sited on overlooks.

The varied topography in the area contributes to an unusual diversity of plant and animal life as eastern and western species mingle. A handout lists some 70 varieties of plants, 24 kinds of mammals, and 60 species of birds. *Open year-round. Admission charged.*

3. Agate Fossil Beds National Monument. The vast open prairie here seems so stark and timeless that it doesn't take a quantum leap of the imagination to populate it with herds of the extinct mammals described at the visitor center. About 22 million years ago this was a grassy savanna that was home to great numbers of small

two-horned rhinoceroses and the tiny *Stenomylus*, a graceful, deerlike creature only two feet tall. The dominant beast was doubtless the *Dinohyus*, or "Terrible Pig," 7 feet tall and 10 feet long, with fearsome tusks in its large head. The oddest looking was the *Moropus*, with the head and neck of a horse, front legs of a rhino, hind legs of a bear, and large claws for feet.

Proof that these beasts ranged freely here lies in layers of sandstone where great numbers of fossil bones, including many complete skeletons, have been unearthed.

A narrow, mile-long blacktop path leads from the visitor center to the Carnegie and University hills, where you can see under Plexiglas covers partially excavated fossils as the paleontologist sees them during the early stages of excavation. Along the way you will cross the Niobrara River, a remnant of the waterway that scoured the valley here and exposed the fossil beds. Only about 25 percent of the fossil-bearing sediment has been quarried, and further excavations are planned.

Colorful wildflowers are sprinkled

1. *You are looking at about a million years of nature's handiwork, modeled in clay.*

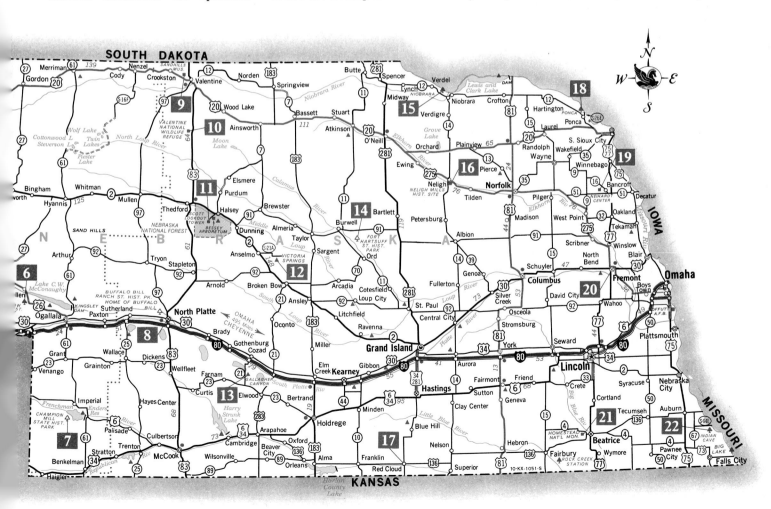

among the prairie grasses, and many are identified along the pathway. Livestock share these wide-open spaces with mule deer, pronghorns, and antelope. You may see rattlesnakes along the path; if you respect their privacy they won't bother you, but be alert. *Open daily May–Sept.; weekends only, remainder of the year.*

4. Scotts Bluff National Monument.
This bluff takes its name from a trapper who met his end here around 1828. But long before that the prominent, 800-foot-high landmark, which the Plains Indians called "the hill that is hard to go around," served as a guide for travelers, signaling the location of Mitchell Pass. Much of the history here centers around the pass, which proved to be the best way through these steep, eroded bluffs and became part of the Oregon Trail.

Thousands of westward-bound families came through here, and the ruts made by their wagons can still be seen. At the visitor center, photographs, artifacts, slide presentations, and living-history demonstrations help to dramatize the westward passage through this forbidding land.

The bluff's summit is accessible by road and by a steep hiking trail that's better walked down than climbed. From the north overlook there's a spectacular view of the North Platte Valley, with Chimney Rock on the horizon to the east and Laramie Peak to the west. Part of the Oregon Trail can be seen from the south overlook.

Even more compelling than the view is the stark evidence of the power of erosion. By standing on the bluff's highest point and extending an imaginary line to the tops of the surrounding hills, you can establish the level of the original mile-high grassy plains that were once here. Everything from where you stand down to the rugged land below has been ground down and washed away to distant deltas, seas, and shorelines. To consider the passage of time in this context can be a humbling experience. *Open year-round. Fee to drive up bluff Apr.–Sept.*

5. Wildcat Hills Game Preserve and Recreation Area.
The stealthy, nocturnal bobcats for which the area is named are seldom seen and are now few in number. But you will probably spot some elk, deer, and buffalo venturing near the fence in the adjoining enclosed game preserve. Wild turkeys are sometimes seen; falcons, eagles, and vultures often wheel overhead.

Although the area is just off Route 71, it is not heavily used—probably because there are no lakes and streams. This makes it an excellent choice for those seeking solitude and natural beauty.

In the recreation area there are several steep-walled canyons laced with about three miles of hiking trails. The trails cross two footbridges and lead to three shelters built of native stone in the early 1930's by the Civilian Conservation Corps. Particularly inviting is the group shelter, with large picnic tables, two fireplaces, and a spectacular view down a canyon to the plain with the great monolith of Scotts Bluff far in the distance. Scatterings of ponderosa pine bring accents of green to the brown, arid ridges and canyon walls. Here too are mountain mahogany trees, rare in Nebraska, along with yucca, cactus, grasses, and wildflowers.

If you're pulling a trailer, leave it in the parking lot, at least until you explore the area. The roads are rough, and several are dead-end with little or no room to turn a trailer around. Sledding and snowtubing are popular here in winter. *Open year-round. Admission charged.*

6. Ash Hollow State Historical Park.
Archeological evidence indicates that the freshwater springs in this canyon have attracted visitors for some 8,000 years, including Plains Indians who used a rock shelter here for nearly 3,000 years. Even earlier, skeletal remains show, prehistoric mastodons and other mammals that roamed these plains found their way here.

More precise are the records of the pioneers who sought out this well-watered oasis with shady groves of ash trees as a place to rest, refresh their livestock, and repair their wagons and other trail-worn gear. The visitor center features relevant displays, an audiovisual presentation, and literature on the site. A short walk takes you to the rock shelter, and a steep paved path leads down the bluff to the spring itself, reputed to have the best water on all the Overland Trail.

Wagon trains entered the hollow from Windlass Hill about 2¼ miles to the south, and their tracks can still be seen. Another exhibition center there provides historic background on the challenge of the hill, and a covered wagon shows the size and weight of the equipment that had to be handled on this steep grade.

Apart from the historical interest of the site, the 1,000 acres of upland prairie here are brightened by wildflowers in their season. From late November until March, bald and golden eagles winter at nearby Lake McConaughy and frequently use the updrafts at Ash Hollow to reach their cruising altitude. On U.S. 26 east of Ash

Hollow you will see cowboy boots upside down on the fence posts. No one has offered a satisfactory explanation for this curious Nebraska custom. *Grounds open year-round; visitor center open Memorial Day–Labor Day. Admission charged.*

7. Champion Mill State Historical Park.

Champion. In the 19th century small feed and flour mills often changed owners as the local economy changed and were frequently remodeled as machinery wore out and improved equipment became available. This mill, built in 1893, is no exception; it stands today as the last functional water-powered mill in Nebraska.

The three-story, white clapboard structure, the 10-acre millpond, and seven acres of land were taken over by the state in 1969, the year after the mill stopped commercial operation. Most of the original machinery has been removed. But the penstock and turbine are in place, and if the pond's water level is high enough, the mill can still work. When the operator turns a control that resembles a ship's wheel to tighten the main drive belt, the

6. A "soddie" built in recent times memorializes the ingenuity of the early pioneers. The Nebraskan custom of displaying old boots is less explicable.

whole complex of belts, shafts, and pulleys starts moving, and the ingenuity involved in putting one power source to many uses is clearly evident.

A small milling machine has been installed and is run by the turbine. Milling demonstrations can be given on request, and bags of whole-wheat flour are for sale.

From the beginning the millpond has been used for recreation. It was at its most popular in the 1920's, when it boasted a boathouse and diving tower. Today the facilities are less elaborate, but the pond can be used for fishing, swimming, boating, and skating, and there are camping and picnic areas along the shore. The site attracts waterfowl and other birds. *Grounds open year-round. Mill open Memorial Day–Labor Day. Admission charged.*

8. Lincoln County Historical Museum.

2403 N. Buffalo Bill Ave., North Platte. To contemplate the small collection of restored frontier-era buildings on the museum grounds here is to sense the feeling of isolation and interdependence that the early settlers must have had. And here too is the urge to grow. The founders of the museum have plans and high hopes for creating a complete frontier town, just as their forebears worked to provide more amenities for their growing communities. The structures now include a depot, Pony Express building, army headquarters, log homestead, and pioneer house. A church and schoolhouse have appropriately furnished interiors, and a barn is filled with farm and ranch equipment.

In the museum building itself the displays recall many aspects of pioneer life on the plains. Weapons, Indian artifacts, tools, and barbed wire attest to the more demanding tasks; while gentler pursuits are represented by fashions, jewelry, musical instruments, toys, artworks, and room settings. Also there are replicas of a post office, doctor's office, judge's chambers, barber and beauty shop, telephone switchboard, and a country store. The most unusual re-creation is a World War II-era canteen that provided hospitality and entertainment for the men on passing troop trains.

Most of the objects were donated by local residents, which accounts for the aura of informal charm. The museum is likely to be crowded during Nebraskaland

Days, the third week in June. *Open Memorial Day–Labor Day. Admission free but donations accepted.*

9. Sandhills Museum. *On Rte. 20 near the west edge of Valentine.*

It is hard to think of anything that at one time or another does not become a "collectible." Here in the unprepossessing metal shed of Sawyer's Sandhills Museum can be seen the result of one man's lifelong interest in Americana and antique automobiles.

Such rare and all-but-forgotten makes as Patterson, Flanders, Jeffery, Imperial, Rattler, and a spiffy 1928 Whippet roadster are on display, as well as a one-cylinder Cadillac and a two-cylinder Buick, and all are in running condition.

Few collectors of Americana can resist Indian artifacts and old firearms, and Mr. G. M. Sawyer is no exception. Among the weapons are the proud products of Remington, Smith and Wesson, Colt, and Winchester. This area's ranching and farming interests are represented by equipment and a stuffed two-headed calf. There are also displays of clothing, dishes, lamps, pianos, and music boxes, including a model reputed to be the first one made in America. An early jukebox opens a curtain on a miniature animated band that plays along. *Open daily Memorial Day–Labor Day. Admission charged.*

10. Valentine National Wildlife Refuge.

The rolling dunes that give the entire Sandhills region of north-central Nebraska its name were created by deposits of windblown sand from an ancient seabed to the west. Native grasses invaded the dunes, the water table rose, marshes and lakes were formed, and the grass became even more abundant.

The unusual environment was threatened by settlers who drained the marshes to obtain more cropland. But in 1935 this refuge of some 70,000 acres was established to preserve a part of the Sandhills, with its unique character. In 1976 it became a national natural landmark.

Since the refuge was created primarily for the preservation of wildlife, anyone with an interest in nature will find it a fascinating place to visit. Trails for hiking or horseback riding lead to the more remote areas and to some of the lakes, nine of which are open to fishermen. Among the animals occasionally seen are pronghorn antelope, white-tailed and mule deer, coyotes, and badgers.

The most compelling attractions are the great flights of waterfowl that take refuge here. In fall and spring, up to 300,000 migrating ducks may inhabit the refuge. Most prevalent are teals, mallards, pintails, shovelers, and gadwalls; but many other species can be seen, including the trumpeter swan, once nearly extinct.

Flocks of wild turkeys may be seen, and shorebirds are abundant. Pheasants range on the higher ground, and there are blinds from which the intricate mating dances of the grouse and the prairie chicken can be observed. *Open year-round.*

11. Bessey Arboretum and Scott Lookout Tower, Nebraska National Forest. *Off Rte. 2 two miles west of Halsey.* Even native Nebraskans find it strange to come upon a huge, sprawling forest in the middle of the otherwise bleak Sandhills prairie; and indeed, these woods are unusual and have their own special beauty, for they are man-made.

The Nebraska National Forest was established by presidential proclamation in 1902 at the urging of Dr. Charles Bessey, a professor of botany at the University of Nebraska, who believed that forests could survive on the plains. In April 1903, 85 acres were planted with ponderosa pine, eastern red cedar, and jack pine. Today more than 22,000 acres of planted woodlands flourish on the 90,000 acres of this national forest property.

At the inviting, spacious Bessey Arboretum, which was established to demonstrate the wide variety of plants that can survive in the Sandhills area, more than 100 species are identified for visitors.

The road through the arboretum continues on to a high bluff and the Scott Lookout Tower, a fire-watch station offering splendid views of the rolling countryside. When there's a ranger on duty, the tower can be climbed. But even the view from the base is well worth the drive.

The arboretum offers campgrounds, a picnic area, canoeing in the Middle Loup River, and a swimming pool. A three-mile hiking trail leads from the campgrounds to the lookout tower. Backpack camping is generally allowed, and in winter the

14. *High-flying flag over the parade ground proclaimed the fort as a bastion of order on a wild frontier. Stable, below, housed the horsepower for the escort wagons.*

area is open for snowmobiling and cross-country skiing. *Arboretum open year-round. Tower open summer weekends.*

12. Victoria Springs State Recreation Area. The history of this picturesque 70-acre park capsulizes the rapid social change on the plains in the late 19th and early 20th century. Settlers first came in the early 1870's, an era represented here by two rough-hewn log cabins; one served as the first post office in Custer County.

The pioneers endured devastating grasshopper infestations, Sioux Indian uprisings, and a range war with cattlemen. But the next generation lived quite a different life. A flourishing health resort grew up around the small lake and natural springs here, complete with a large bathhouse and a plant that bottled not only the "medicinal" local mineral waters but also champagne and soda pop.

Today the remnants of this commercial era are gone, and the area has returned to its natural beauty. Fishing is allowed in the lake and in Victoria Creek, where trout is the common catch. Paddleboats can be rented, but swimming is prohibited. Herons may be observed from the shady lakeside picnic area.

A real treasure is a one-room schoolhouse in use from 1889 until the 1960's. Wall maps, books, and folded flag look as they did when the last teacher locked up. Borrow the key at the park office. *Open year-round. Admission charged.*

13. Gallagher Canyon State Recreation Area. *Off Rte. 21.* This secluded camping and picnic area on a small lake is truly far off the beaten path. It is reached only by a labyrinthine but well-marked journey down winding backcountry roads, including one that cuts through a cornfield.

Once you get there you'll be on your own; the park is unstaffed. The rustic facilities include shady picnic sites, a dirt boat-launching ramp, a swimming area, and a large, grassy campground. Fishing is permitted in the lake, which is part of the area's water supply system. Catfish, white bass, and walleye are likely catches.

Many kinds of birds are attracted to the area by the abundance of wild berries and grapes. Orioles, cardinals, finches, blue jays, magpies, and others may be seen flitting through the cover of cedar, ash, cottonwood, and Russian olive trees. *Open year-round.*

14. Fort Hartsuff State Historical Park.

The frontier army post was established in 1874 to protect settlers and friendly Pawnees from the Teton Sioux. Of the original main buildings, nine still stand, stationed around a spacious, grassy parade. The two others are to be rebuilt.

With gravel more readily available than lumber, most of the buildings were made of grout—which was scribed to give it the more fitting appearance of stone. Such symbolism was important: the soldiers organized an expedition to Long Pine, some 70 miles to the north, to cut a pine more than 100 feet tall for a flagpole. The flag they hoisted was 20 feet long.

Times were hard when the fort was built, and the settlers were thankful for the construction work. Close ties with civilians continued, and the fort became the social center of the Loup Valley.

The garrison had only one major encounter with the Sioux, in 1876. As more settlers moved in and the Sioux's power waned, the need for the fort diminished. It was abandoned in 1881, and the grounds eventually became farmland; but because of their solid construction, most of the buildings were left in place. Now, after considerable restoration and refurbishing, the barracks, officers' quarters, and the other buildings look much as they did when they were built more than a century ago. It's especially convincing when living-history demonstrations are given. These take place on Sundays and holidays from Memorial Day to Labor Day. *Open year-round. Admission charged.*

15. Niobrara State Park.

This quiet byway in a gentle landscape of rolling hills and beautiful valleys centers around a long, narrow lagoon. Non-powered boats are permitted, and paddleboats may be rented. Fishermen try for bass, crappies, catfish, and bluegills. There are inviting grassy areas for picnicking and a fine pool for swimming. Morning and afternoon trail rides through the park on horseback are led by a wrangler.

The park area, about 400 acres, is slowly reverting to marshland, and an additional 1,200 acres of adjoining land higher in the hills have been acquired for new park facilities. The present area may become a wildlife refuge. Crowding can be a problem on holiday weekends. *Open year-round. Admission charged.*

16. Neligh Mills Historical Site.

N St. and Wylie Dr., Neligh. Of some 550 mills that have served Nebraska farmers over the years, this three-story brick mill with branching annexes added at different times is one of the few that remain with all their machinery intact.

The building was started in 1873, and the mill began grinding in 1874. In 1886 the original millstones were replaced with steel rollers. The mill operated successfully with waterpower through World War I, but in 1920 a flood broke the millpond dam, and electricity had to be generated to keep it running. Unlike many other local mills, this one survived the Great Depression and continued in the flour business until 1955. It was sufficiently automated to produce 500 barrels of flour a day with a crew of only five or six. Although flour has not been ground here for a long time, one is reminded of the persistence of dust by the little piles of white stuff that still collects in various places under the machines. Rather tangible ghosts of a more prosperous past.

The warehouse and power-plant additions have exhibits relating to the mill's history. The old office, with its original furnishings, serves as a visitor center and bookstore. *Open Mon.–Sat. and P.M. Sun., Apr.–mid-Nov.*

16. *Mill is a study in unpremeditated architectural elegance. Flume carries water.*

17. Willa Cather Historical Center. *338 N. Webster St., Red Cloud.* The Pulitzer Prize-winning author (in 1922 for *One of Ours*) lived in Red Cloud only from the ages of 11 to 17. But in subsequent years she returned regularly to visit her parents and sometimes stayed the summer. The people and places in this town appeared in many of her books.

How specifically and accurately she wrote about the places she knew is demonstrated in the house rented by the Cathers from 1884 to 1904. Passages from her books are narrated while you view the rooms she described. The house itself, she wrote, had "everything a little on the slant." Here too you will see the wallpaper that Willa took as pay for working in Dr. Cook's drugstore and installed by herself. The drugstore building still stands and is included in a pamphlet listing more than a score of houses, streets, business and municipal buildings, monuments, and churches that have appeared under one guise or another in Willa Cather's books.

There is also a self-guiding tour of Cather landmarks in the surrounding countryside. Pamphlets are available at the historical center headquarters, a fanciful red brick structure that was once the Farmers and Merchants Bank. The center has a small museum and research library, and tours of the Cather home originate here. Other buildings administered by the center are open from time to time. *Open Tues.–Fri. and P.M. Sun.*

18. Ponca State Park. Anyone who thinks of Nebraska as a vast expanse of flatness is in for a pleasant surprise here on the shores of the mighty Missouri amid the hills where the Ponca tribe once roamed. The hills rising directly from the river give the roads a roller-coaster effect and from some favored places provide superb views. At Three State Overlook, for example, parts of Nebraska, South Dakota, and Iowa can be seen.

Rocky outcrops and an extensive hardwood forest add to the park's appeal. The forest boasts a magnificent oak more than 350 years old. Winding through some 900 acres are about 15 miles of hiking trails, and in winter cross-country skiing is popular. Many small picnic sites are scattered through the woods and along the river. The wrangler-led horseback rides traverse some of the most scenic areas of the park. Hikers and riders watch for white-tailed deer, raccoons, wild turkeys, eagles, and other wildlife.

The Missouri beckons anglers, and there's a boat ramp, but the swift current precludes swimming in the river. The park has a modern pool, however. Both are likely to be crowded on weekends in good weather. The 100-site campground offers full facilities, and there are 14 housekeeping cabins as well. *Open year-round. Campground open May–Oct.; other facilities open Memorial Day–Labor Day. Admission charged.*

19. The Neihardt Center. *Elm and Washington Sts., Bancroft.* The Nebraska poet, teacher, writer, and historian John C. Neihardt was posthumously designated the state's Poet Laureate in Perpetuity in 1982. This center, in his memory, has a research library largely dedicated to his life and works, along with tape and slide presentations.

But a major theme here relates less to the man himself than to his lifelong interest in the American Indians and his deep respect for their beliefs. A special feature is the Sioux prayer circle. The circle, traditionally inscribed in the soil, represents the world. The world is divided by two roads. The east-west line marks the hard road of life, the north-south line is the road of the spirit. From the center, where they cross, grows the tree of life, and each quarter of the circle has further symbolic meaning. This concept is elegantly memorialized with a large prayer circle formed in the tiered brick floor of the circular exhibition gallery. The garden is also fashioned into a prayer circle and has signs explaining the symbolism.

Other displays in the center illustrate highlights from Neihardt's remarkably productive career. First published at the age of 19, he wrote, lectured, and taught continually, compiling a very impressive list of honors. He was working on the second volume of his autobiography when he died in 1973 at age 92.

In striking contrast to the modern center with its curved, windowless brick walls is the humble, one-room frame building where Dr. Neihardt worked; it was brought here from his Bancroft home and restored under his supervision. An old typewriter, kerosene lamp, potbellied stove, and comfortable rocker evoke thoughts of a homely, unhurried era that contrasts dramatically with the age of the word processor. *Open Mon.–Sat. and P.M. Sun., May–Oct.; Mon.–Fri. the rest of the year. Admission charged.*

20. Louis E. May Museum. *1643 N. Nye Ave., Fremont.* When in 1874 Theron Nye, the first mayor of Fremont, chose

17. Befitting a famous citizen, a former bank is now the Willa Cather Historical Center. The modest home where she lived as a child is above.

21. *The logs, cut in 1867, speak eloquently of their resistance to conformity.*

the Italianate Revival style for his new house, he was obviously out to make an impression. Upon his demise the big red brick house was left to Ray Nye, who, like father like son, chose to remodel, expand, and make it even more imposing. Young Nye's taste ran to the classical, and he added a stately portico with two-story fluted white columns with Ionic capitals.

The structure itself is an architectural museum piece, and today it appropriately serves the Dodge County Historical Society as its headquarters and museum. The museum, named for the benefactor who made its purchase possible, features changing displays of antiques, decorative arts, and historic photographs from the latter 19th and early 20th centuries and presents exhibits of similar items from other museums. Outstanding details in the house itself include carved oak and mahogany paneling, art glass windows, decorative mantels, and some remarkable tilework in the master bathroom. *Open P.M. Wed.–Sun., Apr.–Dec.*

21. Homestead National Monument. On May 20, 1862, President Abraham Lincoln signed the Homestead Act, enabling people to become farm owners by paying a small fee and living on the land for five years. This 160-acre park commemorates the act and pays tribute to the gritty endurance of courageous men and women who pursued the opportunity. The offer peopled the prairie with thousands of rug-

gedly determined Americans as well as countless European immigrants. Displays in the large visitor center illustrate their hardships and joys.

The park itself is located on the former homestead of Daniel Freeman, one of the first settlers to file a claim under the provisions of the act. A well-maintained, 1½-mile path loops through a woods and through an extensive stretch of restored tall-grass prairie that gives a good sense of the terrain the early pioneers faced. A tiny log cabin, built in 1867, vividly evokes the character of their daily lives.

A guide to the wildlife you may see along the path is available at the visitor center. A quarter-mile away stands a furnished one-room schoolhouse. Built in 1872, it served the community as both an educational and a social focal point for nearly a century. Check at the visitor center for information about seeing the school. *Open year-round.*

22. Indian Cave State Park. This magnificent area—3,000 acres of oak-clad hills and bluffs along the Missouri River—takes its name from a deep overhang of rock that provided Indians with a natural shelter. At the cave are large rocks incised with images of the hunt and the surrounds. Local residents call this area the

Little Ozarks and come to see the lovely displays of redbud flowering in spring and the blazing colors of the hardwood forest in the fall. In fact, October tends to be the park's busiest month.

A scenic road and some 20 miles of trails for day walks and backpacking provide panoramic views. Horseback trail rides are also available. From the bank of the Missouri anglers catch bass, catfish, bullhead, carp, and the occasional sturgeon. In winter, 16 miles of trails are marked for cross-country skiing, and some steep hills provide excellent sledding. There are 225 campsites.

Also within the park are the reconstructed schoolhouse and general store and the two graveyards that remain from the town of St. Deroin. This unusual community was established in the mid-1800's on land set aside for the homeless offspring of white traders and trappers who had married Indian women and then moved on. The town was named for Joseph Deroin, who ran a trading post. The "St."—which he purportedly was not—was added to the name in a vain attempt to attract more settlers to the new town. The store and school are the site of living-history demonstrations given daily in summer and on weekends in fall. *Open year-round. Admission charged.*

22. *Hiking trails crisscross these woodlands on a gentle bend of the Missouri River.*

Kansas

Among the wooded hills and rolling plains are memories of Spanish adventurers, Indians, pioneers, and those who stayed to work the land.

The first white men in this area were the conquistadors who came seeking gold—unsuccessfully—in 1541. Their peaceful meeting with the Indians is commemorated in a museum in Lyons. Also recalled, in other museums and the army posts, are the inevitable conflicts between the Indians and the pioneers heading west and those who settled here. An original Pony Express station, remnants of the Santa Fe Trail, and a vast expanse of unplowed prairie are further reminders of the early days in Kansas.

Another important highlight is the Agricultural Hall of Fame, recalling the men and machines that helped make this state the Breadbasket of the Nation.

1. Last Indian Raid Museum. *258 S. Penn Ave., Oberlin.* The "last Indian raid" in Kansas refers to the tale of some 300 displaced Northern Cheyenne Indians wanting to return to their ancestral home.

Forcibly removed to a camp in what is now Oklahoma, they were sick, hungry, and desolate. In September 1878 some 100 warriors with their wives and children escaped and headed north through Kansas with the U.S. Army in pursuit. As they approached Sappa Creek, they recalled that three years before, 27 of their people had been slaughtered there. On September 30–October 1, the Cheyennes raided the area, killed 30 people, and moved on. A number of the Indians were later killed, and the survivors were sent to a reservation in Montana.

The five-building museum contains a few relics from the raid, such as war clubs, arrowheads, and a settler's revolver. The museum also houses a variety of late 19th- and early 20th-century displays: rooms with typical period furnishings, a doctor's and dentist's office, a barbershop, and a music room with a player piano. A sod house pays tribute to pioneer life, while a large collection of military uniforms and weapons shows their evolution from Civil War times to Vietnam. One of the museum buildings was previously the 1885 Burlington Northern depot for Oberlin and is now furnished with a collection of railroad memorabilia. *Open Tues.–Sun., Apr.–Nov. except holidays. Admission charged.*

2. Hill City Oil Museum. *Hill City.* This museum, featuring items devoted to the petroleum industry, lies in the heart of the oil-producing area of Graham County, which boomed in the late 1930's and 1940's. The look of the "oil patch" is evident in the yard, where cable-tool equipment and a pumping jack (one of the first in the local field) are installed.

Inside, a replica of a cable-tool derrick and other equipment from Neodesha, Kansas (1892 vintage), contrast dramatically with the working scale model of a modern rig. Early boom days are depicted by outstanding photos of the Spindletop Field (Beaumont, Texas) and pen-and-ink drawings of other notable fields.

One display of a geological cross section shows how wells were cored from the different rock formations. Of equal interest is a diorama of geological history portraying oil and gas formations from the Paleozoic to the Cenozoic eras, and showing the different procedures in oil exploration.

Nostalgia is provided with a replica of an old-time service station and a group of various oil company signs from years gone by. *Open daily year-round. Borrow key at Western Hills Motel across the street.*

3. Pawnee Indian Village Museum. *Republic.* Built on a grassy knoll overlooking the tree-lined Republican River, this museum encloses the site of an excavated Pawnee two-family dwelling. Of the 30 to 40 houses in a village of some 1,000 people, this was one of the largest, with nearly 2,000 square feet of floor space.

The village was probably abandoned in the 1830's when its inhabitants decided to join other Pawnees in what is now Nebraska. Ashes from the residents' last fire still remain in the hearth, and tools, weapons, and corn lie exactly as found during the excavation; in the fire-hardened earth floor you can see the 218 holes for the posts that supported a framework of willow poles and covering of earth and grass.

Exhibits representing various aspects of Indian life include artwork, bone and metal tools and weapons, pipes, and a buffalo-robe painting of a battle between

5. *The false front served widely in the West to enhance the most modest of structures.*

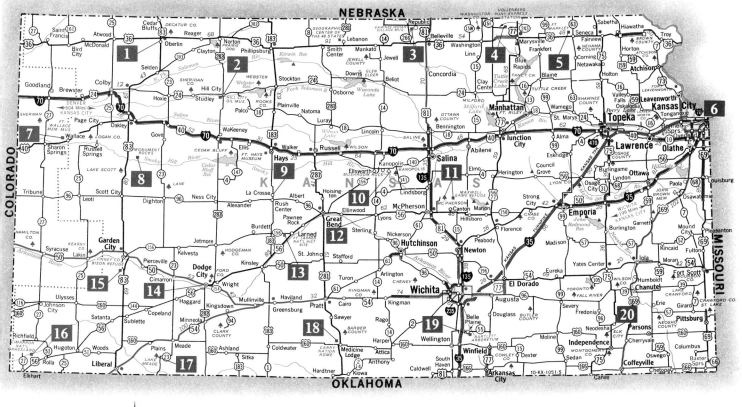

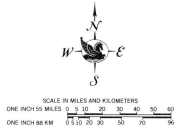

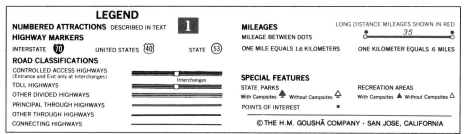

Pawnee and Kansas warriors. One diorama depicts a buffalo hunt (in spring and fall the braves rode southwest to the High Plains in quest of these animals), and another shows the village, with a cutaway model of an earth lodge.

In the six-acre fenced area behind the museum you can see 22 other lodge sites and the remains of a sod and timber wall that had surrounded the village. *Open Tues.–Sun. except holidays.*

---

4. Hollenberg Pony Express Station. *On Rte. 243.* During the 18-month operation of the Pony Express (April 1860–October 1861), its wiry young riders galloped into the history and folklore of America.

In 1859 St. Joseph, Missouri, was the western terminus of telegraph and railroad communication, and mail destined for the West Coast depended upon stagecoaches and mule trains. The Pony Express feat of delivering mail from St. Joseph to Sacramento in 12 days (less than half the previous best time) required 120 riders, 1,500 horses, and a relay station every 10 to 15 miles. It was an efficient but costly operation and terminated when the transcontinental telegraph line was completed.

This national historic landmark is the only unaltered station still standing in its original location, close by Cottonwood Creek. Built in 1857 by rancher Gerat Hollenberg, the sturdy, weather-beaten structure served as home, general store, post office, hotel, and stagecoach stop on the Overland Trail. It was also the westernmost Pony Express station in Kansas.

Here you can get the feel of the Pony Express and stagecoach businesses and see the general store with its ox shoes, bows and arrows, powder horns, kitchen utensils, and branding irons. Climbing the steep steps to the rough-planked attic, you follow the bootsteps of the Pony Express riders and stagecoach passengers who slept there. There are picnic tables and a small playground in a beautifully wooded eight-acre setting. *Open daily except Thanksgiving Day, Christmas, and New Year's Day.*

---

5. Fort Markley. *Seneca.* Approaching Fort Markley, one might think it an old frontier ghost town and would not be far wrong. The livery stable, general store, bank, and other vintage buildings have all been moved here from extinct pioneer towns. Behind their rough lumber exteriors are thousands of intriguing artifacts.

The owner of the rustic Buffalo Café, J.E. Markley, is one of the nation's experts on the Pony Express era and can prove it with a fund of frontier stories. The café, looking like an old western saloon, displays numerous pioneer relics and has several life-size mannequins of Indians sitting in chairs.

The nearest Pony Express station was less than a mile away in Seneca, and the trail crossed the Fort Markley property. A short walk across the pasture takes you to the place where a creek had been dammed to create a watering spot for Pony Express horses. The creekbed is lined with willows and cottonwoods. Nearby is an area with a small buffalo herd.

A campground adjacent to the frontier buildings has sites with electrical hookups and a small lake. *Open year-round. Admission charged for frontier buildings.*

---

6. Agricultural Hall of Fame and National Center. *630 N. 126th St., Bonner Springs.* The center pays homage to the skillful, hardworking farmers who have made American citizens the best fed in the world. It honors the people who led the way as well as the tools they used, and presents a nostalgic case for the agricultural way of life. The exhibits are housed in three main buildings and several auxiliary buildings set on 270 acres of beautiful rolling countryside.

In the center, which claims to have the greatest collection of agricultural equipment in the country, you can see Harry Truman's plow, a 307-piece set of antique woodworking tools, hand-operated milk-processing machines, and numerous other farm items.

Hall-of-Famers include George Washington, Thomas Jefferson, Cyrus McCormick, George Washington Carver, Eli Whitney, and 14 other agriculturists.

You can also visit "Grandmother's House," with its nostalgically furnished rooms, and make a trip to "Ye Olde Country Towne" to see a smithy, country store, harness shop, horse collar factory, telephone office, veterinarian and dental offices, and a broom factory, all as they would have been in grandmother's day.

For a change of pace, one can climb aboard the narrrow-gauge railroad that circles a lake on the grounds or amble down a mile-long wooded nature trail. *Open Mon.–Sat. and P.M. Sun, Apr.–Dec. Admission charged.*

8. Horizontal striations left by sediments of an ancient inland sea are here revealed.

7. Fort Wallace Memorial Museum. *Wallace.* Fort Wallace was one of a string of army posts established to control the Plains Indians and protect travelers along the Smoky Hill Trail. Active from 1865 to 1881, it was built for about 500 soldiers and was the busiest bastion in Kansas.

Nothing remains of the old fort except the cemetery. The museum, located about 1½ miles from the fort site, is a treasury of locally found artifacts from the days of the Indian wars. Here you'll see old military equipment—uniforms, insignia, cartridges, a horn from the post band, saddles—as well as a painted Indian buffalo robe, a player piano, a collection of barbed wire, and cowboy equipment.

Also on view are a Union Pacific depot from Weskan, complete with telegraph, switch equipment, and signal tower, and a stage station from Pond Creek, which contains period relics. *Open Tues.–Sun., mid-May–Labor Day. Admission free but donations encouraged.*

---

8. Monument Rocks. *From Rte. 83 go 6 miles SE on a gravel road.* Rising abruptly above the treeless plain of the Smoky Hill River, the 60-foot-high "monuments" look like lonely sentinels. Sculpted by years of wind and water erosion, many have crenellated tops like castle battlements. They graduate in color from pale

grey at the bottom (matching the soil in the nearby fields) to tan, to gold at their peaks. The rocks are composed of soft Cretaceous chalk from the sediment of an ancient sea, and their layered formations abound with fossils.

Numbering fewer than a dozen, the towers are found in an area about a quarter-mile long and 200 yards wide. These distinctive formations served as landmarks for early wagon trains and military parties as they trekked westward from Kansas to Colorado along the Smoky Hill Trail. The area has now been designated as a national natural landmark. About a mile to the north there are dramatically eroded peaks of sandstone.

The plain, a semiarid prairie covered with native grasses, sage, thistle, yucca, sunflowers, and tumbleweed, is home to various animals, including antelope, jackrabbits, and small lizards as well as a few cattle in fenced pastures. Cottonwoods and elms can be seen half a mile away along the Smoky Hill River, looming above the flat landscape.

---

9. Barbed Wire Museum and Post Rock Museum. *La Crosse.* When Joseph F. Glidden patented a barbed wire "lighter than air, stronger than whisky, and cheaper than dirt," the fate of the Great Plains was sealed. The open range was transformed into fenced farmland, and the sod-busting farmer was now able to confine his livestock and protect his homestead and crops from free-ranging cattle.

Glidden's success spurred innovative competition to create new patterns, and by 1883 40 companies were making barbed wire. The museum presents this history together with more than 500 varieties of the wire and related exhibits.

Of equal importance to frontier life were the posts used to support the wire. Wood was too scarce in 19th-century Kansas to use for fence posts. Creative settlers found a solution by making posts of soft limestone, which hardens in the sun. Slabs of the limestone, which is abundant in Kansas, were quarried and split into stone posts averaging 9 inches square and 5 to 6 feet long. About 40,000 miles of post-rock fence cross this section of Kansas, bestowing upon the region a distinctive character.

In the Post Rock Museum you'll see tools used to make the posts, as well as a miniature quarry showing how the limestone was stripped from the earth and cut to size. The museum itself is a restored house built from the same rock. *Barbed Wire Museum open Mon.–Fri. year-round except holidays. Post Rock Museum open daily mid-Apr.–mid-Oct.*

---

10. Mushroom Rock State Park. *From Rte. 141 go 2.3 miles west on signed gravel road.* The effects of wind erosion are widespread in the Great Plains but nowhere more apparent than at this 5½-acre site. Swooping off the wheat fields and pastureland, these persistent and sometimes violently swirling winds have gradually shaved away the ground of soft sandstone, leaving small islands of resistant sandstone and gradually sculpting them into dramatic mushroom shapes. The two largest are about 25 feet tall with caps about 15 feet wide. The mushroom rocks are in open fields that are blanketed in the spring with the beauty of penstemon, oxalis, scarlet gaura, wild roses, and milkweed.

A gentle brook murmurs through the area, shaded by oaks, cottonwoods, and elms. North of the brook you'll find some man-made art—a rock carving of a U.S. flag with 15 stripes—probably the work of pioneer travelers pausing on their westward trek. The small park has picnic tables and a hand-pumped well for drinking water. A few miles to the south are the two

divisions of the widely popular Kanopolis State Park. The extensive recreational facilities in its 1,585 acres include swimming, boating, and fishing on Kanopolis Lake. *Both parks open year-round except holidays. Admission charged for Kanopolis.*

---

11. Maxwell Game Refuge and McPherson State Lake. *From Canton go 3 miles north on county road, then left 1.2 miles to refuge headquarters.* Descendants of the American buffalo are still at home on this range of rolling grassland. Indeed, they thrive so well in this habitat that their numbers are controlled, kept to about 200 by auctioning off the surplus following the annual roundup. The auction is held at the refuge corral the third week of November, and visitors are welcome.

From the observation tower just outside the fenced territory of the buffalo you have a good chance of seeing the animals, and perhaps glimpsing some of the 40 elk that also roam these 2,254 acres. Elk are shy and are less frequently seen.

The gravel roads provide excellent views of this Kansan landscape— rolling prairie and wooded ravines. Along the 1½-mile nature trail are spiderwort, oxalis, wild roses, black-eyed Susans, and other native flowers. Birds are numerous. The 46-acre lake on the refuge (made by damming Gypsum Creek) has a boat dock and a ramp; anglers are rewarded with

bass, crappie, catfish, pike, and bluegill. A campground is pleasantly situated on the lake's western shore. *Open year-round. Admission free.*

---

12. Rice County Historical Museum. *221 East Ave. South, Lyons.* Lured by the lust for gold, the Spanish conquistador Don Francisco Vasquez de Coronado carried his quest for the Seven Cities of Cibola, the fabled golden cities, northward from Mexico into what is now New Mexico. He found no gold, but the native Pueblo Indians encouraged him to go on to the "Kingdom of Quivira." Pushing on, Coronado made his way into central Kansas to the promised kingdom and further disappointment. There was no gold at all.

This museum commemorates that expedition with exhibits of Quivira pottery, arrowheads, stone tools, and beads, as well as chain mail, a helmet, spurs, and other items left behind by Coronado's soldiers. Also shown are a model of a Quivira-Wichita Indian dwelling and a large collection of Papago Indian baskets made from devil's-claw and yucca leaves.

The walls are hung with two outstanding mural-sized paintings. The "Dawn of a New Era" depicts Coronado meeting with the Quivira Indians by their grass-hut village. The other painting shows the Spanish adventurer leading his men. The area's later history is conveyed by maps of

11. *In the woodsy confines of the refuge, this bull elk can safely strike a classic pose.*

great cattle trails from Texas to the rail-heads in Kansas, stone trail markers, and various other relics. *Open Tues.–Sun. year-round except major holidays.*

13. Fort Larned National Historical Site.
Six miles west of Larned on State Rte. 156. As a principal guardian of the Santa Fe Trail, Fort Larned provided military escort for wagon trains, stagecoaches, and travelers from 1860 to 1878.

The original sod and adobe structures were replaced in 1868 with nine durable sandstone and timber buildings enclosing the traditional parade ground. Still standing much in their original condition, they offer a glimpse of military life on the western frontier.

One of the barracks, converted into a museum and visitor center, features numerous relics, infantry and cavalry uniforms, a life-size model of a 10th Cavalry soldier leading his mount with all equipment and regalia, and some excellent Indian artifacts and photographs of prominent chiefs. The fort's colorful past is presented in a slide show.

An easy mile-long history trail takes you past the sites of the old barracks and other abandoned buildings, the corral, the station for the stage mail, and for a short distance approximately follows the Santa Fe Trail. *Open daily except Thanksgiving Day, Christmas, and New Year's Day.*

14. The Santa Fe Trail at Dodge City.
The best preserved section of the fabled Santa Fe Trail remains carved in the windswept, grass-covered prairie nine miles west of Dodge City.

In the mid-1800's this trail, stretching 780 miles from Independence, Missouri, to Santa Fe, New Mexico, was the most important artery of commerce in the development of the Southwest. A single wagon train might number 400–500 wagons and carry more than a million dollars' worth of merchandise for the settlers in this part of the country and in Mexico.

Despite a century's erosion, the trail is still clearly marked. In some places here, the grooves are as much as three feet deep. It is apparent that the trail was not one single lane but numerous parallel tracks, so that several ranks of traffic—freight wagons, stagecoaches, horses, soldiers,

and cattle—could travel side by side for protection. In fact, more than a dozen separate pathways are evident in the 300-foot width of the trail.

Now listed in *The National Register of Historic Sites,* this area has never been plowed, and with the native grasses, thistle, wild gaillardia, sage, sunflowers, yucca, and prickly pear, it probably looks much as it did when the trail was at its busiest. *Accessible year-round.*

15. Finney County Bison Refuge.
In what was once the heart of the great American bison range, these 3,529 acres shelter a herd of about 60 buffalo, as they are commonly called.

Officially designated the state animal, these "monarchs of the plains" once numbered some 60 to 70 million, but their wanton slaughter during the 19th century reduced them to only a few hundred. This herd was established in 1924 with one bull and two cows. Thanks to similar refuges and privately owned herds in the United States and Canada, there are now more than 30,000 of these great shaggy beasts grazing in safety.

Headquartered on the south bank of the Arkansas River, the refuge spreads southwest over sandhills covered with sage, bluestem, tumbleweed, and yucca. The herd usually grazes at some distance from the headquarters, but visitors can get a close look and take photos on a tour in a pickup arranged with the supervisor. Buffalo are not loners. They roam and graze in herds, but are wary of people and unpredictable in behavior.

Along the way you may see pheasants, mule deer, coyotes, quail, prairie dogs, and prairie chickens, some of which graze with the buffalo. Thriving in a density of sage, tumbleweeds, and yucca, ragwort, sand lilies, and wild gaillardia brighten the prairie in their season. *Accessible Mon.–Fri. year-round except major holidays.*

16. Cimarron National Grassland.
After the bitter lesson of dust bowls in the 1930's, the U.S. government established this and similar reserves to protect native plants and wildlife and restore badly eroded land to its natural state.

Here on 108,175 acres divided by the Cimarron River, native grasses have been

seeded and new sources of water developed. More than 400 oil rigs and gas wells coexist with some 5,000 head of cattle grazed by permit. Elk, white-tailed and mule deer, antelope, coyotes, wild turkeys, and pheasants are among the creatures at home here.

The area is also a natural habitat for the lesser prairie chicken, and on a spring morning or evening the chickens' colorful courting ritual may be seen from observation blinds. Prairie dogs have staked out several of their fascinating towns, and scaled quails have established coveys near prominent landmarks.

You can see it all, including 126 windmills, on a three-hour, 50-mile self-guiding auto tour. An overlook at Point of Rocks offers views of the grassland itself and the Cimarron, which is dry most of the year. A short distance east is Middle Spring, a life-saving oasis on the Santa Fe Trail, where wagon ruts can still be seen.

Cottonwood, elm, willow, and tamarisk trees grow along the riverbanks, and primroses, yucca, spiderwort, and coneflowers are mixed in with wild and cultivated grasses.

Visitors are permitted to camp anywhere but are asked to avoid watering spots used by animals in order not to disrupt them. A picnic ground on the banks of the Cimarron has drinking water and rest rooms. Maps and information are available at the Forest Service office in Elkhart, just south of the reserve. *Open year-round.*

17. Lake Meade State Park. *Meade.*
Amid vast wheat fields and rolling, gullied pastureland lies this welcome park with the waters of Lake Meade nestled in a heavily wooded glen.

The park affords excellent camping, swimming, boating, and fishing; anglers cast for bass, catfish, bluegill, sunfish, northern pike, and crappie in the 80-acre lake. Picnic facilities are available at several spots around the lake and in the secluded wildlife reserve where the grounds are shaded by cottonwoods, locusts, hackberries, towering elms, and red cedars. Of special interest is a 100-gallon-per-minute artesian well.

Hiking along the park roads, one can enjoy views of the lake and woods and watch for woodpeckers, owls, kingfishers,

19. *Trees and shrubs, both formal and informal, are combined for the celebration of fall.*

ducks, and small mammals. Adjacent to the park is a state wildlife refuge. *Park open year-round. Admission charged.*

18. Carry Nation Home. *West Hwy. 160, Medicine Lodge.* This yellow brick house was home to Carry A. Nation, the indomitable crusader for temperance, from 1890 to about 1903. She was away from home for extended periods, however, on her self-appointed rounds, combating the "demon rum" by smashing up saloons with her ever-ready hatchet and satchel full of rocks and brickbats.

Carry Nation began her personal vendetta after her first husband, a brilliant doctor, died of alcoholism, leaving her with a daughter and a burden of debts. She later married David Nation, a preacher and lawyer, but her itinerant campaign took most of her time and she was divorced on grounds of desertion in 1901. Her lecture tours took her to England and Scotland, and she was recognized for her

many charities, especially the home she established in Kansas City for the wives and families of alcoholics. Although jailed a number of times, she pursued her calling with particular zeal in Kansas and the Oklahoma Territory.

On view in the seven-room house are her personal effects, along with the infamous hatchet, brickbats, and a valise. Turn-of-the-century furnishings include her huge oak bed, a pump organ used in a local church, an early wind-up phonograph, and a foot-pedal sewing machine. Visitors are greeted in the entry hall by an oil painting of Mrs. Nation, trusty hatchet in one hand, Bible in the other. *Open daily May–Oct. Admission charged.*

19. Bartlett Arboretum. *Rte. 55, Belle Plaine.* Described as one of the world's loveliest gardens, this 20-acre arboretum is a living museum of flowers, trees, and shrubs from many parts of the world. Started in 1910 by Dr. Walter E. Bartlett, a local physician, its varied gardens, lagoons, marshes, meadows, and woodland

areas inspire with their serene beauty.

Quiet pathways weave through myriad beds of annuals and perennials beneath an equally beautiful canopy of trees—cypresses, Chinese and Japanese maples, dogwoods, 10 kinds of redbuds, pistachios, ornamental pears, and many others. The old carriageway that formerly served the Bartletts' home crosses a Japanese bridge over one of the lagoons.

Each spring, from mid-April to mid-May, 25,000 tulip bulbs, imported and planted the previous fall, burst into colorful bloom. And during the last two weeks of October, thousands of chrysanthemums put on a show, mixing brilliantly with the golds and browns of autumn and the rich greens of conifers.

The entire growing season provides a kaleidoscopic display of hyacinths, phlox, daffodils, marigolds, petunias, wisteria, forsythia, spirea, peonies, jasmine, and roses. Combining native plants with exotic specimens from other countries, the arboretum helps determine which ones can survive the varied climate in this section of the Sunflower State. Crowded on weekends, especially in tulip time. *Open daily Apr.–mid-Nov. Admission charged.*

20. Elk City State Park. *Reached by County Rd. 3900 off Rte. 75 or by County Rd. 3325 off Rte. 160.* Located in the gently rolling terrain of southeastern Kansas, this 857-acre park blends the wheat and cattle country of the western area with the more verdant eastern part of the state. From the moment you enter the park the diversity of Kansas is apparent in the shrubs, trees, and grasses.

Along any of three nature trails through the slightly hilly woodlands one can see most of the deciduous trees found in the Great Plains, including post oak, blackjack oak, elm, pecan, walnut, hickory, cottonwood, and red cedar. Two of the trails are designated as national recreation trails. The extensive wooded areas and native grasses provide a haven for deer, bobcats, armadillos, occasional coyotes, and other wildlife.

The lake and the broad, mowed, grassy areas along the roadways and camping and picnic grounds are among the attractive features here. *Open year-round. Admission charged.*

Oklahoma

Highlights relate to the Indian and pioneer heritage, preservation of endangered species, and a variety of inviting parks and trails.

The earliest foragers on these grassy plains are documented by dinosaur footprints and fossilized remains of the mastodon and mammoth. Under the same roof is the legacy of the Plains Indians and the five flags that have flown over this land. Elsewhere, ancient Indian mounds can be seen, a famous Wild West show is recalled, and a sod house is preserved. The Trail of Tears is remembered, and there's a memorial to Sequoyah, inventor of the Cherokee alphabet.

There are parks featuring a mesa, a cavern, waterfalls, and boulders as well as hiking and nature trails. Buffalo, elk, and longhorns are safe in their sanctuaries, and the Chisholm Trail is immortalized.

1. Black Mesa and Black Mesa State Park. A dark, brooding countenance dominates the arid countryside of the extreme northwestern Oklahoma Panhandle. Rising some 700 feet in relief above a stark plain, Black Mesa extends for about 45 miles from Oklahoma into Colorado and New Mexico. Its highest point above sea level in Oklahoma, 4,972.97 feet, is marked by a granite slab. At its western edges, in Colorado, the mesa reaches an altitude of 6,600 feet. The geologists believe the mesa was formed by basaltic lava flows originating at what is today Piney Mountain, Colorado, five miles from the Oklahoma border.

There are no marked trails to the summit, but in several places the slopes are gentle enough for hiking or riding a horse to the top. The lure here, as in much of the West, is the awesome majesty of the American land.

Black Mesa State Park, about nine miles southeast of the mesa, offers a splendid base for exploring the area. The 349-acre park is also noteworthy in its own right for its huge rock pinnacles suggesting human profiles and figures, and for the flora and fauna thriving in its rugged landscape. A small lake offers boating and fishing. *Open year-round.*

2. No Man's Land Historical Museum. *Sewell St. and Agee Ave., Goodwell.* Oklahoma's Panhandle, a 34- by 168-mile strip, was for many years unclaimed by any state or territory. When Texas, a pro-slave state, joined the Union, it refused to include lands north of latitude 36°30′ be-cause, according to the Missouri Compromise, such territory would be free. The boundary of Kansas had already been set at the 37th parallel, and thus the long, narrow area that remained became known as No Man's Land. The settlers here asked that Congress name it the Cimarron Territory. But Congress refused and in 1890 designated the area as part of the Oklahoma Territory.

The museum, on the campus of Panhandle State University, has outstanding exhibits depicting the history of this region from prehistoric times to the tragic Dust Bowl days of the 1930's. The paleontology displays include mastodon and mammoth bones and teeth, a dinosaur track, and intriguing fossil freshwater fish. The William E. Baker Archaeological

LEGEND

NUMBERED ATTRACTIONS DESCRIBED IN TEXT ▮1▮
HIGHWAY MARKERS

INTERSTATE ⑦   UNITED STATES ㊵   STATE ㉝

ROAD CLASSIFICATIONS

CONTROLLED ACCESS HIGHWAYS
(Entrance and Exit only at Interchanges)
                        Interchanges
TOLL HIGHWAYS
OTHER DIVIDED HIGHWAYS
PRINCIPAL THROUGH HIGHWAYS
OTHER THROUGH HIGHWAYS
CONNECTING HIGHWAYS

MILEAGES   LONG DISTANCE MILEAGES SHOWN IN RED
MILEAGE BETWEEN DOTS   *35*
ONE MILE EQUALS 1.6 KILOMETERS   ONE KILOMETER EQUALS .6 MILES

SPECIAL FEATURES

STATE PARKS   RECREATION AREAS
With Campsites ⛺ Without Campsites △   With Campsites ▲ Without Campsites △
POINTS OF INTEREST ■

© THE H.M. GOUSHA COMPANY · SAN JOSE, CALIFORNIA

SCALE IN MILES AND KILOMETERS
ONE INCH 50 MILES   0   5   10   20   30   40   50
ONE INCH 80 KM   0   5 10   20   30   40   60   80

1. Black Mesa, in the background, overlooks the lazy meanders of the Cimarron River.

Collections, housed in the museum, contain artifacts of the Basket Maker Indians, early occupants of these lands, the Plains Indians, who formerly roamed the region, and white pioneers. Over the main entrance to the museum are the flags of Spain, France, Mexico, Texas, and the United States, all of which have flown over the territory. *Open Tues.–Fri. and P.M. Sat. and Sun. except holidays.*

---

3. Alabaster Caverns State Park. *Freedom.* The feature here is a 2,300-foot-long cavern sectioned into chambers by spectacular formations of alabaster and glittering selenite crystals. (Alabaster is a fine, translucent gypsum.) Its formation began some 200 million years ago when a great inland sea receded, leaving huge deposits of gypsum. Underground streams slowly tunneled the rock, creating the series of chambers. Today a murmuring stream continues the ancient process of erosion on a humble scale.

The entrance to the cavern is in rugged

Cedar Canyon. Short tours take visitors into chambers given such descriptive names as Gun Barrel Tunnel, Devil's Bathtub, Echo Dome, and Bridal Room. Bring comfortable walking shoes and a light jacket. For years the cavern was known as Bat Cave for the host of winged mammals that still reside here, hanging harmlessly from the rock ceiling by day, leaving by night to feed upon insects.

A quarter-mile trail runs along Cedar Canyon to the park's Natural Bridge, an arch rising 150 feet above the canyon floor. Campsites, picnic grounds, and a swimming pool are available. The park is usually crowded in early July and late August. *Open year-round. Admission charged.*

---

4. Homesteader's Sod House. *Aline. Two and a half miles south on Rte. 8.* In September 1893, the Cherokee Outlet, a strip of land purchased by the U. S. government from the Cherokees, opened to

homesteaders. More than 100,000 "Sooners" and "Boomers" rushed to make claims. Among them was one Marshall McCully, who had lost an earlier claim because of a dispute, moved south, filed again, and one year later was building his sod house at this location. For the two-room homestead he plowed about a half-acre of turf strips from a field of buffalo grass. The sod strips were then cut into 18-inch-long blocks and laid like brick, but in double rows. To support the roof a ridgepole was placed across the sod walls, carrying short rafters of split logs set close together; the rafters were then covered with more sod. In these parts, sod was plastered with a claylike material from nearby alkali deposits. Typically, ceilings were covered with flour sacks sewn together to catch dirt, snakes, and insects.

About a million "soddies" were eventually built on the Great Plains. They were not intended for long-term use, and only a few still stand today. But McCully built especially well, and his family occupied his sturdy house for some 15 years. The

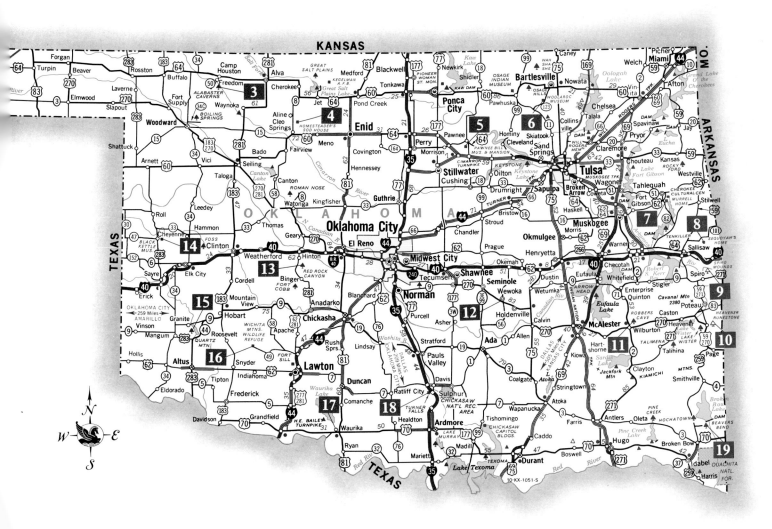

soddy withstood the elements for another 55 years before the Oklahoma Historical Society restored it. Household relics and farm implements of the pioneer days are displayed. *Open Tues.–Fri. and P.M. Sat. and Sun. except holidays.*

5. Pawnee Bill Museum and Mansion. *Pawnee.* Gordon William Lillie, pioneer rancher, sometime partner of Buffalo Bill, and "white chief" of an Indian nation, chose Blue Hawk Peak, a hill in Pawnee Indian country, for the site of this handsome sandstone mansion. The sprawling, two-story structure, built in 1910 of locally quarried stone, is maintained by the Oklahoma Historical Society.

Lillie had lived among the Pawnees, who appointed him their white chief, naming him Pawnee Bill. With his wife May, an expert rider and sharpshooter, he formed the Pawnee Bill Wild West Show in 1888. For a quarter of a century he toured the United States and many foreign countries—part of the time with the famous Buffalo Bill. When his show finally closed in 1913, Lillie indulged his interests in buffalo and longhorn cattle, enlarging his herds to assure the preservation of these already endangered species.

His mansion today contains the original furnishings and treasures from his travels,

7. Hunter's Home reflects builder George Murrell's taste for understated elegance.

including a table and set of chairs inlaid with mother-of-pearl given to him by the Chinese emperor. The museum contains memorabilia of the family and prominent guests, a miniature replica of the Pawnee Bill Wild West Show, and a collection of Indian artifacts. A pleasant picnic area is located on the grounds. *Open Tues.–Sat. and P.M. Sun., May–Oct.; Wed.–Sat. and P.M. Sun., Nov.–Apr. except Thanksgiving Day and Christmas.*

6. Woolaroc. *On Rte. 123.* This lovely 3,500-acre property in the rugged Osage hill country was acquired in the 1920's by Frank Phillips, co-founder of Phillips Petroleum Company, for a wildlife sanctuary and a family retreat. Now owned and managed by a foundation created by Phillips, Woolaroc (*Woo*ds, *la*kes, and *roc*ks) is open to the public. On the grounds are a world-renowned museum established by Phillips, the National Y-Indian Guide Center, and the rustic but spacious lodge, where the Phillipses entertained the nation's leaders and celebrities.

The museum is reached by a road that curves from the grounds' entrance and picnic area through the refuge, a forest of blackjack oaks, post oaks, and sycamores, where buffalo, deer, elk, and longhorn cattle graze. For safety, visitors are required to stay in their cars.

The museum, which portrays the story of man in the New World, contains 55,000 items from the times of the earliest Indians up through the era of the pioneers. Its displays of Indian blankets and Navajo and Plains Indian jewelry are outstanding. A permanent exhibit of western art (one of the world's finest) includes works of Frank Tenney Johnson, Charles M. Russell, and Frederic Remington.

Adjacent to the museum is the National Y-Indian Guide Center, a longhouse with exhibits illustrating Indian culture and achievements. From the center the Enchanted Walkway leads to the 1½-mile-long Thunderbird Canyon Nature Trail. Labels posted along the loop identify the flora and the various geological features. *Open Tues.–Sun. and summer holidays; closed Thanksgiving Day and Christmas. Admission charged.*

7. Murrell Home and Nature Trail. *Tahlequah. Drive two miles south on Rte. 82 and follow signs.* Vintage Americana, echoes of old Indian lamentations, and a state government's first attempt to provide self-guiding nature explorations for the handicapped combine at this unusual setting. The quiet, elegant atmosphere of the antebellum South pervades a mansion built around 1845 by George Murrell at Park Hill, the cultural center of the Cherokee Nation after being displaced from Georgia in 1838–39. Murrell, a longtime friend of the Cherokees, married a niece of the great chief John Ross in Tennessee in 1834, and after her death, her sister. He himself died in New Orleans in 1894.

Hunter's Home, so named because of Murrell's fondness for hunting, has high-ceilinged rooms, each with a fireplace, is impressively furnished in antebellum style, and displays portraits of Murrell and his Cherokee wives. Outbuildings on the 38-acre grounds include a springhouse, log cabin, and smokehouse. The three-quarter-mile nature trail, paved to accommodate the handicapped, winds through dense stands of sycamore, Osage orange, willow, and hickory. Birders come especially for the flycatchers, vireos, and kingfishers. There is a shaded picnic area and playground. *Open Tues.–Sat. and P.M. Sun., May–Oct.; Wed.–Sat. and P.M. Sun., Nov.–Apr. except Thanksgiving Day and Christmas.*

8. Sequoyah's Home. *Sallisaw. Off Rte. 101.* In 1829, some ten years before the Cherokee Nation's travail on the brutalizing "Trail of Tears" from Georgia and Florida to Oklahoma, where they were resettled, George Guess, better known as Sequoyah, came to the new territory and built a log cabin near Big Skin Bayou. Today the restored cabin, which is enclosed in a museum, is an intriguing historical attraction.

Sequoyah is best remembered for his invention of the Cherokee alphabet—a syllabary of 86 characters. He labored diligently for 12 years to develop his major contribution to tribal literacy.

Another cabin on these 10 acres, built of logs taken from an addition to Sequoyah's home, houses the museum office and visitor center. Both cabins display artifacts of the early days of the Cherokees in

11. *Trees have found a foothold in the rock, adding further shelter to this retreat.*

absolute proof, some scholars believe that the runestones were left by Viking explorers almost 500 years before Columbus arrived in the New World.

The Vikings' route to the location may have been from the Gulf of Mexico to the Mississippi River, up the Arkansas and Poteau rivers, and into nearby Morris Creek. The Heavener stone is protected with plastic and is housed indoors.

A hilly one-mile nature trail meanders through the 50-acre park. Hickory, dogwood, redbud, oak, cedar, and pine trees provide cover for raccoons, beavers, armadillos, and deer, and the woods and sky resound with the cries and wingbeats of hawks, blue jays, quail, and brown thrashers. A picnic area and playground are easily accessible. *Open year-round.*

11. Robbers Cave State Park. This heavily forested 8,246-acre park, set in the Sans Bois Mountains, was named for the cave that allegedly served as a hideout for such notorious outlaws as Belle Starr, Bill Dalton, Jesse James, and the Younger brothers. The labyrinth of enormous boulders that surround the smoke-blackened cave, making it easily defensible, gives credence to these tales, as does the difficult climb to the cave's mouth.

The park's three lakes—Carlton, Wayne Wallace, and Coon Creek—offer swimming, boating, and fishing for bass, perch, and catfish. Three trails—a three-quarter-mile nature path, a two-mile Lost Lake Trail, and for hardy hikers a moderately difficult 12-mile route—wind through woodlands of pines, cedars, oaks, sycamores, cottonwoods, and spring-blooming dogwoods and redbuds. Deer, opossums, raccoons, beavers, owls, eagles, blue jays, and woodpeckers abound. Rappelling is a popular activity. Areas are reserved for recreational vehicles and tent camping, and there is also an equestrian camping site. *Open year-round.*

12. Seminole Nation Museum. *524 S. Wewoka Ave., corner of Sixth St., Wewoka.* "I fought in the Civil War and have seen men shot to pieces and slaughtered by thousands," wrote a Georgia militia veteran, "but the Cherokee removal

Indian Territory, including the constitution and laws of the Cherokee Nation (1892) and a Bible and a hymnbook in the Cherokee language. Also on display are a Cherokee-language typewriter, reed baskets, fabrics, and beadwork. A film depicts Sequoyah's life. *Open Tues.–Fri. and P.M. Sat. and Sun. except state holidays.*

9. Spiro Mounds Archeological State Park. *Spiro. From Rte. 271 go north 4½ miles on Lock and Dam Rd. 14.* One of the four greatest centers of the Mississippian Indian culture—and the most mysterious of them all—flourished here at this wide bend in the Arkansas River from the ninth to the 15th century. The park includes 140 acres and 12 mounds.

In the 1930's the great Craig Mound, which contained more than 1,000 burials and a charnel house, was ruthlessly excavated and looted. Since then archeologists have worked to salvage and restore the mound. Among the rich grave goods taken from it were stone effigies, copper breastplates, textiles, pottery, wooden fig-

urines, wooden masks with shell inlays, and delicate shell cups. Some of the artifacts were engraved with skulls, body parts, falcons, and the plumed serpent, the deity of earth and sky. Because of the strange symbolism of the mortuary art, some believe that for a time Spiro was a religious center where elaborate funerary practices were observed.

Many of the artifacts are displayed at the interpretive center. A 1½-mile-long trail winds among the mounds and passes a replica of a thatched-roof dwelling. *Open Tues.–Sat. and P.M. Sun., May–Oct.; Wed.–Sat. and P.M. Sun., Nov.–Apr. except Thanksgiving Day, Christmas, and New Year's Day.*

10. Heavener Runestone State Park. *Three miles north of Heavener.* By a small mountain creek in a tree-shaded glen halfway up Poteau Mountain stands the Heavener Runestone, a 12-foot-high slab with eight Nordic runes (alphabet characters) representing the date of the carving—November 11, 1012. Although there is no

16. *Colorful lichens have begun the process that turns stone to soil. Trees will ultimately dominate this boulder-strewn landscape.*

was the cruelest work I ever knew."

For the Seminole Indians, this tragic journey in the 1830's led from the farms of Florida's Everglades to Wewoka on the Oklahoma prairie, the new capital of the Seminole Nation. The museum here chronicles the transition of the tribe from its southeastern roots to life in a new region. Displays range from a replica of a *chicke*—the traditional Seminole Everglades dwelling built of logs, palm leaves, and hides—to the reconstructed façade of the Wewoka Trading Post, the enterprise from which the new Indian capital grew. Historic photographs recall daily life in the 19th-century Indian Territory and the oil boom of the 1920's. Also shown are examples of the patchwork clothing for which the Seminoles are still famous. *Open P.M. Tues.–Sun., Feb.–Dec.*

13. Red Rock Canyon State Park. Encircled by cliffs of soft red sandstone, the canyon was a rendezvous on the California Trail, which ran from Fort Smith, Arkansas, to the goldfields of California. Here prospectors and settlers rested their animals, restocked on water, repaired their wagons, and replenished their supplies of food and other necessities before heading on. Wagon wheel ruts still visible on the east and north walls show the difficulty

they had entering the canyon. The entrance today is via a steep but negotiable roadway that has two hairpin turns.

Willow, cottonwood, red cedar, walnut, and pecan trees grow in the canyon, for centuries a favorite wintering place for nomadic Indian tribes, who found plenty of wild game and protection from winter winds within its 80-foot-high walls.

Today the 310-acre park is enjoyed for its campsites, picnic areas, and swimming pool. The stream flowing through the ravine provides good fishing, and hikers can climb a two-mile trail around the canyon rim. *Open year-round.*

14. Black Kettle Museum. *Intersection of Rtes. 283 and 47, Cheyenne.* In the cold morning twilight of November 27, 1868, Lt. Col. George Armstrong Custer led his 7th Cavalry in a surprise attack on a sleeping Cheyenne Indian village on the shore of the Washita River. The chief of the village was Black Kettle, an outstanding Indian statesman who just days before had gone to Fort Cobb attempting to negotiate the safety of his people. Figures vary concerning the number of Cheyennes slaughtered, but many women and children died. Black Kettle and his wife were killed

while attempting to escape on their pony.

Black Kettle Museum displays artifacts from the battle and from pioneer and Indian cultures of the period 1860–80. Poignant exhibits recount the antagonists' sad history of misunderstanding. The actual battle site is accessible two miles west of Cheyenne on Route 47A. *Open Tues.–Sat. and P.M. Sun. during daylight saving time; open Wed.–Sat. and P.M. Sun. during central standard time.*

15. Quartz Mountain State Park. Set in the lee of the rugged Quartz Mountains, whose enormous red granite boulders seem to be tumbling down the hillsides, this park was once the winter campground of Kiowa and Comanche Indians. Today its 4,284 acres lure vacationers with a fine resort lodge, cabins, campsites, and picnic grounds along the shore of Lake Altus-Lugert, a large reservoir formed by a dam across the North Fork of the Red River. Fished for its bass, crappie, walleye, and catfish, the lake also offers excellent boating, canoeing, and swimming.

A nature center displays wildlife, plants, and items of local history. Native birds include vultures, hawks, kingbirds, cardinals, bluebirds, and scissor-tailed flycatchers. The half-mile New Horizon hiking trail scales the park's highest peak through live oak, yucca, prickly pear cactus, and stands of cedars. Swimming pools, a golf course, and a rugged backcountry area for off-road vehicles are additional attractions. *Open year-round.*

16. Wichita Mountains Wildlife Refuge.
Reached from Rte. 49. Comanche Indians, Spanish conquistadors, outlaws, and prospectors have prowled the boulder-strewn hills and surrounding grasslands of this 59,000-acre wildlife sanctuary. Created in 1901 to protect endangered prairie animals, the refuge is roamed by a buffalo herd maintained at around 600 head. Other protected species include longhorn cattle, elk, and wild turkeys. A prairie dog town may be seen just east of Quanah Parker Lake.

Portions of the refuge are fenced off for the protection of wildlife and visitors, but much of it can be explored by car or on foot. The public use area (which totals about 22,400 acres) offers fine fishing, boating, swimming, camping, picnicking, and hiking. Mount Scott rises 1,000 feet to the summit from its base, and the drive is worth it for the views. Fifteen miles of hiking trails lead into remote regions, including the Charons Garden Wilderness, where backpack camping is allowed by permit. The challenging 900-foot ascent of Elk Mountain brings the hiker to a labyrinthine plateau pocked with passageways and small caves among huge boulders. *Open year-round.*

17. Chisholm Trail Historical Museum.
One mile east of Waurika near junction of Rtes. 70 and 81. The trail through the center of the old Indian Territory, from Texas north to Kansas, was named for Jesse Chisholm, a part-Cherokee trader who opened up the famous route just after the Civil War. With good grazing and plenty of water along the way, it was ideal for the great herds of Texas longhorns that were driven to a Kansas rail terminal for transshipment east. The Chisholm Trail was used for about 20 years, from 1867 until the end of the 1880's, when the railroads reached Texas. Near Monument Hill, about six miles north of Waurika, you can see a wide depression in the landscape,

thought to be a remnant of the old route.

At the museum entrance a mural portrays cowboys herding half-wild longhorns. Exhibits include saddles, hats, guns, lariats, guitars, playing cards, branding irons, a stained glass window mapping the trail, railroad exhibits, Indian artifacts, and a number of pioneer farm implements. A 15-minute slide presentation dramatizes the trail's history. *Open Tues.–Fri. and P.M. Sat. and Sun. except major holidays.*

18. Turner Falls Park. *Off Rte. 77.* Cascading over Honey Creek's 77-foot-high limestone rocks into a wide, natural plunge pool, these falls (named for Mazzepa Turner, who was a rancher and state representative of the early 1900's) are the centerpiece of a 720-acre park in the heart of the Arbuckle Mountains. The upward thrust of the terrain exposes many rock formations in nearly vertical positions so dramatically that the area is renowned as a geological window on the past. In spring the slopes and fields along the roadways turn a brilliant yellow as myriads of black-eyed Susans begin to bloom.

A short walking trail to the bottom of the falls winds through Honey Creek Canyon, shaded by oak, poplar, cottonwood, locust, and walnut trees. The area is the habitat of deer, raccoons, and opossums and is frequented by many common and gregarious birds. Miles of more difficult hiking trails are also available, as are camping sites and picnic grounds. From

an overview on a rocky bluff off Route 77, visitors can see the falls and the forested canyon. *Open year-round.*

19. Beavers Bend State Park. Named for John Beavers, who once owned much of the land, this park borders the meandering Mountain Fork River deep in the Ouachita Mountains. Forested with pine and hardwood, accented by mistletoe, dogwoods, and bald cypresses along the riverbanks, the park is home to deer, small mammals, quail, wild turkeys, and many species of birds.

Forest Heritage Center, a rustic circular building, contains dioramas and other exhibits, including a slice of trunk from a 325-year-old bald cypress. A group of live southern flying squirrels can be seen in the nature center.

The David L. Boren Hiking Trail extends for 26 miles through the forest to nearby Hochatown State Park, with two backpacking campsites along the way. Beavers Bend has four nature trails threading its 3,482 acres, and the river and Broken Bow Lake are stocked with trout, catfish, bass, crappie, and perch. Activities include swimming, boating, waterskiing, and horseback riding; scattered in the woods are cabins, campsites, and picnic grounds. *Open year-round.*

18. Falling waters find various routes to the swimming hole at the base of the cliff.

Texas

The long and colorful history of the Lone Star State is well represented, as are its varied scenery and natural resources.

Some of the oldest evidence of technology in North America can be seen in a flint quarry here. A number of museums feature the many facets of Texas history, including prehistoric Indians, conquistadors, conflicts with Mexico, Indian wars, cattle ranching, the railroads, the oil boom, and turn-of-the-century nostalgia.

Several cavalry forts serve to recall the Plains Indians' determined resistance to the settlement of the land; and a petroleum museum, silver-mining ghost town, and a plantation are reminders of nature's bounty here in the Southwest.

There's a presidential museum, the home of a renowned Congressman, and the restored courtroom-saloon of a legendary judge. A variety of parks reveals the beauty of the natural scene from the hill country to the shores of the Gulf.

1. Alibates Flint Quarries National Monument. *On Rte. 136, about six miles south of Fritch. Watch for signs to Bates Canyon and the quarries.* To walk along the bluff here is to walk in the footsteps of the prehistoric people who first came to this place some 12,000 years ago in search of stone that was hard enough to kill the mammoths and buffalo upon which their subsistence depended. The Paleo-Indians, who discovered Alibates flint, used it for spear points, arrowheads, knives and scrapers, axes and awls, and other necessities. It was the only wealth they knew.

Flint is usually a solid color, but the type found here is rainbow-hued in infinite variations and patterns. The craftsmanship shown in the ancient articles made of this material is usually so superior to that of objects made of ordinary flint that the early artisans must have been responding to its beauty.

The quarries are shallow pits in the ground from 5 to 25 feet across, not much to see—except that they are the source of some of the oldest evidence we have of human technology in the continental United States. The only access to the site is by a two-hour guided walking tour from the information station at spectacular Bates Canyon on Lake Meredith. Tours start at 10 A.M. and 2 P.M. You'll need sturdy shoes and a hat for protection from the hot sun. There's no water, so a canteen is a good idea. Visitors are allowed to pick up a handful of the flint in the nearby Lake Meredith Recreation Area. *Open daily Memorial Day–Labor Day. For off-season tours call (806) 857-3151.*

---

2. Carson County Square House Museum. *Rte. 207 at 5th St., Panhandle.* The centerpiece of this 10-structure historic complex is indeed a square house. Of a distinctive colonial stick style and measuring 24 by 24 feet, it was built on the N Bar N Ranch in the mid-1880's. The white pine for its construction was brought by oxcart from the nearest railroad terminal, which was then at Dodge City, Kansas. The oldest house in town, it has been the residence of several important citizens. It now stands near its original site.

The museum's dugout dwelling, with its dark, cramped space, is more typical of housing in early Texas days, when lumber and building stone were in short supply and there was barely enough water to make good adobe. Water finally did come from wells pumped by windmills—and the Eclipse windmill here is a fine example of this important piece of equipment.

In one building are dioramas of native wildlife; another features antique farm and ranch equipment. A bank, circa 1927 (with a display of cattle brands), recalls that era of local financing. There's a blacksmith's shop, and transportation is represented by a Santa Fe Railroad caboose. The art gallery offers a variety of changing exhibits. *Open Mon.–Sat. and P.M. Sun. year-round.*

---

3. Panhandle Plains Historical Museum. *On 4th St., Canyon.* The long and varied history of the northernmost section of Texas is exquisitely captured in this well-conceived museum. One panoramic presentation, in chronological order, covers Paleozoic fossils, the culture of early man, the coming of the conquistadors, the Indian-frontier era, ranching, the petroleum boom, and modern industry. And featured in the Hall of the Southern Plains Indians is a superb collection of artifacts from the vigorous and creative Arapaho, Apache, Cheyenne, and Kiowa tribes.

Ranch life in the Panhandle is represented by saddles, branding irons, an excellent gun collection, and a chuck wagon complete with a kerosene lantern for nighttime meals. In the Pioneer Village are reconstructions of buildings that were once essential to frontier towns; all are authentically equipped and furnished.

A century-long parade of fashions (1850 to 1950) is presented in a series of realistic settings. These displays change, as do those in the center's art galleries. One building is devoted to buggies, sleighs, wagons, and automobiles. Also on the grounds is the headquarters of the T-An-

SCALE IN MILES AND KILOMETERS
ONE INCH 84 MILES 0 10 25 50 75 100
ONE INCH 135 KM 0 10 25 50 75 100 150

LEGEND

NUMBERED ATTRACTIONS DESCRIBED IN TEXT **1**

HIGHWAY MARKERS

INTERSTATE **70** UNITED STATES **40** STATE **53**

ROAD CLASSIFICATIONS

CONTROLLED ACCESS HIGHWAYS Interchanges
(Entrance and Exit only at Interchanges)

OTHER DIVIDED HIGHWAYS

PRINCIPAL THROUGH HIGHWAYS

OTHER THROUGH HIGHWAYS

CONNECTING HIGHWAYS

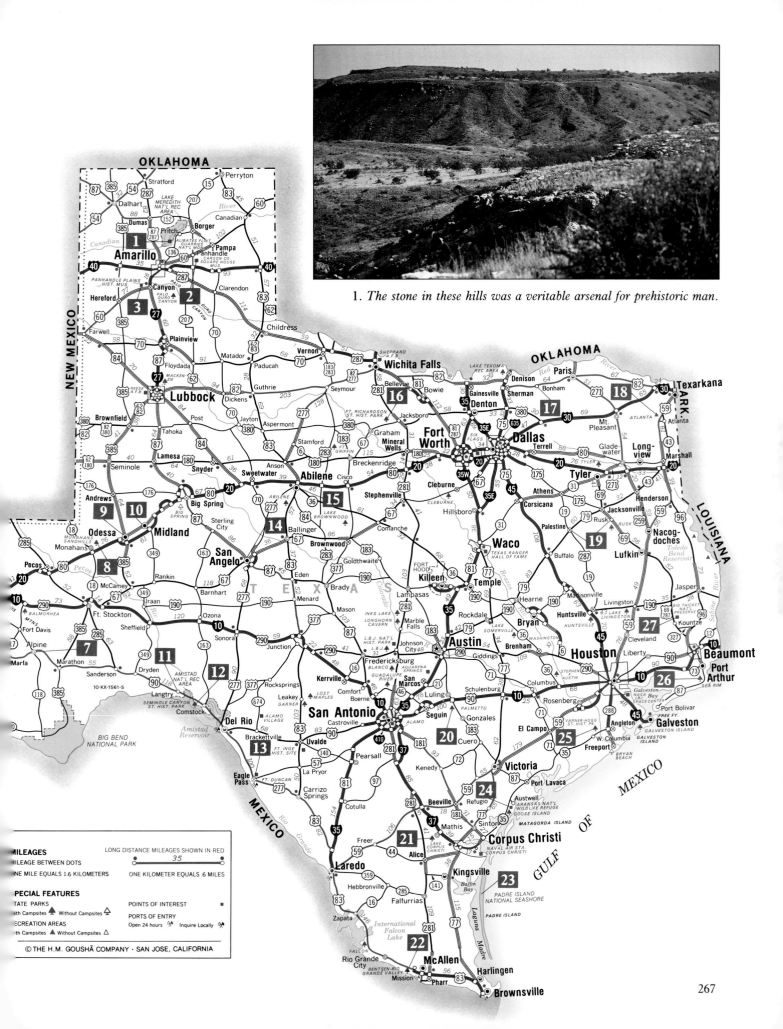

1. *The stone in these hills was a veritable arsenal for prehistoric man.*

MILEAGES

MILEAGE BETWEEN DOTS

ONE MILE EQUALS 1.6 KILOMETERS

LONG DISTANCE MILEAGES SHOWN IN RED

35

ONE KILOMETER EQUALS .6 MILES

SPECIAL FEATURES

STATE PARKS

With Campsites ⛺ Without Campsites ⛺

RECREATION AREAS

With Campsites ▲ Without Campsites △

POINTS OF INTEREST ■

PORTS OF ENTRY

Open 24 hours ⚓ Inquire Locally ⚓

10-KX-1561-S

chor Ranch, the oldest original structure in the Panhandle, and some outbuildings once found on working ranches. *Open Mon.–Sat. and P.M. Sun. except Thanksgiving Day, Christmas, and New Year's Day. Admission free but donations accepted.*

---

4. McDonald Observatory. *Fort Davis.* The drive to this mountaintop observatory, home of one of the most powerful telescopes in the world, is exciting in itself. The steep but well-maintained road offers superb open vistas as it climbs to an elevation of 6,800 feet—the highest point in Texas accessible by public road.

At the summit a short self-guiding walking tour leads to the enormous white dome that houses the University of Texas's 107-inch reflecting telescope. The measurement represents the diameter of the telescope's primary mirror. (Three other domes house smaller telescopes.)

The main dome's viewing gallery, reached by climbing five flights of stairs, is dominated by the massive telescope. It weighs 160 tons and is driven hydraulically. Its giant mirror gathers some 250,000 times more light than the unaided human eye, and a great deal more than could be gathered by optical lenses. Also noteworthy are the large control console and the removable floor, which makes it possible

to lower the mirror for a reapplication of its reflective aluminum coating. An enormous spectrometer used for studying free-floating gas and particles in the Milky Way occupies the third and fourth floors of the dome.

Doors in the dome ceiling are opened on clear nights (and sometimes for infrared observations during the day), and the telescope is rotated so that scientists can observe a particular part of the sky. Indeed, this whole part of Texas is excellent for astronomical research. The air is clear and dry; the view is unobstructed; there are no city lights in the vicinity to compete with the luminosity of the stars. Nearby Mount Fowlkes is the probable site of a new 300-inch telescope that is projected as the world's largest.

The visitor center at the base of Mount Locke offers colorful, well-designed exhibits and slide shows. On the last Wednesday of every month the giant telescope is available for public viewing—an extraordinary opportunity for which reservations must be made six months in advance. Write to the observatory's Visitor Information Center, Box 1337, Fort Davis, Texas, 79734, and enclose a stamped, self-addressed envelope for confirmation of your requested date. The least crowded months here are January and February. *Open daily except Thanksgiving Day, Christmas, and New Year's Day.*

---

5. Fort Davis National Historic Site. *Fort Davis.* For nearly 40 years U. S. cavalry from this frontier outpost escorted travelers moving westward in wagon trains and stagecoaches along the San Antonio–El Paso road, fending off Apache and Comanche raiders. The Apache leader, Geronimo, surrendered in 1886, and the fort was decommissioned in 1891.

The restored fort stands with its face toward an open plain and its back against a cliff. Davis housed some 500 people in its more than 50 buildings, which included extensive living quarters, storehouses, a hospital, bakery, laundry, sawmill, and jail. The corrals accommodated some 475 horses for eight troops of cavalry.

Some of the buildings have been restored inside and out. The most striking of these are the 13 homes along Officers' Row. Arranged in geometric precision, the gleaming white buildings with their columned façades suggest a rank of soldiers standing at permanent attention.

The visitor center, a former barracks, offers slide shows and exhibits of military uniforms, Indian dress, and historical events. In summer, costumed interpreters conduct tours and give demonstrations in the commanding officer's quarters, the kitchens, servants' quarters, and the commissary; uniformed soldiers convey a vivid sense of frontier life.

Extending up a nearby canyon are the ruins of an earlier fort, ravaged by Indians during the Civil War. Visitors interested in nature can explore the Tall Grass Trail and other well-marked paths. *Open daily except Christmas and New Year's Day. Admission charged.*

---

6. Shafter Ghost Town. Many a traveler has sped by Shafter, noticing only the dramatic view of the Chinati Mountains from the steeply banked road. Ghost towns like this one call for curiosity, initiative, and imagination: there are no tourist facilities to beckon, nor do any interpretive signs tell the story of how a once-thriving town came upon hard times and, for all practical purposes, disappeared.

From about 1875 to 1942, Shafter was a rowdy silver-mining center, with about 3,000 residents and enough tough *hombres* to require the year-round presence of three Texas rangers. As its richest veins were mined out and the price of silver fell at home and abroad, the town of Shafter began its decline. There remain only the evocative ruins of an old smelter, a church, a schoolhouse, and crumbling stone and adobe buildings. The old cemetery lies in the southeastern part of town across the creek. The ground here is so hard that it could be dug only to a depth of three feet; stones were piled up for the remaining three feet to make graves of the traditional depth. The hillside, honeycombed with tunnels and holes, is dangerous for walking and should be observed only from a distance. There's still silver "in them-thar hills," and if silver prices increase, Shafter could rise again from its ghostly state.

---

7. Museum of the Big Bend. *Sul Ross State University, Alpine.* An attractive desert garden grows at the entrance to this historical museum, located on the campus of Sul Ross State University. The muse-

4. *The first of the domes built here has a charming residential character.*

um's mission is to record the life and times of the people who have lived in West Texas during the past 12,000 years.

Dioramas and exhibits document thousands of years of prehistoric buffalo and mammoth hunts. When the local climate became drier, subsistence depended on hunting smaller prey and food gathering. Also depicted is the influence of Mexico's culture, which evolved partly from Spanish roots in that country. Graphic displays show how the region's economy has extended to cattle ranching, silver and mercury mining, and wax extraction from the stems of candelilla plants for products such as car polish and chewing gum.

Among the museum's intriguing items are a bullet-riddled stagecoach, a lady's sidesaddle, a ceremonial headdress said to have belonged to Geronimo, a medicine man's equipment, and a high-wheeler that a bicyclist rode from Ohio to Texas in 1885. Other displays recall the Texas rangers and the Mexican revolutionary, Pancho Villa. To avoid crowds, you should plan your visit for fall or winter. Big Bend takes its name from the curve of the Rio Grande about 80 miles south of Alpine on the border with Mexico. *Open daily Tues.–Sat. and P.M. Sun.; closed on university holidays.*

---

8. Monahans Sandhill State Park. Undulating dunes rise to heights of 70 feet above a table-flat landscape, remnants of a sea that was here in the Permian period some 280 million years ago. Part of a vast dune field extending for several hundred miles into New Mexico, most of the 3,840-acre park is now stabilized by vegetation; many dunes, however, are still active—they are shaped and reshaped by the incessant winds.

An interpretive center displays local natural history, including mammoth and mastodon bones, a rattlesnake exhibit, insect specimens, and a hive of living bees. A self-guiding trail begins at the interpretive center. Among the highlights of this short walk are sand sagebrush, mesquite, and the useful prairie yucca. Indians used yucca fibers for rope, the roots for soap, and other parts of the plant for food. Shin oaks, diminutive trees less than four feet tall when fully mature, spread their roots as far as 70 feet to find water.

The desert pond on the interpretive trail is man-made, but there are many natural stands of water in the dunes, especial-

8. *Surrounding evidence suggests that the struggling heliotropes will not prevail.*

ly after a rain. Willows and reeds grow in these places, creating a habitat for birds. Scaled quail, Harris's hawks, cactus wrens, and other desert birds are seen year-round, and many migratory birds stop off. The park's field checklist includes some 80 species. Trailer sites and picnic spots are located among the dunes. Most crowded in the Easter season. *Open year-round.*

---

9. The Presidential Museum. *662 N. Lee St., Odessa.* Not long after President John F. Kennedy's assassination in November 1963, a group of Odessa citizens decided to dedicate a new museum to those who have held the nation's highest office. In the Hall of the Presidents there are portraits of each chief executive along with personal memorabilia. Exhibits show the evolution of ideas, techniques, and materials that have been used in campaigning for office, including banners, buttons, posters, and bumper stickers that feature the names and faces of winners—as well as losers all but forgotten today.

The important breakthrough of radio and television campaigning is documented. Another advance, not as obvious but important, was the advent of campaign buttons made of celluloid. With this then newfangled material it was possible to show the candidates' likenesses in color instead of black and white. An interesting curiosity was the use in 1896 of "soap babies": baby-shaped cakes of soap colored either silver or gold as reminders of an important monetary question.

America's First Ladies are represented by a collection of exquisite, beautifully displayed dolls. Each is shown in her Inauguration ball gown, with matching jewelry, fans, and other accessories, and coiffed in the hairstyle worn on that memorable occasion. Of further interest to the fashion-conscious is a model of the official dress worn by the Texas "Ladies for Lyndon" (Johnson). *Open Tues.–Sat. year-round except major holidays.*

---

10. Permian Basin Petroleum Museum. *Midland.* This extraordinarily creative and surprising museum will fascinate people of all ages—whether or not they have an

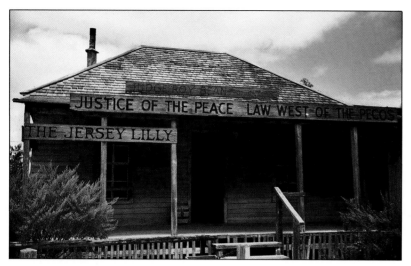 

11. *The building, plain and simple, is in keeping with the brand of justice—as well as the drinks—dispensed by the judge.*

interest in the subject of oil. Exhibits move, talk, and invite participation. The persons in old photos recount in local accents anecdotes from their lives. A spin of a dial allows you to win or lose a theoretical fortune in oil wells. A fascinating film takes you on a plane ride, looking for leaks in a pipeline, while a full-size plane nearby sways along with the film.

Highlights in one of the museum's three wings are the rooms that re-create the boomtown experience of the 1920's, and an enormous walk-through replica of a coral reef, with nearly 200,000 realistic models of coral, fish, and other marine creatures—all of which bear upon the geology of petroleum deposits. More than 200 million years of time and unimaginable pressure within the earth converted the materials in reefs like this one to the oil and natural gas we use today.

Displays in another wing feature the human history of the area and include branding irons, barbed wire, windmills, tepees, and an old-fashioned bicycle. Historical paintings are complemented by audiotapes. The North Wing, the newest section, shows an oil-well blowout that no visitor will ever forget.

Outside the museum, in the Oil Patch Exhibit, you'll find the world's largest collection of obsolete oil-drilling equipment. The rough-and-ready reputations of oilfield workers are understandable in the light of such tools and equipment. *Open Mon.–Sat. and P.M. Sun. except Thanksgiving Day, Christmas Eve, and Christmas Day. Admission charged.*

11. Judge Roy Bean Visitor Center. *Langtry.* In the last decades of the 19th century this part of Texas was still very much the Wild West, and law enforcement was a continuing problem. A former Pony Express rider and saloonkeeper named Roy Bean was appointed justice of the peace and soon became known as the "Law West of the Pecos" (the Pecos River is about 10 miles distant).

Where Bean dispensed his quick version of justice along with hard liquor in his combination courtroom, billiard hall, and saloon, the modern visitor center now dispenses travel information and features dioramas with earphones. Listeners hear about the life and times of the hard-bitten judge, including such colorful stories as that of the world championship Maher-Fitzsimmons prizefight he staged on an island in the Rio Grande in defiance of the governmental authorities in the United States, Texas, and Mexico.

Behind the visitor center is the restored courtroom-saloon with its potbellied stove, antique bottles, and photographs of Bruno, the judge's pet bear. The saloon is named the Jersey Lilly, for the English actress Lillie Langtry, whom Bean greatly admired. (She was called the Jersey Lily after her birthplace, and the misspelling of Lily is a sign painter's error.) Actually, the town was probably called Langtry for a railroad worker of that name, but Bean convinced the actress that it had been named for her, and she accepted his invitation to visit in 1904. The judge died, however, months before she arrived. In addition to Bean's establishment and the

visitor center, there's a five-acre garden with more than 100 species of cacti and other native plants. The peak bloom is in April. The place may be heavily visited in June and July. *Open year-round except Dec. 24–26 and New Year's Day.*

12. Seminole Canyon State Historical Park. *Comstock.* Water can erode rock into spectacular formations, and paradoxically, its effect may be most dramatic where it is scarce, as in this rugged area. Near the park a high bridge offers a magnificent view of the Pecos River Canyon, and visitors to the park can explore Seminole Canyon itself. The moderately strenuous hike down to the canyon floor should only be made on the guided tour. The streambed will most likely be dry, but the effect of its flow of water through the ages is evident in the width of the canyon and in the polished surface of its limestone.

The works of mankind are also in evidence here. In the Fate Bell rock shelter are the treasures of Seminole Canyon—layer upon layer of large, colorful pictographs that were painted on the rocks from 6,000 to 8,000 years ago. They depict animals, people, and some mysterious figures that may never be puzzled out.

Exhibits at the visitor center, where the guided hikes begin, include a realistic, life-sized representation of a family living in a rock shelter; another reproduces a 15-foot panther painted in a cave accessible only by boat.

Other displays depict local sheep- and goatherding—about half the world's mohair is from this region. Visitors can enjoy the desert garden, especially attractive in spring, and a gentle three-mile walk to an overlook above the Rio Grande. The 2,173-acre park has a picnic area overlooking Seminole Canyon and shaded campsites. *Open daily year-round. Canyon tours Wed.–Sun. Admission charged.*

13. Fort Duncan Park. *Eagle Pass. Follow Main St. toward toll bridge to Mexico; turn left on Adams St.; go one-half mile to Bliss St. and turn left into park.* Fort Duncan is in a pleasantly landscaped recreational park separated from the main part of Eagle Pass by Eagle Creek.

At the fort are nearly a dozen buildings that were part of a military garrison established in 1849 as a frontier outpost. For a time during the Civil War the fort was occupied by the Confederate Army, and Eagle Pass was the only port open for the export of cotton from the South. Later, during American involvement in the Mexican Revolution in 1916–17, 10,000 U.S. troops were housed here.

The restorations include the blacksmith's shop, the commanding officer's headquarters, and the small, square, windowless powder magazine.

Inside the post headquarters is a small museum with a delightfully diverse collection of objects from the past. Some exhibits recall the military presence; others, such as an old-fashioned tuba, a handmade baby carriage, and a glamorous dress from the 1890's, are mementos of civilian life. Reminders of the Indian heritage, primarily of the Kickapoo tribe, include a fishing net made from bulrushes, an oversized mortar and pestle, and a jacket impressively beaded with a peacock design. The Kickapoos, who were fierce warriors, were forced into this area from their ancestral lands in present-day Illinois and Wisconsin. *Fort open year-round; museum open (as of this writing) by appointment only. Call (512)773-2241. Admission free but donations accepted.*

14. Fort Concho National Historic Landmark. *213 E. Ave. D, San Angelo.* The Comanche and Kiowa Indians, in a last desperate effort to maintain their lands and freedom, were unwitting contributors to the settlement of the Southwestern Plains. The forts that were established to protect the pioneers became the nucleus for settlements throughout the area. Fort Concho is a good example. Started in 1867, it grew from a tent city to an establishment of stone structures built by German artisans from Fredericksburg, some 130 miles to the southeast. The cavalry based here eventually drove away the last of the Comanche Indians, and the two communities that grew up close to Fort Concho merged, becoming San Angelo, the leading town.

At this writing there were more than 24 restored buildings and others being worked on, with the goal of 36 buildings on a 20-acre site. On the 90-minute guided tour you will see barracks, a chapel, a school, a powder magazine, and outbuildings. Scores of exhibits and collections in the headquarters building relate the settlement of the land, the role of the U.S. Army, and other historic highlights. Here too are displays of natural history and local minerals. *Open Mon.–Sat. and P.M. Sun. except Thanksgiving Day, Christmas, and New Year's Day. Admission charged.*

15. Dyess Air Force Base. *Exit south off Rte. 80/84 onto Hwy. 312 (Arnold Blvd.) just west of Abilene; continue one mile to the base.* Twenty-two aircraft significant in the development of American military aviation are on display here, making this one of our nation's richest collections of historic military planes.

12. *This rugged panorama, seen from Fate Bell rock shelter, must have looked the same to those who were here some 7,000 years ago.*

Among the bombers are a World War II B-17 Flying Fortress and a huge B-52 Stratofortress—a plane first built in the 1950's and still the backbone of our strategic bomber forces. An F-86 Sabre jet fighter of the type flown in the Korean War is on display, and there are several supersonic planes from the later F-100 Century series, ranging from an early F-100 Super Sabre to an F-105 Thunderchief of the Vietnam era.

There are also amphibious planes, reconnaissance craft, tankers, trainers, interceptors, and troop carriers. Among the latter is a classic C-47 Skytrain, or "Gooney Bird," complete with the camouflage and "invasion stripes" used for the Normandy assault in June 1944. The collection and subsidiary exhibits continue to be expanded, and there are plans to build an extensive museum and military archive. *Open year-round. Inquire at base entrance about planes' locations.*

16. Fort Richardson State Historical Park. *Jacksboro.*

This is another of the forts in north-central Texas established for protection from Comanche and Kiowa raiders coming down from Indian Territory (now Oklahoma) north of the Red River. The fort was named for Union Gen. Israel B. Richardson, who was killed at the battle of Antietam, and troops were first stationed here in 1867. Soon after they arrived, the small town of Jacksboro experienced a predictable boom as saloonkeepers, gamblers, and camp followers moved in to help relieve the troopers of their boredom—and their pay.

At the fort today, several of the original fieldstone buildings are preserved or restored. The officers' quarters, powder magazine, guardhouse, commissary, bakery, and the hospital and morgue can be viewed from the park grounds. These buildings, the parade area, and the displays in the barracks are reminders of the forces that had to be marshaled to wrest this land from the Indians.

The fort is set in a 396-acre park, and a 1.7-mile hiking trail loops through the same arid landscape that confronted the soldiers when they were here. *Barracks display open daily Memorial Day–Labor Day; Fri.–Sun. and by special request the rest of the year. Park open year-round.*

17. Sam Rayburn House and Fort Inglish. *Both off Rte. 82 West, Bonham.*

Sam Rayburn, although Tennessee-born, was a dedicated Texas Democrat for a long political career comprising 25 consecutive terms in the U.S. House of Representatives—17 of those as speaker of the House. At the time of Rayburn's death in 1961 at the age of 79, no other person had served—in either capacity—for so long. Both records still stand.

Rayburn had this house built in 1916 and lived here the rest of his life. On view are many personal and family items, such as his famous 1947 Fleetwood Cadillac. The Rayburn Library, a large, imposing structure of Georgia marble, is also in Bonham. It contains a replica of the speaker's Washington office and houses his official and private papers.

Just a short way down the road from the Rayburn house is a replica of the Fort Inglish stockade, which was built in 1837. Life on the early Texas frontier is vividly evoked here by the stark outbuildings and the primitive furnishings displayed in the blockhouse. *Rayburn house open Tues.–Fri. and P.M. Sat. and Sun. year-round except Thanksgiving Day, Christmas, and New Year's Day. Fort Inglish open Mon.–Fri. and P.M. Sat.–Sun., Apr.–Sept. Admission charged to Fort Inglish.*

18. Atlanta State Recreation Area.

The main attraction of this tranquil 1,475-acre park is Lake Wright Patman, which curves some 25 miles from end to end and is about five miles across at its widest point. But the rolling woodlands of mixed pine and oak and the bottomlands of Wilkins Creek add welcome diversity for campers and hikers. There are some lovely picnic areas in the pine glades bordering the lake. In addition to the 3½-mile hiking trail there's a woodland nature trail and an area set aside for minibikes.

Fishing for crappie, bass, and catfish is considered to be excellent, especially in the fall. Waterskiing is popular, and sailing is becoming increasingly so. In the spring and fall one may be fortunate enough to see migrating waterfowl in numbers sufficient to darken the sky. *Open year-round. Admission charged.*

19. Texas State Railroad State Historical Park and Rusk-Palestine State Park.

The romance of the rails is colorfully captured in these unique parks. Even at the height of the steam-train era, it is unlikely that the rolling stock was as brightly painted or lovingly maintained as are the trains that run between Rusk and Palestine.

21. *The lake, which was once a small river, silhouettes a yucca called Spanish dagger.*

The 25 miles of track between the two towns traverse typical East Texas pastureland and picturesque, unspoiled forests of loblolly pine and hardwoods. The line crosses some 30 wooden trestles, and the right-of-way is billed as the longest and narrowest state park in the nation. The Rusk-Palestine State Park includes the two terminals and provides picnic grounds at both places. But the facilities indicated by the symbols below refer to the Rusk unit, the larger of the two. The Rusk depot, a handsome, turn-of-the-century reconstruction built of native stone, has a small theater featuring films of the railroad's history. The maintenance shops are at this end of the line.

The Palestine depot, of wood construction, is in keeping with the fine Victorian houses in this old railroad town.

The train ride is a popular attraction, and reservations should be made three to four weeks in advance. Trains start from each station at 11 A.M. The round trip takes about four hours, including the one-hour layover at the far end. *Trains run Thurs.–Mon., June–Aug; weekends only, Sept.–Oct., Mar.–May. Fare charged. For reservations call (214) 683-2561. In Texas only, call (800) 442-8951. Rusk-Palestine State Park open year-round.*

20. Palmetto State Park. *Off Rte. 183 north of Gonzales.* In this part of Texas, where the land is flat or gently rolling and the horizon is expansive, this park comes as a delightful surprise, with its unusual mixture of natural environments and its 550 species of eastern and western plants, including the dwarf palmetto.

The two-mile scenic roadway from the park entrance to the San Marcos River climbs a small hill above a rich green pasture dotted with cattle and interspersed with woodland, in striking contrast to the sculptural forms of the cactus nearby. From the hilltop the road continues through a natural arcade of pecan, elm, and oak to the trails, campsites, and picnic grounds built on the banks of the river, which flows through the 268-acre park.

Birding is best in winter; more than 240 species have been spotted, including kingfishers, cardinals, red-shouldered hawks, and the caracara, or Mexican eagle. All three short hiking trails, none more than half a mile long, are gravel-surfaced and

23. *Both beauty and function are served by black-eyed Susans that stabilize the dunes.*

easy to walk. Swimming, tubing, and boating are enjoyed in the river, and fishermen appreciate the small oxbow lake for its bass, crappie, and catfish. The park is a checkpoint on the Texas Water Safari, a 419-mile canoe race held in July. *Open year-round. Admission charged.*

21. Lake Corpus Christi State Recreation Area. In this peaceful environment dominated by Lake Corpus Christi, it is hard to imagine that the Nueces River was once a disputed boundary between the United States and Mexico. Not until after the Mexican War, which ended in February 1848, was the Rio Grande River, some 120 miles to the south, established as the official border.

The Nueces was dammed to create the lake and its 200 miles of shoreline. The park's 350 acres border a deep cove. Swimming and waterskiing are popular, and there's good fishing (especially for catfish) from the pier or from boats, which can be rented. A half-mile nature trail wends through shrubs and trees, and birders have compiled a checklist of more than 300 species observed here.

Pleasant lawns slope to the shoreline, and plantings between the picnic shelters (screened for protection from insects) provide privacy. The busy season in this popular campground: April to August. *Open year-round. Admission charged.*

22. Bentsen–Rio Grande Valley State Park. *Mission.* An oxbow lake (also called a resaca) is a cutoff section of a meandering river. The two oxbows in the park recall the wayward past of the restless Rio Grande. Here they bring to the typical dry brush of mesquite and prickly pear a moist habitat of hackberry, cedar elm, Mexican ash, and other woodland plants. The banks of the Rio Grande add yet another ecological dimension—the northernmost range of many subtropical plants and animals native to Mexico.

Professional naturalists and nature lovers are attracted by the remarkably varied flora and fauna in the park's 585 acres of river-bottom woodlands. The field checklist available at headquarters includes more than 270 species of birds. Some of the exotics are the chachalaca, pauraque, rose-throated becard, tropical kingbird, tropical parula, kiskadee flycatcher, and Mexican crow. Among the animals are the ocelot and jaguarundi (both endangered species in Texas) and the javelina, coyote, bobcat, and armadillo. Many plants and birds can be seen on the mile-long Singing Chaparral Nature Trail or on the longer hiking trail at the south end of the park. Many of the animals are nocturnal feeders and are most likely to be seen in the late evening or early morning. *Open year-round. Admission charged.*

23. Padre Island National Seashore. *Corpus Christi.* Looking at the hard sand beach and grass-covered dunes of the 67-

mile-long island, one might think that this is a stable environment. But as on all barrier islands between the sea and the mainland, the scene is ever changing. And this, of course, is part of the attraction.

Also ever changing (but annually consistent) is the great variety of birds seen here in their season. Winter residents include sandhill cranes, snow geese, and redhead and pintail ducks, while in spring falcons and a variety of songbirds return from their winter sojourn to the south. Great blue herons, gulls, terns, and brown and white pelicans may be seen year-round. All in all, from 350 to 400 species have been sighted.

The northern part of the island, around Malaquite Beach, is sometimes crowded. Swimming is good here, and there are lifeguards on duty from June through August. Ordinary passenger automobiles can go several miles farther on the beach, but south of that point a four-wheel-drive vehicle is required. Beachcombing and fishing are popular, and there are some good shell beaches between 10 and 20 miles south of the ranger station. Glass, nails, and the stinging purple jellyfish (Portuguese man-of-war) make bare feet inadvisable. *Open year-round.*

26. *A boardwalk to the beach bridges the shrubby growth to help prevent erosion.*

24. Aransas National Wildlife Refuge. At

this preserve on San Antonio Bay the plants, the birds, and the other Gulf Coast wildlife are protected from the incursion and depredation of mankind. Fittingly enough, the refuge has played a major role in the saving of the whooping crane, a magnificent bird that hunters had reduced to near extinction. Only 15 were here in 1940. By 1985 there were 69 adults and 14 young (a record number) on the refuge and from 150 to 180 in America. A platform with mounted telescopes provides an overview of the otherworldly waterscape and distant grassy islands.

The 54,829 acres are none too many for their purpose. Up to 350 species of birds winter here, and there are deer, javelinas, wild hogs, raccoons, armadillos, alligators, and turtles, while frogs thrive in the lakes and sloughs. Live oak, red bay, and hackberry are the dominant trees along the 16 miles of roadway through the preserve. Intriguingly, even the sturdiest oaks are stunted and shaped by the prevailing wind. On the well-marked nature

trails be sure to wear sturdy shoes and keep an eye out for rattlesnakes.

There are excellent wildlife displays at the visitor center, and on weekends films of wildlife on the refuge are shown. Whooping cranes linger from November through March. The refuge is least crowded in midweek in early spring and early fall. It is hot in summer and mosquitoes are abundant. Insect repellent is recommended. *Open year-round.*

25. Varner–Hogg State Historic Park.

West Columbia. The aura of grace, charm, peace, and quiet that one encounters on this former plantation is surely a reflection of its long and productive past as part of Texas and southern culture. In 1824 Martin Varner was one of 300 applicants granted land when Texas was still a province of Mexico; he built a cabin, worked the land, and raised stock for about 10 years before heading on to the less populated parts of northeast Texas. Under a succession of subsequent owners this remained a working plantation until 1901, when James Stephen Hogg, a former governor of the state, bought the place to use

as a country estate. His belief that there was oil on the land was substantiated in 1917, nine years after his death. Income from the well goes to the University of Texas, which owns mineral rights.

The main house was extensively remodeled by Hogg's daughter Ima and his three sons in 1920. In 1958 the plantation was deeded to the state by Miss Hogg and named for its first and last owners. The house is furnished in the style of prosperous planters of the mid-19th century.

Near a grove of stately pecans a large planting of paper-white narcissus blooms gloriously in December and January. *Open Tues., Thurs.–Sat., and P.M. Sun. year-round. Admission charged.*

26. Sea Rim State Park. With the Gulf of

Mexico on one side and a vast stretch of salt marsh on the other, this park is truly a natural wonder. The name is derived from the so-called sea rim marsh, the section of the marsh grass that extends into the neighboring surf.

The park is composed of some 15,000 acres along Route 87, a vulnerable ribbon of pavement that occasionally disappears under the high tides spawned by tropical storms and hurricanes. Within its borders are three miles of sandy beach and more than 3,000 acres of marshland inhabited by alligators, muskrats, nearly 300 species of birds, and in spring and fall an amazing variety of waterfowl.

Along part of the coastline here, the tidal marshlands meet the waters of the Gulf to create an important nursery ground for shrimp, crab, and other marine life. The beach unit headquarters behind the dunes offers interpretive exhibits. The ⅔-mile-long Gambusia nature trail, also in this section of the park, is a boardwalk that affords an intimate perspective of this fascinating environment.

The nearby Marshlands Unit provides access to boat trails in the marsh, and there are some platforms for observing the wildlife. *Open year-round except during hurricane threats. Admission charged.*

27. Big Thicket National Preserve. *Visitor information station on Rte. 420, off Rte. 69/287.* In the meadows and swamps and the pine and hardwood forests here, one is reminded of many different regions in the United States. Aptly described as "the biological crossroads of North America," the 12 units of this 84,550-acre preserve have overlapping habitats that support an extraordinary variety of flora and fauna.

Bogs and cypress trees of the southeastern swamplands, grasslands and meadows of the Central Plains, Southwest desert cactus and yucca, and the trees of eastern hardwood forests are all found within a 50-square-mile area. Nearly 1,000 kinds of flowering plants grow in the thicket, including four of North America's five species of insect-eating plants.

This ecological anomaly is a remnant of the continent's last major Ice Age, which ended more than 10,000 years ago. As the glaciers pushed south, they carried the seeds of numerous plants—and forced animals—from northerly regions into this area. Many of these species adapted to their new environment, with its varied climate and soil, and continue to thrive here.

The preserve is referred to as "an American ark," for the unusual diversity of wildlife it accommodates. Such unlikely neighbors as wood ducks and roadrunners, armadillos and bobcats are seen here and some 300 species of birds.

Fishermen enjoy the many creeks and sloughs, and hikers take to the trails. Those who prefer to see Big Thicket by car follow the self-guiding, 74-mile auto tour, which has both paved highways and one-lane dirt roads and must be driven in a counterclockwise direction. Allow about 2½ hours plus time for stops to explore this world of haunting beauty. *Open year-round. Visitor information station open daily except Tues.–Wed. in Jan.–Feb.*

27. *The barred owl and the lovely pink orchid are among the many fascinating creatures and plants found here in the Big Thicket. At left is a typical section of upland pine and hardwood forest.*

Montana

The Old West of song and story is recalled here in a variety of ways, as are some admirable works of man and nature.

A superb museum is dedicated to the Indians who once dominated the plains, and a refuge protects a herd of buffalo descended from the millions that once thundered across this land. Here too is the battlefield where the Indians won a victory that led to their ultimate defeat.

Another side of life on the plains is revealed in a historic site where one can savor the good life of a successful rancher. There's also the home, the studio, and the works of an artist who captured the very spirit of the Old West.

The early days of mining are remembered in a preserved ghost town and two others restored to life. The unpredictable forces of nature are exemplified in an underground fantasyland, a devastating landslide, and some marvelous sandstone formations carved by wind and water in a prehistoric riverbed.

1. Hungry Horse Dam and Reservoir.

One of the world's highest dams, 3,565 feet above sea level, rises in the magnificently wild country of the Columbia River's Montana drainage basin. It spans the south fork of the Columbia's tributary, the Flathead, and helps to control flooding on the Columbia farther downstream. Visitors may drive along the dam's crest and take self-guiding tours of the power plant, where, at peak capacity, 80 tons of water per second turn each of four massive generator turbines. These produce about 1 billion kilowatt-hours of electricity annually for the entire Pacific Northwest; audiotapes and an automated display explain this truly remarkable feat of engineering.

Behind the dam lies Hungry Horse Reservoir, 34 miles long and 3½ miles wide at its maximum. A 115-mile Forest Service road through the Flathead National Forest circles the reservoir, providing solitude and wonderful views of the surrounding mountains (especially of the towering bulk of Great Northern Mountain); it also offers access to campsites and to the reservoir for boating, waterskiing, swimming, and fishing. *Open daily Memorial Day–Labor Day; weekdays only, May and Sept.–Nov.*

2. Museum of the Plains Indian and the Bob Scriver Museum of Montana Wildlife and Hall of Bronze. *Browning. The two museums are at the intersection of U.S. Hwys. 2 and 89.* The Museum of the Plains Indian, managed by the U.S. Department of the Interior, contains superb collections of costumes and accessories from 10 tribes of the northern plains, as well as dioramas showing Indian lifestyles before the coming of the white man in the 1800's. Weapons, beadwork, ceremonial objects, toys, and other crafts are shown. The associated craft center also displays contemporary Indian work.

The nearby Museum of Montana Wildlife celebrates North America's other natives, her wild creatures. The animals—moose, buffalo, predatory and game birds—are mounted in dioramas showing their natural environments. Some handsome bronzes by sculptor Bob Scriver portray western themes. *The Museum of the Plains Indian open daily June–Sept.; weekdays Oct.–May. The Museum of Montana Wildlife open daily May–Oct.; no set schedule rest of year; admission charged.*

3. Fort Peck Dam and Fossil Museum.

Fort Peck. Among the world's largest earthfill dams, Fort Peck Dam is a major prototype for virtually all other such dams now in existence. Begun in 1933 for flood control, improved navigation along the Missouri River, irrigation, and the creation of hydroelectric power, it was finished seven years later and is an astonishing colossus: 250.5 feet high, 3.96 miles long, and .96 of a mile wide at the base. The cutoff wall is two miles long and consists of 17,000 tons of steel sunk to a maximum depth of 163 feet. The main wall contains enough earth and gravel to cover a square mile to a depth of 125 feet.

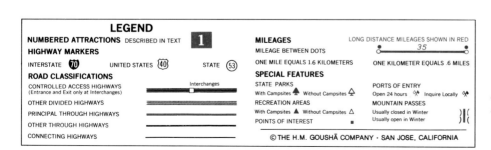

During the construction many fossils were excavated. At the museum in the dam's powerhouse you can examine more than 400 fossils, including the horn core of a 63-million-year-old *Triceratops* dinosaur. While you are there be sure to take the guided tour of the powerhouse itself.

Fossil hunting is a popular activity in this area, which has remained virtually unchanged for some 65 million years, but to find fossils requires some experience. For maps of the most likely places and information about summertime fossil-hunting expeditions (conducted by universities, which usually allow visitors to go along), write to the U.S. Army Corps of Engineers, Montana Area Office, Fort Peck, Montana 59223.

Walled up behind the dam are the gleaming waters of Lake Fort Peck: 134 miles long and up to 16 miles wide. Its 1,520-mile shoreline is surrounded by the million-acre, buffalo-grazed Charles M.

2. Eleven notable deeds in the life of Blackfoot Mountain Chief (in yellow) are depicted on this buffalo robe. That he lived to the age of 93 is evidence of his prowess.

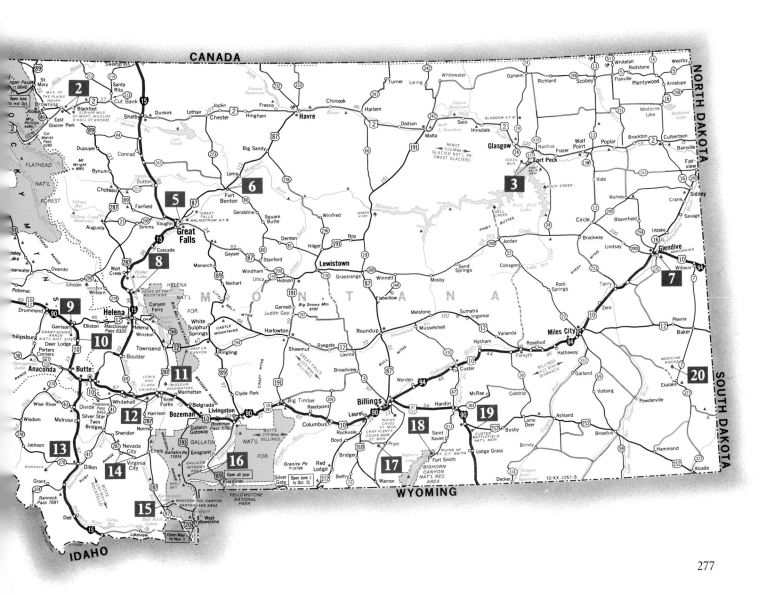

Russell National Wildlife Range. Fishing, boating, and swimming are allowed in the lake, and several public recreation areas offer boat-launching ramps, campgrounds, and picnic facilities. *Powerhouse tours given daily, June–Aug.*

4. National Bison Range. Possibly as many as 50 million bison (the scientifically correct term for the American buffalo) once roamed the American prairies, but hunters so reduced their numbers that by 1900 fewer than 100 were known to exist in the wild. In 1908, at the instigation of the American Bison Society and with President Theodore Roosevelt's help, the National Bison Range was founded: some 19,000 fenced acres of high prairie, forest, and bottomlands in the Flathead Valley. On October 17, 1909, the first seven of these majestic creatures were introduced: two from Texas, two from Montana, and another three from New Hampshire. Today the refuge's herd of 350 to 450 is one of the country's largest. Annually, during the first week of October, excess animals are rounded up for auction.

Two self-guiding auto tours provide a safe and leisurely way to see this untamed country, which is colorful with wildflowers and flowering shrubs in late spring and rich with animal and bird life at all seasons. The shorter auto tour, the Buffalo Prairie Drive, takes only about 20 minutes. The two-hour, 19-mile Red Sleep Mountain Scenic Drive (open mid-May into October) is in some places steep and winding, but its views range from mountains clad with ponderosa pine and Douglas fir to high, rolling grasslands and streamsides thick with alder, birch, and willow. Golden eagles soar at the higher elevations, where elk, mule deer, mountain goats, and bighorn sheep range; pronghorn antelopes wander the high grasslands, and white-tailed deer and water birds frequent the marshy spots. Mission Creek, north of the range, is favored by migrating waterfowl in fall.

There's a nature trail near the visitor center. Fishing is allowed along stretches of Mission Creek. *Range open year-round; visitor center open daily in summer and weekdays in winter.*

5. Charles M. Russell Museum. *400 13th Street North, Great Falls.* Charlie Russell, "the cowboy artist" who came to Montana from Missouri in 1880 when he was 16 years old, during the days of the great cattle ranches, has given his name to this authentic western museum. Working as a rider and wrangler, Russell made his first sketches to entertain his fellow cowboys. His first nationally famous painting was "Last of the Five Thousand," showing a starving cow in the dreadful winter of 1886–87. In 1914 an exhibition of his work was shown in London, and one of his last paintings, still unfinished, sold for $30,000 after his death in 1926.

The museum stands next to the artist's log-cabin home and studio, built in 1903 and authentically furnished. In the museum are some of Russell's most famous paintings and sculptures, including "Jerk Line" and "Buffalo Hunt," which recall a legendary period in the American West. Among the personal memorabilia shown are Russell's letters, some of them illustrated with sketches. *Open Mon.–Sat. and P.M. Sun., June–Aug.; Tues.–Sun., Labor Day–May.*

6. Fort Benton. Founded in 1846, Fort Benton is called the birthplace of Montana. Standing at the farthest extreme of the Missouri's navigable waters, and at the crossroads of important 19th-century pioneer trails, the river port attracted fur traders and, some years later, miners making for western Montana's goldfields. In 1867, an extremely busy year, some 8,000 tons of supplies and several thousand steamboat passengers were landed on Fort Benton's levee, and the steamboat *Richmond* was hijacked.

Today Fort Benton's waterfront, with its many historic monuments, is a fascinating reminder of those roistering days. In old Fort Park on Front Street are the ruins of Old Fort Benton, an outpost of the American Fur Company and later the garrison of the 21st Infantry and the

4. The number of calves in this herd is encouraging evidence that the future of the buffalo, once threatened, is now assured.

Blackfoot Indian Agency. Also located in the park is the Museum of the Upper Missouri, which re-creates both the vigor and the excitement of mid-19th-century life and the community's importance in America's westward expansion. *Museum open daily June–Labor Day; P.M. only, May and Sept.*

7. Makoshika State Park. The Montana badlands are dramatically beautiful (especially at sunset and dawn or after a light snowfall) and severely inhospitable. In Makoshika State Park the land has been stripped to the bone, its 8,000 acres gnawed by the elements into gulches and steep-walled valleys, spires, pinnacles, and table-topped buttes.

A maintained road brings visitors to a trailer campground three miles within the park. From there a nine-mile self-guiding drive (closed in winter) leads to several panoramic lookouts. Many fossils have been found here, and it's easy to believe that the bones of ancient creatures are part of this parched and rocky terrain, which is tinted with every bold and delicate hue in the palette of earth colors. The region is windswept, baked, and frozen by endless successions of weather extremes.

Hiking trails and the scenic drive are used for cross-country skiing and snowmobiling in winter. In the hot summer, shaded picnic areas atop its buttes are cooled by refreshing breezes. *Open year-round but water is turned off in winter.*

8. Gates of the Mountains. *From I-15 about 16 miles north of Helena, take Gates of the Mountains exit and continue to Lewis and Clark Landing.* Some 300 million years in the making, Meriwether Canyon (through which the Missouri River flows) is spectacular to see. Limestone cliffs, intricately folded and studded with fossil remains from the ancient Mississippian Sea, rise sheer above the river to 1,200 feet. Their "singular appearance" so impressed the explorer Meriwether Lewis in 1805 that in his journal he called the canyon "the Gateway to the Rocky Mountains."

Cruises of the nearly six miles of gorge are available from Gates of the Mountains Landing. From the boat you can see ancient Indian pictographs and with luck glimpse bighorn sheep, Rocky Mountain

9. *Prosperity as afforded by a well-managed cattle ranch is clearly indicated here.*

goats, ospreys, and bald eagles. The boat stops at the Lewis and Clark campsite—now a lovely picnic ground—before making its return run. *Cruises are offered daily Memorial Day–Sept. Fare charged. For information call (406) 458-5341.*

9. Grant-Kohrs Ranch National Historic Site. *Deer Lodge.* In the 1850's a Canadian fur trapper named Johnny Grant abandoned his traplines and started raising cattle in Montana. By 1866, when he sold his ranch to Conrad Kohrs, he had 2,000 head of cattle and the finest house in the state. Kohrs became one of the great cattle barons of the American West. His wife, Augusta, whom he brought to Montana when she was 19 years old, made her frontier home a model of 19th-century elegance, importing the best furnishings from St. Louis and Chicago.

Although the ranchland has been reduced from its original 25,000 acres to only 266, the main house and its original furnishings are preserved intact, along with the bunkhouse, stables, barns, sheds, and workshops dating as far back as the 1860's. Park rangers conduct tours of the main house; the 13 outbuildings are on the route of a self-guiding tour. A former barn for thoroughbreds now houses a collection of horse-drawn vehicles. *Open year-round except Thanksgiving Day, Christmas, and New Year's Day. Fee may be charged for house tour.*

10. Towe Ford Museum. *Deer Lodge.* One of the world's largest collections of antique Ford automobiles, this museum includes about 75 different models produced between 1903 and 1952, with examples of the major changes in the evolution of Ford cars, all in gleaming, immaculate condition and ready to run. Among the highlights are a carmine red 1903 Model A, a red 1906 Model N with brass trim, and a well-equipped 1922 Leland Lincoln camper that Henry Ford used on trips to the wilderness.

The museum is adjacent to the Old Montana Prison, a grandiose, chateaulike structure that was in active use from 1871 to 1979 and is now in *The National Register of Historic Places.* A self-guiding tour presents the story of confinement here from the inmates' point of view. You'll see a cell house with 200 cells, some having such descriptive names as Siberia East, The Black Box, and Turkey Pete Cell, after one of the prison's most colorful characters. *Ford Museum presently open year-round except Thanksgiving Day and Christmas; admission charged.*

11. Deep Creek Canyon. *Along Hwy. 12 east of Townsend.* This seldom frequented area of the Helena National Forest offers the solitude of primeval woodland: magnificent groves of lodgepole pines and towering Douglas firs. One senses here that nature has fulfilled herself; that time and the mountains, free from human intervention, have brought forth their best. Eagles and peregrine falcons soar above the heights; elk, deer, black bears, mountain goats, and moose roam the nearly 1 million acres of preserve; and streams like Deep Creek flicker with trout. The U.S. Forest Service maintains a day-use area four miles west of the campground on Highway 12. *Area accessible year-round; campground open Memorial Day–Sept.*

12. Lewis and Clark Caverns State Park.

Although the caverns were not discovered until 1892, they are named for the explorers Lewis and Clark, who passed this way in the first decade of the 19th century. The caverns, a series of corridors and chambers, reach 326 feet below the entrance. A long flight of steps descends to the Spiral Staircase Room, graced by perfectly formed fluted pillars—opaque stalactites and stalagmites. One continues to the Cathedral Room, from whose floor stalagmites rise to a domed ceiling. Corridors filigreed and draped with mineral deposits lead to the Garden of Gods, which has stalactites, stalagmites, and helictites resembling twisted tree roots coming out of the walls. The long chamber also contains the Crystal Pool, tinted green by the oxidation of pennies tossed in by tourists. The last stop on the two-hour walk is the Paradise Room, where you can see cavern formations that are still active. *Open daily May–Sept. Admission charged.*

13. Bannack State Park. *Dillon.* On July 28, 1862, a small band of prospectors led by John White found gold in Grasshopper Creek, and by the fall of the year Bannack had sprung up, a mining town with a population of 400 to 500. According to Lucia Darling, the observant niece of Montana's first territorial governor, it was a "tumultuous and rough" place, "the headquarters of highwaymen" where "lawlessness and misrule seemed the prevailing spirit." Nevertheless, in 1864 Bannack became Montana Territory's first capital.

Today Old Bannack is a ghost town, preserved as a state park but not restored. Along its dusty streets is a fascinating collection of weathered and decaying buildings—the Meade Hotel, which once served as the county courthouse, Skinner's saloon, and the first jail in Montana—all in their own way more eloquent of the frontier than perfect restorations

20. *Some aspect of resistance to the forces of erosion accounts for this imposing monolith.*

would be. There is also a replica of the gallows where Henry Plummer, sheriff of Bannack, and his henchmen were hanged in 1864. He and his "road agents," who murdered more than 100 travelers along the route between Bannack and Virginia City, had for their secret identification a special cut of the beard, a particular knot in the necktie, and the password "I am innocent." The vigilantes who tracked them down also had a code, the mysterious numbers 3–7–77, which are worn today on the shoulder patches of the Montana highway patrol; at Bannack, reminders of the past are especially vivid.

Adjoining the townsite is a well-equipped campground in a grove of cottonwoods frequented by magpies. The creek is fished for trout. *Open year-round.*

14. Nevada City and Virginia City. In 1863 the biggest gold strike in Montana's history took place at Alder Gulch. Within three years the deposits yielded some $30 million in gold, and Montana was declared a territory. Virginia City, a brand-new mining town at the hub of an area where population boomed to more than

10,000, became territorial capital in 1865.

Today Virginia City and nearby Nevada City, another frontier mining town, are restored to look as they did in their heyday in the late 1800's. Along Nevada City's five streets are shops, a Chinese neighborhood, a music hall containing a notable collection of mechanical "music machines," and a hotel offering today's guests both airy Victorian rooms and restored miners' cabins, some with sod roofs. The Alder Gulch Short Line Steam Railroad Museum has vintage rolling stock and once-luxurious passenger cars.

A narrow-gauge railway line carries passengers along the 1½-mile route between Nevada City and Virginia City. Along the tree-lined boardwalks of the latter are authentically furnished stores—an assay office, a jeweler's shop, and Montana's first newspaper office. The Fairweather Hotel is striking for its Victoriana. *Open year-round. Nevada City guided walking tours Apr.–Sept.; fee charged.*

15. Madison River Canyon Earthquake Area. This unusual site is a monument to a recent natural disaster, one that hap-

pened suddenly the night of August 17, 1959: in but 30 seconds, 40 million cubic yards of rock and earth, an entire mountainside, broke loose from the south side of Madison River Canyon and, traveling at a speed of about 100 miles per hour, piled up 400 feet high against the canyon's northern wall.

The mile-long landslide was caused by an earthquake measuring 7.1 on the Richter Scale. In an instant the earth cracked open, Hebgen Lake fell 100 feet, and huge waves oscillated on its surface for more than 11 hours; behind the landslide a new lake 150 feet deep—called Earthquake Lake—was formed. Twenty-eight people lost their lives; 250 others, campers in the canyon, miraculously survived on the ridge now known as Refuge Point.

You can see the results of the quake from several sites and follow a short trail to a dolomite boulder that floated across the canyon. In summer the visitor center, built on the landslide, explains the event with a slide show. *Open year-round.*

---

16. Gallatin Petrified Forest. *From Rte. 89 about 17 miles north of Gardiner, turn onto Tom Miner Rd.; continue 12 miles to National Forest Campground.* The petrified forest here is overwhelming in its grandeur: 40 square miles of ancient stone trees buried millions of years ago by volcanic ash. More than 100 species of trees and shrubs have been identified in the remains of 27 successive forests, each in turn destroyed by volcanic eruptions.

From the improved campground in the Tom Miner area (a beautiful setting with a stream), it is about a two-mile hike on a good trail to the forest. The trails from Route 191 are longer and more rugged.

For the price of a $5 permit, one can collect up to 25 pounds of petrified wood per day, with a limit of 100 pounds per person per year. While picking up the pieces, keep in mind that you'll be carrying them out on a trail that will seem longer than it did walking in. The permits and maps showing the legal collecting areas are obtained from Gallatin National Forest District Rangers in Gardiner, Livingston, and Bozeman. *Auto access is usually possible from June 16 to Sept. 15.*

---

17. Chief Plenty Coups State Monument. *Pryor.* Chief Plenty Coups was held in such esteem by the Crow Indians that they voted not to have any chief after him. Despite the disgraceful treatment of his tribe by the federal government and the steady erosion of reservation lands, he counseled peaceable coexistence.

When Plenty Coups was 12 years old, he visualized a place "where the plums grow." Twenty-five years later, in 1885, his vision materialized in a 319-acre tract allotted to him by the government, and here he made his home for the rest of his life. In 1928, four years before his death, he and his wife deeded 190 acres of the land for a "Nations Park, to be enjoyed by everyone without discrimination."

Today the park contains a picnic ground and a museum depicting the culture of the Crow Indians and housing the personal belongings of Plenty Coups. *Open daily May–Sept.*

---

18. Bighorn Canyon National Recreation Area. In 1968 the completion of the Yellowtail Dam across the Bighorn River created 71-mile-long Lake Bighorn, which extends south into Wyoming. Edging both sides of the lake, the national recreation area encompasses some of the most spectacular canyon scenery in the world.

There are three boat launches: one near the dam, another at Barry's Landing, and the third at Horseshoe Bend in Wyoming. Route 37, which goes to Barry's Landing, not only gives good access to the area for those without boats, but offers wonderful views, most especially from Devil Canyon Overlook. The road traverses the beautiful Pryor Mountain Wild Horse Range, paralleling the old Bad Pass Trail, which was used for centuries by the Shoshones traveling north to the buffalo grounds.

Backcountry campgrounds at Black Canyon and Medicine Creek are accessible only by boat; those at Fort Smith Village, Barry's Landing, and Horseshoe Bend (in Wyoming) can be reached by car. *Campgrounds open year-round.*

---

19. Custer Battlefield National Monument. Few American military engagements are as famous as the battle of the Little Bighorn, where on June 25–26, 1876, Col. George Armstrong Custer, hero of the Civil War and Plains Indians campaigns, and more than 225 of his troops were killed by Sioux and Cheyenne warriors under the command of Chief Crazy Horse and Chief Gall. News of Custer's disaster shocked a nation, and within months a strongly reinforced army destroyed the last remnants of the Indians' resistance to the seizure of their hunting grounds in the Black Hills.

The battlefield monument is in two parts. The larger, which also contains a national cemetery, includes the site of Custer's "last stand." Small white marble markers indicate where the dead may have fallen. The other site is the Reno–Benteen area, where troops led by Maj. Marcus Reno, Custer's second-in-command, and by Capt. Frederick Benteen were pinned down by Chief Gall. Several paths cross the battlefield. At the visitor center is a scale model of the engagement and other excellent interpretive materials. Lectures and guided tours are also offered. *Open year-round.*

---

20. Medicine Rocks State Park. *North of Ekalaka.* Here is one of the strangest landscapes in Montana: the sandstone of a prehistoric riverbed has been eroded by wind and water into an amazing gallery of surreal formations, some rising 80 feet above the plain. Here are arches and columns, caves and pinnacles, and flat-topped mountains up to 200 feet wide, pocked with holes and crannies. Tan colored by day, the bizarre formations are silvery and eerie in moonlight. Fossils of mammals that roamed the area 50 million years ago have been found, and there is evidence of human habitation dating back more than 11,000 years.

Theodore Roosevelt thought the Medicine Rocks "fantastically beautiful" and is said to have left his initials on the soft stone. The rocks take their name from the Indian medicine men who performed ritual dances here. The park has primitive campgrounds, a six-mile guided nature trail, and a steep half-mile walk down to the badlands. *Open year-round, but may be inaccessible by car in winter.*

Idaho

The Gem State offers recollections of its vigorous past and a wondrous variety of places to visit and things to see and do.

The ghost towns stand as poignant reminders of soaring hopes, hard labor, and the broken dreams of those who came here to make their fortune. On a positive note is a town that survived those days and now, returned to vibrant life, retains only the charm of its ghostly aura. The oldest structure in the state was built to serve God, not Mammon, and (with or without heavenly intervention) is beautifully preserved.

Some of the wonders in these parts seem to have been touched by the supernatural: here are sand dunes in an unlikely place, waterfalls that spring from a canyon wall, a surreal cityscape of huge megaliths, a cave where mounds and pillars of ice never melt, and another where the fossil remains of creatures from an ancient tropical sea remind us that the face of the earth is ever-changing. Not so surprising, but with great appeal, are the rivers, lakes, hot springs, canyons, wildlife and wildflowers, and a park that boasts 24 different historic sites.

1. Priest Lake State Park. *Coolin.* The park's three campgrounds give access to an aqueous jewel: a 26-mile-long sapphire-blue mountain lake. Priest Lake takes its name from the indefatigable Jesuit missionary Pierre Jean De Smet, who in 1846, according to legend, became the first white man to see it. The surrounding forest is so thick that until logging roads were put through in the 1950's most travel through the area was by boat.

Fishing is excellent, with Mackinaw and rainbow trout among the likely catches. The lake's several remote, undeveloped islands, at once peaceful and intriguing, all invite exploration.

Just north of Priest Lake is Upper Priest Lake, a wilderness area accessible only by boat or foot trail. The two lakes are connected by a meandering two-mile stream known locally as the Thoroughfare, which provides an enjoyable and picturesque route for a day trip by powerboat or canoe from the Lionhead Campground at the northeastern end of Priest Lake.

A three-quarter-mile hiking trail beginning at the Indian Creek Campground,

located near the center of Priest Lake's eastern shore, leads through a cedar forest to a promontory from which there are magnificent views. There are also longer backpacking trails into the Selkirk Mountains. The area is accessible in the winter and offers miles of snowmobile and cross-country ski trails. *Indian Creek Campground open year-round; day-use fee charged. Lionhead and Dickensheet campgrounds open May–Sept.*

2. Old Mission State Park. *Take exit 39 off I-90, Cataldo.* The former Jesuit mission that is the focal point of this park is the oldest building in Idaho. It was built between 1848 and 1853 by members of the Coeur d'Alene Indian tribe under the direction of Father Anthony Ravalli, and its design reflects a pragmatic blend of Old World ideals and the building materials available in the Idaho wilderness.

The walls of the mission are rough-hewn logs covered with a wattle and daub lattice. In 1865, after a sawmill was built on the mission's grounds, siding and interior paneling were added, which made the walls 24 inches thick. European-style chandeliers were fashioned from tin cans, and wooden altars and crosses were painted to imitate gilt and marble. Many of the wall hangings were made of cloth from the Hudson Bay Trading Post, and others were made by painting newspapers. A thriving Coeur d'Alene farming village was established at the mission, and about 40 Indians lived here until the tribe was forced onto a reservation in 1877. The park also contains the old parish house (1895) and part of the original cemetery. *Open daily Mar.–Oct. Admission charged.*

3. Wallace. To visit this remarkably preserved town is to step back to the turn of the century and be immersed in the aura of a time gone by. Indeed, the entire downtown district, a virtual compendium

of architectural styles, is listed in *The National Register of Historic Places.*

One can take a self-guiding walking tour of 38 historic buildings constructed between 1890 and 1930: small-town banks, hotels, lodges, churches, stores, offices, and homes in styles including Victorian Commercial, Neoclassical, Renaissance Revival, and Art Deco. The tour can be done in about 45 minutes, but there is a wealth of finely crafted detail to linger over, and many of the interiors are as fascinating as the exteriors; anyone particularly interested in architecture could spend several hours exploring the town's buildings in depth.

Wallace has long been a mining and trade center, and the Coeur d'Alene District Mining Museum here should not be overlooked. It has an interesting collection of tools, equipment, rock samples, and memorabilia, as well as informative dioramas and displays showing various mining methods. The area still produces almost half the nation's newly mined silver. *Museum open daily May–Sept.; weekdays only the rest of the year.*

4. Heyburn State Park. *Six miles east of Plummer on Hwy. 5.* From a roadside vantage point about two miles inside this 8,000-acre park, you can view a sight so strange that it seems almost impossible: a river flowing between narrow natural levees as it crosses another body of water. What you are looking at is part of "the river between the lakes," a section of the St. Joe River that seems miraculously, like Moses, to divide the waters of not only one but four separate lakes. Actually, the explanation for this mind-boggling view is simple. In 1906 a dam was built at Post Falls on the Spokane River. The backwaters from the dam inundated the low-lying land around the St. Joe River, creating a series of shallow lakes along its banks. Since the St. Joe was here before the lakes were formed, it does divide their waters, but it doesn't have to perform any miracles to do it.

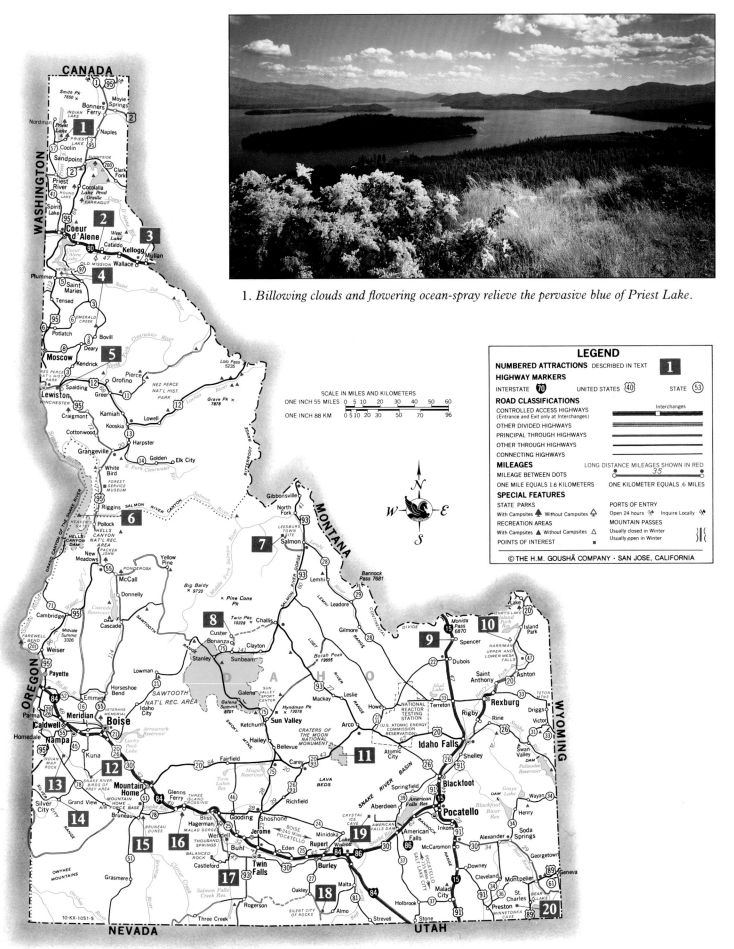

1. *Billowing clouds and flowering ocean-spray relieve the pervasive blue of Priest Lake.*

5. *Here at White Bird Battlefield it is not hard to understand why the Nez Perce fought so hard to retain their ancestral land.*

Wild rice in these shallow lakes makes this an outstanding habitat for waterfowl, and the bass, trout, and kokanee attract not only anglers but also a large colony of ospreys in the summer. The park has camping and picnic areas, beaches, lodges, and boat launches. There is water access to Lake Coeur d'Alene. Hikers on the extensive system of trails are rewarded with spectacular views.

You might want to try a day trip from Heyburn to the Emerald Creek Garnet Area, 10 miles west of Route 3 and 24 miles south of St. Maries. For a $4 daily fee you can dig as much as five pounds of garnets here. In addition to a strong back, you'll need a shovel, a bucket, and a mesh screen to sift and wash the stones. *Heyburn open year-round. Emerald Creek open Memorial Day–Labor Day.*

5. Nez Perce National Historical Park.
Visitor center: Rte. 95, Spalding. For centuries the Nez Perce Indians lived in the valleys of the Snake and Clearwater rivers. In 1805 they welcomed Lewis and Clark

and told them of the great water route to the Pacific along the Snake and Columbia rivers. The tribe lived in relative peace with the influx of American settlers until gold was discovered on tribal lands in the 1860's and the government proposed to limit the Indians to a reservation one-tenth the size of the territory they had been guaranteed. The war of 1877 eventually led to the Nez Perces' defeat. Their brilliant leader, Chief Joseph, is famous for the lucid eloquence with which he expressed the finality of his people's tragic surrender: "From where the sun now stands, I will fight no more forever."

The park comprises 24 separate historically significant sites scattered over four counties, most of them within the Nez Perce reservation. They commemorate not only the Nez Perces but also explorers, missionaries, traders, and gold miners. The park headquarters at Spalding has a visitor center that offers films and interpretive talks and includes a museum portraying the Nez Perce culture with beautiful examples of the Indians' dress, beadwork, and other artifacts as well as early photographs. Within a short drive of Spalding you can see the various sites of

the 1836 mission, a gristmill, the early Indian Agency, and Fort Lapwai. If you're headed south on Route 95, you might pause below Grangeville to enjoy Camas Prairie and the spectacular scenery along the auto tour of the White Bird Battlefield, where the U.S. Army was defeated in the first engagement of the Nez Perce War. In the surrounding area camping, boating, swimming, hiking, and fishing are available. *Visitor center open daily except Thanksgiving Day, Christmas, and New Year's Day.*

6. Heaven's Gate, Hells Canyon. *About one mile south of Riggins, exit west off Rte. 95 onto Forest Service Rd. 517; continue 19 miles to road's end.* It is easy to understand why this scenic vantage point in the Snake River valley is called Heaven's Gate. From the parking area it is only a 350-yard hike to a Forest Service lookout and a truly spectacular view of the glories of Idaho's wilderness—seemingly endless serrated ridges, forested slopes, craggy peaks, and the vast, plunging chasms from which Hells Canyon takes its name.

Hikers can make their base at the Windy Saddle or Seven Devils campgrounds, two miles back down the road. Horses are available near Windy Saddle, but all supplies must be brought in. Elk, bears, cougars, and bighorn sheep roam the surrounding countryside, which is at its most colorful from July to early August, when more then 150 varieties of wildflowers are in bloom. In fall the forests are dappled with yellows and reds.

The area's 21 lakes are too cold for swimming, and most are too distant to bring in boats; nonetheless, they are popular with fishermen, who angle for trout. The road to Heaven's Gate is steep and winding, and it is not recommended for trailer touring or for cars with automatic transmissions. *Road generally open late June–Oct.*

7. Leesburg Town Site. *Exit U.S. Rte. 93 at Williams Creek Rd., about five miles south of Salmon. Follow signs for Cobalt; watch for the sign to Leesburg.* Although the Civil War had ended when gold was discovered in these mountains and veterans streamed into the area, regional feelings still ran high. Former Union soldiers settled about a quarter-mile to the north and called their community Grantsville, while the Confederates established Leesburg in honor of Robert E. Lee. Almost nothing of the Union village remains, but the Leesburg townsite, with some 15 log structures, is listed in *The National Register of Historic Places.*

Leesburg is high in the mountains above the Salmon Valley, and the journey to it makes an interesting day trip. The 33-mile road from Salmon is flanked with spectacular scenery as you move from picturesque farmland upward along a series of switchbacks to an elevation of 6,000 feet. Midway there is a wooded picnic area and a mile and a half farther on, a pleasant campground. Most of the drive is along a relatively smooth road of compacted dirt and gravel, but the final canyonlike section is narrow and steep and should not be undertaken by trailers or low-slung cars. *Open year-round but may be inaccessible by car Nov.–May or after heavy rains.*

8. Custer. Remains of mines and mining camps are scattered throughout this part of the Challis National Forest, where gold and silver were found during the last quarter of the 19th century. By the 1890's Custer was the central town—with a peak population of 600 to 700 and a mill that crushed some $12 million worth of ore. Today, not many of the abandoned town's structures still stand, but the ruins of the jailhouse, bawdy house, livery stable, dance hall, blacksmith's shop, general store, and several other buildings all are labeled and still evoke their spirited past. The schoolhouse and the Empire Saloon now serve as a museum, which tells the story of various Yankee Fork mines. Outdoor exhibits show the tools and equipment used for panning, dredging, and placer and hard-rock mining. An interpretive pamphlet, available at the schoolhouse, guides visitors on a walking tour of the entire village.

The nearby ghost town of Bonanza, just to the south, is also of interest. On the way you'll pass the Yankee Fork gold dredge, which was used to extract the last of the area's retrievable gold in the 1940's and early 1950's. Former workers give tours of the dredge and explain its operation. The Forest Service runs four campgrounds along the road leading from Sunbeam to Custer. *Custer Museum and gold dredge open daily July 4–Labor Day. Fee charged for gold dredge tour.*

9. Spencer Opal Mines. *Headquarters: north end of Main Street, Spencer.* Unlike most gems, opals have no crystal structure; rather, they are a solidified silica jelly, in some cases being as much as 21 percent water. A regular array of holes between the microscopic globules of silica creates a diffraction grating, which breaks white light into the rainbow of color that plays upon the stone's surface. However, their composition gives the gems a tendency to crack, and opals should therefore be moistened occasionally to prevent them from drying out.

Here in Spencer is a different kind of mine, not worked by professional crews but by individual rockhounds who pay a daily fee of $17.50 for the pleasure—and labor—of digging up as much as five pounds of opal material: a mass that may contain gems worth many times that price. There are, however, no guarantees. Anyone can join in, and the necessary

6. *"Hells Canyon" and "Snake River" seem like misnomers in this beautiful region.*

hammers, chisels, and safety glasses can be rented at the headquarters or at the mine site some eight miles outside the town. Water for washing the stones is available at the mine, but visitors should bring their own food and drinking water. *Open Sat.–Mon., May–Sept. Daily use permits available 8:30–11 A.M.*

---

10. Harriman State Park of Idaho. *North of Ashton.* Many Idahoans still call this the Railroad Ranch, the name the estate had for over 75 years as a summer retreat for New York's rich, railroad-owning Harriman family (especially Roland Harriman) and their wealthy colleagues. An area of high-mountain sage and grass meadows flanking the meandering Henrys Fork of the Snake River—and the habitat of such big game as moose, elk, antelope, and black bears—it was a private hunting preserve and a working ranch where the owners enjoyed their version of roughing it and playing cowboy.

Given to the state by the Harrimans, the 4,300-acre park was opened in 1982. The park and the adjoining 10,000 acres of national forest lands form a vast refuge rich in wildlife, which can be viewed along the park's nine miles of hiking trails. In addition to the many large animals, among them buffalo, numbers of waterfowl thrive here, including the rare trumpeter swan, a winter resident.

In summer, the ranch's log buildings may be toured, and the old ranch roads are open to horses and bicycles. There is outstanding trout fishing, with flies only, on Henrys Fork. In winter cross-country skiing is excellent. No camping is permitted, but there are campgrounds nearby. *Open year-round. Vehicle entry fee charged.*

---

11. Craters of the Moon National Monument. At first glance this 83-square-mile park appears to be a stark and forbidding wasteland of black rock as desolate as the moon itself. But it is actually a fascinating geological wonder—a volcano field complete with spatter cones, fissure vents, cinder gardens, and lava flows, with tunnels, caves, and the molds of trees that were once encased in molten lava. All this is the work of more than two dozen volcanoes and eight major eruptions over the past 15,000 years.

Many of the most intriguing features can be seen along a seven-mile loop road from which paved paths lead to points of special interest. In addition, a hiking trail runs south for three miles to the Great Rift, a long volcanic fissure. Along the trail one can detour to the top of Big Cinder Butte—the highest cone—for panoramic views of the entire park. The trail ends near Echo Crater, where many backpackers camp for protection from the area's often harsh winds. Overnighters should obtain a free permit at the visitor center. Throughout the park, use care off the trail. Carry drinking water on hikes and a flashlight to explore the caves.

The best time to visit is mid-June, when the wildflowers bloom. Later in the summer the heat-absorbing black lava can become uncomfortably hot. *Open May–Oct. Admission charged.*

---

12. Snake River Birds of Prey Area. *Best auto access: take Exit 44 off I-84 (Meridian Exit) and continue south to Kuna. Follow Swan Falls Rd. from Kuna to Swan Falls Dam.* Nearly half a million acres along a remote 80-mile section of the Snake River have been declared a protected habitat for one of the densest populations of nesting birds of prey anywhere in the world. Over 700 pairs of raptors, as birds of prey are called, nest here annually—14 different species in all, including some 200 pairs of prairie falcons, 30 pairs of golden eagles, and even a few turkey vultures and Swainson's hawks. In addition, bald eagles, peregrine falcons, ospreys, and several other species stop here during migration.

Binoculars are a must for viewing the birds, which can be seen most easily during the courting and nesting period from mid-March through June. After that, high summer temperatures and the scarcity of food drive many birds to other areas. With advance reservations, local wilder-

11. *There can be no question that a river of molten rock once flowed like water here.*

12. *The keen-eyed golden eagle will see any prey that moves in the valley below.*

ness outfitters offer canoe and raft trips along the Snake River, providing visitors with a vivid sense of the raptors' wild domain. For information call the Bureau of Land Management in Boise: *(208) 334-1582. Open year-round.*

13. Indian Map Rock. *From Nampa go 16 miles south on Rte. 45. Turn west onto Map Rock Rd. and continue eight miles to the site.* Indian petroglyphs are found on many of Idaho's canyon walls, often in places where the tribes hunted, fished, or gathered food. Here on the northern bank of the Snake River is one of the largest examples of this rock art ever found. The markings, inscribed on a lava rock measuring approximately 8 by 10 feet, are quite well preserved. They were made by the Shoshone branch of the Shoshone-Bannock tribe, and are thought by some to be a remarkably accurate map of their seasonal migration routes in the Snake River area. A battle fought some 300–400 years ago between the Shoshones and Bannocks is depicted, and so are some of the plants that grow in the valley. There are other petroglyphs to be seen along the Snake River, but be careful when exploring: this is a prime rattlesnake habitat.

Fishing is quite good in the Snake River, where catfish, bass, crappies, and trout are likely catches. Sturgeon may also be caught, but they must be released. The area offers boating and swimming, but the waters are unpredictable and care should be taken. *Open year-round but may be inaccessible in winter.*

14. Silver City. In 1863 Michael Jordan discovered gold along the creek that today bears his name and started a rush of prospectors into the Owyhee Mountains. Besides gold, the miners found rich slabs of silver, including one that is said to have weighed 500 pounds. Silver City boomed and quickly became the county seat. According to conservative estimates, over $40 million in silver was taken from the area, a volume of production exceeded only by Nevada's Comstock Lode. By the early years of this century, however, these glory days were over. As the mines closed, people drifted away.

Today approximately 75 stark and weathered buildings of this historic mining town still stand on the rugged hillsides. The once colorful streets such as Deadman's Alley, the scene of several gunfights, are eroded and overgrown. The old school is now a museum devoted to the area's varied history. In the former drugstore one can inspect old-time pharmaceutical, dental, and medical equipment, and buy camping supplies.

Silver City's centerpiece now, just as it was in the 1860's, is the five-story Idaho Hotel. With advance reservations you can spend the night here in a room with original furnishings, chamber pots, and kerosene lamps. Bring your own linen or a sleeping bag. Payment is by donation, and family-style meals are served. Wood stoves provide heat. For reservations call (208) 495-2520 or 2402.

Dominated by 8,000-foot War Eagle Mountain to the south, the surrounding countryside offers ample opportunity for hiking and other recreation. Abandoned mills, mine shafts, old townsites, and half a dozen historic cemeteries are spread throughout the area. Jordan Creek is still panned for gold, although most people now prefer to try for the trout. Snowmobiling and cross-country skiing are popular in the winter.

Visitors should note that few supplies are available in Silver City. Gasoline and other necessities should be purchased before driving in. Also the dirt road from Route 78 is rather rough. Allow an hour or more to complete the 23-mile journey. Heavy snow can fall as early as October, and the road may be impassable as late as Memorial Day. Check with the Owyhee County sheriff for road conditions early or late in the season. *Generally open June–Nov. and by special arrangement in the winter. Admission charged to some buildings.*

14. *With simple materials, aspirations of elegance are gracefully displayed.*

15. *The undulating sculptured shape of these scenic mountains of sand dramatically reveals the precise flow of the prevailing winds.*

15. Bruneau Dunes State Park. *Bruneau.*

The two enormous mountains of sand that form this park's centerpiece are in striking contrast to the high, flat plateaus that dominate the landscape here. Covering some 600 acres of the 4,800-acre park, the picturesque dunes give way at their base to lakes and marshland, creating an interesting ecological anomaly.

Eagle Cove, where the dunes stand, was formed by the meandering Snake River about 30,000 years ago. The sand was blown in from the surrounding plateau and trapped by opposing winds, which still keep the dunes from moving far or dramatically changing their shape. The lakes and marsh began to form in 1950, when a nearby reservoir caused the underground water table to rise.

Climbing the dunes is the park's chief attraction. At first glimpse the tallest dune, which is 470 feet high, does not seem particularly challenging. But the hike through shifting sand with no firm footholds and no well-trod trail is surprisingly strenuous. It can also be fun, and the crest offers rewarding views. Sand skiers will find the dunes especially inviting. In summer the sand can be extremely hot and dry, and it's best to climb in the early morning or late afternoon. The climb is predictably gritty; cameras and food should be sealed in plastic bags.

Wildlife here includes waterfowl, and coyotes are common. Fishing (from non-motorized craft) is mostly for largemouth bass, bluegill, and channel cats. May and June are the best months for wildflowers and flowering shrubs, including the vivid primroses, penstemons, and tamarisks. *Open year-round. Admission charged.*

16. Three Island Crossing State Park.

Glenns Ferry. Thousands of westbound pioneers on the Oregon Trail in the 1840's and 1850's crossed the Snake River at this ford, where midstream islands and gravel bars made it possible (though treacherous) to get their teams and wagons through. Today the visitor to this 500-acre riverside park can see a replica of a Conestoga wagon, an informative visitor center exhibit, and well-marked historic sites.

Now slowly fading into the soil and beneath the desert underbrush are traces of the original trail: the wheel ruts and the footpath where families trudged 15 or 20 miles a day alongside the wagons to lighten the load for their beasts of burden. Across the river from the park one can see ruts etched more deeply. The trail's length in Idaho was some 500 miles.

Many of the park's other attractions are along the river, where bass, trout, and catfish can be caught. There is a large picnic and day-use area. A pasture at water's edge contains a few buffalo and long-horns, and the cliffs across the river are home to golden and bald eagles as well as to swallows. Antelope, deer, and bobcats are sometimes seen, and at night packs of coyotes can be heard. *Open year-round. Visitor center open Memorial Day–Labor Day. Campground open year-round with full facilities Apr.–mid-Oct.*

17. Thousand Springs. *Best viewed from Rte. 30 north of Buhl.* The dozen or more waterfalls that spout suddenly from the wall of the Snake River Canyon here were long a puzzle to geologists as well as laymen. Now scientists believe that their source lies 150 miles to the northeast, where the Big and Little Lost rivers vanish into the lava beds that cover much of the region. Increased greatly in volume by melting snow and seepage, the underground streams course through the porous lava until they reach this canyon and plunge into the Snake River.

The springs assume a dramatic variety of forms—wispy curtains, slender columns, foamy, rushing cascades, and raging torrents. Binoculars are helpful—and a telephoto lens for photographers—since the viewing area is across the river at a commercial resort. The viewing area, however, is open and free to the public, and visitors are welcome to use the picnic tables without charge. The resort also offers a swimming pool, hot baths, boat ramps, and camping facilities.

Trout thrive in the cool, clear, aerated water pouring from the springs, making this the state's prime area for trout fishing. Facilities for boaters and campers are available all along this beautiful stretch of U.S. 30, justly known as the Thousand Springs Scenic Route. The area has other spectacular cascades at Twin Falls and Shoshone Falls as well as the picturesque gorge of the Malad River and the remarkable Balanced Rock. *Open year-round.*

18. Silent City of Rocks. *Four miles west of Almo.* These huge natural megaliths, silently dominating the plain like a procession of brooding and forgotten prehistoric gods, are as startling to visitors today as they were to pioneers on their way to California in the middle 1800's. Numerous pioneer diaries comment on the "wild and romantic scenery . . . all manner of fantastic shapes . . . ," which held the visitors "spellbound with the beauty and strangeness of it all." Many immigrants, their individual fates now lost to history, were moved to leave their names marked with axle grease on these ancient stones.

Perhaps, confronting the frailty of their own lives on the difficult way west, they sought to connect themselves with something timeless.

Among the hundreds of rocks here, some 30 are so strikingly evocative that they have been given colorful names, such as Squaw and Papoose, Giant Toadstool, King on the Throne, Kaiser's Helmet, and Devil's Bedstead. A descriptive pamphlet and map, giving the names of many of the formations and the best angles from which to view them, is available at the Chamber of Commerce in Burley. The area is remote and undeveloped, and the access road has a rough, unpaved surface. *May be inaccessible in wet weather or when the road is muddy.*

19. Crystal Ice Cave. *Exit Rte. 39 onto N. Pleasant Valley Rd. northwest of American Falls; continue 20 miles to the cave.* This is the only place in North America where you can take a guided tour down the throat and into the chamber of a fissure volcano. Crystal Ice Cave is 160 feet below the earth's surface. Filled year-round with formations, it is part of the 43-mile-long Great Rift—the longest and deepest open volcanic rift in North America, created

2,100 years ago by violent volcanic eruptions. After the eruptions a backflow of lava plugged the fissure, creating a natural freezer that traps whatever cold air sinks to the bottom of the draftless cave.

The cave is reached by a gently graded 1,200-foot tunnel with high ceilings. The delicate ice crystals fringing the walls sometimes melt, but the great translucent pillars, mounds, and other strangely sculpted shapes—now protected by insulating glass—have survived for centuries. Wear sturdy shoes and dress warmly. The temperature in the cave is 32° F.

Aboveground, a paved path leads to the King's Bowl. Around 80 feet across and 150 feet deep, it is the largest explosion pit along the Great Rift. Other volcanic cones, vents, and caverns dot the surrounding area. The terrain is rugged, and it's easy to get lost if you wander off the trails. In the visitor center there is a specimen of a blind beetle that lives in the cave; it's found nowhere else on earth. *Open May–Sept. Admission charged.*

20. Minnetonka Cave. *West of St. Charles.* More than a half-mile of well-lit paths and stairways leads through nine subterranean rooms, the largest over 300 feet in diameter and 90 feet high. In the cave giant limestone stalactites and stalagmites glisten like melting wax.

Despite this ephemeral appearance, the cave's formation took thousands of years. Water absorbed carbon dioxide as it slowly filtered through the ground, forming carbonic acid, a solution that dissolves limestone into calcite. As this solution dripped through cracks and fissures in the stone, large caverns were gradually hollowed out and filled with calcite deposits—the bizarre formations you see today. Marine fossils from a prehistoric tropical sea are embedded in the cavern walls.

Tours take about an hour. The pathway, damp in some places, is for the most part gently graded; however, there are spots where you'll need to climb fairly steep stairs. Warm clothing should be worn, since the temperature inside stays at 40° F. Picnic and camping areas are a few minutes' drive away. *Open daily mid-June–Labor Day. Admission charged.*

16. Oregon Trail pioneers dreamed of fields green as those that now flank the river.

Wyoming

Here is the essence of the Old West, where Indians, cowboys, trappers, miners, soldiers, and settlers all had their day—and are still remembered.

The Plains Indians dominated this land long before the coming of the white man; and their costumes, weapons, and ceremonial objects can be admired in a variety of excellent museums. Also recalled, in museums, historic forts, and an (almost) ghost town, are westward-bound pioneers, miners who stayed while the digging held out, ranchers and farmers who settled down, and the soldiers sent to protect them all.

The prehistory of this land is documented by dinosaur footprints, the fossils of ancient birds and fish, and an archeological dig. Wildflowers abound in their season, many parks have inviting trails, and in an understatement unusual for scenic attractions, Hells Half Acre is 640 times that size. There are remarkable on-again, off-again waterworks to ponder, and natural splendors on every side.

1. Teton Canyon Campground, Targhee National Forest. *Seven miles east of Alta.*

This small, isolated campground is nestled picturesquely along Teton Creek at the base of striking mountain palisades. Several trails, ranging from easy to difficult, are accessible from here. The Devil's Stair, beginning about 2½ miles up the canyon, climbs steeply along cliffs to the wide, flat area called Teton Bench, offering spectacular views of the Tetons. Less difficult routes include Table Mountain Trail, leading to a popular lookout, and the Alaska Basin Trail, an easy, scenic path about eight miles long.

Deer, elk, and moose roam the area year-round. In midsummer hundreds of hummingbirds flock to the myriad wildflowers, and the creek offers excellent trout fishing. Insects can be annoying, however, so bring a repellent. Snowmobiling and cross-country skiing attract winter visitors. *Park open year-round; trails open June–Sept., weather permitting.*

2. Buffalo Bill Historical Center. *720 Sheridan Ave., Cody.*

With the exploration and development of the West came an inevitable conflict of cultures. What was lost—and some of what was gained—is memorialized in this superb complex of four museums. The most poignant is the Plains Indian Museum, which displays the beauty, elegance, and craftsmanship of costumes, weapons, headdresses, beadwork, and ceremonial objects created by the Plains Indians before the coming of the white man. The tribes represented include the Sioux, Cheyenne, Shoshone, Crow, Arapaho, and Blackfoot.

The Whitney Gallery of Western Art houses paintings, drawings, and bronzes by many renowned American artists, including Frederic Remington, N. C. Wyeth, and Charles M. Russell. A re-creation of Remington's studio contains a number of his works, a collection of Indian artifacts, and other memorabilia.

Military and sporting arms of many nations are shown in the Winchester Arms Museum. Started about 1860 by Oliver Winchester, the famous gun manufacturer, this varied collection today contains more than 5,000 pieces.

The Buffalo Bill Museum depicts the life and times of William "Buffalo Bill" Cody, flamboyant Pony Express rider, buffalo hunter, Wild West showman, and founder of the town of Cody. Among the exhibits are trophies, posters, and a saddle once used by Annie Oakley. *Open daily May–Sept.; Tues.–Sun., Mar., Apr., Oct., Nov. Admission charged.*

3. Medicine Wheel Indian Relic. *Off Alt. Rte. 14, east of Lovell.*

In 1776, when the Crow Indians first occupied this mountain on the western edge of Bighorn National Forest, they discovered the great Medicine Wheel, a circle of limestone slabs and boulders with a circumference of 245 feet, 28 stone spokes, and a round pile of stones about three feet high as a hub. Its origin and purpose remain a mystery, as much for the Indians as for the white man. Speculation is that the wheel was built by a sun-worshiping people. The hub supposedly symbolizes the sun, and the spokes indicate the 28 days of the lunar month. Radioactive carbon dating by the University of Wyoming of wood found inside a rock pile puts the construction of the wheel at 1760, but it is conjectured that

1. *The snow here in Alaska Basin near Teton Canyon is, appropriately, the last to go.*

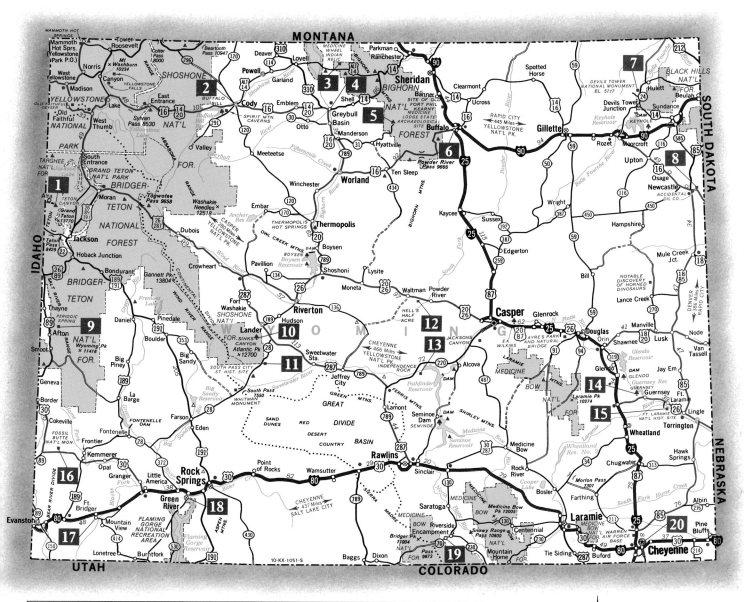

LEGEND

NUMBERED ATTRACTIONS DESCRIBED IN TEXT `1`

HIGHWAY MARKERS

INTERSTATE `70`   UNITED STATES `40`   STATE `53`

ROAD CLASSIFICATIONS

CONTROLLED ACCESS HIGHWAYS
(Entrance and Exit only at Interchanges)   Interchanges

OTHER DIVIDED HIGHWAYS

PRINCIPAL THROUGH HIGHWAYS

OTHER THROUGH HIGHWAYS

CONNECTING HIGHWAYS

MILEAGES   LONG DISTANCE MILEAGES SHOWN IN RED

MILEAGE BETWEEN DOTS   35

ONE MILE EQUALS 1.6 KILOMETERS   ONE KILOMETER EQUALS .6 MILES

SPECIAL FEATURES

STATE PARKS   POINTS OF INTEREST ▪

With Campsites ▲ Without Campsites △

RECREATION AREAS   MOUNTAIN PASSES

With Campsites ▲ Without Campsites △   Usually closed in Winter
Usually open in Winter

© THE H.M. GOUSHA COMPANY • SAN JOSE, CALIFORNIA

N W E S

SCALE IN MILES AND KILOMETERS

ONE INCH 51 MILES 0 5 10 20 30 40 50 60

ONE INCH 82 KM 0 5 10 20 30 50 70 96

---

the relic may be quite a bit older. Some Indians still use the site during the summer for their own ceremonies.

The wheel is reached by a steep and winding three-mile dirt road offering glorious views of surrounding mountains and valleys. In spring wild geraniums, violets, and many other kinds of wildflowers carpet the slopes. *Open year-round; but the entrance road may be impassable in wet or winter weather.*

4. Greybull Museum. *325 Greybull Ave., Greybull.* Located in the Greybull Library building, this small local museum offers an engaging cross section of the history and remarkable geology of the Bighorn Basin. Dinosaur bones were discovered in the hills east of town, and the basin's eroded terrain abounds in Indian and pioneer artifacts and semiprecious minerals. Sheep Mountain, just to the north, is famous among geologists as an anticline ridge, formed as the mountain's slopes slowly

eroded away to leave a towering central spine of older and harder rock. The town is named for the nearby river, which in turn is named for a large white buffalo that roamed this region long before the white man arrived. Pictographs on nearby cliffs represent this legendary creature.

Colorful collections of Indian robes and beadwork and an interesting assortment of pioneer household goods and weapons give a view of man's presence here. But the highlight is an extensive geology and archeology display, including exhibits of fossils and minerals. *Open Mon.–Sat. and P.M. Sun., June–Labor Day; P.M. Mon.–Fri., Sept. and Oct.; P.M. Mon., Wed., Fri., Nov.–Mar.; P.M. Mon.–Fri., Apr. and May. If museum is closed, call (307)765-2627.*

5. Medicine Lodge State Archaeological Site.

Seven miles NE of Hyattville off Cold Springs Road. Ten thousand years of human habitation have been documented at this location—a sheltered valley on the western slope of the Bighorn Mountains, near the confluence of Medicine Lodge and Dry Medicine Lodge creeks. The prehistoric site had long been recognized as an important one because of the outstanding petroglyphs and pictographs that had been incised and etched on a sandstone bluff here 1,000 years ago.

But in the early 1970's even more significant finds were made. Digging at the base of the bluff, archeologists uncovered more than 60 cultural levels and thousands of artifacts, ranging from bones and projectile points to hearths and traces of shelters. The finds are helping scholars to reconstruct the lifeways of man from the end of the Ice Age to today.

In 1972 the area was purchased by the Wyoming Game and Fish Department for a wildlife refuge, and today it is a park. Campgrounds and picnic tables and grills are set among the willows and cottonwoods. A trout fishery at the creek nurtures rainbows and browns, and fishing is excellent. *Open year-round, but roads may be impassable in winter snow.*

6. The Johnson County Jim Gatchell Memorial Museum.

10 Fort St., Buffalo. Jim Gatchell, a druggist in the town of Buffalo from about the turn of the century to the 1950's, was an authority on the history of the Northern Plains Indians and the Powder River country, the area that extends between the Bighorn Mountains and the Black Hills. Gatchell was also an avid collector—Indian and pioneer relics and firearms—and his fine examples of Indian craftwork, many given him by his Indian friends, form the nucleus of the more than 5,000 items exhibited here.

Cheyenne and Crow war bonnets, beaded rifle scabbards, and a scalping

7. The word "awesome," frequently misused, is the best description of this phenomenon.

knife from Custer's last stand recall the days of strife on the western frontier. There is also an excellent diorama of the famous 1867 Wagon Box Fight, when Capt. James Powell removed 14 wagon boxes from their wheels and used them as a barricade against an attack by the great Sioux chief Red Cloud. *Open daily June–Labor Day except July 4.*

7. Devils Tower National Monument.

About 60 million years ago, molten magma from the earth's core forced its way upward into the softer sedimentary rock here. The magma cooled underground and formed a huge plug of hard igneous stone. Slowly the sedimentary rock eroded away, exposing the plug. Known as Devils Tower, it rises abruptly from its base and looms 1,267 feet above the Belle Fourche River. The tower's many vertical fissures give it the appearance of a melting

column of rock. In 1906 the imposing formation was designated the nation's first national monument. Each year expert climbers edge their way to the top, a flat area of 1½ acres.

The surrounding park offers hiking trails, cross-country skiing routes, tent and trailer campsites, picnic grounds, and excellent fishing and tubing spots. Birding is quite good, since the park is at the juncture of wooded mountains and plains. Over 90 bird species have been sighted here, including bald and golden eagles. Prairie falcons sometimes are seen preying on the rock doves that nest on the tower. White-tailed deer inhabit the woodlands, and inquisitive prairie dogs pop up from their towns near the park entrance to pose for photographers. *Park open year-round; campground open mid-May–Sept.*

8. Accidental Oil Company. *Four miles east of Newcastle on Rte. 16.* Al Smith, a lifetime oilman, was convinced that oil could be found at shallow depths as well as at the usual depth of 4,000 feet or more. Seeking oil on land he had leased from the government in 1966 and unable to find a rig, he began to dig by hand, using only a pick and a shovel and a few sticks of dynamite. About four weeks later he astounded the experts by striking oil at a depth of 24 feet. At the peak of its production the well yielded a little more than five barrels of crude oil per day.

A 120-foot ramp leads to a viewing room at the bottom of the 24-foot well. In the ultraviolet lighting the oil oozing from cracks in the 100-million-year-old rock appears to be a bright fluorescent yellow, and the process of seepage is easy to see.

Antique drilling equipment, including a 1912 steam-powered cable-tool drill rig, is displayed on the grounds. An 1880 derrick stands on a hill above the gift shop, which is located in an oil storage tank. *Open daily Memorial Day–Labor Day. Admission charged.*

9. Periodic Spring, Bridger-Teton National Forest. *Afton. Off Second Ave., five miles east of Rte. 89.* Known locally as the Geyser, this frigid mountain spring seems truly magical. For a few minutes it gushes torrentially from a 10-foot-wide opening in the wall of Swift Creek Canyon. Then suddenly it stops, and the streambed, 7,100 feet below, dries up. A few minutes later the water bursts forth from the rock again with all its earlier vehemence.

The duration of these cycles varies with the level of the water table. During dry months—particularly August, September, and October—the spring flows for perhaps 8–18 minutes, shuts off for a similar interval, and then flows again. During the snowmelt in May and June, however, or after heavy rains, it flows continuously with only minor periodic changes in volume. No one is certain what causes this phenomenon, but geologists believe the water is drawn and discharged by a natural siphon from an underground lake.

The spring can be reached only by a steep and narrow trail that offers stunning views of soaring chimney rocks and dizzying glimpses of the creek far below. A profusion of wildflowers blooms in spring. A five-mile road leads to the trailhead. Campsites and picnic areas are located nearby. *Trail open June–Oct.; campground open mid-June–mid-Sept.*

10. Sinks Canyon State Park. This ecologically diverse park takes its name from its most noted natural phenomenon. The Popo Agie River "sinks" here into a limestone cave, proceeds underground for half a mile, and resurfaces into a pool known as The Rise. The area around The Rise contains two strikingly different ecosystems, reflecting the amount of sunlight received on the canyon's slopes. The shadier north-facing slope is a lush forest of Douglas fir, limber pine, and aspen, while the arid south-facing slope supports primarily juniper, sagebrush, and grasses.

Black bears, beavers, mule deer, moose, and bighorn sheep range the hillsides, and the river abounds in trout. A nature trail with 21 stops can be walked easily in an hour. Each stop is interpreted in a booklet, which also describes the canyon's geology and wildlife. Both of the park's campgrounds are situated in picturesque clearings along the river.

The park road is part of a 60-mile loop through scenic mountain backcountry between Lander and South Pass City. Pamphlets describing highlights of the drive are available at the park. *Park open year-round, weather permitting; visitor center open Memorial Day–Labor Day.*

11. South Pass City State Historic Site. Situated at the southern end of the Wind River Range, where the Oregon Trail crossed the Continental Divide, South Pass City is one of the scores of communities established during the search for "the yellow metal that drives the white man crazy," as one wise Indian put it. Gold was discovered here in 1867; within a year 28 mines were established, and the area's population boomed to about 3,000. But five years later no one had yet hit a mother lode; discouraged, the miners moved on to more promising locations, and the town rapidly declined.

Now restored, South Pass City is a living ghost town with a handful of residents, its bustling past still visible in 30 or so buildings that were once of vital importance; the 1868 Sherlock Hotel, cattleman J.W. Iliff's bank, the Miner's Exchange Saloon, and the claim recorder's office are among them. Giving authenticity to the scene, a few optimistic prospectors still work the mines. *Visitor center open daily May 15–Oct. 15.*

12. Hells Half Acre. *East of Waltman off Rte. 20-26.* The pioneers who named this region rather underplayed its size, but its hellish aspects obviously impressed them. Hard rains and winds have carved a 320-acre chasm in an otherwise flat terrain, sculpting pinnacles, gulches, and fantastic shapes out of the bed of white clay and shale. The freakish landscape was regarded with superstitious awe by both Indians

11. Remnants of mining machinery are as broken as the hopeful dreams they represent.

and trappers, who often avoided the area. But it is also a scene of striking beauty, with bands of yellow, pink, white, and orange striating the canyon walls.

A restaurant at the rim of the chasm has viewing platforms open to the public, and there are hiking trails down into the canyon, which is maintained as a county park. But be careful: what may appear to be hard rock underfoot is crumbly baked clay. A campground is located nearby. *Park open year-round, weather permitting.*

13. Independence Rock State Historic Site. *West of Alcova off Rte. 220.* A famous landmark on the Oregon Trail, the huge granite mound found here reaches 193 feet above the Sweetwater River valley and extends over 27 acres. William Sublette, fur trader and guide, is generally credited with naming the rock on July 4, 1830, in honor of the anniversary of the Declaration of Independence.

Wagon train travelers found Independence Rock a convenient resting and camping stop on the trail. The names and dates carved on its face by these early pioneers prompted the Jesuit missionary Pierre Jean De Smet to dub the rock "the Great Register of the Desert" as early as 1841. More than 5,000 inscriptions were carved here, and many of them are still visible. A paved path takes visitors from the parking lot to the rock and a picnic area. *Open year-round.*

14. Guernsey State Park. In 1927 the Bureau of Reclamation dammed the North Platte River here. The resulting 2,400-acre Guernsey Reservoir is the centerpiece of this lovely park. Ancient sandstone cliffs rise defiantly from the placid shorelines, surrounded by rolling, grassy hills dotted with stands of juniper and pine. The four-mile Lakeshore Drive offers outstanding panoramic views and provides access to four of the park's seven campgrounds. The other camping areas are in the park's backcountry, where deer, antelopes, bobcats, and coyotes occasionally may be spotted. A sandy beach can be used by swimmers, and picnic areas and two boat ramps are available. Fishing, however, is poor because the reservoir is drained annually to remove silt.

The park buildings and other facilities are an added attraction. These sturdy sandstone masonry structures, built during the Great Depression of the 1930's, are excellent examples of the Civilian Conservation Corps's skill and craftsmanship. The most impressive building (with heavy cypress doors and hand-wrought iron lighting fixtures) is the visitor center and museum, where there are displays about regional geology, archeology, and history. Several mementos of the CCC also are shown. *Park open year-round; visitor center open P.M mid-May–mid-Sept.*

15. Fort Laramie National Historic Site. *Three miles SW of Fort Laramie off Rte. 26.* In 1834 William Sublette and Robert Campbell, two fur traders, established their headquarters and a trading post here near the confluence of the Laramie and North Platte rivers. As more and more wagon trains creaked westward, the Indians became increasingly angry, and the settlers' need for protection along the Oregon Trail grew. Finally in 1849 the U.S. government bought the trading post and turned it into a military fort. In 1938 it became a national historic site.

Several buildings have been restored, including the commandant's home, the surgeon's quarters, the bakery, the guardhouse, the post store, and "Old Bedlam," Wyoming's oldest surviving military structure, which provided housing for the post's officers. Park staff members in the dress of the 1870's demonstrate cannon firing, baking, and other fort activities, and give a parade in full uniform each afternoon. Displays in a small museum include 19th-century army uniforms, weapons, and saddles. Park rangers conduct tours. *Open daily except Christmas and New Year's Day.*

16. Fossil Butte National Monument. *Eleven miles west of Kemmerer off Rte. 30N.* Violent land upheavals here 50 million years ago created a lake where the forerunners of many modern mammals, birds, fish, and reptiles flourished in a subtropical climate. When these creatures died, their remains were protected by layers of sediment. Later, under enormous pressure, the sediment turned to lime-

13. Fresh water and the trailside landmark were long anticipated by weary pioneers.

stone, preserving the animals' fossilized skeletons in almost perfect condition.

At the visitor center of this 8,180-acre monument, fossils of fish resembling perch, catfish, and herring are exhibited along with rare fossils of a stingray, an early crocodile skull, a boa constrictor, and a prehistoric bird. A somewhat demanding one-mile trail, with 13 interpretive signs, climbs 700 feet on its way to the fossil quarries. An automobile route winds for almost four miles through sagebrush and native grasses to a small picnic area in an aspen grove.

You may have cows for company in this open range country, and you may see a few mule deer, pronghorn antelopes, and moose. In winter cross-country skiing and snowshoeing are popular. The park may be crowded on summer weekends. *Park open year-round; visitor center open daily mid-May–Sept., staff availability and weather permitting.*

---

17. Fort Bridger State Historic Site. *Fort Bridger.* Jim Bridger, justly famous beaver trapper, trader, and guide, established a trading post here in 1843 with his partner Louis Vasquez and supplied the needs of wagon trains on the Oregon Trail. Twelve years later the Mormons bought the post as a resting place for their people emigrating westward, but after a dispute with the federal government they burned it and went on to Salt Lake City. United States troops arrived in 1857 and built what was to remain an important fort until 1890, putting up 29 buildings.

Stables used by the Pony Express and the sutler's complex (post store), stocked with goods and fashions from the 1880's, may be seen. Army uniforms, buffalo robes, and the evidence of a poker party are shown in the bachelor officers' quarters. The commandant's residence has been restored with period furnishings, including a moosehorn chair.

A Mountain Man Rendezvous is held annually on Labor Day weekend, when traders come dressed in early 1800's garb and set up their tepees for business. The park is very likely to be crowded during this event. *Open daily Apr.–Oct.; weekends the rest of the year.*

16. *Documenting evolution in Wyoming is a fish that lived here 50 million years ago.*

18. Sweetwater County Historical Museum. *County Courthouse, corner of Center St. and Flaming Gorge Way, Green River.* Through the ages Sweetwater County has had a series of inhabitants, from dinosaurs and other prehistoric creatures to various Indian tribes, and eventually to white settlers and to the Chinese laborers who came in the 1870's to work in the mines.

The museum illustrates this stream of history with such exhibits as a rare fossil of a palm leaf, a dinosaur footprint, and the mounted heads of buffalo, deer, and a trumpeter swan. Excellent examples of Sioux quillwork and beadwork may be seen, as well as gongs, pottery, garments, and other items that belonged to the Chinese immigrants.

The large collection of historic photographs shows early miners, mining sites, mountain men, pioneers, and the coming of the railroad. *Open Mon.–Fri. year-round except holidays. Also open P.M. Sat., May–Aug.*

---

19. Grand Encampment Museum. *Encampment.* The discovery of a copper lode in 1897 brought affluence to the ranch town of Grand Encampment. However, the prosperity lasted only 11 years—the mines were closed in 1908, when the owners were accused of fraud. Although the town survived, the "Grand" was dropped from its name for the sake of honesty.

The aura of the mining community has been re-created at this museum complex—a cluster of weatherbeaten buildings almost overtaken by the desert. On a guided tour you can inspect a doctor-dentist office, an 1870's stagecoach station, a saloon, and a general store equipped with a huge coffee grinder and a brass cash reg-

ister. A group of nostrums sits on the shelves. The Doc Culleton Building displays old-time photographs and other reminders of the copper-mining days. Also of interest is a two-story outhouse designed for use when deep snows and drifts buried the lower unit. *Open P.M. Memorial Day–Labor Day; P.M. weekends Sept.–Oct., weather permitting.*

---

20. Wyoming State Museum. *Barrett Building, Central Ave. at 24th St., Cheyenne.* Wyoming's colorful heritage, from Plains Indians and mountain men to cowboys and miners, is vividly presented in this spacious museum, aptly located in the state's capital city. Cheyenne was founded in 1867 as a major depot along the Transcontinental Railway, and less than a year later the Territory of Wyoming was created by Congress. The museum itself was started in 1895, just five years after Wyoming was granted statehood.

Life on the range is recalled with a 1911 line shack that once sheltered cowboys during their fence-riding chores, along with trailside cooking equipment and 21 different branding irons. And of course there are displays about the Old West's desperadoes. Two of the more slippery characters are George "Big Nose" Parrott, a train robber and murderer, and Ella "Cattle Kate" Watson, who once rustled steers with the best of the boys. Both were lynched. An extensive collection of artifacts from Wyoming's Indian tribes gives emphasis to the Arapahos and the Shoshones, and an art gallery exhibits the work of leading artists and photographers. *Open Mon.–Sat. year-round except holidays; also P.M. Sun., Memorial Day–Labor Day.*

Utah

There are few places in the world where so many different sculptural forms created by wind and water are so dramatically displayed.

Here you'll find spectacular cliffs and cathedrallike domes, soaring sandstone spires, monumental natural bridges, and a stunning panorama of a devastated land where wild mustangs roamed. The gooseneck meanders of the San Juan River must be seen to be believed.

Aspects of the ancient past are preserved in the fossilized bones of dinosaurs that once walked this land and in the petrified fallen timbers of a forest that stood here 140 million years ago.

From our own era are a museum dedicated to the automobile and the historic site where the driving of two golden spikes tied a nation together with bands of steel. Here too there's an inviting variety of places for fishing, swimming, boating, hiking, and birding.

2. *Trains recall the historic day when East and West were joined by bands of steel.*

1. Bear Lake State Park. *Garden City.*

There are two separate areas in this lakeside park, each of them offering access to the turquoise waters of 70,500-acre Bear Lake, which is surrounded by exquisite mountain scenery. Sailing, powerboating, and fishing are the main attractions at the state marina in the northern section. Eleven miles to the south, at Rendezvous Beach, the emphasis is on swimming, although here too boats may be rented or trailered in. Three campgrounds—Willow, Cottonwood, and Big Creek—are attractively situated along the shore.

Fishermen hook cutthroat trout here and Mackinaws that can weigh up to 30 pounds. Ice fishing for smeltlike ciscoes is popular in winter. Sandhill cranes are common in the park's meadows and wetlands from late May to early June. *Marina open year-round, campgrounds open June–Oct. Admission charged.*

2. Golden Spike National Historic Site.

Promontory. Shortly past noon on May 10, 1869, two locomotives—Union Pacific's *119* and Central Pacific's *Jupiter*—met face to face here amid the barren hills at the summit of the Promontory Mountains. Executives from both companies stepped forward and symbolically drove four ceremonial spikes into a polished laurel tie. Two of the spikes were gold (from which the site takes its name), one was silver, and one was an alloy of iron, gold, and silver. To conclude the ceremony a final, ordinary spike was driven into an ordinary tie. Some people have called this "the most significant event of the 19th century." While one might quarrel with that claim, there can be no doubt that the completion of the nation's first transcontinental railroad was a monumental achievement of engineering, willpower, and backbreaking work.

Although the entire enterprise took six years from start to finish, most of the track was laid in four years by gangs of laborers toiling from dawn to dusk six days a week. The Central Pacific crew of Chinese laborers pushed eastward through the towering Sierra Nevada, with rock cuts, deep fills, trestles, switchbacks, 37 miles of wooden snowsheds and galleries, and 15 tunnels through 6,213 feet of solid granite. The westward-driving Union Pacific workers, mostly Irishmen, had easier terrain but a no less hostile environment, for the Cheyennes and Sioux, well aware of what this railroad would mean to their territory and way of life, fought against it. All together, these unsung heroes, who at best earned

$2 or $3 per day ($10 to $15 if they provided their own horse or mule team), laid 1,776 miles of track, permanently linking America's East and West.

Replicas of the two engines, with polished brass and gleaming red paint, stand facing each other in the same spot as did the originals. A visitor center offers a 20-minute film about the epic undertaking and displays artifacts, photographs, and a map of the transcontinental route. Nine miles of the original track bed can be toured by car, and a three-quarter-mile hiking trail leads to the remains of the Big Fill and Big Trestle, two structures that vividly evoke the heroic labors needed to complete the route. *Open daily except Thanksgiving Day and Christmas. Locomotives on display May–Sept.*

3. Bonneville Speedway Museum. *1000 State Hwy., Wendover.* Named for the nearby Bonneville Salt Flats, famed for the speed trials held there, the museum features automobiles. Among these is a famous Bonneville performer, the *Goldenrod*, which in 1965 set the land speed record for wheel-driven automobiles at 409 miles per hour. This speedster is 52 feet

long and looks like a rocket. Its winning run is shown on videotape.

The oldest classic car here is a 1909 Rauch and Lang electric; the newest, a 1975 Chevrolet. Others include a 1915 Dodge, a 1937 Ford pickup, a 1955 gull-wing Mercedes, and a 1963 Rolls-Royce Silver Cloud III. All the machines are in beautiful condition, and the collection changes as additions replace cars that are out on loan or being used in other ways.

The museum also houses a variety of objects reflecting its owner's other wide-ranging interests. This eclectic assemblage includes Pima Indian baskets and pottery, a 1906 French piano, a Tiffany marble mantel clock, a Blizzard oak icebox, and a late 19th-century folding bathtub. *Open daily May–Oct. Admission charged.*

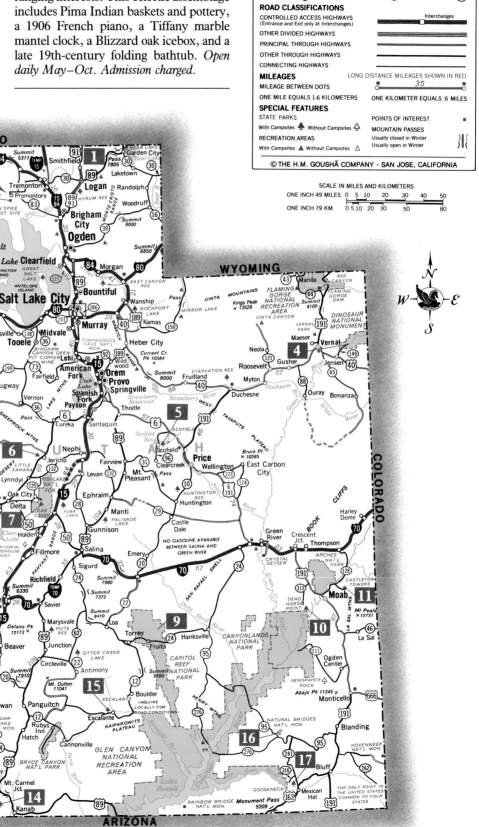

4. Dinosaur National Monument. *Fossil Quarry off Rte. 149 north of Jensen.* One hundred forty-five million years ago, this now arid land was a low-lying plain inhabited by dinosaurs. When they died most of their skeletons decayed. But in one place flooding rivers buried many of their bones in sandbars, and in time these bones became fossilized. The north wall of the Quarry Visitor Center is actually the quarry face, which dramatically reveals fossils of turtles, crocodiles, and 14 species of dinosaurs, including some almost complete skeletons.

A few miles east, at Cub Creek, well-preserved petroglyphs may be seen. These animal, human, and geometric designs were pecked into the sandstone about 1,000 years ago by the Fremont People, whose prehistoric culture was first studied along the Fremont River.

A paved, self-guiding scenic drive begins at monument headquarters, 25 miles east of Jensen near Dinosaur, Colorado, and runs north for 3l miles through sagebrush-covered plateaus and verdant canyons. More remote backcountry areas can be explored along several rugged, unpaved roads. In addition, opportunities exist for backpacking and river trips; information and the necessary permits can be obtained at monument headquarters or the Quarry Visitor Center. Two developed campgrounds and several backcountry camping areas are accessible by car. *Quarry Visitor Center open year-round except Thanksgiving Day, Christmas, and New Year's Day; scenic drive generally accessible May–Oct; campground near Quarry Visitor Center open year-round.*

![icons: picnic, tent, RV, hiking, cross-country skiing, binoculars, bicycling, swimming]

5. Scofield State Park. *Scofield.* Here is a small, relaxing park that is ideal for fishermen, birders, and other nature lovers. The picnic area and campground are set on a small rise above glistening Scofield Lake, overlooking the tree-covered mountains of the Wasatch Plateau on the opposite shore. Hikers along the moderate trails throughout the park's 400 acres may with luck see moose, deer, elk, coyotes, and hardworking beavers who have built dams along the lake's feeder streams. Red-tailed hawks nest on parkland, and from late summer into November bald eagles and Canada geese may be seen.

Boating access to the seven-mile-long lake is provided by a ramp and dock suitable for both powerboats and sailboats. Swimming is popular and so is fishing, with plentiful rainbow and cutthroat trout commonly growing to 12 inches or more.

A triathlon race (running, swimming, and bicycling) is sponsored here late in July, and even casual cyclists will appreciate the surrounding open country roads. The winter season is also popular, bringing people for excellent ice fishing, and for snowmobiling and cross-country skiing on groomed trails. *Open daily May–Nov. Trailheads and ice-fishing areas open in winter. Admission charged May–Oct.*

![icons: picnic, RV, hiking, binoculars, bicycling, swimming, fishing, boating, waterskiing, cross-country skiing]

6. Little Sahara Recreation Area. *Jericho.* It's easy to see where this 60,000-acre park with its vast sand dunes got its name; and like the African Sahara, it is a harsh environment that limits the scope of the flora and fauna. Only sagebrush, June grass, and gnarled junipers reaching little more than 20 feet high manage to survive here—and one plant that is singular in these dunes: the giant four-wing saltbush, which can grow four feet in one season. The distant surrounding mountains often are surmounted by dramatic cloud formations in the deep blue sky.

One of the three campgrounds and picnic areas caters to dune buggy and dirt bike enthusiasts, who roar up and down the rolling sand dunes with abandon. People interested in a more pastoral environment will prefer the Jericho and White Sands campgrounds and the 10,000-acre Rockwell Natural Area, where dune driving is prohibited. The dunes are most crowded in spring and fall. *Campgrounds open daily; visitor center open Fri.–Sun., spring through fall.*

![icons: picnic, tent, RV, hiking, binoculars]

7. Oak Creek Campground. *East of Oak City.* Situated in a canyon at an elevation of 5,900 feet, where Oak Creek threads its way among maples, oaks, and cottonwoods, this site has been a favorite recreation area for more than 75 years. People came here for fishing, hunting, camping, and just plain enjoying the outdoors. In the 1920's it became a popular dance resort, and people arrived by horse and wagon on a summer evening for a whirl on the floor to the "catchy music" of the Foot Warmers Orchestra.

Today the dance floor is gone, but the natural setting is as invigorating as ever. The 29-acre area offers a picnic ground and campsites. More primitive and dispersed campsites are available a quarter-mile up the road just beyond the Big Spring Campground.

Oak Creek is stocked annually with rainbow trout, and fishing is generally quite good. Hiking is limited by the surrounding steep canyon slopes, but the inveterate walker will find either the Lyman Canyon Trail or the South Walker Trail enjoyable routes into Dry Creek. Both of these trails are slightly more than three miles long, and the trailheads for each are

4. *The time and place of dinosaurs is dramatically documented in this sandstone wall.*

10. *Conditioned as we are to the human life span, the time required to create this landscape is literally incomprehensible.*

within a three-mile drive up the road from the campground. *Open daily, May–Oct. Admission charged.*

8. Frisco. During much of the late 19th century, Frisco was a vibrant community of miners working a rich lode: by 1885 tens of millions of dollars worth of gold, silver, copper, lead, and zinc had been extracted. But the mineral deposits were eventually depleted, and the boomtown sank back into the desert. By the 1920's Frisco was a ghost town, occupied only by the swift lizards scurrying across its dusty yards and rocky ruins.

Today the only indications of its former activity are the mine entrances at the base of the San Francisco Mountains. A cemetery provides sparse clues about people who lived and died here, for the inscriptions on many of the wooden grave markers have weathered away. Though the riches are gone from the mines, you can see the huge heaps of tailings, cone-shaped stone kilns, pithead machinery, and clusters of derelict buildings threaded together by narrow dirt roads best suited to vehicles with high suspension and four-wheel drive. *Open year-round.*

9. Capitol Reef National Park. *Visitor center 12 miles east of Torrey on Rte. 24.* Magnificent canyon landscapes, well-maintained hiking trails, ancient Indian sites, a preserved 19th-century Mormon orchard, remote dirt roads, and a 25-mile round-trip scenic drive make this desert park a backcountry enthusiast's delight. The primary feature of its rugged wilderness is a 100-mile-long ridge, or "reef," created by a buckling of the earth's crust as it was thrust upward by subterranean pressure. Millennia of erosion and other geological forces have carved in the terrain a stunning gallery of canyons, arches, towers, and buttes. One particularly striking dome, which is reminiscent of the top of the U.S. Capitol in Washington, inspired the reef's name.

On the canyons' sandstone walls one can still see the glyphs carved by the Fremont People, who inhabited the area from roughly A.D. 800 to 1200. Later the Paiute Indians lived here, and in the 1880's Mormon settlers planted orchards that were so successful their community eventually came to be called Fruita. Today the Mormons' 1896 schoolhouse can be toured, and the orchards, about a mile from the visitor center, are maintained by park personnel and are open to visitors in season, when apples, cherries, peaches, apricots, and pears can be purchased on a "pick your own" basis.

A gravel road, following the path of a pioneer wagon trail, provides a scenic drive through the canyons into Capitol Gorge. A guidebook to the drive is available at the visitor center. Hiking trails and rugged backcountry roads also abound; bring plenty of water and insect repellent. A developed campground is maintained near the visitor center, and primitive sites are located at Cedar Mesa in the park's southern wilderness. *Open year-round.*

10. Dead Horse Point State Park. *Moab.* Toward the end of the last century packs of wild mustangs roamed the mesas around what is now called Dead Horse Point, a stone promontory surrounded by high cliffs overlooking the Colorado River 2,000 feet below. Cowboys fenced the narrow neck of land leading onto the promontory to use it as a natural corral for the mustangs. Once they had selected the best horses for personal use or sale, the gate was opened and the unwanted culls were allowed to find their way off the point and onto open range. One group never made it; according to legend, those broomtails died of thirst within distant view of the Colorado River.

Dead Horse Point is just one of the breathtaking overlooks in this 7,000-acre state park. Paved and primitive trails radiate outward from the visitor center to six

14. *Eroding cliffs determined the color of the sand. The flowers are mule ears.*

points overlooking the river and the heavily eroded cliff walls, with their towering spires and steep bluffs.

The park offers self-guiding hikes and, in summer, short ranger-guided tours through a wilderness of piñon pine, Utah juniper, single-leaf ash, and a wide variety of colorful wildflowers and cacti. Rock climbers and hang gliders occasionally pursue their sports along the precipice. *Open year-round. Developed campground open Apr.–Oct. Winter camping allowed on the point. Admission charged.*

11. Castleton Towers. *South off Rte. 128 east of Moab; follow signs for Castle Valley.* Sandstone spires reach skyward like ancient cathedrals ruined by the elements. Massive boulders split from sun-baked walls lie strewn about the steep hillside like marbles scattered by a petulant giant. Above the flat crowns of monstrous canyons, dramatic cloud formations sweep

across a clear blue sky and work their ever-changing magic on the palisade walls. Here is a primeval scene of nature in magnificent disarray.

This unsupervised area has many roadside blanket-picnic spots with panoramic views. It also presents an open invitation to hikers, backpackers, birders, and photographers to explore the ancient hills and canyons of a unique and beautiful landform. *Open year-round.*

12. Gunlock Lake State Beach. *Gunlock.* Containing a 266-acre man-made reservoir, this small recreation area offers an array of water activities in a beautiful environment. Surrounding the beach are tall, eroded canyon walls dotted with Utah junipers and cacti. In summer the gigantic white, bell-shaped flowers of the sacred datura add, by way of contrast, a pleasing and fragile softness to the scene. Birders will particularly enjoy this 548-acre area.

Canyon wrens are common, and their strange, tubular nests can be spotted in the cottonwood trees.

Primitive campsites are scattered among the sagebrush on a slope overlooking the water. Boating, waterskiing, and fishing are popular. Spring and fall have the best weather. Holiday weekends are likely to be crowded. *Open year-round.*

13. Kolob Canyons, Zion National Park. Spectacular geological formations and a wide variety of environments make Kolob Canyons a place of exceptional beauty and interest. Within this less-used section of Zion National Park are the park's highest peak, 8,726-foot Horse Ranch Mountain, and the world's longest freestanding natural span known, the Kolob Arch.

A 5½-mile paved auto route into the five Finger Canyons of the Kolob is marked by 14 numbered stops keyed to an accompanying pamphlet available at the visitor center. The road winds between canyon walls of reddish Navajo sandstone sculpted by 13 million years of geological upheaval and erosion into the numerous buttes, arches, and ridges that we see today. Part of the road follows Hurricane Fault, a 200-mile-long fracture in the earth's crust, which elevated the land to the east nearly a mile. The change in altitude from valley to clifftop creates temperature differences averaging between 10° and 15° F. As a result, three distinct ecological zones can be observed in the canyons, from the valley's semiarid piñon and juniper woodland to the lush forests of aspen, fir, and pine crowning Timber Top Mountain.

Mule deer, coyotes, and mountain lions frequent the area, as do peregrine falcons, ravens, and golden eagles. A strenuous hiking trail, requiring eight hours for a round trip, leads from the canyon road to Kolob Arch. Backcountry camping is allowed with a permit. The area may be crowded in spring, especially on holidays and weekends. *Open year-round.*

14. Coral Pink Sand Dunes State Park. *South of Mt. Carmel Junction.* You'll know you've arrived when you hear the sound of revving motors, for the 2,000 acres of rolling dunes in this 3,730-acre reserve attract dirt bike and dune buggy enthusiasts from far and wide. The sand is extremely fine, and off-road vehicles should have paddle-type tires.

The coral pink dunes are beautiful to see and photograph, especially just before sundown, when they come alive with shifting shadows. Backpackers will find the campground here an excellent staging point for challenging, unmarked hikes through butte and mesa country. Be wary, however; rattlesnakes, black widow spiders, and scorpions thrive in this desert climate. Birders are likely to see scrub jays and hummingbirds in an adjacent area studded with piñon pine, Utah juniper, and yucca. Sunflowers grow wild here, along with blue-flowering sophoras. June and July are the best months to enjoy the spectacular wildflower display. The park may be crowded on summer holidays and weekends. When winter snow cover is sufficient, the dunes are excellent for tubing. *Park and campground open year-round. Admission charged.*

15. Escalante State Park. *Escalante.* The petrified forest in this 2,100-acre park is among the most remarkable in the country. In the late Jurassic Period 140 million years ago, the area was a wetland washed by streams powerful enough to transport whole fallen trees. The trees grew heavier as they became waterlogged and eventually sank to the river bottoms, where they were covered with gravel and silt. Over the ages water percolated through the soil, and as the wood cells dissolved they were replaced by silica as well as oxides of iron and manganese. The results can be seen in the startling reds, yellows, purples, and other colors in the petrified logs scattered throughout the park.

Hikers enjoy the moderately difficult one-hour climbs along the Wide Hollow and the Bailey Wash trails. Numbered stops along the trails correspond to entries in a printed guide available at the campground office. The 110-acre reservoir here offers opportunities for swimming, wind surfing, and fishing for rainbow trout. Ice fishing is popular in the winter. *Open year-round. Admission charged.*

16. Natural Bridges National Monument. Until 1904 the three huge sandstone bridges here were called Caroline, Augusta, and Edwin, names given them by prospectors who explored the area in the 1880's. They were rechristened with native American names by President William Howard Taft in 1909 shortly after the site was designated a national monument. He chose Hopi words, presumably because of the prehistoric cliff dwelling that stands nearby, rather than words of the Paiutes or Navajos, who inhabited the area in historic times. The oldest bridge is called *Owachomo* ("rock mound"); the longest is *Sipapu* ("the place of emergence"); and the youngest is *Kachina,* named for the masked divinities of the Hopi religion. All three bridges were formed by the erosive action of streams as they flowed through the switchback bends of a canyon. Eventually the streams wore through the canyon walls where they turned, and thus the bridges were formed.

An eight-mile loop road, suitable for bicycles as well as cars, links the starting points of the short trails to the three bridges and provides access to overlooks offering splendid views of the surrounding canyon scenery. For those seeking longer hikes, nearly six miles of trail traverse the canyons' floors and connect the bridges. The terrain here, however, may be hazardous, and hikers should be alert for flash flooding. A campground near the visitor center has 13 primitive sites, but drinking water is not provided.

Electricity for the facilities here is produced by a large array of photovoltaic cells. These solar energy collectors cover nearly an acre, and when the installation was dedicated in 1980, it was the largest of its kind in the world. *Open year-round, but some trails may be closed in winter. Visitor center open Memorial Day–Labor Day. Admission charged.*

17. Goosenecks State Park. *Rte. 316 west off Rte. 261, north of Mexican Hat.* The dramatic beauty of Utah's precipitous landscape is epitomized by the view from this 10-acre park set atop a towering mesa. From an overlook four "gooseneck" bends can be seen in the muddy San Juan River as it wends 1,000 feet below. These bends, for which the park is named, are important examples of a geological phe-

nomenon known as an entrenched meander: a curving streambed that by gradual water erosion or land upheaval is cut deep below the surface of the valley in which the river flows. Here the meanders have worn so deep that they have exposed layers of sandstone, shale, and limestone dating back more than 300 million years.

The mesa's vegetation has evolved to derive maximum moisture from the arid land. The Indian ricegrass, Mormon tea, prickly pear, and other sandy lowland plants provide cover and food that is too sparse to support much indigenous animal life; jackrabbits, skunks, and lizards are about the only creatures that manage to sustain a living in this landscape. Birders will find the overlook rewarding, however, and it's an excellent place to stop for a picnic lunch amid magnificent surroundings. *Open year-round.*

16. *The cross-bedded sandstone of Sipapu Bridge soars to a height of 67 feet and measures more than 80 feet in length.*

Colorado

The splendor of the Rockies, vast sand dunes, and ancient Indian ruins blend with memories of mining camps, pioneers, and the Santa Fe Trail.

In one grand wilderness straddling the Continental Divide, and studded with magnificent peaks, there are 200 miles of hiking and horseback trails. In other areas trails traverse foothills and prairies, canyons and mesas.

Watery settings include a reservoir, a spectacular falls, and a 15,000-acre lake that is shared with New Mexico. The Great Sand Dunes, in their unlikely inland location, are the tallest in America.

Indian culture is recalled by some 11th-century dwellings and a museum devoted to the Utes, the last Indians to roam freely here. Other museums document the lives of the soldiers, miners, farmers, and ranchers who settled this rugged land.

1. Browns Park National Wildlife Refuge. This wilderness area, a river valley with sagebrush flats overlooked by slopes sprinkled with junipers and piñon pines, has changed little in the century since Butch Cassidy and other cattle rustlers came here to hide their stolen steers. Even before that, Browns Hole, as the valley was then known, was a favorite haunt of Indian hunters and fur trappers. Not only did it offer shelter from winter winds, but the Green River made it a habitat for a relatively large number of animals in the midst of an arid region. Today the silence and grandeur of the 6,000-acre wildlife refuge make it a superb setting for hikers, backpackers, campers, and stoppers-by who take the four-mile river drive.

The park is primarily a nesting and stopping place for migratory waterfowl, including canvasbacks, redheads, mallards, and Canada geese, but wading, songbirds, and even coastal birds also come here. Nearly 200 bird species have been sighted, including sage grouse and chukar partridge. Pronghorn antelopes, mule deer, and bighorn sheep sometimes appear in spring. Trout, catfish, and carp can be caught in the river.

Primitive camping facilities are located at a deep bend of the river. Bring your own drinking water as well as food and fuel. The nearest supplies are 50 miles away. *Open year-round.*

2. Mount Zirkel Wilderness, Routt National Forest. *Easiest access: at Steamboat Springs take County Rte. 129 north 19 miles to Clark, then follow Seedhouse Rd. (Forest Rd. 400).* Visitors to this 140,000-acre wilderness will find nature's splendor and solitude in its most primeval magnificence. Spreading along the Continental Divide, the area contains more than a dozen peaks around 12,000 feet high, more than 65 small lakes—many of them too remote to be named—and countless cascading streams. The terrain includes stands of spruce, pine, and quaking aspen, mixed grasslands below the tree line, and more rugged territory above it. Elk and deer graze in the meadows during summer, and coyotes, grouse, and ptarmigan are occasionally seen.

Two hundred miles of hiking and riding trails lead to some of the area's most spectacular scenery, and there are ample opportunities for experienced backpackers to venture from the trail into untracked wildness. Several backcountry outfitters in nearby Clark offer horseback excursions and guided hunting trips in season. Anglers will take brook, rainbow, and cutthroat trout. Two campgrounds are maintained by the Forest Service along Seedhouse Road. *Open year-round but often inaccessible in winter; campgrounds usually open June–Sept.*

3. Lory State Park. *Off Rte. 287, Bellvue.* A former cattle ranch, this 2,600-acre park is true Rocky Mountain high country, ranging in elevation from 5,000 to 7,000 feet. In a dramatically scenic setting sagebrush and prairie grassland valleys are flanked by orange sandstone hogback ridges. Moving upward, slopes covered with low-growing mountain shrubs give way to imposing ponderosa pine forests with patches of bare rock.

The varied vegetation provides habitats for many animals. Wild turkeys, red-tailed hawks, and blue grouse are often sighted, as are the mule deer and Abert squirrels with their long, tufted ears.

The park has 25 miles of trails, open to both hikers and horseback riders, and tent camping is permitted at eight backcountry sites along them. A cross-country horse

2. A rich backdrop of evergreens sets off the flamboyant seasonal tracery of aspens.

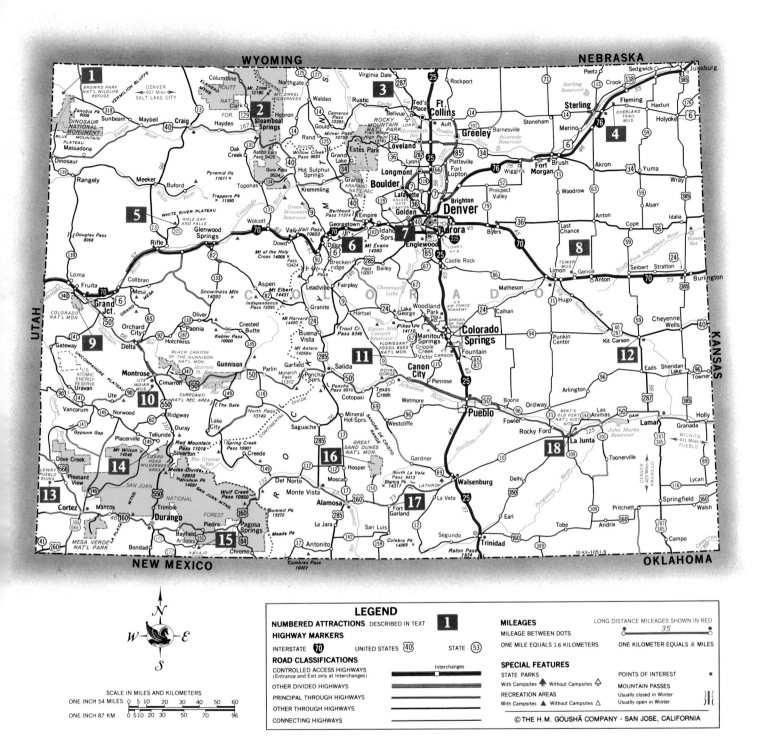

UTAH

COLORADO

KANSAS

NEW MEXICO   OKLAHOMA

LEGEND

NUMBERED ATTRACTIONS DESCRIBED IN TEXT [1]

HIGHWAY MARKERS

INTERSTATE (70) UNITED STATES (40) STATE (53)

ROAD CLASSIFICATIONS

CONTROLLED ACCESS HIGHWAYS
(Entrance and Exit only at Interchanges) Interchanges

OTHER DIVIDED HIGHWAYS

PRINCIPAL THROUGH HIGHWAYS

OTHER THROUGH HIGHWAYS

CONNECTING HIGHWAYS

MILEAGES LONG DISTANCE MILEAGES SHOWN IN RED

MILEAGE BETWEEN DOTS 35

ONE MILE EQUALS 1.6 KILOMETERS ONE KILOMETER EQUALS .6 MILES

SPECIAL FEATURES

STATE PARKS POINTS OF INTEREST
With Campsites ▲ Without Campsites △

RECREATION AREAS MOUNTAIN PASSES
With Campsites ▲ Without Campsites △ Usually closed in Winter
 Usually open in Winter

© THE H.M. GOUSHA COMPANY · SAN JOSE, CALIFORNIA

SCALE IN MILES AND KILOMETERS

ONE INCH 54 MILES 0 5 10 20 30 40 50 60

ONE INCH 87 KM 0 510 20 30 50 70 96

jumping course is also available. Three days of trials are held here during the third week in May—the only time the park draws a crowd.

Rock climbers challenge the routes up Arthur's Rock, which rises to 6,780 feet. Whether reached by rope or trail, this promontory provides a breathtaking view of Fort Collins and surroundings. *Open year-round. Admission charged.*

4. Overland Trail Museum. *U.S. Rte. 6, east of Sterling.* In the 1860's the Overland Trail was one of the most heavily used routes in the nation. Long lines of covered wagons and frequent runs by the coaches of the Overland Stage Line carried settlers and adventurers westward by the thousands. The starting segment of the trail along the South Platte River here was notable as an easy-to-follow natural highway with a sure supply of water and game.

The stone structure that houses the museum is a replica of Fort Sedgwick, a

stronghold established for protection from Indians. The westward-bound emigrants are commemorated by a collection of household items they carried with them, including an 1861 sewing machine and a handsome hand-carved cherry rocker. The cattle business that later flourished on the vast surrounding plains is recalled by displays of spurs, chaps, saddles, more than 400 kinds of branding irons, and an array of early farm implements.

The area's earliest history is represented by cases of mastodon and mammoth

303

bones and arrays of Indian arrowheads. *Open daily May–Sept. Admission free but donations accepted.*

---

5. Rifle Gap and Falls State Recreation Area. This remote mountain recreation area has two parts, and—surprisingly in this dry region—the most notable feature of each is water. The Rifle Gap Reservoir is a 350-acre lake created by the damming of East and Middle Rifle creeks in 1965. The other part is Rifle Falls, where East Rifle Creek takes a spectacular plunge.

Filled with mountain runoff, the reservoir has clear turquoise water that makes it an exceptionally inviting place to swim, boat, sail, and water-ski. Scuba divers, especially, will rejoice in the water's sparkling clarity. Anglers are likely to catch walleyes, bass, and trout. The trout come from a hatchery just five miles up the road that is open to visitors. Surrounding the reservoir are knolls of cedar piñon. A small herd of buffalo can be seen grazing in a field along the western shore, and deer can be spotted throughout the year, especially in April and May.

About four miles north of the reservoir, Rifle Falls not only has an impressive trio of 90-foot cascades side by side, but its limestone cliff has a number of small caves, the largest about 70 feet long and 25 feet high. The caves' walls and ceilings are covered with an amazing pattern of small crisscrossing stalactites resembling a cobweb. *Open year-round but may be inaccessible in winter. Admission charged.*

---

6. Hotel De Paris. *409 Sixth St., Georgetown.* Situated in a historic landmark district notable for its Victorian structures, this hotel was one of more than a dozen establishments that catered to visitors when Georgetown was a booming silver-mining center. And in the rugged new land it was an isle of refinement, with carved walnut furniture, diamond-dust mirrors, paintings, etchings, fine china, lace curtains, and tapestry draperies.

People came from far and wide to sample the elegant food, wine, and service provided by the hotel's founder, Louis Dupuy. A Frenchman from Normandy, Dupuy had been apprenticed to a chef in Paris before working his way across the Atlantic. He traveled west by enlisting in the U.S. Cavalry and then deserting.

The hotel, restored by the Colonial Dames of America, has lost none of its charm. Indeed, it has a freshness that suggests it still caters to guests. The dining room is set for dinner with a cruet and a vase of flowers on every table. Ten guest rooms boast marble-topped sinks, mirrored dressers, and carved headboards.

Georgetown has other refurbished buildings you can visit, and a restored railroad that runs to a nearby mining area. *Open daily Memorial Day–Sept.; P.M. Tues.–Sun. in winter. Admission charged.*

---

7. Golden Gate Canyon State Park. Lumberjacks, settlers, and miners with pack animals in tow once trudged the network of trails crossing this rugged mountain terrain. For hikers who follow in their footsteps today, this is the jewel of Colorado parks, a place of quiet forests, rushing streams, and magnificent scenery. The mountains—green and fragrant with spruce, pine, and fir, and spangled in early autumn with the bright yellow of quaking aspen—are the domain of mule deer, elk, black bears, bobcats, and mountain lions. Golden eagles and sharp-shinned hawks soar above.

Some 40 miles are covered by 13 trails, ranging in length from just over a mile to nearly six miles. Some are strenuous, with steep climbs, but other trails proceed easily along valley floors and ridges and may be used for horses. The best vista, however, is not far from the road: Panorama Point offers nearly a 100-mile view of the towering Continental Divide.

Reverend's Ridge Campground has such amenities as hot showers; Aspen Meadows Campground is for tents only. July and August provide the most favorable weather for hiking and camping, but it is best to avoid weekends then. *Open year-round; campgrounds open June–Sept. Admission charged.*

---

8. Tower Museum. *Take Exit 371 from I-70 at Genoa; continue half a mile west.* One of the first things the visitor to this offbeat 20-room museum encounters is a puzzling array of some 300 artifacts. Anyone who can identify 10 in a row gets an admission refund. Few people today, however, can recognize such items as a buggy-whip holder, a buffalo cud, and a magician's knife. But it is fun to try, and it is a good introduction to the truly eccentric nature of the place and its collection.

The 75-foot wooden tower and the sprawling complex of rock rooms at its base are the brainchild of C. W. Gregory, sometimes known as Colorado's P. T. Barnum. He put up the tall structure to attract visitors and dubbed it the World's Wonder View Tower; from its knolltop site it does offer a spectacular view extending into five states on a clear day.

The museum's chief attraction, however, is its collections of archeological materials, antique items, and oddities. These include 75,000-year-old mammoth bones, 8,500-year-old buffalo bones, 20,000 Indian arrowheads, a thousand paintings by the Indian princess Ravenwing, and collections of old firearms, telephone and telegraph insulators, and barbed wire. *Open year-round. Admission charged.*

---

9. Colorado National Monument. The wild vastness and beauty of this series of canyons and mesas have been preserved, thanks to one man, John Otto, a turn-of-the-century maverick who campaigned tirelessly for a national park.

Sculpted by wind and rain and ancient seas over millions of years, the magnificent formations of orange, yellow, and red sandstone can be enjoyed not only by campers and backpackers but by day visitors. The 35-mile Rim Rock Drive that snakes through the park can be covered on a short outing. The road is narrow, with precipitous drop-offs, but it offers excellent vantage points as well as spots for picnics and short hikes.

Longer trails proceed across mesas and zigzag up and down the canyon walls. Golden eagles, turkey vultures, and several hawk species are among the birds that swoop overhead. Spring and fall are the best times for hiking. In the summer heat a hat and a supply of water are essential. Rock climbers and overnight backpackers should register at the visitor center and ask about restrictions. *Open year-round. Admission charged.*

9. *This vista, called Grand View, must have been named by someone who was understandably at a loss for the suitable words.*

10. Ute Indian Museum. *17253 Chipeta Dr., Montrose.* The Utes were a diverse, widely scattered people who lived throughout the Rockies, in Colorado as well as Utah, the state named for them. They are believed to be the only tribe native to Colorado; the Cheyennes and other Plains tribes were pushed westward into the state by white settlements.

In the late 1800's and early 1900's Thomas McKee, a photographer, lived among the Utes, documenting their lives in pictures and acquiring artifacts. His collection is effectively displayed in this small but fascinating museum run by the Colorado Historical Society. Examining the articles, one is impressed by the artistry and workmanship revealed.

In one of the two galleries you'll find traditional and ceremonial items used by the various branches of the tribe. Two fine dioramas depict a pre-reservation encampment and the bear dance ceremony.

The second gallery features famous Utes, most notably the great chief Ouray, who led the tribe in signing a treaty with the United States in the 1860's. Ouray's wicked-looking horn-handled knife and a beaded buckskin shirt made for him by his wife, Chipeta, are on display. *Open Mon.–Sat. and P.M. Sun., Memorial Day –Labor Day. Admission charged.*

11. Town of Victor. Located only six miles from Cripple Creek, the site of a world-renowned gold strike in the 1890's, this once-thriving mining town now has a population of a few hundred rather than the thousands it had at its peak. Pit scaffolding and tailings are the only visible remains of the 400-odd mines that filled more that 70 trains per day with ore. But the many structures still standing speak with a hushed eloquence of the town's prosperous past.

Most of the buildings are brick, and many date from 1899, when Victor was rebuilt after fire leveled the original wooden structures. Among them are a school, a hotel, a railroad station, fraternal lodges, and the city hall. There are also the remains of a mine where gold was found while the foundation for a hotel was being dug. A museum displays mementos of the town's colorful past, along with items relating to the newscaster Lowell Thomas, a Victor native. The town's even more famous son was the prizefighter Jack Dempsey, who worked in the mines and trained for his early fights in the firehouse.

Visitors should stay well away from mines, which are rife with rotting timbers, loose rocks, vertical shafts, and sometimes poisonous gases. *Open year-round.*

12. Kit Carson Museum. *Rte. 40, Kit Carson.* This museum's name is somewhat misleading. It is not dedicated to the legendary Western hero but rather to the town here that was named after him. In its glory days more than a century ago, Kit Carson was a thriving railhead, a town of Western legend with saloons, dance hall girls, and a six-shooter on every hip. But little survives from that town, which burned to the ground, and the museum's collection concentrates on the relatively quiet high plains farming and grazing center that replaced it.

The museum is housed in a 1904 Union Pacific depot, still furnished with an old-fashioned telephone, a telegraph key, and signal levers. Several displays re-create

14. *Amazing in this rock setting at Navajo Lake are the delicate blue columbines.*

14. Lizard Head Wilderness Area. Straddling the spectacular, snowcapped San Miguel Mountains, this 31,000-acre preserve encompasses some of Colorado's most impressive peaks. Three rise more than 14,000 feet; several others, over 13,000 feet. Although mining once made a brief foray into the basins, this wilderness remains a land of unspoiled beauty and a delight for backpackers and mountain climbers who want to experience real wilderness in the high Rockies.

No vehicles are allowed in the area. Trailheads for the five established hiking routes can be reached along forest roads leading off Route 145. The most popular is the Navajo Lake Trail, which cuts through meadows and forests of spruce and aspen and then climbs steep switchbacks before it descends to the lake. Backpackers are asked not to camp by the lake, however, in the interest of environmental protection. Detailed topographical maps are essential and can be obtained at local book and sporting goods stores. Novice backpackers should travel with an experienced companion. The high mountains can be difficult and dangerous. And even on lower pinnacles, a climber should be prepared for razor-edge ridges above the timberline and permanent snowfields near the summits.

Snow remains on some trails until mid-June, and the temperature can drop below freezing on midsummer nights. Heavy downpours are common on summer afternoons. The preserve can also be explored by day hikers staying at nearby campgrounds. Most areas have little or no firewood, so bring a cookstove. Horseback riders are welcome once the trails are fully dry, around the end of June. *Open year-round but usually inaccessible in winter.*

late 19th-century rooms with period furnishings and costumed mannequins. There is a small doll collection and another of farm implements ranging from horse-drawn planters to harrows and hay rakes. Among the other diverse items that outline the community's history are Indian arrowheads and grindstones, a bear trap, branding irons, and a caboose stove, all donated by townspeople. *Open daily Memorial Day–Sat. after Labor Day.*

13. Lowry Pueblo Ruins. For centuries the Anasazi Indians dominated the Four Corners region (the meeting place of Utah, Colorado, Arizona, and New Mexico), where they built pueblos and cliffside

dwellings. But long before the time of Columbus they left their homes, letting them fall into ruins. One of these is Lowry Pueblo, a complex of three dozen rooms and nine kivas, or ceremonial chambers, built on a mesa around the end of the 11th century. Probably it accommodated a farming community of about 100 people, but it was abandoned after 50 years or so, and its stone walls were not discovered until this century.

Now a national historic landmark, the ruins are open to visitors. The unique feature at Lowry is the painted kiva, now protected with a roof. Its plastered walls are neatly painted with a zigzag motif suggesting lightning. *Open year-round.*

15. Navajo State Recreation Area. Fed by melting snow, Navajo Lake is a giant reservoir with some 15,000 acres of sparkling turquoise water. More than three-quarters of the lake is in New Mexico, backed up against a dam about 20 miles to the south. This Colorado recreation site—located on the lakeshore close to the state line—offers perfect access to the water, however, and to all the water-sports activities that it invites. Indeed, the park boasts a quarter-mile-long boat ramp, the largest in the state. It also has a good marina and dock where boats can be rented. Water-skiing, sailing, and windsurfing are all popular, and fishing is especially attractive. There is also a small, unguarded inlet for swimming.

Short hikes can be taken along an old stagecoach road and an abandoned railroad track bed. Ducks, geese, songbirds such as thrushes and meadowlarks, and lizards are among the most commonly observed wildlife. The visitor center has a collection of Indian artifacts rescued from the area before it was flooded. *Park open year-round with full campground facilities mid-Apr.–Oct.; marina open Apr.–Sept.; visitor center open daily May–mid-Sept. and irregularly rest of year. Admission charged.*

16. Great Sand Dunes National Monument.

The "Great" in the name of this fascinating natural phenomenon is more than appropriate. Not only are these ever-changing dunes ranked as the tallest in North America but the dune field stretches impressively over 150 square miles of high mountain valley floor. The vast expanse of sand was formed over millions of years by the action of glacial meltwaters and shifting rivers.

The park itself encompasses the main dune field nestled at the foot of the rugged Sangre de Cristo Mountains. Because of the mountains, the sand here is caught in a wind trap, and in spots, peak piles upon

peak, to form 700-foot-high dunes that look like miniature mountains.

Not surprisingly, this unusual park appeals to sand skiers as well as to hikers, backpackers, and campers, who stay in a campground in an area of cottonwoods and pines at the dunes' edge. Some visitors venture onto the dunes at night with flashlights in hopes of spotting the kangaroo rats and the giant sand-treader camel crickets that manage to survive in this arid environment. The crickets are not found anywhere else on earth.

The best weather is generally in spring and fall. In summer, even though the air temperature is moderate, the sand can get uncomfortably hot. The park tends to be crowded on Memorial Day weekend with visitors from the region. *Park open year-round; campground open Apr.–Oct.*

17. Fort Garland.

Rte. 159. For a quarter of a century, beginning in 1858, this remote frontier garrison provided protection for settlers in the San Luis Valley from the Ute Indians. It was opened only a few years after the first pioneers arrived and was abandoned when the Utes were forced to settle on a reservation.

The fort's rectangular array of low adobe structures housed up to two companies of 100 men each. Many different army units and territorial militias manned the fort. But it is best known for being the last

command (1866–67) of the famed frontiersman Kit Carson, then a colonel with the 1st New Mexico Cavalry.

At the restored fort, the commandant's quarters have been set up to look as they did during Carson's stay, and a life-size diorama shows him meeting with Utes in his office. In the officers' quarters and enlisted men's barracks, dioramas illustrate the Spanish conquest of the region, the early fur trade, an army pack train, and a stage holdup. There are also displays of uniforms, weapons, flags, and the Mexican woolen cloaks known as serapes. The fort may be crowded in July. *Open Mon.–Sat. and P.M. Sun., Memorial Day–Labor Day. Admission charged.*

18. Bent's Old Fort National Historic Site.

Hard on the heels of the first American explorers, trappers and traders eagerly extended their range into the high plains and mountains of the Southwest. Among the trading posts that sprang up in their wake, the most important was this one, built in the early 1830's by two Missouri brothers, William and Charles Bent, in partnership with a reputed French nobleman, Ceran St. Vrain.

Located on the Mountain Branch of the Sante Fe Trail, a fairly safe, easy route following the Arkansas River, the adobe fort soon became a hub for trade radiating south to Santa Fe and Mexico, west to the Pacific, and north into Wyoming.

For years the three men controlled a huge commercial empire. But the Mexican War and the designation of the post as a U.S. military base, the decline in trade, the death of Charles Bent, the departure of St. Vrain, and a cholera epidemic led William Bent to abandon the fort in 1849. Tradition holds that Bent was so irked by the army's refusal to buy the fort that he blew it up.

This national historic site is a reconstruction of the post as it appeared in its heyday around 1845. Within thick, high walls an open plaza is ringed by furnished living quarters, warehouses, workshops, and even a billiard room. Staff members dressed as trappers, Indians, and Mexicans demonstrate frontier activities. *Open year-round.*

18. This reconstruction reveals the unexpected architectural beauty of the frontier fort.

New Mexico

From its prehistory to the atomic age, ice caves to lava flows, arid deserts to snowcapped mountains—this is a land of incredible contrast.

In settings of superlative scenery is dramatic evidence of an ancient people who built 500-room complexes, created communities connected by an extensive network of roads, and practiced sophisticated methods of agriculture.

Recent accomplishments, with untold implications for the future, are celebrated in museums dedicated to the atomic age and space exploration. The 19th century is recalled in a famous landform where pioneers literally left their mark, a historic army fort, a town that time forgot, and the mansion of a lucky miner. Great sand dunes, sculpted monoliths, a 6,000-acre lake, hiking trails and nature walks, a wildlife refuge, a treasure field for rockhounds, and a magnificent folk museum further contribute to the contrast here.

1. National Atomic Museum. *Kirtland Air Force Base.* A visit to this modest museum is fascinating, terrifying, and unforgettable. Here one is brought face to face with a class of weapons that may have the capacity to destroy all mankind.

The Energy Horizons Room is devoted to the peaceful uses of energy. There are explanations of the various ways that fossil fuels, solar energy, nuclear fission, and the wind and tide are used to produce power. There's also a library and a theater that shows films related to the development and use of energy. The 53-minute feature, *Ten Seconds That Shook the World,* is a documentary on the secret Manhattan Project, which led to the production of the first atomic bomb.

Displayed in a separate section are aerodynamic containers in which atomic and nuclear warheads can be delivered—by land, sea, and air. Of course, most of what is seen here has been superseded by more efficient models. Outside the museum are rockets, missiles, and a B-52 aircraft that was used for testing nuclear weapons in the atmosphere. *Open year-round except Easter, Thanksgiving Day, Christmas, and New Year's Day.*

2. Aztec Ruins National Monument. The ruins here were discovered in the 1870's and mistakenly named for the Aztec Indians of Mexico. The 500-room structure, built in the early 1100's by the Chacoan Anasazis, was one of many outlying communities linked to Chaco Canyon by a network of excellent roads.

Eventually the Chaco people abandoned the site, and by 1225 it was reoccupied by the Mesa Verde Anasazis from the north. Differences in masonry techniques and architectural styles distinguish their additions and modifications from the original construction. An easy trail leads through part of the ruins, allowing you to study the masonry and the interiors of the rooms. The ceilings here are original, and the green sandstone band running the length of the west wall is unique to this structure. The visitor center exhibits weaving, basketry, and some fine Anasazi pottery. *Open daily except Christmas and New Year's Day. Admission charged.*

3. Heron Lake State Park. *On Rte. 95.* Located near the Continental Divide, the park includes scenic Heron Lake, a watery expanse of some 6,000 acres created when Willow Creek was dammed in the mid-1970's. The surrounding 4,910 acres of parkland are ideal for camping and hiking. Four general camping areas are maintained, and more primitive sites can be reached by a dirt road that goes most of the way around the lakeshore. A hiking trail through the wilderness connects Heron Lake with El Vado Lake State Park, about five miles away. Deer and elk may be glimpsed in the evergreen forests, and in winter bald and golden eagles may be seen against the spectacular backdrop of snowcapped mountain peaks.

Sailing, swimming, and fishing are popular on the lake in the summer, and two boat ramps are provided. The most likely catches for fishermen are rainbow trout and kokanee. The most agreeable weather is from May into October. *Park open year-round. Visitor center open Memorial Day–Labor Day.*

4. Red River. For an off-season stay in the majestic Sangre de Cristo Mountains (the southern end of the Rocky Mountain chain), try this small alpine resort village

2. This remnant of the 500-room original reveals the superb quality of the masonry.

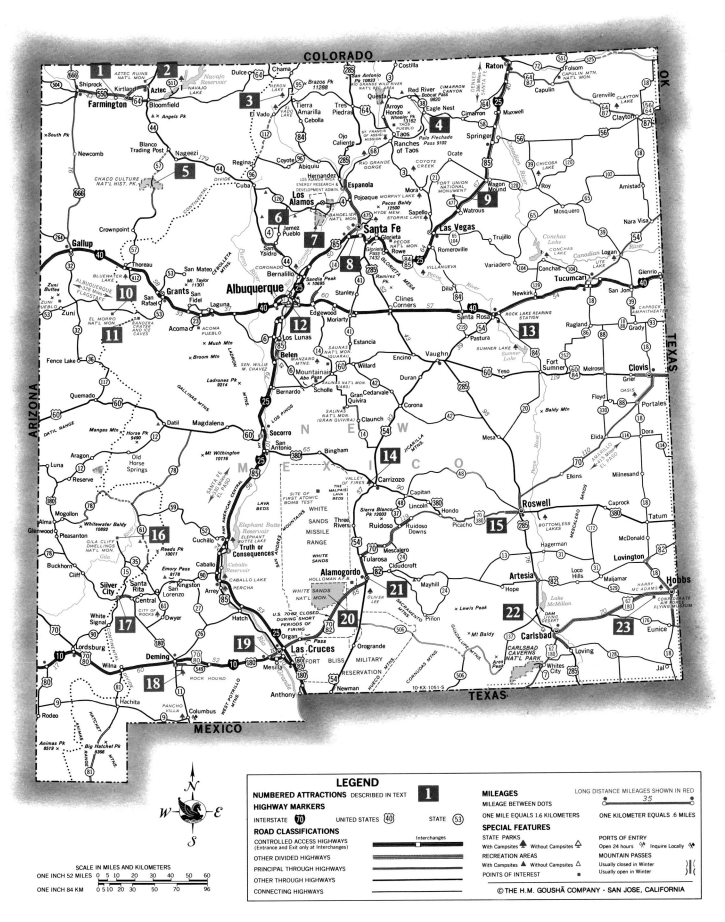

OK

TEXAS

ARIZONA

MEXICO

TEXAS

LEGEND

NUMBERED ATTRACTIONS DESCRIBED IN TEXT ☒1

HIGHWAY MARKERS

INTERSTATE 🛡70   UNITED STATES ⬢40   STATE ⬡53

ROAD CLASSIFICATIONS

Interchanges

CONTROLLED ACCESS HIGHWAYS
(Entrance and Exit only at Interchanges)

OTHER DIVIDED HIGHWAYS

PRINCIPAL THROUGH HIGHWAYS

OTHER THROUGH HIGHWAYS

CONNECTING HIGHWAYS

MILEAGES   LONG DISTANCE MILEAGES SHOWN IN RED

MILEAGE BETWEEN DOTS   ●————35————●

ONE MILE EQUALS 1.6 KILOMETERS   ONE KILOMETER EQUALS .6 MILES

SPECIAL FEATURES

STATE PARKS

With Campsites ♣ Without Campsites △

RECREATION AREAS

With Campsites ▲ Without Campsites △

POINTS OF INTEREST ■

PORTS OF ENTRY

Open 24 hours ✗ Inquire Locally ✗

MOUNTAIN PASSES

Usually closed in Winter

Usually open in Winter

© THE H.M. GOUSHÁ COMPANY · SAN JOSE, CALIFORNIA

SCALE IN MILES AND KILOMETERS

ONE INCH 52 MILES   0 5 10   20   30   40   50   60

ONE INCH 84 KM   0 5 10 20 30   50   70   96

N
W ✦ E
S

309

nestled in a narrow valley at an altitude of 8,700 feet. The village, which has fewer than 300 permanent residents, bulges with vacationers during the summer months, the Christmas season, and the spring college recess (when students come for downhill skiing), but the rest of the year it is nearly deserted.

Skiing is only one attraction here. For those beckoned by the great outdoors, late spring and early autumn are perfect times to explore the trails and narrow dirt roads twisting up the mountainsides, green and fragrant with ponderosa pines, Douglas firs, cedars, and hemlocks. In June and July the slopes are bright with primroses, mountain orchids, bluebells, and columbines, and around the first of October the quaking aspen reaches its golden glory. Elk, black bears, mountain lions, bobcats, and coyotes roam the forest, and at the higher altitudes marmots and mountain pikas are frequently seen.

From mid-May through October you can arrange a pack trip up to six days' duration to camp at a high mountain lake and fish for trout. A Carson National Forest campground along the highway just a mile west of the village provides an idyllic picnic spot on the banks of the Red River. For another picnic outing, drive to the Rio Grande Wild and Scenic River Recreation Area about 13 miles away (off Route 3 near Cerro), where you can view the Rio Grande far below as it catapults through a sheer-walled canyon.

5. Chaco Culture National Historical Park. One might think, near the end of 20 some miles of dirt road, that this site is *too* far off the beaten path. But for anyone interested in architectural design or the history of prehistoric Indians, Chaco Canyon is a place to stimulate and reward the imagination. The standing evidence of a sophisticated culture existing here about 700 to 1,000 years ago is overwhelming.

On a dozen major sites in the park, where several thousand Anasazis once lived and farmed, are the remains of their multistoried structures, built in the 10th and 11th centuries and completely vacated by 1300. The largest and most remarkable is Pueblo Bonito ("the beautiful village"), a stone edifice covering nearly three acres. Its 660 or so rooms rise like steps to four or five stories and curve around two great

stone-paved plazas. Sunk in the plazas are 32 kivas, round chambers that probably had a religious function.

The Park Service's printed guide to Chaco has photographs of the five distinctive types of masonry used, so that you can compare them, descriptive information, and a trail map. A road winds through the canyon, and trails lead to many of the ruins, including Casa Rinconada, a great kiva (63½ feet in diameter) that may have been a community center. Beyond Casa Rinconada, at Tsin Kletsin, is a magnificent view of the valley, an area that was once the hub of the Chacoans' world and is now a vast silent space.

There are picnic tables at the visitor center; a campground a mile away lacks water and utilities. *Open year-round. Check road conditions with park headquarters: (505) 786-5384.*

6. Bradbury Science Museum. *Los Alamos.* The Los Alamos National Laboratory was built for the Manhattan Project, which was responsible for designing and building the atomic bomb. The project's director, J. Robert Oppenheimer, chose the site not only for secrecy and scientific considerations, but also because he thought the ruggedly scenic country would appeal to his team of scientists.

Among the memorabilia in the museum is the influential letter from Albert Einstein to President Franklin D. Roosevelt in 1939 apprising him of the potential

power of atomic fission and urging authorization for immediate development.

Most of the museum is devoted to contemporary energy research and use. There are displays on geotechnology, solar energy, America's energy future, and such nuclear reactor technology as magnetic and laser fusion. Various aspects of weapon design, testing, and world deployment are also shown. There are some 35 hands-on displays, buttons, knobs, and dials to work with, and computers to lead you through minicourses of instruction. In the museum theater are continuous films on scientific subjects. *Open Tues.–Fri. and P.M. Sat.–Mon. except major holidays.*

7. Bandelier National Monument. The road to Bandelier takes you through some of the most spectacular country in New Mexico, offering enormous vistas of mountains, mesas, cliffs, and canyons. The monument itself covers nearly 50 square miles, almost all of it undisturbed wilderness. Some 66 miles of maintained hiking trails lead into and out of steep-walled canyons, bringing you to Pueblo ruins, cave rooms hewn out of rock cliffs, petroglyphs and pictographs, waterfalls, and scenic overlooks.

An easy self-guiding walk described in a pamphlet leads from the visitor center along the floor of Frijoles Canyon, where Anasazi Indians once farmed, passing the ruins of a circular pueblo. A fork in the trail—somewhat steep, with a number of steps—takes you to cave rooms and dramatic rock formations. From here one has

9. The far horizon suggests the distances these carts and wagons had to traverse.

10. *Black-eyed Susans—about knee-high—bring human scale to the mighty bluff.*

a magnificent view of the valley, with a stream lined with cottonwoods and box-elder maples that turn to a brilliant yellow in the early autumn.

A much longer, more demanding trail takes you down-canyon to two beautiful waterfalls and eventually to the Rio Grande as it courses through White Rock Canyon. The great variety of trees, shrubs, and flowering plants adds to the appeal of Bandelier. Since the monument is at an altitude of 7,000 feet and the terrain is rugged, one should be in good physical condition to explore. Permits are required (free at the visitor center) for backcountry hiking, horseback riding (bring your own steed), and cross-country skiing. *Park and visitor center open daily except Christmas.*

8. Museum of International Folk Art. *Santa Fe.* This fine collection, a part of the Museum of New Mexico, contains more than 120,000 objects from both hemispheres, making it the world's largest repository of folk art. Ceramics, furniture, toys, jewelry and amulets, textiles, folk costumes, and religious and ceremonial objects are included, with such diverse artifacts as Bhutanese and Indonesian textiles, several pieces of Palestinian costume jewelry, and a collection of American weather vanes and whirligigs.

Some of the most remarkable displays are the strikingly realistic dioramas of street scenes, marketplaces, and theaters from around the world. A memorable highlight is the miniature bull ring, rendered in perfect detail and populated by hundreds of tiny costumed figures.

One is captivated by the ingenuity and playfulness demonstrated throughout, even in sober historical scenes and religious pieces. It was the goal of the founder, Florence Dibell Bartlett, to promote world peace and understanding through the study of material culture, especially the joyful medium of folk art. This superb museum justifies her optimism. *Open daily mid-Mar.–mid-Oct.; Tues.–Sun. rest of the year, except holidays. Admission free but donations encouraged.*

9. Fort Union National Monument. Fort Union has had three incarnations. The first fort, built in 1851, was a key station on the Santa Fe Trail. After the outbreak of the Civil War a star-shaped earthen fortification was constructed in anticipation of a Confederate attack, which never came. The third and last installation, whose ruins you may tour, was the largest in the Southwest upon its completion in 1869. Troops stationed here waged several campaigns against the Indians of the southern plains, finally defeating them in 1875. In 1879 the railroad replaced the Santa Fe Trail, and in 1891 the fort was finally abandoned.

Enough remains of the fort to indicate how very extensive it once was. From the visitor center at the parking lot a 1¼-mile interpretive walk leads through its two units: the Post, where the troops and their officers were garrisoned, and the Depot, where those responsible for supplies, commissary, transportation, and equipment were stationed. Neatly symmetrical in their layout, the two areas were carefully planned for their separate functions.

Along the trail are photographs showing the fort when it was in use and recorded dialogues on subjects the men might have discussed 100 years ago. Watch out for rattlesnakes. Exhibits in the visitor center relate to life at the fort and conflicts with the Indians. *Open year-round except Christmas and New Year's Day.*

10. El Morro National Monument. El Morro, or the "headland" or "bluff," is the massive point of a sandstone mesa rising some 200 feet above the valley floor. A waterhole fed by rain and snowmelt at the base of the bluff has long attracted travelers passing through the desert. Members of three civilizations—Zuni Indians, Spanish soldiers and priests, and American settlers, soldiers, and adventurers—have left hundreds of records, from scratchings to elegant script, inscribed in the soft yellow stone, making El Morro one of the great historical graffiti walls in America. The first inscription by an American is dated 1849.

A trail leads from the monument headquarters up the side of the mesa, passing many inscriptions. Along the way are markers keyed to a self-guiding booklet, which identifies petroglyphs and gives translations of Spanish inscriptions, including an eight-line poem elegantly incised in 1629. A steep climb continues to the windswept top, where there are two

A Trail Ride in the Rockies

"This is your horse; his name is Tequila," said Jerry, the wrangler and owner, as I walked into the small corral just outside Red River. Having been on a horse only once before, I approached the sorrel a little apprehensively and managed (with some pride) to hoist myself into the saddle without help. The ground seemed far below. As he adjusted the stirrups, Jerry instructed me, "Keep the balls of your feet on the stirrups, and don't let your feet slide through." I was glad I had worn sturdy oxfords and not sneakers. "Hold the reigns at the knot and pull gently to the left or right to guide him." We sauntered out of the corral into a meadow where I was given a couple of minutes to practice. To my relief, Tequila was entirely obedient.

In single file our small party began its three-hour ride, which was to take us to an altitude of 10,400 feet. We forded Red River and headed up the mountainside. It was mid-October: the air was light and heady, the sky a dazzling blue, and the sun warm and caressing as it beamed down through the towering pines and firs. My heart sang.

I marveled at Tequila's surefootedness as he clambered over rocky stretches and an occasional fallen tree.

Gradually I relaxed enough to let go of the saddle horn and use my camera. "Elk have been on the trail in the last 10 minutes, but don't expect to see them," Jerry called back. I looked hard, and he was right. Zigzagging upward, we reached a small alpine meadow crusted with snow and paused to enjoy the eye-level view of the mountain peaks across the valley. We went on to a gold prospector's log cabin, collapsed from the weight of its sod roof. Tethering our horses to trees, we sat on the logs and had refreshments.

Our return trip took us down the other side of the mountain past an abandoned gold mine. The altitude was no problem (the horse was doing all the work), but during the last half-hour of the downhill trek it became impossible to find a comfortable way to sit. Back in the corral I dismounted and staggered on legs that seemed permanently bowed. But recovery was quick, and my exhilaration was boundless. Feeling like a Girl of the Golden West, I patted my trusty steed and promised to ride these hills once more. —*N. Barron.*

For information call (505) 754-2518.

large Indian ruins and expansive views of the valley and the Zuni Mountain Range.

For weather El Morro is best from July through September; for wildflowers, June is more rewarding. The monument may be heavily visited on both Memorial Day and July 4 weekends. *Open year-round. Admission charged.*

11. Bandera Crater and Ice Caves.
Grants. Represented here, in remarkably close proximity, are the extremes of natural phenomena—fire and ice.

You arrive at a ranch and think you've erred, but you haven't. This land is private property, owned by one family for 100 years. The trail to Bandera Crater is a half-mile long and ascends 100 feet. At an altitude of 8,000 feet one walks slowly, and distances seem greater than they are.

At the end of the trail you are on the Continental Divide, looking into a dormant crater 800 to 1,000 feet deep. Clumps of piñon pine grow among the cinders of its interior. From the lip of the crater there's a splendid view of the surrounding countryside, dotted with ponderosa and piñon pine, juniper, oak, and aspen.

When the volcano erupted some 5,000 years ago, molten rock coursed down the mountainside and created many lava tubes as it cooled. Sections of tubes collapsed by an earthquake have formed small caves; with a constant temperature of 31°F, ice has slowly accumulated in them. You can reach one of these ice caves by a short, level trail across a lava field that still shows its flow. Mounds of ice, shot through with hues modulating from bright green to soft blue, glisten on the cave floor, and icicles hang from the ceiling, glittering in reflected sunlight.

Oddly enough, this strange, moonlike

area draws an abundance of hummingbirds. These feathered jewels are best seen in August and early September, a rainy season when many flowers are in bloom. *Open year-round. Admission charged.*

12. Rio Grande Nature Center. *Albuquerque. Take I-40 to Rio Grande Blvd.; exit north to Candelaria Blvd. and continue a few miles.* This new park and preserve is on the east bank of the Rio Grande. Two easy walking loops, each about a mile long, lead from the visitor center to the river, crossing sandy grassland and brush, passing densely vegetated ponds, and entering woodland with large deciduous trees that you don't expect to find in New Mexico. Purple asters, prairie sunflowers, and globe mallows grow along the trails, and occasionally a coyote, roadrunner, or

quail appears. Beavers have dropped many large trees along the Rio Grande.

Beside the visitor center is a pond favored by water birds, turtles, and other creatures. A heron decoy has been placed here to lure live companions. The best months for watching migratory birds are November and February. Science programs for children and nature films are offered in the visitor center. *Open daily except Thanksgiving Day, Christmas, and New Year's Day.*

13. Rock Lake Rearing Station. *On River Rd. off U.S. 84, Santa Rosa.* Two kinds of fish are raised here: walleyed pike and rainbow trout. The walleyes must be released within one to five days after they hatch; they are carnivorous and if confined will eat their own kind. Half of the fish are transported to New Mexico's lakes and streams; the rest are traded to other states for warm water fish. About 33 million pike are hatched here each year.

The rainbows are brought here as fingerlings and reared to a length of 8¾ to 10 inches, which takes about 10 months. As they grow they are moved from one tank to another. Aerated flowing water allows the fish to live in incredible density. They are packed in so tightly that from some angles they seem to be a single mass. Sardines come to mind. The trout feed themselves by pushing a feeder wire. The plant is so automated that it needs only a staff of four to run it. Some 140,000 rainbows per year are raised here for release in southeastern New Mexico. *Open year-round.*

14. Valley of Fires State Park. Here you can see one of the youngest lava beds in the United States, the Carrizozo Malpais (badlands). An estimated 1,500 years ago red-hot lava flowed for 44 miles from Little Black Peak, visible to the northeast, covering 127 square miles of valley floor, in some places to a depth of more than 150 feet. As it flowed it began to cool and solidify, forming a ropy, corrugated crust.

The Malpais Trail leads into the park, a rugged 463-acre field of fissured black lava. Thick-soled shoes are recommended. A brochure describing the highlights on the trail is usually available near the trailhead. Along the loop trail, a very pleasant, easy, and dramatic walk, one

sees a remarkable variety of shapes and textures—whorls, eddies, and bubbles—created by the cooling, moving lava, and, where domes formed by escaping gases have collapsed, gaping black pits.

For all the forbidding aspects of this landscape, many plants have established themselves in the soil that has blown into the cavities and depressions in the lava crust. It is remarkable to see yucca, juniper, hackberry, prickly pear, beargrass, and squawbush, to name a few, growing out of this seemingly impermeable substance. A number of animals—mice, snakes, and lizards—have also found the lava field to be a viable environment.

The Sierra Blanca Mountains to the south and east provide a superb backdrop for this landscape. For best weather go in spring or summer. *Open year-round.*

15. Roswell Museum and Art Center. *Rte. 70/285, Roswell.* Devoted to art, science, and history, the eclectic collection in this well-organized museum provides a fascinating view of southwestern culture. Colorfully outfitted mannequins in the history section portray the full range of people significant in the region's development: conquistadors armed with maces and battle-axes, warriors from local Indian

tribes, cowboys, hunters, and soldiers. Among the cowboy displays is a surprisingly large collection of chaps.

The science area features the works of Robert Goddard, the Father of Modern Rocketry, who lived near Roswell in the 1930's and did many of his pioneering experiments in this area. The earliest devices look as though they had been made by a surrealist plumber, and it's very difficult to believe that less than 40 years after these early models were built their successors carried man to the moon.

The art collection, which focuses on southwestern painters, has a canvas by Georgia O'Keeffe and an entire room devoted to works by Peter Hurd, whose portrait of President Lyndon B. Johnson won special attention. There are also small bronzes depicting life in the Southwest, a collection of kachina dolls, and some splendid Pueblo pottery. *Open Mon.–Sat. and P.M. Sun. and holidays except Christmas and New Year's Day.*

16. Gila Cliff Dwellings National Monument. *Because of poor road conditions from Silver City, cars with trailers over 20 feet should take Hwys. 61 and 35, a route reached from Hwy. 90 at San Lorenzo.* Five natural caves high in the face of a cliff contain the ruins of dwellings built and occupied by the Mogollon Indians be-

16. *To enclose their dwelling, the people who lived here had only to add the façade.*

tween A.D. 1170 and 1350. A diligent farming people, they were also skillful weavers and artistic potters.

One of the ruins can be reached by a trail that climbs about 180 feet in its mile-long loop. A short flight of steps reaches up to the cave, which is very large, with an arched ceiling. Gazing out from its cool, dark recesses and seeing the West Fork of the Gila River as it flows past fields where crops once grew, one has a sense of having entered another era. Wandering through the rooms, one finds structural timbers dating back to the 1280's, as well as the remains of food that was stored centuries ago.

This is a popular site, but it is usually uncrowded from March to mid-May and in September and October. The visitor center offers relevant information, exhibits, and an audiovisual presentation. Guide booklets may be purchased. The Gila River Recreation Area has picnic sites and campgrounds about a quarter-mile away. It is advisable to carry water with you. *Open year-round except Christmas and New Year's Day.*

17. Silver City Museum. *312 W. Broadway, Silver City.* The eclectic charm of this little museum aptly recalls Silver City's rich and varied history. The hand-some Victorian house with its square tower and mansard roof was once the home of Henry B. Ailman, a young prospector who struck it rich in the 1870's. The building, listed in *The National Register of Historic Places,* is filled with furniture, clothing, household goods, musical instruments, and decorative objects typical of the era. One room in particular evokes the heyday of the area's mining boom with stylish mannequins in period attire and historic photographs that vividly recall impressions of both the profits and the considerable dangers of silver mining.

The area's ranching heritage is represented by a fine display of cowpuncher's clothing and gear. Artifacts from southwestern Indian tribes are also displayed, including an excellent collection of Casas Grandes pottery. *Open Tues.–Sat. and P.M. Sun. year-round except holidays.*

18. Rock Hound State Park. *Nine miles off Rte. 11.* The park is dedicated to the genus rockhound, that special breed that savors the dusty challenge of the search and the thrill of discovery. The parkland, on a mountainside formed of volcanic rhyolite, is rich in semiprecious stones, primarily jasper, opal, blue agate, and psilomelane. Visitors can dig their own stones here and take away up to 20 pounds per visit.

You must bring your own equipment, but you can count on the park staff to provide helpful tips on methods and places for digging. A small exhibit in the visitor center displays many of the minerals found here, often showing the ways they can be finished as gems. Summer is quite hot; the most comfortable season for digging is winter.

The 250-acre park is also a worthwhile destination just for the scenery. The campground and picnic area offer sweeping views of Deming and the valley below. *Open daily year-round. Admission charged weekends, April–Labor Day.*

19. Mesilla. For scores of early western towns, it was a disaster when the railroad laid its tracks elsewhere. In this case it was nearby Las Cruces rather than Mesilla that got the railroad line in 1881. Today this is considered by many to be a blessing, for the bypassed town has retained its tranquil charm and historic interest, unmarred by the progress the railroad would have ushered in.

The first settlers arrived by wagon train in about 1847, during the Mexican War, when Mexican troops were stationed here. In 1854 the American flag was raised in Mesilla Plaza, and four years later the Butterfield Stage put the community on the map. Captured by Texans during the Civil War, Mesilla served briefly as the capital of the Confederate Territory of Arizona. Some years later Union forts dominated the life of the town. Famous and infamous visitors included the Mexican revolutionary Francisco "Pancho" Villa and the outlaw Billy the Kid, who was condemned to death here. In 1957 Mesilla was declared a state monument.

Around the plaza and elsewhere in the town are some fine old adobe buildings, many dating from the mid-19th century. Highlights are the twin-towered church of San Albino, where the Angelus is rung three times daily, the Gadsden Museum, with displays of historic items from the area, and Mesilla Plaza.

20. White Sands National Monument. Ever changing and ever beautiful, these vast, brilliantly white dunes owe their existence to the layers of gypsum in the surrounding mountains. Seasonal rains and snow dissolve the gypsum and carry it to Lake Lucero, southwest of the dunes.

17. Victorian charm is expressed in the windows and tower and the decorative details.

When the lake bed is dry, the prevailing southwest wind grinds the gypsum crystals into tiny grains and deposits them in these undulating waves of sand. The dunes shift slowly to the northeast, some by more than 20 feet per year, and new dunes are formed behind them.

From the park entrance a gypsum roadway leads for some eight miles into the sands. Numbered signs along the way are keyed to a pamphlet, available at the visitor center, which describes the area's remarkable geology, flora, and fauna. The outer dunes are covered with such desert plants as four-wing saltbush and iodine bush. But the vegetation gradually thins out until there is nothing but the pristine sand. The dunes are especially beautiful in moonlight, and the roadway remains open summer evenings until 10 P.M.

Hiking and sand surfing are popular in the dunes. Picnic sites are provided near the end of the roadway, but water is available only at the visitor center eight miles away. With a permit, camping is allowed in a primitive backcountry site. *Open year-round except Christmas. Admission charged.*

20. *Ripples on gypsum last longer than those on water—which are gone with the wind.*

---

21. International Space Hall of Fame. *Off U.S. 70 in Alamogordo.* Much of the development of rocketry in America took place in the New Mexico desert. Appropriately, this ancient lunar landscape is the setting for a modern museum dedicated to those who introduced the space age.

Some 100 international scientists are presently honored here. The inductees include Johannes Winkler, a German rocket pioneer; Robert Goddard, the Father of Modern Rocketry; the famous test pilot Chuck Yeager, the first man to fly faster than the speed of sound; American and Soviet astronauts such as Neil Armstrong and Yuri Gagarin; and Sir William Congreve, who introduced a solid-propellant artillery rocket in 1805.

Among the exhibits are satellites and capsules, lunar vehicles, and a great variety of rocket engines and guidance systems. One of the favorite attractions is a "physics playground" where visitors explore the laws of aerodynamics, using a device popularly called a Bernoulli blower to balance a ball on a jet of air. The highlight, however, is a walk-through space station. One can also purchase dried food like that used on spaceflights. The Omni-

max Theater has a 70-millimeter projector and a 40-foot wraparound screen on which special films are shown with startling realism. A sophisticated planetarium and laser concerts with choreographed lights add to the excitement. *Open daily except Christmas. Admission charged.*

---

22. Living Desert State Park. *Carlsbad.* Set on a rise above the town, this park is a showcase for the plants and animals native to the New Mexico desert. Paths bordered with hundreds of desert plants, all clearly marked, lead to the various buildings and enclosures. Cacti in an amazing variety of shapes and sizes grow in a large greenhouse, and in the spring many burst forth with brilliant flowers.

Enclosures flanking the park contain larger animals, including antelope, buffalo, mule deer, wolves, and elk. There is also a prairie dog town, a bear den, a reptile house, a nocturnal house with such animals as the kit fox, kangaroo rat, and coatimundi, and an aviary that provides a close look at hawks, owls, roadrunners, and other desert birds. At the far end of the park is a small lake for waterfowl and mammals that prefer wet places.

During the summer season here—from April to September—it is more comfortable to visit in the cool of the morning or

evening. The park is usually crowded during the Easter season. *Open year-round. Admission charged.*

---

23. Confederate Air Force Flying Museum, New Mexico Wing. *Lea County Airport, Hobbs.* The Confederate Air Force is an organization of small units (wings) of airplane enthusiasts dedicated to the preservation of World War II vintage planes, with the motto "Keep 'em Flying." Centered in the Southwest, the organization now has more than 70 wings and worldwide membership. Various wings sponsor air-power demonstrations throughout the United States.

The 12 or so aircraft here are appropriately housed in a hangar of World War II vintage, fittingly cluttered with parts and tools. Considerable maintenance is required to keep these planes in flying condition—which nearly all of them are. The most impressive craft is the American B-25 medium bomber, the type used by Lt. Col. James H. Doolittle in the famous 16-plane raid on Tokyo in April 1942. Also on view are American transports and trainers and a German Messerschmitt 108. If the hangar is locked, airport security guards will let you in. *Open year-round. Admission free but donations requested.*

Arizona

Ghost towns and prehistoric ruins are juxtaposed with forests of cacti, Joshua trees, and petrified logs.

For centuries this seemingly arid land was home to seminomadic agrarian Indians who built cliff dwellings and other communities; although these now stand in ruins, they still evoke a sense of wonder.

The architectural heritage of the early white settlers is of another character. There are a few towns where the aura of the rough-and-ready miners still prevails, and three are included here.

Nature's bold design is revealed in sizable tracts of the dramatic saguaro cactus, the organ-pipe cactus, and the Joshua tree. These and many other fascinating desert plants are displayed in two excellent arboretums. There are also inviting canyons where desert plants and lush greenery grow almost side by side. Further visual delights are a great display of erosional sculpture and a forest of trees turned to stone.

1. Navajo National Monument. *Rte. 564, Kayenta.* Although the Navajos have become one of the most powerful tribes in the Southwest, they are relative newcomers who migrated south from their Canadian homeland in the 1400's. Sometime later they found the ruins of villages built by the Anasazis and moved in.

A half-mile trail (open year-round) leads to an overlook with a fine view of Betatakin ("ledge house" in Navajo) across the canyon. Nestled in a great alcove in the face of a sheer sandstone cliff, it looks like a fairy-tale setting, rosy-colored and tucked into its niche as if by the hands of a giant. You can visit the ruin itself only on guided tours conducted by park rangers. Tours are given from May through September. The outing requires a strenuous three-hour round-trip hike; keep in mind that the elevation here is 7,300 feet.

The ruins of Keet Seel ("broken pieces of pottery" in Navajo) are even more remote and are open only from Memorial Day through Labor Day. The trail in is an arduous eight miles, but arrangements can be made for horseback excursions. You can go and return in a day or camp near the ruins overnight. Only 20 people per day are allowed to visit the site, and

permits and reservations are required. Call (602) 672-2366.

Inscription House, the other ruin here, has become so fragile that it is closed to the public. The visitor center museum presents the history and lifestyle of the Navajos with a slide show and various displays. *Park and visitor center open daily except Thanksgiving Day and Christmas.*

2. Canyon de Chelly National Monument. *Headquarters three miles east of Chinle on Rte. 64.* Of all the spectacular canyons in Arizona, Canyon de Chelly is in the eyes of many the most breathtakingly beautiful. Two scenic roadways branching from the monument headquarters lead to overlooks offering magnificent views of deep, vertical-walled canyons, sandstone spires towering from 700 to 800 feet, the Rio de Chelly as it flows through the winding valley floor, and the mellow Anasazi ruins snugly sheltered in pockets along the face of the cliffs or beneath massive rock overhangs.

Since Navajos live and farm within the monument, visitors are allowed in some areas only when accompanied by an authorized guide. An exception is the White House Trail, which zigzags down the cliff to the canyon floor 700 feet below. Impossible though it seems from above, the path is perfectly safe provided you are wearing appropriate shoes. Toward the bottom the trail goes through a short tunnel carved out of rock. Don't be surprised if a small flock of domestic goats, herded by a dog, rushes past you along the way.

For a close-up view of Anasazi cliff dwellings, wade across the Rio de Chelly and follow a path along the river for about 100 yards. You'll find some ruins at the base of the cliff near the river's edge. Overhead you'll see the White House ruins (so called because one of the houses is finished with a white plaster) perched on a deep ledge in the towering wall of sandstone. The climb back up the cliff is a little arduous, but the entire adventure is memorable. Check at the visitor center for flash

1. *Ruins in the large arched opening reveal how well the site was chosen.*

flood warnings before you begin the trek.

Hiking trips and four-wheel drive excursions can be arranged. Reservations should be made in advance. Call (602) 674-5436. *Visitor center open daily.*

3. Hubbell Trading Post National Historic Site. *Rte. 264, Ganado.* A visit to the trading post on this 160-acre homestead evokes its heyday, when the post was the social center for Navajos, ranchers, and farmers scattered in the surrounding hills and mesas. Established in 1878 by John Lorenzo Hubbell, it is the oldest continuously active trading post on the Navajo Reservation. Now owned by the National Park Service, it sells not only groceries and other supplies, but also Navajo, Zuni, and Hopi crafts—turquoise and silver jewelry, rugs, blankets, and baskets. Both English and Navajo are spoken.

You can take a self-guiding tour of the compound to see the bunkhouse, storage buildings, bakery, corral, barn, and the yard, with its assortment of old buggies and farm equipment. Free guided tours are given of the Hubbell home, which looks much as it did 100 years ago. It has rough-hewn timbered ceilings and is filled with excellent Indian craftwork.

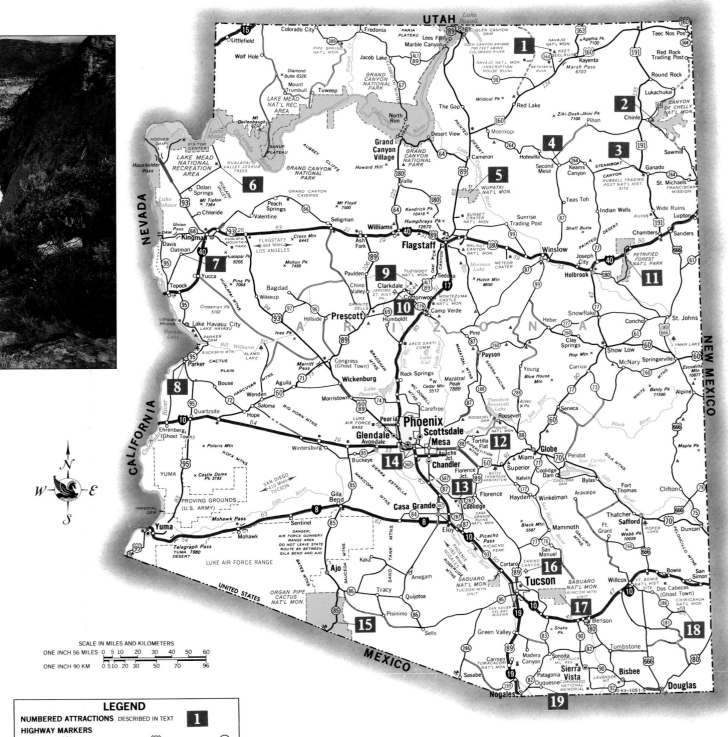

Demonstrations of rug weaving and silversmithing are given in the visitor center. *Open daily except Thanksgiving Day, Christmas, and New Year's Day.*

---

4. Hopi Cultural Center. *Second Mesa.*
The Hopis are believed to be descendants of a farming people who first settled in the Southwest some 1,500–1,600 years ago. Today the Hopi villages, a fascinating mixture of modern technology and ancient architecture, are centered on three towering desert mesas.

The Hopi Cultural Center at Second Mesa has a museum that also serves as an informal visitor center for the entire reservation. The displays recount the tribe's long history, from the earliest times through the Navajo, Spanish, and Ameri-

317

can invasions of its homeland. One of the most popular exhibits concerns the kachinas, deities central to the Hopi religion. Exquisite craft displays include Hopi bridal clothes and finely wrought jewelry, pottery, and basketry. Both the museum and the nearby Hopi Arts and Crafts Guild offer opportunities to observe craftsmen at work.

Tours to various Hopi villages are available. Inquire at the museum to find which places welcome tourists. *Museum open daily, but the schedule may be erratic during Nov.–Jan. Admission charged.*

---

5. Wupatki National Monument. In 1065 a nearby volcanic eruption sent clouds of ash and cinders into the sky, causing the local Sinagua Indians to flee. The ash settled over 800 square miles, and when the Indians returned they found that it retained moisture, improved the soil, and made their farms more productive. The area attracted Indians from neighboring regions and became a cultural melting pot. Wupatki grew to be a major pueblo, eventually rising to four stories in some places and containing more than 100 rooms. But about 150 years later the residents were forced to leave again, probably because of severe drought. By 1225 Wupatki and the surrounding villages had been abandoned.

At the 56-square-mile Wupatki National Monument you may tour the pueblo ruins and see the amphitheater, the ball court, and several typical rooms. A roadway leads to other archeological sites, among them several fortified pueblos, and continues 18 miles to Sunset Crater National Monument, the site of the volcanic eruption in 1065. Mineral deposits around the crater's rim give the upper slopes the glowing coloration of a sunset—from which the crater takes its name. Although no hiking is allowed on the volcano's cone, a one-mile loop trail leads through the lava beds. A campground is maintained near the visitor center. *Monuments open year-round; visitor centers open daily except Christmas and New Year's Day. Campground open mid-Apr.–Oct.*

6. Hualapai Valley Joshua Trees. *Turn east off Rte. 93 onto the dirt road for Dolan Springs.* Believe it or not, these odd-look-

ing prickly trees are members of the lily family. They can grow to 40 feet and bear beautiful greenish-yellow or cream-colored flowers in spring.

According to legend, the Mormons gave the tree its biblical name because its form, with upraised branches, suggested the prophet Joshua at prayer.

You'll spot the first Joshua trees slightly beyond Dolan Springs. As you continue, the trees become larger and more frequent until finally, some 20 miles down the road, you find yourself in a veritable forest. The strangeness of the scene is enhanced by the spectacular backdrop of the Grand Wash Cliffs. There are no facilities; you are completely on your own in the desert's solitude. The elevation is about 4,000 feet, so the heat is not oppressive. The area is named for the Hualapai Indians, who have a reservation nearby. *Road may be impassable in wet weather.*

---

7. Oatman. Founded in 1906 on the western slopes of the Black Mountains, Oatman was an important mining town and served as the business center for several surrounding communities. By 1931 the area is said to have had 15,000 inhabitants, to have produced 1.8 million ounces

7. Corrugated iron siding on the church sustains the vertical architectural idiom.

of gold, and even to have engendered its own stock exchange. But in 1942 the mines were closed for good.

The town has become something of a tourist center, with cafés, artists' studios, craft shops, and snack bars now occupying many of the original buildings. Along Main Street, which stretches up a hillside, there are boarded-up entrances to the old mines, and wild burros, descendants of those brought by the first prospectors, roam the street looking for handouts. Film companies, taking advantage of the spectacular mountain scenery and the turn-of-the-century buildings, have produced several movies here, including *How the West Was Won.*

From the main highway, the 28-mile drive to Oatman includes eight miles of rough mountain road with sharp switchbacks that can be treacherous if one is distracted by the scenery.

---

8. Colorado River Indian Tribes Museum. *Second Ave. and Mojave Rd., Parker.* Four different tribes live on the Colorado River Indian Reservation, which spreads into California. The Mojaves, Navajos, Hopis, and the southern Paiutes, known here as Chemehuevis, share a tract of nearly 300,000 acres. The purpose of the museum is to depict the characteristic lifestyles, histories, and cultural attributes that distinguish the varied heritages of these four.

Costumes and models of the traditional homes of each tribe are shown, along with historic artifacts. Among the outstanding crafts displayed are Mojave beadwork, Hopi kachina dolls, Navajo rugs, and Chemehuevi baskets. Many crafts are for sale. *Open Mon.–Fri. and midday Sat. except holidays.*

---

9. Tuzigoot National Monument. Atop a barren ridge 120 feet above the Verde Valley are the ruins of a town constructed by the Sinagua Indians, farmers and artisans who moved into the valley about 1125. Around 1200 they began building the pueblo at Tuzigoot using stone and adobe. Originally it housed about 50 people, but by 1300 it had grown to more than 90 rooms and accommodated a population of several hundred. Even at this point there were few doorways; the rooms were entered by ladders through holes in the ceilings. The village flourished for another

9. *Obvious here is the space that can be saved by entering rooms through the roof.*

Rainbow Museum, at the southern end of the 29-mile road traversing the park, has exhibits explaining the area's geological and human history. Extraordinary specimens of petrified logs are on the grounds, and just behind the museum a half-mile trail leads to Giant Logs, one of the largest concentrations of these fallen petrified trees. Less than a mile away by road are Agate House, the colorful ruins of a pueblo built from petrified wood, and Long Logs, where the ancient timbers have remained remarkably intact.

One of the most beautiful areas is Blue Mesa, 12 miles north along the park road. Here erosion has left the petrified logs resting on sandstone pedestals. Trails lead from the mesa top to the desert floor.

Indian reminders are everywhere. Five miles north of the turn for Blue Mesa you come to Newspaper Rock, a huge boulder covered with Indian petroglyphs. A mile farther up the road are the Puerco Indian ruins, the remains of a pueblo built before 1400. You can drive the road in either direction. *Open daily. Admission charged.*

12. Boyce Thompson Southwestern Arboretum. *Rte. 60, west of Superior.* This collection of cacti and other hot-climate plants was started in the 1920's by William Boyce Thompson, a mining magnate. The 1,000-acre site has become an outstanding botanical garden and research center containing over 1,500 species of plants from various parts of the world.

More than two miles of intersecting paths, most of them level and easy, wind through the gardens, and the scenery changes dramatically as you walk. Desert plants, including yuccas, paloverdes, chollas, and a towering 200-year-old saguaro cactus, seem almost out of place when you encounter the lush vegetation around tiny Ayer Lake or the pomegranate, olive, and Chinese pistachio trees clustered along a stream. A shady eucalyptus grove provides a pleasant resting place and picnic area.

The plants are delightfully fragrant, and at practically any time of year some of them are in bloom. The best time to visit, however, is from October to May. In summer the temperature here can reach a sizzling 118° F. Living among the plants are many of their natural companions: some 70 species of animals and nearly 175

100 years before the Sinaguas abandoned the valley; their descendants were probably absorbed by pueblos to the north.

The small visitor center displays an extensive collection of artifacts recovered from the site. A furnished reconstruction of a typical pueblo room vividly portrays Sinagua daily life. An easy quarter-mile loop trail leads from the visitor center to the ruins, where the interior of the pueblo may be viewed. *Open year-round. Admission charged.*

10. Jerome State Historic Park. Once a booming mining town at what was thought to be the richest copper deposit in the world, Jerome is now a booming ghost town. After the last large mining operation closed in 1953, a few residents stayed on and kept the town alive. Today its Main Street is eager for tourists, with craft shops, art galleries, and cafés behind its picturesquely weathered and dilapidated storefronts. But relics of old mining operations are seen on all sides.

Begin your visit at the Jerome State Historic Park. This hilltop estate was the home of James S. "Rawhide" Douglas, the owner of one of the two major mines. Exhibits in the museum here tell the en-

tertaining story of a town that went from boom to bust about as often as other towns elect mayors—mine claims, money crises, great finds, great losses, price crashes, fires, and buy-outs were commonplace.

Historic photographs trace Jerome's development from a tent camp to a town of 15,000 with an opera house, theater, baseball fields, churches, and especially saloons. A model depicts one of the mines and shows the volume of ore removed.

The short drive from the highway to Jerome is magnificently scenic, and from the town's precarious perch on the steep slopes of Cleopatra's Hill, at an elevation of more than 5,000 feet, there are panoramic views across the Verde Valley to the far-off San Francisco Peaks. *Museum open daily. Admission charged.*

11. Petrified Forest National Park. The park's geological story began some 200 million years ago, when pinelike trees died here and were buried in the silt of a huge floodplain. The silica-rich waters slowly penetrated the logs' cell tissue. Eventually the silica hardened, turning the logs into a stony substance aglow with a rainbow of colors. An upthrusting of the earth's crust, followed by millions of years of erosion, created the area's magnificent sandstone buttes and exposed the logs.

species of birds have been sighted in the arboretum. The gift shop has a large variety of ornamental plants for sale. *Open daily except Christmas. Admission charged.*

13. Casa Grande Ruins National Monument. One of the most mysterious of the Southwest's Indian ruins, Casa Grande was built around 1350. Clearly it served an important purpose. The three-story earthen structure sits like a crown on a high foundation at the center of a walled village, and the placement of windows in the upper stories suggests that it may have been used in part as an astronomical observatory. But beyond that, its function is lost in the past.

The building was constructed by the Hohokam, proficient farmers who built more than 600 miles of canals to irrigate their crops of corn, cotton, squash, and beans. They lived in small villages of one-room mud dwellings and were known for their earth-colored pottery and their skill in carving stones and shells. About a century after Casa Grande was built, they abandoned their Gila Valley villages for reasons that are still unknown.

On display at the visitor center are ceramics, implements, jewelry, and other artifacts found here. A self-guiding hiking trail leads through the ruins of Casa Grande and the surrounding village. The ruins of a second Hohokam village, which includes a ball court, can be viewed from the picnic area of this 472-acre park. *Open year-round. Admission charged.*

14. McCormick Railroad Park. *7301 E. Indian Bend Rd., Scottsdale.* Miniature trains, modeled after actual equipment at a scale of five inches to a foot, wind through this 30-acre park on a seven-minute trip past the station house, a water tower, and road-crossing signals—all at the same scale. Passengers are carried for a nominal charge. In addition, a group of local railroad buffs known as the Maricopa Live Steam Club meets at the park on Sundays and operates smaller-scale equipment, offering free rides to visitors. Standing exhibits include a full-sized 1907 Baldwin steam engine, a 1914 Pullman baggage car that saw service on the Santa

15. *The multistemmed organ-pipe stands in contrast to the single saguaros here.*

Fe Railroad, and the *Roald Amundsen*, a 1928 Pullman luxury car used by visiting VIP's, including U. S. presidents. Two reconstructed turn-of-the-century railroad stations serve as shops for memorabilia.

Part of the park is a small arboretum containing some 60 species of trees, shrubs, and vines, among them paloverde, desert willow, Mexican ebony, and Chilean mesquite, as well as varieties of acacia and eucalyptus. The park was the gift of Mr. and Mrs. Fowler McCormick, and most of the 5:12-scale trains were the gift of their son, Guy Stillman, a local civic and business leader. The park may be crowded on weekends and holidays. *Open daily year-round except Thanksgiving Day and Christmas.*

15. Organ Pipe Cactus National Monument. "Organ-pipe" is an apt name for a cactus whose slender stems curve upward in clusters to a height of 20 feet. During May and June the pale lavender flowers at the ends of the branches bloom at night and attract the nocturnal insects required for pollination. The red egg-shaped fruit matures in July, splitting open as it ripens to disclose the black seeds that are consumed by many of the 250 species of birds observed here. Fruit that drops to the ground provides food for coyotes, peccaries, foxes, and other animals. The park, 500 square miles of Sonora Desert, is this rare plant's northernmost habitat.

Ajo Mountain Drive, a 21-mile loop, and the 51-mile Puerto Blanco Drive wind through the southern section of the monument. Along each route there are picnic areas. The park has several hiking trails, some through the desert and others into the Ajo Mountains. A 208-site tent and trailer campground is located south of the visitor center. Campers should bring their own fuel. *Open year-round.*

16. Sabino Canyon Recreation Area.

Tucson. Take Exit 256 (Grant Rd.) east off I-10 and continue eight miles. Turn northeast onto Tanque Verde Rd., go one mile and turn north onto Sabino Canyon Rd. Two natural environments meet here in juxtaposition. Desert plants, such as giant saguaro cacti, speckle the desolate canyon walls, while lush riverine greenery flourishes along Sabino Creek on the canyon floor. The overall effect is that of a desert oasis following the twisting creek up into the Santa Catalina Mountains.

Motorized vehicles are not allowed in the canyon, and both the main roadway and its southern spur are ideal for hikers and bicyclists, although the times for bicycling are restricted. Each road is serviced by a shuttle bus that stops at the trailheads, picnic sites, and scenic overlooks. The Telephone Line Trail on the south slope of Sabino Canyon provides glorious views of the valley floor, and the Bear Canyon Trail follows Bear Creek to Seven Falls in the area's more remote southern section. One of the most beautiful ways to see the canyon is by moonlight, and evening shuttle bus rides are offered the last three days before a full moon. *Open daily. Fee charged for bus.*

17. Saguaro National Monument, Rincon Mountain Unit.

The giant saguaro cactus, with its huge upright arms extending from a sturdy trunk, may after some 200 years reach a height of 50 feet. The distinctive branches, in fact, do not develop until the cactus is about 75 years old, depending on available moisture. Literally thousands of these towering plants fill the Sonora Desert here in the eastern section of the national monument's two units.

The saguaros are a great boon to desert wildlife. During May and early June clusters of creamy-white blossoms appear at the tips of their trunks and branches. These are followed by three-inch red fruits, which the birds enjoy. When the fruit ripens and drops, it is eaten by mule deer, coyotes, and peccaries. Woodpeckers drill holes in the fleshy arms for nests, which are often used later by screech owls, purple martins, and sparrow hawks.

The plants and creatures of the desert can be studied closely on an eight-mile drive that loops through the heart of the saguaro forest and also on a one-mile nature trail leading to a sheltered picnic area. For those seeking the backcountry, over 50 miles of hiking and horseback-riding trails traverse a 58,000-acre wilderness and ascend to the summits of the fir-forested Rincon Mountains at an altitude of 8,700 feet. Six wilderness camping areas are managed by the park. Each requires an overnight-use permit, which can be obtained without charge at the visitor center. *Open year-round. Admission charged.*

18. Chiricahua National Monument.

Strangely beautiful pinnacles, towers, spindle-thin columns, spires, and balanced boulders are huddled together here in the Chiricahua Mountains in such numbers that they seem almost surreal. The basic materials were laid down millions of years ago, when the landscape was covered with layers of volcanic ash, which eventually hardened into rock. When the volcanic action finally ceased, the earth's crust slowly lifted, and the rock began to crack and split, creating the curious forms that were further shaped by millennia of wind and rain.

For centuries these mountains were a formidable stronghold of the fierce Chiricahua Apache Indians. The range in altitude here, from about 5,000 to more than 7,300 feet, helps to create a hospitable environment for a wide assortment of plants. Mexican piñons, Apache pines, and Douglas firs thrive on the upper slopes, cottonwoods and wildflowers mark the course of the canyon streams, and yucca and cacti grow in the open, sunny places.

The park has 17 miles of hiking trails, a campground, and a picnic facility. Exhibits about the history and wildlife of the area may be seen at the visitor center at monument headquarters. From here a paved, six-mile scenic drive leads through a maze of canyons to Massai Point, which offers exquisite views of the surrounding valleys and has an exhibit building where displays describing the region's dramatic geology may be seen. *Park open year-round; visitor center open daily except Christmas. Admission charged.*

19. Duquesne.

Take Rte. 82 NE from Nogales; turn right at sign for Kino Springs. Once a thriving mining center of about 1,000 inhabitants, Duquesne is now a place of such ghostly desolation that eeriness seems to waft like a specter among the trees and through the decaying houses. Vultures circle overhead, while the rustling of wild turkeys, roadrunners, and other small creatures among the underbrush from time to time shatters the all-pervasive silence.

Despite the haunting vestiges of the past, the town's setting—on a hillside overlooking a stream—is cheerfully pleasant. Evergreens, hardwoods, and various shrubs, left undisturbed for almost 100 years, clothe the slopes and soften the sight of mining equipment abandoned by the last of the town's residents. Zinc, copper, lead, and silver are still to be found here, but the cost of extracting the ore and shipping it to processing centers is said to be prohibitive. The 15-mile road from Route 82 is winding, steep, and rugged. *Road may be impassable in wet weather.*

17. *The black-tailed jackrabbit is maintaining its running gear—and lifeline.*

Washington

From wave-lashed Tatoosh Island to the lofty heights of Mount Rainier, you'll find historic sites, geologic marvels, and scenic wonders.

The well-watered land and mild climate have long been hospitable to man. One excellent museum shows evidence of 9,000 years of habitation in the area, while on the northwest coast are the remains of an Indian settlement that prospered more than 500 years ago. There are ghost towns, remnants of mining camps, pioneer settlements of varying size and authenticity, a homestead that delineates the daily life of the early settlers, and a palatial art museum in an unexpected place.

The incomparable forces of nature are demonstrated in the devastation wrought by the eruption of Mount St. Helens—and in the regeneration now under way. In other places are dramatic landforms sculpted by unimaginable torrents of water released during the last Ice Age. A limestone cave reveals fascinating formations, and a petrified forest invites inspection. There are scenic viewpoints and places for bird-watching, hiking trails to waterfalls and limpid lakes, and an inland cruise penetrating the North Cascades.

1. Neah Bay. Famous for its scenery and salmon, Neah Bay also has one of the finest museums of Indian culture in the United States. The $2 million Makah Cultural and Research Center houses the best of more than 55,000 archeological items from the remains of Ozette, a nearby Makah Indian village that was buried and preserved by mud slides about 500 years ago. The exhibits—totem poles, seagoing canoes, a wealth of exquisitely crafted artifacts, clothes, household articles, and a reconstruction of a tribal longhouse—give a complete picture of an ancient and highly developed lifestyle.

Cape Flattery, the most northwestern point in the lower 48 states, is a half-hour hike from Neah Bay through dense forest on a trail that may be quite muddy. The cape is noted for rugged headlands, crashing surf, and its view of Tatoosh Island. Koitlah Point and Hobuck Beach, each a short drive from Neah Bay, also offer stunning scenery. Whale watching is popular, and birding is excellent. *Museum open daily June–mid-Sept.; Wed.–Sun., mid-Sept.–May. Admission charged.*

2. Deer Park Campground, Olympic National Park. *Exit south off U.S. 101 at Milepost 253 onto Deer Park Rd. and continue 17 miles.* Situated among firs and pines at the end of a steep, narrow, and tortuous dirt road—unsuitable for trailers or unsure drivers—Deer Park has 10 primitive campsites near the summit of 6,007-foot Blue Mountain. The hike of about a mile along the dirt road climbing from the camping area to the summit is rewarded by a superb panoramic view of the Olympic Range, Puget Sound, Vancouver Island, and the massive barrier of the Cascade Mountains. Other trails, which are steep and arduous in places, lead through wooded valleys and alpine meadows where one is likely to see half-tame deer, for which the area is named, as well as marmots and raccoons. With luck you may spot a mountain goat on a distant ridge. Piper's bellflowers, Flett violets, and a species of astragalus, all unique to Deer Park, bloom here in the summer as well as swathes of Indian paintbrush, lupines, and avalanche lilies.

In this fragile environment campfires and wood gathering are prohibited. A ranger station is manned here during the summer. *Road generally open late June–Oct. Campground open as snow permits.*

3. Baker Lake Recreation Area. *North off Rte. 20, Concrete.* Here is the essence of the Pacific Northwest: a land of dense, dark green aromatic forests, snowcapped mountains, large lakes lying in wooded valleys, and highland lakes fed by glacial streams. Although Baker Lake and Lake Shannon are man-made (created by power-company dams), they sit beautifully and naturally at the base of majestic Mount Baker. At nine-mile-long Baker Lake, which is the more accessible, boating, waterskiing, and fishing are the main activities; prior to July 4 each year it is stocked with 50,000 rainbow trout. Whitefish, salmon, and steelheads are also caught here.

Hikes range from short strolls to treks requiring several days into rugged backcountry and up the slopes of Mount Baker. For an introduction to the region's

3. *In this idyllic wooded setting, nature features her remarkable palette of cool colors.*

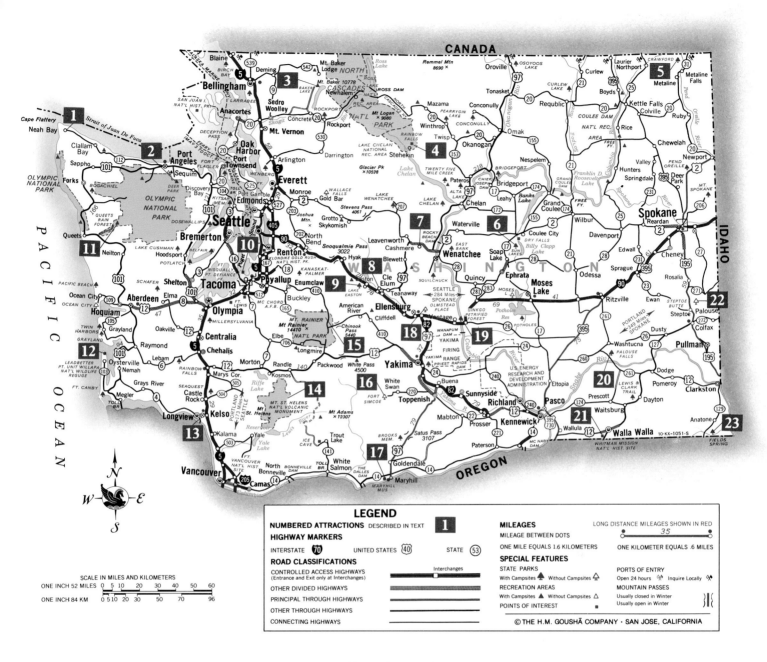

LEGEND

NUMBERED ATTRACTIONS DESCRIBED IN TEXT **1**

HIGHWAY MARKERS

INTERSTATE **70**   UNITED STATES **40**   STATE **53**

ROAD CLASSIFICATIONS

CONTROLLED ACCESS HIGHWAYS (Entrance and Exit only at Interchanges) — Interchanges

OTHER DIVIDED HIGHWAYS

PRINCIPAL THROUGH HIGHWAYS

OTHER THROUGH HIGHWAYS

CONNECTING HIGHWAYS

MILEAGES   LONG DISTANCE MILEAGES SHOWN IN RED

MILEAGE BETWEEN DOTS   • 35 •

ONE MILE EQUALS 1.6 KILOMETERS   ONE KILOMETER EQUALS .6 MILES

SPECIAL FEATURES

STATE PARKS   PORTS OF ENTRY

With Campsites ▲ Without Campsites △   Open 24 hours ⊗ Inquire Locally ⊗

RECREATION AREAS   MOUNTAIN PASSES

With Campsites ▲ Without Campsites △   Usually closed in Winter

POINTS OF INTEREST ■   Usually open in Winter

© THE H.M. GOUSHA COMPANY · SAN JOSE, CALIFORNIA

SCALE IN MILES AND KILOMETERS

ONE INCH 52 MILES 0 5 10 20 30 40 50 60

ONE INCH 84 KM 0 5 10 20 30 50 70 96

---

plant life, take the Shadow of the Sentinels Nature Trail (near the main entrance highway), which has interpretive signs along the way. Some of the Douglas firs on the trail are more than 600 years old. At the mouth of Swift Creek, near the north end of Baker Lake, agates and jaspers can be found. Several campgrounds are maintained along the access road, and the area may be heavily visited in summer. *Access road open year-round.*

4. Stehekin Village and Rainbow Falls.

Accessible from Chelan. Stehekin is the Indian term for "the way through," and it aptly describes the narrow, fjordlike val-

ley in which 55-mile-long Lake Chelan lies, providing a way through the almost impenetrable mountain barrier of the North Cascades. At the upper end of the lake is the quiet, isolated village of Stehekin; settled in 1885, it has fewer than 100 residents. Even today there are no roads to Stehekin, but it can be reached by a delightful four-hour cruise from Chelan on the *Lady of the Lake*, a diesel-powered boat. Floatplane trips are also available. A shuttle bus runs 23 miles up the valley from the village to various campsites and trailheads. Shuttles also make the 3½-mile journey to Rainbow Falls, which plunge 312 feet. The falls are dramatic the year-round, and especially so during the torrential spring runoff, when clouds of mist catch the sunlight and create rainbows.

The meadows and woods are richly adorned with wildflowers from spring through summer, and in early autumn the foliage is at its height.

Stehekin is a popular starting point for backpacking into the North Cascades; horses can be rented here, and there are numerous trails to explore. Motorbikes are also available for use on the road.

Spring and fall are the best times to visit; in summer the place is often crowded. Lodgings are limited, and if you plan to stay over, reservations are recommended. *Boat operates daily mid-May–mid-Oct.; Mon., Wed., Fri. rest of the year. For information call (509) 682-4711.*

6. One can almost visualize the incredible volume of water that thundered over the cliffs and scoured this basin 500,000 years ago.

5. Gardner Cave, Crawford State Park.

Twelve miles north of Metaline. Shortly beyond the collapsed sinkhole that serves as the entrance to this 2,000-foot-long cavern, you will find a glistening world of flowstone, dripstone formations, and gours, which are dishlike basins in the cave floor. Their names—Christmas Tree, Queen's Throne, Fried Eggs—aptly suggest the strange shapes and effects created by rainwater laden with carbon dioxide as it slowly dripped through the 500-million-year-old metaline limestone here. Perhaps the most striking feature is a speleothem, a floor-to-ceiling column of calcite formed by the union of a stalactite and a stalagmite.

About 500 feet of the cave is equipped with lighted stairways and walkways and may be viewed on hour-long guided tours conducted by the park staff. Wear warm clothing, since the cave temperature remains at about 40°F, and bring a flashlight to peer into darker corners.

To reach the cave, which is the featured attraction of the 40-acre park, you follow a 200-yard paved walkway up a small hill from the parking lot. The walk serves as a nature trail, with plaques identifying the flora. There is also a small picnic area. *Open Wed.–Sun., May–June; daily July–Sept. Admission charged.*

6. Sun Lakes State Park.

What gives this park its awesome beauty is an extinct waterfall. Long ago, as the glaciers of the Ice Age melted, Dry Falls was the largest waterfall on earth. Five times wider than Niagara and more than twice as high, the surging wall of water dropped 400 feet over a triple crescent 3½ miles wide. As the glaciers that had dammed the Columbia River retreated and its waters returned to their original bed, the falls were left literally high and dry.

The interpretive center on the rim of the falls explains the geologic story of the Grand Coulee country and Dry Falls and also has exhibits detailing the flora and fauna of the area, including the elephants and rhinoceroses that once lived here.

Most of the park's 4,000 acres (and its facilities) are within the canyon formed by the waters of Dry Falls, which left 400-foot-high cliffs on the east and 800-foot-high walls on the western side. Ten small lakes are contained within the park, as well as several natural springs and creeks. It has 17 miles of hiking trails plus 12 miles of equestrian trails. Horses, bicycles, and boats may be rented.

The park is especially lovely in early spring, when melting snows create a series of temporary waterfalls that tumble from the clifftops. Numerous wildflowers cover the ground with splashes of color from mid-April through May. Large populations of deer and marmots reside here,

and in the autumn and winter great numbers of Canada geese arrive. *Park open year-round. Dry Falls Visitor Center open Wed.–Sun., mid-May–mid-Sept.*

7. Pioneer Village and Chelan County Historical Museum.

Cottage Ave., Cashmere. Deservedly renowned, this museum and pioneer village traces life as it has been lived in this area for more than 9,000 years with imaginative, insightful displays of Indian and pioneer artifacts.

Touring the museum, one marvels time and again at the artistry and ingenuity of the American Indians. Visitors learn, for example, that as early as 5,000 years ago they practiced a form of brain surgery using fermented herbs that were similar to penicillin. No less impressive are the tiny beads carefully drilled with primitive stone tools, the basketry, and the fine leather and feather work.

The Hudson's Bay Company display gives a vivid view of what went on in the fur business here in the early 1800's. One not only sees an assortment of trade goods but learns the rates of exchange: a one-foot-high metal bucket, for instance, bought a one-foot-high stack of fur pelts.

The museum serves as a primer for the 19 buildings of the reconstructed village. Each is amazingly complete, down to the stacks of period-labeled canned goods on the shelves of the general store and the books and inkwells in the schoolhouse. Many buildings have fascinating stories. The jailhouse, you learn, was originally designed as a home by an escaped convict from Leavenworth Prison. A waterwheel used for irrigation, incorporating the drive shaft of an old Columbia River paddle steamer, is an interesting symbol of the pioneers' ingenuity. There is so much to see here that you may wish to bring a lunch: a picnic area overlooks the village and a river. To avoid crowds come in April, May, or October. *Open Mon.–Sat. and P.M. Sun., Apr.–Oct.*

8. Cle Elum Historical Museum. *Corner of First and Wright Sts., Cle Elum.* On April 5, 1901, when store owner Theron Stafford made the first phone call in Cle Elum, he had some 10 numbers to choose from. In 1966, when the dial system was installed—completing the transition to dial phones in the towns served by Pacific Northwest Bell—he would have been able to reach 96 million in the United States alone. To commemorate this extraordinary development, the Pacific Northwest Bell Telephone Company gave the original telephone exchange building to the city, along with a fine selection of historic equipment ranging from an 1894 model with a crank to the touch-tone designs of today.

The museum, however, is not solely devoted to the telephone. A collection of photographs from newspapers and other sources, supported by a miscellany from home and workplace, depicts the life and times of this small coal-mining town. One oddity is a camera owned by Etta Place, who, with Butch Cassidy and the Sundance Kid, tried to rob a nearby bank. *Open Mon.–Fri. and P.M. weekends, Memorial Day–Labor Day; P.M. Tues.–Thurs. the rest of the year.*

9. Lake Easton State Park. *Easton.* Tucked in a glacial valley high in the Cascade Mountains, this pleasant woodland park offers year-round recreation. In summer mile-long Lake Easton attracts boaters, fishermen, and swimmers—despite its cold waters. A boat-launching ramp is provided, and the lake is stocked twice a year with rainbow trout. Other likely catches include whitefish, silver trout, Dolly Varden, and cutthroat. Six miles of hiking trails traverse 196 acres of relatively level forest terrain and connect with trails leading into the surrounding mountains. Nearby trails for all-terrain vehicles also are maintained. Birders will see ducks and, with luck, the pair of ospreys that nest on the lake's western shore. Mushroom gathering, picnicking, and camping also are popular.

In winter the main roads through the park are plowed, although the snow may be three to four feet deep. It's a great setting for snowshoers and cross-country skiers, and children find the gently sloping hills perfect for sledding and tubing. Snowmobiling is allowed on designated trails adjacent to the park, and dogsled races are held periodically on the nearby Milwaukee Road Trail. *Open year-round.*

10. Fort Nisqually, Point Defiance Park. *Tacoma. Take the Sixth Ave. exit off Hwy. 16 and continue north on Pearl St.* In the deep wilderness where beaver trapping was a lucrative business and the arm of the law was remote, the British Hudson's Bay Company built forts to safeguard its money and stock of furs. Such was the case in 1833 when Fort Nisqually was built, a lonely post on Puget Sound.

The fort here today is a reconstruction of one that stood about 17 miles to the south, and it has an authentic look and feeling. Of the 10 buildings inside the stockade, three can be toured: the 1843 Granary (the oldest standing structure in Washington State), the blacksmith's shop, and the Large House, a reconstruction of the factor's quarters displaying artifacts from the old fort. You can climb the stairs inside the three-story bastions and see a six-pound cannon with the British royal crown markings of the 1830's. *Park open year-round. Large House open P.M. only, Wed.–Sun., Mar.–Apr.; Tues.–Sun. in May; daily June–Sept.*

11. Queets Valley Rain Forest, Olympic National Park. The cooling of moisture-laden ocean air as it is driven upward by mountain slopes is responsible for the unusually heavy annual precipitation—about 145 inches—in this remote part of the Olympic National Park. The result is a temperate rain forest that grows with almost tropical intensity. Sitka spruces and western hemlocks are the dominant trees, along with Douglas firs and western red cedars. Club moss hangs everywhere in

11. *The abundance of mosses and ferns is living evidence of the special climate here.*

festoons, and licorice fern grows in the shade of big-leaf maples. There is scarcely a square inch of soil that does not support vegetation of some kind. A well-maintained 14-mile dirt road following the Queets River gives access to the valley.

The most famous inhabitants here are the noble Roosevelt elk, frequently seen in meadows along the easy three-mile loop trail, which begins at the campsite at road's end. You might also glimpse black-tailed deer or a pileated woodpecker. Other hikes involve fording the river, but this should be done only in summer when the water is low.

Trout and salmon fishing is good, and float trips are popular from April through June. Be careful of submerged logs and overhanging boughs, however. There are launching places for boats, canoes, and rafts along the access road and at the campsite. *Park open year-round. Campground open June–Sept.*

12. Leadbetter Point Unit, Willapa National Wildlife Refuge. *Stackpole Rd., Oysterville.* The three-mile-long refuge at the tip of Long Beach Peninsula is a world of mud flats, sand dunes, saltmarsh, and oyster beds—a home or way station for more than 200 species of birds, especially during the migratory seasons. Virtually every kind of shorebird in Oregon and Washington congregates here at some time during the year. Black brants by the thousands stop on their way north from Mexico in April and May, and scores of sooty shearwaters en route to New Zealand drop by in August. In January the point is a good place to glimpse such rarities as gyrfalcons and snowy owls.

On the ocean side of the point you may see seals sunning themselves. In summer the 500-acre Salicornia Saltmarsh, which has never been dredged, produces a rich display of grindelia, jaumea, asters, and other wildflowers. The refuge is accessible only by foot trails from the parking lot. Mosquitoes are numerous and repellent is recommended. *Open year-round.*

13. Cowlitz County Historical Museum. *405 Allen St., Kelso.* This well-organized museum chronicles the main themes of

19th-century life in the Pacific Northwest. Fish traps intriguingly made from roots, canoe anchors, hunting bows, arrowheads, and carrying baskets reflect the Indians' mode of survival in this abundant land, while the hardships of pioneers on their overland journey and the struggles of early settlers are recalled by displays of weapons, early-day tools and equipment, and a tableau of a fur-clad pioneer standing in his cramped but sturdy log cabin. The all-important logging industry is also portrayed. The rapid changes in lifestyles of the Northwest are depicted in colorful tableaux of a doctor's office, a general store, and a parlor, which unlike the earlier pioneer's cabin is furnished with a pump-organ, an Edison phonograph, and a stereoscopic viewer. An exhibition of local birdlife completes the collection. *Open Tues.–Sun., Memorial Day–Labor Day; Tues.–Sat. and P.M. Sun. rest of the year. Closed major holidays.*

14. Windy Ridge, Mount St. Helens Volcanic National Monument. *From Rte. 12 at Randle go south for 35 miles on Forest Service Rds. 25 and 26 to Windy Ridge.* On May 18, 1980, a volcanic erruption blew out the northern face of Mount St. Hel-

ens. The stupendous explosion threw almost a cubic mile of rock and ash some 14 miles into the atmosphere, devastated 154 square miles of forest, river, and lake, and took 57 lives.

The most dramatic view of the destruction is from Windy Ridge. On the way the road passes through dense forests of Douglas fir and then abruptly enters the devastated area of blown-down timber and valleys filled with ash. At Windy Ridge you are only four miles from the crater; directly below you lies Spirit Lake, choked with logs.

For an even closer look into the crater and at the growing lava dome, stop at Norway Pass, just off Forest Service Road 26, and take the 2½-mile hike leading through the downed forest to a fine viewpoint. Along the way you'll notice evidence of the recovery process as lupines, fireweed, and pussytoes grow up through the blanket of ash.

Naturalists at Windy Ridge give interpretive lectures several times a day during the summer. Further information is available at the Iron Creek Information Station on Forest Service Road 25, south of Randle, and there are explanatory displays at Seaquest State Park on Silver Lake, east on Route 504 off Interstate 5 at Castle

Rock. A new Mount St. Helens Visitor Center is planned at Castle Rock. *Forest Service access roads to Windy Ridge generally open June–Oct.*

15. Sunrise Area, Mount Rainier National Park. *Off Rte. 410.* Among America's most ravishing sights is the 14,410-foot volcanic peak of Mount Rainier with its 27 glaciers reaching down like fingers to subalpine meadows carpeted in summer with wildflowers. The Sunrise Area, seven miles east of the summit at an elevation of 6,400 feet, is an excellent place to admire this majestic mountain, and to explore a region where a variety of plants and animals manage to survive in extremely marginal circumstances. The 14-mile paved access road to Sunrise climbs through breathtaking mountain scenery.

Hiking trails start at the Sunrise Visitor Center and lead through subalpine firs, whitebark pines, and Alaska cedars. At the timberline are gnarled and dwarfed trees, some of which may have taken 75 years to reach a height of 18 inches. Rainier's famous meadows of wildflowers bloom in two stages on the eastern slope. In late June or early July you can expect to see pasqueflowers and lilies; these are fol-

17. *Wildflowers, flowing river, and rolling hills add their charm to the works of man.*

lowed by cinquefoils, blue lupines, asters, and Indian paintbrush.

There are no accommodations at Sunrise; the nearest campsites are 10 miles away at White River Campground. *Accessible late June–Sept. Admission charged.*

16. Fort Simcoe State Park. Work on Fort Simcoe began in the summer of 1856 amid growing hostility between the local Yakima Indians and the settlers and gold seekers whose quest for a better life often led them to encroach upon tribal lands. After the defeat of the Yakimas in the war of 1858, the fort served as an Indian agency headquarters for 63 years.

Of the original 35 buildings, five still stand: three captains' dwellings, a squared-log blockhouse, and the quite un-military-looking commander's house, which is restored and furnished as it was in 1858. A log barracks and two additional blockhouses have been reconstructed. A small museum has displays about the history of the fort and the Yakimas, including a life-size diorama of a Yakima winter house made of tule matting.

The fort occupies a commanding rise where the foothills of the Cascade Mountains yield to the plain along Toppenish Creek. Traditionally the site was a meeting place for the Yakimas, who called it

mool-mool, meaning "bubbling water," because of the nearby spring. As you stroll through the oak groves of the 200 acres here, don't be surprised if you hear a rat-a-tat-tat overhead. This is a favored breeding site for Lewis's woodpeckers. The park has an extensive picnic ground and a play area for children. *Open daily Apr.–Sept.; weekends only, Oct.–Mar.*

17. Maryhill Museum of Art. *Hwy. 14, Goldendale.* The palatial stone mansion, set high on a remote spot overlooking the Columbia River, was built by the multimillionaire Samuel Hill, the son-in-law of railroad magnate James J. Hill and an international peace promoter, world traveler, and friend of royalty. Sam Hill, of Quaker parentage, had intended to start a Quaker agricultural community here with Maryhill as his residence. The colony did not materialize, and he was persuaded by Loie Fuller, an avant-garde dancer, to turn the building into a museum. Later his friend Queen Marie of Romania dedicated the museum to beauty and peace as a symbol of her gratitude for American aid after World War I. In 1935, four years after Hill's death, the wealthy art patroness Alma Spreckels donated part of her own art collection to the museum.

The centerpiece of the museum is Sam

14. *The devastation soon after the eruption of Mount St. Helens, as seen from Norway Pass. Pearly everlastings and fireweed affirm hope for the future.*

19. The spirit of the chase—graven in stone by a prehistoric hunter-artist.

Hill's collection of "Rodin's Rodins"— bronzes, plasters, and sketches that the famous sculptor kept in his studio for reference. Among them is a plaster cast of a reduced version of "The Thinker," the only one in existence. After the Rodin collection, take time to browse and see the rest of Maryhill's displays, which include 19th-century American and European paintings, weaponry, icons, American Indian baskets, antique chess sets, 1940's French fashion mannequins, and the Queen Marie Room, where you'll find her throne, a coronation gown, and many of her personal belongings.

Maryhill is as much a curiosity as it is a museum of fine art. Nothing really quite prepares you for this imposing structure—filled with priceless art and artifacts—literally in the middle of nowhere. An eccentric added attraction is a concrete model of England's Stonehenge, visible from the highway leading to Maryhill: it was built by Hill as a memorial to the men of Klickitat County who died in World War I. *Museum open daily mid-Mar.– mid.-Nov. Admission charged.*

18. Olmstead Place State Park. *Ellensburg. Take Exit 109 off I-90 and continue north to Mountain View Ave. Turn east on Mountain View, which becomes Kittitas Hwy., and continue to Squaw Creek Trail Rd.* Samuel and Sarah Olmstead, attracted by the grasslands and rich soil of the Kittitas Valley, arrived here in 1875, built a 40- by 30-foot cabin, and began farming a 160-acre homestead. Their family lived here for two generations, including the year 1878, when the cabin was used as a fort in the Nez Perce War.

Today this historical park offers an intriguing opportunity to see how a Kittitas Valley family farm developed from the 1870's through the 1950's. Touring the four rooms of the original cabin, you'll see a long rifle owned by a neighbor and the saddles, crockery, cookware, china, storage chests, organ, stove, and desk that were the stuff of the family's daily life.

A house built in 1908 is more elegantly appointed, with wrought-iron lamps, carved desks, and a library furnished with a red plush velvet love seat. The red barn—originally used for grain storage— now houses a huge clover huller. Much of the vintage farming equipment seen on the grounds is operated during the Threshing Bee held the second weekend after Labor Day. You can also tour the granary, wagon shed, and dairy barn.

The three-quarter-mile Altapes Creek Trail leads along the tree-lined creek to the picturesque Seaton Schoolhouse, a small log cabin built more than 100 years ago. *Altapes* is an Indian word meaning "most beautiful creek in the valley." *Open weekends and by appointment weekdays, Apr.–Oct.; open by appointment only the rest of the year. Call (509) 925-1943.*

19. Ginkgo Petrified Forest State Park. *Vantage.* Specimens from one of the world's most spectacularly varied fossil forests can be seen here on a 7,400-acre site that encompasses prehistoric swamp and lake beds repeatedly inundated by lava. Felled trees from the dense forests of the Miocene Epoch—not just the ginkgo for which the park is named, but some 200 other species—were preserved beneath the solidified basalt, gradually turning to brilliantly colored stone as mineral deposits replaced their cell structure. Ice Age erosion brought them to light again.

Now cross-sections of the fossilized logs can be seen in the park's Heritage Area Interpretive Center along with an array of intelligently planned explanatory exhibits. The area also contains a number of delicate Indian carvings incised in black basalt: not to be missed. You can see logs in their original setting by taking either of the hikes through the Natural Area, the first a three-quarter-mile interpretive trail, the second a 2½-mile trek.

It's a good idea to make your camping headquarters at Wanapum Recreation Area, which is located within the park three miles south of Vantage on the shore of the Columbia River. Wanapum provides excellent facilities for fishermen and other outdoor enthusiasts. *Park open year-round. Interpretive Center open daily, Memorial Day–Labor Day.*

20. Palouse Falls State Park. The grace, beauty, and power of Palouse Falls, as it drops 195 feet into a horseshoe-shaped basin, create one of Washington's most spectacular sights. From the park viewpoint you can photograph the awesome surge of water and the rainbows created by its sun-struck mist. Sure-footed visitors hike 250 feet down to the basin for a water-level view (or to try for catfish, which spawn in the canyon pools). Others walk the path that meanders around the bluffs above the falls for a bird's-eye view. The hike takes about 20 minutes. Below the falls the wild waters of the Palouse rush through its natural canyon, which extends for eight miles, and then wind among rolling bluffs to empty into the Snake River.

The falls and canyon have a long history. Twenty thousand years ago a glacial lake spread from northern Idaho to northwestern Montana, covering more than 3,000 square miles. As the climate warmed, the ice dam burst and a tremendous flood of water and debris roared down the Snake and Columbia rivers, rearranging the landscape as it went. The canyon attracts many bird species, including owls that nest in the cliffs.

You'll find picnic tables and a small campground. Campsites are also available at nearby Lion's Ferry State Park. *Open Mar.–Sept. Admission charged.*

21. Whitman Mission National Historic Site. This pastoral setting of open fields with a millpond, a memorial obelisk, a reconstructed covered wagon, some ruins, and a grave site is the scene of a tragic conflict of cultures that took place in 1847.

Marcus and Narcissa Whitman, along with their companions, Henry and Eliza Spalding, came west in 1836 to convert the Indians to Christianity. The mission that they built here at Waiilatpu soon became an important way station for other emigrants. Whitman's efforts to convert the Indians, however, achieved far less success. The nomadic Cayuses were not interested in settling in a farming village and attending the mission school. Their tenuous trust of whites collapsed when an epidemic of measles brought in by the pioneer children wiped out half the tribe. Although Dr. Whitman treated both Indians and whites alike, the Indians had no resistance to the disease, while many of the white children survived. Believing they were purposely being poisoned by the white people, a band of desperate Cayuses attacked the mission on November 29, 1847, killing the Whitmans and 11 others and taking 50 captives who later were ransomed. The settlers' punitive campaign against the Cayuses drove the Indians from their land and into the mountains. Two years later the tribe surrendered.

The visitor center at this 98-acre site displays implements belonging to the Whitmans and some beautiful Cayuse garments, including a feathered headdress, a beaded leather shirt, and dresses ornamented with shells. The tomahawk that may have been used to kill Dr. Whitman is also beautifully decorated, and looks more like a treasured gift than a lethal weapon. A short audiovisual show describes the mission's history. In summer, craft demonstrations are presented. *Open year-round except Thanksgiving Day, Christmas, and New Year's Day.*

22. Steptoe Butte State Park. At an elevation of 3,613 feet, the top of the magnificent butte here is frequently above the clouds. A three-mile paved roadway leads from the peaceful orchards at its base to its spectacular summit, from which (on a clear day) there is a lovely view of the patchwork of surrounding farmland. The great grain elevators in the distance appear as tiny silver towers and the towns as colorful clusters of toy blocks.

The butte is named for Lt. Col. Edward J. Steptoe, who on May 6, 1858, set forth from Walla Walla with a detachment of 130 lightly armed cavalry to show the local Indians that the U.S. Army was a serious force in the area. A group of some 600 Coeur d'Alene, Palouse, Spokane, and Nez Perce Indians, fearing further incursion on their land, prevented the soldiers from crossing the Spokane River and forced them to retreat. The troops took a defensive position on the broad butte here and held out until nightfall, when they buried their dead and slipped away. Perhaps the colonel's most significant achievement stemming from the campaign was to have his name pass into the vocabulary of geology as a term for this particular type of butte: a *steptoe* is an island of rock surrounded by a flow of lava. *Open year-round, but summit road may be impassable in snow.*

23. Fields Spring State Park. Named for an early homesteader who developed a spring as a water supply for his nearby ranch, this pleasant 445-acre park is situated on a trail once used by the Nez Perce Indians. The prime attractions today are the splendid view of three states from the top of Puffer Butte and the excellent birding. Seven kinds of woodpeckers have been observed, and ruffed grouse, hawks, great horned owls, and various warblers are common. The complete bird list includes some 90 species.

Puffer Butte is aptly named, since the mile-long trail to the 4,450-foot summit is fairly strenuous as it climbs through meadows and woodlands of fir, spruce, and ponderosa pine. Deer and elk are occasionally seen along the trail. From the top of the butte you can look directly down into the canyon of the Grande Ronde River 3,000 feet below. To the west lie the forests and rolling hills of Washington, to the south Oregon's Wallowa Mountains, and to the east the Snake River and the mountains of Idaho.

The park has a campground and recreation areas. In winter a sled run provides downhill thrills, and the park is a popular departure point for cross-country skiers. *Open year-round.*

22. Wheat fields in their various stages of growth carpet the rolling Palouse hills.

Oregon

Created largely by volcanic action, with a western edge sculpted by the raging sea, the varied and dramatic landscape is inevitable.

By the Pacific Ocean, the goal of Lewis and Clark's historic expedition, you can learn how the explorers spent a winter before heading back east. Also to be seen along the coast are the justly famous sea stacks, promontories, dunes, beaches, and driftwood, as well as formal gardens, birds, and fields of wildflowers.

Oregon's fiery geologic past is revealed in a bleak and forbidding lava bed, a butte of black volcanic glass, a lava tube that swallows a river, and a fabulous lake in the caldera of a collapsed volcano.

There is old-time logging equipment to examine and a goldfield steam train to ride; in another mining area, where the Chinese outnumbered the Occidentals, there's a fascinating collection of Oriental artifacts. Other museums feature cowboy, Indian, and pioneer memorabilia. You'll also find some truly rugged scenery to explore and a variety of places to see incredible numbers of waterfowl and, perhaps, to catch some fish.

2. From an unknown forest this sculpture was transported by the raging wind and water.

1. Fort Clatsop National Memorial. *Astoria.* Arriving on the West Coast in December 1805, the explorers Lewis and Clark decided to make their winter camp here by the edge of the river now named for them. Game was abundant and, with the ocean close by, they could make salt. They built a 50-foot-square log stockade with two rows of cabins to accommodate their party of 33 and named it for a friendly local Indian tribe. Here they stayed until the spring of 1806, when they started their journey home.

When the Oregon Historical Society purchased the site in 1901, not a trace of the fort remained. Its reconstruction in 1955 was based on a diagram drawn by Captain Clark on the cover of his journal.

In addition to the fort, the 125-acre site includes a splendid visitor center. Among its fascinating displays are paintings of major events on the expedition's journey, a reprint of Clark's map, and an elkhorn-handled knife that may actually have been made by a member of the expedition.

Short walks with historical markers lead to the fort, to a spring that presumably supplied the men with water, and to a canoe landing on the riverbank. Well-kept lawns and a forestlike setting of Sitka spruce and hemlock add to the attractiveness of the place. In summer costumed attendants demonstrate pioneer tasks. *Open daily year-round.*

---

2. Cape Meares State Park and Cape Meares National Wildlife Refuge. *Off Three Capes Scenic Drive.* In 1788 Capt. John Meares, exploring the coast, came upon this imposing headland and named it Cape Lookout. When the coast was surveyed in 1850, a point 10 miles to the south was erroneously designated Cape Lookout, and by 1857 the name had become so well known that the original site was renamed Cape Meares. The 40-foot octagonal lighthouse, perhaps built here by mistake, operated from 1890 to 1964.

The park and lighthouse sit atop Cape Meares, a 217-foot-high bluff with sheer cliffs dropping straight to the sea. A sturdy fence along the 250-yard path to the lighthouse protects visitors from a possibly fatal tumble.

Some 2½ miles of trail cross the 232-acre park. From the trail on the south side of the cape you can view the Three Arches Wildlife Refuge, three islands of rock about 2½ miles to the south. With binoculars you may catch a glimpse of the sea lions inhabiting the marine refuge.

To find the Cape Meares Wildlife Refuge, take the Oregon Coast Trail east from the parking lot. The trail leads through the refuge and down to the beach. On the way you'll pass the Octopus Tree, a Sitka spruce that is striking for its enormous size and candelabra branching. Its six limbs extend horizontally from the trunk for 30 feet before turning upward. From early February through July trilliums, skunk cabbage, lilies of the valley, and other wildflowers add color to the landscape. Tufted puffins and pelagic cormorants are among the numerous seabirds nesting on the 139-acre refuge, where black-tailed deer are also seen.

The Three Capes Scenic Drive, about 35 miles long, offers spectacular views of coast, dunes, and picturesque villages. *Park open year-round; lighthouse open Thurs.–Mon., June–Sept.*

3. Sea Lion Caves, Inc. *Twelve miles north of Florence on Rte. 101.* Both California sea lions, which are black and have a sharp bark, and Steller's sea lions, brown with a deep roar, are found here. During fall and winter as many as 400 gather in the cave, their only permanent year-round home on the American mainland. In spring and summer they often bask on the rocky cliffs.

Entrance to the cave (despite the official name, there is only one) is by an elevator that descends 208 feet from the visitor center to the observation window. The 300-foot-wide cavern, about two acres in size with a dome 125 feet high, is believed to be America's largest sea cave and the world's largest rookery for Brandt's cormorants, which usually arrive about April first and stay until the middle of August. As many as 2,500 nests have been found on the cliffs. The view from the visitor center makes this a popular place for whale watching. *Open year-round except Christmas. Admission charged.*

4. Jessie M. Honeyman Memorial State Park. Sand dunes, ocean beaches, two freshwater lakes, and a forest of Douglas fir, spruce, hemlock, and cedar await visitors to this splendid 522-acre park.

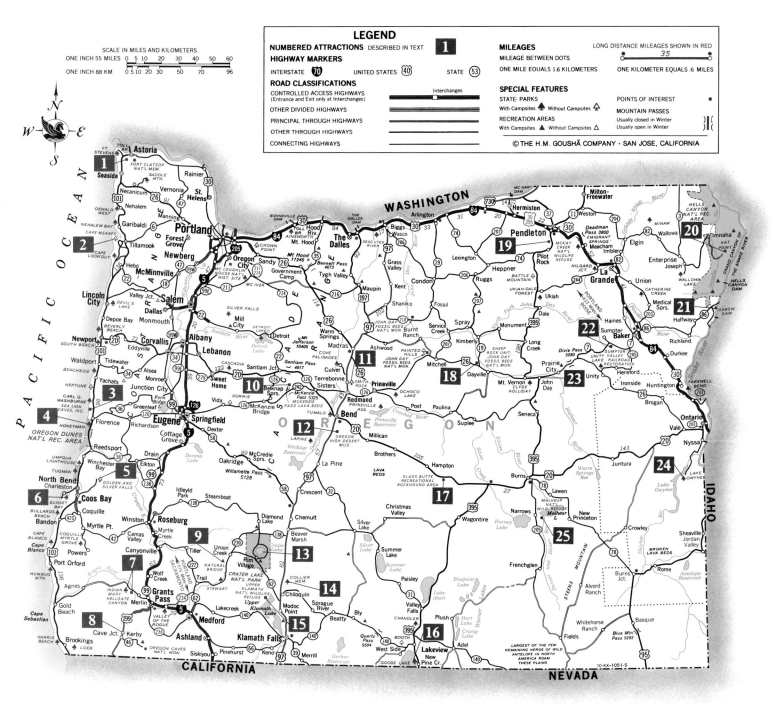

The dunes, mere infants by geologic reckoning, were formed during the last 10,000 to 15,000 years by the erosive power of the sea. Cleawox Lake, with dunes to the west and woodlands to the east, has a sandy swimming beach and a picnic area. Freshwater swimming is also available at Woahink Lake, east of Route 101.

Other summertime activities include boating, waterskiing, canoeing, and fishing for bluegill, bass, and trout. In fall the park attracts mushroom hunters. Winter brings storm watchers, flocks of geese and other birds, and rockhounds hunting for agates; during March visitors climb the dunes for whale watching.

The park, named in honor of Mrs. Jessie M. Honeyman, an early supporter of Oregon's conservation movement, has several picnic grounds, camping sites, and a boat-launching ramp. Hiking trails range from short walks through the forest to longer treks over the dunes to the ocean. *Open year-round.*

5. Golden and Silver Falls State Park.
Twenty-two miles NE of Coos Bay. The two falls, located at opposite ends of the 157-acre park, are about three-quarters of a mile apart. Golden Falls (named in honor of an early visitor) drops over a rounded ledge of lava; Silver Falls (named to complement its "sister") cascades from a basalt amphitheater over a series of boulders and divides into two streams that become Silver Creek.

A parking lot and picnic ground are halfway between the two falls. To reach Golden Falls, follow a half-mile path along the canyon through stands of evergreens; the trail offers a pleasant view of Glenn Creek. Silver Falls is reached by a quarter-mile path along the canyon floor among ferns and moss-draped trees.

The park, which has been left in its natural state, is notable for its grove of myrtles—rare and beautiful hardwood trees that flourish in southern Oregon. Chipmunks, porcupines, and black bears are found here, with elk and deer coming to forage in winter. Trout fishing in both Glenn and Silver creeks is excellent in early summer. Picnic tables and grills are provided. *Open year-round.*

6. Sunset Bay State Park.
Three and a half miles SW of Charleston. When trapper Jedediah Smith arrived at Sunset Bay in 1828, he found it inhabited by Indians who fished its waters and gathered shellfish from the intertidal zone. People still come to Sunset Bay to fish, particularly for sea perch, rockfish, and sea trout. Swimming is popular too in the calm, warm, cliff-encircled bay. A fish-cleaning station, a pine-sheltered campground, and a boat-launching ramp are provided.

You can enjoy lunch beside a small creek, on a grassy point overlooking the beach, or under a roofed pagoda. Picnic tables and grills are scattered throughout the park.

Afterward you can walk along the beach or hike through a woodland inhabited by deer, raccoons, and seldom-seen bobcats. If you really wish to explore the shoreline, take the Oregon Coast Trail, which begins at Sunset Bay's parking lot, winds for 3½ miles along the shore, and continues through the Shore Acres gardens to Cape Arago's beaches.

For an outstanding view of the bay's rugged sandstone cliffs, drive about a mile south on the Cape Arago highway to a stairway that crosses the guardrail and leads to a lookout at the very edge of a cliff. *Park open year-round; camping mid-Apr.–Labor Day.*

7. Indian Mary Park and Hellgate Canyon.
Eleven miles north of Merlin on Merlin Galice Rd. Indian Mary Park and Hellgate Canyon are side by side on Oregon's Rogue River. Novelist Zane Grey, who owned a cabin on the river, wrote of Hellgate in several of his stories. A portion of Indian Mary Park was once the smallest Indian reservation (40 acres) in the United States, granted by the government in 1855 to Umqua Joe, Mary's father, for warning

5. *The sight and sound of Golden Falls are sheer delight in this fern-fringed setting.*

white settlers of an impending massacre. The reservation is now a 65-acre park with exotic trees and shrubs planted among native ponderosa pine and Douglas fir. Spring brings extra touches of beauty, when the trees and shrubs, complemented by azaleas, lupines, and yellow monkey flowers, burst into bloom. In autumn the foliage is brilliant.

The park has shaded picnic grounds, playgrounds, and campsites with hookups. The river, wide and calm near the park, is popular with swimmers and fishermen. The Indian Joe Trail, a steep 3½-mile route, leads to a lookout from which you can see the forested hills and grasslands of the Rogue River valley.

Hellgate Canyon, a jumble of sheer cliffs and overhanging rocks, is a favorite with rafters, kayakers, and tubers. An excursion boat, which departs from Hog Creek a mile above the canyon, also weaves through the chasm. Sandbars here attract gold panners as well as picnickers. *Open year-round. Admission charged.*

8. Josephine County Kerbyville Museum. *Kerby.*

Following the discovery of gold on the banks of Josephine Creek in 1851, several towns, including Kerbyville (since shortened to Kerby) mushroomed. Few of these towns remain, but the heirlooms, tools, and mementos of many of the people who once lived in them have been donated to the Kerbyville Museum.

In the main museum building you'll see a colorful facsimile of an old-time country store interior, Indian handiwork, quilts, rugs, blankets, and a collection of women's clothing illustrating that the apparel of a well-dressed lady could weigh as much as 100 pounds.

The complex also includes a quaint one-room log schoolhouse, a barn-sized blacksmith's shop, farm equipment, and the 1871 Stith-Naucke House. The two-story building is charmingly furnished with Victoriana and other antiques that belonged to early Josephine County families. Both creek and county were named for the daughter of an early prospector. *Open Wed.–Sun., mid-May–mid-Sept.*

9. Natural Bridge, Rogue River National Forest. *Fifty-five miles north of Medford off Rte. 62.*

Natural Bridge is visible during summertime periods of low water; it's also a spectacular sight at other times, when the Rogue submerges it in swift whitewater rapids. The bridge is a large, intact lava tube that channels the river underground for about 200 feet before the waters resurface. Its origins date back to the eruption of Mount Mazama, which formed Crater Lake nearly 7,000 years ago and sent lava flows raging across the surrounding countryside. As their surfaces cooled and hardened, tunnels, or tubes, formed underneath. Unlike the giant stone-arch variety of natural bridges, the Rogue River bridge is virtually level with the shoreline and lower than the sides of the gorge channeling the river.

Natural Bridge campground has sites for tents and small trailers, each with a picnic table and grill. There are several hiking trails, one to Woodruff Bridge, a favorite spot for catching rainbow trout, and another to Big Bend.

Avoid wading near the opening of Natural Bridge and walking on its slippery-smooth surface. Tales are told of people and pets being dragged into the rushing subterranean waters and never seen again. *Open Memorial Day–Labor Day.*

10. McKenzie Pass Lava Beds. *Off Rte. 242 between McKenzie Bridge and Sisters.*

Stretching for some 75 square miles on both sides of McKenzie Pass Road are the jumbled lava beds that resulted from thousands of years of eruptions along the High Cascade volcanic chain. Markers along the half-mile Lava River Trail, which starts at the summit of the pass, explain lava gutters, pressure ridges, cooling cracks, crevasses, and other formations, and identify the fascinating dwarf trees—among them mountain hemlock, lodgepole pine, and Pacific silver fir—that manage to cling to the landscape.

Except for the Belknap Crater flows, which are rolling, graceful rivers of rock, the lava is a broken, jumbled mass of rocks, like ice breaking up on a river, the result of its surface cooling over molten turbulence. An easy quarter-mile trail leads to Proxy Falls; a 7½-mile route, quite steep in places, takes you from the highway at Windy Point to Black Crater.

Wright Observatory at the summit of McKenzie Pass offers views of Cascade peaks. Nine campgrounds are situated

10. Hemlock seedling is a bright accent of life in a forbidding field of lava.

along the road, which is closed from October to late June because of snow and is not recommended for trailers or campers at any time. *Open July–mid-Oct.*

11. Smith Rock State Park. *Three and a half miles east of Terrebonne.*

The keynote here is color: 623 acres of spectacular sandstone formations—boulders, cliffs, crags, and pinnacles—in magnificent pale yellows, burnt reds, rich greens, and purples that change with the shifting sunlight. The Crooked River, a ribbon of blue, twists among them. Legend has it that the park was named for a soldier named Smith who fell to his death here during the Indian troubles of 1863. In fact, it is named for its discoverer, John Smith, a

Kentuckian who came to Oregon in the 1850's and rose to political prominence.

Picnic sites are scattered throughout the park. Several paved pathways lead from the parking lot to the river's edge and across a footbridge, where a network of trails spreads out among the formations. *Open year-round.*

12. Oregon High Desert Museum. *Six miles south of Bend on U.S. 97.* "Hands-on" exhibits, both indoors and out, and a series of educational programs bring the natural and cultural history of this region of mountains and valleys alive.

Displays at the visitor center include branding irons, spurs, guns, a settler's cabin, a full-scale wickiup, and a variety of animal pelts.

Paths wind through desert shrubs and ponderosa pine past a porcupine cage, a birds-of-prey demonstration area, a weather station, and an otter pond that has viewing areas above- and below-ground. The Forestry Learning Center recounts the history of logging and forest management in the region. *Open year-round except Thanksgiving Day, Christmas, and New Year's Day. Admission charged.*

13. Crater Lake National Park. *Fifty-seven miles north of Klamath Falls off Rte. 62.* Crater Lake is particularly beautiful in winter, and despite an annual snowfall of 600 inches, easy to visit. The road is kept clear, and a 30-mile ski trail circles the crater rim. On weekends from Thanksgiving to April you can join snowshoe hikes led by a park ranger.

Crater Lake is the deepest (1,932 feet) and probably the bluest lake in the United States, set like a sapphire in the bowl-shaped caldera of old Mount Mazama, a volcano that erupted and collapsed nearly 7,000 years ago.

Traces of past volcanic activity can be seen at The Pinnacles, reached by Sand Creek Highway, a 10-mile paved road passable from late summer until heavy snow. These pumice and scoria formations, 75 to 100 feet tall, rise like an army of obelisks from a 200-foot-deep canyon.

Some 30 trails (ranging from less than a mile to 35 miles) crisscross the park.

13. *This unusual view of the lake and Wizard Island is from Watchman Peak Trail,*

Hikes up Watchman Peak (.8 mile) and Mount Scott (2.5 miles) provide the best views of the lake. There are two campgrounds, at Mazama and at Lost Creek, both accessible by road from Rim Drive. And with a permit you can camp in the backcountry. *Park open year-round; visitor center open June–Oct., weather permitting. Admission charged in summer.*

14. Collier Memorial State Park. *Chiloquin.* The 650-acre park's main attraction is a logging museum founded by Alfred and Andrew Collier, who donated most of the acreage to the state in 1945 as a memorial to their parents.

Two years later the brothers began to round up the museum exhibits, many of them drawn from a time and technology that no longer exist. Equipment on display ranges from ox yokes and horse-drawn wagons to a modern generating plant capable of supplying enough power for an entire sawmill. A wood-burning locomotive, 19th-century steam tractors, chain-saws, and a wealth of other logging and pioneering artifacts are housed in the museum buildings, which include a turn-of-the-century logger's homestead, a

blacksmith's shed, and a group of authentic pioneer cabins.

A spacious day-use area is set among pine and aspen where the Williamson River and Spring Creek come together. A second, more secluded picnic area is located on the creek's west shore. You can rent canoes or rafts for the fun of exploring the river, which is also a superb spot for trout fishing. The camping area has 68 sites, 50 with full hookups. *Museum and day-use areas open year-round. Campground open mid-Apr –Oct.*

15. Upper Klamath National Wildlife Refuge. There is only one way to tour this vast wetlands preserve: by boat. More than 14,000 acres of marsh and open water here provide food and nesting sites for some 250 species of birds. The small village of Rocky Point on the western edge of the refuge at Pelican Bay offers access to the marshes and a fine viewing spot on the shore. From here you can follow a six-mile self-guiding canoe trail through the marshlands, a trip that provides a unique opportunity for watching birdlife, particularly the pelicans, egrets, herons, and Canada geese. The best time for viewing

which may be snowbound until late July.

these birds (and perhaps raccoons, deer, otters, and minks) is at sunrise. Bald eagles and ospreys nest nearby and can occasionally be seen fishing the waters.

During the waterfowl nesting season (spring through fall) much of the refuge is closed to visitors. Both hunting and fishing are permitted in season on 5,700 acres of the refuge territory. Trout average four or five pounds, and six- to ten-pounders are fairly common. Perch is another likely catch. Hunting is limited to geese, ducks, coots, and snipe.

The Forest Service maintains campgrounds near Rocky Point, and from April into November several sportsmen's resorts in the area offer marina facilities, cabins, and motorboat and canoe rentals. *Campgrounds open Apr.–Oct.*

16. Goose Lake State Park Recreation Area. *Off U.S. Rte. 395.* Perched on the eastern shore of Goose Lake, a body of water that extends well into California, this pleasant 60-acre park attracts large numbers of migrating fowl, most notably the Canada honkers from which the lake takes its name. For part of the year the lake resembles a grassy marsh. As the wa-

ter ebbs in summer, it becomes almost shallow enough to walk across; tules and bulrushes sprout even in the lake's center.

Among the other waterfowl here, Chinese ring-necked pheasants, introduced by the state park service, can sometimes be spotted in deep grass and brush.

For anglers, the lake offers bluegills and lampreys; and there's a creek boasting Goose Lake striped trout, unique in its ability to survive in warm water. Swimmers often enjoy the lake, but windy days stir up the silt. The park campground has sites ranging from primitive to full hookup. *Open Apr.–mid-Oct.*

17. Glass Butte Recreational Rockhound Area. *Off U.S. Rte. 20, 25¾ miles west of intersection with U.S. Rte. 395.* Serious rockhounds come from near and far to dig at Glass Butte. Formed by a volcanic eruption nearly 5 million years ago, the 6,400-foot mountain has some of the world's largest outcrops of obsidian—a black volcanic glass that forms when lava with a high silica content cools quickly.

American Indians prized the brittle, easily chipped obsidian and turned this area into a virtual factory for axes, scrapers, chisels, and weapon points.

While ordinary jet black obsidian is appealing and makes attractive jewelry, the material can also be streaked with gold, silver, and other colors, or have an iridescent rainbow sheen. Even the rare fire obsidian is found here. Some 7,000 acres have been set aside for rockhounding, and in the valley chunks can be kicked up with a boot or found lying loose in the roadbed. Anyone seeking the more valuable varieties, however, should bring shovels, picks, and rock hammers.

The road to the site is rutted and rough and best traversed with four-wheel drive. The area is primitive, with no facilities, although overnight camping is permitted. Camping or not, visitors should bring food and water. *Open year-round.*

18. Sheep Rock Unit, John Day Fossil Beds National Monument. *Rte. 19.* Twenty-five million years ago, saber-toothed cats pursued dog-sized horses across the plains here, while piglike entel-

odonts and rhinoceroses grazed the lush meadows. You can see evidence of these and other exotic prehistoric mammals preserved in the stratified layers of this remarkable area's volcanic and sedimentary rock. The best place to examine the fossils closely is the Cant Ranch Visitor Center, where there are also exhibits on the scientific methods used to investigate the beds.

Hiking trails, some fairly easy, lead through spectacular "badlands" scenery where fossils are still being found. The John Day River crosses the area and provides good fishing for catfish in the summer and steelheads in the fall and winter. *Open daily year-round; Cant Ranch Visitor Center open daily mid-Mar.–Oct.*

19. McKay Creek National Wildlife Refuge. *Off U.S. Rte. 395.* Established as a refuge and breeding ground for wildfowl, this preserve is almost completely inundated for much of the year. In spring and early summer, the reservoir is a serene, mirror-smooth lake covering more than two-thirds of the 1,800-acre refuge—the only dry land a rim of shoreline. During these seasons it attracts boaters, fishermen, and water-skiers and serves as the major source of water for nearby cropland. By August, however, it shrinks to less than one-fifth its former size, exposing mud flats that sprout vegetation, providing food for wildlife.

Birds found here include great blue

14. *Heavy construction of the logging equipment bespeaks the labor involved.*

herons, American coots, long-billed curlews, ring-billed gulls, and red-winged blackbirds. Spring and fall bring an increase of waterfowl—mallards and Canada geese, with some American widgeons, green-winged teals, and pintails. Their population peaks at 33,000 in winter. *Refuge open Mar.–Sept.; 600 acres remain open during state waterfowl hunting season.*

20. Hat Point Overlook, Hells Canyon National Recreation Area. *Twenty-four miles SE of Imnaha via one-lane dirt road.* Hat Point Overlook is really only for those with four-wheel-drive cars. The trip, however, is extremely rewarding, because of the views of Hells Canyon—the deepest gorge on the North American continent.

The 24-mile trip on a one-lane dirt road from Imnaha takes 2½ hours, not counting stops, and goes from an altitude of approximately 1,700 feet to 6,982 feet—a vertical distance of slightly more than one mile. At Five Mile Viewpoint the road levels out and goes through pine forests and wildflower-filled meadows inhabited by a variety of wildlife.

Besides Hells Canyon, the view from the summit includes the Snake River, more than a mile below, and across the canyon in Idaho, the craggy peaks of the Seven Devils Mountains. For an even more panoramic vista visitors can climb

the 100-foot tower, which is manned in summer. A hiking trail begins in the picnic area and winds through meadows and down the cliff to the canyon far below.

Campgrounds are provided for tents and light campers. No running water is available. *Road open July–Nov.*

21. Oxbow Dam, Hells Canyon National Recreation Area. *Seventy miles east of Baker at junction of Oregon Rte. 86 and Idaho Rte. 71.* When Hells Canyon Power Development Complex was completed in 1968, three dams spanned the Snake River Canyon—Oxbow, Brownlee, and Hells Canyon—their backwaters forming three man-made lakes and a recreation area 90 miles long. Oxbow is the center of the complex and the smallest of the three.

Twenty-minute tours of the Oxbow Power Plant, noisy but interesting, include a look at the generating equipment in action, a decompression machine, and the oil recycling equipment. In addition, Oxbow has a fish hatchery, where steelheads can be seen from September through the end of April.

All three dam areas are popular with powerboaters, water-skiers, swimmers, and fishermen, who try for bass, catfish, steelheads, and crappies. Here too are large populations of deer, elk, and bighorn sheep, as well as chukars, quails,

Hungarian partridges, bald and golden eagles, cranes, geese, grouse, swans, and a variety of ducks and songbirds.

A scenic highlight of the entire recreation area is the 22-mile Hells Canyon Drive, which begins at Oxbow. Several miles of hiking trails and camping and picnic areas are available. *Park open year-round; Oxbow plant tours P.M. daily; hatchery open daily.*

22. Sumpter Valley Railroad Restoration. *At Railroad Park on Dredge Loop Rd. off Hwy. 7, five miles east of Sumpter.* Travel back to the glory of eastern Oregon's turn-of-the-century lumber and mining industry aboard the open-air cars and original caboose of this restored narrow-gauge railway, driven by an authentic wood-burning Heisler locomotive.

The Sumpter Valley Railway Company, started in 1890 by lumber magnate David Eccles, was a highly prosperous operation by the time its tracks were extended to the Sumpter gold mines in 1896. During the 1930's, however, business declined, and in 1947 the railroad, known as the Stump Dodger, ceased operation.

Since 1970 local volunteers have been restoring the track bed and offering rides through the picturesque countryside. Occasionally a run is attacked by "bandits," provided by the Baker Chamber of Commerce, who add to the colorful illusion of the Old West. While you're waiting for the trip to begin, browse through the historic photographs and railroad memorabilia in the depot's museum, or visit the engine cab, where the crew is happy to explain how the steam locomotive works. *Usually open Memorial Day–Sept. For schedule call Baker Chamber of Commerce (503) 523-5855. Admission charged.*

23. Kam Wah Chung & Co. Museum. *NW Canton St., John Day.* Here's a reminder of the days when Chinese laborers outnumbered white miners and ranchers nearly three to one in eastern Oregon. Kam Wah Chung & Co., built in the 1860's as a trading post, was bought in 1887 by two young immigrants, Lung On, a merchant, and Ing Hay, a herbalist. They lived and worked there until the

20. At the edge of this meadow of alpine firs is the deepest canyon in North America.

25. *Trumpeter swans and antelopes are among the many appealing species that thrive in the Malheur Wildlife Refuge.*

1940's, having grasped the "Golden Flower of Opportunity" implied by the store's Chinese name.

Kam Wah Chung & Co. became a center for the Chinese community: a general store, doctor's office, pharmacy, temple, gambling and opium den, and speakeasy. Today the tiny herbal dispensary is jammed with boxes, tins, and jars full of traditional remedies. The building's shrines are still hung with effigies, paper cutouts, and peacock feathers. Joss sticks and fortune sticks survive along with shriveled offerings of fruit.

And there's more: bootleg-whiskey bottles, fireworks, playing cards and dominoes, gold-mining pans and scales. There are also pieces of handmade furniture built in traditional style by members of the local Chinese community.

A visit to this well preserved place of multifarious business evokes the history of Chinatowns throughout the West. It's a cultural and historical experience that's fun. *Open Mon.–Thurs. and P.M. Sat. and Sun., May–Oct. Admission charged.*

---

24. Lake Owyhee State Park. *Thirty-six miles SW of Nyssa.* You can boat the 52-mile length of Lake Owyhee and never be more than a half-mile from its shoreline's spectacular scenery. The lake is really a reservoir backed up behind Owyhee Dam (completed in 1935). Its 310 miles of shoreline are the steep sides of the rocky

gorge through which the Owyhee River runs; its name comes from a 19th-century spelling for Hawaii (the story goes that two Hawaiians died here at the hands of Indians in 1819).

You cruise past stone pinnacles and spires, multicolored layers of bent and broken strata, soaring red-rock outcrops. Some visitors may prefer to concentrate on fishing what has been called the most overstocked and underfished lake in Oregon. Tournaments meet here to take the renowned largemouth and smallmouth bass, and there is plenty of crappie, perch, and catfish—as well as a smaller population of coho and trout.

About two miles above the dam you'll find a picnic area and campground. The rest of the shoreline is virtually inaccessible, although there are a few trails leading from the campground, and 70 miles of dirt roads (four-wheel drive only) twist through the terrain. Boaters and water-skiers should keep to the center of the lake to avoid offshore boulders. *Park open year-round; camping mid-Apr.–mid-Nov.*

---

25. Malheur National Wildlife Refuge. *Off Rte. 205, 32 miles south of Burns.* This 183,000-acre wetlands preserve, situated in desert uplands covered with sagebrush and juniper, encompasses two large, shallow lakes (Harney and Malheur) and a

number of ponds, ditches, dikes, and canals. The refuge's permanent bulrush marshes and seasonally flooded meadows provide ideal habitats for both nesting and migrating birds. The best way to see it all is by car, starting at refuge headquarters. Here the George M. Benson Museum offers an impressive array of mounted birds, from common flickers to cranes and eagles, as well as tip sheets on current bird-watching hot spots.

Spring brings pintail ducks, sandhill cranes, tundra (whistling) swans, and snow and Canada geese, and fall draws mallards and warblers as well. May and August are the prime months for songbirds. Ducks, geese, and trumpeter swans are winter stay-overs. Birds of prey spotted here include great horned owls and golden and bald eagles. Beavers and muskrats in the marshes and mule deer in the uplands are among the 58 mammal species seen.

Cross-country hiking is not allowed until August, when spring and summer nesting seasons are over. But a couple of short trails, open year-round, lead to vantage points. Flooding in the refuge's northern lowlands can limit access and require detours. It's best to call first: (503) 573-2026. *Refuge and museum open year-round; some roads may be impassable in spring and winter. Headquarters open weekdays.*

Nevada

In the land whose geologic wonders and scenic beauty now reign supreme, the ghost towns remind us how transient was the frantic quest for wealth.

Some mining camps and towns have been spruced up, while others, gone to seed, have nearly disappeared. They are, however, the unique legacy of an era, and represent the reality of dust, mud, privation, high jinks, and random violence bred by gold fever in cramped quarters where the stakes were high.

It is unlikely that many miners took time to lay down their picks and shovels to contemplate the greater wealth of the magnificent mountains, valleys, deserts, and volcanic landscapes here. As visitors soon find, there's much more to see than atmospheric ghost towns. There are otherworldly landscapes —including a cave still in the process of creation—as well as wildlife areas where hikers and horseback riders, fishermen and swimmers come for the rejuvenation that can only be found in the great outdoors.

1. Tuscarora. Tuscarora is a sleepy scattering of tumbledown buildings left over from the mining town's 19th-century heyday. They're interspersed with the shiny campers and trailers in which many of the present-day residents (fewer than 20 old-timers) prefer to live.

A visitor's first stop might be the town museum, housed in one of the original buildings along Main Street. Photographs and other memorabilia displayed here evoke Tuscarora's boomtown past, along with a collection of minerals and ore samples—many once displayed in the town saloon, the gifts of proud miners to the barkeeper. A second stop could be the Tuscarora Tavern, housed in the former Masonic and Oddfellows Hall, where in hunting season the once bustling corner of Weed and Main comes alive again.

Tuscarora, named for a Union gunboat, was founded a couple of years after the Civil War but didn't hit its stride until the big silver strike of 1876. The rush was on then, the town's hard-to-work placer mines abandoned to the large and industrious Chinese population. "It's a lively little camp," noted one reporter. "Particularly in this case on Sundays, when men charge up and down the streets on bucking mustangs, riding . . . into saloons."

Yet by the First World War mining in Tuscarora was mostly a memory, and today it is a place of dusty charm.

---

2. Unionville. Perhaps 20 people still live along the main street of Unionville, which winds nearly three miles deep into Buena Vista Canyon. The road is flanked with ruined walls and foundations that recall earlier days of hope and even, in the 1870's, a certain prosperity.

The camp was settled in 1861 by silver miners of divided loyalties: Southern sympathizers named it Dixie, but when the Northern faction gained the upper hand, they changed it to Unionville. Mark Twain came to do some prospecting the year the town was founded. But he and his partners got involved in buying up shares in dozens of other mining operations and left after a week or two.

As the mines petered out in the decades after 1880, Unionville's residents headed one by one for better diggings, until by the 1940's the town's fate was sealed. Little remained. Today, for the visitor, there's just enough: a bed-and-breakfast place surrounded by a picket fence and a garden, and at the upper end of town, a shady park with picnic tables. Bring your

own lunch—for the charm of Unionville and places like it is that you can't *do* anything, not even shop.

---

3. Giant Tufa Park. *From Lovelock take Central Avenue north 1½ miles; turn west onto Pitt Road and drive 2½ miles; turn right onto an unmarked gravel road; and continue for slightly over a mile.* Many and varied are the rock forms of the West, but none more curious in their makeup than the lumps, clumps, columns, and pillars of tufa rising from the flatlands here. To walk between and around them is like taking a trip to another planet. Some "tower" tufas are 10 to 20 feet tall, some exotically blotched with colorful patches of lichen. And on the summits of the tallest a hawk will often perch while stalking its prey.

No less fascinating than the aura of science fiction surrounding the formations are their geologic origins. At the close of the last Ice Age water rich with calcium carbonate interacted with shoreline concentrations of algae and bacteria to form tufa (from an Italian word for "soft stone"): porous, limestonelike deposits eventually sculpted by wind, waves, and

4. Unexpected in this elegant structure are the courtroom, jail, and blacksmith's shop.

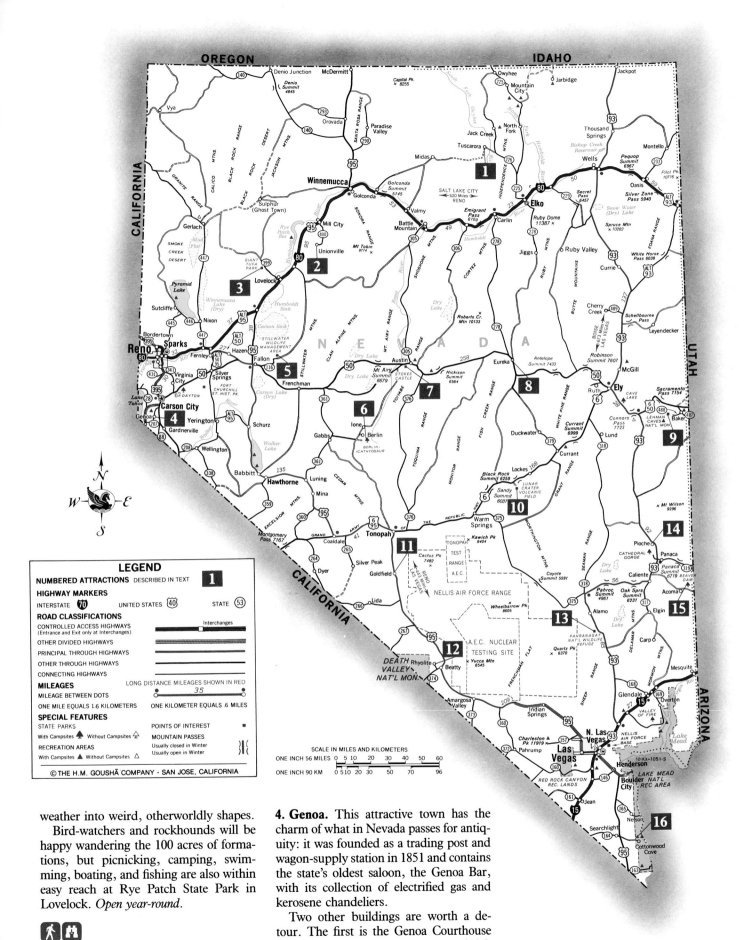

weather into weird, otherworldly shapes.

Bird-watchers and rockhounds will be happy wandering the 100 acres of formations, but picnicking, camping, swimming, boating, and fishing are also within easy reach at Rye Patch State Park in Lovelock. *Open year-round.*

4. Genoa. This attractive town has the charm of what in Nevada passes for antiquity: it was founded as a trading post and wagon-supply station in 1851 and contains the state's oldest saloon, the Genoa Bar, with its collection of electrified gas and kerosene chandeliers.

Two other buildings are worth a detour. The first is the Genoa Courthouse Museum, an elegant two-story brick

6. *For all practical purposes, the mining machinery is as extinct as the fossilized ichthyosaur shown at left.*

building dating from 1865 (like the Genoa Bar, it is said to be the oldest building of its kind in Nevada). Washo Indian artifacts and other exhibits are on display, and you can wander through the old courtroom, the original jail cells, a period kitchen, and a blacksmith's shop.

Across the street is the Mormon Station Historic State Monument, which looks like a Wild West fort but is simply a reconstruction of the 1851 log-cabin trading post and its compound. The original burned in 1910; this replica (which houses a small museum devoted to pioneer life and Nevada history) was built in 1947. You can picnic here. *Courthouse open daily, Memorial Day–mid-Oct. Mormon Station open daily, May–mid-Oct.*

5. Stillwater Wildlife Management Area. *Fallon.* The marshy remnant of an ancient inland sea, this important waterfowl food and rest stop on the Pacific Flyway is sustained by an irrigation project begun in 1948. Over 34,000 acres of marshland have been reclaimed: a vast, irregular mosaic of reeds and low, grassy peninsulas and islands that seem to float in the shallow waters. The environment changes, however, at the northern end of the management area, where there are sand dunes and flats of saltbush and greasewood.

There's fishing for catfish, bullheads, and crappies in the Indian Lakes. But the major attraction, of course, is the great number of birds that thrive in the area. Local bird species include 161 that are seen in season, 75 of which nest here. In March and April great flights of ducks stop off. Shorebirds come winging in during August and September, and hundreds of thousands of ducks put down again in October and November. Tundra (whistling) swans stay over during the winter. Variations in water level affect the bird population, but when conditions are right, as many as 15,000 young get their start in the area's marshes.

If flooding is not a problem, take the 26-mile loop drive, which goes north on Hunter Road, passing the wildlife refuge, and penetrates a large expanse of primary marsh with several places to park. Be sure to have your binoculars and camera with you. *Open year-round.*

6. Berlin–Ichthyosaur State Park. *Gabbs.* The company town of Berlin, established in 1897, is now a classic ghost town. The wood shacks and the remains of the mill and gold mine look much as they did in 1910, when the town was virtually abandoned. Except for the ranger who lives there and an occasional prospector, the town is empty. Some of the buildings have new roofs, but otherwise they show the effects of standing for some 90 years on the open hillside. Inside, a few remnants of furniture and utensils and an old bathtub reinforce the feeling that the miners just picked up and moved on.

The ranger leads tours of the town on summer weekends. If he's not there, take a self-guiding tour, following the signs that identify such sites as a miner's cabin, a boardinghouse, the stamp mill, an assay office, and a stage station. The stage driver often stayed in town on Monday nights to attend the dance at the Union Hall. When the weather was bad he shared the station with the horses.

The ichthyosaur fossils are in Union Canyon in the heart of the Shoshone Mountains, a two-mile drive from Berlin. In the fossil shelter the remains of 11 of these huge "fish-lizards" (which became extinct 70 million years ago) are shown just as they were found. Predators, despite their resemblance to today's whales and porpoises, they were the largest animals of their time, ranging up to 50 feet in length. Their remains have turned up all over the world, but these are the biggest ichthyosaurs ever excavated. If the shelter is closed, you can see these fossils through an observation window. Picnic tables are nearby, and a nature trail leads to a campground. *Both sites open year-round. Rangers on duty daily Memorial Day–Labor Day, and usually Fri.–Mon. the rest of the year. Fossil shelter open when ranger is on duty. Fee charged for tours.*

7. Stokes Castle. *Austin.* Whether or not Stokes Castle is the replica of a tower on the outskirts of Rome that locals claim it to be, it is a striking sight reminiscent of the Scottish Highlands. It stands on a promontory midway up the western flank of the Toiyabe Mountains, overlooking the Reese River valley and the far-off Shoshone Mountains.

The three-story "castle," a touching reminder of brave beginnings and lost dreams, was built in 1897 for Anson Phelps Stokes, an owner of the 92-mile Nevada Central Railroad (defunct since 1936). Stokes intended the structure as a summer retreat for his family, but they spent only a single summer there. The walls are hand-hewn granite; the floor joists, lengths of steel rail that extend to support now-vanished balconies. The flat roof was designed to serve as a terrace, and even from ground level it's easy to imagine the incomparable view (the house, now floorless and stairless, is closed to visitors). Curtains could be drawn, as in Roman houses, to shut out sun and wind.

The entrance road from Austin, a quarter-mile long, is narrow, winding, and impassable in snow: not recommended for large recreation vehicles or cars pulling trailers. But there is an RV campground in Austin, and within a 12-mile radius, a couple of Forest Service campsites. Other camping, hiking, riding, and fishing facilities are available along the area's creeks and canyons. *Open year-round.*

8. Eureka. Of the many Nevada mining towns whose fortunes have waxed and waned over the years, Eureka is a well-preserved gem with a statewide reputation. It didn't suffer the usual cycle of boom-and-bust because almost all the profits from its lead mines went to their English owners. There wasn't enough left over to build the flamboyant Victorian structures so prominent in Virginia City and elsewhere. There was always money to keep the town going, but never enough to justify tearing down and building anew.

It is a small, quiet place. The people are friendly, and you can sense in them an almost palpable pride in the restoration work lavished on buildings like the courthouse and the Jackson House.

At the courthouse, the finest building in town, you can pick up a guide map to Eureka's attractions. A major one is the Sentinel Newspaper Museum, located in what is possibly the oldest existing newspaper building in the state. It's a graceful, arcaded structure housing an old press and exhibits ranging from newspaper publishing to fire fighting by way of music. For there's an opera house in Eureka too, which, perhaps because it has never been restored (old graffiti festoon the walls), retains a special creaky charm. *Sentinel Museum open daily, June–Sept. Opera house open year-round by appointment; admission charged.*

9. Lehman Caves National Monument. *Baker.* Imagine the amazed look on Absalom Lehman's face the day in the early 1880's when he let himself down a rope into the hole he'd discovered on a rocky hillside of his ranch. His coal-oil lamp illuminated a fantastic array of elongated formations that looked as though dripping water had been frozen into solid stone. That's almost what happened, of course, and deposits carried by calcite-laden water seepage still harden into stone formations along the caves' mile-and-a-half system of tunnels and rooms.

An unhurried 90-minute tour covers two-thirds of a mile, winding past formations ranging from the expected stalactites and stalagmites to elegant, rippling drapery and the rare pallets, or shields—smooth disclike formations with streamers of flowstone. One of these, known as the Parachute because of its balanced shape, has become a symbol of the cave. Lacy, frostlike crystals of aragonite and nodules of calcite and cave coral enhance the beauty of the subterranean scene. The tour provides an eerie, inspiring experience, and a chilly one: bring a jacket.

Back aboveground, there's a picnic area, café, and gift shop near the cave entrance and visitor center, and a quarter-mile nature trail. The visitor center can supply information about the wealth of hiking, riding, and camping opportunities in the adjacent 28,000-acre Wheeler Peak Scenic Area. The monument is usually crowded on Labor Day, Easter, Memorial Day, and July 4. *Open daily except Thanksgiving Day, Christmas, and New Year's Day. Admission charged.*

10. Lunar Crater Volcanic Field. *Off Rte. 6.* As close to a moonscape as most of us will ever get, Lunar Crater and the adjacent 100 square miles of volcanic terrain are similar to features found on the moon: before the 1969 moon shot, the area was used to test lunar-expedition equipment. Thanks to the stable, dry climate here, there's been little change since the volcanic activity that began 2 million years ago ended—in geological terms, relatively recently—only a few millennia ago.

It's a fascinatingly desolate place, dotted with saltbush and greasewood. But in the years when rainfall exceeds the four- to six-inch annual average, the wildflower displays after the rainy season (about mid-May to early July) can be magnificent, particularly when globe mallow slashes the desert with scarlet.

Lunar Crater sets the scale for the field's formations: nearly four-fifths of a mile across, it's 430 feet deep. The smaller Easy Chair Crater, four miles to the north,

9. *Mineral-laden water, drop by drop, created all of these fabulous forms.*

gets its name from its situation on the edge of a tall cinder cone—together the two formations look like an overstuffed chair.

Other features in the area include The Wall, a steep face of fused volcanic ash; Lunar Lake, a shallow lake in the midst of alkali mud flats; and (two miles north of Route 6) Black Rock Lava Flow, a 1,900-acre basalt plateau.

There are no trails, but it's not difficult to hike cross-country. Remember to carry drinking water, be on the alert for rattlesnakes, and avoid hazards like abandoned mine shafts and unstable crater slopes. *Open year-round.*

11. Goldfield. When Goldfield was going strong, the streets indeed seemed paved with gold. From its founding in 1902 until 1910, it was one of the most celebrated boomtowns in the country and the largest community in Nevada. A lot of people got rich quick. Goldfield boasted banks, breweries, hospitals, newspapers, and the fanciest hotel in the West. Built in 1908 for $450,000, the 154-room Goldfield had a 22-karat gilt ceiling (still intact) in the mahogany-paneled lobby, carpets, brass

12. *The old Cook Bank expresses the height of its success and depth of failure.*

beds, and an electric elevator. Jack Dempsey sparred here, and there's a local story that Theodore Roosevelt, when he was campaigning on the Bull Moose ticket, spoke from a hotel balcony.

The gold began to run out after 1910, and the death knell was sounded in 1923, when a fire razed 52 city blocks.

Today the remnants of past glories are not so obvious, but with some patience and imagination you can get a sense of what Goldfield used to be. The place to begin is the historical society, at the Gloryhole antique and gift shop across from the Goldfield Hotel. Here you can book a tour of the hotel and obtain walking-tour maps and other brochures.

Besides the hotel, there is the courthouse, still used and well maintained, with polished woodwork and Tiffany lamps. The stone schoolhouse, though boarded up, still retains an aura of scholastic discipline. Anyone interested in things mechanical will be fascinated by the 1920's machine shop at the Brown-Parker Garage, its belt-driven machinery in perfect working condition.

12. Rhyolite and the Bottle House. When Rhyolite, one of Nevada's last great gold rush towns, was founded in 1905, the earlier Nevada mines were closing and thousands of prospectors headed here for another fling with lady luck.

During the boom years the town, with a floating population of about 16,000, had its own stock exchange, the Spanish-style railroad depot was the finest in the state, and the main street bustled with business and twinkled with electric lights. By 1911, however, it became evident that the quality and quantity of ore was less than expected. The miners and speculators began to leave as quickly as they had arrived. The census in 1910 recorded a population of 675; now it's less than 50.

One of the principal business streets, wishfully named Golden, is lined with the foundations and broken walls of once-proud stone buildings. But the train depot has been restored, and there are somewhat utopian plans afoot to restore the town. Until then, these haunting ruins stand as a unique memorial to a town that built too well too soon.

On the way into Rhyolite stands a house with walls made of 51,000 bottles (most of them Anheuser-Busch beer bottles) set in clay. When it was built in 1905,

no-deposit bottles provided a cheap alternative to lumber. Restored in 1925 for a movie setting, it is now maintained as a historic relic. The interior is a hodgepodge of curios, memorabilia, and odds and ends of household furnishings. The owner (who lives elsewhere) shows visitors through. *Bottle House open daily "if there are enough people." Admission charged.*

13. Pahranagat National Wildlife Refuge. These 5,380 acres not only provide a welcome fall and spring stop-off for waterfowl on the Pacific Flyway but also attract fishermen, birders, campers, and drivers seeking quiet just off the main highway.

The refuge is unusual here in the Nevada desert. It lies in a fertile valley watered by two natural aquifers: Ash Springs and Crystal Spring. Upper and Lower Pahranagat lakes get most of their water in the winter months. During the spring and summer, farmers in the valley divert the lakes' sources for irrigation, and the lake levels fluctuate with the seasonal supply and demand.

Come spring, finches, warblers, and orioles inhabit the cottonwood trees. Meadowlarks and blackbirds are seen in the meadows. The great blue heron rookery at the north end of the refuge usually numbers some 50 birds, including double-crested cormorants. You might see some sandhill cranes in the spring and fall and some bald eagles in the winter. The waters, which are stocked with white crappie, also yield black bullheads, carp, and Florida largemouth bass. Boats without motors (except electric) may be used on Upper Lake, Middle Pond, and Lower Lake. Boats are not allowed on North Marsh. If you are interested in Indian petroglyphs, a ranger at headquarters can tell you where to see them off the Black Canyon Road. *Open year-round.*

14. Pioche. Silver was found near Pioche as early as 1863, and after the mines opened in 1869, the settlement boomed. It also gained notoriety as a trigger-happy, lawless town, the toughest in the West. Even today, the residents of Pioche take perverse pride in pointing out that not a single one of the first 70 or so men buried

13. *In this desert setting the quiet waters of Lower Lake are appealing, even without the myriad waterfowl that often stop here.*

in the cemetery's Boot Hill died in bed. The Chamber of Commerce includes among its useful visitor brochures a list of their sensational obituaries.

The recently restored Boot Hill is one of Pioche's official "historical points of interest"; another, lawbreaking having called for justice to be done, is the so-called Million Dollar Courthouse (also restored). Costs, estimated at $26,400 in 1871, ballooned until by the time the final debt was paid off in 1937, corruption and refinancing had raised them to nearly $1 million. In 1948 the courthouse was sold at auction for $150.

In contrast to many boomtowns, Pioche thrives today, and in addition to such reminders of days gone by as the Masonic Hall (1872), Thompson's Opera House (1873), and the exhibits in the Lincoln County Museum, the town's shaded, gently winding streets afford such amenities as shops, cafés, and overnight accommodation. Pioche sponsors three annual celebrations: Burro Days (June), Heritage Days (July), and a third on Labor Day weekend; crowds can be expected. Nearby, Eagle Valley Dam, Echo Dam, and Cathedral Gorge offer picnicking, camping, fishing, and boating. *Courthouse open daily mid-May–Oct. Museum open Tues.– Sat. and P.M. Sun. year-round; admission free but donations appreciated.*

15. Beaver Dam State Park. *Caliente. Follow sign from Rte. 93. The 28-mile drive into the park, along a dirt road with steep inclines and hairpin turns, should not be attempted in bad weather. Trailers and motor homes are inadvisable.* The park's mile-high canyon landscape is one of the most rugged and remote in Nevada, but the rewards for getting there are considerable. The scenery is breathtaking. Flashing streams run through deep canyons and forests of piñon pine and juniper.

Hiking and riding are favored activities in these 203 acres, with two short interpretive trails (both under a mile) for nature lovers. There's also swimming in the 15-acre Schroeder Reservoir, and watercraft without motors are allowed. The lake is stocked with trout, and fishermen usually do quite well. There are 43 campsites scattered in the area. Be prepared for variations in temperature. After a summer's day in the 90's the 50° nights can seem amazingly cold. *Open year-round.*

16. Cottonwood Cove. Lake Mohave, created by Davis Dam on the Colorado River, has superimposed a watery area on the dry domain of the Mojave Desert here on the border of Nevada and Arizona. This juxtaposition of contrasting environ-

ments appeals to swimmers, boaters, and fishermen, and to rockhounds (who look for agate and turquoise), backcountry explorers, and other desert fanciers.

The road in from the highway cuts through a forest of cholla cactus, and at the visitor center these and other local cactus species are identified. On a nature trail you will be introduced to a number of other plants native to the desert.

There are some 100 miles of backcountry roads to be explored in the area; maps are available at the visitor center. Along the roads keep an eye out for wild burros, jackrabbits, and coyotes. The birds most often observed are roadrunners, Gambel's quail, owls, and hummingbirds. The trees that gentle the desert landscape with their welcome soft greens include cottonwoods, olives, palms, and the lovely paloverde.

Fishing for striped and largemouth bass, crappie, rainbow and cutthroat trout, and channel catfish is reported excellent. Boat rentals, including houseboats, are available at the marina. From the water you sometimes see bighorn sheep on the red bluffs of Black Canyon north of Cottonwood, or Pyramid Canyon to the south. Cottonwood Cove is usually crowded on Memorial Day weekend and Easter time. *Open year-round.*

California

For all its popularity as a travel destination, the Golden State still has many interesting and attractive out-of-the-way places to savor.

A variety of intriguing landscapes and sculptural forms, including cinder cones, spatter cones, lava tubes, caves, and lavacicles, owe their existence to volcanism. Other fanciful shapes, in clay, sandstone, and tufa, were sculpted by the forces of erosion. The sea has also shaped the land, and along the coast are tide pools to inspect and sandy stretches where nature's portable bounty of agates, shells, driftwood—and clams—can be gathered. Rocky coves are inhabited by seals and sea lions; and from the headlands whales and porpoises can be seen. On the sea-girt Channel Islands one is literally surrounded by these denizens of the deep.

Among the remarkable variety of trees that grow here are redwoods, the largest living things; bristlecone pines, the oldest living things; and the strange and wonderful Joshua trees.

Birds can be seen by the millions, as can uncountable numbers of migrating butterflies, great expanses of wildflowers, and two interesting species of elk. Mankind's contributions—from tools 200,000 years old to a model of a space station—are also to be contemplated.

1. Prairie Creek Redwoods State Park. *Orick.* Driving north on Route 101, travelers are almost certain to notice the sudden appearance of the majestic Roosevelt elk roaming Boyes Prairie near the park headquarters and visitor center.

A display at the center features a month-by-month account of the life cycle of this magnificent creature—the largest wild animal in California. Like the elk, the rest of the area's flora and fauna tends to call forth superlatives, and other equally elaborate displays do them justice: an entire room is devoted to the ecology of the mighty redwoods, for instance.

The 1,400-acre park is a preserve for these trees (*Sequoia sempervirens*), the tallest species on earth. Some specimens here soar 300 feet. They and their companion plants can be seen in closeup on more than 30 trails that range from easy to strenuous, and from one-tenth of a mile to seven miles long. Some lead down to Gold Bluffs Beach. The James Irvine Trail, for

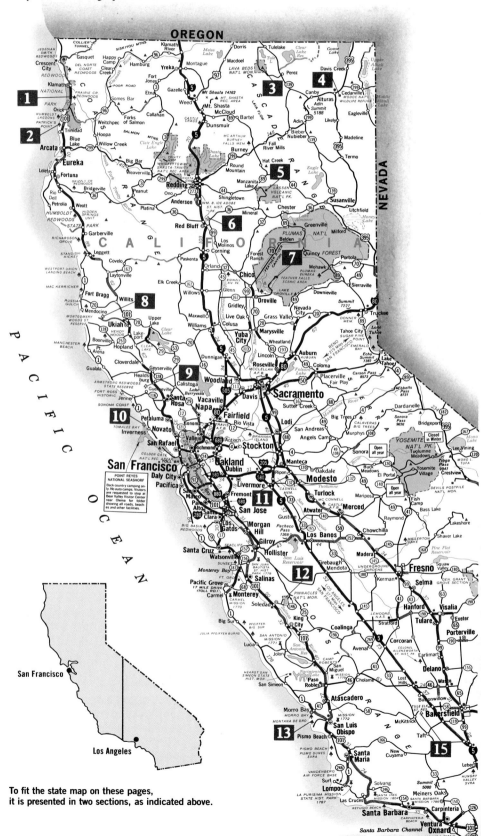

To fit the state map on these pages, it is presented in two sections, as indicated above.

example, is a 4.2-mile hike through redwoods and a lush undergrowth of hemlock, laurel, and alder. It connects with the Fern Canyon Trail, where eight species of ferns cling to the steplike ledges of the canyon wall. Frogs and Pacific giant salamanders inhabit the streambed here. A herd of elk roams the beach and should be given a wide berth. They are wild and unpredictable. You can camp at the beach or near park headquarters at Elk Prairie. *Open year-round. Admission charged.*

2. Patrick's Point State Park. Land meets sea here with dramatic results. The fringes of this headland, covered with evergreen

forests and berry- and wildflower-carpeted meadows, are battered and fragmented: worn offshore rocks called sea stacks bear testimony to the thundering, pounding force of the ocean.

In the tide pools of the "crash zone" between surf and cliff you can find sea anemones, starfish, mussels, and snails. The surf's ceaseless throb is occasionally interrupted by the hoarse, hollow call of

the California sea lions, which congregate on the rocks in great numbers.

Plenty of trails crisscross the park. Rim Trail, which begins at the campground, is an agreeable two-mile walk that affords good views of the coastline. In season (December–April) you can watch for gray whales. Agate Beach Trail leads down from the campground to Agate Beach, an agreeable sandy crescent. The ocean is too

1. *The subtle blend of colors suggests that the elk are in their native habitat.*

LEGEND

NUMBERED ATTRACTIONS DESCRIBED IN TEXT **1**

HIGHWAY MARKERS

INTERSTATE **70**   UNITED STATES **40**   STATE **53**

ROAD CLASSIFICATIONS

CONTROLLED ACCESS HIGHWAYS
(Entrance and Exit only at Interchanges)   Interchanges

OTHER DIVIDED HIGHWAYS

PRINCIPAL THROUGH HIGHWAYS

OTHER THROUGH HIGHWAYS

CONNECTING HIGHWAYS

MILEAGES   LONG DISTANCE MILEAGES SHOWN IN RED

MILEAGE BETWEEN DOTS   35

ONE MILE EQUALS 1.6 KILOMETERS   ONE KILOMETER EQUALS .6 MILES

SPECIAL FEATURES

STATE PARKS   PORTS OF ENTRY

With Campsites 🛖 Without Campsites △   Open 24 hours ⚙ Inquire Locally ⚙

RECREATION AREAS   MOUNTAIN PASSES

With Campsites ▲ Without Campsites △   Usually closed in Winter
                                         Usually open in Winter
POINTS OF INTEREST ▪

© THE H.M. GOUSHA COMPANY · SAN JOSE, CALIFORNIA

SCALE IN MILES AND KILOMETERS

ONE INCH 65 MILES   0 5 10 20 30 40 50 60 70

ONE INCH 105 KM   0 5 10 20 30 50 70   113

cold and treacherous for swimming, but this is a happy hunting ground for agate and driftwood collectors. You can fish for lingcod and sea trout off the rocks at the south end of the beach. There are several more trails, most of them steep descents to the shore or climbs to spectacular lookouts. *Open year-round. Admission charged.*

3. Lava Beds National Monument. *Off Rte. 139, south of Tule Lake.* A vast, majestic stretch of high desert ringed with purple mountains, the monument preserves the special beauty and strangeness of land marked by volcanic activity. From the northeast entrance the park road winds through scrubby sagebrush and rolling hills dotted with juniper and finally with stands of yellow pine. Jagged lava rocks, deep orange in color, lie amid the wispy sage. As the road climbs, one sees the distant snowy peaks of ancient dead volcanoes. The sky is deep blue, and the wind is scented with sage and cinders.

At the visitor center near the southeast entrance, information is available on the area's turbulent volcanic origins and its plant and animal life, and a rock garden illustrates the variety of minerals found here. An interpretive trail in the adjacent, illuminated Mushpot Cave explains lavacicles, spatter cones, balconies, and other formations found in the monument's 200 lava tube caves. More than a dozen of these are accessible from Cave Loop Road, which begins at the visitor center. If you want to explore them, the center will lend you portable lights.

The lava caves provided refuge for the Modoc Indians in the Modoc War of 1872–73, an Indian rebellion whose history is recounted at the visitor center. Petroglyphs 300 to 800 years old, found on cliffs, remind one that to the Modocs this area was the center of the world.

While you are here, take the Wildlife Refuge Tour along the northeast edge of the monument: the route overlooks Tule Lake in the Klamath Basin National Wildlife Refuge, frequented by literally millions of waterfowl in autumn. Falcons and other predators congregate along the cliffs here, including the largest number of bald eagles south of Alaska. *Open year-round.*

4. Modoc National Wildlife Refuge. *Alturas.* An expanse of golden desert with a managed system of marshes, lakes, and ponds, this 6,000-acre refuge on the Pacific Flyway is specifically designed for waterfowl, and is a bird-watcher's delight. But even the most avid birder will want to take time to savor the desert air and lively landscape surrounded by low mountains.

While geese, herons, ducks, egrets, and a variety of shorebirds and warblers are the most frequently seen here, some 220 species have been recorded. A drive around Teal Pond is a good way to see them at close range. Grassy, tufted islets dot the pond, and herons and egrets often stand motionless along their shores. Great numbers of whistling swans may also be seen gliding on the placid blue waters.

The refuge is the summer home for the largest population of sandhill cranes in California. This wading bird with blue-gray body and bright red patch on the head grows about four feet tall and is easy to spot. If birding is your special interest, April and September are the best times to see the greatest number of species.

Among the mammals seen here the year-round are rabbits, muskrats, minks, raccoons, coyotes, and mule deer. Fishing is allowed in Dorris Reservoir, and part of the refuge is set aside for seasonal hunting. *Open year-round.*

5. Butte Lake Area, Lassen Volcanic National Park. Fifty wilderness lakes lie within the shadow of Lassen Peak, but tucked away in the northeast corner of the park is a network of half a dozen that are easy to reach from the uncrowded Butte Lake Campground. Their names—Bathtub, Widow, Juniper, Horseshoe, Jakey, and Snag—all evoke a pioneer past.

It was in fact settlers following the Emigrant Trail in 1851 who discovered the just-formed cinder cone in this area. The cone's double crater is a two-mile hike from Butte Lake, much of it through ponderosa pine and fir, but the final half-mile is a steep and dusty climb through loose cinder. Views from the summit are rewardingly glorious.

For a view of the cone itself you can hike to Prospect Peak, which, at 8,338 feet, is approximately 1,400 feet taller than the cinder cone. To the west, Lassen Peak looms over all. Another trail, south-

5. Butte Lake and the cinder cone owe their existence to Lassen Peak in the distance.

7. *When a small stream changes from the horizontal plane to the vertical, the transformation can be spectacular.*

ward to Snag Lake (formed in 1851, when lava dammed Grassy Creek), skirts the base of the 1851 lava flow, a basalt formation appropriately called the Fantastic Lava Beds. *Park open year-round, but snows may close Butte Lake road in winter. Admission charged.*

6. William B. Ide Adobe State Historic Park. *Off I-5, at 21659 Adobe Road, Red Bluff.* Shaded by two towering specimens of Sacramento Valley oak, the 1850's home of William Brown Ide is a focus for year-round programs aimed at giving visitors a firsthand feel for pioneer life. Ide, fresh from Illinois, served as president of the short-lived Republic of California from June 14, 1846, when a small band of American settlers revolted against Mexican rule, until July 10, when the republic was declared a U.S. protectorate.

Two years later, with money earned in the goldfields, Ide and his sons built this house of adobe brick, faced on the outside with glossy ocher mud. The state acquired the compound in 1951, embarking on extensive restoration of the low-roofed main house, carriage house, well, smokehouse, and corral (now complete with one frisky black burro).

Typical of the living-history park programs is Adobe Day, the third Saturday in August, when visitors not only watch adobe bricks in the making but pitch in to help. Other pioneer skills and crafts are also demonstrated. *Open year-round.*

7. Feather Falls Scenic Area. *From Rte. 162, east of Oroville, turn right on Forbestown Rd.; continue to Feather Falls turnoff on left.* Gleaming as a glass skyscraper, the three tiers of Feather Falls plunge 640 feet into a rugged valley cut into the Sierra foothills. The easiest way to see the falls is to follow the signs to the scenic overlook at Bald Rock. Even from this vantage point, the base of the falls is hidden by a jutting granite hillside.

For another perspective, hikers can take the steep, rocky, but well-marked trail leading through sparse manzanita and pine chaparral to a point overlooking the churning green water at the base of the falls. Count on an afternoon to make the seven-mile round trip.

The scenic area, which encompasses 15,000 acres in the Plumas National Forest, includes a number of other hiking trails, scenic spots, and campgrounds. The three branches of the Feather River (whose middle fork is fed by the falls) afford some of the most challenging white-water rafting in the state. Downstream are calmer stretches that are fine for canoeing and swimming. *Open year-round.*

8. Montgomery Woods State Reserve. *At Ukiah, off Rte. 101, take State St. to Orr Springs Rd.* Montgomery Woods is a fine place to see giant redwoods in their primeval state. A clearing ringed with the largest trees—10 to 15 feet in diameter—opens about four-fifths of a mile along the steep loop of Memorial Grove Trail, which begins at the reserve pullout. From

a carpet of their red-brown needles, redwoods rise like temple columns, and any stage designer would envy the hazy amber light and vivid green of the ferns in this setting. Silence is deep, civilization distant. Camping is prohibited in the 1,350-acre reserve, but there are picnic tables near the creek that borders the trail.

An added aspect of the woods' appeal is the pleasure of getting there. Orr Springs Road winds through barren, rocky hills with views of rolling hills and pasturelands and glimpses of the emerald Napa and Mendocino valleys. Narrow, steep, and full of hairpin turns, the road is an exciting experience, but one should not attempt it with a trailer or mobile home in tow. *Open year-round.*

9. Armstrong Redwoods State Reserve. *Off Rte. 116 north of Guerneville.* This 700-acre reserve, dense with the noble coast redwood, was established in the 1870's by Col. James B. Armstrong, an early lumberman and conservationist. It is seen at its best from Pioneer Trail, which begins at the ranger station.

The first of the remarkable specimens here is the Parson Jones Tree: at 310 feet, taller than an upended football field. Next comes Burbank Circle, a ring of smaller trees "only" eight to ten feet in diameter. But the Armstrong Tree, farther along, soars 308 feet and measures 14½ feet across. If the frequent rain so vital to the redwoods keeps you in the car, you can still see many of the grove's landmark trees from the road.

Beyond the reserve picnic grounds the narrow road continues into the Austin Creek State Recreation Area. Here the changing altitudes in the 4,200-acre park induce changing vegetation, climaxing at the higher and drier levels in laurel, manzanita, madrona, and oak. Below them spreads a magnificent view of the redwoods and coastal mountains. Some 20 miles of trails are open to both hikers and horses. Camping and hiking facilities are excellent, birds and other wildlife abundant, wildflowers splendidly profuse in the spring. Rainy season: November to April. *Reserve and recreation area open year-round. Admission charged.*

12. *Rewards reserved for hikers only are boldly displayed here on High Peaks Trail.*

10. Tomales Bay State Park. *Turn right on Pierce Pt. Rd. off Rte. 1 beyond Inverness.* From clearings in the dense, aromatic undergrowth above the sandy crescent of Hearts Desire Beach (at the end of Pierce Point Road), there are endless views beyond the circling gulls and hawks to the golden hills across the bay. If you don't mind chilly water, you can swim here, then warm up with a hike along the Johnstone Trail at the east end of the beach: a corridor lined with huckleberry, oak, giant fern, and braids of green lichen. Or take the Indian Nature Trail at the west end to Indian Beach, where with a California fishing license you can dig for littleneck clams and the occasional giant four-pound horseneck.

Off Route 1 on the way into the park, stop at the Bear Valley Visitor Center for a wealth of information on the history, the plants, and the wildlife of Tomales Bay. A word about the weather: vital for sustaining the park's abundant vegetation through the March–September dry season are the picturesque but damp and chilly fogs that roll in the rest of the year. *Open year-round. Admission charged.*

11. Caswell Memorial State Park. *2800 S. Austin Rd., Ripon.* Entering the grove of ancient valley oaks on the banks of the Stanislaus River is like entering an oasis. The temperature in the dense green shade is often 20° below that of the dusty expanses of the surrounding San Joaquin Valley. You get a good idea here of how central California looked back in the days when valley oak *(Quercus lobata)* covered much of the region.

From the parking area sandy paths wind through underbrush that makes an excellent refuge for bright blue Steller's jays, chipmunks, squirrels, and quick little lizards. They feed on wild grapes hanging from the oaks. There are wild roses and fat wild blackberries too.

One path (marked) leads to a swimming beach. But the river, where largemouth and smallmouth bass are caught in the summertime, as well as salmon and steelheads in the autumn, is easily accessible throughout the park. Branching off the beach path, the Oak Nature Trail leads to a vantage point from which the park's great blue heron rookery can be observed through binoculars. Picnic and camping facilities abound within these 260 acres. *Open year-round. Admission charged.*

12. Pinnacles National Monument. *On Rte. 146 east of Soledad.* It's a surprise, driving through the gentle coastal hills of Monterey County, to come suddenly upon the jagged red spires and rugged canyons of Pinnacles National Monument. The rich soil here, on the weathered remains of an ancient volcano, helps support a variety of plant and animal life, and the Pinnacles' high, open terrain is well suited to hiking. There are 35 miles of tended trails against a backdrop of the endlessly changing hues and textures of eroded volcanic rock. "Wilderness treks" are for experienced hikers, cave trails for would-be spelunkers (don't forget a flashlight). Scaling the Pinnacles' sheer pink cliffs, however, demands experience and specialized equipment.

Several trailheads are accessible from Bear Gulch Visitor Center, where excellent annotated maps are available. The Moses Spring Self-Guiding Trail, for instance, climaxes with a visit to Bear Gulch Caves. Other caves lie near the Balconies Trail, reached from the western entrance to the park. Hikers who want even more of a challenge can take High Peaks Trail, a two-mile ramble among the higher reaches of the Pinnacles.

Heat can be intense in season, and weekends are crowded. The most relaxed times to use the picnic facilities and the Chaparral Campground, located in a fragrant stand of digger pine, are weekdays. *Open year-round. Admission charged.*

13. Montana de Oro State Park. This stretch of seaside plateau is known as the Mountain of Gold for the blaze of orange and yellow California poppies, monkey flowers, fiddle-necks, and gold fields that carpet its easy contours when spring arrives (in mid-April). At water's edge the land crumbles into cliffs that plunge into an abundance of rocky inlets and tide pools along the four miles of shoreline in this 7,969-acre park. At one point the shoreline edges inward to form a crescent pebble beach, a good place to set off on an investigation of the rocks and pools. The water is too cold and rough for swimming.

The beach itself is littered with treasures: sand dollars, driftwood, colored pebbles, popweed (a seaweed whose air-bubbled stems explode with a loud crack when stepped on). The pools teem with snails, limpets, sea anemones, and hermit crabs. Whale spotting is a favorite pastime from November to March, and the area is a wintertime stop for migrating monarch butterflies, which can turn entire trees into fluttering fantasies.

Add to all this year-round good weather, good picnic and camping facilities, a

13. *How artfully nature combines the globe gilia, golden eriophyllum, and mimulus.*

would be encyclopedic, but most people come to see the seals and sea lions, pelicans, and foxes, as well as the porpoises and dolphins. Whales may be seen offshore from December through March.

Anacapa is only a 90-minute boat ride from the coast; Santa Barbara lies 40 miles south. San Miguel, navy-administered, requires special visiting permits, as do Santa Cruz and Santa Rosa, the biggest and most varied of the islands but in private hands. With permits (available at the visitor center) one can hike, camp, dive, or fish. Dress to ward off penetrating sea spray and hot sun, and bring your own food and water. *Boats go to Anacapa (weather permitting) year-round; to Santa Barbara, summer only. Fare charged.*

15. Tule Elk State Reserve. *Off Stockdale Rd., Buttonwillow.* Oil derricks may seem to be the only things moving in the lazy heat that lies over the cotton fields for so much of the year in this area. But then you come to Tule Elk State Reserve, where small, shaggy elk are seen grazing. Given the top-heavy three- by four-foot span of mature antlers on adult bulls that measure only four feet from hoof to shoulder, no wonder they seem to move some-

network of easy trails—and tonic sea air mingled with the restorative scents of coastal sage and pine. *Open year-round.*

14. Channel Islands National Park. *Access from Spinnaker Dr., Ventura.* The park's mainland visitor center—which is in Ventura—provides an enticing view of what to expect and is well worth a visit. It adjoins a dock from which commercial boats depart regularly for Anacapa and Santa Barbara. Of the five Channel Islands, these two are the most easily accessible. Once the excitement of the channel crossing is over (it can be rough), the real adventure begins.

The islands, never crowded, offer an unrivaled opportunity to observe the overwhelming diversity of marine, bird, animal, and plant life sustained in the park and the surrounding National Marine Sanctuary. Any list of what to look for

14. *Anacapa Island's rocky ramparts stand firm (so far) against the relentless sea.*

Houseboating on Lake Shasta

Lake Shasta is attractive from any point of view, but to float freely on its deep green surface in a sturdy craft with all the comforts of home is to have the best of both worlds.

On our *Flagship 6* houseboat, here am I at the helm, recently promoted by a dockside briefing from landlubber to captain of all we survey. There's a slight breeze, the air is fresh and sweet, the lake sparkles, green-clad mountains slope to the water's edge, and rising serenely in the near distance is the gleaming white summit of Mount Shasta.

Motoring past the many inlets and coves, we soon understand how Shasta can have 370 miles of shoreline. And on seeing the anglers in action we readily believe the claim that 17 species of fish are in residence here.

After an hour or so under way, we find a pleasant stretch of open water, cut the engine, secure the helm, and in the boatman's vernacular "let her drift." A blessed silence descends, and we become at one with our surroundings. From the topside sundeck the surrounding mountains are perfectly reflected in the water, space recedes in all directions, and nothing moves but an occasional soaring hawk. The blue water is inviting and the temptation to dive from the rooftop is irresistible. Ladders on the decks fore and aft make it easy to get back on board.

Between these two spacious decks is the cabin. There's a dinette with a picture window—view guaranteed—a range, refrigerator, sink, ice chest, barbecue grill, and cabin heater. The head has a shower, sink, and toilet. In the sleeping area are upper and lower double bunks, and the dinette converts to a bed for two. Other models sleep 10. All necessary linens, dishes, utensils, and safety equipment are supplied. One could hardly ask for more.

Before starting out we had studied the chart and conferred with the concessionaire to find destinations where we could hike, and where we could avoid the noise and commotion inherent in the sport of waterskiing, which is very popular here. We finally decided on Frenchman Gulch. Mooring our craft according to instructions, we have a leisurely dinner and do some serious stargazing from the top deck before turning in. The next morning a short hike to Green Mountain stimulates a hearty appetite for breakfast.

This lazy pattern of motoring, drifting, swimming, reading, sunbathing, listening to our stereo-cassettes—and eating and snacking more frequently (and hiking less) than we had planned—ends all too soon.

We head back to home port with mixed emotions. Here we are floating above thousands of acres of once-magnificent woodlands, the habitat of countless plants and animals. Places where the Indians roamed are gone forever, and the old boomtown of Kennit lies deep under water. Much has been sacrificed in the name of progress; even so we cannot deny the pleasures that the lake affords. —*B. Roether.*

For reservations call (213) 691-2235

what gingerly. They also often click their antlers in a dancelike rhythm, or otherwise communicate in strange blowing sighs or grunts.

There are some 35 of these engaging animals in the reserve herd, but tule elk were once so plentiful in the formerly rich San Joaquin Valley floodplains that Sir Francis Drake described them as appearing to "flow from the foothills to the seas." Then 19th-century ranchers encroached on their grasslands, and hunters and traders shot them for fur, food, and tallow. By 1874 their numbers were down to a single pair. Intensive conservation efforts, however, have increased the national population to a reassuring 1,500.

The elk are sensitive to scrutiny, so quiet is advisable. Some of the best viewing can be had in the summer, when they love wallowing in their water hole, or in the cool spring, when they are friskier. Fortunately, their feed trough is near the viewing-area fence. *Open year-round.*

16. Mono Lake Tufa State Reserve. *Lee Vining*. Mark Twain called the fantasy landscape of Mono Lake a "sullen, silent, sail-less sea," and indeed the 700,000-year-old lake, formed during the last Ice Age, is three times saltier than the ocean and has a forbidding mien. It is fed by melting snow and underwater springs and dotted with dramatic and intricately fili-greed white limestone towers, knobs, and spires produced when calcium-laden fresh water wells up through alkaline lake water, precipitating calcium carbonate, or tufa. As the lake level drops (through natural evaporation), and as freshwater sources are diverted to provide drinking water for the Los Angeles area, the lake bed's tufa formations are exposed.

No fish can live in the concentrated minerals and salts of Mono Lake, but brine shrimp and brine flies thrive in the trillions (*mono* is the Yokut Indian word for "fly"). They provide food for the thousands of gulls and other migratory birds that flock here in spring and summer.

The lake's South Tufa area features a one-mile nature trail that clearly explains the lake and its peculiarities. Other attractions in this immense reserve (17,000

18. Here's architecture without an architect—which can frequently be the best kind.

acres) include exceptionally buoyant swimming at nearby Navy Beach, boating, and if you arrive at the right time—dusk, say—a glimpse of the awesome alpenglow, the strange phenomenon of reflected light that bathes the High Sierra with rose and gold long after the sun's rays have vanished. *Open year-round.*

17. Ancient Bristlecone Pine Forest. *Big Pine*. Suspended eerily on the rugged slopes of the White Mountains, at an altitude of 10,000 and more feet, is a stand of one of the planet's oldest living trees: the bristlecone pine (*Pinus longaeva*). The most ancient specimen is the 4,700-year-old Methuselah, which stands in a grove of pines growing here for 4,000 years or more. It can be found about a 4½-mile walk beyond the Schulman Grove Information Center. Twelve miles farther along the road that crosses the forest is the world's largest bristlecone pine. Here in the Patriarch Grove, at 11,000 feet, is the Old Patriarch itself, which measures more than 36 feet in circumference.

The bristlecones' tortured shapes reflect the barren, windswept conditions amid which they persevere, jutting out from the mountainside like bleached bones or driftwood. Many branches appear dead, while others are thickly furred with green needles. Drippings of clear, bluish sap perfume the air. For all the seeming aridity of the land, there are lovely stands of wildflowers in the Patriarch area in August.

In most weather conditions, the steep road to the forest provides breathtaking views across Owens Valley to the sheer white face of the Sierra Nevada. But after big snowfalls, cars must turn back at Sierra Vista lookout, which is at an elevation of 10,000 feet. In good weather, take advantage of miles of trails and picnic grounds beautifully sited in and around this great forest. *Open year-round, but road closed to vehicles beyond the Piñon picnic area (elevation 7,500 feet), Dec.–mid-May.*

18. Wildrose Charcoal Kilns and Mahogany Flat, Death Valley National Monument. *Off Rte. 190, take either Emigrant Canyon Rd. or Panamint Valley Rd.* At Wildrose Ranger Station a narrow and sometimes treacherous gravel track climbs through Wildrose Canyon to Thorndike Campground at 7,500 feet, near which looms a strange colony of what look like giant beehives or prehistoric dwellings. These are the Wildrose Charcoal Kilns, 10 perfectly aligned stone-and-mortar structures some 30 feet in diameter at the base and rising to a height of about 25 feet. They were built in the 1870's to turn local juniper and piñon pine into charcoal for the lead and silver ore smelters near the Modoc and Minnietta mines. Nobody has used the kilns for at least a century, but their sooty, conical interiors remain architecturally and acoustically fascinating. When you speak inside one, the echo seems to come from many places at once.

17. Sun-bleached deadwood on the living tree records its struggle for life.

A mile beyond the kilns lies Mahogany Flat (with campground), the site of a thick forest of sinewy mountain mahogany, and the trailhead for the strenuous eight-mile climb to Death Valley's highest point, Telescope Peak (11,049 feet). *Open year-round, weather conditions permitting; check with park ranger.*

19. Red Rock Canyon State Park. The smoothly sculpted clay, sandstone, lava, and tuff formations in the canyon form a natural divide between the Sierra Nevada and the Mojave Desert. At Red Cliffs Preserve (on the eastern side of Route 14, which runs for about seven miles through the park), erosion has carved the stone into corrugated ripples whose shades range from pristine white to peppermint-candy reds. The entire area is a geological treasure-house, but rockhounds may be happiest in Opal Canyon (first right after Red Cliffs Preserve); the local miners can provide opal-hunting tips.

At Red Cliffs, where the bluffs crumble into dunes, Joshua trees offer shelter to the ubiquitous jackrabbits. Much rarer (and slower) and well worth looking for are desert tortoises, the official state reptile. You can glimpse them here from March into June, when they venture out of their burrows morning and evening.

On the opposite side of the highway from Red Cliffs loom the appropriately named and colonnaded White House Cliffs. A campground nestles beneath their white walls, and Hagen Canyon Preserve Trail—for hikers only—commences at the nearby ranger station. There are, however, many other sandy tracks suitable for horses, and a few are open to cars.

Despite such easy accessibility, the park's reaches are usually so invitingly empty that it's hard to believe Los Angeles's teeming millions are only a few hours distant. *Open year-round.*

20. Mojave River Valley Museum. *Barstow Rd. at Virginia Way, Barstow.* Situated at the heart of the Mojave region, the museum is packed with a miscellany of objects related to valley history and geology. Ancient Indian artifacts stand next to models of NASA space stations. There's a large section devoted to the Calico Early Man Archeological Site discoveries, including 200,000-year-old chipped stone tools. Dr. Louis Leakey, among others, believed that the Mojave may be one of the earliest sites of human habitation in the New World, and until his death in 1972 he supervised the Calico dig.

Material from other archeological sites is on display, including the 15-million-year-old bones of a three-toed horse at the Barstowian fossil beds and the teeth of a 15-million-year-old camel. There are also objects from the Chemehuevi Indian culture, and a gruesomely fascinating case containing the remains of a mysterious "headless horseman" and the rusting weapons that apparently belonged to him. Collections of precious and semiprecious stones provide milder excitement for rock lovers (the mineralogy exhibits also include borax miners' tools and artifacts).

A block from the museum is the Barstow Way Station, an information center where tours of the Calico Early Man Site can be arranged. *Open year-round.*

21. Providence Mountains State Recreation Area and Mitchell Caverns Natural Preserve. For 16 miles leading north from Route 40, a glistening blacktop is the sole evidence of human intrusion into this windswept desert vista, rimmed on the horizon by the jagged Providence Mountains. The views as you climb have a calm, eerie quality and a rare dimension of spaciousness and mystery. The road ends at a primitive campground and visitor center on the side of a 4,330-foot mountain.

From here tours of the Mitchell Caverns are conducted by a ranger who points out interesting features along the three-quarter-mile trail, which is steep and rocky but offers fantastic scenery. Wooden doors in the mountainside admit visitors to two of the caverns, illuminated to set off the calcite formations.

Most of the park's 5,250 acres are open for hiking, and in this clear atmosphere many amateur astronomers set up their telescopes for days at a time. But remember that water is scarce and the nights are cold. Wildflowers are a major attraction in March and April, but the desert blooms in September too. Checklists of the area's plants, birds, amphibians, and reptiles are available. Rattlesnakes are common, so be on the lookout. *Open year-round. Cave tours daily, mid-Sept.–mid-June.*

22. Even the smallest Joshua trees (in background) proclaim their distinctive character.

23. *Similar natural forces have shaped the sculptured sandstone and the Torrey pines.*

cific winds. Mojave yucca and mission manzanita also thrive here. The sandy track of Razor Point Trail, which begins near the handsome old adobe visitor center, winds its fragrant way seaward among a profusion of trees and other plants.

From the smooth red stone of Razor Point itself, the loftiest spot in the reserve, there are spacious views of the pines, Los Penasquitos Marsh, and the graceful sweep of the beach—protected and warm the year-round. Another path descends rugged yellow cliffs to Flat Rock, sometimes frequented by surfers. Dolphins can frequently be seen from the beach, and in season (December through March), gray whales. *Open year-round. Parking fee.*

24. Anza-Borrego Desert State Park.
Ocotillo. Only the toughest plants and animals survive in this 600,000-acre section of the Colorado Desert, with its bleached sands and desolate landscape of eroded ridges. The campground in the Bow Willow area makes an agreeable headquarters: never crowded, it's only about 10 miles from the park's southern entrance. You can stroll in any direction through open sand and savor unimpeded vistas beneath the dome of a turquoise sky.

Nearby trails, more ambitious, skirt the Carrizo Badlands on the park's eastern edge, or to the west, lead into Bow Willow Canyon along the route the Kumeyaay Indians followed to the uplands in the spring. Evidence of these vanished people (their village sites and petroglyphs) is scattered throughout the park.

Just north of Bow Willow Canyon, near Mountain Palm Springs, the scene changes at the Palm Bowl, where a magical ring of more than 100 palms could be a vision from the *Arabian Nights.* Look for rare specimens of the squat elephant tree near here too: it has the gray, wrinkly appearance of an elephant's trunk. If you drive still deeper into the park, stop at Agua Caliente Hot Springs, which are fed into scrupulously clean, covered swimming pools, or penetrate northward as far as the elaborate visitor center at Borrego Springs. It's an excellent introduction to exploring the rest of this vast and enormously varied park. *Open year-round.*

22. Joshua Tree National Monument.
Twentynine Palms. Here is the very essence of the desert: clear skies; crisp, clean, sparkling air; and some half-million acres of fascinating landforms, plants, and animals. The area is in fact the conjunction of two deserts—the Colorado to the east and the higher, cooler, and moister Mojave in the western part of the monument, where the Joshua trees grow.

These strange trees—with their shaggy bark resembling a pelt of rough fur and their contorted branches bearing clusters of spiny leaves—could hardly be imagined, but once seen, they can never be forgotten. Great jumbled mounds of gigantic rounded boulders appear randomly among the trees, adding to the surreal character of the landscape.

Don't miss Keys View, at the end of a paved road from Ryan Campground. Here a serene expanse of purple and gray mountains fills the horizon, the valleys below lost in olive and amber shadow.

At the monument's northeast entrance is the Oasis Visitor Center, where there is indeed an oasis—Twentynine Palms.

From the center a road heads south through the Colorado Desert, where cholla cactus and scarlet-flowering ocotillo thrust their thorny limbs above patches of creosote bushes, the prevailing form of plant life here. Near the south entrance a four-mile trail beginning at Cottonwood Spring (a man-made oasis bird-watchers will find rewarding) leads to Lost Palms, the largest of the monument's four oases. There are nine campgrounds, mainly in the central section of the monument, and a variety of hiking trails. Water is scarce, so bring your own. *Open year-round.*

23. Torrey Pines State Reserve and State Beach.
Torrey pines, which grow only here and on Santa Rosa Island, far to the north, cover the reserve's rocky headland like dense green jade set against golden sandstone. They extract moisture from fog and mist through exceptionally long needles and have an extensive root system that holds them firm against the fierce Pa-

Alaska

Essence of wilderness: mountains, valleys, and fjords; realm of glaciers, icebergs, bears, and eagles—where nature reigns supreme.

For most residents of the so-called lower 48, all of Alaska is off the beaten path. But the relatively few roads and accessible places are all in fact quite well known. Facilities are limited, and reservations should be made well in advance.

What people come for is the indescribably magnificent scenery, the abundance and variety of wildlife—on land and sea and in the air—and the near-mystical aura created by such vast reaches of wild, uninhabited space. Hikers can explore many facets of the wilderness—from tide pools to rain forests and glaciers—and observe unparalleled concentrations of the dominant birds and animals.

Excellent museums document the history of the state and feature the totem poles, masks, and other ceremonial objects for which the native peoples are justly famous. The early Russian presence is evidenced by some handsome churches; the gold rush days are specifically recalled; and historic military installations can be visited, as well as a lush valley where 75-pound cabbages are the norm.

1. Kotzebue. A tour of this Eskimo town north of the Arctic Circle includes a visit to its colorful waterfront, an introduction to the surrounding flowery tundra, and a visit to the Living Museum of Arctic Culture. The museum, one of the state's most sophisticated, helps to explain and maintain the unique Eskimo traditions. Authentic Eskimo dances are given, and visitors can participate in a lively blanket toss. This seemingly playful exercise originated as a technique for lifting hunters up to look for game in the flat, treeless terrain. Outside are a replica of an Eskimo sod igloo and the frame of a skin boat.

In the same building as the museum is a factory where the natives carve blocks of jade into jewelry, figurines, and other items. The jade is quarried at distant Jade Mountain by the local native corporation and barged to Kotzebue.

The museum building also contains the National Park Service offices from which Kobuk Valley National Park, the Noatak National Preserve, and Cape Krusenstern National Monument are administered.

Each of these wildernesses can be reached by aircraft from Kotzebue.

In the Kobuk Valley are archeological sites that provide evidence of human habitation here 12,500 years ago. Here, where the climate and archaic flora still approximate the glacial period, the Great Kobuk Sand Dunes cover 25 square miles, with dunes up to 100 feet high and summer temperatures reaching 100° F.

Noatak National Preserve contains the largest complete river system in the United States to remain unaltered by man; it has been declared a UNESCO International Biosphere Reserve.

At Cape Krusenstern are some 114 beach ridges laid down successively over the past 5,000 years, each one a repository of artifacts that together form a chronology of Eskimo culture in Arctic prehistory. *Museum open daily late May–mid-Sept.*

2. Pribilof Islands. More than a million fur seals on the beaches and 2.5 million seabirds on easy-to-observe nesting cliffs comprise one of the most wondrous wildlife spectacles in North America. Two of the volcanic Pribilof Islands, St. Paul and St. George, 270 miles out in the Bering Sea, are inhabited by Aleuts, whose ancestors were brought here by Russians to kill seals for their pelts. Today the Aleuts provide food and lodging for tourists, who fly in on days when the fog is not too thick for landings. Blinds are available from which to watch the bull, cow, and pup seals interact, all barking and roaring loudly.

Neither is it quiet on the cliffs, where bird-watchers have close-up views of unafraid black-legged kittiwakes, tufted and horned puffins, red-faced cormorants, common and thick-billed murres, and three species of auklet. The red-legged kittiwakes, which also nest on the cliffs, are rarely seen away from the Pribilofs. *Accessible early June–late Aug. For information and reservations call (800) 426-0600.*

4. Caribou stands its ground with the snowy mass of Mount McKinley in the distance.

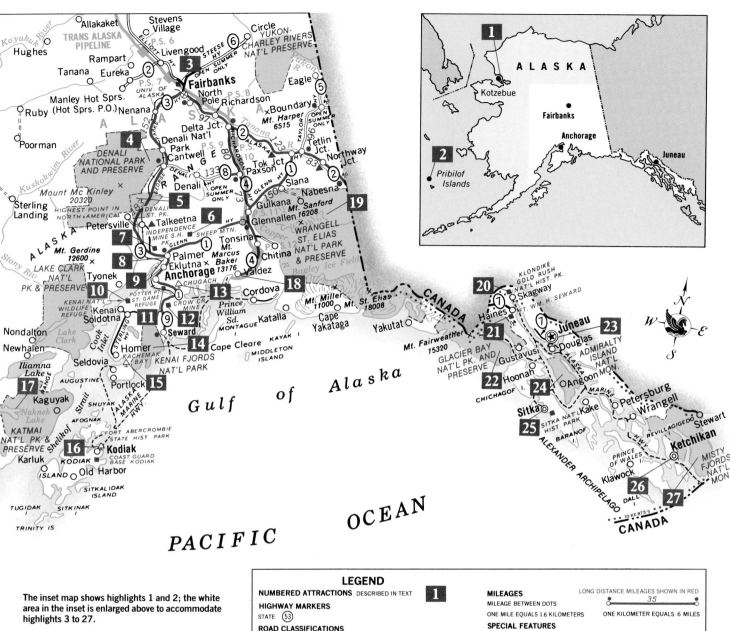

ALASKA

The inset map shows highlights 1 and 2; the white area in the inset is enlarged above to accommodate highlights 3 to 27.

SCALE IN MILES AND KILOMETERS

ONE INCH 128 MILES 0   50   100   150

ONE INCH 206 KM 0   50   100   240

LEGEND

NUMBERED ATTRACTIONS DESCRIBED IN TEXT   **1**

HIGHWAY MARKERS

STATE   (53)

ROAD CLASSIFICATIONS

PRINCIPAL THROUGH HIGHWAYS

OTHER THROUGH HIGHWAYS

© THE H.M. GOUSHA COMPANY · SAN JOSE, CALIFORNIA

MILEAGES   LONG DISTANCE MILEAGES SHOWN IN RED

MILEAGE BETWEEN DOTS   ●――― 35 ―――●

ONE MILE EQUALS 1.6 KILOMETERS   ONE KILOMETER EQUALS .6 MILES

SPECIAL FEATURES

STATE PARKS   POINTS OF INTEREST   ■

With Campsites ▲   Without Campsites △

RECREATION AREAS   PORTS OF ENTRY

With Campsites ▲   Without Campsites △   Open 24 hours ⚓   Inquire Locally ⚓

3. University of Alaska. *Fairbanks. From University Avenue, which becomes Farmers Loop Road, turn into campus on Taku Drive. Large Animal Research Station is Mile 1 Yankovich Road, reached by way of Ballaine Road from Farmers Loop.* Modern sculpture, a Russian blockhouse, hard-rock mining equipment, and a nature trail surround the new university museum. Here superb exhibits explain aspects of Alaska's wildlife, geology, and history, as well as the culture and crafts of the native peoples. A unique display is an Ice Age bison that was well preserved in perma-nently frozen ground for 36,000 years be-fore it was unearthed by gold miners.

Other Ice Age creatures still very much alive—musk oxen, moose, caribou, and reindeer—are pastured at the university's Large Animal Research Station. These animals can be watched from an elevated platform that gives an unobstructed view of the area. Binoculars are recommended.

The subarctic agricultural research gardens of the university experimental farm demonstrate the productiveness possible when there are 20 hours of summer day-light. Sandhill cranes can be seen feeding in the experimental fields. *University open year-round. Museum open daily May–Sept.; P.M. daily Oct.–Apr. except Thanksgiving Day, Christmas, and New Year's Day; ad-mission charged.*

4. Denali National Park and Preserve. Alaska's best-known attraction, this park was created as Mount McKinley National Park in 1917, primarily to protect the Dall sheep and other wild animals. Mount Mc-

Kinley, the highest peak in North America (20,320 feet), is usually wreathed in clouds, but this remains one of the nation's most magnificent parks, and perhaps the easiest place in Alaska to observe a variety of wildlife.

To avoid undue disturbance of the animals, private vehicles are banned from the park road most of the year unless they are headed for a reserved campground spot or one of the private lodges at the end of the road. The best way to see the park is via the free shuttle bus from Riley Creek Visitor Center. Along the 85-mile park road, which traverses a glorious natural tapestry of stunningly colorful tundra wildflowers and offers marvelous scenery, visitors are likely to spot Dall sheep on Igloo Mountain, grizzlies (brown bears) at Sable Pass and many other sites, moose along the eastern section of the road, caribou, hoary marmots, Arctic ground squirrels, and Alaska's state bird, the willow ptarmigan. Less common but not unusual are sightings of red foxes and golden eagles. It is a rare privilege to see wolves; but other canines, the park's sled dogs, used for winter patrols, demonstrate their work three times daily from Memorial Day to Labor Day. *Open year-round. Park road passable only in summer and early fall.*

5. Denali State Park. *George Parks Hwy. (Hwy. 3).* The Tanaina word for Mount McKinley was *Denali,* "the great one." The peak itself was named in 1896 for the presidential nominee, William McKinley, but this 324,420-acre park is called by the Indian name. From the highway bisecting the park, particularly from the Ruth Glacier overlook, you can see the snow-mantled upper slopes of the great mountain and its companion peaks and the many glaciers flowing from them. But in summer, clouds veil Mount McKinley's soaring summit most of the time.

Nonetheless, with the perpetual snow line at just 8,000 feet, the other white-topped peaks of the Alaska Range create magnificent views along the highway and park hiking trails. Byers Lake is the center of most recreation in the park. A five-mile trail circles the lake and provides hiking access to another scenic path up Curry Ridge. Black bears and grizzlies inhabit the park, together with moose, wolves, and smaller mammals such as foxes, lynx,

8. *Barren mountains contrast with the fields and meadows of the Matanuska Valley.*

and beavers. Bears can be troublesome along Troublesome Creek Trail, when they gather here for the salmon that spawn in July and August. All posted precautions regarding bears should be carefully followed. *Open year-round.*

6. Sheep Mountain. *Mileposts 107 to 123 on Glenn Hwy.* Dall sheep, cousins of the Rocky Mountain bighorn, are easy to spot here, for in spring and summer their white coats stand out sharply against the green vegetation or rust and yellow rocks of this highly mineralized mountain just north of the highway.

The sheep are most numerous in early and late summer. If you don't have a good pair of binoculars, you might want to use the viewing telescope at Sheep Mountain Lodge (Milepost 113.5). From Caribou Creek (Milepost 107) a hiking trail winds up the 6,300-foot mountain, and you can look down on the valley from the sheep's perspective. *Road passable year-round.*

7. Independence Mine State Historic Park. *Seventeen and a half miles along Fishhook-Willow Rd. (10 miles unpaved) from Glenn Hwy.* Hard-rock mining—in this case wresting ore from the heart of a mountain—is a difficult operation, as evidenced by these gold mine buildings,

ruined and reconstructed, perched above the tree line in the Talkeetna Mountains.

The first lode claim in the Willow Creek drainage area was staked in 1906 in the quartz veins high along the west side of Fishhook Creek, and became the Alaska Free Gold Mine; nearby claims, staked on the east side of Granite Mountain in 1908, became the Independence Mine.

By 1938 both mines were controlled by the Alaska-Pacific Consolidated Mining Company. In 1941, its biggest year, the 200-man camp produced gold worth $1,686,790. Second only to Juneau's AJ Mine in producing hard-rock Alaskan gold, Independence brought forth a total of 10,300 pounds before closing in 1951.

In 1980 new gold mining nearby stimulated the creation of the state historic park here and the renovation of the existing buildings. The red-roofed mine manager's house, restored to its 1942 appearance, has old photos, artifacts, a simulated gold mine tunnel, and displays showing how the gold was extracted, milled, and shipped. Other buildings include mess halls, bunkhouses, the sheet-metal shop, and the old assay office, now a hard-rock mining museum. *Park open year-round. Visitor center open Wed.–Sun., June–mid-Sept.; weekends rest of the year.*

8. Matanuska Valley. *Palmer.* Nineteen hours of summer sun and loamy soil promised rich harvests when the federal government established the Matanuska Valley Colony in 1935. In May of that year, 203 families who had lost their farms in the economic turmoil of the Great Depression were selected to go north to build new lives. Most of them came from Minnesota, Michigan, and Wisconsin, where they were assumed to have become familiar with farming in very cold climates. Some of the colonists failed, but others were successful. Many of the latter, or their children, still live in the Matanuska Valley, and a few are still on their original farms. Some of the original structures from the pioneer colony, including a church and a typical barn, have been moved to Colony Village on the Alaska State Fairgrounds at Palmer.

More significant as a memorial are the lush crops flanking the country roads backed by rugged mountains. If you happen to be here for the state fair in August, you'll see Matanuska Valley cabbages weighing in at 75 pounds or more. The Matanuska Glacier, one of Alaska's largest, can be viewed from Mile 100 on the Glenn Highway, 58 miles east of Palmer. *Accessible year-round.*

9. Eklutna. The name of this small Tanaina Indian village means "mouth of river between two hills," but today it is tucked away beside the active Glenn Highway. Here is the St. Nicholas Russian Orthodox Church, the second oldest in Alaska, built in Anchorage in the 1830's and later moved to its present location. What makes this place especially distinctive are the brightly painted "spirit houses" that mark the graves in the churchyard. Some of the little structures are multistoried and some have glass windows; they contain a variety of objects that belonged to the deceased but have no letters or dates to identify the dead person. Rather, each spirit house follows a particular family's design, and this is how the parishioners know who is buried where. A tiny, hand-hewn log prayer chapel also stands in the churchyard.

10. Kenai National Wildlife Refuge. This refuge used to be called Kenai National Moose Range. Although the name has changed, there are still thousands of these fascinating animals (the largest of which can weigh 1,400 pounds) roaming the area. They are most commonly seen along the Swanson River and Skilak Loop roads (both gravel), and smaller roads that branch from the Sterling Highway.

Some 1,200 lakes spangle this wilderness of nearly 2 million acres. Many, such as Bottenintnin Lake, reflect the Kenai Mountains, glacier-accented peaks on the refuge's boundary with Kenai Fjords National Park. Large, graceful trumpeter swans glide across the lakes, and the haunting call of the loon can be heard.

Dall sheep and mountain goats are common above a marked observation point near Kenai Lake, on the Sterling Highway east of the refuge boundary. Beluga whales are often seen from Fort Kenay Overlook, above the mouth of the Kenai River in the town of Kenai.

Waterproof boots are suggested for hikers, for many of the 200 miles of trails are often swampy. Berry picking is popular in late summer and fall. Designated canoe routes wind along the refuge river and lake system, and chartered floatplanes provide access to some of the lovely remote lakes. *Open year-round.*

11. Potter Point State Game Refuge. *New Seward Hwy. (Hwy. 1), 12 miles south of downtown Anchorage.* This bird-watching area within Alaska's largest city is host to trumpeter swans, bald eagles, Canada geese, ducks, gulls, terns, and shorebirds, as well as mink, muskrats, and salmon. Migrating birds make spring the best time to visit, but wildlife enthusiasts with cameras and binoculars will likely be rewarded at any time of the year.

The refuge attracts its many species of birds primarily because there are four distinct habitats within the 2,300 acres. Geese are drawn to the salt marsh along Turnagain Arm. Mallards and other ducks flock to the freshwater marsh created in 1917, when the Alaska Railroad was constructed and its roadbed became a dike. Muskegs in the transition area between marsh and dryland harbor snipe, grouse, and sandpipers. Such deciduous trees as birch, alder, willow, and cottonwood support warblers, thrushes, and other songbirds in the wooded areas. And of course these habitats each support a distinctive community of plants. The refuge is served by Anchorage's bus system, and there are turnouts overlooking Potter Marsh. *Open year-round.*

9. In this Russian Orthodox churchyard, the "spirit houses" serve as grave markers.

12. Crow Creek Mine. *Along Crow Creek Rd., which branches off Alyeska ski area road 1.9 miles from junction with Seward Hwy. (Hwy. 1).* Placer gold mining began on Crow Creek around 1895; at its peak the area produced more than 700 ounces per month. Although owner Cynthia Toohey maintains that there is still more gold available than ever was removed, her mine has not been operated commercially in more than 20 years. Visitors from all over the world, however, still pan for "color" here, and half-ounce nuggets may still be found glittering in the gravel. All the necessary gold-panning equipment can be rented at the mine.

Listed in *The National Register of Historic Places*, the mine preserves its original equipment and buildings, which were the first non-Indian structures in the Anchorage area. Today, the rugged authenticity of the site is softened somewhat by the mine's beautiful flower gardens. They splash bright color against the dark greens of the surrounding spruce and hemlock rain forest—a welcome function today, but one the old-timers, feverishly panning for color of another kind, would probably have found incomprehensible. *Open daily spring through fall. Admission charged.*

---

13. Chugach State Park. This awesome wilderness in the Chugach Mountains, almost half a million acres of jagged peaks and alpine meadows, lakes, glaciers, and marshy tidal flats, shelters an abundant variety of wildlife. Its outstanding trails include part of the Old Iditarod Trail, used by dogsled teams to speed diphtheria serum to Nome in 1925. The segment of the trail outside the park is part of the course for the grueling Iditarod Dogsled Race, held annually in commemoration. Although the trails are easily accessible from heavily populated Anchorage, they are sufficiently numerous to remain peaceful even in summer.

Wildlife here includes beluga whales seeking fish in Turnagain Arm (an inlet of spectacular beauty) and mountain goats scaling the nearby precipices. Telescopes at the Eagle River Visitor Center (reached from the Glenn Highway) focus on surrounding steep slopes where Dall sheep and black bears are normal sightings. Moose are plentiful, and there is a salmon-viewing deck a short way down a fine nature trail that begins at the attractive log visitor center.

The altitude in the park ranges from sea level to 8,000 feet, and the annual rainfall

from 70 inches in the east to 15 inches in the west. The resulting climatic zones nurture an astonishing and beautiful variety of trees, shrubs, wildflowers, lichens, and mosses. *Open year-round.*

---

14. Kenai Fjords National Park. The gateway to the 580,000 acres of glaciers, mountains, ice fields, and some of the world's most spectacular coastline is the picturesque town of Seward. The park offers easy access to the groaning spires and ice-blue tongues of Exit Glacier, and to Bear Glacier, the largest of the more than 36 named glaciers flowing from the broad Harding Ice Field, and a popular destination for kayakers.

But the main attractions here are the deep, narrow fjords, which can be viewed on day-long boat trips from Seward. From scenic Resurrection Bay the boats pass tide-carved Three Hole Arch and enter Aialik Bay, where bald eagles dive for fish. At Chiswell Islands, in the Alaska Maritime National Wildlife Refuge, as many as 63,000 seabirds may nest, including black-legged kittiwakes, tufted and horned puffins, and black oyster catchers

with carrotlike bills. Sea mammals often seen in the fjords include harbor seals and Steller's sea lions, killer and humpback whales, porpoises, and sea otters. *Park open year-round. Boats run mid-May–mid-Sept.; fare charged. For information and reservations write P.O. Box 881, Seward, Alaska 99664, or call (907) 224-3664.*

---

15. Kachemak Bay State Park. Wild and undeveloped, this 120,000-acre park offers majestic peaks, glaciers, and forests, and a rugged coastline with tides among the highest in the world. Access is by boat or floatplane from the fishing community of Homer across the bay.

Perhaps the best introduction to the park's ecology is on a boat tour conducted by the China Poot Bay Society to their Center for Alaskan Coastal Studies. Twice daily a tour boat leaves Homer for a 45-minute ride to Gull Island, nesting site for thousands of puffins, murres, gulls, and cormorants. On the way, sightings of sea mammals (sea otters, seals, porpoises, whales) are common. The tour pauses near a bald eagle nest in a spruce tree atop a wave-battered cliff.

14. *Among the many marvels in the park are the icebergs spawned by Bear Glacier (above) and the Steller's sea lions disporting themselves on the sea stacks in the fjord.*

At the center in Peterson Bay, a naturalist leads an exploration of pools teeming with life—giant sunflower starfish, bright sea anemones, sea urchins, and moon snails—all revealed by a 15- to 28-foot drop of the tide. At high tide, the tour ascends to trails in the rain forest and archeological sites of ancient Tanaina Indians. The boat back to Homer may pause while the crew pulls up crab pots to harvest some of the bounty of Kachemak Bay, which is among the world's best producers of seafood. *Park open year-round. Boat runs summer only; fare charged. For reservations write P.O. Box 2225, Homer, Alaska 99603, or call (907) 235-6667.*

16. Fort Abercrombie State Historic Park. *Off Rezanoff Dr. East, Kodiak.* Alaska's largest island has attracted a variety of invaders. Koniag people supplanted Kachemak Eskimos, and were themselves subjugated by Russian fur traders in 1784. In 1867 America broke tradition by buying the island from Russia, along with the rest of Alaska. During World War II another invasion threatened when the Japanese occupied Attu and Kiska islands in the western Aleutians in the spring of 1942. In response to this, building began in earnest at Fort Abercrombie.

Concrete bunkers, gun pits, and a massive eight-inch gun barrel, occasionally shrouded in Kodiak's ghostly fogs, are all that remain of this installation, where rust and the Sitka spruce rain forest now mount an invasion of their own. Although the site had little charm for the 8,000 soldiers stationed in Kodiak, its green, mysterious mood, a small meadow vibrant in summer with wildflowers, the crash of waves, and the cries of seabirds echoing from the cliffs below appeal to visitors today. Abercrombie Lake is stocked with rainbow trout and grayling; rock bass and flounder can be caught near its outlet into the Pacific Ocean.

The Baranof House Museum, built around 1793 near Kodiak's harbor, and a Russian Orthodox church on the hill above preserve the Russian heritage here. A drive south of town along the island's only road reveals an extremely lovely stretch of rugged coast. *Open year-round.*

17. Katmai National Park and Preserve. *Fly from Anchorage to King Salmon, then hop a floatplane to Brooks Lodge on Naknek Lake.* On June 6, 1912, Novarupta Volcano exploded from the flank of Mount Katmai, scattering seven cubic miles of ash and pumice around the Northern Hemisphere and filling the nearby Ukak River valley 700 feet deep with ash; the summit of Mount Katmai collapsed, forming a caldera that now holds the blue waters of Crater Lake.

This was the second largest eruption in recorded history, but because of its remote location, there were no known casualties. Expeditions over the next few years explored the region, including the steaming Ukak River valley, which was named Valley of Ten Thousand Smokes. The area, made a national monument in 1918, has been enlarged into a national park and preserve. The ash has cooled now, the fumaroles are depleted of their water vapor, and the valley no longer smokes. But a 24-mile van tour or a "flightseeing" trip to the valley reveals a landscape that is still incredibly awesome.

Beyond the sheer vast beauty of the wilderness, the major attraction here is perhaps the great number of grizzly bears that come in the summer to feast on the abundant salmon. On their protein-rich diet, these magnificent, dangerous animals can attain a weight of 900 pounds; they are common around Brooks Lodge and the nearby Park Service campground during the July and late August salmon runs. Visitors should pay careful attention to the advice available in Park Service leaflets about how to behave in bear country. *Open daily June–early Sept. Fees for van and plane tours.*

18. Valdez. Port Valdez is one of the most northerly ice-free harbors in the Western Hemisphere, and huge tankers come here from around the world to take on oil at the marine terminal of the 800-mile trans-Alaska pipeline. At its completion the pipeline was the most expensive structure ever built by private endeavor, and one can visit its impressive terminal on two-hour bus tours from Valdez.

Set at the end of an 11-mile fjord, the town is encircled by the dramatically saw-toothed peaks and shining glaciers of the Chugach Mountains. Sea otters and seals

17. *The brown bear, shown with cub, is the undisputed monarch of all it surveys.*

are common in the inlet, and kittiwakes, puffins, and bald eagles are abundant.

Valdez is also a terminus for a state ferry, the *E. L. Bartlett*, which crosses Prince William Sound past Columbia Glacier. This, the second largest tidewater glacier in Alaska, is retreating rapidly and drops many icebergs into the sound. A private tour boat, the *Glacier Queen*, also makes this run and detours to observe wildlife, including the large nesting colony of kittiwakes near the town of Whittier. Several campgrounds are found near Valdez. *The* Bartlett *sails Valdez–Whittier daily except Tues. and Thurs. mid-May– mid-Sept; Valdez–Cordova two to four days a week year-round. Boat and pipeline terminal tours in summer only. Fees charged.*

19. Wrangell-St. Elias National Park and Preserve. This is our largest national park, overwhelming in its size (its 12.4 million acres stretch north for 170 miles from the Gulf of Alaska) and in the wild, astonishing grandeur of its scenery. To the east it adjoins Canada's vast Kluane National Park and Territorial Game Sanctuary, and the two together have been declared a United Nations World Heritage area. Between them they include 10 of the continent's highest peaks and the greatest wealth of mountains, canyons, and glaciers in North America. The park's highest peak is the towering 18,008-foot Mount St. Elias.

Road access to the wilderness is from Slana in the north and from Chitina near the central section. From Slana the normally well-maintained gravel road crosses the tundra to Nabesna, a small mining settlement. Inquire locally about conditions on this lovely 45-mile trip, which requires some stream fording. About 10 miles off Nabesna Road is Tanada Lake, where the fishing, especially for grayling, is as rewarding as the scenery and the views of wildlife. The hiking trail to the lake may be muddy and difficult, and the easiest access is by charter floatplane. A lodge and cabins are available in summer.

From Chitina the dirt road toward McCarthy runs for 65 miles (five hours) through superb scenery along an old railroad route. Vehicles with high clearance should have no trouble in summer, though flat tires can be a problem on such back roads. Good highways follow the western border of the park and offer spectacular views of extinct volcanoes: Mount Drum, more than 12,000 feet high, and Mount Sanford, 16,237 feet.

ADVENTURE—Off the Beaten Path

The Cruise to Tracy Arm

We boarded the *Riviera,* a comfortable 50-footer, at her berth in Juneau for the day cruise to Tracy Arm and Sawyer Glacier and headed down Stephens Passage. The fog shrouding the passage made the surrounding mountains even more dramatic. Then we turned east at Holkham Bay to enter Tracy Arm, the mist faded in the warming sun, and the majesty of Mount Sumdum and Sumdum Glacier proclaimed that all preceding glory was merely prelude.

We cruised for 25 miles between precipices of smooth granite rising to heights of 2,000 feet from the water's edge. The vertical walls were broken occasionally by U-shaped glacial valleys, and wherever it was not too steep, the slopes were clothed with a dense forest of spruce.

On the way up the fjord, whose glacier-carved bottom has been sounded at more than 1,200 feet, the *Riviera* took a zigzag course to get a closer look at a pod of killer whales on one side of the mile-wide waterway, then back to inspect an iceberg shot through with crystalline light, and back again to do justice to a view of a bald eagle. Seals popped up and stared wide-eyed as if to see what kind of cameras we were using, porpoises paced our progress, and mountain goats appeared as small white accents on distant cliffs.

At the head of the fjord, the skipper cut the engines at a safe distance from the giant bergs that roared off the jagged white face of Sawyer Glacier, towering hundreds of feet above. Floating here freely and silently, we were at one with the bobbing chunks of ice surrounding us.

There are two glaciers feeding into Tracy Arm, and both are retreating. North Sawyer loses about 85 feet a year, and South Sawyer gives up about 300. As we marveled in the warm sunshine at this frigid world of blue and white, the crew served a delicious lunch of fresh Dungeness crab. We cooled our drinks with ice that had been stored for hundreds of years in nature's own deep freeze; netted now for our pleasure, it was clear as diamonds.

Cruising back down the fjord to the outposts of civilization, one could only contemplate the obvious: how brief is our time on earth and how paltry our works—compared to the grandeur of the wilderness. —*K. and D. Dannen.*

For reservations call (907) 586-9888.

19. *Fishermen who come to remote Tanada Lake are further rewarded by the beauty of the Wrangell Mountains reflected here.*

Summers are cool and can be rainy and foggy. July is the warmest month, but the mosquitoes are out in force. August may have more rain and fewer bugs. *Open year-round. For information on accommodations and charter flights in the park, write Superintendent, Wrangell-St. Elias National Park and Preserve, P.O. Box 29, Glennallen, Alaska 99588.*

20. Klondike Gold Rush National Historical Park. *Skagway.* When gold fever struck in 1897–98, some 20,000 to 30,000 adventurers came through Skagway to brave the Chilkoot and White Pass trails on their way to the Klondike goldfields. They suffered immense hardship, many died, and only a very few got rich. But Skagway prospered, as did nearby Dyea at the head of the trail that crosses the Chilkoot Pass into Canada.

The park commemorating the gold rush includes the Skagway Historic District, Dyea (now in ruins), and the American portion of the Chilkoot Trail, as well as Pioneer Square in Seattle, where so many dreamers made plans for the trip north. For many, the dreams ended here in Skagway, where some 80 saloons and gambling halls and the notorious "Soapy" Smith and his cronies were all willing and able to relieve the unwary of their grubstakes.

The aura of those days pervades the Skagway Historic District, with its boardwalks and old false-fronted buildings. A walking tour includes the restored railroad depot (home of the park visitor center), the Mascot Saloon, Goldberg's Cigar Store, and the Arctic Brotherhood Hall, whose Victorian facade is uniquely embellished with thousands of bits of driftwood.

The Skagway Museum in the city hall houses relics of pioneer days and the gold stampede. The native cultures in Alaska are represented by the arts and crafts of the Eskimos, Aleuts, Athapaskans, and the coastal Tlingit and Haida Indians.

The Chilkoot Trail, open when weather permits, is an extremely strenuous 33-mile hike that takes from three to five days, and is recommended only for the most experienced backpackers. There are, however, several other hiking trails into the hills outside Skagway. *Historic district open year-round.*

21. Fort William H. Seward. *Haines.* With a growing salmon industry and the gold rush, Alaska's population doubled in the 1890's. In 1903 the U.S. Army began construction of a fort at Haines on land deeded to the government by the Presbyterian Board of National Missions. It was dedicated the following year as Fort William H. Seward, honoring the Secretary of State whose "folly" it had been to pur-chase Alaska from Russia in 1867. The first contingent of soldiers arrived in September, and the fort became the regimental headquarters for all of Alaska. In 1922 it was renamed Chilkoot Barracks to avoid confusion with the town of Seward. World War II saw new military installations in Alaska, and Chilkoot became an induction center and rest camp. Later it was deactivated in favor of newer, more strategically placed installations.

Now in *The National Register of Historic Places*, its stately white buildings and nine-acre parade ground, backed by the awesome peaks of the Chilkat Range, still form an imposing sight. Several buildings have been put to new uses: an artist's studio, a crafts workshop (where you can see totem poles being carved), and an arts center where the well-known Chilkat Dancers perform traditional dances of the Northwest Coastal Indians. New additions include Totem Village, with totem poles and a Tlingit tribal house.

The Haines area is noted for its eagles. At the 48,000-acre preserve about 20 miles up the Haines Highway, as many as 3,500 bald eagles, the largest gathering in the world, feed on the spawning salmon. Although the best time to see them is from October through January, they are also numerous in spring and early summer. *Fort open year-round.*

22. Glacier Bay National Park. This primeval wilderness of more than 1.3 million acres is accessible from Juneau or Haines. It is a short flight from Juneau to Gustavus and a half-hour bus ride to the lodge and headquarters at Bartlett Cove. From Haines it's 45 minutes by air. Sixteen glaciers feed into the inlets of the bay, and there are daily boat trips to the glacier "snouts," precipitous ice cliffs that "calve" 220-foot-high bergs into the tidal inlets. Park naturalists explain how glaciers are formed, and how they advance and retreat. In this area most of the ice is now retreating (200 years ago it was up to 4,000 feet thick here), and in its wake have come many seabirds and such mammals as mountain goats, brown and black bears, marmots, river otters, mink, harbor seals, whales, and porpoises. Black bears are most readily observed on the floatplane "flightseeing" trips from the lodge. Also near the lodge are trails leading through the moss-draped rain forest to the beach: be sure to bring waterproof footwear and rain gear.

Among the birds that favor the forest are grouse, woodpeckers, thrushes, and golden-crowned kinglets. In the park as a whole more than 200 species have been observed. When the 25-foot tides in Bartlett Cove are out, they reveal a fascinating variety of starfish, sea urchins, and other tide-pool creatures. *Open year-round. Glacier Bay Lodge open late May–late Sept. For reservations in season, write Glacier Bay Lodge, Gustavus, Alaska 99826. Off-season, write Glacier Bay Lodge, 312 Park Place Bldg., Seattle, Wash. 98101.*

23. Juneau. Long before 1880, when Joe Juneau struck gold here, the Tlingit Indians knew the area, with its spectacular scenery and plentiful fish. Today a cosmopolitan port where bears roam freely within a 10-minute walk of the state capitol, Juneau offers a unique mix of cultural and wilderness attractions.

The Alaska State Museum reflects the area's diversity with displays on wildlife, the region's Indian and Russian heritage, and the gold rush of the 1880's and 1890's. At the octagonal St. Nicholas Russian Orthodox Church, built in 1894, you can see handsome icons and other church relics. The U.S. Forest Service Information Center at Centennial Hall gives information about hiking, camping, and other outdoor recreational opportunities, and has logging, fishing, and mining displays.

Tour buses run to Mendenhall Glacier, making it one of the continent's most accessible ice fields. Its cold blue face rises some 100 feet above the waters of Mendenhall Lake. Telescopes at the nearby visitor center enable you to get a detailed look at the glacier and, with luck, a view of mountain goats atop Mount Bullard in the distance. Hiking trails lead back into the woods. Arctic terns perform aerial acrobatics during the spring nesting period, and in autumn bald eagles fish for salmon in nearby Steep Creek.

For information about "salmon bakes" (uniquely Alaskan seafood feasts), scenic plane rides, charter fishing, Glacier Bay tours, and other area activities, check with the visitor center in the Davis Log Cabin. Located at 134 Third Street, this building is a re-creation of the 1881 cabin that was Juneau's first church.

24. Admiralty Island National Monument. The Tlingit Indians call this island *Xootsnoowu*—"Bear Fortress"— and certainly the name is apt. Almost 100 miles long and 30 wide, the island is indeed a

25. *This impressive totem is but one of many in the National Historical Park.*

unique place of thick forest, lakes, streams, inlets, estuaries, bogs, alpine meadows, and snowcapped peaks rising above the tree line. Relatively few trails penetrate its nearly 1 million acres, and there are no roads of significant length. Most travel is by boat.

The island's dominant residents are some 1,000 huge Alaskan brown bears. Frequently bears can be observed fishing near a viewing stand at the mouth of Pack Creek. Some 500 to 600 bald eagles are hatched here annually, more than in the entire lower 48 states. Deer, seals, sea lions, and river otters are often seen. The waterways yield an abundance of fish, crabs, and shrimp.

The main access to the monument, which is administered by the United

23. *Crosses on the dome and bell tower mark this as a Russian Orthodox church.*

States Forest Service, is through the Tlingit village of Angoon, served both by the state ferry and by floatplane from Juneau, about a 30-minute flight away. Accommodations, boat rentals, and guide services are available. Because the island is a remote and vast wilderness, careful preparations should be made before you visit. *Open year-round. For information write the U.S. Forest Service, P.O. Box 2097, Juneau, Alaska 99803.*

25. Sitka. In 1804 Alexander Baranof, the manager of a Russian fur trading company, burned the Tlingit Indian fort here and reestablished the Russian colony the Tlingits had destroyed two years earlier. Sitka became the foremost city on the North American Pacific Coast, the capital of a colonial empire founded on sea otter pelts. Eventually, however, overhunting ruined the fur trade, and in 1867 the Russians sold Alaska to the United States for $7,200,000 in gold. The official transfer took place on Castle Hill overlooking Sitka's harbor on October 18—Alaska Day, celebrated annually in Sitka with three days of pageant and ceremony.

Today Sitka retains much of its czarist and Tlingit heritage. Russian cannon face the harbor from atop the Castle Hill National Historic Site, and the colorfully costumed New Archangel Dancers perform Russian folk dances at the Centennial Building. St. Michael's Russian Orthodox Cathedral dominates the downtown area, and the Bishop's House, built in 1842 for Alaska's first Russian Orthodox bishop, is restored as part of Sitka National Historical Park. Also within the park are the site of the Tlingit fort and a lovely two-mile forest trail lined with magnificent totem poles. Crafts and artifacts of the Tlingits and other regional tribes are displayed at the park's Indian Cultural Center, and a world-famous collection of tribal masks is found at the nearby state-run Sheldon Jackson Museum. The park's visitor center features exhibits on Sitka's history. *Park open year-round except Thanksgiving Day, Christmas, and New Year's Day.*

26. Tongass Historical Society Museum and Totem Heritage Center. *Ketchikan. Museum at 629 Dock St.; Heritage Center at 601 Deermount St.* Anyone interested in Northwest Indian art should not miss the excellent collections in these museums. The material in the Tongass Historical Society Museum is largely from three highly creative peoples: the Haidas, Tlingits, and Tsimshians. The totems, tools, baskets, and ceremonial objects displayed here are among the best of their kind. Also shown is equipment from the gold rush days and the salmon-fishing industry.

In the Totem Heritage Center some 30 totem poles, house posts, and fragments from Tlingit and Haida villages can be seen in their unrestored state. These great totems, carved from the trunks of red cedar trees, indicate personal status and clan relationships and serve as memorials. They are unique to the Pacific Northwest and are widely celebrated for their emotional power and strength of design.

The center presents lectures and films on subjects related to the area and conducts workshops where established artists teach the traditional skills of carving, basketry, and engraving. On the grounds there's a nature trail where local plants are identified. *Museum open daily mid-May– Sept.; P.M. Wed.–Sun., Oct.–mid-May, except Thanksgiving Day and Christmas; donations welcome. Heritage Center open daily mid-May–Sept.; P.M. Tues.– Fri., Oct.–mid-May; admisssion charged.*

27. Misty Fiords National Monument. Nearly 13 feet (that's 156 inches) of precipitation drench Misty Fiords annually, adding to the abundant water provided by melting glaciers and ice fields. The fjords are narrow ocean inlets carved by Ice Age glaciers. The nearly vertical granite cliffs lining their shores tower spectacularly to a height of 3,000 feet. Cloud-wreathed waterfalls spangle the soaring precipices.

All but the steepest slopes are covered by an evergreen rain forest broken only by glacially excavated lakes and muskegs. Even above the tree line (2,000 to 3,000 feet above sea level), the land is covered with shrubs and grasses that provide summer pasture for Sitka black-tailed deer. Other wildlife includes bears, bald eagles, and mountain goats, and the waters abound with trout, salmon, sea lions, porpoises, and whales.

Most visitors arrive by boat or floatplane from Ketchikan, about 30 air miles away. There are no roads, but seven short hiking trails penetrate the rugged terrain of this 2.3-million-acre wilderness. The U.S. Forest Service maintains 14 rustic cabins scattered throughout the monument at such appealing places as Big Goat Lake. *Monument accessible year-round. For information and cabin reservations write to Tongass National Forest, Box 6137, Ketchikan, Alaska 99901.*

27. True to its name, Misty Fiords provides enough moisture to grow trees on granite.

Hawaii

For all the similarity of their volcanic origin and temperate climate, each of the five main islands has a character all its own.

Although Hawaii is a tourist haven, there are still interesting out-of-the-way places to see. On each island there are beautiful beaches, scenic waterfalls, and hiking trails, as well as lookouts and viewpoints that reveal panoramas ranging from the merely spectacular to the breathtaking. Some of the waterfalls are reached by inviting trails, and some offer the pleasure of a swim in the pools at their base.

Four of the islands have outstanding botanical gardens where a remarkable variety of plants and birdlife can be enjoyed. Museums present the natural history and culture of the islands, and one has a fascinating eclectic collection of artifacts.

Bringing one from the ancient to the more recent past are petroglyphs, a temple site, a royal retreat, and lava flows that wreaked various kinds of havoc. A modern attraction is a minibus tour among rare and endangered exotic animals.

KAUAI—*The Garden Isle*

1. Ke'e Beach and Kalalau Trail.
Ke'e Beach, at the very end of Route 56, is protected by an offshore reef and, un-

like other beaches in the vicinity, provides safe wading, swimming, snorkeling, and scuba diving even in winter. Ke'e is part of Haena State Park, a "scenic wildland" that includes Maniniholo Dry Cave, an ancient lava tube, and Waikapalae and Waikanaloa wet caves, containing pools of glowing green water. Hawaiian legend says that chiefs of old used to gather here.

There's much to see, and you can camp, but the real attraction is Kalalau Trail, used since prehistoric times to reach Kalalau Valley, 11 miles away. Beginning at Ke'e Beach, the trail follows the spectacular Na Pali Coast. You can backpack and make overnight stops at Hanakapiai, Hanakoa, and Kalalau, or settle for a day trip to Hanakapiai Beach at the two-mile mark. Side trails lead to waterfalls and lush valleys, and hikers won't go hungry or thirsty: the way is lined with delicious wild yellow guavas. The coast is treacherous; swimming is not recommended, and in wet weather hiking the entire trail calls for caution. *Open year-round.*

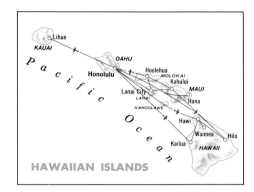

HAWAIIAN ISLANDS

2. One could hardly expect more of a waterfall than three cascades and a misty rainbow.

2. Wailua Falls. *At the end of Rte. 583, Kapaia.* Even if you knew there was a natural wonder on the scale of Wailua Falls in the vicinity, you'd never dream this prosaic little road past a Buddhist cemetery and through four miles of waving sugarcane would be the way to reach it. The double torrent that feeds the falls (*wai* means "fresh water," *lua*, "two") drops 80 feet to a flower-ringed pool. The plunge is especially dramatic after heavy mountain rains—a comparatively frequent occurrence, since 5,000-foot Mount Waialeale, which dominates the center of Kauai, is considered the wettest spot in the world, with a yearly rainfall of almost 500 inches. Unfortunately, there's no safe way to climb down to the base of the falls, so your view is limited to what can be seen from just one place. However, the next time you catch a rerun of *Fantasy Island,*

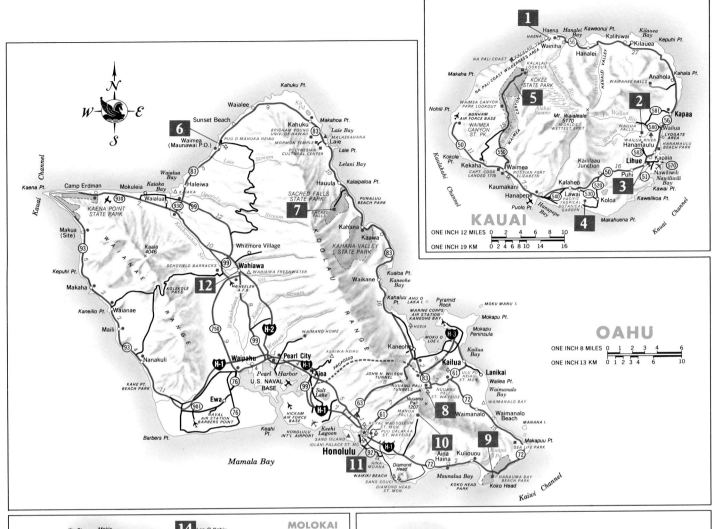

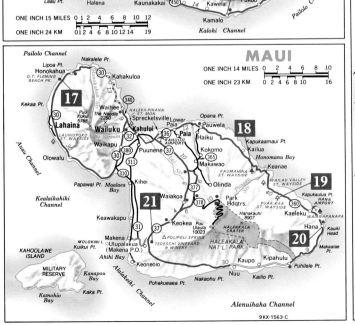

5. *Ferns in foreground echo the colors of the rain-carved walls of Kalalau Valley.*

note the opening shots: filmed from a helicopter, they give a different perspective of this lovely cascade. *Open year-round.*

3. Kauai Museum. *4428 Rice Street, Lihue.* The informative and well-organized material here includes exhibits on the history of both Kauai, the "garden island," and the nearby "forbidden isle" of Niihau. You'll find almost everything worth knowing about the islands' natural history and Hawaiian culture before westerners came. The displays range from *poi*-pounding tools to weapons. Recorded history begins with Captain Cook's landing on Kauai at Waimea in 1778, moving through the little-known Russian attempt to dominate the island, and finally to the impact of Protestant missionaries. Other periods covered include the islands' plantation heyday (when labor was imported from Japan and elsewhere), the Hawaiian monarchy, and contemporary times. There are two charmingly unexpected exhibits worth a detour: an assortment of Hawaiian quilts and a collection of bowls made from the calabash gourd. The work of local artists is frequently shown here. *Open Mon.–Fri. Admission charged.*

4. Pacific Tropical Botanical Garden. *Lawai. Exit south off Rte. 50 onto Rte. 530; exit south off Rte. 530 onto Hailima Rd. and continue to the garden.* You reach the garden by way of unpaved cane-har-

vesting tracks, so in threatening weather call first to make sure your tour hasn't been canceled. When you get there, you will see many tropical plants and flowers not grown elsewhere in the 50 states. The spectacular specimens include Indian pickle trees, giant Victoria water lilies, Panama hat plants, Tahitian chestnuts, bottlebrush trees, 500 species of palm, and a group of plants used in ancient Hawaiian medicine. Many exhibits are edible, and you're encouraged to taste.

The 186-acre private, nonprofit garden was opened in 1971 to foster tropical research and preserve rare and endangered species. Since then, the Pacific Garden has developed extensive education and training programs—and an international reputation. Tours usually include a visit to the neighboring Allerton Gardens, a private estate whose stately decorative plantings were begun by Queen Emma, wife of Kamehameha IV, in the 1870's. *Tours Mon.–Fri. by reservation only; call (808) 332-8131 or 332-8901.*

5. Kokee State Park. At nearly 4,000 feet, the park's 4,345 acres are considerably cooler than lower elevations, and rainfall can be heavy, which accounts for the different character of the scenery here. Pines and other temperate plant life replace palms and tropical vegetation. Along the road there are views from Kokee's luxuri-

ant green surroundings into red-walled Waimea Canyon, and at the northernmost point of the park Kalalau Lookout affords a sweeping overview of Kalalau Valley.

The park contains several trails, some leading into the 30 square miles of Alakai Swamp. Bird-watching is excellent, and in August and September you can catch trout. From June to August delicious Kokee plums are here for the picking, and all year long there are *lilikoi* (passion fruit) and guavas.

Just outside the park headquarters museum, note the Polynesian jungle fowl begging for handouts: they're descended from birds that Polynesians brought from Tahiti and now survive only on Kauai. *Open year-round.*

OAHU–*The Gathering Place*

6. Puu o Mahuka Heiau. *Exit Rte. 83 at Pupukea Homestead Rd.; continue 7/10 mile and exit right onto unmarked road; continue 7/10 mile to the temple.* The isolation of this ruined sacrificial temple (*heiau*), a state historical site and one of Oahu's largest and oldest structures, simply serves to make its ties to Hawaii's pagan past more tangible. The wooden statues of the old gods may have been destroyed here in 1819, when the old religion was abolished, but ancient customs survive: you'll note, for instance, that some of the stones used to reconstruct the *heiau*'s rectangular platform (one wall measures 520 feet) have been wrapped—perhaps that very morning—in leaves from the sacred *ti* plant. Then there are the stories. Some are violent: it's said that three sailors from Capt. George Vancouver's crew were sacrificed here in 1792. Some are not: women from the old nobility came here to give birth, and the *heiau* is supposed to have been a center for *kahunas* (priests) who practiced a form of telepathy. In 1780 one famous *kahuna* at Puu o Mahuka Heiau even predicted the coming of the *haole* (white men), whose arrival marked the beginning of the end of the rites for which these structures were originally built.

7. Sacred Falls State Park. *One mile south of Hauula on Rte. 83.* The two-mile trail to the falls isn't an easy one, but the hike is worth it, particularly on a weekday in fine weather. On weekends, despite the hazards of flash-flooding, falling rock, slippery spots, and drop-offs, one might find an entire Boy Scout troop swimming in the pool at the base of the 80-foot falls.

The trail follows Kaluanui Stream through dense vegetation (which includes guava and mountain apple trees) into a valley that narrows down to a width of only about 50 feet near the falls. The valley walls loom above you to heights of between 1,200 and 1,600 feet. Not long before you reach the falls you'll see a gouge in the cliff face that legend says is a mark left by the giant pig demigod Kamapuaa when he leaned against the rock so that his family could escape their enemies by climbing over his body. The gouge is probably a huge pothole. Wear good walking shoes and plan on spending at least two hours to make the round trip. *Open year-round.*

8. Nuuanu Pali State Wayside. *Off Hwy. 61; follow signs at Nuuanu Pali Summit.* Although this dramatic view over the mountains, hills, and bays of windward Oahu is at its magnificent best in the morning, you might want to time your visit for lunch or later to avoid the crowds and tour buses. The viewing platform, recently enlarged to accommodate the crowds, also detracts from the area's original wilderness atmosphere, so descend to the ledge just below it (about 1,000 feet above sea level).

Because the lookout is at a low point in the Koolau Range crest, trade winds drive so forcefully through the gap that you can virtually lean into them. There are stories of would-be suicides blown right back onto the top of the *pali* (cliffs), and when the wind is from the opposite direction it can be dangerous. When the battle of Nuuanu was fought here in 1795, pitting Kamehameha I against Kalanikupule, king of Oahu, whole battalions of warriors (estimates range from 400 to 10,000) were said to have been driven—or blown—over the *pali. Open year-round.*

9. Hanauma Bay Beach Park. What makes this beach unique are shallow waters filled with rock and coral that provide shelter for hundreds of varieties of colorful reef fish. With a snorkel mask you can observe them even at wading distance. Toss out a morsel of bread, and whole schools will swim up virtually within reach. Snorkel- or scuba-equipped divers can venture out for even more spectacular fish-watching. It goes without saying, of course, that neither fish nor coral can be taken from this protected area.

Many tourists speeding along Kalanianaole Highway (Route 72) miss this ravishing spot. The locals know about it, though, so it's best to avoid weekend visits. But if you come with a mask and a snorkel on a winter weekday, be prepared for a marvelous experience. The almost perfectly semicircular beach and bay are what remain of a volcanic crater breached

7. The 80-foot fall seems like less in the context of cliffs that are 20 times higher.

by the sea thousands of years ago. The descent to the beach from the parking area is therefore steep. *Open year-round.*

10. Manoa Falls. *Manoa Rd., Honolulu.* Manoa Falls and the mile-long trail leading to them provide a surprising plunge into wilderness only minutes from the bustle of Honolulu. The falls, about a half-hour walk through shady forest from the end of Manoa Road, drop an astonishing 200 feet into a pool in which swimming is allowed—though in dry weather the water isn't really deep enough. There are other swimming holes, however, in Waihi Stream, which borders the trail.

The hike is an easy one unless the weather is wet, when slippery, moss-covered rocks and twisted banyan roots pose a hazard. But on a fine day the indigenous plant life makes this an attractive trip. This opinion is shared by locals, and it's best to avoid weekends. Plants include banana palms, bamboos, African tulip trees, *ape-ape* (pronounced *ah-pay ah-pay*), ferns, and guava bushes. *Open year-round.*

11. Puu Ualakaa State Wayside. *Round Top Dr., Honolulu.* Many *malihini* (newcomers) miss this glorious view because it's not easy to find. But look for Makiki Street on a detailed street map, and you'll see that it connects to a scenic drive to this mountaintop wayside. A second, longer route—Tantalus Drive—begins further west off Puowaina Drive. Honolulu residents usually ascend by one drive, descend by the other. The heights tend to be much cooler than the lowlands, and the wayside is an ideal spot to visit on a hot summer day.

When you get here, the expected facilities make it seem like just another park: trees, grass, picnic tables, comfort stations. But then there's the view: no other area open to the public boasts anything like it. The city is spread out before you from Pearl Harbor and the airport in one direction to Diamond Head and Koko Head in the other.

Puu Ualakaa (known locally as Round Top) means "hill of the rolling sweet potatoes." It got its name, according to the story, because Kamehameha I ordered sweet potatoes to be planted here—and when they were dug up, they rolled down the hill. *Open dawn to dusk year-round.*

12. Wahiawa Botanic Garden. *California Ave., Wahiawa.* This verdant, secluded—and educational—haven is missed by the many tourists who go as quickly as possible through Wahiawa, an "army town" near the famous Schofield Barracks which, it must be admitted, is not one of the island's most attractive settlements. It is worthwhile, however, to stop and see the splendid collection of plants in the botanic garden.

In the 1920's the wooded gulch in which the garden is situated was used by the Hawaii Sugar Planters' Association as a nursery and for forestry experiments. In 1950 the 27-acre plot was turned over to the city and county of Honolulu; and although the area is still being developed, it's a charming and informative place to visit. Following the self-guiding tour folder, you enter past Australian tree ferns 40 feet tall, and native tree ferns (*hapu'u*) whose stalks are covered with a woollike substance (*pulu*) once exported for pillow and mattress stuffing. Other native plants in the Hawaiian Garden range from hibiscus (the state flower) to loulu palms. The last of the indicated stops (No. 23) is given over to a collection of small plants and vines of the aroid family ranging from the decorative anthurium to the edible taro. As you might imagine, birds abound in this garden environment. *Open daily except Christmas and New Year's Day.*

MOLOKAI–*The Friendly Isle*

13. Molokai Ranch Wildlife Park. *Accessible only by guided tour from the Sheraton Molokai Hotel, Kaluakoi Resort, Kepuhi.* Passengers on small planes flying over the western "heel" of this slipper-shaped island are sometimes startled to see giraffes cavorting on the hills below. The animals are some of the more than 500 residents of Molokai Ranch Wildlife Park, a 2,000-acre reserve that is home to aoudads (Barbary sheep), axis deer, Indian black bucks, elands, oryxes, impalas, and the greater koodoo. Birds include the ostrich,

the rhea, and several kinds of pheasants, quail, and other fowl.

The privately run park was established to raise the animals, many of which are rare or endangered, in order to supply zoos and animal parks around the world. One-hour minibus "safari" tours are available daily from the Sheraton Molokai. The obliging driver, who's also the guide, stops when it seems appropriate for visitors to break out cameras or binoculars. Sometimes the animals come right up to the bus for handouts, but feeding them is strictly prohibited. Instead, they're encouraged to forage the park's rolling terrain, which bears a strong resemblance to the African veld. *Open year-round. Admission charged.*

14. Kalaupapa. This settlement on Molokai's north shore lies some 2,000 feet below "topside," which is what residents call the rest of Molokai. The difficulty of reaching it was one reason why the leprosy victims, who were treated by the Belgian priest Father Damien, were exiled here in the 19th century. Today there are only about 100 former patients left, living amid touching reminders of Father Damien and his mission. To visit this settlement one needs permission from the state of Hawaii Department of Health and must be 16 or older. Tour sponsors can make the necessary arrangements.

A steep trail leads down from Palaau State Park, and there's also a mule train that wends its way down a trail that (at this writing) is rather poorly maintained. But there's reliable air-taxi service from Molokai Airport, and charter flights are available from Oahu and Maui.

Once you've reached this remote but beautiful spot, a guided tour, on foot or by mule, is the only way to see the historic sites in the village where the remaining residents now live and the virtually deserted hospital, abandoned buildings from the days when thousands were treated here. The affliction now called Hansen's disease can be controlled by modern drugs.

On the eastern side of the peninsula you'll find Father Damien's church, St. Philomena's, a grassy cemetery, and a monument to the heroic priest who, in his service to the patients, contracted the disease and died here. This is Kalawao, the original site of the colony, and the park here is an ideal place to lunch (bring your own) as you contemplate the dramatic 3,000-foot-high cliffs along Molokai's windward shore. *Open year-round. To reserve for on-site tours call (808) 567-6171.*

15. St. Joseph's Church. *Kamalo.* Father Damien ministered to needs beyond those of the Kalaupapa leprosy colony. He also built five churches for his parishioners on Molokai's uplands, or "topside," and

13. An exotic gathering suggests Edward Hicks's "Peaceable Kingdom" paintings.

14. *St. Philomena, a symbol of order and hope in a wild and tragic setting.*

made his ecclesiastical rounds by horseback. St. Joseph's, built in 1876, is a white one-room building with a churchyard that contains several graves. One small but poignant stone is incised partly in Hawaiian: "Margarita Kameekua, *hanau* Honolulu March 1, 1914, *make* Kamalo February 27, 1915." *Hanau* means "born," and *make* means "died."

A life-size black metal statue of Father Damien stands just outside the tiny church, which, like St. Philomena's at Kalawao, is kept in good repair but used only for special occasions. Farther east along Route 450, near Mapulehu Stream, is Our Lady of Sorrows (1874), another of Father Damien's topside churches. *Open year-round.*

16. Halawa Valley and Hipuapua and Moaula Falls. The steep descent into Halawa Valley looks dangerous, but by the time you get here you will be accustomed to the valley's remote ruggedness, so follow it carefully to the bottom. Hundreds of families lived here in former times (you'll see traces of stone boundary

walls), but now only intrepid weekenders are willing to forgo electricity and telephones to build valley retreats.

From the end of the paved road—a picturesque spot with winding stream, church, and rocky beach (good for picnics, unsafe for swimming)—follow the dirt road into the forest. The water pipes at the left of the stream are your guide. Follow them for about an hour and you'll reach the 500-foot Hipuapua Falls; the final 10 minutes are rough going over rocks. Another option is to diverge from the main trail after about a half-hour at the place where a pipe crosses the stream. Follow this pipe and you'll find it somewhat easier to reach the pool at the base of 250-foot Moaula Falls—a good place to swim if you follow local ritual first: throw in a *ti*-plant leaf; if it floats, fine. If it sinks, stay out: the lizard living at the bottom of the pool is angry and swimming is dangerous. In rainy weather, or when the stream is high, the trails themselves are risky. *Open year-round.*

MAUI–*The Valley Isle*

17. D. T. Fleming Beach Park. *Honokahua.* Nearby Kapalua Beach used to be called Fleming Beach (in honor of a local ranch manager, David T. Fleming) until the name was reassigned to this county beach farther north along Route 30. Although confusion about the names has kept the park off the beaten path, it has long been a favorite with locals. Fleming is one of the most convenient of the rugged area's picturesque beaches, with showers, barbecue grills, and picnic tables—at least one of which always seems to be available (on weekdays, anyway). There's even a public telephone.

Winds ruffle the ironwood and palms at the top of a sandy crescent, which slopes down to a usually gentle swell and good swimming. When the waves pick up, body and board surfers turn out in force. Stay on the beach, though, when heavy winter waves roll in, setting up rip currents and undertows. And when you stroll the beach, wear rubber sandals (*zoris*): fallen ironwood cones can be rough on bare feet. *Open year-round.*

18. Puohokamoa Falls and Kaumahina State Wayside. *Falls parking area is at an unmarked pull-off along Rte. 360 two miles west of Kaumahina State Wayside; look for a green picnic table and low stone wall.* Visitors tend to drive right by this site, unaware of the lovely falls, which cannot be

17. *When the "surf's up," this is a splendid place to marvel at the wave riders' skill.*

19. Spectacular flower of the ginger lily dramatizes a classic Hawaiian setting.

seen from the road. Park, and follow the sometimes muddy path. You can eat yellow guavas that may be seen along the way, but avoid the oily *kukui* (candlenuts), which the ancient Hawaiians used for light—and as a strong laxative.

There's another table and a barbecue pit at the falls. If you decide to refresh yourself in the pool at the base of the falls, be prepared to find yourself a target for tourists' cameras—except in the late afternoon. If picnicking is a must and the tables at the falls are taken, drive a little farther to Kaumahina, where there are plenty of facilities and good views of the ocean and Keanae Peninsula. Watch for the *hala* (pandanus) tree and several types of eucalyptus (including the shaggy paperbark). At least one African tulip tree may be in bloom. *Open year-round.*

19. Puaa Kaa State Wayside. Puaa Kaa is a delightfully intimate park with two modest 25-foot waterfalls. A paved pathway takes you across the top of the first falls,

then leads along a stream to the second. Both tumble into pools that are fine for swimming, though few visitors seem to take advantage of this opportunity.

Both pools are bordered by picnic tables, and conveniently situated a little farther along the road, near a second parking lot, are rest rooms. The road crosses a small bridge, and if you walk across, you can see still more falls and pools, though they're not really a part of Puaa Kaa Wayside. *Puaa kaa* is an ancient Hawaiian name meaning "rolling pig."

Tropical foliage is abundant here: banana palms, guava trees (often bearing ripe, ready-to-eat fruit), heliconia flowers, ferns, African tulip trees, red and green varieties of *ti* plants, and the giant-leaved *ape-ape. Open year-round.*

20. Helani Gardens. *Off Rte. 360 about a mile west of Hana.* The beneficence of the Hawaiian climate is beautifully demonstrated here. H. F. Cooper established these gardens as a wholesale nursery in 1975; now he has opened them to visitors, who are free to wander the five-acre lower gardens along paths called Main Drag or Six Bridges to Heaven. The 65-acre upper gardens are also open but are of primary interest to botanists, horticulturalists, and plant collectors.

The specimens, tropical and subtropical plants and trees from throughout the world, are generally well marked. But Mr. Cooper has added his own fillip to the expected common, genus, and species names. Here you will find aphorisms, Bible and poetry quotations, or anonymous quotes he feels ought to be passed on to visitors. Near a bed of spider lilies, for instance, we learn that "Knowledge is power only when it is translated into direct and positive action."

In addition to the plants and flowers, there's a pond of Japanese carp (*koi*), whose churnings and gulpings are in noisy contrast to the peace that reigns in the rest of this quiet place, where the only other sound is likely to be the rhythmic clatter of bamboo blowing in the wind.

Picnic facilities and rest rooms are located in the lower gardens. *Open year-round. Admission charged.*

21. Tedeschi Vineyard and Winery. *Off Rte. 37, Ulupalakua.* Few tourists heading for Haleakala National Park think of stopping off in the cool, bucolic up-country region; and thus they miss the green, rolling ranchland and the surprising experience of Hawaii's only true wine country.

Pardee Erdman, owner of Ulupalakua Ranch, has turned over 15 acres and the former estate jail to Emil Tedeschi to raise grapes, make wine, and run a tasting room. All who stop are invited to try a glass of Maui Blanc, a "light, dry pineapple wine," which was the first Tedeschi product in 1977.

When Emil and Joanne Tedeschi moved here from California's Napa Valley in 1974, they and their partner Erdman entertained high hopes of reviving the island's wine industry. These have been fulfilled. After Maui Blanc in 1977 came a sparkling wine in 1983, Blanc de Noir, produced from Carnelian grapes. The year 1985 saw the turn of a light, fruity red, Maui Nouveau; now a more full-bodied red is being introduced. Visitors are free to stroll the grounds and visit the warehouse and fermentation room when open. The wines are of course for sale. *Open year-round.*

HAWAII—*The Big Island*

22. The Puako Petroglyphs. *Take the Puako turnoff from Rte. 19 and continue three miles; the path to the petroglyphs connects with the road about 100 yards before road's end.* In keeping with their reputation as one of Hawaii's major mysteries, the cryptic inscriptions left by the ancient Hawaiians aren't easy to find, let alone decipher. Stick figures, boats with sails, warriors with weapons, circles within circles—they continue to elude the anthropologists who study them.

Routes to petroglyph sites are seldom clearly marked, since so many have been vandalized. But to find the extensive Puako fields, follow the road through the village, and at 152 Puako Drive look for a hand-lettered sign on the inland side of the road. It announces "PETROGLYPHS" (or did at this writing). Follow its arrow through the fence gate and continue along the lava path for 15 or 20 minutes. Make the trip early or late in the day, when temperatures are lower and longer shadows make the carvings easier to distinguish. You can make rubbings by stretching cloth over them and rubbing with charcoal (don't use crayons; wax damages the carvings). *Open year-round.*

---

23. Kamuela Museum. *West of Waimea near junction of Rtes. 250 and 19.* The appeal of this family-owned museum lies in the fact that it looks like someone's home, with objects selected and juxtaposed by personal preference rather than by curatorial categories. It's a delightful hodgepodge in which the discerning visitor can expect to find something of interest: a rare example of the temple idols that were supposed to have been destroyed by royal and missionary edict long ago, or paintings and furnishings from Iolani Palace, the residence of the royal family at Honolulu. Another exhibit related to royalty is a travel clock presented by Queen Victoria to Hawaii's last reigning monarch, Queen Liliuokalani. A unique Hawaiian object is the ancient canoe breaker, a hammer designed specifically to put an invader's fleet out of commission.

The collection, some 50 years in the making, was assembled by Albert K. and Harriet K.M. Solomon. Mrs. Solomon is a descendant of John Palmer Parker, founder of the Parker Ranch on land granted by Kamehameha I. *Open year-round. Admission charged.*

---

24. Waipio Valley. In a state whose islands seem to provide panoramic vistas at every turn, here on the Big Island it is easy to miss the spectacular view across Waipio Valley. It is, however, worthwhile to take the nine-mile Route 240 to Waipio Valley Lookout. From this vantage point you can see the island's largest valley some 2,000 feet below. This was once home to the ancient Hawaiian kings—and to as many as 50,000 Hawaiians, who gradually abandoned the valley settlements for fear of *tsunamis* (tidal waves). Today there are taro patches and rice paddies, but their owners usually live outside the valley.

The steep, narrow road down to the valley is restricted to vehicles with four-wheel drive, but there's an hourly shuttle tour into the valley from Kukuihaele. There's a five-room hotel in this hauntingly desolate place, and for a modest charge you can get a bed and a kerosene lantern to light the way to your room. *Open year-round. Charge for shuttle tour.*

---

25. Akaka Falls State Park. *Rte. 220, Honomu.* You reach the park after a six-mile drive west, passing through the little plantation town of Honomu and its fields of sugarcane. Here in a setting of tropical foliage and flowers are Akaka Falls, which plunges a sheer 442 feet down black volcanic rock, and its neighbor, Kahuna Falls, which tumbles about 100 feet. They are visible from a slippery, sometimes steep but paved pathway that loops a half-mile through deep forest greenery. Rest benches are set among ginger (notice the magnificent torch ginger), orchids, heliconias, azaleas, and bird-of-paradise.

24. *In this view of the verdant Waipio Valley, the fringe of white surf that separates the islands from the sea is beautifully defined.*

Where the path begins, there are giant monkeypods sheltering picnic tables. But the spectacular drop of Akaka Falls is the big attraction here. No swimming is allowed, and it would be difficult indeed to make your way to the base of either falls. *Open year-round.*

26. Kapoho. *Follow Rte. 132 east from Pahoa to the junction with Rte. 137.* The Hawaiian Islands were created by volcanic action. This is the positive side. On the negative side is the destruction that has been—and may still be—wrought. In January 1960, for example, the community of Kapoho all but disappeared under a flow of molten rock. Known today as the Ghost Village, it is interesting not for what you see here, but for what you don't. Road signs still show the way to the village, but once you're there, all you find jutting from the black, dusty lava is an occasional fragment of corrugated metal roof. Continue through the intersection of Routes 132 and 137 toward the ocean, and on your left is Kapoho Cemetery, where, as the wind whistles through a stand of ironwood, you can contemplate the few graves that weren't overrun. Beyond the cemetery hill you will see the cinder cone from which fire and molten rock spewed that January day.

Farther along the road to the ocean stands Kumakahi Lighthouse. Inexplicably, the lava flow stopped just short of the lighthouse, encircled its base, and pushed on to the ocean. Thus, as if to compensate for the destruction of a village, it added half a square mile to the island's land surface. The six-foot-high edge of the frozen flow is a thought-provoking sight. But as is usually the case in Hawaii, the lava moved slowly (here it flowed from the East Rift Zone, which runs from Kilauea Volland to the sea). Residents had ample time to remove their belongings, and no lives were lost.

27. Kaimu Black Sand Beach. *Intersection of Rtes. 130 and 137, Kaimu.* This crescent of pulverized-lava beach, bordered by coconut palms and pandanuses, has subsided since a 1975 earthquake, but it's still a dramatic sight. Violent waves have been grinding its glassy black lava particles ever since 1750, when molten rock

27. The refreshing surf is the antithesis of the molten lava from which the sand derives.

poured into the sea here and was blasted into bits by steam explosions. Although local residents familiar with the currents go surfing here, visitors would be foolish to try to swim off Kaimu. It's an idyllic spot for a picnic, however. Incidentally, it is against the law to take any of the sand, even the smallest amount, from the beach.

There are many other black sand beaches in Hawaii, but Kaimu is probably the most impressive of all. It is also possibly the blackest, and you'll want to wash your feet in the little freshwater pool on the island side of the highway before getting back into your car. *Open year-round.*

28. Kipuka Puaulu (Bird Park). *Mauna Loa Rd. NW, off Rte. 11.* The northern edge of Hawaii Volcanoes National Park has a quiet 100-acre oasis that provides a habitat for a number of unusual plants and birds, native and imported. This haven, Kipuka Puaulu, better known as Bird Park, was created when a lava flow parted and came together again, sparing a 100-acre island of forest in between (*ki-*

puka is the Hawaiian name for this phenomenon). Note, however, that Kipuka Puaulu's woodland isn't in its primeval state: life introduced by settlers flourishes—ranging from wild pigs and goats to nasturtiums and the grasses that cover large areas. There's an interesting mile-long, self-guiding loop trail. You'll see the giant *koa*, *papala-kepau*, *mamani*, and thickets of *pilo* trees.

The birds flitting through Kipuka Puaulu's treetops include exotics like the Japanese white-eye and Chinese thrush and such natives as the wrenlike *elepaio* and the *amakihi*, *i'iiwi*, and *apapane*—three members of the nectar-gathering honeycreeper family. You may not see all of them, but you will certainly hear their chatter. *Open year-round.*

29. Footprints Trail. *Accessible by foot from the Maunaiki trailhead on the east side of Rte. 11.* A half-hour trek from Route 11 brings you to the spot where in 1790 a hapless band of Hawaiian warriors and their families were overtaken by a volcanic eruption as they moved through the Ka'u Desert. Overcome by poisonous gases, they were trapped by the heavy fall of ash, which soon turned to mud and later hardened. Some of their footprints are preserved about a mile before Maunaiki Trail joins Ka'u Desert Trail, also called Footprints Trail. Many of the prints are eroded, others covered and uncovered by shifting sands. But their outlines are touchingly unmistakable. Especially poignant are prints that were obviously made by a fleeing child.

It's reassuring to know that in modern times only one person has been killed by a volcanic eruption in Hawaii: a photographer who took one too many chances as he tried to record an eruption in 1924. *Open year-round.*

30. *This remote grave is not inappropriate for the premier world explorer of his time.*

30. Kealakekua Bay. Today Kealakekua Bay, on the Kona Coast, is a marine reserve and a state underwater park: a popular place for skin and scuba diving, with glass-bottomed boat tours for the less athletic. But in 1779, when the bay was an important anchorage, it achieved undying notoriety as the place where Capt. James Cook was killed. It is ironic that the great navigator who discovered Hawaii for the western world, and who was honored as a god by the Hawaiians, should die at their hands in a skirmish over a stolen boat. The Captain Cook Monument, an obelisk on the northwest side of the bay, marks the spot where he fell. It's reached only by boat, though you may drive almost up to the beach on the bay's south shore. From here you can walk to the ruins of Hikiau Heiau. It was at this temple that Cook conducted (for a member of his crew) the first Christian burial service in the islands. *Accessible year-round.*

31. Kamakahonu and the Ahuena Heiau. *On the grounds of the King Kamehameha Hotel, off Alii Dr., Kailua.* It was to this 11-acre compound of land, beach, and bay—a kind of retreat for the Hawaiian highborn, or *alii*—that King Kamehameha I and his court came shortly after leaving Honolulu in 1812. They made it the center of the islands' civil and religious government. Recently, with the assistance

of the Bishop Museum in Honolulu, the precincts have been restored to an approximation of their state during the years 1813 to 1819, when the king and his priests ruled from here.

In the background you can see one of Hawaii's most historic sites: Ahuena Heiau, an ancient temple rebuilt by Kamehameha, who dedicated it to Lono, god of peace, prosperity, and agriculture. But

at the king's death in 1819, when his favorite wife Kaahumanu became regent for his son Liholiho (Kamehameha II), the *heiau* and all it stood for was destroyed, including the *kapu* system of taboo. In 1820 the first Christian missionaries were welcomed. *Open year-round.*

31. *Early Hawaiians, using native materials, expressed a strong sense of sculptural form.*

Acknowledgments

Driver-Reporters

Alabama–Richard Marshall
Alaska–Kent and Donna Dannen
Arizona–Daniel Weiss
Arkansas–Ross Harlan, Robert Lancaster
California–Barbara Roether
Colorado–B. Cory Kilvert, Jr.
Connecticut–Richard Marshall
Delaware–John Baker, Barbara Braun
Florida–B. Cory Kilvert, Jr.
Georgia–B. Cory Kilvert, Jr.
Hawaii–Robert Bone
Idaho–Susan Moore, Thomas Barr
Illinois–B. Cory Kilvert, Jr.
Indiana–Richard Marshall
Iowa–B. Cory Kilvert, Jr.
Kansas–Ross Harlan
Kentucky–Richard Marshall
Louisiana–Margaret Perry
Maine–B. Cory Kilvert, Jr.
Maryland–John Baker, Barbara Braun
Massachusetts–Richard Marshall
Michigan–Richard Marshall
Minnesota–Richard Marshall
Mississippi–Richard Marshall
Missouri–Richard Marshall
Montana–Susan Moore
Nebraska–Robert C. Guenzel, Jr.
Nevada–Deborah Bull, Robert Bull
New Hampshire–B. Cory Kilvert, Jr.
New Jersey–Deborah Bull, Robert Bull, Noreen Church, Rebecca Rass
New Mexico–Daniel Weiss
New York–Noreen Church, Richard Marshall
North Carolina–B. Cory Kilvert, Jr.
North Dakota–B. Cory Kilvert, Jr.
Ohio–Richard Marshall
Oklahoma–Ross Harlan
Oregon–Thomas Barr
Pennsylvania–Mark Gasper
Rhode Island–Richard Marshall
South Carolina–B. Cory Kilvert, Jr.
South Dakota–Susan Moore
Tennessee–Richard Marshall
Texas–Carroll Calkins, Robert Lancaster, Susan Wernert
Utah–B. Cory Kilvert, Jr.
Vermont–B. Cory Kilvert, Jr., Harriet W. Riggs
Virginia–Richard Marshall
Washington–Thomas Barr
West Virginia–Richard Marshall
Wisconsin–Richard Marshall
Wyoming–B. Cory Kilvert, Jr.

Picture Credits

Cover: *top to bottom right*: Camerique; Doris Gehrig Barker; Imagery; FPG International; © David Muench; *bottom left*: FPG International; *spine* Shostal Associates. **1** © David Muench. **2–3** © David Muench. **4** *top to bottom left*: © Jim Schafer 1985/View Finder; © David Muench; © David Muench; James P. Rowan: Click/Chicago; © David Muench; Tom Algire; *top to bottom right*: © David Muench; Garry D. McMichael/Southern Images; © David Muench; © David Muench; Doris Gehrig Barker; Tom Algire. **5** *top to bottom*: © Jim Brandenburg/DRK Photo; © David Muench; Jerry Hardy; © Jim Schafer 1985/View Finder; Doris Gehrig Barker; Ken Dequaine. **8–9** Voscar, The Maine Photographer © 1980. **10** © Kip Brundage/Woodfin Camp & Associates. **11** Dover-Foxcroft Historical Society/Photo by Neal Mallett. **12** *left* © L. Lorusso/The Picture Cube; *right* © Joe Devenney 1983. **13** © Robert Perron 1985. **14** *left* Richard Rowan; *right* The Jones Gallery of Glass and Ceramics. **15** © Ira Block/The Image Bank. **17** *top left* © David Muench. **18** © Richard Berenson 1982. **19** Eric Sanford Photography. **20** Fred Sieb Photography. **21** Genii Sanford Photography. **23** *lower right* © 1985 George A. Robinson from f/Stop Pictures. **24** Photographs by Hanson T. Carroll. **25** Forward's Color Productions. **26** *top* Forward's Color Productions; *bottom* Vyto Starinskas. **27** Doris Gehrig Barker. **28** Paul Rocheleau. **29** *left* © Joe Viesti/The Col. John Ashley House, Ashley Falls, Mass., property of The Trustees of Reservations; *right* Paul Rocheleau. **32** *top* Jerry Howard/Positive Images; *bottom* Fredrik D. Bodin. **33** Jerry Howard/Positive Images. **34** R. Krubner/H. Armstrong Roberts. **35** H. Armstrong Roberts. **36** Jack Spratt/The Image Works. **38** *upper* Jerry Howard/Stock, Boston; *bottom* © Karen Bussolini 1983. **39** *top* © John T. Hopf; *bottom* © Arthur Swoger 1985/Frederic Lewis, Inc. **40** © Karen Bussolini 1985. **41** *bottom* Connecticut Department of Economic Development. **41–42** © Karen Bussolini 1982. **42** *right* Steven Murtha. **44** Robert Perron. **45** *top* Robert Perron; *lower* Connecticut Department of Economic Development. **46** Kenneth A. Wilson. **48** Doris Gehrig Barker. **49** © David Muench. **50** Courtesy Frederic Remington Art Museum, Ogdensburg, New York, all rights reserved. **51** George Buctel. **52** Sandy Tambone. **53** Stuart L. Craig, Jr./Bruce Coleman Inc. **54** *top* Barbara Lipton/Courtesy of the Jacques Marchais Center of Tibetan Art; *bottom* Doris Gehrig Barker. **55** Gilbert Nielsen. **57** *top left* E. R. Degginger/Imagery. **58** Imagery. **59** *top* Anne Heimann; *bottom* Imagery. **60** E. R. Degginger/Imagery. **61** Gilbert Nielsen. **62** *left* Ralph Krubner; *right* Gilbert Nielsen. **63** © David Muench. **64** Gilbert Nielsen. **65** David M. Campione. **67** *top*, **68, 69** © Jim Schafer 1985/View Finder. **70** © David Muench. **71** Gilbert Nielsen. **72** © H. Scott Heist 1985. **73** © John K. Bachmann 1984. **74** Gilbert Nielsen. **76** Larry Lefever/Grant Heilman Photography. **78** *top* Tony Florio; *bottom* Michael Dunn. **79** © David Muench. **80** Michael Dunn. **82** *top* Michael Dunn. **82–83** *bottom* M. E. Warren. **83** *top* M. E. Warren; *bottom right* Gilbert Nielsen. **84** © David Muench. **85** *top* Michael Dunn; *bottom* Maryland Division of Tourist Development. **86** Gerald S. Ratliff/West Virginia Department of Natural Resources. **88** *top* West Virginia Department of Commerce, Marketing/Tourism Division; *bottom* Arthur C. Prichard. **89** Arthur C. Prichard. **90** Robert Harrison/Whetstone Photography. **91** *left* Gerald S. Ratliff/West Virginia Department of Natural Resources; *right* Arnout Hyde, Jr. **92** Virginia Division of Tourism. **94** *top* © David Muench; *bottom* David Forbert/Shostal Associates. **95** Virginia Division of Tourism. **96** Photri. **97** © David Muench. **99** *top* © David Muench. **100** *top* Aerial Photography Services; *bottom* Danny C. Booker. **101** Danny C. Booker. **102** © David Muench. **103** *top* North Carolina Department of Cultural Resources; *bottom* Jack Dermid. **104** *top* © David Muench; *lower* Jack Dermid. **105** *left* Chip Henderson; *right* Ken Dequaine. **106** Carolina Sandhills National Wildlife Refuge. **108** *top* B. Cory Kilvert, Jr.; *bottom* South Carolina Department of Parks, Recreation & Tourism. **109** Williams-Brice Museum, Sumter, South Carolina. **110** *top* Jack Dermid; *bottom* © David Muench. **111** Jack Dermid. **112** Buford C. Burch. **114** Big Shanty Museum, Kennesaw, Georgia. **115** B. Cory Kilvert, Jr. **116** Buford C. Burch. **117** Fred Sieb Photography. **118** *left* © David Muench; *right* Jodi Cobb/Woodfin Camp, Inc. **119** *top* John Earl; *lower* Jack Dermid. **120** Grant Heilman/Grant Heilman Photography. **122** *top* B. Cory Kilvert, Jr.; *bottom* Kris Bolte. **123** *bottom right* Wendell D. Metzen; *remainder* Florida Division of Tourism. **124** D. Muench/H. Armstrong Roberts. **125** *left* Wendell D. Metzen; *right* Florida Division of Tourism. **126** *left* Z. Leszczynski/Earth Scenes; *right* William D. Griffin. **127** © Mike Barrs 1986/SharpShooters. **128–129** *bottom* Ken Dequaine. **131** E. Cooper/H. Armstrong Roberts. **132** Ken Dequaine. **133** Tom Algire. **134** John Shaw. **135** Joseph P. Messana. **136** Kent and Donna Dannen. **138** Wolfgang Weber. **139** Ohio Travel Bureau. **140** Wolfgang Weber. **141** Heidi Wood/Bruce Coleman Inc. **142** Kent and Donna Dannen. **143** Heidi Wood/Bruce Coleman Inc. **144** Ruth Chin. **146** *top* Doris DeWitt: Click/Chicago; *bottom* Cathlyn Melloan: Click/Chicago. **147** *left* James P. Rowan: Click/Chicago; *right* Doris DeWitt: Click/Chicago. **148, 149, 150, 151** Ruth Chin. **152** Robert S. Spann. **154** Lee Boltin/Courtesy of the Tyler Collection, John James Audubon Museum, Henderson, Kentucky. **155** *top* J. Blank/H. Armstrong Roberts; *bottom* Kent and Donna Dannen. **156** © David Muench. **157** John Earl. **158** *top* P. Beney/FPG International; *bottom* Doris DeWitt: Click/ Chicago. **159** John Earl. **160** Kentucky Department of Travel Development. **161** © David Muench. **163** *top* D. Muench/H. Armstrong Roberts. **164** Bob Schatz. **165** James M. Frey/Photo Fair. **166** *top* Robin Hood; *bottom* Peg Davitt/Photo Fair. **167** Wesley F. Walden. **168** Donald Dudenbostel. **169** John Netherton/Cumberland Valley Photographic Workshops. **170** © David Muench. **172** © David Muench. **173** *top* Dennis Holt/Bruce Coleman Inc.; *bottom* Alabama Bureau of Tourism and Travel. **174** Alabama Bureau of Tourism and Travel. **175** *top* Tuskegee Ranger District, U. S. Department of Agriculture; *bottom* From The Warner Collection of Gulf States Paper Corp., Tuscaloosa, Alabama. **176** Richard F. Raber. **177** *top* W. Metzen/H. Armstrong Roberts; *lower* Fred Myers. **178** Franke Keating. **180, 181** Courtesy of the Mississippi Division of Tourism. **182, 183** Garry D. McMichael/Southern Images. **184** Annie Griffiths/DRK Photo. **186** Mike Magnuson. **187** Ann L. Berg/Bruce Coleman Inc. **188** *left* Ken Dequaine; *right* Daniel J. Cox. **189** Jeannine R. Lunder/Bruce Coleman Inc. **190, 191** Les Blacklock. **193** *top right* Tom Algire. **194, 195, 196** Ken Dequaine. **197** *left* George Buctel; *right* Kenneth S. Vreeland/Bruce Coleman Inc. **198** S. J. Krasemann/DRK Photo. **199** Ken Dequaine. **200** © David Muench. **202** Michael Whye. **203** B. Cory Kilvert, Jr. **204** © David Muench. **205** Michael Whye. **207** *top left* Dwight Ellefre/Bruce Coleman Inc. **208** Ken Dequaine. **209** *left* Ken Dequaine; *right* David Hiser/Aspen. **210** *left* B. Cory Kilvert, Jr.; *right* © Todd V. Phillips/ Third Coast 1985. **211** *top* Ken Dequaine; John Gerard. **212** Jane Shaw/Bruce Coleman Inc. **213** Richard F. Raber. **214** Cathy Meddin. **216** Ken Dequaine. **217** Robert Lee II/Bruce Coleman Inc. **218** Grant Heilman/Grant Heilman Photography. **219** *top* James P. Rowan/The Marilyn Gartman Agency; *bottom* Kent and Donna Dannen. **220–221** Kent and Donna Dannen. **222** © David Muench. **224** Robyn Horn/Arkansas Department of Parks and Tourism. **225** Garry D. McMichael/Southern Images. **226** R. Bullard/Bruce Coleman Inc. **227** Tim Ernst/Southern Images. **229** *bottom* Pictures of Record. **230** B. A. Cohen. **231** C. C. Lockwood. **232** Margaret Perry. **233** Louisiana Office of Tourism. **234** Kent and Donna Dannen. **236–237, 237** Kent and Donna Dannen. **238** *left* North Dakota Tourism Promotion; *right* B. Cory Kilvert, Jr. **239** B. Cory Kilvert, Jr. **240** Courtesy of South Dakota Tourism. **242** *top* W. Marc Bernsau; *bottom* Jim Brandenburg/DRK Photo. **243** Tom Bean. **244** W. Marc Bernsau. **245** Courtesy of South Dakota Tourism. **247** *top* © David Muench. **248, 249** Kent and Donna Dannen. **250, 251** Michael Whye. **252** Willa Cather Historical Center, Nebraska State Historical Society. **253** *top* © David Muench; *bottom* Indian Cave State Park. **254** Dick Herpich. **256** © David Muench. **257** Kent and Donna Dannen. **259** Jim Meyer/Mark MacLaren, Inc. **260** Garry D. McMichael/Southern Images. **261, 262** Bob Taylor. **264** © David Muench. **265** Bob Taylor. **267** *top* Lake Meredith Recreation Area/National Park Service. **268** Robert and Linda Mitchell. **269** © David Muench. **270** *left* Robert and Linda Mitchell; *right* Sullivan and Rogers/ Bruce Coleman Inc. **271** Robert and Linda Mitchell. **272, 273** Kent and Donna Dannen. **274** Garry D. McMichael/Southern Images. **275** *left* © David Muench; *remainder* Gwen Fidler. **277** *top* © David Muench/Courtesy of the U. S. Dept. of Interior, Indian Arts and Crafts Board, Museum of the Plains Indian and Crafts Center. **278** Thomas Peters Lake. **279** Jeff Gnass/West Stock. **280** Montana Promotion Division. **283** *top* Will Hawkins. **284, 285** © David Muench. **286** Bob Clemenz Photography. **287** *top* David Boehlke/Idaho Travel Council; *bottom* Bob and Ira Spring. **288, 289** © David Muench. **290** Boyd Norton. **292** © David Muench. **293** The Wyoming Travel Commission. **294** © David Muench. **295, 296** Kent and Donna Dannen. **298** B. Cory Kilvert, Jr. **299** Thomas Peters Lake. **300** Dick Dietrich. **301** Joura/H. Armstrong Roberts. **302** Boyd Norton. **305** Jim Adams/Amwest. **306** © David Muench. **307** Thomas Peters Lake. **308** Harvey Caplin. **310, 311** © David Muench. **312** Jerry Hardy. **313** © David Muench. **314** Daniel Weiss. **315, 316, 318** © David Muench. **319** David Hiser/Aspen. **320** D. Muench/H. Armstrong Roberts. **321** John Shaw. **322** Duane D. Davis. **324** Michael Dunn. **325, 326** Bob and Ira Spring. **327** *top* Ray Atkeson; *bottom* Jay Lurie. **328** Charles Gordon/West Stock. **329** J. Gleiter/H. Armstrong Roberts. **330** Bob Clemenz Photography. **332, 333** © David Muench. **334–335** *top* D. Muench/H. Armstrong Roberts. **335** *bottom*, **336, 337** Ray Atkeson. **338** Richard Moreno/Nevada Commission of Tourism. **340** Kenneth L. Miller. **341** Ray Atkeson. **342** © David Muench. **343** Dennis Brooks. **345** *right*, **346** © David Muench. **347** D. C. Lowe. **348, 349** © David Muench. **350** Jeff Gnass/West Stock. **351** *top* Ron E. Pickup/Amwest; *bottom* Bob Clemenz Photography. **352** © David Muench. **353** George Wuerthner. **354** Mark Newman/West Stock. **355** *top right inset* George Buctel. **356** Richard Rowan. **357** Steve McCutcheon. **358** George Wuerthner. **359** *top* Kent and Donna Dannen; *bottom* Martin W. Grosnick. **360** Steve McCutcheon. **361** George Wuerthner. **362** *left* Keith Gunner/est Stock; *right* Kent and Donna Dannen. **363** Tom Bean/DRK Photo. **364** Pat O'Hara. **366, 367** © David Muench. **368** Paul Chesley/Aspen. **369** Douglas Peebles. **370** E. Cooper/H. Armstrong Roberts. **371, 372** © David Muench. **373** *top* Ray Atkeson; *bottom* © David Muench.

INDEX

*Page numbers in **bold** type refer to illustrations and captions. The entry numbers of featured attractions appear in brackets [ ].*

377

Horseshoe Bend National Military Park, Ala., 174 [12], **174**
Hotel De Paris, Georgetown, Colo., 304 [6]
Howard Steamboat Museum, Jeffersonville, Ind., 151 [19], **151**
Hualapai Valley Joshua Trees, Ariz., 318 [6]
Hubbell Trading Post National Historic Site, Ganado, Ariz., 316–317 [3]
Hudson's Bay Company, 324, 325
Huguenot Street, New Paltz, N.Y., **52,** 53 [19]
Hungry Horse Dam and Reservoir, Mont., 276 [1]
Hunter's Home, Tahlequah, Okla., 262, **262**
Huntsdale Fish Cultural Station, Carlisle, Pa., 73 [18]
Huron City Museums, Port Austin, Mich., 134 [19]
Hurricane Fault, Utah, 300

I

Ice Caves Mountain National Landmark, N.Y., 53 [20]
Idaho, 282–289, 283 (map)
Idaho Hotel, Silver City, Idaho, 287
Ide, William B., Adobe State Historic Park, Red Bluff, Calif., 347 [6]
Illinois, 206–213, 207 (map)
Illinois Railway Museum, Union, Ill., 206 [3]
Illinois River, 208, 209
Independence Mine State Historic Park, Alaska, 356 [7]
Independence Rock State Historic Site, Alcova, Wyo., 294 [13], **294**
Indiana, 144–151, 144–145 (map)
Indian Cave State Park, Nebr., 253 [22], **253**
Indian Map Rock, Idaho, 287 [13]
Indian Mary Park, Merlin, Oreg., 332–333 [7]
Indian Motocycle Museum, Springfield, Mass., 30–31 [7]
Indian Museum of the Carolinas, Laurinburg, N.C., 101 [7], **101**
Indian Petroglyphs, Bellows Falls, Vt., 26–27 [16]
Ingraham, Edward, Library, Bristol, Conn., 43
Ingram's Pioneer Log Cabin Village, Kinmundy, Ill., 212 [17], **213**
Inscription House, Kayenta, Ariz., 316
Inscription Rock, Kelleys Island, Ohio, 136
International Peace Garden, N.Dak., 234–235 [3]
International Space Hall of Fame, Alamogordo, N.Mex., 315 [21]
Iowa, 200–205, 201 (map)
Ipswich River Wildlife Sanctuary, Topsfield, Mass., 33–34 [17]
Iron County Museum, Caspian, Mich., 130 [6]
Iroquois National Wildlife Refuge, N.Y., 46 [1]
Island Beach State Park, N.J., **62,** 63 [16]
Island Pond, Vt., 22
Isle La Motte, Vt., 22

Isleños Center, Chalmette, La., 233 [17]

J

Jack Daniel Distillery, Lynchburg, Tenn., 165–166 [9], **165**
Jackson, Andrew, 169, 170, 174, 175
Jacksonport State Park, Ark., 224 [5], **224**
Jackson–Washington State Forest, Brownstown, Ind., 150 [15]
Jamaica Bay National Wildlife Refuge, New York, N.Y., 54–55 [23], **54**
James, Jesse, 205, 212, 214, 263
Jane's Island State Park, Crisfield, Md., 85
Jefferson Telephone Company Museum, Jefferson, Iowa, 202–203 [8]
Jerome State Historic Park, Ariz., 319 [10]
Jessup's Neck, N.Y., 55
Jewel Cave National Monument, S.Dak., **242,** 243–244 [10]
Jim Thorpe, Pa., **72,** 73 [20]
Jockey Hollow, Morristown, N.J., 58–59
Johnson County Jim Gatchell Memorial Museum, Buffalo, Wyo., 292 [6]
Johnson–Humrickhouse Museum, Coshocton, Ohio, 140 [10]
Jones, Casey, Home and Railroad Museum, Jackson, Tenn., 164 [4]
Jones, Casey, Museum, Vaughan, Miss., 180 [8]
Jones, Sam Houston, State Park, La., 231 [11]
Jonesborough Historic District, Jonesboro, Tenn., 169 [22], **169**
Jones Gallery of Glass and Ceramics, Maine, 14–15 [18], **14**
Josephine County Kerbyville Museum, Kerby, Oreg., 333 [8]
Joshua Tree National Monument, Twentynine Palms, Calif., **352,** 353 [22]
Juneau, Alaska, 362 [23], **362**
Jung, Wesley W., Carriage Museum, Greenbush, Wis., 198

K

Kachemak Bay State Park, Alaska, 358–359 [15]
Ka'u Desert, Hawaii, 373
Kaimu Black Sand Beach, Kaimu, Hawaii, 372 [27], **372**
Kalalau Trail, Kauai, Hawaii, 364 [1]
Kalalau Valley, Hawaii, 366, **366**
Kalamazoo Nature Center, Kalamazoo, Mich., 135 [21], **135**
Kalaupapa, Hawaii, 368 [14], **369**
Kamakahonu, Kailua, Hawaii, 373 [31], **373**
Kamuela Museum, Waimea, Hawaii, 371 [23]
Kam Wah Chung & Co. Museum, John Day, Oreg., 336–337 [23]
Kandiyohi County Historical Society Center, Willmar, Minn., 189–190 [15]
Kansas, 254–259, 255 (map)
Kapoho, Hawaii, 372 [26]

Katmai National Park and Preserve, Alaska, 359 [17], **359**
Kauai, Hawaii, 364–366, 365 (map)
Kauai Museum, Lihue, Hawaii, 366 [3]
Kaumahina State Wayside, Hawaii, 369–370 [18]
Kealakekua Bay, Hawaii, 373 [30], **373**
Ke'e Beach, Hawaii, 364 [1]
Keet Seel, Kayenta, Ariz., 316
Kelleys Island, Ohio, 136–137 [2]
Kenai Fjords National Park, Alaska, 358 [14], **358**
Kenai National Wildlife Refuge, Alaska, 357 [10]
Kennedy, John F., Space Center, Fla., 124
Kenosha Public Museum, Kenosha, Wis., 199 [19]
Kent Iron Furnace, Kent, Conn., 40
Kent Museum, Calais, Vt., 24 [7]
Kentucky, 152–161, 152–153 (map)
Kerbyville Museum, Kerby, Oreg., 333
Kershaw–Cornwallis House, Camden, S.C., 108
Kimball, Heber, House, Nauvoo, Ill., 210
Kimball Wildlife Refuge, R.I., 39 [10]
Kimmey House, Westminster, Md., 81
King and Queen Seat, Rocks State Park, Md., 81
Kings Gap Environmental Education and Training Center, Carlisle, Pa., 73
Kingsland Bay State Park, Vt., 24–25 [9]
Kiowa Indians, 264, 266, 271, 272
Kipuka Puaulu (Bird Park), Hawaii, 372 [28]
Kirtland Air Force Base, N.Mex., 308 [1]
Kisatchie National Forest, La., 230 [8], **231**
Kittatinny Mountains, N.J.–Pa., 56, **57,** 58
Klamath Basin National Wildlife Refuge, Calif., 346
Klein Museum, Mobridge, S.Dak., 240 [2]
Klondike Gold Rush National Historical Park, Skagway, Alaska, 361 [20]
Kluane National Park and Territorial Game Sanctuary, Alaska, 360
Knife River Indian Villages National Historic Site, N.Dak., 237–238 [11]
Kobuk Valley, Alaska, 354
Kodiak, Alaska, 359
Kokee State Park, Hawaii, 366 [5], **366**
Kokomo, Ind., 146–147
Kolob Canyons, Zion National Park, Utah, 300 [13]
Kolomoki Mounds State Park, Blakely, Ga., 116–117 [14]
Kotzebue, Alaska, 354 [1]
Kumakahi Lighthouse, Hawaii, 372

L

Lacreek National Wildlife Refuge, S.Dak., 244 [13]

Lafayette State Trout Hatchery, Lafayette, R.I., 37 [5]
Lafitte, Jean, National Historic Park, La., 233
Lake Chautauqua State Park, N.Y., 46 [2], **46**
Lake Claiborne State Park, La., 228 [2]
Lake Corpus Christi State Recreation Area, Tex., 272, 273 [21]
Lake Easton State Park, Easton, Wash., 325 [9]
Lake Francis State Park, N.H., 16 [1]
Lake Gogebic State Park, Mich., 130 [4]
Lake Maria State Park, Minn., 189 [14]
Lake Meade State Park, Meade, Kans., 258–259 [17]
Lake Meredith Recreation Area, Tex., 266
Lake of the Ozarks State Park, Mo., 218 [12], **218**
Lake of the Woods, Minn., 184
Lake Ouachita State Park, Ark., 225–226 [11]
Lake Owyhee State Park, Nyssa, Oreg., 337 [24]
Lake St. George State Park, Maine, 13–14 [15]
Lake Vesuvius Recreation Area, Ohio, 143 [20], **143**
Lakota, Lake, S.Dak., 245
Landsford Canal State Park, S.C., 107 [4]
Lanier House, Monticello, Ky., 159
Lapham–Patterson House, Thomasville, Ga., **117**
Lassen Volcanic National Park, Calif., 346–347 [5], **346**
Last Indian Raid Museum, Oberlin, Kans., 254 [1]
Lava Beds National Monument, Calif., **346** [3]
Lawnfield, Mentor, Ohio, 138 [4]
Lea County Airport, Hobbs, N.Mex., 315 [23]
Leadbetter Point Unit, Willapa National Wildlife Refuge, Oysterville, Wash., 326 [12]
Leesburg Town Site, Salmon, Idaho, 285 [7]
Leffingwell Inn, Norwich, Conn., 45 [16], **45**
Lehman Caves National Monument, Nev., 341 [9], **341**
Letchworth State Park, N.Y., 48 [5], **48**
Lewes Historic Area, Del., 78 [6]
Lewis, Meriwether, 153, 214, 217, 237, 240, 279, 284, 330
Lewis, Miles, House, Bristol, Conn., 42–43
Lewis and Clark Caverns State Park, Mont., 280 [12]
Lily Bay State Park, Maine, 10 [5]
Lincoln, Abraham, 25, 116, 138, 140, 150–151, 156, **156,** 158, **158,** 169, 199, 211, **211,** 212, 253
Lincoln, Abraham, Birthplace National Historic Site, Hodgenville, Ky., 156 [10], **156**
Lincoln, Nancy Hanks, 150, 156, 158
Lincoln, Sarah Bush, 211
Lincoln, Thomas, 150, 156, 158, 211

Page numbers in **bold** *type refer to illustrations and captions. The entry numbers of featured attractions appear in brackets [ ].*

381

*Page numbers in **bold** type refer to illustrations and captions. The entry numbers of featured attractions appear in brackets [ ].*

383

Page numbers in **bold** *type refer to illustrations and captions. The entry numbers of featured attractions appear in brackets [ ].*